Special Edition, Using Novell® PerfectOffice® 3

Bill Bruck, Ph.D., with
Judy Felfe
Steve Mann
Sue Plumley
Patrice-Anne Rutledge
Brian Underdahl

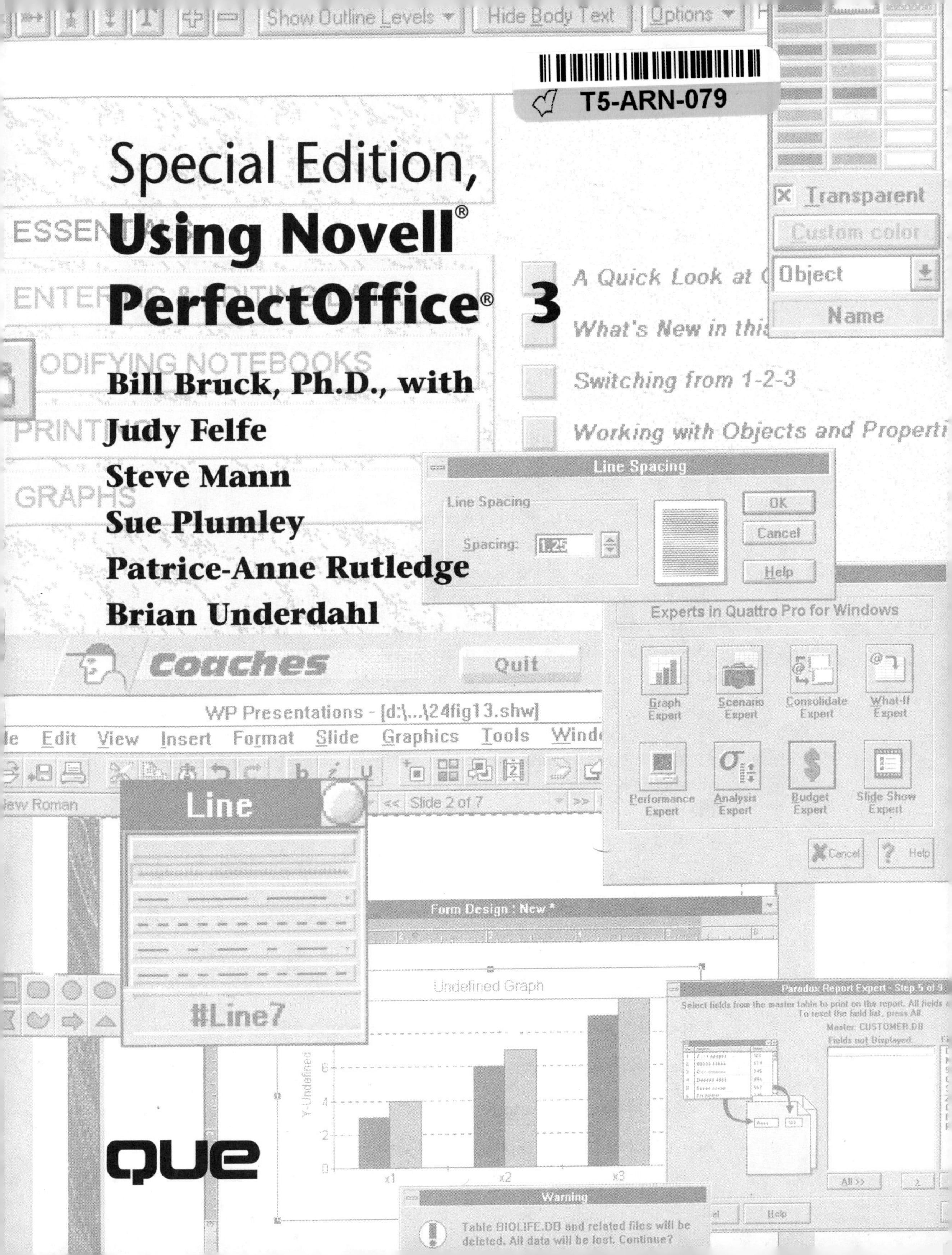

QUE

Special Edition, Using Novell PerfectOffice 3

Library of Congress Catalog No.: 94-69622

ISBN: 0-7897-0089-1

98 97 96 95 4 3

Interpretation of the printing code: the rightmost double-digit number is the year of the book's printing; the rightmost single-digit number, the number of the book's printing. For example, a printing code of 95-1 shows that the first printing of the book occurred in 1995.

Screen reproductions in this book were created with Collage Complete from Inner Media, Inc., Hollis, NH.

Publisher: David P. Ewing

Associate Publisher: Don Roche, Jr.

Associate Publisher—Operations: Corinne Walls

Managing Editor: Michael Cunningham

Product Marketing Manager: Greg Wiegand

Assistant Product Marketing Manager: Kim Margolius

Credits

Acquisitions Editor
Deborah F. Abshier

Product Director
Kathie-Jo Arnoff

Product Development Specialists
Joyce J. Nielsen
Lisa D. Wagner

Production Editors
Jeanne Terheide Lemen
Lynn Northrup

Editors
Charles Bowles
Nicole Rodandello
Maureen Schneeberger

Technical Editors
Edward Hanley
Robert W. Hartley
Gabrielle Nemes
David Rippy

Figure Specialist
Cari Ohm

Book Designer
Sandra Schroeder

Cover Designer
Jay Corpus

Production Team
Amy Cornwell
Chad Dressler
Lorell Fleming
Daryl Kessler
Bob LaRoche
Steph Mineart
Alan Palmore
Kaylene Riemen
Clair Schweinler
Jon Swain
Allan Wimmer
Jody York

Indexer
Kathy Venable

Acquisitions Coordinator
Tracy Williams

Operations Coordinator
Patricia J. Brooks

Editorial Assistant
Jill L. Pursell

Composed in *Stone Serif* and *MCPdigital* by Que Corporation

About the Authors

Bill Bruck, Ph.D. is a Certified Novell Instructor and owner of Bill Bruck & Associates, a training and consulting firm in Falls Church, Virginia. BB&A delivers customized training services in PerfectOffice, WordPerfect, GroupWise, and other applications to clients nationwide. Bill's consulting work focuses on process reengineering, automating business processes utilizing the latest generation of PC applications. A counseling psychologist by training, Bill comes from academia, having taught at the University of Florida, Seattle University, and West Georgia College. He is currently Professor of Psychology at Marymount University in Arlington, Virginia. Bill is also an author of several other Macmillan books on WordPerfect and WordPerfect Office.

Judy Felfe is the owner of Felfe Consultants, a personal computer training company in Houston, Texas. Judy has been a WordPerfect Certified Instructor since 1988. She has coauthored WordPerfect 6.0 DOS and WordPerfect 6.0 Windows books for Que Corporation.

Steve Mann is the Group Leader for the Suite Development team at WordPerfect, the Novell Applications Group. His team is responsible for cross-product integration in PerfectOffice 3.0. Steve specializes in product automation, scripting languages, custom solutions, and problem solving. He has written articles for various computer magazines and served as managing editor of *PC Today*. He also founded two successful software companies during his 12 years in the PC industry. Steve has an M.A. in Experimental Psychology from the University of North Dakota.

Sue Plumley owns and operates Humble Opinions, a consulting firm that offers training in popular software programs and network installation and maintenance. Sue is the author of 10 Que books, including *Crystal Clear DOS*, *Crystal Clear Word 6*, and *Microsoft Office Quick Reference*, and coauthor of 12 additional books, including *Using WordPerfect 6 for DOS*, *Using OS/2 2.1*, Special Edition, and *Using Microsoft Office*.

Patrice-Anne Rutledge is a computer trainer and database developer who works for an international high-tech company in the San Francisco Bay area. She writes frequently on a variety of topics, including technology, business, and travel. Rutledge discovered computers while pursuing her original career as a translator and was quickly hooked. She holds a degree from the University of California and has been using Paradox for the past six years.

Brian Underdahl is an author, independent consultant, and custom application developer based in Reno, NV. He's the author of over 10 computer books, including *Using Quattro Pro 6 for Windows*, an excellent source of more detailed information on Quattro Pro. He has also been a contributing author to nearly 20 additional computer-related books, and has acted as a product developer and as a technical editor on many other Que books.

Acknowledgments

I would like to extend my thanks and acknowledgment to my coauthors on this book: Judy Felfe, Steve Mann, Sue Plumley, Patrice-Anne Rutledge, and Brian Underdahl. Their professionalism in getting chapters written, working as a team, and putting up with the vagaries of beta software is greatly appreciated.

Publisher's liaison Lesa Carter at WordPerfect, the Novell Applications Group, has been very helpful in supplying beta software; various anonymous technical support staff have been uniformly courteous, knowledgeable, and helpful with a variety of questions and concerns.

Thanks to Que staff, including Associate Publisher Don Roche, Acquisitions Editor Deborah Abshier, Product Director Kathie-Jo Arnoff, Product Development Specialists Joyce Nielsen and Lisa Wagner, and Production Editors Jeanne Lemen and Lynn Northrup for their support, the extra week they granted me to write this, and the work they put in on this book.

Finally, my deepest appreciation to my mother, Lucy Bruck, for everything—but most recently, for putting me up while I'm between houses, and providing all sorts of motherly things that have enabled me to write day and night on this book!

Contents at a Glance

Contents

II Using WordPerfect 83

5 Getting Started with WordPerfect 85

6 Formatting Text and Documents 103

8 Customizing WordPerfect 153

9 Organizing and Formatting Large Documents 167

10 Working with Tables and Graphics 189

Introduction

by Bill Bruck

PerfectOffice is the most integrated, powerful suite of desktop applications you can buy. It includes many best-of-class applications, including the latest versions of WordPerfect for word processing, Quattro Pro for spreadsheet analysis, Presentations for drawing and presentation graphics, GroupWise for e-mail and scheduling, InfoCentral for personal information management, and Envoy for document publishing and distribution. The professional version of PerfectOffice adds the powerful Paradox database and AppWare for creating custom applications.

With the power of PerfectOffice comes both simplicity and complexity. Individuals can load it on their stand-alone machines at home, and let QuickTasks and Coaches guide them through sending correspondence, making family budgets, and maintaining a Christmas list. Multinational corporations can load PerfectOffice on LANs, and conduct enterprise computing through powerful groupware such as GroupWise, maintain corporate documents electronically through Envoy, keep corporate databases in Paradox, and create custom interfaces and automated tasks with AppWare.

Who Should Use This Book?

WordPerfect, the Novell Applications Group, has created an easy-to-use and easy-to-learn product in PerfectOffice. However, the sheer number of included applications, richness of features, variety of shortcuts, and power of its automation functions imply that the new user will not be able to take full advantage of PerfectOffice by mere experimentation.

This book is for everyone using PerfectOffice 3.0.

For newcomers to PerfectOffice and its applications, this book offers a conceptual overview of the suite, outlines of common functionality, and a thorough introduction to each of the included applications.

More experienced users will appreciate the sections on suite integration and customization.

Many readers will find that they use one PerfectOffice application extensively, and the others occasionally. For these users, this book will be their only point of reference for those applications used occasionally. It will also serve as a first point of reference for their major application. Many users will also want to buy a Que book devoted exclusively to that major application, such as *Using WordPerfect 6.1 for Windows*, Special Edition, or *Using Quattro Pro for Windows*, Special Edition.

How This Book Is Organized

This book is organized into seven major parts that take you from the basic design of PerfectOffice, through using each application, and into advanced integration and customization of the suite:

Part I: Working with PerfectOffice

Part II: Using WordPerfect

Part III: Using Quattro Pro

Part IV: Using Paradox

Part V: Using Presentations

Part VI: Using GroupWise and InfoCentral

Part VII: Integrating and Customizing PerfectOffice

Part I, "Working with PerfectOffice," provides a conceptual overview of the suite. It shows you how to perform simple PerfectOffice functions, explains how common tools such as the Speller and Grammatik work, and discusses common file management issues.

Parts II through VI are devoted to the specific applications that make up PerfectOffice. You can turn directly to these sections if you have specific questions to answer or tasks to accomplish.

Part VII, "Integrating and Customizing PerfectOffice," discusses ways in which individual applications work together. You find out how to use QuickTasks to perform common functions, how to use the Desktop Application Director (DAD) to integrate various applications, how to use Envoy to electronically distribute documents, and how to transfer data between applications. You also learn how to create and edit toolbars and custom menus, and how to customize DAD.

Conventions Used In This Book

The conventions used in this book have been developed to help you learn to use PerfectOffice quickly and easily. Most PerfectOffice commands can be entered with either a mouse or the keyboard—for example, choosing menu options or dialog box commands. Instructions are written in a way that enables you to choose the method you prefer. For example, if the instruction says "Choose **F**ile, **O**pen," you can click the mouse pointer on the File menu, then click again on the Open option. Alternatively, you can press Alt+F to access the File menu, then press O; or use the arrow keys to highlight Open, then press Enter.

When you need to hold down the first key while you press a second key, a plus sign (+) is used for the combination:

> Alt+F or Ctrl+M

The Shift, Ctrl, and Alt keys must all be used in this way.

When two keys are pressed in sequence, they are separated with a comma. For instance, the Home key is never held down while pressing another key, but it is often pressed *before* pressing another key. "Press Home, up arrow" means to press and then release the Home key, then press and release the up-arrow key.

When a letter in a menu or dialog box is underlined (shown in bold in this text), it indicates that you can press Alt plus that letter (or that letter alone in submenus and dialog boxes) to choose that command. In "Choose **F**ile, **O**pen" you can access the menu by pressing Alt+F; then with the File menu selected, you can choose Open by pressing the letter O. Often, the underlined letter is the first letter in the word; at other times it is not. For instance, to choose **F**ile, Preferen**c**es, you would press Alt+F, then press the letter C.

If there are two common ways to invoke a command, they are separated with a semicolon (;). For instance, you can access the Print dialog box in two ways, as indicated by these instructions: "Choose **F**ile, **P**rint; or press Shift+F7."

Many times, the quickest way to access a feature is with a button on the toolbar. In this case, the appropriate toolbar button is shown in the margin next to the instructions.

Bold text is used to indicate text you are asked to type. UPPERCASE letters distinguish file names and DOS commands. On-screen messages appear in `monospace` type.

We, the authors, hope you enjoy using PerfectOffice, and find this book to be a valuable tool to assist you in the learning process and for your ongoing reference.

Part I

Working with PerfectOffice

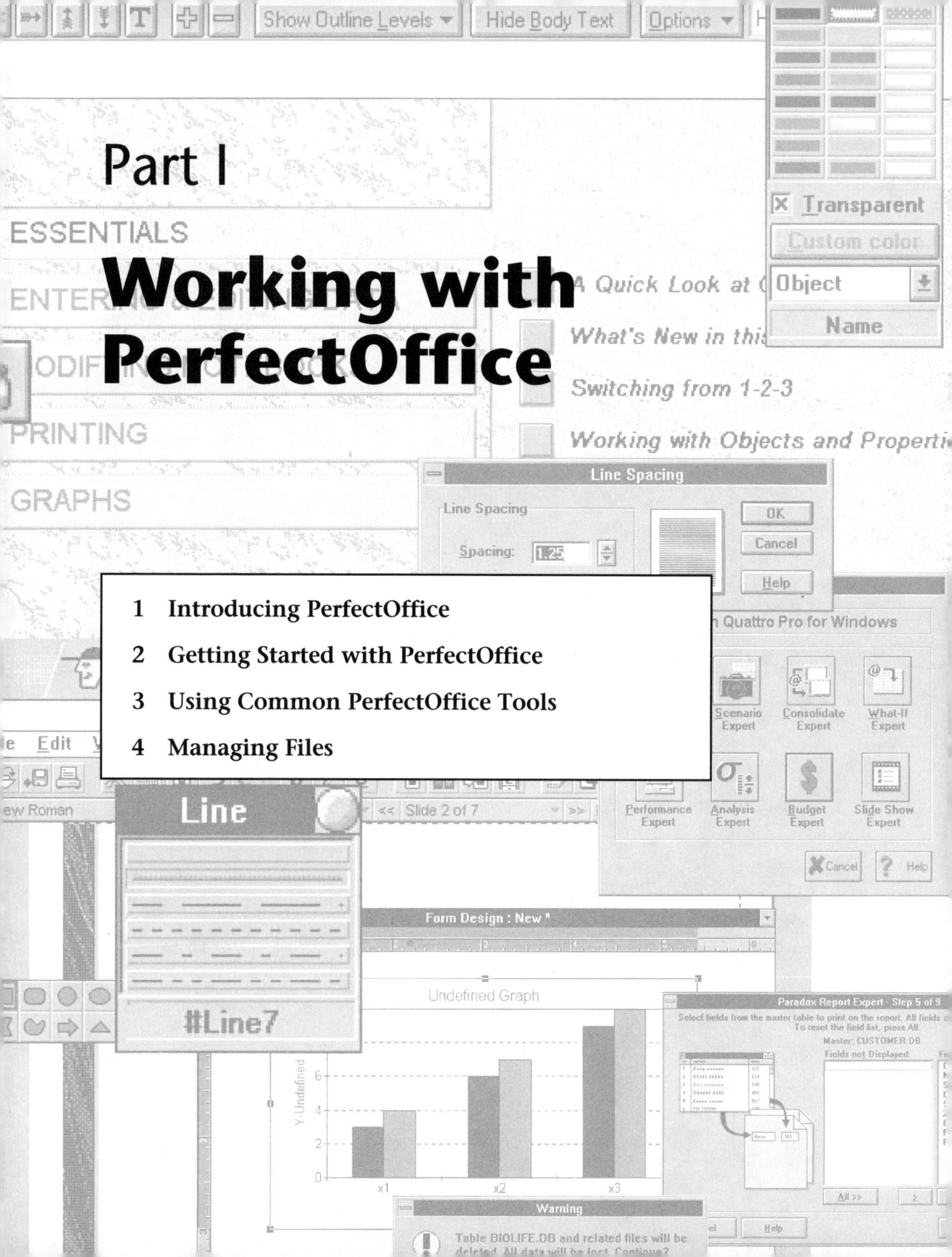

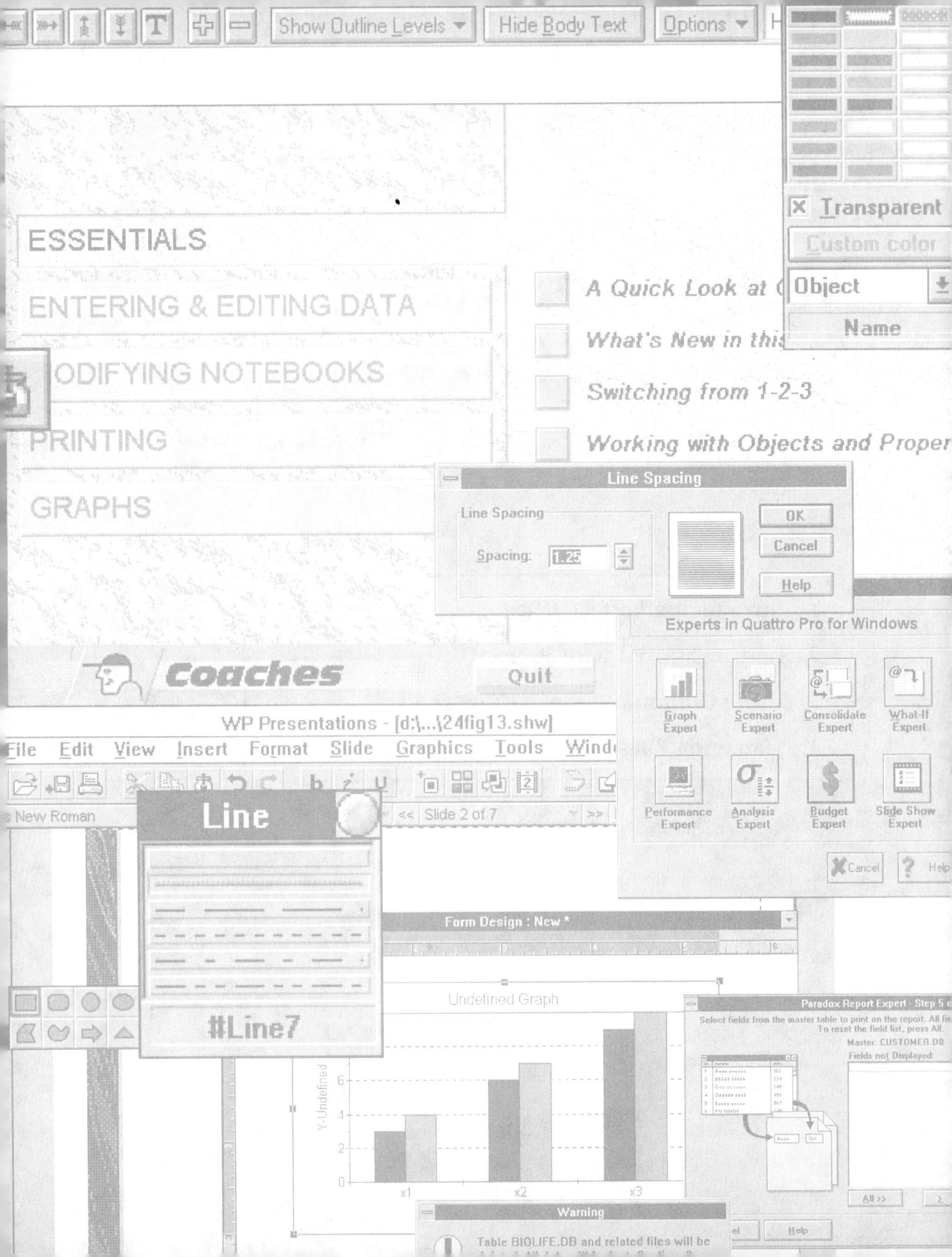

Show Outline Levels
Hide Body Text
Options
Transparent
Custom color
Object
Name
ESSENTIALS
ENTERING & EDITING DATA
ODIFYING NOTEBOOKS
PRINTING
GRAPHS
A Quick Look at
What's New in this
Switching from 1-2-3
Working with Objects and Proper
Line Spacing
Line Spacing
Spacing: 1.25
OK
Cancel
Help
Experts in Quattro Pro for Windows
Graph Expert
Scenario Expert
Consolidate Expert
What-If Expert
Performance Expert
Analysis Expert
Budget Expert
Slide Show Expert
Cancel
Help
Coaches
Quit
WP Presentations - [d:\...\24fig13.shw]
File Edit View Insert Format Slide Graphics Tools Wind
s New Roman
<< Slide 2 of 7 >>
Line
#Line7
Form Design : New *
Undefined Graph
Y-Undefined
x1
x2
x3
Paradox Report Expert - Step 5
Select fields from the master table to print on the report. All fie
To reset the field list, press All.
Master: CUSTOMER.DB
Fields not Displayed:
All>>
Help
Warning
Table BIOLIFE.DB and related files will be

Chapter 1

Introducing PerfectOffice

by Bill Bruck

With PerfectOffice, you have purchased the latest version of the world's best-selling word processor, WordPerfect for Windows 6.1, and a collection of other best-of-class applications such as Quattro Pro, GroupWise, and Presentations. But PerfectOffice is much more than a collection of applications. It is a true integrated suite of products that is aimed at making tasks you do at the office or at home easier.

This chapter provides a conceptual introduction to PerfectOffice. In this chapter, you learn

- What's included in PerfectOffice
- What tools are available to help you learn to use the products
- About the Desktop Applications Director (DAD)
- How PerfectOffice offers an integrated working environment
- About the network features of PerfectOffice
- How to decide which application to use for various tasks

What Is PerfectOffice?

PerfectOffice is a collection of applications for common home and office tasks, integrated with the Desktop Applications Director, that includes powerful tools to build custom cross-program applications.

What's Included with PerfectOffice?

PerfectOffice comes packaged in three different versions, all of which are designed for the Microsoft Windows operating environment:

- Standard
- Professional
- Select

PerfectOffice Standard ships with the following applications:

- WordPerfect 6.1
- Quattro Pro 6.0
- Presentations 3.0
- GroupWise 4.1a QuickLook
- Envoy 1.0
- InfoCentral 1.1

In addition, PerfectOffice Professional adds:

- Paradox 5.0
- Visual AppBuilder 1.0

PerfectOffice Select enables corporations to "pick and choose" which applications they purchase. For instance, if a company has standardized on Excel or Lotus 1-2-3 and prefers not to use Quattro Pro, it does not need to purchase it as part of the suite. In fact, the architecture of PerfectOffice is such that many of the cross-application macros will work with Excel, Lotus, or other applications sold by other vendors!

What Are the Operating Requirements?

To use PerfectOffice, you must have the following system requirements:

- 386 25 MHz or higher microprocessor
- Windows 3.1 or higher
- 90 MB disk space for standard installation
- 8 MB RAM recommended
- VGA display

Understanding the Design Goals of PerfectOffice

As you probably know by now, PerfectOffice isn't just a bunch of stand-alone applications bundled and marketed together. It is a true *suite* of integrated products that is aimed at home and business functionality.

Thus, understanding PerfectOffice isn't merely a matter of learning the features of individual applications. In fact, before you learn about the functions of all the applications, it's important to understand the basic design goals of PerfectOffice. These can be divided into the following areas:

- Ease of learning and use
- Integrated working environment
- Integration with network services

Ease of Learning and Use

PerfectOffice has been developed with extensive input from WordPerfect's Useability Laboratories. Two features that have been incorporated into PerfectOffice as a result of this research are a consistent user interface, and the extensive availability of Coaches and Experts.

Consistent Interface

A consistent interface means that the way you work in one application should parallel how you work in another. In PerfectOffice, this can be seen in several areas:

- *Menu similarity*. As you can see in figure 1.1, menus are similar in PerfectOffice applications. Not only are the names on the menu bar similar, the selections within each menu item parallel each other as much as possible, taking into consideration the differences in every application's features.

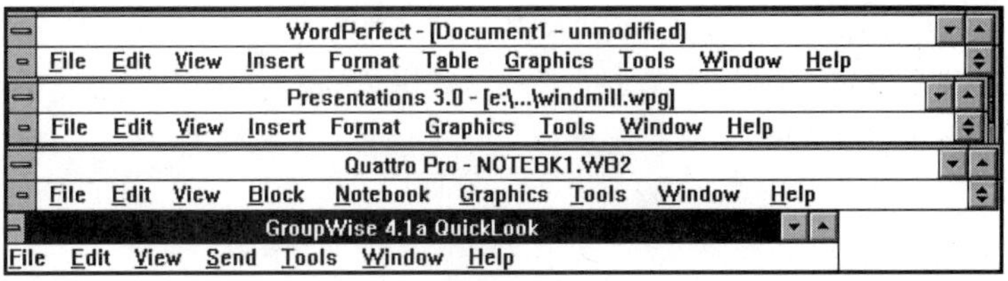

Fig. 1.1
Menus are similar in PerfectOffice applications.

- *Toolbar similarity.* In a similar manner, the same icons are used for basic tools across applications. These are listed in table 1.1.

Table 1.1 Common PerfectOffice Icons

Icon	Function
	New
	Open
	Save
	Print
	Cut
	Copy
	Paste
	Undo
	Redo
b	Bold
i	Italic
U	Underline
	Speller
	Grammar Checker
	Coaches

- *Dialog box similarity.* In addition, similar dialog boxes are used wherever possible throughout PerfectOffice. For instance, the same File Open dialog box is used in WordPerfect, Presentations, GroupWise, Quattro Pro, InfoCentral, and Envoy.

Coaches and Experts

PerfectOffice continues to define the outer limit of how applications can assist you to do common tasks with Experts and Coaches.

Experts are similar to the Wizards found in Microsoft applications. They help you accomplish a task by taking you through a series of choices. For instance, the Table Expert within WordPerfect (see fig. 1.2) shows you a list of predefined table styles, and enables you to pick from among them.

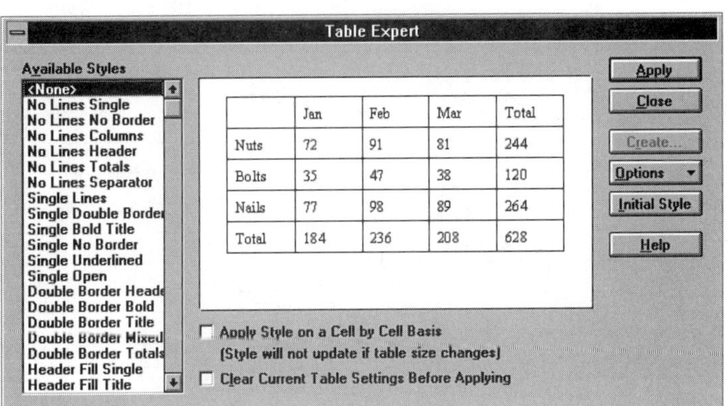

Fig. 1.2
Experts walk you through sophisticated features, like making tables in WordPerfect.

Similarly, the Show Expert in Presentations guides you through the steps needed to create an effective presentation. The Show Expert first asks what type of presentation you are going to make, and to what type of audience (see fig. 1.3).

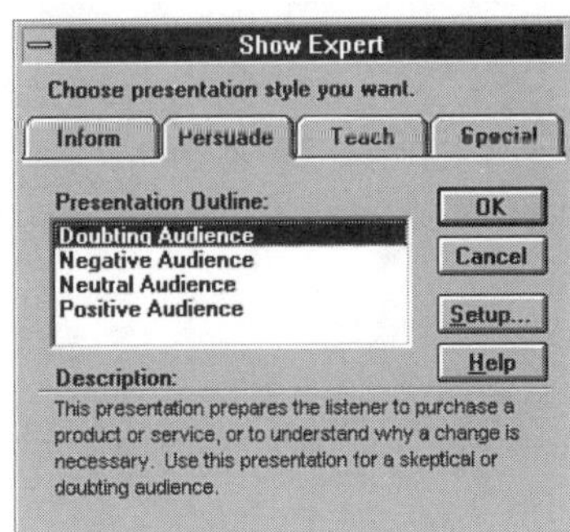

Fig. 1.3
The Show Expert gives you advice on constructing Presentation shows for different purposes.

Depending on your choices, the Show Expert shows you what a sample outline of the presentation might entail (see fig. 1.4).

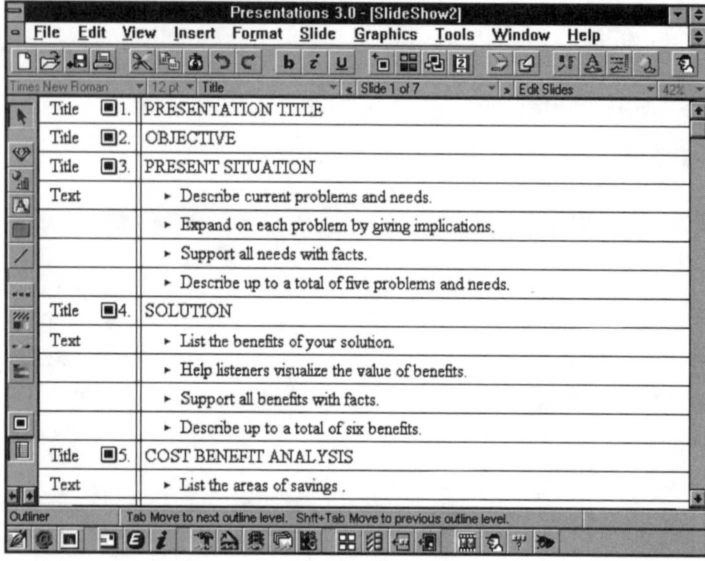

Fig. 1.4
The Show Expert even suggests an outline for your presentation.

Coaches are similar to Experts, but provide more choices for the user. Whereas Experts take you though a task step-by-step, Coaches enable you to deviate from the predefined steps to meet your own needs. For example, the Entering Dates Coach in Quattro Pro asks if you want to use your own notebook, or a sample notebook, to learn to enter dates (see fig. 1.5).

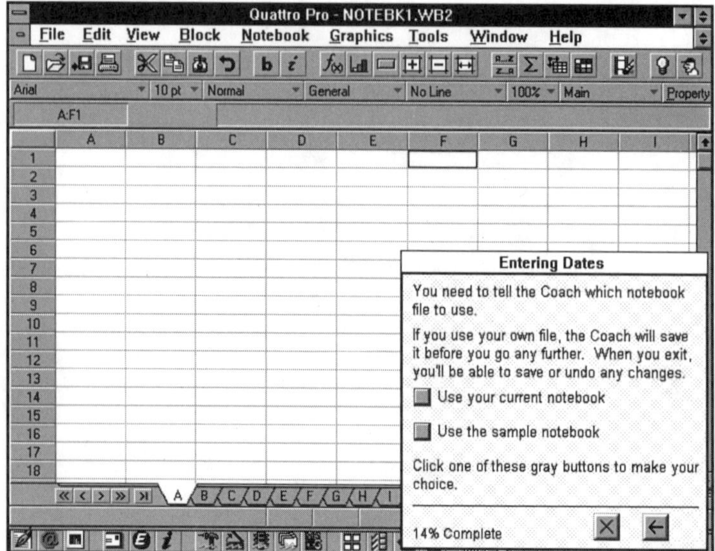

Fig. 1.5
Coaches like the Entering Dates Coach in Quattro Pro enable you to use your own documents or sample data.

Other Coaches provide active assistance in performing the task. Many WordPerfect Coaches, like the Create Bullets & Numbers Coach, provide a Show Me button that will move the mouse pointer and click the appropriate menu items (see fig. 1.6).

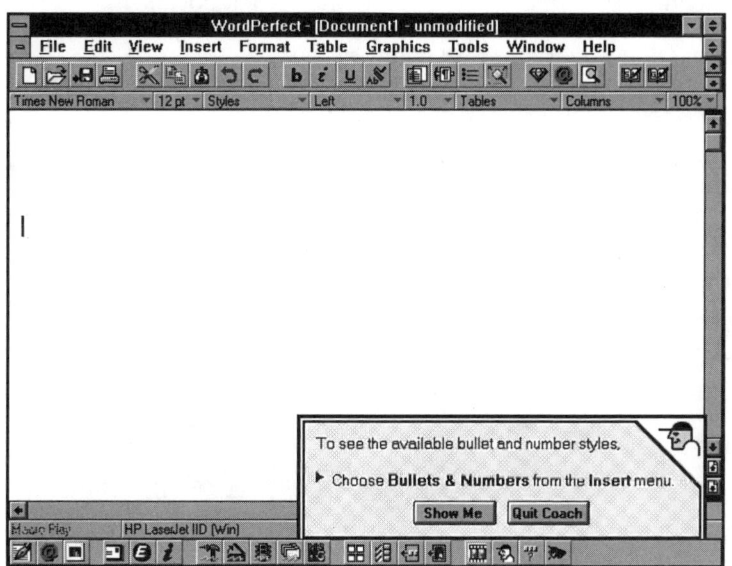

Fig. 1.6
Some Coaches, like WordPerfect's Create Bullets & Numbers Coach, even move the mouse pointer for you when you click Show Me.

Integrated Working Environment

Perhaps PerfectOffice's most powerful feature is the integrated working environment it provides. With PerfectOffice, you can concentrate more on the tasks you need to do, and less on the application(s) you need to do them.

▶ See "Using Help," p. 34

Of course, part of an integrated working environment is the common look and feel of applications. However, with PerfectOffice, this is only the beginning. PerfectOffice offers features that include:

- QuickTasks
- Common tools for file management and writing
- The Desktop Applications Director (DAD)

QuickTasks

You can think of a QuickTask as a Coach that operates across applications. QuickTasks provide guided, step-by-step instructions for common tasks such as:

- Finding a file
- Creating a letter, memo, or fax
- Creating an agenda, calendar, or newsletter
- Sending a file via e-mail or faxing the current document
- Creating a budget or loan amortization
- Checking your e-mail
- Scheduling an appointment
- Adding a person to your mailing list

Even apparently simple QuickTasks can involve several applications. For instance, the Create Letter QuickTask uses WordPerfect to write the letter, and then GroupWise to mail it (see fig. 1.7).

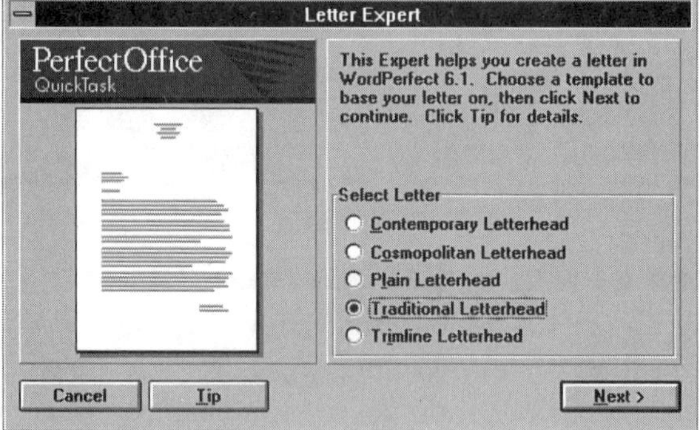

Fig. 1.7
QuickTasks help you with common tasks like creating a letter.

The QuickTask helps you choose a letter format, pick the recipient from an address list, and include common elements (see fig. 1.8).

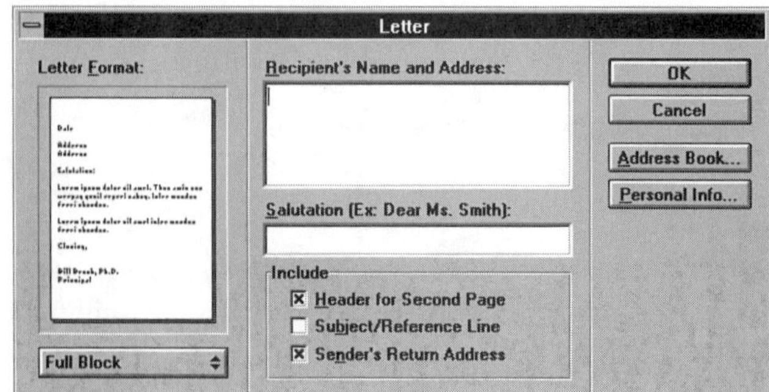

Fig. 1.8
The Create Letter QuickTask even includes a recipient address block, and creates the letter's header, reference line, and return address for you.

After pausing to enable you to type the text of the letter, and then putting in a closing for you, this QuickTask helps you finish the letter by automatically creating an envelope, spell checking the letter, saving it, printing it, or e-mailing it using GroupWise (see fig. 1.9).

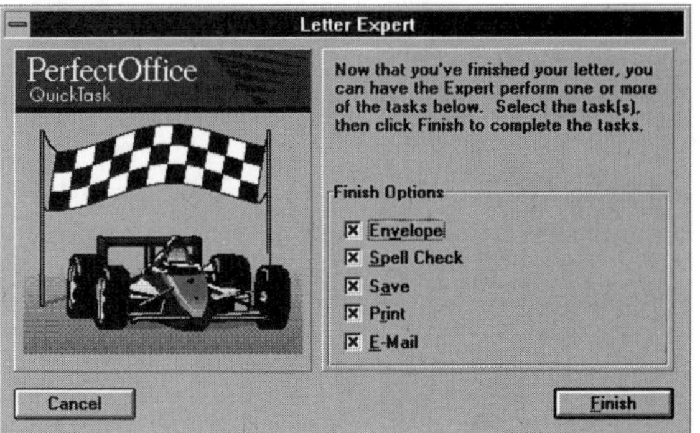

Fig. 1.9
The Create Letter QuickTask can finish the letter for you—even by calling GroupWise to e-mail it!

There are even QuickTasks to run Start Your Day and End Your Day routines, and a QuickTask to help you make your own QuickTasks!

► See "Learning QuickTask Essentials," p. 665

Common File Management Tools

File management is the art of creating an electronic filing system that enables you to store files securely and find files quickly. PerfectOffice offers several tools to assist you in your electronic filing tasks:

- *Common directory dialog boxes*. PerfectOffice applications have common directory dialog boxes (see fig. 1.10). These dialog boxes all have file management capabilities built in. From these dialog boxes, you can copy, move, rename, print, and change file attributes, and create, remove, and rename directories. In fact, there is a directory dialog box—QuickFiles—that is available to you from any application by accessing a pop-up toolbar called the DAD Bar.

- *QuickLists*. Within each directory dialog box you can display a list of directories or selected files within directories. This directory/file list supports English names, rather than the cryptic DOS path names. Thus, you can easily choose "John's Correspondence" or "CRC Proposals" and move to that drive and directory.

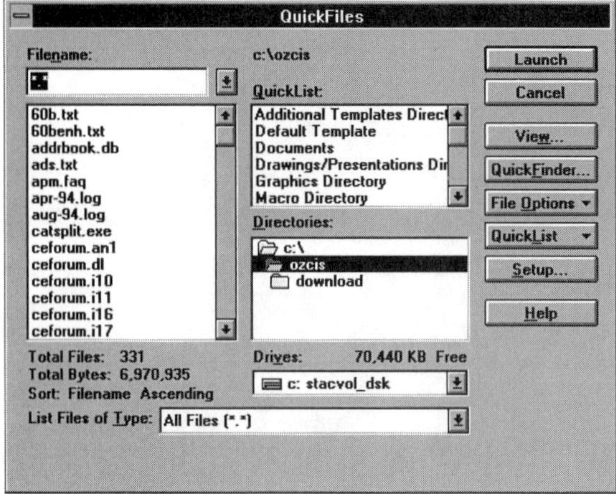

Fig. 1.10
PerfectOffice applications use common directory dialog boxes to facilitate ease of use.

- *QuickFinder*. PerfectOffice also includes the powerful QuickFinder indexing program that enables you to build indexes of your data files. Using these indexes, you can search for all files with specific words in them (for example, Wilson Accounting Group). Almost immediately, all files with these words are listed. You can even search for files containing synonyms of target words (accounting, budgeting), word forms (account, accounted, accounting), and common misspellings (acount).

▶ See "Using QuickOpen," p. 689

- *QuickOpen*. The pop-up toolbar called the DAD Bar that is available in all applications also contains an application called QuickOpen (see fig. 1.11). This application lists the last files you have opened in PerfectOffice applications. You can choose any of these files to quickly open the appropriate application and the selected file. You can now concentrate on your work—instead of worrying about the application that creates it!

Fig. 1.11
QuickOpen enables you to choose from the last ten files opened in PerfectOffice applications.

- *QuickRun*. Ever need to run a program that doesn't have a Windows icon? QuickRun is for you. The QuickRun dialog box (see fig. 1.12) enables you to specify the path and filename of any program you wish to run, or use the **B**rowse button to select the file from a directory dialog box. If you click the right arrow to the right of the **C**ommand Line text box, you can even select the application from a list of the previous programs you have run.

▶ See "Using QuickRun," p. 690

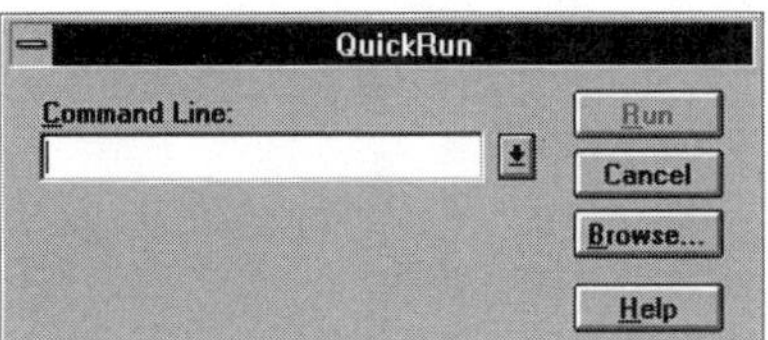

Fig. 1.12
QuickRun enables you to run DOS or Windows programs, and remembers the last programs you have run.

Common Writing Tools

PerfectOffice also provides you with writing tools that make the art of writing easier, and your document more professional. These tools are available not only in WordPerfect, but in Presentations and GroupWise. These include:

- *Speller*. The Speller corrects common spelling errors and catches irregular capitalization, words containing numbers, and repeated words. In WordPerfect, the Speller also remembers words you have told it to ignore in a document, so that future spelling checks of that document will continue to ignore the words.

▶ See "Using the Writing Tools," p. 43

- *Thesaurus*. The Thesaurus provides you with synonyms and antonyms of selected words. It groups synonyms according to the word's meaning and part of speech (noun, adjective, verb).

- *Grammatik*. Grammatik is PerfectOffice's grammar checker. Not only does it flag over a dozen types of errors, it actually rewrites sentences for you! You can select from among ten predefined checking styles, depending on the style of writing you use, or create your own.

- *QuickCorrect*. Would you like for PerfectOffice to correct your spelling as you type? Would you like common abbreviations like LBSB to automatically expand as you type to your firm's name of Luskin, Brankowitsch, Serrandello and Buskin? QuickCorrect is for you! Not only can QuickCorrect correct spelling and abbreviations, it can also automatically capitalize the first word of sentences, correct irregular capitalization, and place the correct number of spaces between sentences.

▶ See "Using the Automation Tools," p. 51

- *PerfectSense Technology*. Novell has incorporated many elements of artificial intelligence into PerfectOffice's writing tools. Some of these are incorporated in Grammatik and QuickCorrect. Others include the ability of the Find and Replace command to search for word forms—thus, when you replace *fly* with *drive*, *flying* and *flown* are replaced with *driving* and *driven*. The move and copy commands incorporate the ability to sense where extra spaces and lines are needed to maintain the format of the document.

These writing tools are discussed further in Chapter 3, "Using Common PerfectOffice Tools."

DAD

DAD, the Desktop Application Director, is the glue that holds PerfectOffice applications together, and makes them a true applications suite.

You can think of DAD as a customizable toolbar, available in every application, that can contain tools to launch applications, perform Windows tasks, and invoke DAD features. Let's look at each part of this definition.

- *Customizable toolbar*. You won't bring up DAD in a window, like you do other applications. DAD has a toolbar called a DAD Bar (see fig. 1.13). There are several different DAD Bars that ship with PerfectOffice, and you can switch between them at will. You can also create and edit your own DAD Bars, so you can have just the features you need within reach at all times.

Fig. 1.13 You control PerfectOffice functions with DAD Bars, like the PerfectOffice DAD Bar pictured here.

- *Available in every application*. When you first load PerfectOffice, the DAD Bar is in the Always Visible mode. It always appears on your screen, as seen in fig. 1.14. Perhaps the most interesting display mode is Auto Hide. In this mode, the DAD Bar does not display, but when you move your mouse pointer to the edge of the screen, it pops up.

> **Note**
>
> There is also a third display mode, Normal. This mode causes the DAD Bar to display like any other Windows application. That is, it will be hidden behind other active windows, and you can switch to it with Alt+Tab.

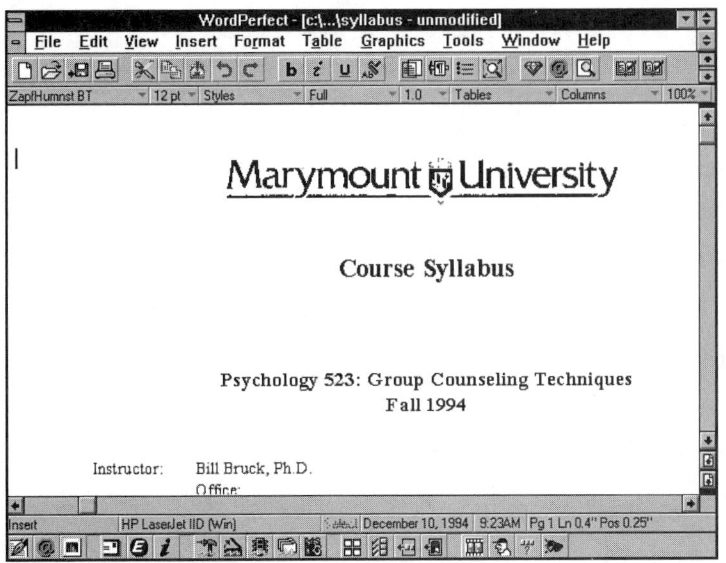

Fig. 1.14
When the DAD Bar is in the Always in Front mode, it does not overwrite your PerfectOffice applications; instead, it makes an extra line for itself.

- *Launch applications*. DAD Bars can launch PerfectOffice applications, or any other application that can be run under Windows. In this respect, they are like the MOM Bar in Microsoft's Office suite.
- *Perform Windows tasks*. DAD Bars can also help you with Windows. In fact, the Control Panel DAD Bar that ships with PerfectOffice has icons for Windows Control Panel functions, including color, fonts, ports, mouse, desktop, keyboard, printer, international, date/time, network, volume, recording, sound, drivers, and 386 Enhanced (see fig. 1.15).

Fig. 1.15
The Control Panel DAD Bar provides icons for Windows Control Panel functions.

- *Invoke DAD features*. The PerfectOffice DAD Bar includes buttons to launch several DAD features discussed above, including QuickTasks, QuickOpen, QuickRun, and QuickFile. The Data Sharing DAD Bar adds buttons for copying Paradox information to WordPerfect, copying Presentations information to WordPerfect, and other data-sharing functions.

More than just an application selector, DAD is a true applications suite manager. As you get used to working in a true suite environment, you will find DAD Bars to be one of your most valuable tools. You can read more about DAD Bars in Chapter 2, "Getting Started with PerfectOffice."

Integration with Network Services

While PerfectOffice is great to use on a desktop, its true power is unleashed on a network. In their public statements regarding PerfectOffice and other desktop applications, Novell has stated that their applications philosophy is that "the network is an essential part of the suite, not an afterthought to be dealt with."

This network integration is seen in many areas, including:

- Performing common network tasks within applications
- Document publishing across Local Area Networks and Wide Area Networks
- Document sharing technology
- Groupware ready
- Integrated code
- Cross-vendor integration
- Custom development environment

Perform Common Network Tasks

Whether you are running Novell, Banyan, Windows NT, or another common network operating system, PerfectOffice enables you to perform common network tasks from any directory dialog box, such as attaching to file servers from any Open File dialog box.

Document Publishing

As time goes on, companies are publishing more and more documents electronically. In this model, master copies of personnel manuals or technical manuals are maintained electronically. They can then be updated as needed by responsible parties, and the updated information is available instantly to all users.

PerfectOffice includes Envoy—a powerful document publishing application that allows you to distribute documents across LANs and WANs, or on diskette. Files can contain bookmarks and hypertext links to assist users in jumping to areas of interest. Documents are "bonded" so that users cannot change them, but can highlight or add notes to areas of interest.

Envoy even includes a run-time viewer, so that documents can be read and annotated by persons who do not have Envoy on their Windows system.

Data Sharing with Client-Server Applications

Users can easily share data between applications with three PerfectOffice features:

- *Shared file formats*. Whether you need to bring a WordPerfect outline into a Presentations slide, or clip a memo from WordPerfect and insert it into a GroupWise message, you will find it easy to do.

- *OLE 2.0*. The latest version of Microsoft's Object Linking and Embedding (OLE) is available in five PerfectOffice applications: WordPerfect, Quattro Pro, Presentations, InfoCentral, and Paradox. OLE 2.0 enables you to drag and drop objects such as drawings or charts from one application window to another. It also enables you to edit objects like Presentations drawings from within WordPerfect by merely double-clicking them.

► See "Techniques for Linking and Embedding," p. 730

- *OBEX*. With Object Exchange Technology (OBEX), PerfectOffice applications can subscribe to data published by another user on his PC. The data you subscribe to is live; when the publisher changes a spreadsheet, changes are reflected on the copies on subscribers' machines.

Groupware Ready

Not only does PerfectOffice include Envoy; it also ships with GroupWise—a powerful groupware tool for e-mail, group scheduling, and workgroup task management. PerfectOffice also supports simple MAPI, so if you are using a competitor's e-mail package, PerfectOffice will probably work with it.

► See "Introducing GroupWise," p. 571

In addition, PerfectOffice integrates with InForms—Novell's electronic forms software. Using InForms, corporations can make electronic forms that support electronic signatures for security, can be routed automatically for approvals, and update any number of popular databases.

PerfectOffice also integrates well with SoftSolutions—Novell's document management application. Legal firms and other organizations can take advantage of SoftSolutions' version tracking, document "check out" system, and other document management features.

Code Integration

PerfectOffice uses the concept of shared code to maximize performance and minimize use of system resources. Common tools such as the Speller, Thesaurus, Grammatik, QuickCorrect, QuickFinder, and QuickLists are shared between applications, thus saving disk space. No matter which application calls them, they are only loaded once, saving system resources.

Cross-Vendor Integration

Recognizing that many individuals and corporations want to "mix and match" applications from several vendors, PerfectOffice offers several features that make cross-vendor integration easy:

- *Support for Visual Basic.* Cross-application macros can be written in Microsoft's Visual Basic, and will work with PerfectOffice applications.
- *PerfectOffice Select.* As mentioned earlier, PerfectOffice Select allows companies to pay only for the PerfectOffice applications they use.
- *PerfectLinks.* A set of Application Programming Interfaces (APIs) provides compatibility with Windows applications made by other vendors. This means, for instance, that if a company wants to use Microsoft's Excel instead of Quattro Pro, the QuickTasks that involve Quattro Pro can use Excel instead. Further, other vendors can write applications that will use PerfectOffice features such as the Speller and QuickFinder.

Custom Development Environment

PerfectOffice's custom development environment enables users to create custom applications in three ways:

- *PerfectScript* is an easy-to-use scripting language. You can think of it as writing a WordPerfect macro, except that PerfectScript works between applications, as well as within them. You can even make your own QuickTasks using PerfectScript.
- *Visual AppBuilder* is used for more complex custom applications. You can think of it, roughly, as a superset of Visual Basic, or Visual Basic Plus. Visual AppBuilder ships with PerfectOffice Professional.
- *Visual Basic* support is also supplied with PerfectOffice, for programmers who already are familiar with this application.

Note

Discussion of these three automation tools—to create custom applications—is beyond the scope of this book.

Many of the foregoing integration features are included in what Novell terms PerfectOffice's PerfectFit Technology. PerfectFit includes PerfectOffice's:

- Common look and feel (menus, icons, toolbars)
- Common tools with shared code (Speller, Thesaurus, grammar checker, file manager)
- Common automation tools (QuickCorrect, quick help, QuickMenus)
- Common scripting language (PerfectScript)

Determining Which Application to Use

Most people have a "home base" program where they generally start out and do the majority of their work during the day. Usually, this is WordPerfect, though many people spend most of their time in Quattro Pro. In the past, people would often try to use their "home base" program well past the limits of its innate capabilities—for example, writing memos in their spreadsheets.

To some extent, software manufacturers encouraged this trend. For instance, WordPerfect incorporates all the elements of WordPerfect Corporation's now defunct spreadsheet, PlanPerfect.

However, when working in an integrated suite environment, you will find yourself more often using multiple applications to produce common documents. For instance, a newsletter may be created in WordPerfect and incorporate Quattro Pro spreadsheets or charts and Presentations graphics. It may be published electronically with Envoy and e-mailed with GroupWise, or mailed to persons using a WordPerfect mail merge relying on a Paradox database.

PerfectOffice sometimes seems to offer an abundance of riches. There are often so many ways to do things that you may get confused! For instance:

- You can maintain a personal calendar or to-do list in GroupWise and InfoCentral; there is also a QuickTask that helps you create an attractive calendar in WordPerfect!
- You can create an address list within WordPerfect to use in conjunction with templates, or create one in InfoCentral, Paradox, or Quattro Pro.
- You can have InfoCentral launch WordPerfect to write letters to persons in the InfoCentral iBase, or you can use WordPerfect templates.
- You can create charts and graphs in Presentations, Quattro Pro, and Paradox.

While these multiple ways of doing things may seem confusing at first, there are some simple criteria you can use to determine which way to go:

- *Use the right amount of horsepower.* WordPerfect's address list is not very feature-rich, and can contain only about 1,000 records. InfoCentral's allows a maximum amount of flexibility in adding fields and relationships, but can only be accessed by one person at a time. Paradox databases are more complex to set up, but can contain thousands of records and be edited by multiple users simultaneously.

  Similarly, InfoCentral allows you to create a relationship between any calendar event and a person or project, so that you can organize information about your activities. However, its ability to schedule recurring events is very weak compared to that of GroupWise.

  In general, match the power of the feature to your needs.

- *Minimize the number of applications you use.* If almost all your work is done in WordPerfect, then perhaps the address list in WordPerfect will suffice. Similarly, if you work in Paradox or Quattro Pro a lot, and have no other reason to use Presentations, you may wish to do your charting in the database or spreadsheet, rather than moving to a dedicated presentation application.

  In general, use the KISS principle—Keep It Simple, Stupid! Minimizing the number of applications you use keeps it simple.

- *If you work alone, use what's familiar.* Even if there is more power in an iBase than maintaining a to-do list in GroupWise, or a Presentations chart has more features than a Paradox one, you may be wise to stick with the applications you know and love, rather than try to do things a new way—if you work alone.

- *If you don't work alone, ignore the last rule.* When I go into organizations as a consultant, I often find people using an application to do something it wasn't designed for. For instance, I often find people keeping time and billing information in WordPerfect, rather than in a database. Why? Because that's what they know, and so as more people start using the system, that's what they use as well.

  If there will be a number of persons involved in a business process, make sure that you pick the application best suited to the task, rather than using the one that the original person was most familiar with.

For example, if you need to send document drafts to several people for annotation, don't just assume that it should be done in WordPerfect, because "everybody knows it." (Many probably don't know how to use the comment feature effectively, anyway!) Consider the advantages and disadvantages of publishing the document in Envoy versus distributing it in WordPerfect before making a final decision.

From Here...

In this chapter, you learned what PerfectOffice is and how it is designed. In the next chapters, you learn more about common PerfectOffice elements:

- Chapter 2, "Getting Started with PerfectOffice," shows you how to enter and exit PerfectOffice, use a DAD Bar, and explore some of the common features shared by PerfectOffice applications.
- Chapter 3, "Using Common PerfectOffice Tools," teaches you to use the different types of toolbars offered in PerfectOffice applications. See how the Desktop Application Director (DAD) can be used to find files, launch applications, and more.
- Chapter 4, "Managing Files," examines PerfectOffice's powerful file management capabilities. Learn how to use directory dialog boxes, the QuickFinder, and QuickLists.

Chapter 2

Getting Started with PerfectOffice

by Bill Bruck

Well, here you are. You've got PerfectOffice loaded and you're ready to get started. Let's do it! In this chapter, you learn how to

- Make sure a DAD Bar is visible
- Select applications with DAD
- Use common PerfectOffice features like toolbars and QuickMenus
- Use various help systems built into PerfectOffice

Introducing DAD

DAD is PerfectOffice's Desktop Application Director. Not being privy to the inner workings of WordPerfect, the Novell Applications Group, I assume that DAD is no relative of Microsoft's MOM, and that the similarity of acronyms is purely coincidental.

Be that as it may, DAD is a powerful entity. In fact, at the risk of being sexist, DAD is much more powerful than MOM. DAD is a true integration tool that welds the applications that comprise PerfectOffice into a true application suite.

◄ See "Understanding the Design Goals of PerfectOffice," p. 9

In learning to use PerfectOffice, it is thus appropriate that you start by learning how to use DAD for simple tasks, like launching applications. In Chapter 33, "Working with DAD," you will learn how to use the full range of features that DAD offers.

Using DAD involves three skills:

- Displaying a DAD Bar
- Launching applications with DAD
- Exploring DAD's capabilities

Displaying a DAD Bar

DAD Bars are toolbars that can appear in any application and are used to access DAD's capabilities. DAD Bars can be set to any of three display modes. To use a DAD Bar, you must first know how to make one appear on the screen, if it isn't there already.

> **Note**
>
> Three different DAD Bars ship with PerfectOffice, and you can create others that keep your most-used programs ready at hand. This discussion assumes you are displaying the default DAD Bar, called the PerfectOffice DAD Bar. The DAD Bar you actually see may be different, if PerfectOffice was customized for your organization.

The first display mode is called Always in Front. This is the way the DAD Bar will display when you first install PerfectOffice. The DAD Bar will always display, no matter what window is active, as shown in figure 2.1. It may be on any side of the screen, but you will know that the DAD Bar is in this display mode because it will, in fact, always be in front. If your DAD Bar is in this mode, you will always be able to access DAD features as described later in the section, "Launching Applications with DAD."

The second mode is Auto Hide. The DAD Bar does not appear at all on the screen; however, it pops up as you move the mouse pointer to the edge of the screen where the DAD Bar is located. Thus, if the DAD Bar is positioned at the bottom of the screen, move the mouse pointer to the bottom of the screen to make the DAD Bar appear. As you move the mouse pointer away from the DAD Bar, it disappears from view. To see whether DAD is in the Auto Hide mode, move the mouse pointer to the top, bottom, right, and left of the screen. If the DAD Bar pops up, you're in the Auto Hide mode and can then access DAD features.

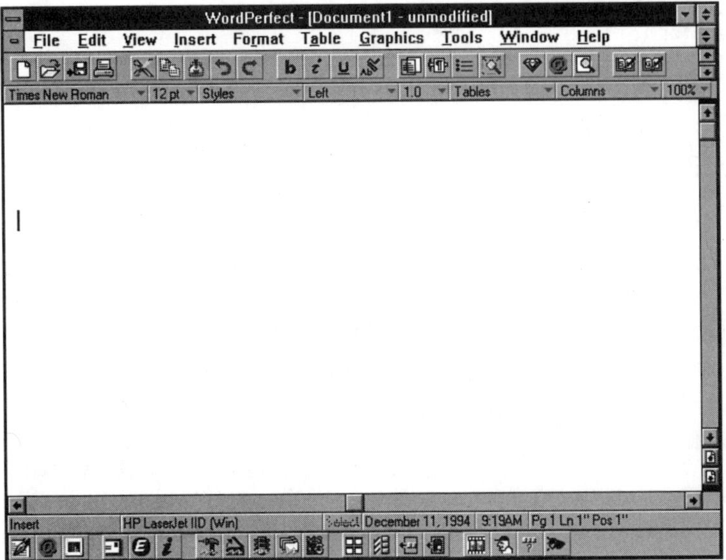

Fig. 2.1
If the DAD Bar is in the Always in Front mode, it will not obscure any of your PerfectOffice applications.

The last mode is the Normal mode. In this mode, the DAD Bar behaves like any other Windows application—that is, it is a window that you can switch to like any other. Perhaps the easiest way to switch to the DAD Bar when it is in Normal mode is to hold down the Alt key, then repeatedly press the Tab key until the Desktop Application Director appears in the pop-up window in the middle of the screen (see fig. 2.2).

► See "Customizing Toolbars and DAD Bars," p. 740

Fig. 2.2
You can switch to the DAD Bar like any other window.

Alternatively, you can press Ctrl+Esc to bring up the Windows Task Manager, and then choose the Desktop Application Director (see fig. 2.3).

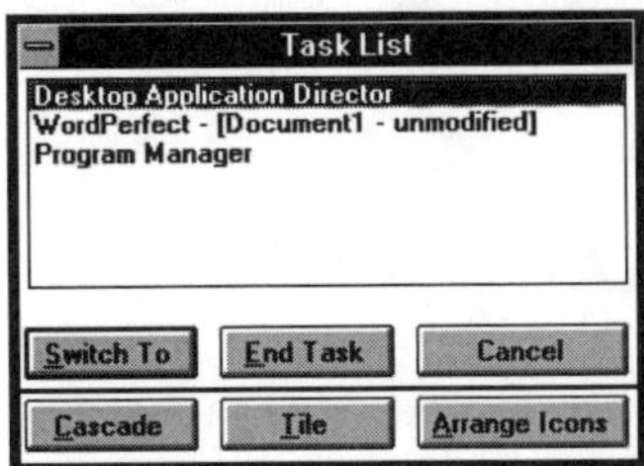

Fig. 2.3
Alternatively, you can switch to the DAD Bar in the Normal mode using the Windows Task Manager.

Troubleshooting

I did all those things and the DAD Bar still isn't showing. What's wrong?

If the Desktop Application Director does not show when you press Ctrl+Esc, then DAD isn't loaded. Restart Windows, and if it still isn't loaded, see the note in the later section, "Opening and Closing PerfectOffice," for directions on how to make PerfectOffice load when Windows starts.

Tip

To see what application a button launches, rest your mouse pointer on an icon for a second or so. You see a pop-up QuickTip that names the application.

Launching Applications with DAD

To launch an application on a DAD Bar, first ensure that the DAD Bar is visible as described in the last section, then click the icon for the application you want.

You can switch between open applications if they are PerfectOffice applications. For instance, if you click the WordPerfect icon on the DAD Bar, then click the Presentations icon, both WordPerfect and Presentations will open. If you click the WordPerfect icon again, you switch back to WordPerfect.

Be careful in using this technique with non-PerfectOffice applications, however. For instance, if Microsoft Word 2.0c is on a DAD Bar and you click it to open it, then click Presentations, then click Word again, *you will open a second copy of Word,* rather than switching back to the first copy.

Exploring DAD

One of the best ways to get to know DAD (so to speak) is to explore DAD's QuickTour. Ensure that the PerfectOffice DAD Bar is visible, then click the QuickTour icon. You will be guided through a tour of many of DAD's features (see fig. 2.4).

You may also wish to click some of the DAD tools that you find on the PerfectOffice DAD Bar (see fig. 2.5).

Before leaving this introduction to DAD, however, there is one more skill you may want to have: switching between DAD Bars.

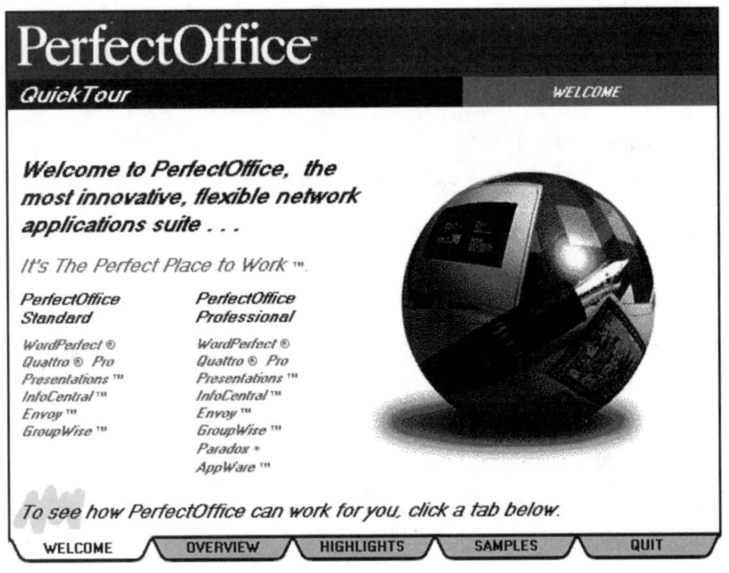

Fig. 2.4
DAD's QuickTour shows you many of its features in a five-minute animated show.

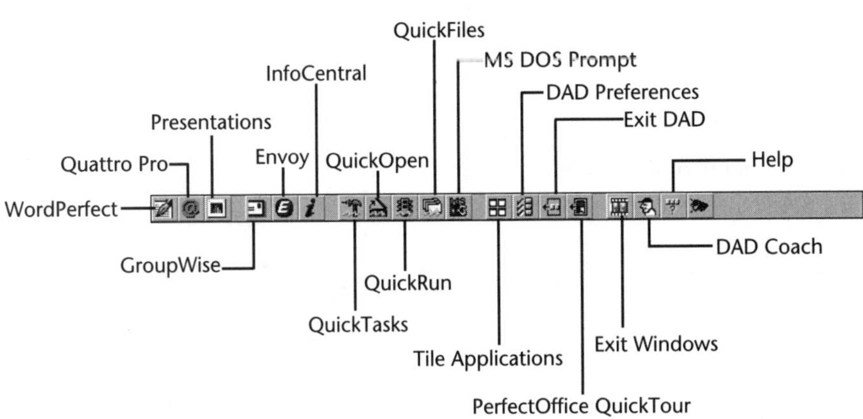

Fig. 2.5
The DAD Bar offers access to PerfectOffice applications and features.

Yes, there are many DAD Bars—not just one. Three DAD Bars ship with PerfectOffice, and you will learn how to create your own in Chapter 36, "Customizing Toolbars, DAD Bars, and Menus." The three that ship with PerfectOffice are:

- *PerfectOffice.* This DAD Bar has icons for all PerfectOffice applications, as well as DAD features including QuickTasks, QuickOpen, QuickRun, and QuickFiles. It also has icons for the MS-DOS prompt, and other DAD assistance features, like the DAD Coach.

- *Control Panel.* This DAD Bar has icons for many of the items found in the Control Panel program group, including Color, Fonts, Port, Mouse, Printer, and so on.

- *Data Sharing.* This DAD Bar has icons for Cut, Copy, and Paste, as well as icons for transferring data between specific PerfectOffice applications.

To switch between DAD Bars, follow these steps:

1. Ensure that the DAD Bar is visible as described earlier.

2. Right-click anywhere in the DAD Bar. You will see a QuickMenu that shows the three standard DAD Bars and one custom DAD Bar called Applications (see fig. 2.6).

Fig. 2.6
Right-clicking the DAD Bar brings up its QuickMenu.

3. Click the name of the DAD Bar you wish to display.

Tip
When DAD is open, you can consider PerfectOffice to be open, because DAD is the integrating tool for PerfectOffice applications.

Opening and Closing PerfectOffice

When you install PerfectOffice, the setup program puts the Desktop Application Director in the Startup program group, so that PerfectOffice loads automatically when you start Windows.

This is by far the best way to use PerfectOffice, because DAD does not use many Windows resources, and it doesn't obscure any other application windows.

If, for some reason, DAD does not load automatically when you start Windows, you can open PerfectOffice by double-clicking the DAD icon in the Novell PerfectOffice program group.

Note

You can make PerfectOffice start automatically by dragging the DAD icon from the PerfectOffice program group to the Startup program group.

Under normal circumstances, you should never need to close PerfectOffice. If, however, you are running short of Windows resources, you can close PerfectOffice by following these steps:

1. Ensure that the DAD Bar is visible.

2. Right click anywhere in the DAD Bar. You see a QuickMenu.

3. Choose Exit. DAD will close and you return to your application or the Program Manager.

Common PerfectOffice Window Elements

Throughout PerfectOffice applications, you will see similar screen elements (see fig. 2.7).

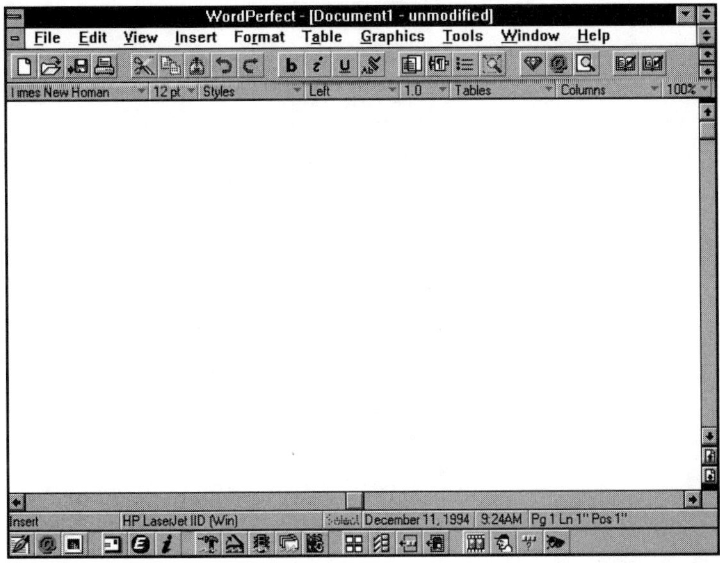

Fig. 2.7
Each PerfectOffice application has similar toolbars, menus, and QuickMenus, as shown in WordPerfect 6.1.

- *Toolbar.* Toolbars appear in all PerfectOffice applications. In some, like WordPerfect and Presentations, more than one toolbar may appear on the screen at once. In all applications, you can rest the mouse pointer on the toolbar to see a QuickTip telling you what the tool is used for. You can always invoke the toolbar feature by clicking the appropriate button. Buttons that are grayed out are for features that are not currently available. For instance, if you have nothing in the Clipboard, the paste icon will be grayed out because there is nothing to paste.

► See "Creating and Editing Toolbars, DAD Bars, and Menu Bars," p. 750

In some applications, you can create and edit your own toolbars.

- *Menus.* All PerfectOffice applications have standard Windows menus. In fact, as discussed in Chapter 1, many of the menu items are identical from application to application.

  You can choose a menu item by clicking it with the mouse, or by holding down the Alt key and pressing the underlined letter of the menu.

  In some applications, you can create and edit your own menus.

- *QuickMenus.* You can right-click different parts of PerfectOffice application windows to see pop-up QuickMenus. QuickMenus offer context-appropriate options to help you do your work more quickly.

  For instance, figure 2.8 shows the QuickMenu that appears when you click the text area of a WordPerfect window. Figure 2.9 shows the QuickMenu that appears when you click the margin.

Paste
Font...
QuickFormat...
Spell Check...
Reveal Codes
Bullets...
Center
Flush Right
Indent

Fig. 2.8
The QuickMenu that displays from the text area of a WordPerfect window helps you with text formatting options.

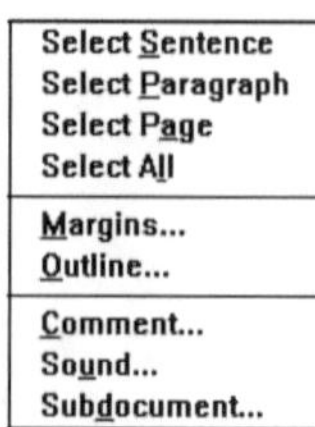

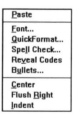

Fig. 2.9
The QuickMenu that appears when you click the margin provides options for selecting text and adding attachments.

Using Help

PerfectOffice offers many different ways to provide help to you. These include:

- An extensive on-line Help system
- Coaches and Experts
- Tutorials

On-Line Help

Help is implemented in a standard Windows Help system. PerfectOffice Help works the same way it does in any other Windows application.

To access the Help system, choose **H**elp from the menu or press F1. What you will see varies slightly between applications. Common choices include:

- *Contents.* This option provides a list of major Help topics. You might think of this as a "main menu" for Help. These often include How Do I, Examples, Search, Additional Help, Macros, and Using Help (see fig. 2.10).

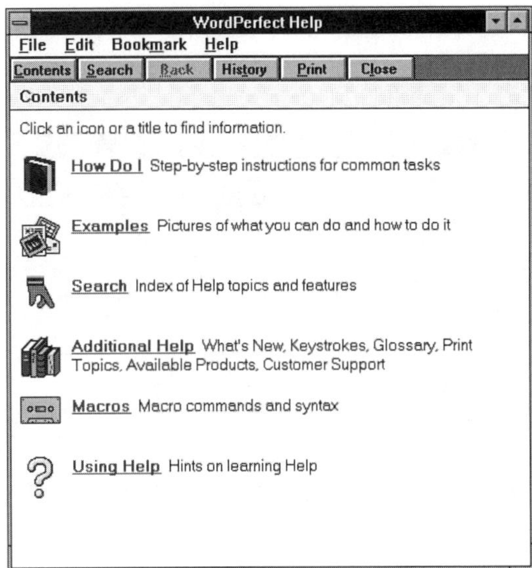

Fig. 2.10
Help Contents serves as a main menu of Help commands.

- *Search for help on.* This option enables you to search for keywords, and shows you a list of topics that relate to the word you have chosen.
- *How Do I?* This provides a list of common tasks that one may wish to do in the application, thus giving you a functional approach to obtaining help.
- *Coaches.* This is a list of coaches available in the product.
- *Experts.* This is a list of experts available in the product (see the following section, "Using Coaches and Experts").

- *Macros.* This takes you to a different Help system—the complete macros manual. This manual provides Help on all macro programming topics and gives examples of each.

Tip
In Help, a term with a dotted underline is a glossary term. You can click it to see its definition.

- *Using Help.* Provides assistance on how to use the Help system.
- *About...* This option provides information on the product, including the version, release date, and other product specific information.

You can also access context-sensitive Help on the function you are selecting by pressing F1 after highlighting a menu choice, by clicking the Help button (if present), or by pressing F1 from a dialog box or window.

While you are in the Help system, the menu offers several options (see fig. 2.11).

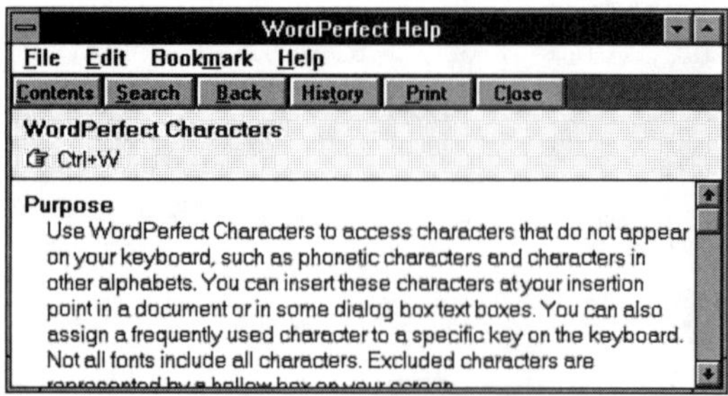

Fig. 2.11
All PerfectOffice Help windows offer similar menu options.

- The **F**ile menu enables you to print a Help topic or open a different Help file.
- The **E**dit menu enables you to copy the Help topic to the Clipboard, where it can be imported into another application. You also can **A**nnotate a Help screen with your own comments. A paper clip indicates the presence of an annotation, which you can then read as desired.
- The Book**m**ark menu enables you to set a bookmark at a Help topic that you use often. Marked topics appear on this menu under the first **D**efine option. Choosing a topic takes you directly to that Help screen.
- **S**earch enables you to search for keywords, and shows you a list of topics that relate to the word you have chosen.
- **B**ack takes you to the last Help topic you have seen.
- His**t**ory shows you a list of all the Help topics you have looked at, and enables you to select one to go back to.

- **P**rint prints the selected Help topic.

- While you are reading a Help screen, you may click an icon to see a definition of that icon. Underlined words are hypertext linked to other topics. You may click an underlined word to jump to help on that topic.

Using Coaches and Experts

You can access the Coaches and Experts available in a PerfectOffice application by choosing **H**elp, C**o**aches or **E**xperts (if they appear). You may also find an option for using an Expert when you perform a function within PerfectOffice. For instance, when you choose **F**ile, **N**ew in WordPerfect, and you choose Publish as the new document group, you see the Newsletter Expert as one of your selections (see fig. 2.12).

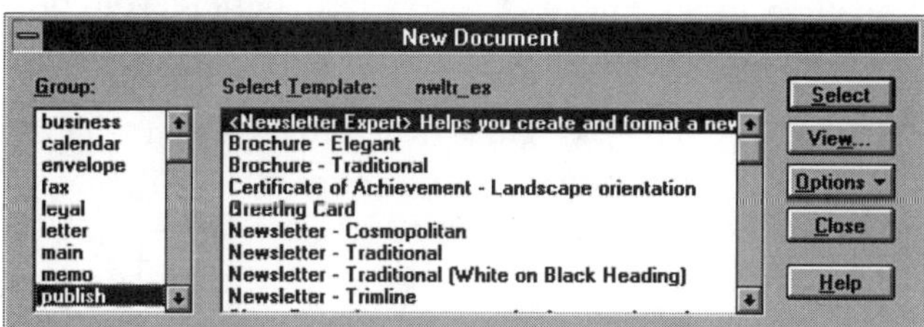

Fig. 2.12
Experts provide context-sensitive Help as you choose options, just as when you choose **F**ile, **N**ew, Publish in WordPerfect.

Similarly, when you create a new document in Presentations, one of the choices in the New Document dialog box is to create a slide show using an Expert (see fig. 2.13).

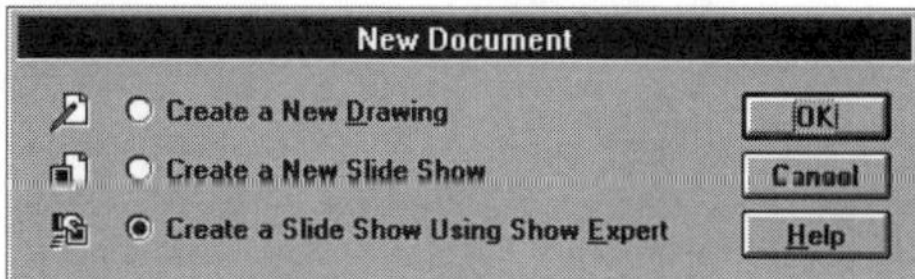

Fig. 2.13
In Presentations, when you create a new slide show, you have the choice of being helped by an Expert.

Using Tutorials

One of the best ways to get to know the PerfectOffice applications is by using the tutorials that come with them. You will find assistance in the different programs in slightly different formats:

- In Quattro Pro and Paradox, choose **H**elp, C**o**aches to learn the basics of how to use the applications (see fig. 2.14).

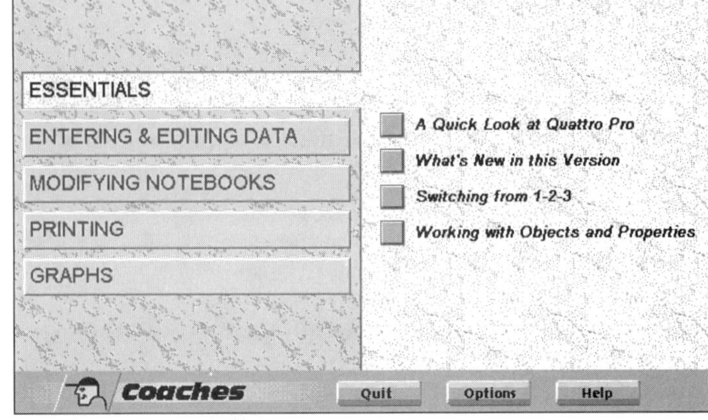

Fig. 2.14
In Quattro Pro and Paradox, choosing **H**elp, C**o**aches helps you learn the new features of the products.

- In WordPerfect, choose **H**elp, **T**utorial to learn the basics. Alternatively, **H**elp, **U**pgrade Expert enables you to select your old word processor, then shows you how to do the same task in WordPerfect 6.1.
- Presentations also has an **U**pgrade Expert in its **H**elp menu that works the same way. Additionally, its Show Expert walks you through creating a new slide show when you choose **F**ile, **N**ew (see fig. 2.15).

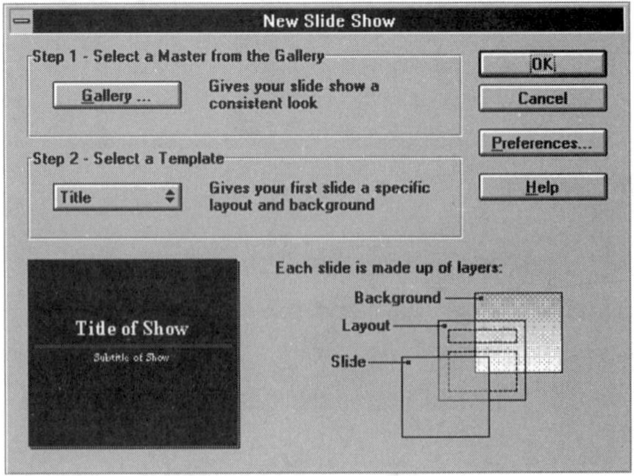

Fig. 2.15
When you create a new file in Presentations, the Show Expert walks you through creating a slide show.

- InfoCentral and the (default) PerfectOffice DAD Bar both have QuickTours. These are interactive screen shows that enable you to see some of the major features of the application. Access the InfoCentral **Q**uickTour from its **H**elp menu. The DAD QuickTour is a button on the PerfectOffice DAD Bar.

From Here...

In this chapter, you were introduced to PerfectOffice, and some of the common features shared by PerfectOffice applications. In the following chapters, you learn about PerfectOffice shortcuts and how to manage files and work areas in PerfectOffice:

- Chapter 3, "Using Common PerfectOffice Tools," teaches you how to use the different types of toolbars offered in PerfectOffice applications. See how the Desktop Application Director (DAD) can be used to find files, launch applications, and more.

- In Chapter 4, "Managing Files," you find out about PerfectOffice's powerful file management capabilities. Learn how to use directory dialog boxes, the QuickFinder, and QuickLists.

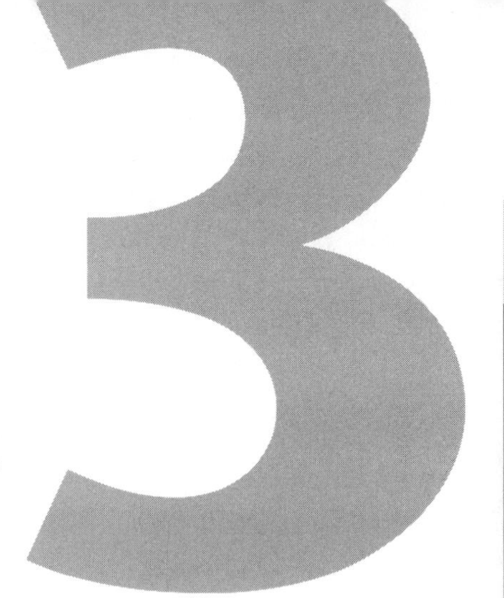

Chapter 3

Using Common PerfectOffice Tools

by Bill Bruck

Even if you will only be using one or two PerfectOffice applications, you might want to read through this chapter. Many things are done similarly in PerfectOffice. This chapter and Chapter 4, "Managing Files," detail these commonalities.

In this chapter, you learn how to

- Use a QuickTask
- Use writing tools including the speller, thesaurus, and grammar checker
- Use QuickMenus and QuickCorrect
- Understand PerfectSense technology

Using QuickTasks

As you learned in Chapter 1, QuickTasks are macros that integrate PerfectOffice applications to assist you in performing common office duties.

To use a QuickTask, follow these steps:

1. Click the QuickTasks button on the DAD Bar. A list of QuickTasks appears, similar to the one shown in figure 3.1.

◄ See "Displaying a DAD Bar," p. 28

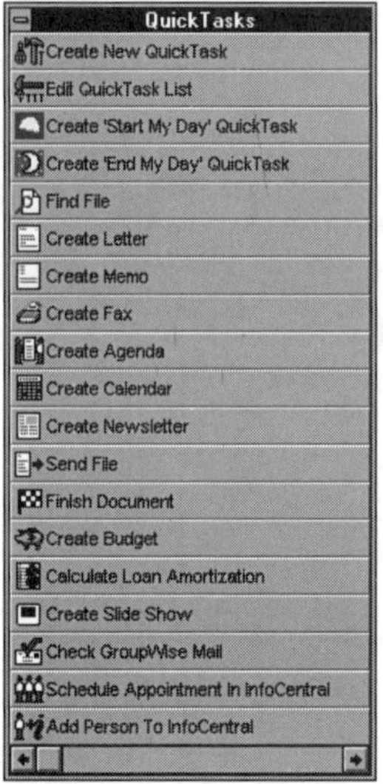

Fig. 3.1
QuickTasks walk you through common office functions with the click of a mouse.

2. Click the QuickTask you wish to use. The appropriate applications will be loaded, and you can follow the prompts to accomplish the task.

For instance, suppose that you are working on a budget in Quattro Pro and you get a phone call. Your boss needs a copy of a WordPerfect memo named C:\MEMOS\PURCHASE.512 that you sent to the Purchasing department last week. You could respond to his request efficiently using the Send File QuickTask by following these steps:

1. Click the QuickTasks button on the DAD bar. You see the QuickTask list.

2. Click the Send File QuickTask. You see the Send a Document QuickTask dialog box (see fig. 3.2).

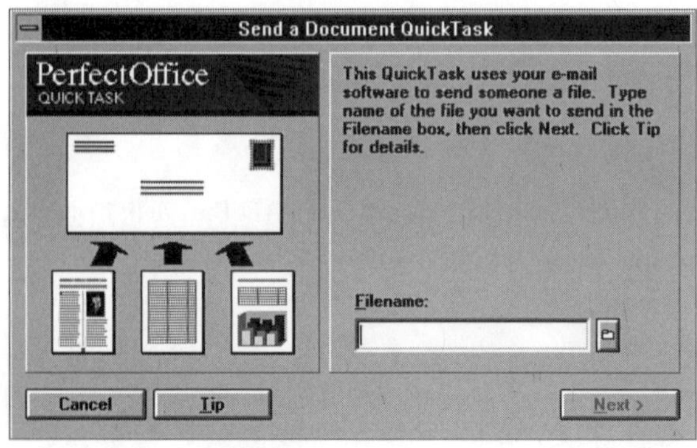

Fig. 3.2
The Send a Document QuickTask automatically e-mails a file you specify.

3. In the **F**ilename box, enter the file name you want to send and click **N**ext.

   GroupWise opens, and you see a Mail To dialog box. The memo is already loaded as an attachment, and your insertion point is right where you need it—in the T**o** box.

4. Enter the UserID of your boss and choose Sen**d**. The memo is sent, and you return to your Quattro budget.

Using the Writing Tools

PerfectOffice offers you powerful tools to assist you in producing a document that looks like it was crafted by a professional. These tools include a spell checker, thesaurus, and grammar checker.

Checking Your Spelling

You can access a common speller from PerfectOffice applications including WordPerfect, Presentations, and GroupWise. Additionally, you can access a speller as a stand-alone application by clicking the Spell Checker icon in the PerfectOffice group in Program Manager.

Note

Quattro Pro uses a different spell-checking interface than other PerfectOffice components. InfoCentral, Paradox, and Envoy have no spell checker.

The Spell Checker checks words in your application against lists of words called dictionaries. There are three different types of dictionaries that the Spell Checker uses:

- *Main Dictionary*. This is the dictionary that ships with PerfectOffice. If you purchase additional language modules, you will have additional main dictionaries for the other languages.

- *Supplementary Dictionary*. When you add a word to the dictionary, it is added to a user-created list of words called the *supplementary dictionary*. You may specify the file that these additional words are added to; thus, you can create any number of supplementary dictionaries. You can also make or purchase such dictionaries for specialty terms.

- *Document Dictionary* (in WordPerfect only). When you use the Skip **A**lways option in the Spell Checker, the word is added to a list of words that is stored with the document itself. Thus, when you check the spelling of the document again, these words are skipped.

You can chain up to nine dictionaries together when you do a spell check. Thus, you can conceivably use your main dictionary, a French dictionary, a medical dictionary, and your own personal list of client names when you spell check a document.

Using the Spell Checker involves three skills:

- Choosing the appropriate dictionaries
- Setting the spell-check options
- Conducting a spell check

Conducting a Spell Check

To conduct a spell check, follow these steps:

1. In WordPerfect, Presentations, or GroupWise, make sure the text you want to check is on-screen.

2. Choose **T**ools, **S**peller or click the Speller button on the toolbar. You see the Spell Checker dialog box (see fig. 3.3).

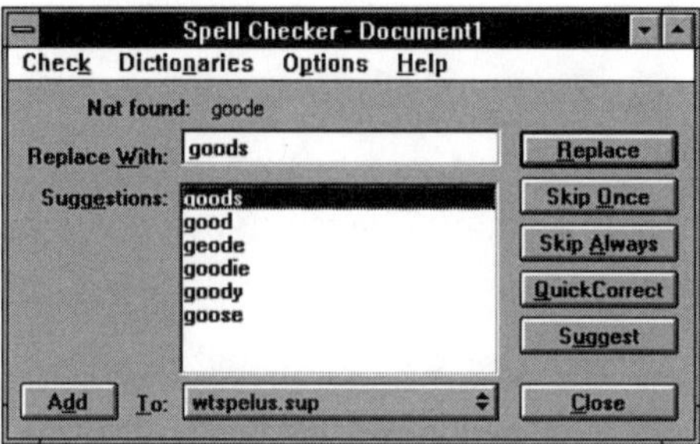

Fig. 3.3
The Spell Checker is available in WordPerfect, Presentations, and GroupWise.

3. The spell-checking procedure may start automatically, depending on how options have been set. If it does not, choose **S**tart.

4. When the Spell Checker pauses at a misspelled word, you have the following options:

   ***R**eplace.* Select a word in the Sugg**e**stions list. It appears in the Replace **W**ith box. (Alternatively, enter a word in the Replace **W**ith box.) Click **R**eplace. The misspelled word in the document is replaced with the specified word.

   *Skip **O**nce.* Skip the word this time, but stop if it appears again in the text being checked.

   *Skip **A**lways.* Skip the word wherever it appears in the text. (In WordPerfect, this will also add the word to the document dictionary.)

   ***Q**uickCorrect.* If you select a word in the Sugg**e**stions list, then choose **Q**uickCorrect; the misspelled word and corrected word are added to the QuickCorrect list. (See "Using QuickCorrect" later in this chapter for details.)

   *S**u**ggest.* This displays any additional possible corrected words in the Sugg**e**stions list box.

   *A**d**d.* This option adds the word to the selected supplementary dictionary file. The word is then always skipped when you spell check any other document.

   ***T**o:* Enables you to change the supplementary dictionary file to which words are added.

5. When the spell check is completed, click **C**lose to close the Spell Checker and return to your application.

Selecting Dictionaries

You may select up to nine dictionaries that the Spell Checker will check potentially misspelled words against. To select dictionaries, follow these steps:

1. Access the Spell Checker as described earlier.

2. Choose Dictio**n**aries, and then choose either **M**ain or **S**upplementary, depending on which type you want to select. You see the Main Dictionaries dialog box (see fig. 3.4), or the Supplementary Dictionaries dialog box, which offers identical functionality.

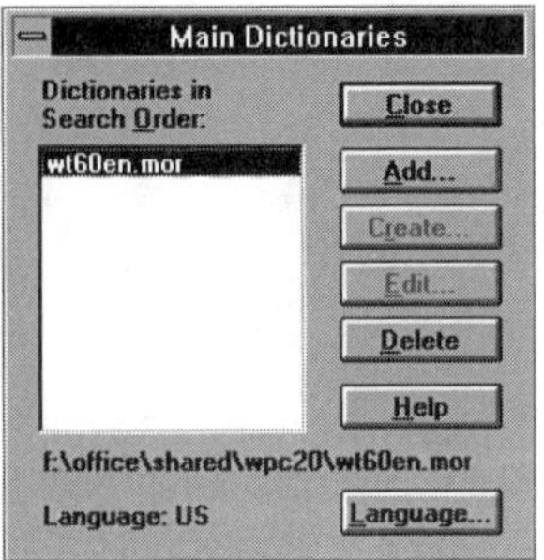

Fig. 3.4
You can chain up to nine dictionaries to be used in spell checking.

3. You may now select from several options:

   - Choose **A**dd to add a new dictionary to the search list, then select the appropriate dictionary from the Select Dictionary dialog box.
   - Choose C**r**eate to create a new supplementary dictionary.
   - Choose **E**dit to edit an existing supplementary dictionary.
   - Choose **D**elete to delete a dictionary from the search list.
   - Choose **L**anguage to specify which dictionaries the Spell Checker should search for.

4. When you are finished selecting dictionaries, choose **C**lose to return to the Spell Checker.

Tip
When editing a supplementary dictionary, you add words, termed *key words*. For each key word you can tell the Spell Checker to skip it, replace it with another word, or specify a list of alternatives.

Setting Spell Checker Options

From the Spell Checker dialog box, if you choose O**p**tions, you can choose from several ways to customize the way the spell checker works:

- *Words with **N**umbers.* When selected, Spell Checker stops at words containing numbers. (This was more often needed when people confused 1's and l's. In some types of modern writing—like computer manuals—many terms do contain numbers, so you might want to disable this feature.)
- ***D**uplicate Words.* When selected, Spell Checker stops when the same word is repeated twice.
- ***I**rregular Capitalization.* When selected, Spell Checker stops at words with odd capitalization, such as ANd or tHe. (Again, computer writers writing WordPerfect books probably wouldn't like this option!)

- *Exhaustive Checking.* This option is only used in foreign languages, where not all suggestions display by default.
- *Auto Replace.* Automatically replaces words that are in a supplementary dictionary and have a replacement term.
- *Auto Start.* Starts spell checking when the Spell Checker dialog box is opened from within an application.
- *Recheck all Text.* Check all text, not just text that has not yet been checked.
- *Document Dictionary.* In WordPerfect, enables the document dictionary that stores words marked Skip Always in previous spell-check sessions.
- *QuickCorrect Dictionary.* Enables the QuickCorrect dictionary to be used along with other dictionaries.
- *Beep on Misspelled.* Beeps when a misspelled word is found.

Using the Thesaurus

You can use PerfectOffice's Thesaurus to find synonyms and antonyms of selected words in several applications, including WordPerfect, Presentations, and GroupWise. You can also open it as a stand-alone application by double-clicking the Thesaurus button in any PerfectOffice program group in which it appears, such as WordPerfect.

To use the Thesaurus in a PerfectOffice application, follow these steps:

1. Place your insertion point in the word for which you want to find a synonym or antonym.
2. Choose **T**ools, **T**hesaurus. You see the Thesaurus dialog box (see fig. 3.5).
3. Highlight the word you want to use as the replacement, and choose **R**eplace. You return to your application, and the selected word is replaced with the one chosen from the Thesaurus.

You may notice that synonyms are arranged in groups within the Thesaurus. A line separates words that are synonyms for the noun, verb, or adjective form of the selected word, or antonyms of the word. Within each of these major groupings, a blank line separates words that deal with variations in meaning of the selected word.

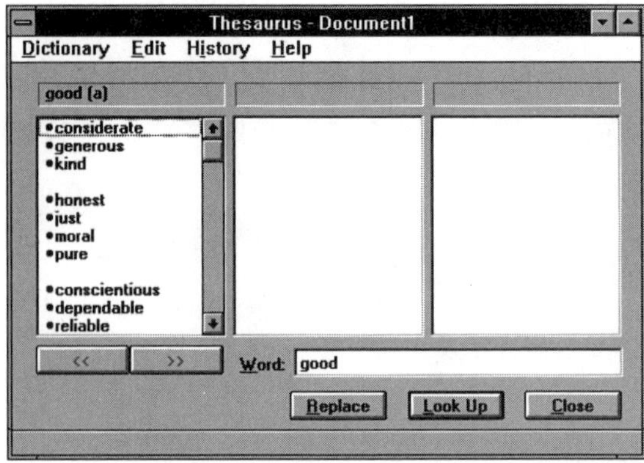

Fig. 3.5
It's easy to choose synonyms with the Thesaurus.

Some words in the synonym list have a dot to the left of them. These are headwords. Headwords are words that you can look up in the Thesaurus to find further synonyms.

While you are in the Thesaurus, you have several options:

- Double-click any word in the suggested word list that has a dot to the left of it to see that word's synonyms and antonyms in the next column. You then can pick a replacement word and choose **R**eplace.

  If you repeat this process several times, you will need more than the three columns provided in the Thesaurus. You can then use the left and right buttons to move from column to column (see fig. 3.6).

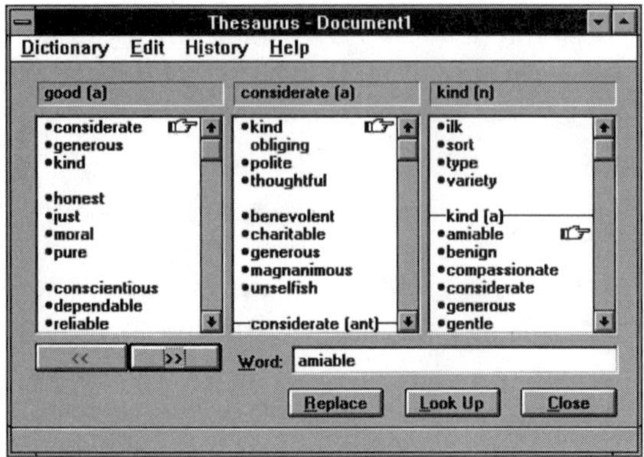

Fig. 3.6
You can find synonyms for any word with a dot to the left of it.

- If you choose **L**ook Up, all columns disappear except the one that is selected.
- You can see a list of all the words that you have shown synonyms for by choosing H**i**story from the Menu Bar.
- Alternatively, you can select **W**ord, then enter in any other word that you wish to look up and press Enter.
- If you select part or all of a term in the **W**ord box, you can choose **E**dit, then cut or copy the selected text. Alternatively, if you have a term in the clipboard, you can choose **E**dit, **P**aste to retrieve this term into the **W**ord box.
- You can also choose an alternative dictionary to use by choosing **D**ictionary, **C**hange Dictionary. You see the Select a WordPerfect Thesaurus dialog box, and all thesaurus dictionaries (files with a .THS extension) are displayed.

Troubleshooting

Why isn't the Thesaurus on the WordPerfect toolbar like the Spell Checker and Grammatik?

I don't know. However, if you use the Thesaurus a lot, you can easily put it on the toolbar in WordPerfect, Presentations, or GroupWise. To do so, right-click the toolbar, then choose **E**dit. With the Edit Toolbar dialog box on-screen, choose **T**ools, **T**hesaurus. The new button appears on your toolbar. Click OK to return to the application.

Checking Grammar

Grammatik, PerfectOffice's grammar checker, can prove to be an invaluable tool to help you refine your writing style. It can be accessed in WordPerfect, GroupWise, and Presentations by clicking its button on the toolbar. You can also open it as a stand-alone application by double-clicking the Grammatik button in any PerfectOffice program group in which it appears, such as WordPerfect.

To use Grammatik in a PerfectOffice application, follow these steps:

1. Open the file you want to check.
2. Choose **T**ools, **G**rammatik. You see the Grammatik dialog box (see fig. 3.7).

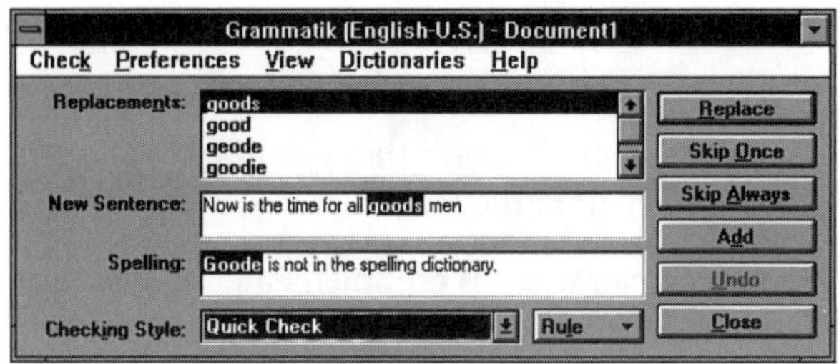

Fig. 3.7
Grammatik will not only flag potential errors, it will suggest corrections for you.

3. Grammatik automatically starts checking your document for grammar and spelling errors. When an error is found, Grammatik will make a change (if possible). You can then choose any of the following:

   - **R**eplace to accept the change to your document.
   - Skip **O**nce or Skip **A**lways to ignore the error one time or throughout the document.
   - A**d**d to add the misspelled word to Grammatik's dictionary.
   - **U**ndo to undo your last change.

4. When you are finished, click **C**lose.

While you are in Grammatik, you may choose from the following options to customize the way the grammar checker works:

- Choose Check**i**ng Style to select from among the ten predefined styles.
- Choose Ru**l**e to turn off a particular grammatical rule, turn it back on, or save the set of rules as a new checking style.
- Choose Chec**k** from the menu bar to check the current **S**entence, **P**aragraph, or **D**ocument. To **E**nd of Document will check from the insertion point forward. Selected **T**ext and Text Entry **B**ox will be grayed out unless text is selected or you are in a text box.
- If you choose **P**references, **C**hecking Styles, you see the Checking Styles dialog box (see fig. 3.8). Choose from ten predefined styles. Each style uses different rules for checking things like spelling, split infinitives, passive voice, long sentences, and so forth.
- Choose **P**references**,** **E**nvironment to set options shown in figure 3.9.

Tip
To see the specifications for each predefined checking style, choose Help from the Checking Styles dialog box. Click Grammar and Writing, and then click the Checking Styles.

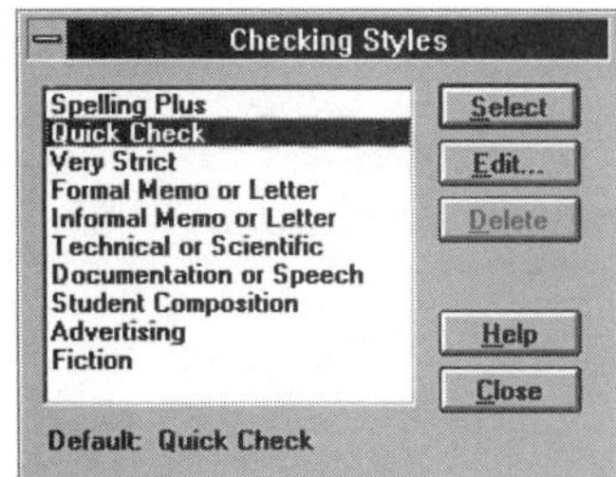

Fig. 3.8
Grammatik comes with ten pre-defined styles that use different rules for grammar checking.

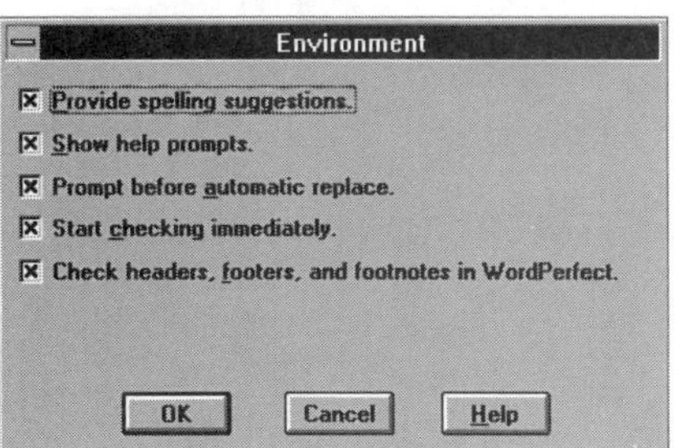

Fig. 3.9
You can specify how Grammatik checks your document in the Environment dialog box.

- You can see some very interesting statistics on your document by choosing **V**iew, **S**tatistics. You can choose among these three types of statistics on your document:

  Basic tells you the total number of syllables, words, sentences, and so on. It also tells the average number of syllables per word, words per sentence and sentences per paragraph.

  Readability compares your document to a Hemingway short story, IRS 1040A instructions, and the Gettysburg Address. You see the Flesh-Kincaid grade level, percent of use of passive voice, sentence complexity, and vocabulary complexity (see fig. 3.10). You can even add sample documents of your own for comparison purposes.

  Flagged statistics list all error classes being checked, and the number of items flagged in each class for your attention.

Using the Automation Tools

In addition to providing writing tools, PerfectOffice offers you tools for improving your efficiency and automating common tasks, including QuickMenus, QuickCorrect, and the PerfectSense technology.

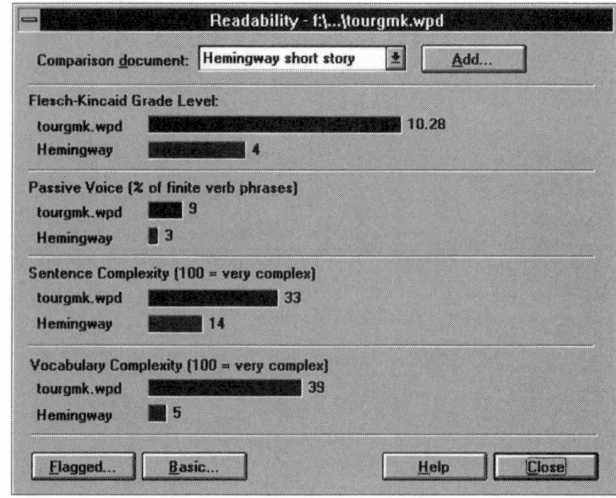

Fig. 3.10 You can compare how your document rates against a story by Hemingway, IRS instructions, or the Gettysburg Address.

Using QuickMenus

QuickMenus are pop-up menus that appear when you click the right mouse button in selected areas within PerfectOffice applications. QuickMenus display context-sensitive options. For instance, the QuickMenu displayed when right-clicking a Quattro Pro cell is shown in figure 3.11. It offers the options most used while entering and formatting data in a spreadsheet.

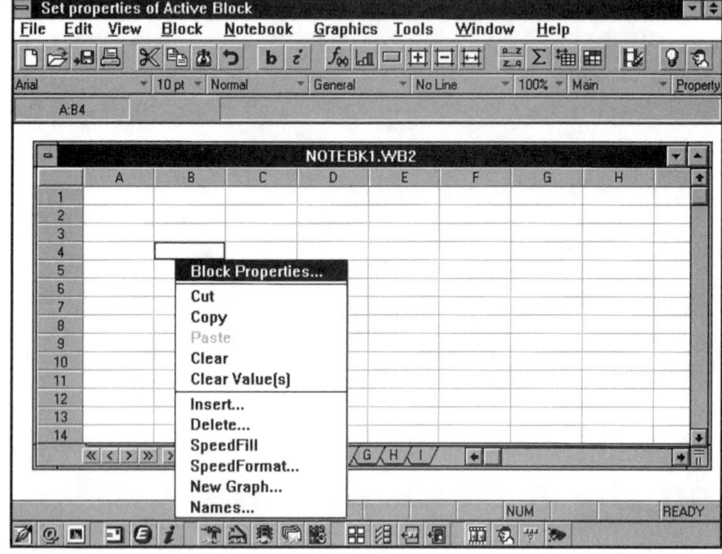

Fig. 3.11 QuickMenus, accessed by clicking the right mouse button, offer context-sensitive options.

Alternatively, the QuickMenu accessible from the main WordPerfect document window is shown in figure 3.12. It provides options used in creating, editing, and formatting text.

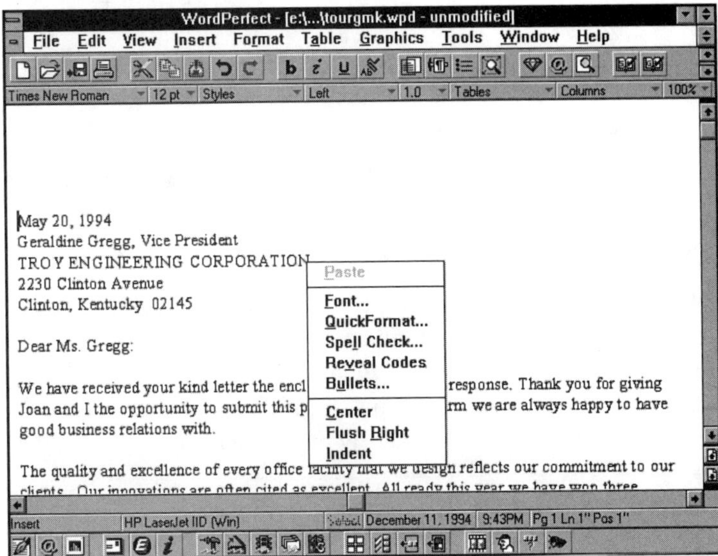

Fig. 3.12
These options are available from the QuickMenu at the main editing window of WordPerfect.

Using a QuickMenu is often more efficient than selecting the same option from a menu or toolbar, since you do not need to move the mouse as much. Though it doesn't seem like much, you will quickly find that once you get used to QuickMenus, they can significantly improve your efficiency.

Using QuickCorrect

QuickCorrect is an intelligent writing tool that helps you avoid common spelling and grammar errors as you type. QuickCorrect is presently found in WordPerfect, Presentations, and GroupWise.

Tip
The same QuickCorrect dictionary is used in all applications. Thus, once you define an automatic correction, it will be made in all applications using QuickCorrect.

QuickCorrect enables you to maintain a list of abbreviations and commonly misspelled words, then automatically replaces these with the correct term or word as you type.

To use QuickCorrect, you need to know how to turn on QuickCorrect, maintain a list of misspelled words, and set options.

To turn on QuickCorrect, choose **T**ools, **Q**uickCorrect. You see the QuickCorrect dialog box (see fig. 3.13). Select the R**e**place Words as You Type checkbox, if there is not already an x in the box. Now, any commonly misspelled words you have identified will automatically be replaced as you type.

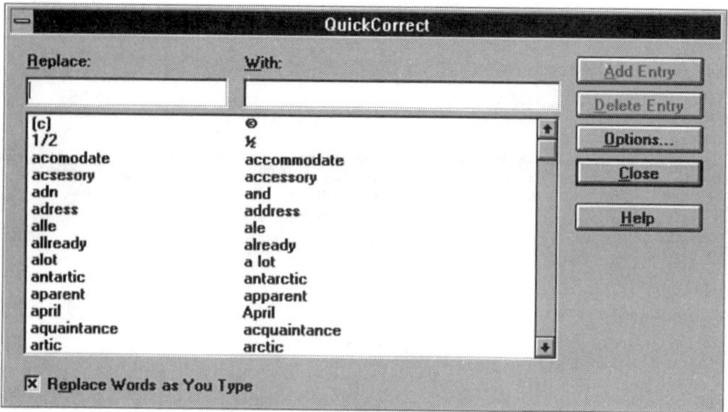

Fig. 3.13
QuickCorrect will correct common spelling errors on-the-fly, as you type.

To add words to the commonly misspelled words list, access the QuickCorrect dialog box. Type a word you often misspell, or an abbreviation you wish to have automatically expanded, in the **R**eplace text box. Type the correct spelling or the expanded term in the **W**ith text box, and then click **A**dd Entry. You see the term in the list of commonly misspelled words.

> **Caution**
>
> Be careful when you add abbreviations to this list. The abbreviation will *always* be replaced by its expanded term; thus, you will not be able to use the abbreviation in the document.

If you choose **O**ptions from the QuickCorrect dialog box, you see the QuickCorrect Options dialog box (see fig. 3.14). You can choose from among the following options:

Tip
Though most people do not know it, typographical convention calls for a single space between sentences when using proportional fonts.

- *Sentence Corrections*. You can automatically capitalize the first letter of each sentence, prevent the first two letters of a sentence from being capitalized, or change any double space in a sentence to a single space.

- *End of Sentence Corrections*. You can change a sentence that ends with a single space to a double space, or change a double space to a single space.

- *Single SmartQuotes*. This option automatically changes apostrophes to single open and single closed quotes. (The first apostrophe is changed to a single open quote; the next to a single closed quote.)

- *Double SmartQuotes*. This option automatically changes the first ' to a double open quote ("), and the next one to a double closed quote (").

- *Use Regular Quotes with Numbers.* This option enables you to use a straight single or double quote following a number.

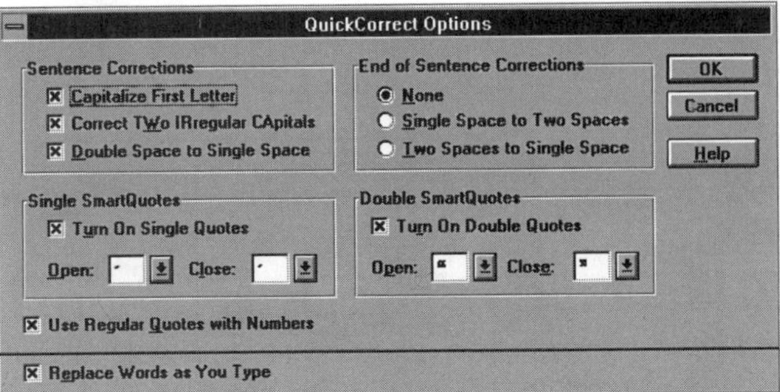

Fig. 3.14
QuickCorrect will even capitalize the first letter of sentences, and adjust the number of spaces after a period for you.

Note

With both the Single and Double SmartQuotes options, you can turn the option on by selecting the appropriate checkbox. You can also specify the character to be used for the SmartQuote symbols.

Tip
Turning on Single SmartQuotes will not cause apostrophes used in possessive words (for example, Sam's) to be turned into SmartQuote symbols.

Troubleshooting

How can I stop QuickCorrect from un-capitalizing PC ATs and PC XTs? It changes them to PC Ats and PC Xts.

You can do this in three ways: First, you can disable irregular case checking by choosing **T**ools, **Q**uickCorrect, **O**ptions, Correct T**W**o Irregular Capitals. However, you may want the feature on for other potential errors.

Second, you can position the insertion point back on the t of Ats or Xts and change it to a T. QuickCorrect will not override this edit.

Third, you can add the terms "Ats" and "Xts" to the QuickCorrect dictionary, and replace them with "ATs" and "XTs".

Understanding PerfectSense Technology

PerfectSense is the term Novell uses for the artificial intelligence built into Grammatik and in the Find and Replace function.

In previous versions, Grammatik could flag errors, but not suggest replacements for them. In its latest version, Grammatik makes the writing process much easier by providing suggestions to correct errors. Thus, in figure 3.15, you can see that the run-on sentence detected in the file is flagged, and by simply choosing **R**eplace, a correct version is substituted.

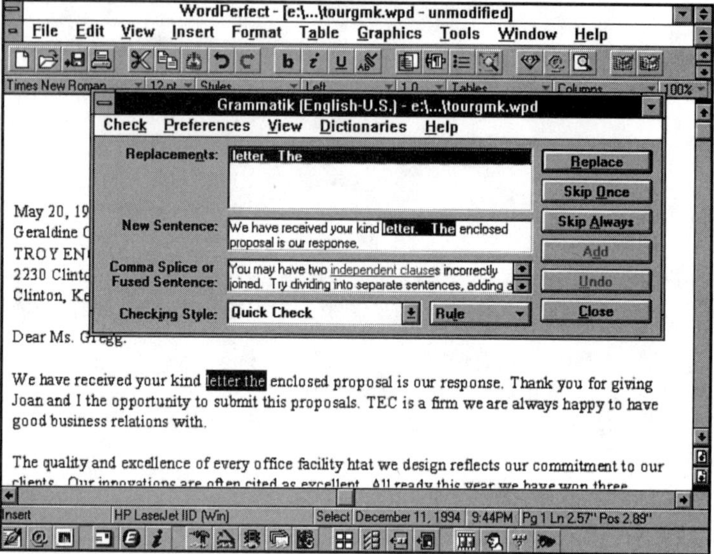

Fig. 3.15
PerfectSense technology enables Grammatik to suggest correct grammar, in addition to flagging possible errors.

Similar intelligence is used in Find and Replace. In the past, you could replace *drive* with *fly*, but if *driving* or *drove* was in the document, no replacement would be made. With PerfectSense technology, searching for *drive* will stop on all forms of the verb, including *driving, drives*, and *drove*. It will replace them with *flying, flies*, and *flown*.

From Here...

You may wish to turn to the chapters on specific applications, but before you do, it might be helpful to look at some of PerfectOffice's powerful file management features:

- In Chapter 4, "Managing Files," you learn about PerfectOffice's powerful file management capabilities. Learn how to use directory dialog boxes, the QuickFinder, and QuickLists.

- See Chapter 5, "Getting Started with WordPerfect," to learn how to use WordPerfect to create common business and personal documents. See how to edit documents, format them, and use a host of shortcuts that will help you automate your word processing work.
- In Chapter 12, "Getting Started with Quattro Pro," you discover how to create everything from simple home budgets to complex spreadsheets involving data analysis and charts.

Chapter 4

Managing Files

by Bill Bruck

Can you imagine an administrative assistant who stacks all correspondence, outgoing letters, internal memos, and other paperwork in one large drawer? What would happen if everyone in a department did this, using a large, common box? We can predict that this organization would not be able to function effectively!

Yet, many of us maintain our electronic files in an equivalent shambles. In this chapter, you learn how to use tools that enable you to create an effective electronic filing system.

In this chapter, you learn how to

- Save, open, and close files
- Use directory dialog boxes
- Create, rename, and remove directories
- Copy, move, rename, delete, print, and assign attributes to files
- Find files using QuickFile, QuickLists, and QuickFinder

Saving, Opening, and Closing Files

When you create a WordPerfect document, Quattro Pro spreadsheet, or Presentations drawing, you are working with a *file*. Files can exist in your computer's memory and on disks. You can think of these electronic files like their paper counterparts.

Your computer's memory is like the surface of a desk that for security reasons is cleared at the end of the day, and everything on it put into the shredder.

You can work on files while they are on your desktop: You can create files, add information to them, or send them to other people. But at the end of the day, unless you put them away, they will be destroyed. Paper files can't stay on the desktop after hours. Similarly, electronic files are destroyed when you turn off your computer, or exit the program that creates them.

Note

For those of you who aren't computer "techies," *memory* is the working area of your computer. When you are using programs, they are loaded into memory. When you open a file, it is loaded into memory. The programs and data that are in memory are lost when you turn off your computer.

Disks are storage areas—whether they're floppy disks, local hard disks (in your own computer), or network drives. You do not "run" programs from the disk. You load a program from the disk into memory when you open it. Then, when it is in memory, you can use it. Similarly, you load data from your disk into memory to access it. Data on disks is maintained even when you turn off your computer.

Tip
Memory is the generic term for Random Access Memory, or RAM.

Your disk is like your file cabinet. You can keep files in it indefinitely—until it gets full. Then, you can add another file cabinet, until your office gets full of cabinets! A better idea is to purge files in your file cabinet periodically, so that you only keep the ones you need. Until you take a file from the file drawer and put it on your desk, however, you can't work on it. Similarly, electronic files can stay on a disk indefinitely, but until you load them into memory, you can't work on them.

In fact, the analogy can be carried further: You can think of each disk drive as a file cabinet. Each disk can contain directories—like file cabinets contain file drawers. Each drawer can contain hanging folders and/or loose sheets of paper, while directories can contain subdirectories and/or files. Each hanging folder can contain manila folders and/or sheets of paper, while subdirectories can contain other subdirectories and/or files.

Thus, whether you are working in WordPerfect, Quattro Pro, Presentations, or other PerfectOffice applications, you need to save your work if you wish to be able to access it after you turn off your computer. You also need to be able to retrieve it from the disk into memory when you want to edit it again.

> **Note**
>
> In most applications, files exist only in memory until they are saved. Thus, if you work on a spreadsheet and add 100 rows of information without saving your work, then the power goes off, you will lose that work. Databases like Paradox and InfoCentral work somewhat differently. Once the database is created, each record is saved on the disk as it is created or edited. Thus, the most information you will lose in a power failure are changes to the current record.

Saving Files

Saving a file is like taking a copy of it from your desktop and putting it into a file drawer. To save a file means storing it on a disk—either a floppy disk, your local hard drive, or a network drive. After you save a file, it exists in two places—in memory and on the disk.

In all PerfectOffice applications, you can save the file you are working on by choosing **F**ile, **S**ave. If the toolbar is displayed, you may also click the Save button. The first time you save the file, you see a Save As dialog box (see fig. 4.1). Type the name of the file in the File**n**ame text box and click OK to save your work.

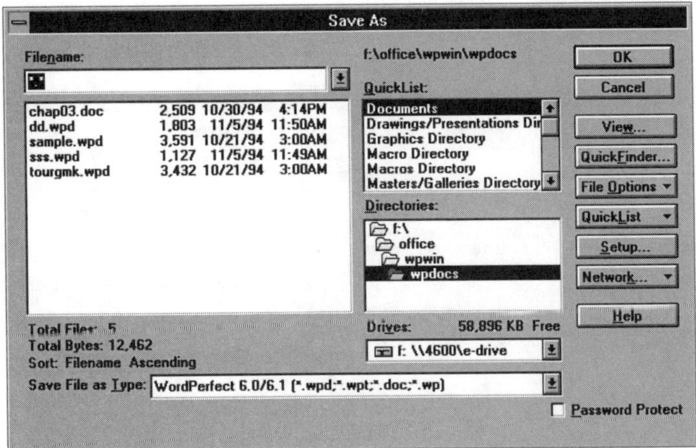

Fig. 4.1
The first time you save a file, you see the Save As dialog box, enabling you to name the file.

You can also save the file in a different drive and/or directory by choosing the appropriate drive and directory, as explained in the section, "Using Directory Dialog Boxes."

> **Tip**
>
> Many people consider it bad practice to store your files in a subdirectory that holds your application files. Consider making a separate WPDOCs directory under the root directory.

When you want to save your work again, choose **F**ile, **S**ave, or click the Save button on the toolbar. You do not see a dialog box. The operation happens immediately. When you re-save your work in this way, the first version is replaced on the disk by the second; thus, the earlier file is lost.

Tip
Be sure you don't mind losing your earlier version before pressing Save on the toolbar. Your new version will replace the old on the disk.

To save both versions, you need to either save the second one with a different name or in a different directory. You cannot have two files with the same name in the same directory. Choose **F**ile, Save **A**s to rename the latter version. You will see the Save As dialog box, and can rename the document prior to saving it.

Opening Files

Opening a file is like taking a copy of it from your file drawer and putting it on your desk. It then exists in two places—in the file drawer and on your desk. When you make changes to it, the original is still safely in the file drawer. The original copy in the file drawer is only changed when you save the edited version again.

Thus, when you open a file in any application except for Paradox and InfoCentral, you are retrieving a copy of the file from the disk to your computer's memory. In all PerfectOffice applications, you can open a file by choosing **F**ile, **O**pen. If the toolbar is displayed, you can also click the Open button. In either case, you see an Open File dialog box similar to the one shown in figure 4.2.

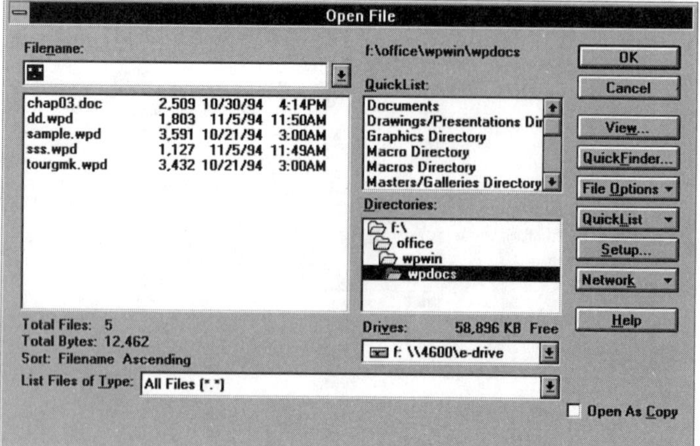

Fig. 4.2
Choose files to open from the Open File dialog box, which also provides many file management capabilities.

Closing Files

Closing a file is like taking it off of your desktop and shredding it. If you have saved it prior to closing it, it is in your file cabinet (or electronically, on your disk). Otherwise, it is gone for good.

Thus, when you close a file in any application except for Paradox and InfoCentral, you are erasing it from your computer's memory. In Perfect-Office applications, you close a file by choosing **F**ile, **C**lose. If the file has been edited since it was last saved, you will be prompted to save it prior to closing it. Unless you wish to lose your work, it's a good idea to do so!

Note

When you close an application, you will also close any open files in that application. Thus, when you close an application that has modified, open files, you will be prompted to save them before the application closes.

Troubleshooting

Why isn't there a button to close a file like there is to save or open a file?

There is—but it's not on the toolbar. You can double-click the control menu button that is on the left side of the Menu bar to close the active document. There are actually two control menu buttons. The one on the left of the Title Bar is the application control menu button. Double-clicking it closes the application. The lower one on the Menu bar is the control menu button that controls the document.

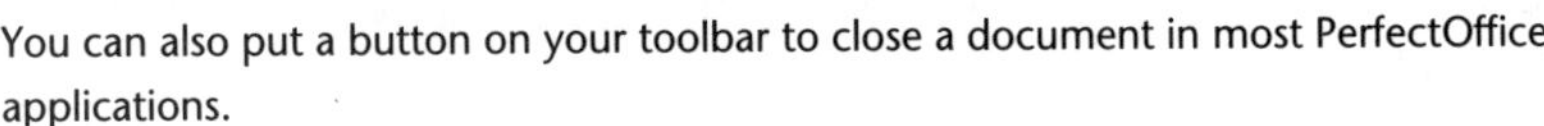

You can also put a button on your toolbar to close a document in most PerfectOffice applications.

Using Directory Dialog Boxes

PerfectOffice offers extremely powerful file management features through *directory dialog boxes*. You see a directory dialog box whenever you use any feature that offers you options while saving or retrieving files—for example, File Open, File Save As, Insert File, Insert Object, and so forth. In fact, any time you can select a file using a Browse button, you will be taken to a directory dialog box. Directory dialog boxes are so helpful for file management, there is even one on the PerfectOffice DAD Bar called QuickFiles.

Depending on their function, directory dialog boxes will have some different options. However, you will see common options in all directory dialog boxes, as exemplified in the QuickFiles dialog box (see fig. 4.3).

Fig. 4.3
All directory dialog boxes have similar file management options.

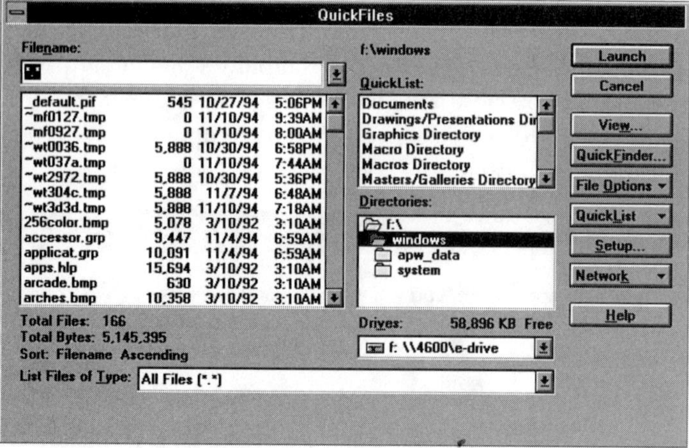

Note

You may see a QuickList list box, a Directories list box, or both, depending on how your QuickList options are set. See "Using QuickLists" for more information.

In this dialog box, notice the following features that appear in all directory dialog boxes:

Tip
You can display a subset of files in the File List box by typing wildcards in the File**n**ame text box, and pressing Enter. For instance, ***.WPD** will show all files with the extension .WPD—that is, WordPerfect Documents.

- *File **n**ame text box.* This text box enables you to type in the name of the file to be saved or opened.
- *File list box.* This box lists all files in the currently selected directory. Choose a file by double-clicking it, or click it and then click Launch. Beneath the file list box, you see the total files meeting the criteria in the File**n**ame box, the total bytes (characters) of disk space taken up by these files, and how the files are sorted.
- ***D**irectories list box.* This box lists the directories on the path to the currently selected directory, and the subdirectories of the currently selected directory. For instance, in the displayed QuickFiles dialog box, the currently selected directory specified near the top of the dialog box is F:\WINDOWS. In the Directory list box, you see the root directory (F:\) and the windows directory, which is highlighted. You also see the subdirectories of windows: apw_data and system.

Note

To choose a different directory, double-click it. The files in that directory will then appear in the files list box. If the directory you desire is not displayed (for example, C:\OFFICE\WPC20), first choose a directory that is common to the currently selected directory and the desired directory. In this case, C:\OFFICE is common to both. Then you see WPC20 displayed as a subdirectory of C:\OFFICE, and you can double-click it to choose it.

- *Drives text box*. This box lists the currently selected drive. To select another drive, click the down arrow to the right of the text box. All available drives will be listed; click the one you want to choose.

- *List Files of **T**ype* (directory dialog boxes that open files). By default, all files (*.*) are listed. You can choose to see only files of specified types by clicking the down arrow to the right of this text box. You see a list of various types of documents, and can choose the desired type—WP Templates, Quattro Pro spreadsheets, and so forth.

- *Save Files as **T**ype* (directory dialog boxes that save files). By default, files will be saved in the format of the application which creates them. You can choose to save the file in another format by clicking the down arrow to the right of this text box. You see a list of various types of formats, and can choose the desired type—WordPerfect 5.1, 6.0, 6.1, Word 2.0, Word 6.0, and so forth.

- *OK* (directory dialog boxes that save or open files); or *Launch* (QuickFiles dialog box). This is the "action" button that opens or saves the appropriate file. In the QuickFiles dialog box, the Launch button opens the file and the appropriate application.

- *Cancel*. Closes the directory dialog box and takes no further action.

- *Vie**w***. Choosing Vie**w** opens a window on the screen that displays the selected file (see fig. 4.4). You can move the Viewer window by dragging the Title Bar, or size it by dragging an edge or corner of the Viewer window. To close the Viewer, double-click the control menu box at the top-left corner of the Viewer window.

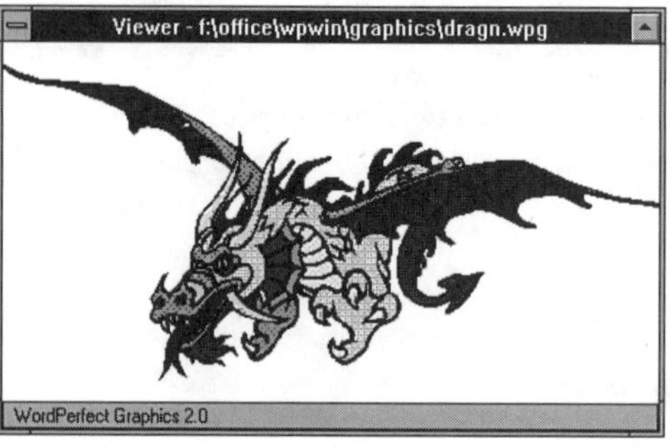

Fig. 4.4
You can preview files prior to opening them by using the Viewer window.

> **Note**
>
> PerfectOffice's viewer technology enables you to view over 130 different types of files. These include all major word processing, spreadsheet, and graphics formats. While viewing a file, you can scroll through it using the scroll bars in the Viewer window. You cannot, however, edit the file.

Tip
Right-click anywhere in the Viewer window to access viewer options. This QuickMenu lets you specify the viewer font, print the viewed file, find words in the file, and several other options.

- *Quick**F**inder.* Use this to rapidly search through the contents of files to find the file you are looking for. See "Using QuickFinder" for more details.

- *File **O**ptions.* Select a file or files, then choose File **O**ptions. You see the pop-up menu shown in figure 4.5. You can then manage your files by copying, moving, renaming, deleting, printing, or changing their attributes. You can perform similar operations on directories.

Fig. 4.5
File Options give you total control to manage your files and directories.

- *Quick**L**ist.* Display a list of commonly used directories with English names using this option. See "Using QuickLists" for details.

- ***S**etup.* Use this option to modify your file list display and sorting order (see fig. 4.6). You can choose to display the filename only, the filename, size, date, and time, the descriptive name (if available) and filename, or to show custom columns.

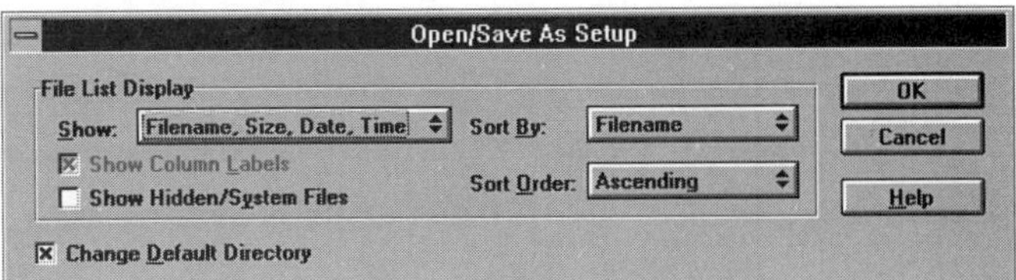

Fig. 4.6
Setup enables you to make default changes to the sort order and what information displays about files.

> **Caution**
>
> Setup options remain as defaults for future PerfectOffice sessions. This can be problematic if you wish to sort files temporarily by date, then forget that this is a permanent change.

- *Network*. If you are on a network, this button appears and (depending on your network type) enables you to log on to and out of the network, change network connections, and perform other network tasks.

> **Troubleshooting**
>
> *Is there any quick way to get to a particular file when there are more files in the list than display in the File list box?*
>
> Sure! Click once in the File list box to select it, then start typing the filename. As you type, your position in the list will move to the first file that starts with the letters you have typed.

Managing Directories

If you remember our original analogy, directories and subdirectories are like the drawers, hanging folders, and manila folders in a file cabinet (disk drive). They are used to organize your work, and enable you to create a system for maintaining your files.

In order to manage the directories that make up your electronic filing system, you need to be able to create, remove (delete), and rename directories. All of these can easily be accomplished from any directory dialog box by following these steps:

1. Access a directory dialog box.
2. Choose File **O**ptions. You see a pop-up menu appear, like the one in the QuickFiles dialog box (see fig. 4.7).

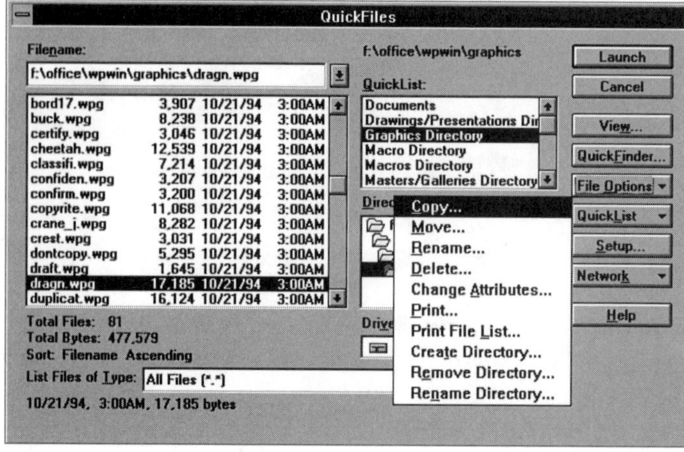

Fig. 4.7
You can create, remove, or rename directories by choosing File **O**ptions in directory dialog boxes.

Tip
You can access these options via a QuickMenu by right-clicking the directory list.

3. Use the following instructions to complete the operation you need:

- To create a directory, choose Crea**t**e Directory. You see a Create Directory dialog box. Type the path name of the new directory and choose Create. The new directory is created, and you return to the directory dialog box.

- To remove a directory, first select the directory by clicking it in the **D**irectories list box, and then choose R**e**move Directory. You see a Remove Directory dialog box with the currently selected directory listed as the Directory to Remove. Choose Remove to confirm the removal. If the directory contains files and/or subdirectories, you will be informed of this fact, and will need to reconfirm the removal of the directory.

> **Caution**
>
> Removing a directory with files in it deletes the files from the disk. These files may not be able to be retrieved after the directory has been removed, even by the system administrator. Use this command with care.

- To rename a directory, first select the directory by clicking it in the **D**irectories list box, and then choose Re**n**ame Directory. You see the Rename Directory dialog box, with the currently selected directory listed in the From text box. Specify a different directory, if needed, by entering it in the From text box, and enter the new name in the To text box. Choose Rename. The directory is renamed and you return to the directory dialog box.

Working with Files

There are two goals of file management:

- To ensure the integrity of data files
- To ensure that data files can be easily found and accessed

The first goal is primarily the job of the system administrator, who must create and maintain backup systems, virus checkers, and other strategies to ensure data integrity.

The second goal is primarily yours. It is achieved through two methods: good organization and file finding tools. File finding tools like QuickFinder and QuickLists are discussed later, but they are no substitute for good organization.

You will primarily organize your files using directories; to keep a well organized electronic office, you will need to delete obsolete files, move files to new directories you create, and copy files from one directory or disk to another. In addition, PerfectOffice gives you the ability to change files' attributes (read-only, archived, and so forth), print files, and print file lists.

To perform these file management functions, follow these steps:

1. Access a directory dialog box.
2. Select the file or files you want to perform operations on:
   - To select one file, click it.
   - To select a number of sequential files, drag the mouse pointer over them.
   - Alternatively, to select a number of sequential files, click the first one, then hold the shift key down and click the last one.
   - To select a number of non-sequential files, click the first one, then hold down the Ctrl key and click the other ones in turn.
3. Choose File **O**ptions. You see a pop-up menu appear, like the one shown earlier in figure 4.7.
4. Choose to copy, move, rename, delete, print, or even change file attributes with File **O**ptions.
   - To copy, move, or rename the selected file(s), choose **C**opy, **M**ove, or **R**ename. You see a dialog box like the Copy File dialog box

Tip
You can also access these options via a QuickMenu by right-clicking the file list.

Tip
Copy files by dragging them to a directory on the directory list or the QuickList. Move files by holding the shift key while dragging them to another directory.

shown in figure 4.8. (The Move and Rename File dialog boxes have similar options.) If only one file is selected, you can specify a different file than the selected one to be copied, moved, or renamed, and a path and/or filename to copy, move, or rename the file to. You can specify a new path, a new filename, or both. (If more than one file is selected, the dialog boxes tell you that you are acting on selected files, and you can only specify the path to copy, move, or rename them to.) When copying, you can also indicate that the command should not replace files with the same size, date, and time to speed up copying by ignoring identical files.

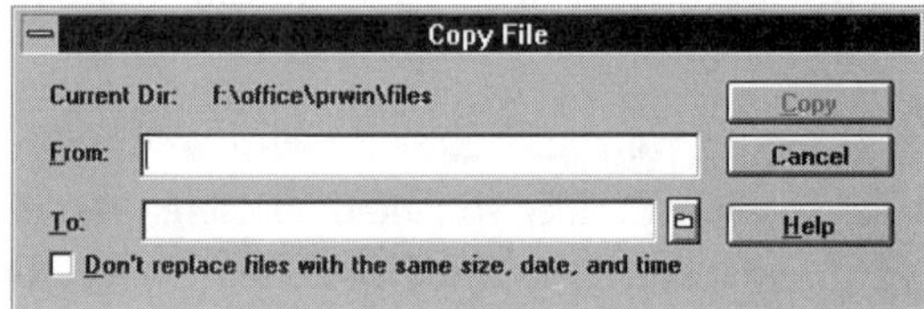

Fig. 4.8
Copy files by specifying the file to be copied, and the directory and/or name for the new file.

- To delete the selected file(s), choose Delete, or press the Del key. You see a Delete File dialog box (see fig. 4.9). To delete the selected file, choose **D**elete. To delete a different file, enter its path and filename then choose **D**elete. (If more than one file is selected, the Delete Files dialog box asks you to confirm the deletion of the selected files. To do so, choose **D**elete.)

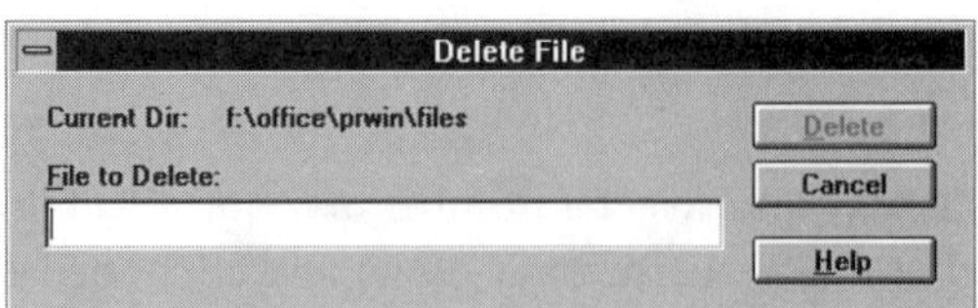

Fig. 4.9
To delete a file, specify its name, and then verify the action by choosing **D**elete.

- To change the attributes of selected file(s), choose Change Attributes. If one file is selected, you see the Change File Attributes dialog box (see fig. 4.10), and you can enter a different filename if desired. If more than one file is selected, the Change File Attributes dialog box does not offer this option. Choose **A**rchive to indicate to backup programs that the selected files need to be backed up (archived); Hidde**n** to prevent selected files from being shown in directory lists or found in QuickFinder searches; **R**ead-Only to ensure that others who open the file cannot edit it; or

System to indicate that the selected programs are part of the operating system and are not be shown in directory lists or QuickFinder searches. When you have chosen the file attributes, click OK to perform the changes and return to the directory dialog box.

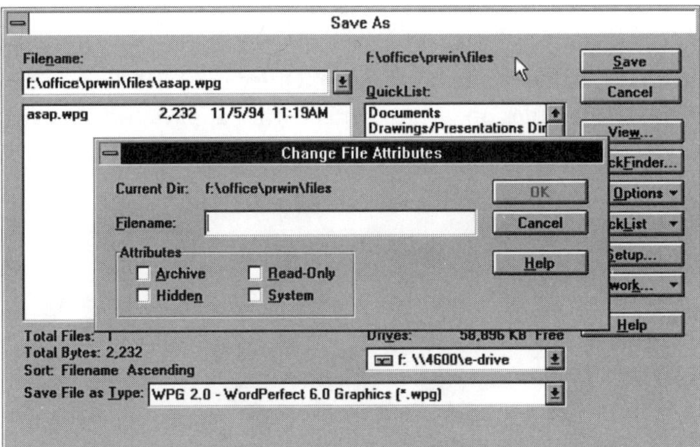

Fig. 4.10
You can use PerfectOffice's directory dialog boxes to change file attributes.

- Choose Print, File List to print a list of the files in the file list box.
- On some directory dialog boxes, you will see a Print option. If available, this option will print the selected files without opening them into a document window.

Finding Files

Sometimes, even with the powerful file management tools at your disposal, you forget where you have filed an important document. Or someone else in your office comes to you and says, "Can you get that memo that I did sometime last month? It was about Providence National Bank." In the past, this could have been a full day job. Not any more!

PerfectOffice is unsurpassed at helping you to find the files you need. It includes three powerful tools to prevent files from getting "misplaced."

- **QuickOpen** lists the last ten files opened in *any* PerfectOffice application.
- **QuickLists** enable you to give English names to commonly used directories and groups of files.

- The **QuickFinder** enables you to search through your files and create a list of all files with specific words or phrases in them.

Using QuickOpen

Useability research by Novell, Inc. shows that a high percentage of people—when they first start up their computer—need to open one of the last ten files they worked on. Realizing this, Novell created QuickOpen.

◄ See "Displaying a DAD Bar," p. 28

QuickOpen is available through the PerfectOffice DAD Bar. It provides a pop-up list of the last ten files opened in PerfectOffice applications (see fig. 4.11). Double-clicking any of these files will launch the appropriate application, and open the selected file in it.

Fig. 4.11
QuickOpen shows you the last ten files opened in PerfectOffice applications.

QuickOpen will show up to the last four files opened in any single PerfectOffice application, and up to ten files for all applications combined. (Files opened in other applications that are not part of the PerfectOffice suite will not be included.)

Using QuickLists

A QuickList is a list of directories and file groups that can be displayed in directory dialog boxes, as shown in the Save As dialog box (see fig. 4.12).

QuickLists enable you to quickly access the files you use most. One QuickList item can be used to display all files for a particular project—for example, H:\PROJECTS\J&D-INC*.*. Another can show all WordPerfect graphics files in a common directory—for example, W:\OFFICE\CLIPART*.WPG.

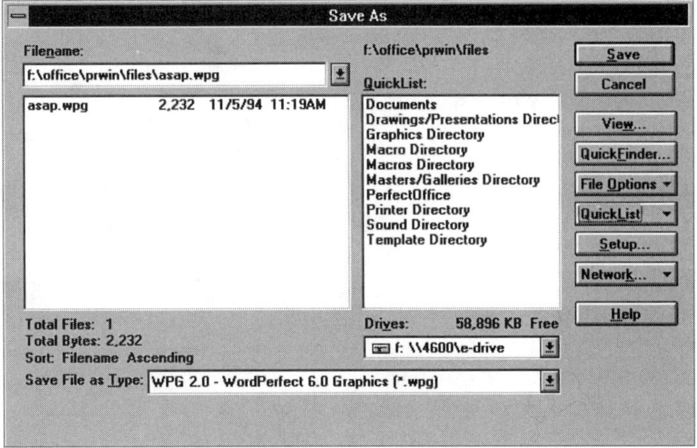

Fig. 4.12
QuickLists can show directories (C:\WPDOCS*.*) or specific groups of files (C:\WPDOCS*.WPG).

One particularly nice aspect of PerfectOffice's integration is that you see the *same* QuickList items in *every* directory dialog box of *every* PerfectOffice application!

To effectively use QuickLists, you need to know how to display a QuickList list box, and add, edit, delete, or print QuickList items.

Displaying QuickLists

The QuickList list box is shown in PerfectOffice directory dialog boxes. While directory dialog boxes are displayed in a variety of circumstances, one of the most common is when you choose **F**ile, **O**pen or click the File Open button on the toolbar.

Tip
You also find QuickLists in the directory dialog boxes you access when choosing a macro, inserting figures or files, and attaching files to messages in GroupWise.

The QuickList list box may not display in your directory dialog box, depending on how you set your QuickList options. Directory dialog boxes can show both QuickLists and Directories, QuickLists only, or Directories only. To modify the display of QuickLists from a directory dialog box, choose Quick**L**ist. You see a pop-up menu such as that shown in figure 4.13. Choose Show **Q**uickList, Show **D**irectories, or Show **B**oth as you prefer.

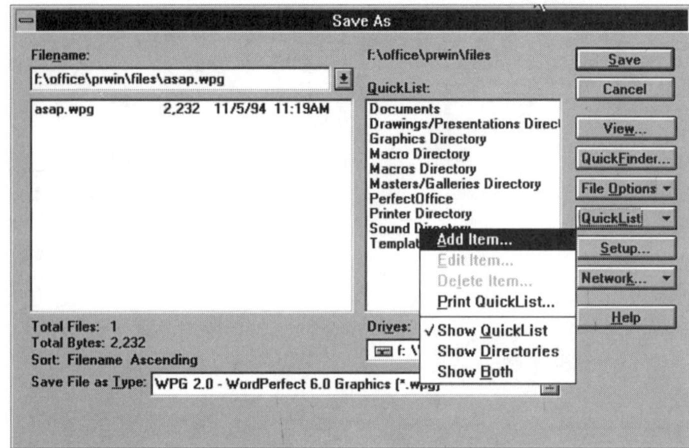

Fig. 4.13
Directory dialog boxes can show QuickLists, Directories, or both.

Tip
Modify the display of QuickList and Directory list boxes by right-clicking in either list box. You can then choose Show **Q**uickList, Show **D**irectories, or Show **B**oth.

Managing QuickList Entries

Once you have QuickLists displayed, you can easily add or edit QuickList entries by following these steps:

1. Access a directory dialog box as described above.
2. Choose Quick**L**ist, and then choose **A**dd Item. You see the Add QuickList Item dialog box (see fig. 4.14).

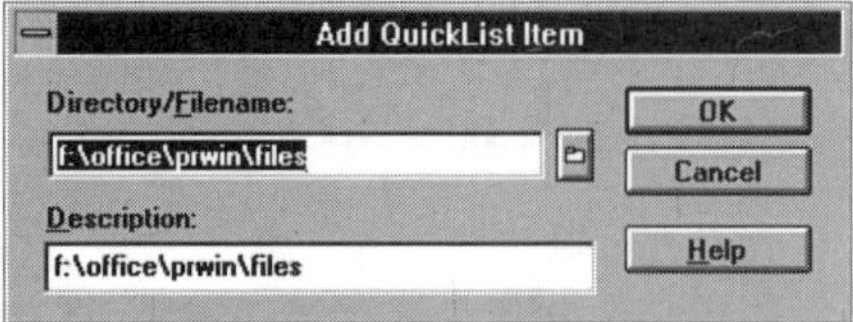

Fig. 4.14
You can add any number of items to your QuickList item list.

3. Specify the Directory/**F**ilename of the QuickList. Type the directory's name, or use the Browse button to access a Select Directory box (see fig. 4.15). You can then choose a directory from the **D**irectories list box.

> **Note**
>
> You can specify a group of files within a directory. For instance, C:*.BAT selects all files with the extension BAT in the root directory of the C: drive. H:\SMITH.R* selects all files in the home directory with the name SMITH, and an extension beginning with R.

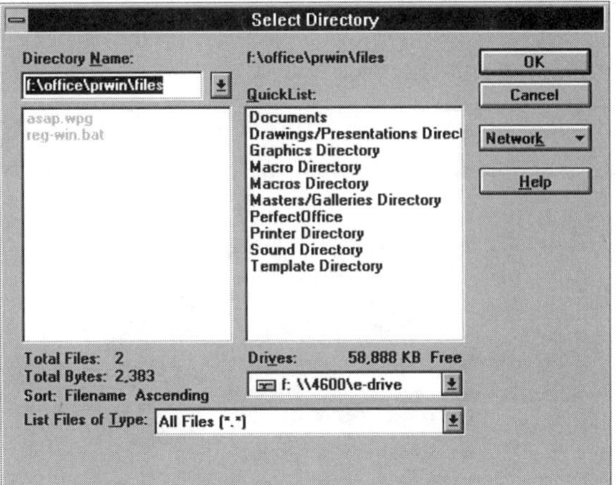

Fig. 4.15
If you prefer not to type the name of a directory for a QuickList entry, use the Browse button to choose the directory from the Select Directory dialog box.

4. Specify a description for your new QuickList item. Items are displayed alphabetically and approximately 25 characters will show in the list box.

5. Choose OK. The new item is displayed in the QuickList list box.

Note

You can edit a QuickList item using the same basic steps used to create an item. From the directory dialog box, select the item to be edited, then choose Quick**L**ist, **E**dit Item. The Edit QuickList Item dialog box works just as the Add QuickList Item dialog box does, except that the current Directory/**F**ilename and **D**escription appear.

To delete a QuickList item, follow these steps:

1. Access a directory dialog box.

2. Select the QuickList item to be deleted.

3. Choose Quick**L**ist, and then choose De**l**ete Item.

4. Confirm the deletion by choosing **Y**es. You return to the directory dialog box, and the QuickList item is deleted. (No directory or file is deleted—merely the QuickList item referring to them.)

To print a QuickList, follow these steps:

1. Access a directory dialog box.

2. Choose Quick**L**ist, then choose **P**rint QuickList. You see a Print QuickList dialog box such as the one shown in figure 4.16.

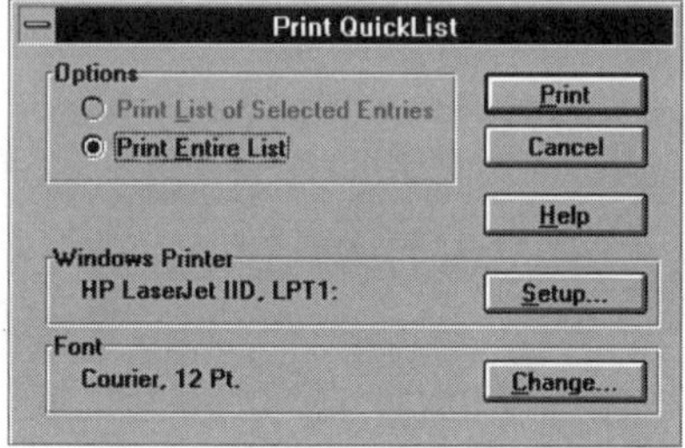

Fig. 4.16
You can print your QuickLists from the Quick**L**ist option in directory dialog boxes.

3. If needed, choose **S**etup to select a different printer, change print orientation, paper size, paper tray, or other print options.

4. If needed, choose **C**hange to select a different font for the printout.

5. Choose **P**rint. The list of QuickList items will print and you will return to the directory dialog box.

Using QuickFinder

QuickFinder is an indexing program that enables you to quickly find files that contain selected text anywhere in them. It does so by creating *indexes*—files that contain a list of the words in each file that you wish included in the index.

Thus, before you can use QuickFinder to find files, you must create an index. You will want to periodically update the indexes that you create.

You may access the QuickFinder from any directory dialog box, by clicking Quick**F**inder. You see the QuickFinder dialog box (see fig. 4.17).

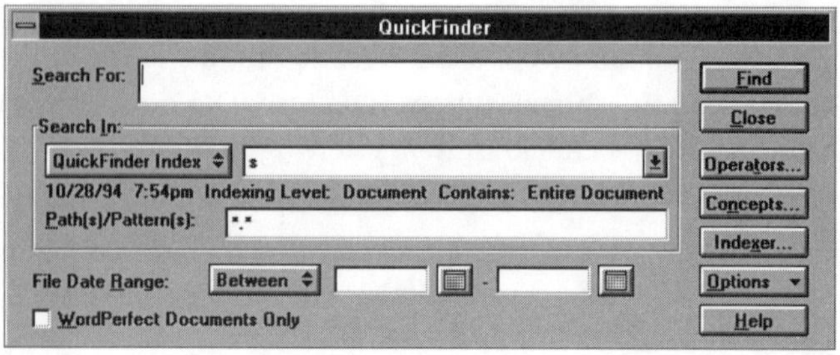

Fig. 4.17
The QuickFinder enables you to quickly find files that contain any text string you specify.

Creating a QuickFinder Index

You can index any or all files on your network and/or local disks. However, index files occupy approximately 10% of the space of the original files; thus, the index of 100 meg of files might take 10 meg of disk space. For this reason, you may choose to index only directories that contain active files that you may wish to search.

Tip
You can also access the QuickFinder File Indexer by double-clicking its icon in any program group that contains it, such as WordPerfect 6.1.

Further, you can create any number of indexes. You could create one index for old, out-of-date files that are stored in an archive directory, another for company policy documents, and another for proposals.

To create a QuickFinder index, follow these steps:

1. From a QuickFinder dialog box, chose Inde**x**er. You see the QuickFinder File Indexer dialog box shown in figure 4.18.

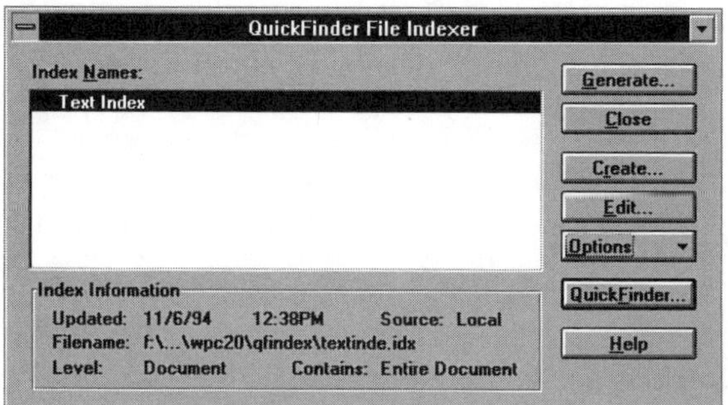

Fig. 4.18
You can create any number of QuickFinder indexes to search through specific areas of your drives.

2. Choose C**r**eate. Give the index a name, and click OK. You see the Create Index dialog box shown in figure 4.19.

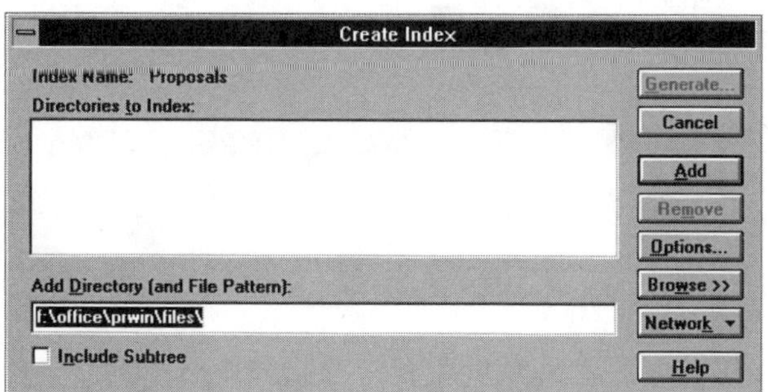

Fig. 4.19
To create an index, specify any number of directories or file patterns (using wildcards).

Tip
Index only specific files in a directory by using a file pattern with wildcards, such as C:\123*.WK1 to index all Lotus spreadsheets that are stored in the C:\123 directory.

3. Type the name of a directory and/or file pattern to be indexed in the Add **D**irectory (and File Pattern) text box. If you want the specified directory's subdirectories to also be indexed, select I**n**clude Subtree.

   Alternatively, choose Bro**w**se to add directories by choosing them with the mouse.

4. Choose **A**dd. The specified directory appears in the Directories **t**o Index list.

5. Continue to add additional directories by repeating steps 3 and 4. If you make a mistake, select the directory and choose Re**m**ove.

6. If you want to exclude .EXE, .COM, and .BAT files; index WordPerfect documents only; or change the level of detail that the index contains, choose **O**ptions.

Tip
You can switch to another task while the index is being generated by pressing Alt+Tab.

7. When you are finished creating the list of directories, choose **G**enerate. You see a Generating Index dialog box, and the progress of the index creation is displayed.

8. You return to the QuickFinder File Indexer, and the new index is added to the list of index files. Chose **C**lose to return to the QuickList dialog box.

Updating a QuickFinder Index

Periodically, you may want to update your QuickFinder indexes, because QuickFinder will only search for text in files that have been indexed. To update an index, follow these steps:

1. From a QuickFinder dialog box, chose Inde**x**er. You see the QuickFinder File Indexer dialog box (see fig. 4.20). Alternatively, double-click the QuickFinder File Indexer icon in the WordPerfect 6.1 program group.

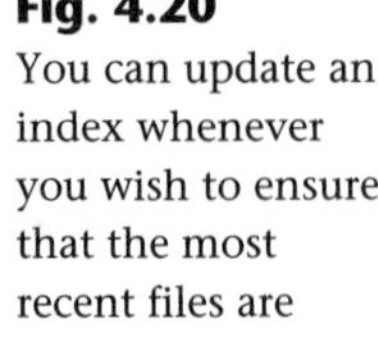

Fig. 4.20
You can update an index whenever you wish to ensure that the most recent files are included in it.

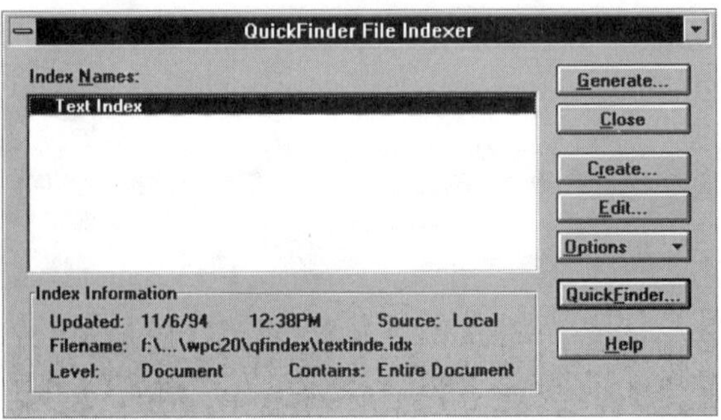

2. Select the index you wish to update.

3. Choose **G**enerate. You see the Index Method dialog box (see fig. 4.21).

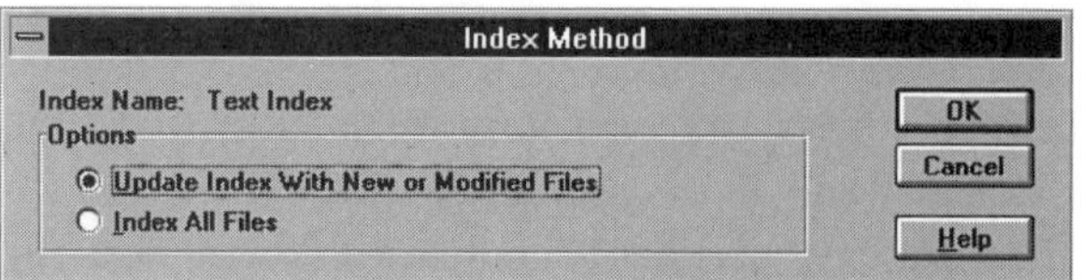

Fig. 4.21
When you regenerate an index, you can re-index all files or just the ones changed since the last generation.

4. To re-index all files, choose **I**ndex All Files. To index only those files not included in the last index, choose **U**pdate Index With New or Modified Files.

5. Choose OK. You see a Generating Index dialog box, which displays the progress of your update.

6. You return to the QuickFinder File Indexer, and the index is updated. Choose **C**lose to return to the QuickList dialog box.

Finding Files with QuickFinder

To search for a file with a specified word or phrase in it, follow these steps:

1. Access a directory dialog box.

2. Choose Quick**F**inder. You will see a QuickFinder dialog box such as that displayed in figure 4.22.

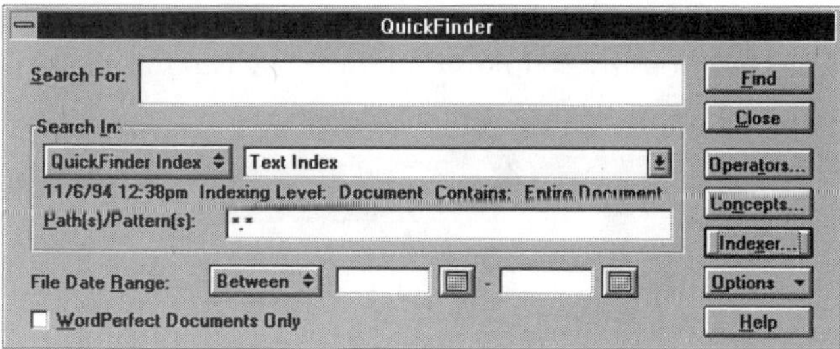

Fig. 4.22
To find files, choose Quick-Finder from any directory dialog box.

3. Select QuickFinder options as discussed below, then choose **F**ind. The files matching your search criteria will appear in a Search Results List dialog box.

   Alternatively, choose **C**lose to return to the directory dialog box without conducting the search.

While you are in the QuickFinder dialog box, you have the following options:

- ***S**earch For* (required). Enter a word or phrase (called a *word string*) in this text box. You can specify operators (below) to conduct a search that combines word strings.

Tip
There are two wildcards you can use. ? stands for one character in a word string; * stands for any number of characters in a word string.

- *Search **I**n.* You can search in the current **D**irectory, the **S**ubtree (the current directory and all of its subdirectories), the entire D**i**sk, or a **Q**uickFinder Index, if one has been defined. You choose the Directory, Subtree, Disk, or QuickFinder Index to search using the text box to the right.

- ***P**ath(s)/Pattern(s).* You can specify paths or filenames to search using the ? and * wildcards. By default, all files (*.*) are searched.

- *File Date **R**ange.* Use the File Date Range pop-up list button to specify whether you wish to search for files last saved **A**fter, **B**efore, Be**t**ween, or **O**n a specified date or dates. Then either type in the dates or select them from a pop-up calendar using the calendar buttons next to the date text boxes.

- ***W**ordPerfect Documents Only.* Use this checkbox to restrict the search to documents created with WordPerfect.

- *Opera**t**ors.* When you choose Opera**t**ors, you see the Search Operators dialog box (see fig. 4.23). QuickFinder enables you to combine word strings to perform very complex searches. You can search for documents in which a word or word string precedes another, a word occurs within a certain number of words of another, and a word or string appears on a given page. Find complete documentation on the use of operators by choosing **H**elp from the Search Operators dialog box.

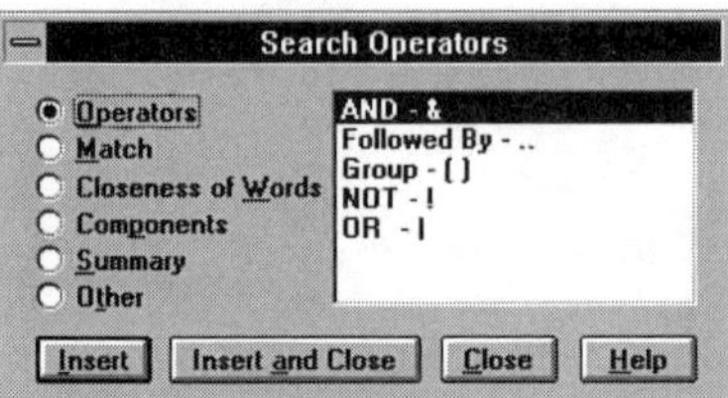

Fig. 4.23
The Search Operators dialog box enables you to create complex search criteria with Boolean logic ("and's" and "or's").

- *Concepts*. The Concept Builder dialog box appears when you choose Concepts after specifying a search word (see fig. 4.24). You have five concept-building tools available to you that make your searches more powerful. **W**ord Forms expands your search to include conjugations and plurals. For instance, the word "counsel" will generate the words counsel, counseled, counselled, counselling, and counsels. **T**hesaurus adds synonyms of the selected word—for example, *advise*, *caution*, and *guidance*. The**s**. - > Word Forms includes the word forms of the selected synonyms, like *advising*. T**y**pographical adds common misspellings of the selected word (*hte* for *the*). **P**honetic adds words that sound like the selected word—for example, *cancel* and *conceal*.

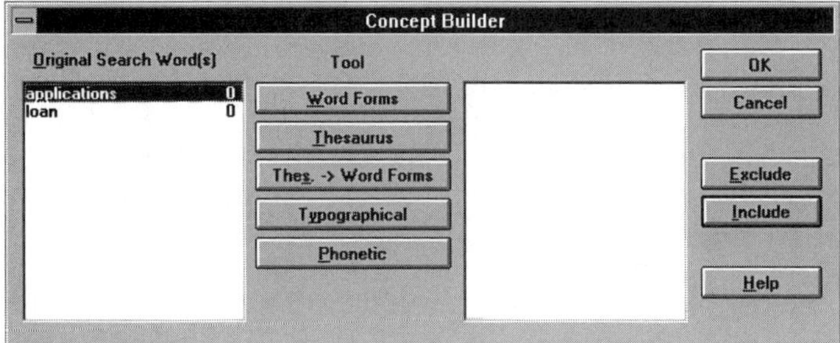

Fig. 4.24
You can search for different forms of words (carry, carrying, carried), synonyms (hauled), and misspellings of the word (cary).

You may exclude any words that appear on the list when you use a concept-building tool by selecting them and choosing **E**xclude. The excluded word(s) will become gray. When you are finished, click OK. You return to the QuickFinder dialog box, and the desired words appear in the **S**earch For text box with "or" symbols (|) between them.

- *Options*. You can choose Es**t**imated Relevance Ranking or **F**ull Word Count Relevance to have QuickFinder rank the files it finds by the number of words contained in the criteria you specify. You can also search through the summary fields of WordPerfect 5.xx and 6.xx documents by choosing **N**o Summary Fields, D**e**fault Summary Fields, or **A**ll Summary Fields.

If you want to recapture your previous search, choose Last Search **R**e-sults. You can also save a search by choosing **S**ave Search Query. If you do, you can also choose **L**oad Search Query and **D**elete Search Query.

From Here...

In this chapter, you learned how to manage files in various PerfectOffice applications, and how to use the common printing features you find in PerfectOffice. Now you're ready to learn about the applications you will use. Each of the following parts is independent; you can turn directly to the part that pertains to the application you need.

- See Chapter 5, "Getting Started with WordPerfect," to learn how to use WordPerfect to create common business and personal documents. See how to edit documents, format them, and use a host of shortcuts that will help you automate your word processing work.
- In Chapter 12, "Getting Started with Quattro Pro," you discover how to create everything from simple home budgets to complex spreadsheets involving data analysis and charts.
- Chapter 19, "Getting Started with Paradox," explores how to use Paradox to create databases for home and business use. Learn how to create queries, design reports and forms, and create crosstabs and graphs.
- In Chapter 24, "Getting Started with Presentations," you can learn all about Novell's premier graphics and presentations program. See how to create slide shows, make charts, and use drawing objects.
- Chapter 28, "Getting Started with GroupWise and InfoCentral," teaches you how to use GroupWise to send e-mail, schedule meetings, and assign and track tasks within a work group. Learn about InfoCentral—Novell's Personal Information Manager.

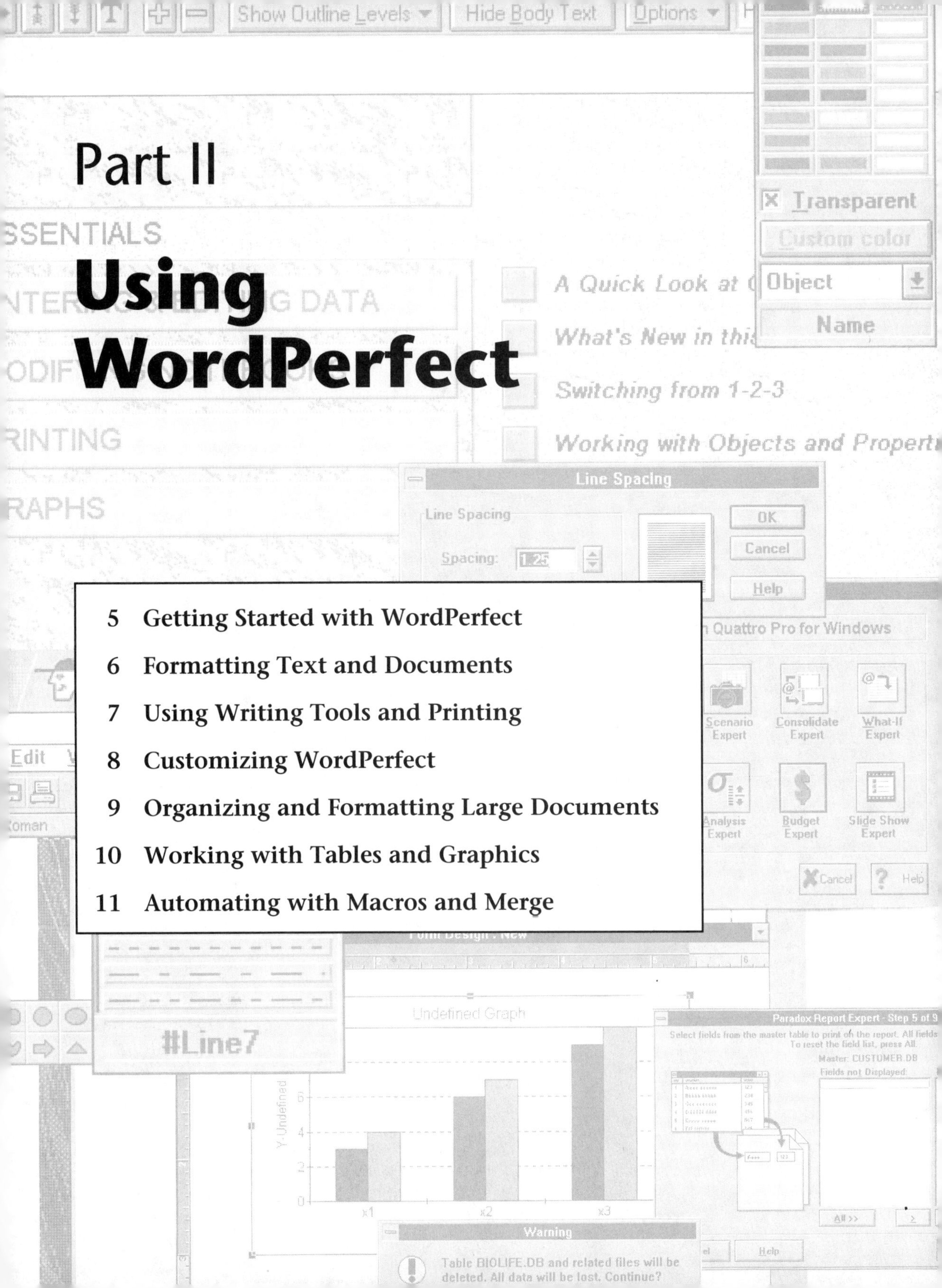

Part II

Using WordPerfect

Show Outline Levels
Hide Body Text
Options
Transparent
Object
Name
ESSENTIALS
ENTERING & EDITING DATA
ODIFYING NOTEBOOKS
PRINTING
GRAPHS
A Quick Look at
What's New in this
Switching from 1-2-3
Working with Objects and Pro
Line Spacing
Line Spacing
Spacing:
1.25
OK
Cancel
Help
Experts in Quattro Pro for Windows
Graph Expert
Scenario Expert
Consolidate Expert
Performance Expert
Analysis Expert
Budget Expert
Cancel
Coaches
Quit
WP Presentations - [d:\...\24fig13.shw]
File Edit View Insert Format Slide Graphics Tools Windo
New Roman
Slide 2 of 7
Line
#Line7
Form Design : New *
Undefined Graph
Y-Undefined
x1
x2
x3
Paradox Report Expert
Select fields from the master table to print on the repo
To reset the field list, pr
Master: CUSTOM
Fields not Displa
All>>
Help
Warning
Table BIOLIFE.DB and related files will be deleted. All data will be lost. Continue?

Chapter 5

Getting Started with WordPerfect

by Judy Felfe

Of all the applications included with the Novell PerfectOffice suite, WordPerfect may be the one you use most. You probably need a word processor to produce letters and envelopes. Using WordPerfect, you can also create memos, fax cover sheets, reports, newsletters, mailing labels, brochures, and many other types of documents.

In this chapter, you learn to

- Understand the WordPerfect editing screen
- Enter text
- Edit text
- Reverse your last action(s)
- Save a document
- Close and open documents

WordPerfect offers many features that help you complete your work quickly and easily. There are features that correct errors automatically, features that add visual interest to your documents, and features that help you organize and manage long documents. WordPerfect provides easy graphics handling, outlining, calculations of data in tables, the capability to create a mailing list, list sorting, and efficient file management. You can perform desktop publishing tasks such as formatting fonts, inserting drop caps, adding graphic borders, and adding shading.

When you use WordPerfect 6.1, you're sharing a common look and feel with other applications in the Novell PerfectOffice suite. Switching to Quattro Pro to perform your spreadsheet work is easily accomplished without drastically changing the way you work. In addition, you can integrate data from another application and edit that data while you stay "in place" (in WordPerfect). For example, when you have embedded a Quattro Pro spreadsheet in a WordPerfect document, you can edit the spreadsheet after double-clicking the embedded object in your WordPerfect document. Then, when you finish editing the spreadsheet, you can return to the WordPerfect document by choosing **F**ile, E**x**it and Return.

This section of *Using Novell PerfectOffice* presents you with an overview of the WordPerfect 6.1 program. In this book, you learn how to use WordPerfect to accomplish most of the business tasks that you would want to carry out with your word processor. For a more comprehensive examination of the WordPerfect 6.1 program, refer to Que's *Using WordPerfect 6.1 for Windows,* Special Edition.

Understanding WordPerfect Basics

◄ See "Using Help," p. 34

If you're familiar with Windows applications, you already know quite a bit about using WordPerfect. You know how to use the Control menu, the File menu, the Window menu, and Help. You also know how to use the mouse with scroll bars and menus, and you know how to use dialog boxes. These features are common to all Windows applications.

This section familiarizes you with some features and screen elements that are particular to the WordPerfect program, as well as with other elements of the editing window that are common to all Windows applications.

When you start the WordPerfect program, you see specific screen elements as defaults, including the title bar, menu bar, the WordPerfect Toolbar, the Power Bar, the status bar, and the scroll bars. You can hide or redisplay these elements or other elements by choosing a command from the View menu. Suppose that you want to display the Ruler bar. Choose **V**iew, **R**uler Bar to display the Ruler bar; choose **V**iew, **R**uler Bar again to hide the Ruler bar.

Note

The scroll bars are turned on or off by choosing **E**dit, Pr**e**ferences, **D**isplay.

Figure 5.1 illustrates the default WordPerfect screen and identifies screen elements.

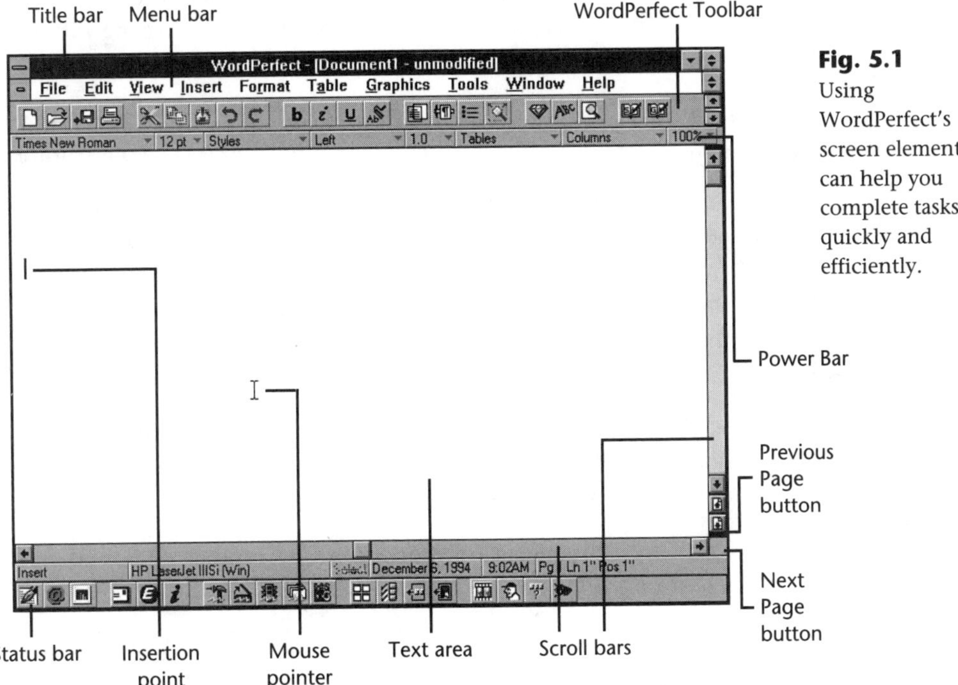

Fig. 5.1 Using WordPerfect's screen elements can help you complete tasks quickly and efficiently.

The following list describes the installed, default screen elements.

- *Title bar.* The title bar identifies the WordPerfect *application* window and the name of the document in the current *document* window. When the mouse pointer is on a button, on the status bar, or on the Previous or Next Page button, or when a menu command is selected, the title bar describes the function of that item.

- *Menu bar.* The menu bar gives you access to the most commonly used WordPerfect features. Each menu contains a specialized list of related commands. Choose commands from the Format menu, for example, to change fonts, to change margins, to create a header or footer, and so on.

- *Toolbar.* By default, the WordPerfect Toolbar is displayed just beneath the menu bar. When you point to a button, its name is displayed beneath the pointer and its function is described in the title bar. The toolbar contains buttons you can use to perform common tasks, such as opening an existing document, saving a document, applying boldface, and spell-checking. When scroll arrows are displayed at the right end of the toolbar, you can use them to see other buttons. When you're performing a specialized task, you can switch to a toolbar with buttons that relate to that task, for example, when you're working with a table, you can display the Tables toolbar.
- *Power Bar.* The Power Bar consists of a series of buttons that give you easy access to commonly used text editing and text layout features.
- *Text area.* The text area consists of a blank "page" in which you can enter text or place pictures, graphics, and so on. By default, the text area is displayed in Page View, which means that you see everything on the page just as it will print, including the margin space at the top of the page (depending on the zoom percentage, you may not see a full page of text at once).
- *Scroll bars.* Use the scroll bars to move quickly to another area of the document. Previous Page and Next Page buttons appear at the bottom of the vertical scroll bar.
- *Status bar.* The status bar informs you of the status of many WordPerfect features.

► See "Creating a Header or Footer," p. 124

► See "Understanding the Outline Feature Bar," p. 171

► See "Working with Tables," p. 190

► See "Creating a Graphics Box," p. 211

In addition to the installed, default screen elements, other toolbars, the Ruler Bar, and various feature bars may be displayed on-screen.

Entering Text

When you start WordPerfect, you are supplied with a new, empty document window (named Document1 in the title bar). You can begin to type at the blinking insertion point (the insertion point is positioned just below the top margin). As you type, text is entered at the insertion point.

This section describes the basic techniques of entering text, moving through a document, and selecting text for editing.

Typing Text

When typing text, you type as you would in any word processor. WordPerfect automatically wraps the text at the end of a line, so you don't have to press Enter to begin a new line. Press Enter *only* when you want to start a new paragraph or create a blank line. WordPerfect defines a paragraph as a line that ends with an Enter keystroke (a hard return).

▶ See "Creating Drop Caps," p. 212

▶ See "Creating a Macro," p. 219

▶ See "Using Merge," p. 226

As you type, certain keys that you press (Enter, Tab, Spacebar, for example) create non-printing characters at the insertion point. You can view these non-printing characters by choosing **V**iew, **S**how ¶.

Figure 5.2 illustrates non-printing characters, with a document containing lines that wrap with hard returns and lines that wrap with automatic word wrap.

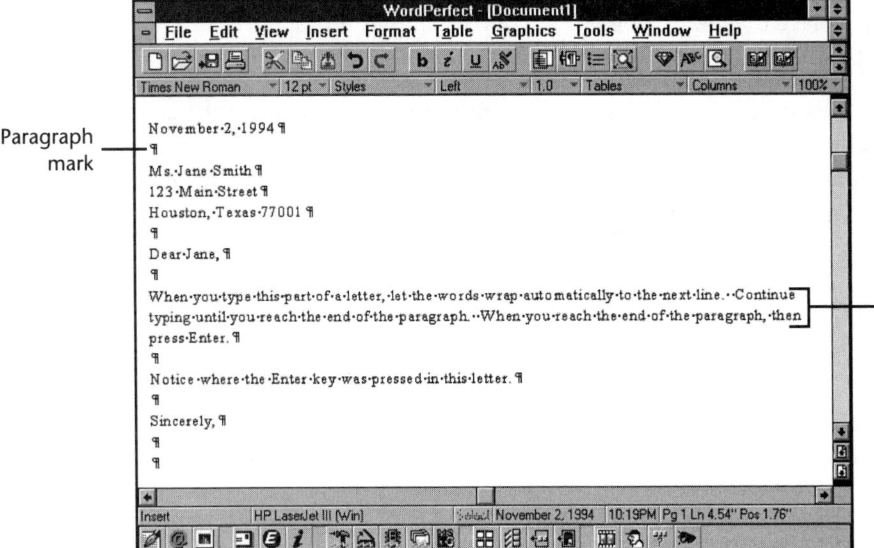

Fig. 5.2 Paragraph marks and spaces are nonprinting characters; they do not print, whether or not they are displayed.

As you type, follow these guidelines:

- If you make a mistake, press the Backspace key to erase the character immediately preceding the insertion point.
- Press the Delete key to remove the character immediately following the insertion point.
- When you're typing a sentence or phrase that extends past the end of the line, let the words wrap to the next line automatically (don't press Enter).

- Use the Tab key or the Indent feature to indent lines (don't use the space bar).
- Press the Insert key to use typeover mode, in which the text you type replaces existing text (you can tell whether Typeover is active by looking at the status bar at the bottom of the screen). Press Insert again to turn off typeover mode.

Positioning the Insertion Point

To move the insertion point, move the mouse pointer (the I-beam) to the new location and click the left mouse button. You can position the insertion point anywhere in the text area, but not past the end of the text.

To move the insertion point to a place that you don't see on-screen, use the scroll bar(s) to move to a new location. When the new location is visible on-screen, place the mouse pointer where you want to position the insertion point and click the left mouse button.

Another way to move the insertion point is by pressing keys on the keyboard. Sometimes, especially when you're already using the keyboard to type text, it's easier and faster to move the insertion point by pressing keys than by using the mouse. The following table lists common keys that you can use to move around in your document.

Key	Moves Insertion Point
Arrow key	One character up, down, left, or right
PgUp/PgDn	One screen up or down
Ctrl+←/→	One word to the left or right
Home/End	Beginning or end of line
Ctrl+Home/End	Beginning or end of document

Selecting Text

After you enter text, you may want to delete a word, sentence, paragraph, or other section of text, or you may want to boldface the text or change its font or size. Before you can perform a formatting or editing action on existing text, you must first select the text. *Selecting*, or highlighting, the text shows WordPerfect where to perform the action.

You can select text with the mouse or with the keyboard, or with a combination of both. The following list describes techniques for selecting text:

- To select a section of text of any length, position the I-beam pointer at one end of the text and drag to the other end of the text with the mouse.

- To select a word, position the I-beam pointer anywhere in the word and double-click. To select multiple words, keep holding down the left mouse button after you double-click, and then drag through the words.

- To select a sentence, position the I-beam pointer anywhere in the sentence and triple-click. To select multiple sentences, keep holding down the left mouse button after you triple-click, and then drag through the sentences.

- To select a paragraph, position the I-beam pointer anywhere in the paragraph and quadruple-click. To select multiple paragraphs, keep holding down the left mouse button after you quadruple-click and drag through the paragraphs.

- To select a sentence, position the mouse pointer in the left margin area. When you point the mouse in the left margin area, the I-beam pointer changes to a right pointing hollow arrow (see fig. 5.3). Click to select a single sentence; to select multiple sentences, keep holding down the left mouse button after you click and drag through the sentences.

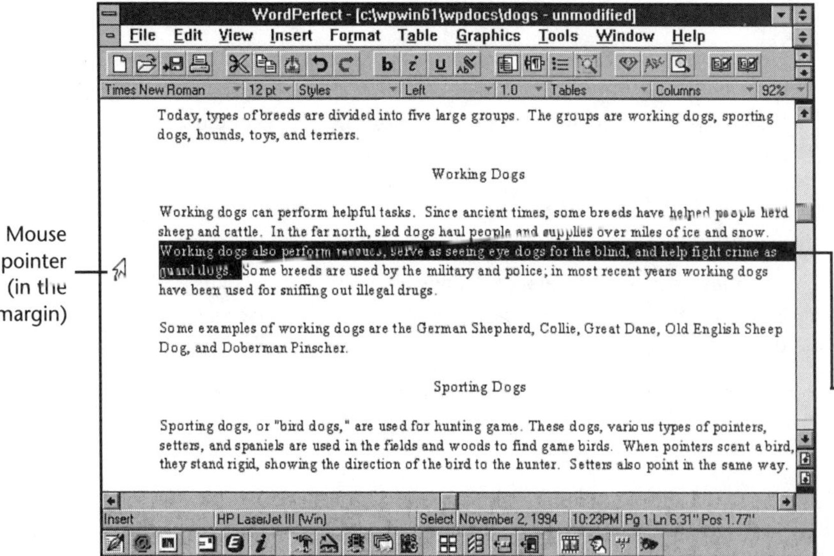

Fig. 5.3
Position the mouse pointer in the left margin and click once to select a sentence quickly; select more than one sentence by dragging the mouse pointer in the margin.

◀ See "Using Quick-Menus," p. 52

- To select a paragraph, position the right-pointing arrow pointer in the left margin area and double-click. To select multiple paragraphs, keep holding down the left mouse button after you click and drag through the paragraphs.
- For multiple selection options, position the right-pointing arrow pointer in the left margin area and right-click. Next, make a choice from selection options on the QuickMenu.
- To select a section of text of any length, position the insertion point at one end of the text. Next, position the I-beam pointer at the other end of the text and hold down Shift while you click.
- To select text with the keyboard, position the insertion point at the beginning of the text, then press and hold down the Shift key while you press the appropriate cursor movement keys. To select from the insertion point to the end of the line, for example, hold down Shift while you press End. To select the character immediately following the insertion point, hold down Shift while you press the Right Arrow (→).

Troubleshooting

I began typing the text, but it didn't appear where I expected it to appear.

Text that you type appears at the *insertion point,* not at the mouse pointer. Before you type text, position the insertion point by clicking where you want the text to appear.

I have trouble controlling the selection when I drag through text with the mouse.

It takes practice to control the mouse when you select text by dragging through it. Try using one of the alternative methods described in this section. For example, position the insertion point at the beginning of the selection and hold down Shift while you press arrow keys to select the text.

I selected some text and made it bold, but when I started typing afterward the text disappeared.

When text is selected, whatever you type *replaces* the selected text. It's a good idea to deselect text as soon as you finish performing any action(s) on the selection. To deselect text, click anywhere in the typing area.

Note

You can use the Shift key to extend (or shrink) a selection. Hold down Shift while you press an arrow key to extend (or shrink) the selection.

To deselect text, click the mouse anywhere in the text area, or press any of the arrow keys.

Editing Text

You can easily make changes and corrections to your document. You can select any text and delete it, copy it, or move it. These are just a few of the operations you can perform on selected text. How often have you typed text only to realize that Caps Lock was turned on? Don't type the text again; use the Convert Case feature to correct the problem. This section shows you how to make basic editing changes quickly and easily.

Undeleting Text

Use Undelete to restore text that you deleted. Undelete will restore any or all of your last three deletions. Don't confuse Undelete with Undo; use Undelete to restore deleted text, and use Undo to undo other operations. To use Undelete, take the following steps:

1. Position the insertion point where you want to restore the text.

2. Choose **E**dit, U**n**delete; or press Ctrl+Shift+Z. The Undelete dialog box appears and the most recent deletion is displayed in the text area. If necessary, drag the dialog box out of the way so you can see the displayed deletion.

3. If the displayed deletion is what you want to restore, choose **R**estore. Otherwise, choose **N**ext or **P**revious to display the deletion that you want to restore, and then choose **R**estore.

Undoing Mistakes

Many mistakes can be reversed with the Undo command. Suppose that you move text to the wrong place. You can undo the move operation with Undo. Click the Undo button on the Toolbar to undo your most recent action. You can also choose **E**dit, **U**ndo, or press Ctrl+Z.

WordPerfect also provides a Redo command (Edit menu) that you can use to reverse the last Undo. The keyboard shortcut for Redo is Ctrl+Shift+R.

The Undo/Redo commands work only on the last action you performed. However, WordPerfect provides lists of Undo/Redo actions and you can undo a series of actions by choosing **E**dit, Undo/Redo **H**istory. Figure 5.4 shows the Undo/Redo History displaying the most recent actions. To undo the last four actions, click the fourth item from the top of the Undo list (this highlights all of the first four items, as shown in the illustration) and then choose **U**ndo.

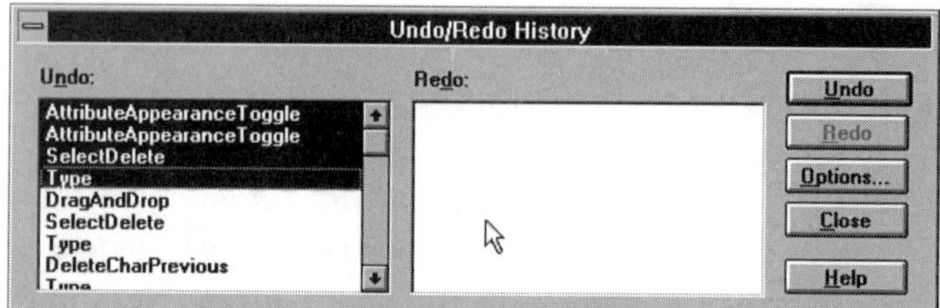

Fig. 5.4
The Undo/Redo History lists a series of the most recent actions that you can undo (or redo).

Deleting and Moving Text

To delete any amount of text, select the text and press the **Delete** key. When you press Delete, the text is erased; you can recall it (or any of the last three deletions) with the Undelete command.

If you're going to move the text to another location, use the Cut command instead of the Delete key. Choose **E**dit, **C**ut, or press Ctrl+X to move selected text to the Windows Clipboard. The text remains on the Clipboard until something else is placed on the Clipboard.

Once you place text that you want to *move* on the Clipboard, the next step is to show WordPerfect where you want to place the text. Do this by positioning the insertion point where you want the text to appear. Then, choose **E**dit, **P**aste, or press Ctrl+V. The text in inserted at the insertion point.

Copying Text

To copy text, select the text and then choose **E**dit, **C**opy, or click the Copy button. WordPerfect copies the selection to the Clipboard. You can then paste the text in another location by positioning the insertion point and choosing **E**dit, **P**aste, or by clicking the Paste button.

Copying text—or other elements in your documents, such as pictures and charts—is a way to share data between applications. The Windows Clipboard is common to all applications running under Windows. You can, for example, create text in WordPerfect, copy it, and paste it in Presentations. You can also copy a spreadsheet from Quattro Pro and paste it into WordPerfect.

Drag-and-Drop Editing

Another technique for moving and copying text is called *drag-and-drop*. Drag-and-drop is especially handy for moving or copying selected text a short distance—to a location that is already visible on-screen. Drag-and-drop can also be used to move graphics.

Tip
To copy the text instead of moving it, hold down the Ctrl key before you release the mouse button at the new location. When you hold down Ctrl, the drag-and-drop pointer includes a plus (+) sign.

To drag-and-drop text or graphics, take the following steps:

1. Select the text or graphics element that you want to move.
2. Point to the selected text or graphic and hold down the left mouse button. The drag-and-drop pointer appears if you are moving text (see fig. 5.5).
3. Drag the pointer until the insertion point is at the new location, and then release the mouse button.

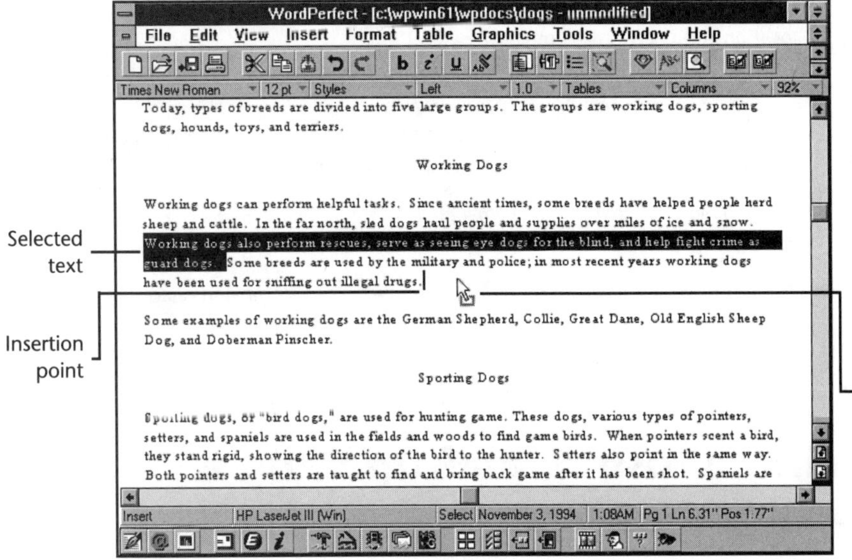

Fig. 5.5
Use the drag-and-drop pointer to drag the selected text or graphic to a new location. When the insertion point is correctly placed, release the mouse button.

Converting Case

WordPerfect includes a handy command that you can use to change the case of selected text. Suppose that you typed a heading with initial caps at the beginning of each word and you decide that it would look better in all upper case. You can use Convert Case to convert it to upper case.

To change the case of existing text, take the following steps:

1. Select the text.
2. Choose **E**dit, Con**v**ert Case.
3. Choose **L**ower, **U**pper, or **I**nitial Capitals.

Troubleshooting

I accidentally deleted text that I didn't mean to delete.

Position the insertion point where you want to restore the text and choose **E**dit, U**n**delete. Display the correct deletion and then choose Restore.

I pasted text in the wrong place.

Click the Undo button, and then position the insertion point in the correct location and press Ctrl+V, or choose **E**dit, **P**aste.

I accidentally get the drag-and-drop pointer when I don't want it.

Press Esc before you release the mouse button. If it's too late, and the text has already been moved, use the Undo command to correct the mistake.

I tried to move selected text to another page with drag-and-drop, but it was very cumbersome to position the insertion point while dragging the selection.

Try using Cut and Paste rather than drag-and-drop when moving or copying to a distant location.

Saving, Closing, and Opening a Document

◄ See "Working with Files," p. 69

This section shows you how to save and close a document, open an existing document, and start a new one. The following discussion is specific to the WordPerfect program.

Saving a Document

As in other Novell PerfectOffice programs, you save a WordPerfect document by assigning it a name and a location in your drive and directory list. After naming the file, you can save changes to the document without renaming it; simply press a shortcut key or click the Save button on the Toolbar.

Tip
Save your documents often as you work on them. If a power failure occurs while you're working on a document and you haven't saved it as a file, you will lose the document.

Naming a Document

The first time you save a document, choose the **F**ile, Save **A**s command. WordPerfect displays the Save As dialog box, as shown in figure 5.6.

When you save a document, the storage location defaults to the directory specified through **E**dit, Pr**e**ferences, **F**ile. In addition, the File Preferences dialog box specifies a default filename extension of .WPD. For information on changing these defaults, see Chapter 8, "Customizing WordPerfect."

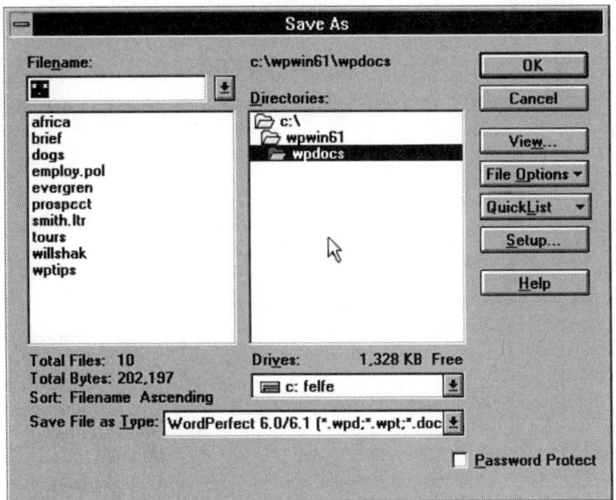

Fig. 5.6
Enter the name of the document in the Filename text box.

You can save a file to a hard drive, floppy drive, network drive, and so on; available drives are in the Drives list. Next, select a directory in the **D**irectories list. Finally, in the Save File as **T**ype box, you can select another format, if desired (in case you want to use the file in another version of WordPerfect or in another application).

Tip
You can customize settings for naming and saving your documents. See Chapter 8 for more information.

To save a document, take the following steps:

1. Choose **F**ile, Save **A**s. The Save As dialog box is displayed.
2. Select the drive, directory, and file type, if you don't want to use the defaults.
3. Enter the name of the file (including an extension, if desired) in the File**n**ame text box.
4. Click OK to save the document. Notice that the title bar displays the location and name and the fact that it is unmodified.

Saving Changes to a Named Document

Once you've saved your document by assigning it a name and a location on the disk, you can continue to work on it. The changes you make are not saved, however, unless you tell WordPerfect to save them.

After modifying or editing an already-named document, choose **F**ile, **S**ave, or press Ctrl+S. WordPerfect saves the changes and you are ready to proceed.

Tip

If the file you want to open was recently edited, it will be listed at the bottom of the file menu when you choose **F**ile. You can select it from the File menu without accessing the Open File dialog box.

Closing a Document

When you finish working with a document, choose **F**ile, **C**lose. The document is removed from the screen and from the computer's memory (but not from storage on disk). If there are changes that haven't been saved, you are given a chance to save them to disk before the close operation is completed.

Opening a Document

To open a saved document in WordPerfect, choose **F**ile, **O**pen, or press Ctrl+O. WordPerfect displays the Open File dialog box (see fig. 5.7).

In the Open File dialog box, select the file name from the list of files, if you saved it in the current default directory. Otherwise, you can change the drive and directory to access the desired file.

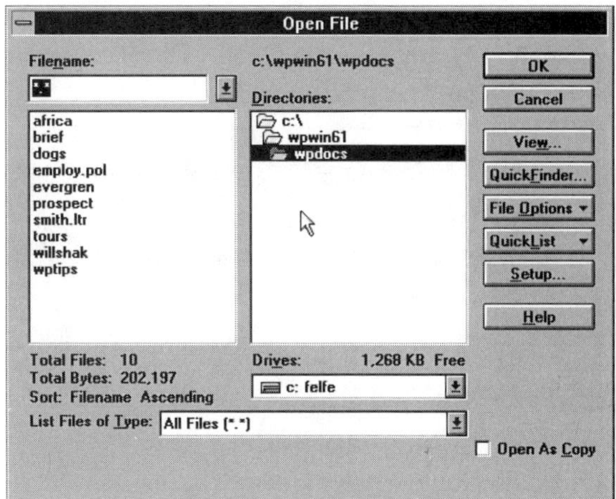

Fig. 5.7
Select the file from the list of files, and then choose OK to open the document.

Starting a New Document

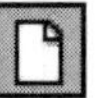

You can start a new document at any time. To start a new, blank document, click the New Blank Document button, or press Ctrl+N. A new, blank document window is displayed.

► See "Formatting the Page," p. 122

When you start a new document with the method above, you accept the Standard template. A template is a preformatted document. All documents are based on a template; Standard is the default template. The Standard template has the following characteristics:

- Uses an 8 1/2 × 11-inch portrait-oriented page
- Includes 1-inch top and bottom margins and 1-inch left and right margins
- Uses the initial printer font for the currently selected printer.
- Uses left justification
- Supplies five heading styles that can be used to format different levels of headings in your document

Another way to start a new document is by clicking the New Document tool, or by choosing **F**ile, **N**ew, or by pressing Ctrl+T. The New Document dialog box appears, with the default template selected (see fig. 5.8).

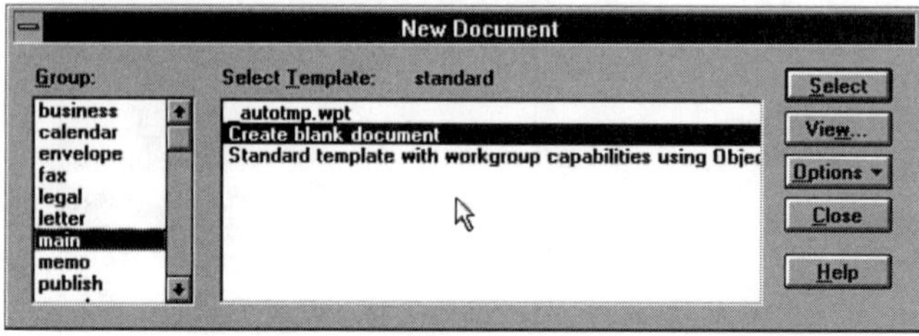

Fig. 5.8
The New Document dialog box enables you to choose from a selection of preformatted, automated templates on which to base a new document.

A template is a basic document design, including text as well as formatting. You can save time and work by using templates for your standardized documents, such as your letters, memos, and fax forms. Many templates prompt you for information when you use them; this saves you the work of positioning the insertion point manually to fill in the information. For more information about templates, see Chapter 7, "Using Writing Tools and Printing."

Troubleshooting

I wanted to save a file with a new name, but when I clicked the Save button or chose File, Save, I didn't have a chance to change the name.

To change the name, storage location, or file type of the document in the active document window, choose **F**ile, Save **A**s. In the Save As dialog box, you can change any of these options.

I wanted to save a file in a different directory, but that directory isn't listed in the directory list.

You may need to select a directory above the selected directory before you can see the desired directory name. For example, if C:\WPWIN61\WPDOCS is the selected directory and you want to look at the files in C:\WPWIN61\MEMOS, first you must select C:\WPWIN61. Then, you can see (and select) the C:\WPWIN61\MEMOS directory. Remember that you should double-click a directory to select it.

I opened a document that was created in another file format, and now I want to save it.

Click the Save button in the toolbar or choose **F**ile, **S**ave. WordPerfect displays the Save Format dialog box, where you can accept the suggested WordPerfect 6.0/6.1 format or select the original format or another format.

In the New Document dialog box, you can choose a template group to display the templates within that group. Use the View button to preview the contents of a template (but not the formatting). Once you select a template, choose Select to open a new document based on that template.

From Here...

In this chapter, you learned to create text in a document and then edit that text by moving, copying, deleting, and so on. Additionally, you learned to save the document and then open that document for further editing. For more information about working in the WordPerfect application, see the following chapters:

- Chapter 6, "Formatting Text and Documents," covers how to change the views of your document, how to format such items as font and font size, how to adjust spacing between lines and paragraphs, indent text, and set tabs, and how to change margins and page orientation.

- Chapter 7, "Using Writing Tools and Printing," covers using templates and using the Spell Checker, QuickCorrect, and Grammatik to proofread your documents. Chapter 7 also tells you how to print documents, envelopes, and labels.

- Chapter 9, "Organizing and Formatting Large Documents," tells you how to create outlines and lists, and how to apply formatting with styles.

Chapter 6

Formatting Text and Documents

by Judy Felfe

Many of WordPerfect's features enable you to change the appearance of your documents, that is, to *format* your documents. You can boldface or italicize text, or you can adjust the spacing between lines, or you can choose from many other formatting features to make your documents more readable and more attractive.

In this chapter, you learn to

- View the document in the way that best suits the task
- Change font face, font size, and font style
- Adjust line and paragraph spacing
- Center text on a line
- Align text in tabular columns
- Indent text
- Change margins and justification
- Create headers and footers and number pages
- Make a document fit on a page
- Change paper size
- Work with formatting codes

WordPerfect makes formatting quick and easy. You can use toolbar buttons and menu commands to make an ordinary business document eye-catching and readable.

Note

When you format a document, WordPerfect records your commands in the form of *embedded codes.* You can avoid formatting problems if you remember to check the position of the insertion point before you make a formatting change. Unless you want to remove specific formatting manually (by removing the code that causes the formatting), you don't need to concern yourself with embedded codes. You can, however, see embedded codes whenever you want by choosing **V**iew, **R**eveal Codes.

In this chapter you learn to format text, lines, paragraphs, and pages, using the easiest and fastest methods.

Understanding Views

WordPerfect enables you to use several different view modes while you're editing your document. You can use Page view, Draft view, or Two Page view. Each view mode offers its own advantages for text editing and formatting. Changing the view mode affects the on-screen appearance of the document; it doesn't affect the actual formatting of the document.

In addition to the choice of view modes, WordPerfect provides various magnification options for viewing a document. You can magnify the view from 25% to 400%.

Finally, you can remove or display various screen elements to produce a customized view. This section describes the views and their advantages and disadvantages.

View modes, magnification options, and the display or removal of screen elements are all set from the View menu; for quick access to magnification options, use the Zoom button on the Power Bar. To switch quickly back and forth to a Full Page view from the current magnification, click the Page/Zoom Full button on the Toolbar.

Using View Modes

When you work in a document, you're working in Page view by default. You can use the View menu to switch to another view mode whenever it suits you.

Tip
You can modify the viewing options to change the default view mode from Page view to Draft view.

Page View

In Page view, what you see on-screen is the entire page, just as it will print (see fig. 6.1). This is a true WYSIWYG (What You See Is What You Get) view of your document. Page view displays headers, footers, page borders, top and bottom margins, and footnotes. Page view is better suited for applying finishing touches to the text and page than for entering and editing text. Keep in mind that working in Page view is slightly slower than working in Draft view.

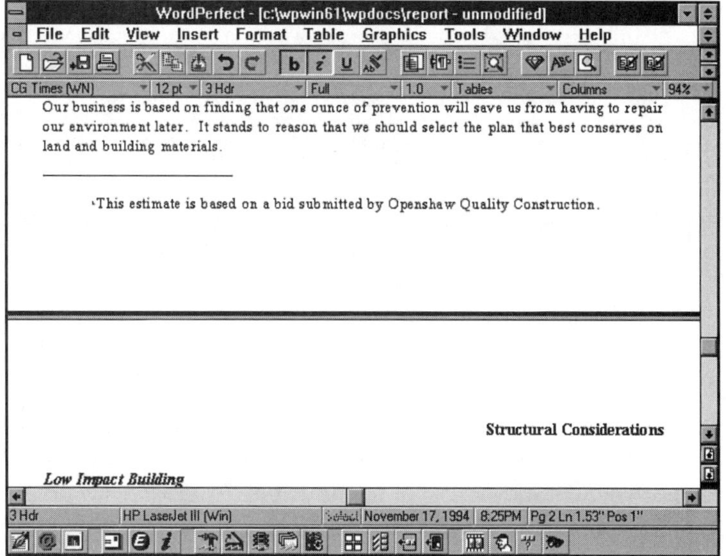

Fig. 6.1
Page view shows you everything on the page just as it will print; this is a true WYSIWYG view.

Draft View

It's fastest and easiest to enter and edit text when you work in Draft view. In Draft view, you see text just as it will print, including variations in font face and font size and graphics elements (see fig. 6.2). You can scroll smoothly from the bottom of one page to the top of the next page without jumping past the gap between the bottom margin of one page and the top margin of the next page. Whenever you want to see everything on the page just as it will print, including margin space, headers, footers, page numbering, and page borders, you can switch from Draft view to Page view. For a quick look at a full page in Page View, click the Page/Zoom Full button on the Toolbar, then click it again to return to your current view mode.

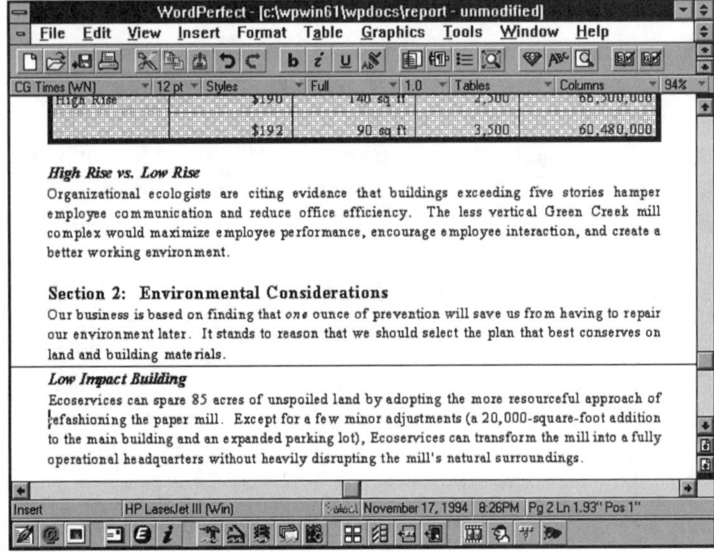

Fig. 6.2
Draft view enables you to enter and edit text smoothly and easily.

Two Page View

Use Two Page view when you want to see two pages on-screen at once. Two Page view is suited for looking at facing pages (when you're printing on both sides of the paper) and for seeing more of the document layout than you can see in Page view. You can edit your document in Two Page view just as you can edit it in Draft view or Page view, although the text is extremely small. Working in Two Page view is even slower than working in Page view.

Figure 6.1 shows you a document in Page view. Figure 6.2 shows you the same document in Draft view.

Magnifying the View

For a better view of your work when you work in Draft view or Page view, change the magnification factor. Choose **V**iew, **Z**oom, or use the Zoom button on the Power Bar. You can set magnification to any value between 25% and 400%.

Troubleshooting
I can't see all of the text on a line on-screen at once.
Change the level of magnification with the Zoom button or after choosing **V**iew, **Z**oom. Experiment with 100%, Margin Width, and Page Width to see what best suits the situation.
It takes too long to scroll through a document.
Maximize the speed at which you're working by using Draft view mode (open the View menu to change the view mode).
When I scroll from the bottom of one page to the top of the next page, the screen takes a big jump and it's difficult to get a continuous view of the text from one page to the next.
Open the View menu to change from Page view to Draft view.

Tip
To set your own magnification, choose Other on the Zoom button drop-down list, then, at the Zoom dialog box, type a percentage in the **O**ther text box.

Formatting Characters

WordPerfect provides many features for formatting characters (for formatting text); you can apply a variety of fonts, sizes, and styles to your text. The Toolbar and the Power Bar both provide buttons for quick and easy text formatting.

You can format text by first selecting the text and then making the formatting changes. Alternatively, you can position the insertion point, make the formatting changes, and then type the text. All text typed from that point on will be formatted according to your specifications until you change the formatting again.

Tip
Another way to format text is to use Styles. You can use the same style to format text over and over again.

Changing Font Face

Font face is the typeface of text. Common font faces are Times New Roman and Courier. Some font faces are built into your printer; Windows offers many TrueType font faces in addition to those that are built into your printer. Choose the font face that suits your work. For an informal flyer you could choose a light italic font, such as Brush. For a more formal effect, you could choose Shelley, or Caslon Openface.

You can quickly select a font from the Power Bar's drop-down list, shown in figure 6.3.

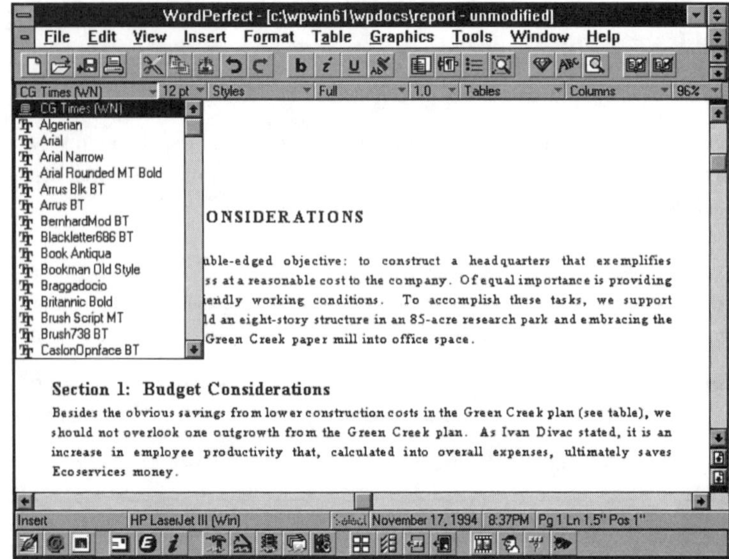

Fig. 6.3
WordPerfect lists the four most recently used font faces at the top of the list so you can find them quickly. The entire list of available fonts is then listed in alphabetic order.

Changing Font Size

◄ See "Starting a New Document," p. 99

Font size is measured in *points*. A smaller point size results in a smaller print; a larger point size results in a larger print. Points and *picas* are typesetter's measurements used for measuring spacing, line thickness, and so on. There are 12 points to a pica and 6 picas to an inch; therefore, there are 72 points to an inch.

All text you enter in a new document that is based on the Standard template is in your printer's initial typeface and size. Most font faces are *scalable*, meaning that you can change the font size. To quickly change the font size, click the Font Size button on the Power Bar, then select a size from the drop-down list.

Changing Font Style

Font styles are *attributes* that are applied to text. The Toolbar provides Bold, Italic, and Underline buttons. You can use the buttons, or you can use keyboard shortcuts Ctrl+B, Ctrl+I, and Ctrl+U (respectively) to apply these attributes.

► See "Using Styles," p. 177

Font styles can be applied either before or after you type text. To apply a style after typing text, you must first select the text, and then click the appropriate button (or press the shortcut key). To apply a style before typing text, click the appropriate button (or press the shortcut key) to turn on the style, type the text, and then click the appropriate button (to turn off the style).

In addition to the bold, italic, and underline attributes, there are a number of other appearance attributes to choose from in the Font dialog box.

Using the Font Dialog Box

You can double-click either of the Font buttons on the Power Bar, you can choose Format, Font, or you can press F9 to display the Font dialog box. Use this dialog box to apply a number of font changes to your text all at once. The Font dialog box (see fig. 6.4) has options for every type of font change that you can make. It also provides a Resulting Font preview box.

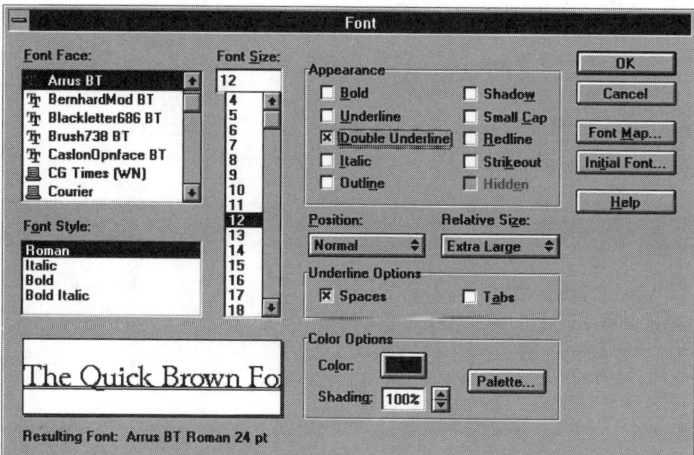

Fig. 6.4
Use the Font dialog box to apply several font changes at the same time.

Note

To select the font that you want for *all* elements of a document, including headers, footers, footnotes, and graphic box captions, use the Document Initial Font feature. Click the Initial Font button in the Font dialog box, or choose Format, **D**ocument, Initial **F**ont. Make your selections in the Document Initial Font dialog box. Note that you can change the default initial font for the selected printer in this dialog box. When you change the default font for the selected printer, that font becomes the default font for the standard template.

Troubleshooting

I changed the font and font size of text, and now I want to return it to its original format.

Choose **E**dit, Undo/Redo **H**istory to undo the changes.

Formatting Lines and Paragraphs

Tip
Use QuickFormat to quickly copy text formats (see "Copying Formats" later in this chapter).

Use Line and Paragraph formatting features for many of the appearance changes that you want to make in a document. For example, you can change line spacing, you can center text on a line, you can indent paragraphs, and you can change margins and justification.

Line and paragraph formatting features are available through the Layout menu. Commonly used features are also available on the Power Bar and the toolbar.

Adjusting Spacing

Tip
You can enter text, select it, and then format it, or you can specify the formatting before you type text. If you format before you type, that format continues until you change it again.

You can adjust the spacing between lines of text when it suits your work, or you can adjust the spacing between paragraphs. Unless you change the defaults, or unless you're using some of the specialized templates, you're using single spacing between lines and between paragraphs.

Note

Line spacing refers to the spacing between lines that are separated by automatic word wrap. Paragraph spacing refers to lines that are separated by a hard return (an Enter keystroke).

Line Spacing

Line spacing refers to the space between the baseline of one line of text and the baseline of an adjacent line of text. WordPerfect adjusts line spacing automatically to allow for the largest font on a line. Enough extra white space is added to make the text readable.

WordPerfect's default line spacing is set to single spacing. When you specify a new number for the line spacing value, the current line height is multiplied by that number. If you choose a value of 1.5 for line spacing, for example, the height of a single-spaced line is multiplied by 1.5. See figure 6.5 for examples of different line spacing values in a document.

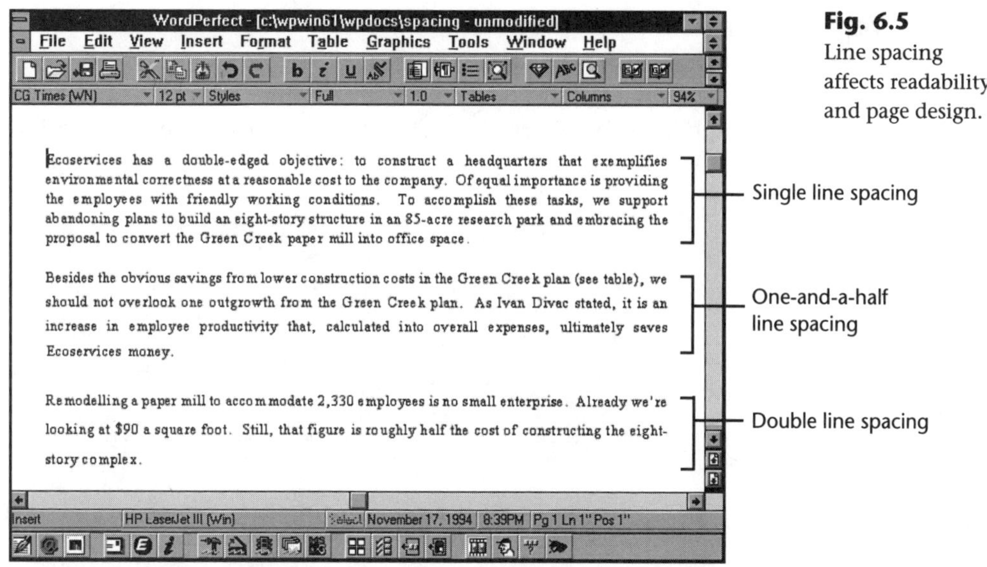

Fig. 6.5
Line spacing affects readability and page design.

To adjust line spacing, click the Line Spacing button on the Power Bar, and then choose a value from the Line Spacing list. If you want a value that isn't on the list, choose Other. Alternatively, choose Fo**r**mat, **L**ine, **S**pacing. In the Line Spacing dialog box (see fig. 6.6), enter a new value in the **S**pacing text box. After entering the value you want for line spacing, choose OK.

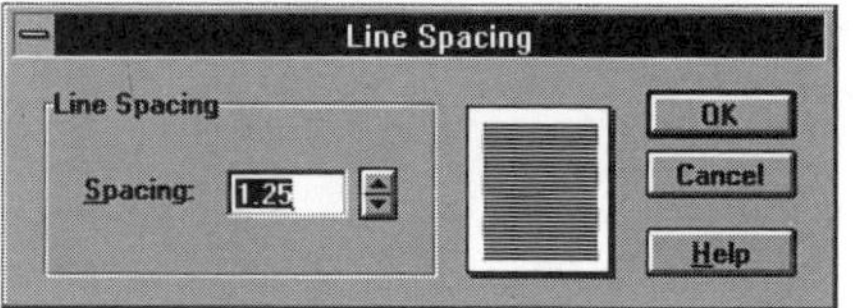

Fig. 6.6
Change the line spacing at the insertion point (or for selected text) at the Line Spacing dialog box.

Paragraph Spacing

Adjust the spacing between *paragraphs* rather than *lines* when you want to adjust the white space between paragraphs (wherever there is an Enter keystroke). You commonly see paragraphs that are separated by a blank line. This appearance is the result of pressing Enter twice. You can add readability to your document with a different approach—by adjusting the spacing between paragraphs. When you set paragraph spacing to 1.5, for example, and you press Enter *once* at the end of a paragraph, the distance between the first paragraph and the second paragraph is 1.5 times the current line spacing value.

To adjust the spacing between paragraphs, click the Paragraph Format button, or choose Format, Paragraph, Format. The Paragraph Format dialog box is displayed, as shown in figure 6.7. Enter a new value for Spacing Between Paragraphs and choose OK. Text with paragraph spacing adjusted to 1.5 is shown in figure 6.8.

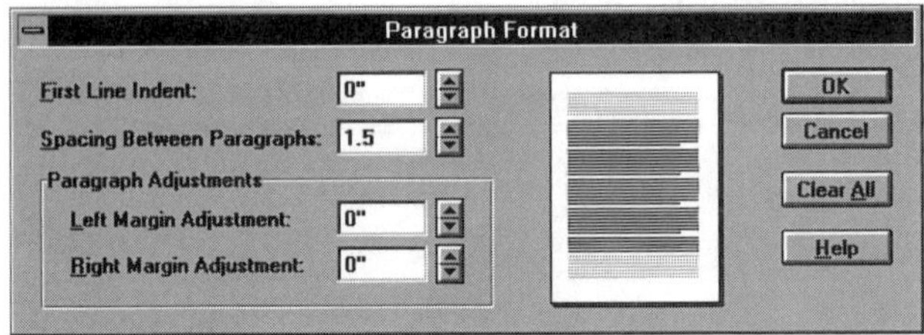

Fig. 6.7
Add extra spacing between paragraphs for readability.

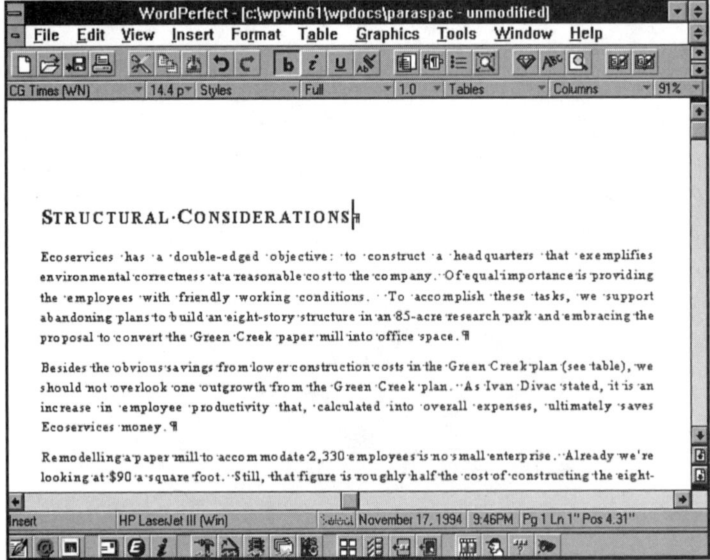

Fig. 6.8
With paragraph spacing set at 1.5, press Enter once between paragraphs to get a result that looks like this.

Tip
When you want a series of lines to be centered or flush right, change the Justification instead of applying Center or Flush Right over and over again.

Centering and Flush Right

You can format individual lines of text with Center or Flush Right. Text that is *centered* is centered between the left and right margins. Title lines are commonly centered. Text that is *flush right* ends at the right margin; it extends "backward" to the left. Page headers and footers often have text that is flush right. Centering and Flush Right apply to single lines only. You must apply either feature separately to every line that you want formatted with that feature.

To apply Center or Flush Right, use the QuickMenu, or press Shift+F7 for Center or Alt+F7 for Flush Right.

◄ See "Using QuickMenus," p. 52

When you apply Center or Flush Right, text following the insertion point is formatted with that feature.

Note

To use Center and Flush Right on the same line, position the insertion point to the left of the text that you want centered and apply the Center feature. Then, position the insertion point to the left of the text that you want flush right and apply the Flush Right feature.

If you accidentally apply Center or Flush Right twice to the same line of text, you will add a line of dots to the left of the text. Apply the same feature a third time to erase the dots.

Using Indent and Double Indent

You can indent one or more paragraphs to emphasize the text, format a long quotation, or create subordinate levels.

► See "Organizing a Simple List with Bullets and Numbers," p. 168

Note

When you create an indent at the beginning of a paragraph, every line in the paragraph has an indented margin; when you Tab at the beginning of a paragraph, only the first line of the paragraph has an indented margin.

To indent a paragraph to the first tab stop from the left margin, position the insertion point at the beginning of the paragraph and choose **I**ndent from the QuickMenu, or press Shift+F7. To indent the margin even further, use multiple indents.

To indent both left and right margins, position the insertion point at the beginning of the paragraph and press Ctrl+Shift+F7, or choose Fo**r**mat, P**a**ragraph, **D**ouble Indent.

To indent several paragraphs at once, first select the paragraphs, and then follow the steps for indenting or double-indenting a single paragraph. Figure 6.9 shows the effects of indents.

Note

Remember that a paragraph ends with a hard return (an Enter keystroke).

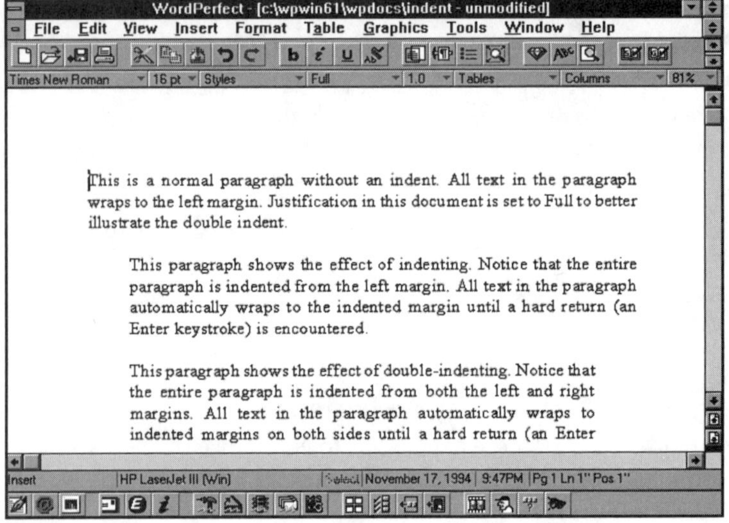

Fig. 6.9
The effects of indents and double indents.

Caution

Don't try to align paragraphs on-screen with the space bar or Enter key. This probably won't look right and it causes editing problems.

Setting and Using Tabs

Unlike indents, which affect all text lines until the next hard return, tabs affect only the current line of text. Tabs are used primarily to indent the first line of a paragraph, to indent one-line paragraphs, and to line up columns of text or numbers.

By default, tabs are set at half-inch intervals across the page. When you use a feature that positions at the next tab stop (Tab, Indent, or Double Indent), the insertion point moves to the next tab stop on the right. You can customize tab stops to suit your work. For example, if you want less space between the bullets in a bulleted list and the text following the bullets, move the tab stop that aligns the text closer to the bullet. You can also set customized tabs to type in columns of text or numbers.

Note

By default, tabs are measured relative to the left margin, not from the left edge of the page. This means that when the left margin is changed, tab settings remain at the same distance from the margin. You can optionally set tabs in absolute measurements, from the left edge of the paper.

Note

Another way to align columns of text or numbers is with a table. Tables make it easy to align text, and there are many formatting features that you can use to enhance the appearance of tables.

▶ See "Working with Tables," p. 190

Setting Tabs with the Ruler Bar

You can quickly set tabs using the Ruler Bar. New tab settings take effect at the beginning of the current paragraph. Be sure to position the insertion point properly (or to select the text for which you want customized tab settings) before you adjust tab settings.

Tip

Before you set new tab stops, position the insertion point and clear all existing tab stops.

Tab settings on the Ruler Bar are indicated by markers that hang down in the bottom area of the Ruler Bar. The shape of the marker indicates the type of alignment (left, center, right align, decimal align) and whether the tab stop has a dot leader. Figure 6.10 shows the Ruler Bar with customized tab settings for several types of alignment.

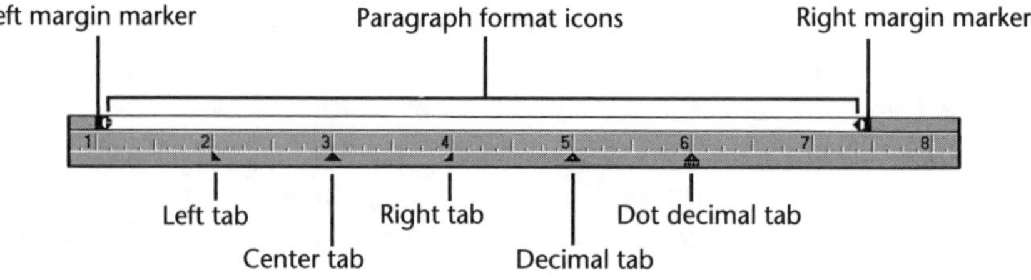

Fig. 6.10
Drag a tab to a new position to move it, or drag a tab below the Ruler Bar to remove it.

- To move a tab, drag it to a new position. As you drag, the position is indicated on the Status Bar.
- To insert a new tab (of the current type), click in the Tab area of the Ruler, beneath the numbered ruler scale.
- To set a different *type* of tab, right-click in the Tab area and choose a type. For example, to set a tab that aligns a column of numbers, first right-click in the Tab area. Choose **D**ecimal, and then click at the desired position on the ruler scale.
- To remove a tab, drag it below the ruler. To remove all tabs, right-click in the Tab area and choose Clear **A**ll Tabs.

Setting Tabs from the Tab Set Dialog Box

The Tab Set dialog box enables you to set tabs precisely, and to specify options that aren't available from the Ruler Bar. Before you adjust tabs, be sure to position the insertion point in the paragraph where you want the new tab stops to take effect, or select the text that you want formatted with new tab stops.

To display the Tab Set dialog box, choose Fo**r**mat, **L**ine, **T**ab Set, or right-click in the Ruler Bar and choose **T**ab Set. WordPerfect displays the Tab Set dialog box (see fig. 6.11).

Fig. 6.11
Use the Tab Set dialog box to position tabs in precise positions.

Tab Set
Settings
Type: Left
Position: 0"
Repeat Every: 0.500"
Position From
Left Margin (Relative)
Left Edge of Paper (Absolute)
Dot Leader Options
Dot Leader Character: .
Spaces Between Characters: 1
Align Character
Character: .
OK
Cancel
Set
Clear
Clear All
Default
Help

- To clear a tab setting, specify the setting in the **P**osition text box, then choose **C**lear.
- Choose Clear **A**ll to clear all tabs. This should be the first step in setting customized tabs.
- To set a tab using the Tab Set dialog box, take the following steps:
    1. Select a tab type from the **T**ype drop-down list.
    2. Specify a position that you want in the **P**osition text box.
    3. Choose **S**et.
- To clear existing tab stops and restore the default tabs, choose **D**efault.

Click OK when you finish working in the Tab Set dialog box.

Setting Margins

You can change the margins at any point in a document. You may want to make the left and right margins smaller to add more room for text in columns, or you may want to set one-half inch top and bottom margins when you use page headers and footers. WordPerfect's Standard template uses 1-inch top and bottom margins and 1-inch left and right margins. Left and right margins can be set by dragging margin markers on the Ruler Bar; all four margins can be set from the Margins dialog box.

Tip
Make your margin change to all elements of the document, including document text, page headers, and footers, by choosing For**r**mat, **D**ocument, Initial Codes **S**tyle before you change margins.

Setting Margins with the Ruler Bar

You can quickly adjust left and right margins using the Ruler Bar. Choose **V**iew, **R**uler Bar to display the Ruler Bar. To adjust the left or right margin, drag the appropriate margin marker to the desired position. The *left* margin marker is the outside marker at the left end of the white space in the Ruler Bar; the *right* margin marker is the outside marker at the right end of the white space. As you drag a marker, its position is indicated on the Status Bar and a vertical dotted line marks its position on the line.

Setting Margins from the Margins Dialog Box

You can specify precise margins from the Margins dialog box. To access the Margins dialog box, choose Format, **M**argins, or right-click in the left margin and choose **M**argins. The Margins dialog box is displayed (see fig. 6.12).

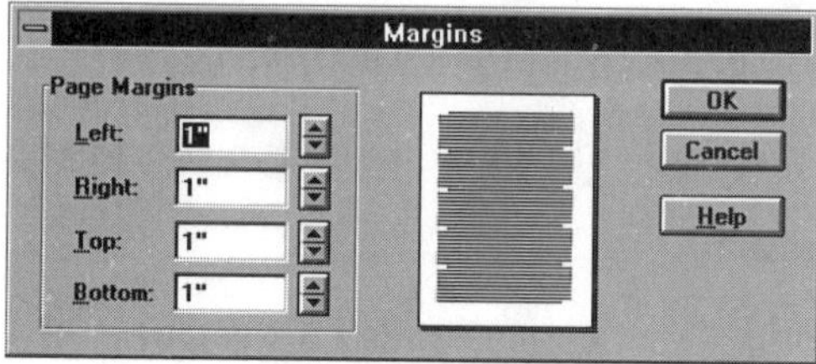

Fig. 6.12
Specify precise margins from the Margins dialog box.

Enter the new margins settings in the appropriate text box areas. When you finish adjusting margins, choose OK.

Setting Justification

Justification is the way that text is aligned relative to the left and right margins on the page. The way you justify text can make the text easy to read, decorative, eye-catching, formal and sophisticated, or casual and flexible. WordPerfect provides four main types of justification: Left (the default), Center, Right, and Full.

Note

If you want all your new documents to use a justification that is different from the default, change the default justification. Choose Fo**r**mat, **D**ocument, Initial Codes **S**tyle. Specify the justification that you want in the **C**ontents area for the style, and ✓ the Use as Default checkbox before you click OK to close the Styles Editor.

Figure 6.13 illustrates the four main types of justification.

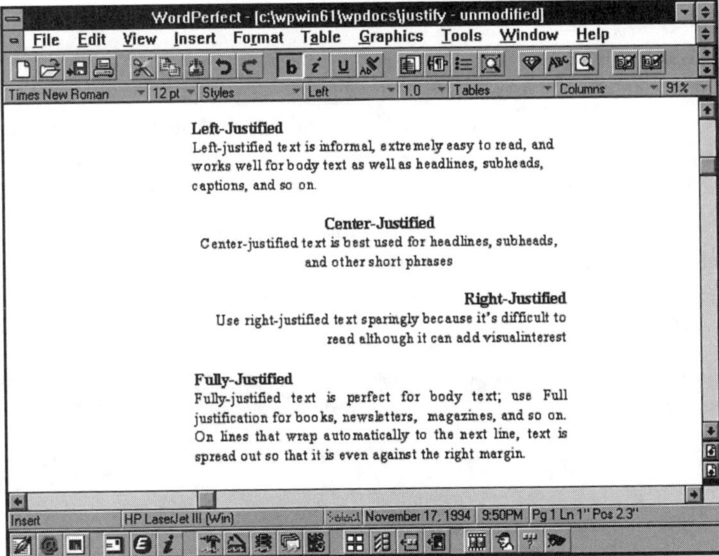

Fig. 6.13
Justify your text in the way that enhances your work.

Troubleshooting

I used a Double Indent to indent a quotation in my document but I want the text to go further in from the margins.

Position the insertion point in front of the indented text and create another Double Indent. This indents the text by one more tab stop.

I set customized tab stops for columns of text and now, at the end of the document, my bulleted list doesn't look right.

Position the insertion point at the end of the columns of text and restore the default tab settings (choose Fo**r**mat, **L**ine, **T**ab Set, **D**efault, OK).

I tried to adjust the customized tab settings that I created for columns of text but now the columns don't line up evenly.

You can undo the damage with the Undo button, or with the Undo/Redo History (Edit menu). Before you adjust tab settings again, be sure to position the insertion point on the first line of the text that you want to adjust.

I used full justification in my document, and now there are big gaps between words.

One way to alleviate the problem is to turn on Hyphenation by choosing Fo**r**mat, **L**ine, Hyph**e**nation, Hyphenation **O**n. For more information on using hyphenation, see Hyphenation in the WordPerfect reference manual.

Copying Formats

QuickFormat makes it easy to copy formats from already formatted text without respecifying each format instruction. Suppose that you took pains to apply several font changes to a subtitle to make it look just right. Now you want to give the same look to other subtitles. Just show QuickFormat where to copy the formats, and it does all of the work for you. When you choose to format "headings," WordPerfect automatically updates all related headings formatted with QuickFormat. If you change your mind about the font face in your heading, for example, you can change the font face in one of the headings, and your change is instantly reflected in the others.

Note

You can apply more than one set of QuickFormat formats in the same document.

To use QuickFormat, first select the text that contains the formats that you want to copy, or place the insertion point in the paragraph whose formats you want to copy. Next, click the QuickFormat button on the Toolbar, or choose Fo**r**mat, **Q**uickFormat. The QuickFormat dialog box is displayed (see fig. 6.14).

Fig. 6.14
Choose Headings from the QuickFormat dialog box to copy paragraph formatting as well as fonts and attributes. Choose Characters to copy fonts and attributes only.

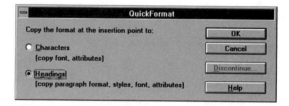

Select Headings to copy fonts and attributes as well as paragraph formatting. When you choose OK, the mouse pointer changes to a paint roller or a paint brush, depending on whether you chose to format characters (brush) or headings (roller). Figure 6.15 shows you the paint roller pointer while QuickFormat is active.

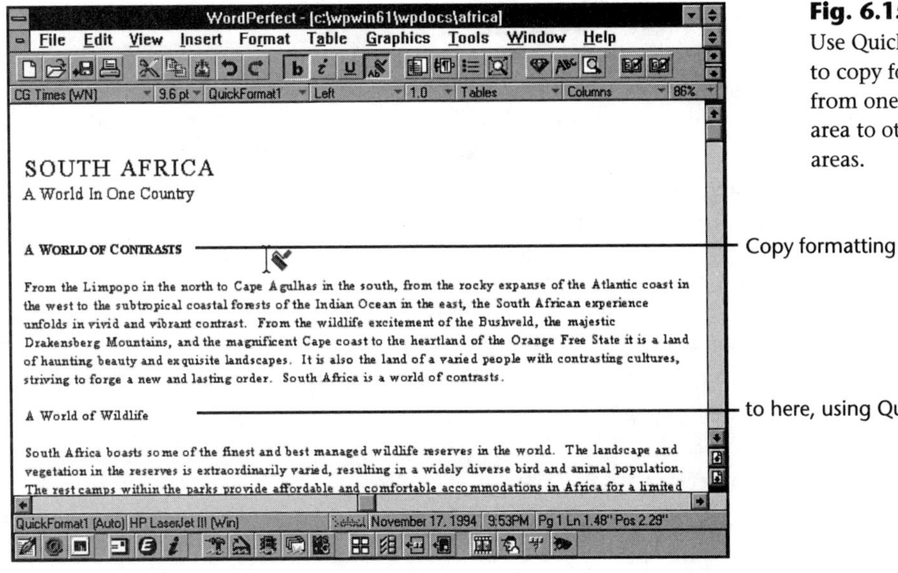

Fig. 6.15
Use QuickFormat to copy formats from one text area to other text areas.

While QuickFormat is active, select any text to which you want to copy formats, or click in a paragraph to which you want to copy formats. Repeat this step as often as desired. When you finish copying formats, click the QuickFormat button to deactivate the feature. The pointer returns to its I-beam appearance.

Troubleshooting

I indented a paragraph, but it doesn't look right.

Remember that you should only use Indent once at the beginning of the paragraph to indent the entire paragraph. If you used Indent again anywhere else in the paragraph, this may be what caused your problem. Either delete the paragraph and retype it, or remove any extraneous `[Hd Left Ind]` codes (choose **V**iew, **R**eveal Codes to turn on Reveal Codes).

I used QuickFormat to copy formats to text in several locations, but after I finished, I accidentally copied them to an extra place.

When you choose **H**eadings at the QuickFormat dialog box, it's easy to copy formats; simply click in the paragraph that you want to format. However, it's also easy to click inadvertently and to format text unintentionally before you remember to turn off QuickFormat. The damage is easily reversed by clicking the Undo button.

Formatting the Page

When you work with multiple-page documents, you may be concerned with the position of page breaks. You also probably want to use page headers and/ or footers, and you might want to number pages. These topics can all be thought of as elements of page formatting. Paper Size can also be thought of as an element of page formatting, although this topic can just as easily apply to a single-page document as to a multiple-page document.

WordPerfect's page-formatting features are flexible and easy to use. You can change the appearance of the page to fit your text so that you present the most professional-looking document possible. This section shows you how to format the page.

Working with Page Breaks

WordPerfect automatically divides your document into pages based on the formatting choices you make. These automatic page breaks are called *soft page breaks*. The position of a soft page break adjusts automatically as you edit a document and cannot be deleted.

Because it's often important to break a page at a specific location, Word-Perfect offers ways to control where pages are divided. The simplest method for ensuring that a page break falls where *you* want it to fall, regardless of format changes, is to use the Page Break feature. A page break created with the Page Break feature is called a *hard page break*.

To create a hard page break, position the insertion point at the beginning of the first line that is to start on a new page, and press Ctrl+Enter, or choose **I**nsert, **P**age Break. All text following a hard page break automatically repaginates.

In Draft view, a hard page break appears as a double line across the screen; a soft page break appears as a single line across the screen. In Page view, soft page breaks and hard page breaks look exactly alike; each of them appears as a heavy line across the page.

Note

When you remove hard page breaks from a document, start at the beginning of the document and work your way toward the end of the document. When you remove a page break, all text from that position on repaginates automatically, and you can adjust subsequent page breaks accordingly.

A hard page break can be removed. To remove a hard page break, position the insertion point just in front of the page break and press Delete, or position the insertion point just after the page break and press Backspace.

Making It Fit

It's easy to make a document fit on the page when you use the Make It Fit Expert. Instead of making endless trial-and-error adjustments to margins, font size, and line spacing, let the Make It Fit Expert do it all for you. You get a perfect fit every time. You tell the Expert what kind of adjustments to make; if you don't like the results, Undo them and try the Make It Fit Expert with another set of adjustments.

To use the Make It Fit Expert, take the following steps:

1. In an open document, choose Fo**r**mat, Make **I**t Fit Expert. The Make It Fit Expert dialog box is displayed (see fig. 6.16).
2. Specify the number of pages to fill in the **D**esired Number of Filled Pages text box. For example, to make a document that is just barely too long for a single page fit on one page, specify **1** as the number of pages to fill.
3. Select the options that you want adjusted in the Items to Adjust area.
4. Choose **M**ake It Fit.
5. Check the results to see if they're satisfactory. Remember that you can Zoom back and forth from a Full Page view with the Page/Zoom Full button. If you don't like the results, click Undo and repeat these steps with different adjustments.

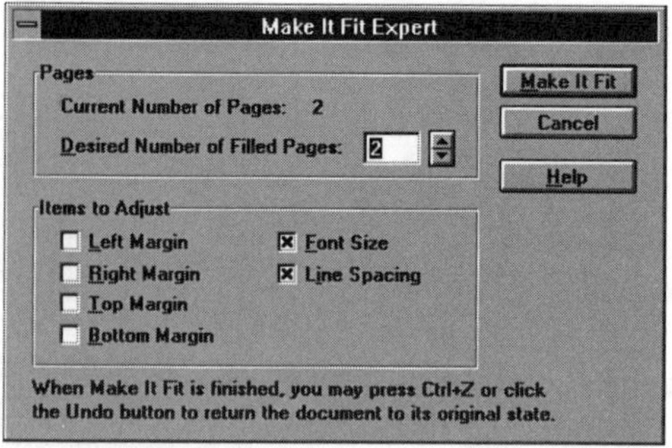

Fig. 6.16
The Make It Fit Expert contracts (or expands) a document to a specified number of pages.

Using Headers and Footers

A header or footer is information that appears at the top or bottom of every page (or just on odd or even pages). You can save yourself a lot of work by creating headers and footers in multiple-page documents.

WordPerfect's headers and footers are easy to use and very flexible. A header or footer can include one or more lines of text, automatic page numbers, the document path and filename, graphic lines, and other graphic elements, as well as formatting such as tables or columns.

The amount of white space at the top or bottom of the page changes only when you change the top or bottom margin, not when you use headers or footers. When you use headers and footers, there is less room on the page for body text. Soft page breaks adjust automatically to allow room for headers and footers.

Headers and footers are visible on-screen in Page view or Two Page view. Even though you can't see a header or footer on-screen in Draft view, it *will* print.

Creating a Header or Footer

The instructions that follow refer to Header A, but are the same as the instructions for Header B, Footer A, or Footer B. WordPerfect provides two headers, Header A and Header B, in case you want different headers on odd and even pages. Unless you're printing on both sides of the paper, you only need one header. To create Header A, take the following steps:

1. Position the insertion point on the first page of body text, or on the page where you want the header to begin.

2. Choose Format, **H**eader/Footer. The Headers/Footers dialog box is displayed. Select Header A, if it's not already selected.

3. Choose **C**reate. You are placed in a special editing screen for Header A (indicated in the title bar at the top of the screen). The Header/Footer feature bar is displayed just below the Toolbar and the Power Bar. If you're working in Page view or Two Page view, you can see the body text on-screen while you're working with your header. The insertion point is placed at the beginning of the header area.

   - Choose **I**nsert, **O**ther, **P**ath and Filename to insert the path and filename.

   - Use the Flush Right (Alt+F7) feature to place information at the right margin.

   - Choose **I**nsert, **D**ate, Date **T**ext; or press Ctrl+D to insert the current date. Alternatively, choose **I**nsert, **D**ate, Date **C**ode to insert a dynamic date.

4. Use the appropriate buttons on the feature bar (see fig. 6.17) to format and to add information to your header. Choose Nu**m**ber, **P**age Number to insert automatic page numbers at the insertion point. Choose Insert **L**ine to insert a horizontal graphics line that extends from margin to margin at the baseline of text on the current line. Choose **D**istance to adjust the distance between text in the header and text on the page.

5. Use the WordPerfect menu bar, the Toolbar, and the Power Bar as needed to format and edit your header.

6. When you finish working in the header editing screen, click the **C**lose button on the feature bar.

Make a letter that prints on your letterhead stationery more attractive and professional-looking by creating a header that prints on all pages after the first page. On the first line of the header is the name of the recipient, on the second line is the date, and on the third line is the page number. Figure 6.17 illustrates a header that follows this format. Although the header is being created on the first page of the letter, it will be suppressed on this page (see "Suppressing Headers, Footers, and Page Numbering" on the following page).

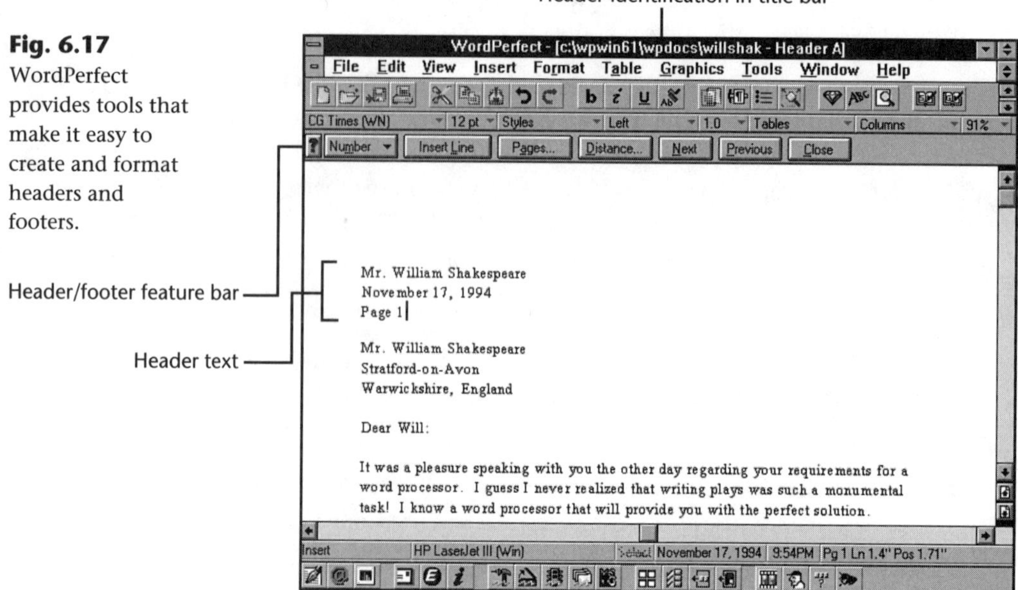

Fig. 6.17
WordPerfect provides tools that make it easy to create and format headers and footers.

Suppressing Headers, Footers, and Page Numbering

To keep a header or footer from printing on a specific page, use WordPerfect's Suppress feature. Typically, a header or footer is created on the first page of body text, although it may be suppressed on that page. Headers and footers are usually suppressed on title pages at the beginning of new sections in a long document.

To suppress headers, footers, and page numbering, take the following steps:

1. Position the insertion point on the page where you want to suppress the header/footer/page numbering.
2. Choose Fo**r**mat, **P**age, S**u**ppress. The Suppress dialog box is displayed (see fig. 6.18).
3. Checkmark the features that you want to suppress on the current page.
4. Choose OK.

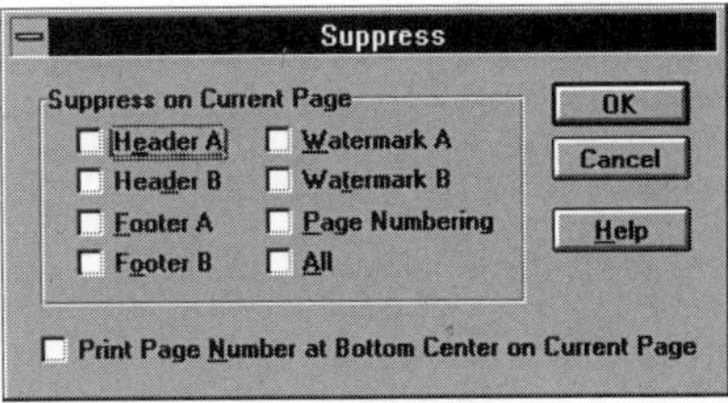

Fig. 6.18
Suppress headers, footers, or page numbering on the current page.

> **Note**
>
> WordPerfect's Delay Codes feature provides you with a method for delaying the effects of headers and footers (and other types of formatting) for a specified number of pages.

Numbering Pages

Although you can insert page numbers in headers or footers, you also have the capability to number pages with the Page Numbering feature. The page number prints in the top or bottom line of the text area. WordPerfect inserts a blank line to separate the number from other text on the page. In Page view, page numbering is visible on-screen. To suppress page numbering, see "Suppressing Headers, Footers, and Page Numbering" in the previous section.

Tip
When you use page numbering within a header or footer, you have more formatting features available than when you use the Page Numbering feature.

Choosing a Page Number Position

To use the Page Numbering feature, you must specify a position for the numbering. Choose Fo**r**mat, **P**age, **N**umbering. The Page Numbering dialog box is displayed. Figure 6.19 illustrates the Page Numbering dialog box with Bottom Center as the selected position. Dashes have been added on either side of the number after choosing **O**ptions and inserting the dashes in the **F**ormat and Accompanying Text text box.

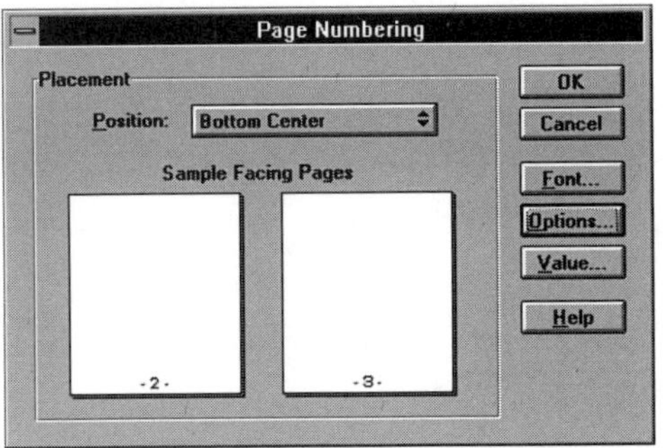

Fig. 6.19
Add page numbers to your document with the Page Numbering feature.

Changing the Page Number Value

By default, WordPerfect uses the physical page number as the page number *value*. The page number value is the number that will print, whether you ask for page numbering in a header or footer or whether you ask for it with the Page Numbering feature. When you have a title page at the beginning of your document, you need to change the page number value on the first page of body text so WordPerfect thinks of that page as page 1.

To change the page number value, position the insertion point on the page to be renumbered, then choose **V**alue at the Page Numbering dialog box, then enter a new value in the New **P**age Number text box.

Changing the Paper Size

Whenever you start a new, empty document with the Standard template, you're using the Letter paper size (8 1/2 × 11-inch paper in a portrait orientation). To use a different physical size or a different orientation, specify another paper size with WordPerfect's Paper Size feature. For example, if you need lots of page width for a table with many columns, you could choose Letter Landscape as your paper size.

To change the Paper Size, take the following steps:

- Position the insertion point on the first page where you want to specify a paper size.
- Choose Fo**r**mat, **P**age, Paper **S**ize. The Paper Size dialog box (see fig. 6.20) appears.
- Select the paper size that you want. Notice that the information area and the Orientation area give you information about and a preview of the selected paper size.
- Choose **S**elect. The selected paper size takes effect on the current page.

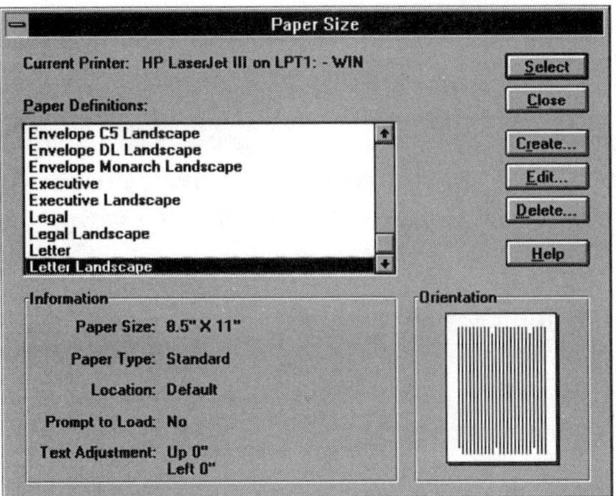

Fig. 6.20
Choose a paper size at the Paper Size dialog box.

Troubleshooting

I created a hard page break but now I have too many page breaks.

Make sure you're working in Draft view so you can see which page breaks are hard page breaks (you can't remove a soft page break). Position the insertion point just in front of a hard page break and press Delete to remove it. Alternatively, turn on Reveal Codes so you can delete the code (see "Working with Formatting Codes" below).

I asked for Page Numbering on the first page where I wanted it and the number that prints is not 1.

Unless you change the page number value, the number that prints is the same as the physical page number. Position the insertion point on the page that you want numbered with a 1 and change the page number value to 1 (after choosing Fo**r**mat, **P**age, **N**umbering, **V**alue).

Working with Formatting Codes

The Reveal Codes screen gives you a behind-the-scenes look at your document. Unless you have formatting problems, there is no need to look at the Reveal Codes screen. Working with Reveal Codes on, however, is an excellent

► See "Customizing Display Preferences," p. 154

method of becoming familiar with codes and formatting! Remember that WordPerfect records your formatting commands in the form of embedded codes. The Reveal Codes screen shows you those embedded codes along with your text. Sometimes, the most efficient way to solve a formatting problem is by working in the Reveal Codes screen and by removing the code that causes a problem. This section shows you how to work in the Reveal Codes screen.

The position of the insertion point determines the placement of codes and where their formatting takes effect. When you select a subtitle and apply boldfacing, for example, boldface codes are embedded at either end of the subtitle. When you change tab settings, a tab set code is embedded at the beginning of the current paragraph.

When you display the Reveal Codes window—by choosing **V**iew, Reveal **C**odes, or by pressing Alt+F3—the screen is split into two windows (see fig. 6.21).

Fig. 6.21
Formatting codes are visible in the Reveal Codes window.

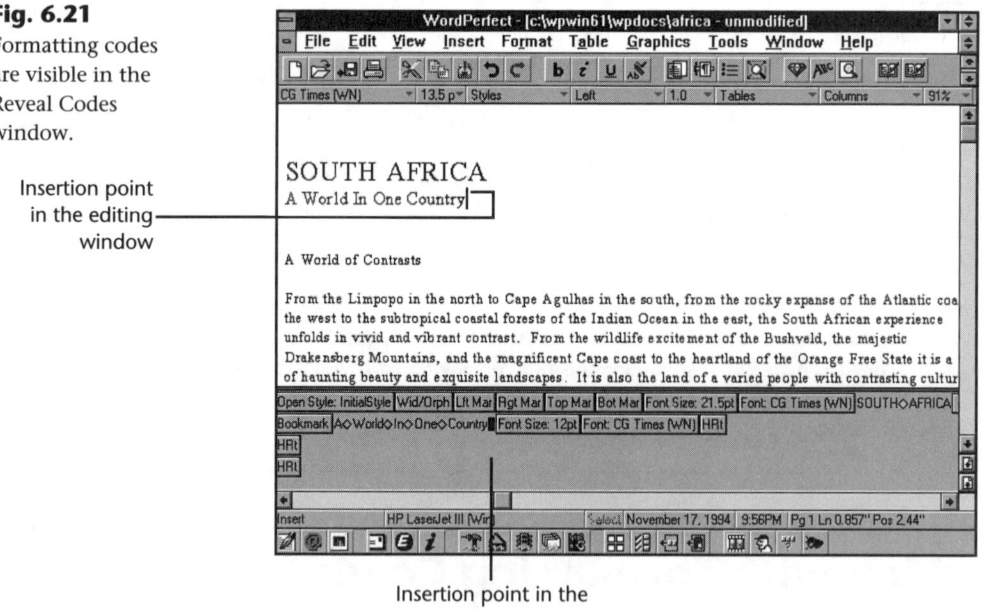

Note

Every document contains an `[Open Style:InitialStyle]` code at its beginning. This code cannot be removed, but it can be edited. Formatting in the Initial Style is a reflection of formatting in the Initial Style for the current template.

► See "Using Styles," p. 177

Notice in figure 6.21 that the insertion point is positioned in front of an `[HRt]` code. To move the insertion point, use the arrow keys or click with the mouse.

◄ See "Positioning the Insertion Point," p. 90

The following pointers will help you work in Reveal Codes:

- To remove a code, drag it out of the Reveal Codes window, or position the insertion point in front of the code and press Delete.
- To edit a code (so you can change the value it contains), double-click the code. To edit a margin code, for example, double-click the code. You are taken instantly to the Margins dialog box, where you can specify a new value.

Troubleshooting

I have difficulty locating the insertion point in the Reveal Codes window.

Press an arrow key while you are looking in the Reveal Codes window. The movement of the insertion point (a small rectangle) should attract your attention.

From Here...

In this chapter, you learned to format characters, lines, paragraphs, and pages by using WordPerfect's commands and buttons. You can now change the font face, font size, and font style; adjust line spacing, change margins and justification, create headers and footers and number pages, make a document fit on the page, and specify a paper size.

For more information about creating documents with WordPerfect, see the following chapters:

- Chapter 7, "Using Writing Tools and Printing," covers the use of templates, checking spelling and grammar in a document, using the thesaurus, printing a document, printing an envelope, and printing labels.
- Chapter 8, "Customizing WordPerfect," shows you how to customize WordPerfect to suit the way you work. You'll learn to customize display preferences, file preferences, environment preferences, Toolbar and Power Bar preferences, Status Bar preferences, and Summary preferences.

Chapter 7

Using Writing Tools and Printing

by Judy Felfe

WordPerfect supplies a variety of tools that make it easy to create professionally finished documents without errors. By simply selecting a template and filling in the blanks, you can quickly create fax forms, memos, daily planners, and many other standard documents. In addition to supplying you with preformatted documents, WordPerfect provides a variety of powerful proofreading tools. You can check spelling and correct errors automatically. You can keep your text from being monotonous and repetitive by finding alternative words with the Thesaurus. You can use the grammar checker to suggest improvements to your writing style.

With all of these writing tools at your fingertips, you can create error-free, well-written documents that look as though they were created by a graphics artist. WordPerfect takes care of much of the tiresome detail work of formatting, manual proofreading, and evaluating your writing style.

Once you finish your document, you can print it. WordPerfect provides features that make it easy to print envelopes and mailing labels as well as documents.

In this chapter, you learn to

- Use templates
- Check your spelling and use QuickCorrect
- Find synonyms with the Thesaurus
- Check your grammar
- Print your document, print envelopes, and print labels

Using Templates

Every new document that you create is based on a template. The standard template (the default template) is generic; *you* provide most of the formatting and all of the text. Other templates often provide text as well as formatting. Many templates are automated. Repetitive information is entered only once, and you can fill in the blanks with a minimum of effort. The template prompts you for necessary information (like the recipient's name), you answer the prompts, and the template places your input in the proper location.

Whenever you create a new document that should have a consistent, specialized appearance, it makes sense to use a template. It's well worth your while to explore WordPerfect's templates, and to see which ones will save *you* time and work. In this section, you learn how to use templates and how to make minor modifications to a template so that it better suits your taste.

Understanding Templates

You already know that templates can contain text as well as formatting. Each template contains its own set of tools, including styles, abbreviations, macros, keyboards, toolbars, and menus. Many templates have customized toolbars so that you have just the right tools close at hand when you create a document based on that template. When you use one of WordPerfect's letter templates, for example, the toolbar has buttons for inserting a prewritten letter into the current document, for selecting your closing from a list of closings, for setting the document initial font, and for spell checking.

A typical *memo* template might contain the company letterhead and logo, and standard text in specific places on the page. A *letter* template, on the other hand, might consist of your company name and address, the date, a standard salutation, and a standard closure. An *expense report* template could include a table complete with formulas that automatically total each category of expense as well as the total expenses.

Although the template feature is complex, learning to make the feature work for you is easy. You can use WordPerfect's predefined templates as is. You can easily make basic editing changes to existing templates, and you can easily create simple templates of your own.

Applying Templates to Documents

When the time comes to create a particular type of document—a memo, for example—take the following steps:

1. Click the New Document button in the middle of the WordPerfect toolbar (the New Document button lets you choose a template to start a new document; the New *Blank* Document button, at the left end of the toolbar, starts a new document based on the standard template).

   Alternatively, choose **F**ile, **N**ew. The New Document dialog box appears. The default selection is the standard template (Main group). Figure 7.1 illustrates the dialog box with memo as the selected group and Memo-Contemporary as the description of the selected template (memo2).

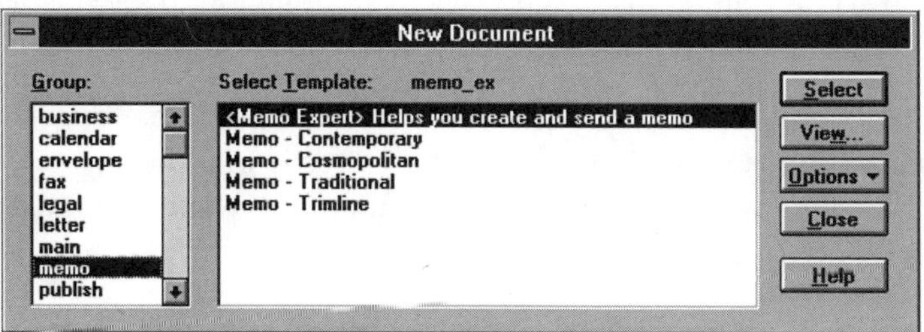

Fig. 7.1
Choose a template as a model for a new document.

2. Highlight a template group, then highlight a description in the Select **T**emplate list.

3. Choose **S**elect. A copy of the selected template opens in a new document window.

4. Enter information as prompted. The first time you use a template that requires personal information, you are prompted to fill in the information at the Personalize Your Template dialog box. The information includes your name, company name, and so on. The information you enter is recorded and is then available for use in all templates. If you should decide at a later time to edit your personal information, click the **P**ersonal Information button at any template's Template Information dialog box (see fig. 7.2).

Tip
To find out more about an existing template, highlight its description, then click the View button. The View window appears, showing you the text and an idea of the formatting of the template.

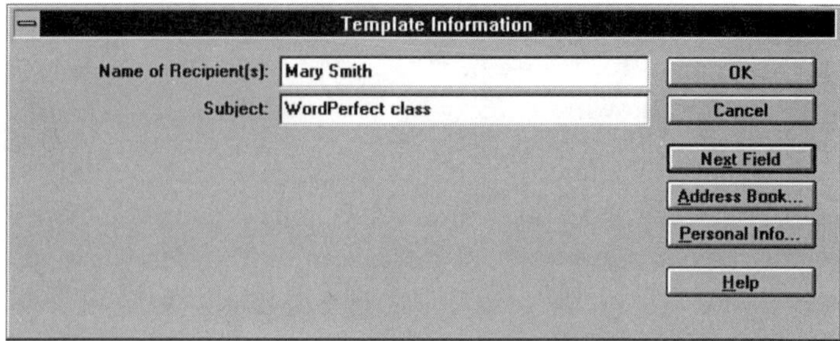

Fig. 7.2
Enter template information for a new document.

5. Depending on the template, you may be prompted for recipient information and any other information required for the template. At a template's Template Information dialog box, you can edit your personal information. If the template requires recipient address information, you can access your template address book information to select a name from your address book or to add a new name to the address book.

6. After you finish responding to prompts, your screen may appear as shown in figure 7.3. Type information directly into the document as desired. You can save the document, print it, or work with it like any other document.

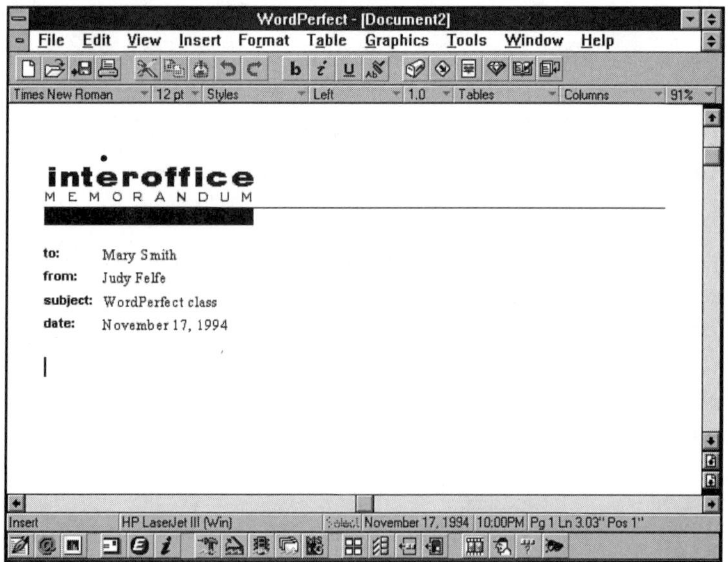

Fig. 7.3
A memo document after responding to prompts for template information.

Making Basic Editing Changes to a Template

Suppose that the Expense Report template suits you almost perfectly, but you'd like it to use a different font face. Or, suppose that you'd like to make a permanent change to a column width in the expense report table. Don't be afraid to edit a template and make basic editing changes.

To edit a template, take the following steps:

1. Access the New Document dialog box (by clicking the New Document button or by choosing **F**ile, **N**ew). Select the description of the template that you want to edit.

2. Choose **O**ptions. At the Options menu, choose **E**dit Template. The template file is opened into an editing window and the Template feature bar is displayed below the Power Bar.

3. Make changes as you would when you edit any document. For example, change the column width in the expense report table. Be careful when editing a template not to delete or modify any of the prompts without using the "build prompts" feature button. Any missing prompts or bookmarks will result in error messages the next time you use the template.

4. When you finish editing the template, choose **E**xit Template (on the feature bar). Answer **Y**es to the prompt to save changes. The changes are saved and will be reflected in all new documents based on this template.

Tip

If you can't remember the filename of the template you want to edit, access the New Document dialog box and highlight the description of the template. The filename is displayed above the Select **T**emplate list.

Note

To create a new template, click the New Document button. At the New Document dialog box, choose **O**ptions, then **N**ew. If you have a previously saved document that you'd like to use for the template, use the **I**nsert File button on the feature bar to insert the document into the template editing window.

Troubleshooting

I entered my personal information the first time I used a template and now I want to change it.

Start a new document based on a memo template (or any other template that uses prompts). At the prompt dialog box, choose **P**ersonal Info. Change the information as desired.

Checking Spelling

Tip

If you select text before starting the Spell Checker, only the selected text is spell-checked.

The Spell Checker is the single most important proofreading tool you can use. No matter how long or short a document is, using the Spell Checker is well worth the time it takes. How do you feel about the person who sends you a letter with a typo or a spelling error? Don't let this happen when someone else receives your letter.

The Spell Checker looks for misspelled words, duplicate words, and irregular capitalization. When it finds a word with one of these problems, it stops and offers suggestions. You can replace the problem word, skip to the next problem, and so on. This section shows you how to work with the Spell Checker.

Additionally, WordPerfect includes a feature called QuickCorrect. Using QuickCorrect, you can instruct WordPerfect to correct spelling mistakes as you make them. If, for example, you often type **teh** instead of **the**, QuickCorrect can correct the error immediately. This section also discusses how to use the QuickCorrect feature.

Using the Spell Checker

To start the Spell Checker, click the Spell Check button, or choose **T**ools, **S**pell Check. The Spelling dialog box appears. It displays the first problem, with a list of suggestions for replacement (see fig. 7.4).

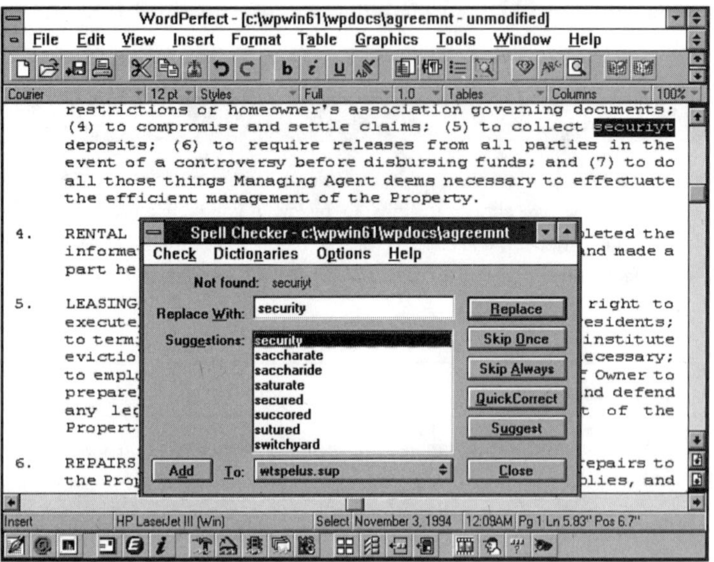

Fig. 7.4
Select a word in the Suggestions list or enter the correct word in the Replace With text box to correct the mistake in the text.

Table 7.1 describes options in the Spell Checker dialog box.

Table 7.1 Spell Checker Options

Option	Description
Not found	Displays the word in question.
Replace **W**ith	Suggests an alternative spelling; you can enter your own new spelling in this text box.
Sugg**e**stions	Select a word in the Sugg**e**stions list box to replace the misspelled word.
Replace	Replace the word with the text specified in the Replace With box.
Skip **O**nce	Skip this occurrence and move to the next problem.
Skip **A**lways	Skip all occurrences of this word in this spell check session.
QuickCorrect	Replace the word with the word in the Replace With box, and add the error and the replacement word to the QuickCorrect list. See the following section, "Using QuickCorrect," for more information.
S**u**ggest	Offer more suggestions, if possible.
A**d**d	Add the word to the supplemental dictionary named in the **T**o box. Use this option to add proper nouns (like your name or street address) so the Spell Checker won't stop on them again.
To	Specify the dictionary to which words will be added (normally, your personal supplemental dictionary).
Close	Close the Spell Checker.

If the problem word is a capitalization problem, WordPerfect displays `Capitalization` instead of `Not Found`. Highlight the correct suggestion, or type it into the Replace **W**ith box, then choose **R**eplace.

If the problem word is a duplicate word, WordPerfect displays `Duplicate words` instead of `Not Found`, and suggests that you replace the duplicate word with a single word. You can replace or skip to the next problem.

Use the menu in the Spell Checker dialog box to change the scope of the spell check or to customize the way the Spell Checker works. Any settings that you change affect future Spell Check sessions.

Using QuickCorrect

QuickCorrect saves time and effort by correcting common spelling errors as you make them. QuickCorrect replaces the error with the correct spelling (or the correct capitalization) as soon as you move past the misspelled word. If, for example, you often type **teh** instead of **the**, QuickCorrect corrects the word as soon as you press the spacebar, or as soon as you press another punctuation key (such as a comma, period, or semi-colon). In addition to correcting spelling errors, QuickCorrect can automatically correct sentence problems, like double spacing between words. QuickCorrect can also be programmed to replace open and close quotes with typesetter-style quotes (called *SmartQuotes*).

QuickCorrect has a built-in list of common misspellings and their correct spellings. You can add your own common misspellings to the list. QuickCorrect is just one of WordPerfect's many features that can be customized for the way *you* work.

To add items to the list of errors and their corrections, or to change QuickCorrect options, choose **T**ools, **Q**uickCorrect; or press Ctrl+Shift+F1. The QuickCorrect dialog box is displayed (see fig. 7.5).

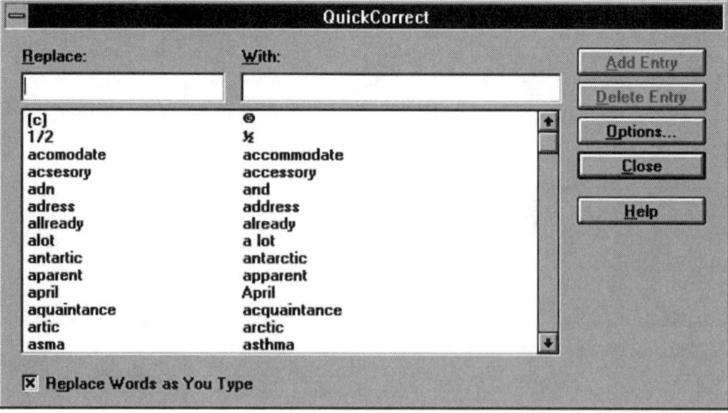

Fig. 7.5
Use QuickCorrect to automatically correct common spelling errors.

Add an entry by typing what you want to correct in the **R**eplace box, typing what you want the correction to be in the **W**ith box, and then choosing **A**dd Entry.

To change QuickCorrect options, click the **O**ptions button. The QuickCorrect Options dialog box appears (see fig. 7.6).

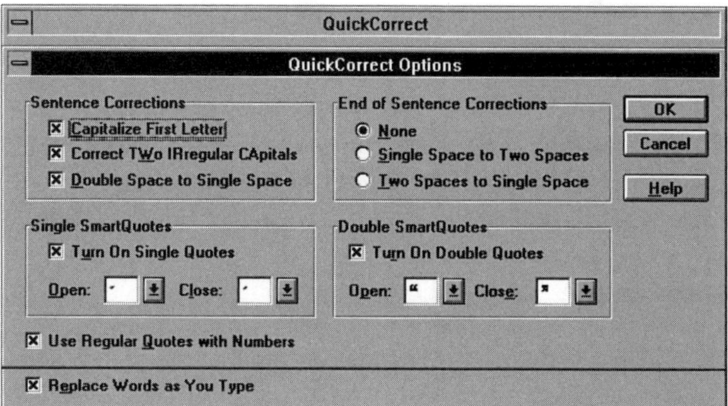

Fig. 7.6
Tell QuickCorrect what kind of corrections you want it to make at the QuickCorrect Options dialog box.

Troubleshooting

I have a lot of words that contain numbers, such as measurements, in my document. I want the Spell Checker to skip these words.

Choose **O**ptions on the Spell Checker menu bar, then deselect Words with **N**umbers.

I want to remove a word that I inadvertently added to my dictionary.

Choose Dictio**n**aries at the Spell Checker menu bar, then **S**upplementary. Highlight the dictionary you want to edit and choose **E**dit. Make the desired changes and choose **C**lose (twice).

Note

For most purposes, deselect "Document Dictionary" in Spell Checks option menu so that added words are stored in the supplemental dictionary rather than a document dictionary. This allows added words to be available for all documents, not just individual documents.

Using the Thesaurus

WordPerfect's Thesaurus can help you improve your composition skills. When you can't think of the word that means exactly what you want to say, or you think that you've used the same word too often, let the Thesaurus help you. The Thesaurus supplies a variety of alternatives (synonyms and antonyms) for the word you're looking up. You can choose the word you want from the list of alternatives and ask the Thesaurus to make a replacement for you.

Tip

You can start the Thesaurus, type the word that you want to look up in the **W**ord box, and choose **L**ook Up.

Suppose that you want to find a synonym for the word *monumental.* Place the insertion point in the word. Choose **T**ools, **T**hesaurus, or press Alt+F1. The Thesaurus appears. Alternatives for *monumental* appear in the first column. The alternatives are divided into adjectives (a) and antonyms (ant) (scroll downward to see alternatives that are not visible). Depending on the word that is looked up, references might include nouns (n), verbs (v), adjectives (a) and antonyms (ant). A word that can be looked up is called a *headword.* Headwords are marked with bullets. To display another column of alternatives, double-click a headword.

Figure 7.7 illustrates the Thesaurus after several lookups have been performed. If you perform more than three lookups, you can use the arrow buttons to scroll to columns that aren't visible. When you decide on the word that you want to use as a replacement, select it and choose **R**eplace. If you decide not to make a replacement, choose **C**lose.

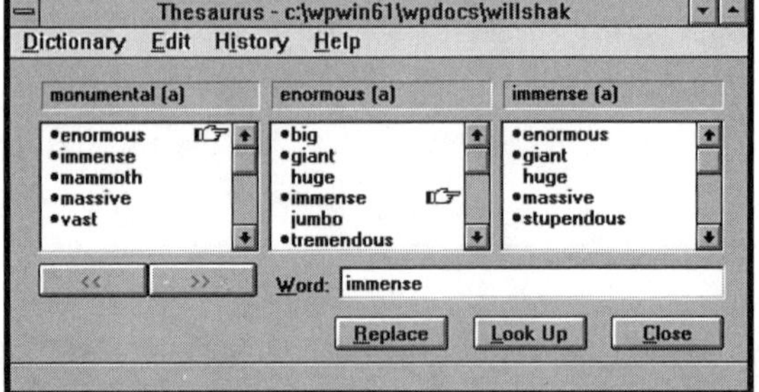

Fig. 7.7

Find alternate words with the Thesaurus.

Troubleshooting

I looked up several meanings, and now I want to go back to the original word I looked up in the Thesaurus.

Use the arrow buttons to scroll back to the column of alternatives for the original word, or choose **H**istory on the Thesaurus menu bar and then choose the word that you want to go back to.

While I was using the Thesaurus, I thought of a different word that I wanted to look up. Can I do it without closing the Thesaurus and typing the word into the document?

Type the word that you want to look up in the **W**ord box, and then choose **L**ook Up.

Checking Grammar

Grammatik is yet another proofreading feature that WordPerfect provides for you. Even if you don't *think* you have problems with your writing style, Grammatik may help you. When Grammatik points out a potential problem and explains the logic behind the problem, you may realize that its suggestions offer real improvement. Grammatik is a built-in grammar checker that checks your document for correct grammar, style, punctuation, and word usage, and thus catches many errors that would be bypassed by the Spell Checker. Grammatik checks both grammar and spelling; so you actually take care of grammar problems and spelling problems all at once.

Tip
To turn off spell checking while the grammar checker is running, choose **P**references from the Grammatik menu, then **E**nvironment. Deselect **P**rovide spelling suggestions, then choose OK.

When Grammatik reports a potential grammar problem, you can review the error and suggestion, then decide whether to change the text.

To proofread your document with Grammatik, click the Grammatik button or choose **T**ools, **G**rammatik. Proofreading begins, as shown in figure 7.8.

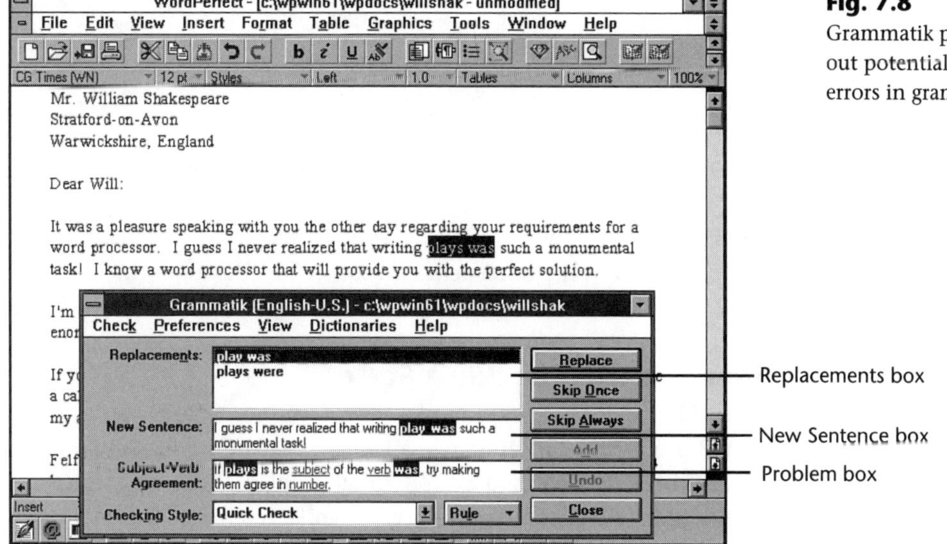

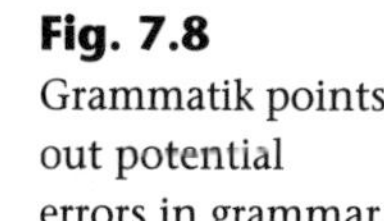

Fig. 7.8
Grammatik points out potential errors in grammar.

Correcting Errors

When Grammatik stops on a problem, you can respond with the options described in table 7.2.

Table 7.2 Grammatik options

Option	Description
Resume	This option appears after you pause Grammatik to edit the document. Click **R**esume to resume proofreading.
Replace	Replace the problem word or phrase with the suggested replacement.
Skip **O**nce	Ignore the highlighted problem and move on to the next problem.
Skip **A**lways	Ignore the highlighted problem for the rest of this proofreading session.
A**d**d	Add the word to your dictionary.
Undo	Undo your last replacement.
Ru**l**e	Turn off the current rule, save current settings to a new style, etc.
Close	End the proofreading session.

In some cases the problem might require manual editing. When this occurs, edit the problem in the document window (after clicking in the document or using the scrollbar). When you finish your manual editing, choose **R**esume.

Changing the Checking Style

The checking style that Grammatik uses determines what is identified as a potential problem. For example, in a formal checking style, a contraction (such as **won't**) is identified as a potential problem. You can change the checking style to one that's best for your work. To change the checking style for this session *and* future sessions, use the **P**references menu, or to change it *just for this session,* use the Check**i**ng Style drop-down list.

To examine the rules for any style, or to edit the style, tell Grammatik that you want to edit the style. Choose **P**references, **C**hecking Styles, select the style that you want to examine (or edit), and then choose **E**dit. In the Edit Rules dialog box, you can see which rule classes are selected for the style and other rules that apply to the style. If you actually do want to edit the style, save your changes with **S**ave (to keep the same style name) or with Save **A**s (to give the edited style a new name).

Performing a Statistical Analysis

Grammatik can display statistics that will help you make your writing easier to understand. To view these statistics, choose **V**iew, **S**tatistics. Figure 7.9 illustrates Grammatik's statistics.

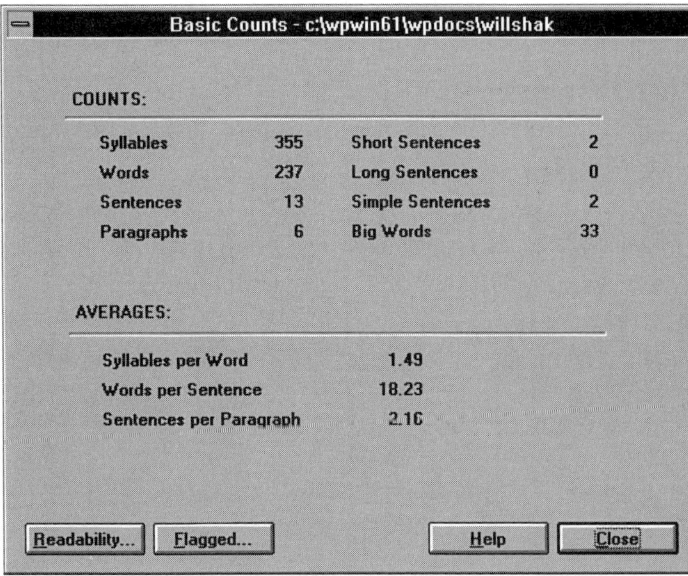

Fig. 7.9
View document statistics with Grammatik.

Tip
The Document Information feature provides a word count, average words per sentence, and other stats that are not provided by Grammatik. To see Document Information, choose **F**ile, Document **I**nfo.

II

Using WordPerfect

Troubleshooting

Grammatik keeps stopping on contractions ("won't," "you're," and so on) and I want it to skip them.

You can either change the checking style to a less formal style, or you can turn off the rule with the **Rul**e button.

I can't see the problem word in the proper context; the Grammatik window is obscuring that portion of the document.

Move the Grammatik window to another position by dragging its title bar. You can also scroll the document window. If you scroll the document window, you need to click the **R**esume button when you're ready to resume grammar checking.

Printing

◀ See "Making It Fit," p. 123

▶ See "Customizing Other Preferences," p. 163

Whether you use WordPerfect to create simple documents or desktop publishing masterpieces, printing is a task that you perform often. Because you are working in a WYSIWYG environment, what you print is not the mystery it was a few short years ago. If you're working in Draft view, you can see almost everything just as it will print. You can click the Page/Zoom Full button to get a quick look at a full page in Page view. Alternatively, you can use the View menu to switch to Page view.

Printing a Document

To print the document in the active window, click the Print button, or choose **F**ile, **P**rint. The Print dialog box is displayed.

When you print a document, most often you will print using the default options in the Print dialog box. The default options print one copy of all the pages in the document. Figure 7.10 shows the Print dialog box.

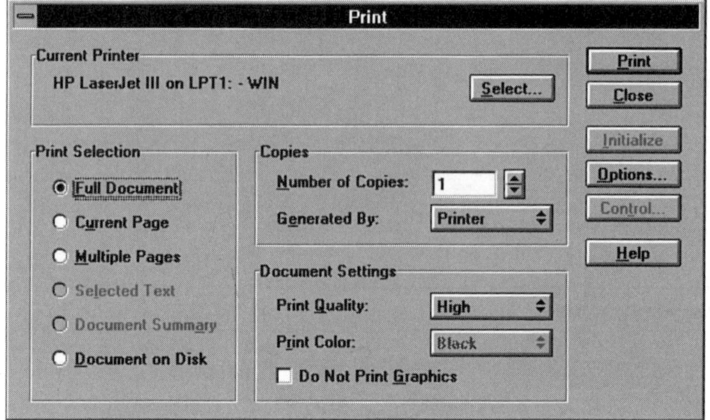

Fig. 7.10
To print using the default options in the Print dialog box, click the Print button.

Table 7.3 describes options in the Print dialog box.

Table 7.3 Options in the Print Dialog Box

Option	Description
Select	Change the selected printer to the one you want to use. For example, before you send a fax, change to the printer that has been defined as your fax printer.
Full Document	Print all pages in the document.

Option	Description
C**u**rrent Page	Print only the page in which the insertion point is located.
Multiple Pages	Print more than one page. For example, you can specify a range of pages 5-7 to print pages 5 through 7, or a range of 18- to print from page 18 through the end of the document.
Se**l**ected Text	Print the selected text (this is the default if text is selected when you tell WordPerfect to print).
Document Summ**a**ry	Print the document summary only.
Document on Disk	Print a document stored on a hard disk or floppy disk or network drive without opening it into a document window.
Number of Copies	Specify the number of copies.
G**e**nerated By	When this option is set to Printer rather than WordPerfect, multiple copies are not collated, but print time is faster, especially when the document contains graphics.
Print **Q**uality	When you print draft copies, use Medium or Draft to save time.
P**r**int Color	This option is available only when the selected printer is capable of printing in color.
Do Not Print **G**raphics	Save printing time by checking this box but sacrifice the printing of table lines, graphics lines, page borders, and any graphics images in the document.
Options	Print the document summary, print a booklet, etc.
Con**t**rol	Monitor the progress of a print job, or cancel a print job.

Note

If you want to print a document on disk, consider using File **O**ptions in WordPerfect's Open File dialog box. You can select multiple files and print them all at once.

Printing an Envelope

Note

The font on an envelope is automatically taken from the document initial font (Fo**r**mat, **D**ocument, Initial **F**ont). To save yourself the work of changing fonts twice—once in the document text and once in the envelope window—make sure that the document initial font is what you want both for the letter and the envelope.

WordPerfect's Envelope feature automatically formats and addresses your envelope for you. If you have already typed the inside address into a letter, and you want an envelope for the letter, just choose Fo**r**mat, En**v**elope.

To address an envelope after typing a letter, follow these steps:

1. Choose Fo**r**mat, En**v**elope to open the Envelope dialog box (see fig. 7.11).

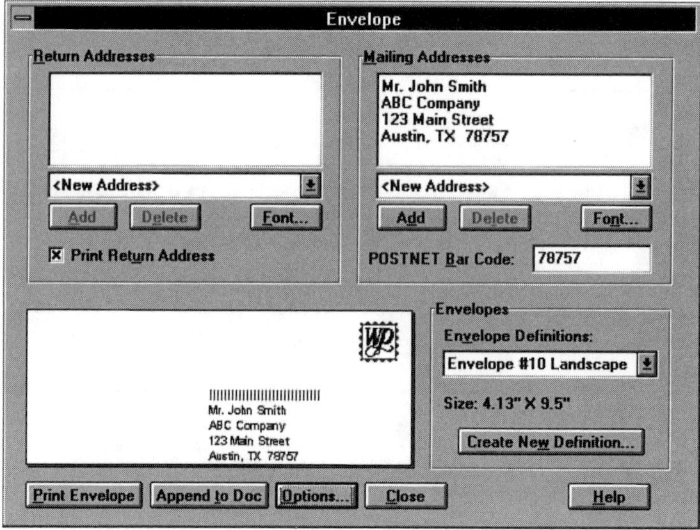

Fig. 7.11
WordPerfect's Envelope feature automatically formats and addresses your envelope.

2. Choose **R**eturn Address to place the insertion point in the text box, then type the return address.

   To change the font face or size used in the return address, choose the **F**ont button in the return address section.

If you type a return address, you can choose **A**dd so you can use the address in future envelopes.

3. To enter or add a mailing address, choose **M**ailing Address and type the mailing address or edit the available text.

   As with the return address, you can change the font face or font size used in the mailing address.

   You can add the mailing address shown to the envelope address list by chosing A**d**d.

4. If you want a POSTNET bar code printed on the envelope, but the POSTNET **B**ar Code option is not displayed under the mailing address, choose **O**ptions and select one of the "include" options in the USPS Bar Code Options section.

5. To print the envelope immediately, choose **P**rint Envelope; to add the envelope to the document, choose Append **t**o Doc.

Printing Labels

WordPerfect makes it easy to print labels by showing you each label on-screen exactly as it will appear on the printed sheet. All that you have to do is to find and select the brand name and item number on WordPerfect's list of label types and then enter the names and addresses.

If you're printing three-across labels, you probably want to select a font that is smaller than the font you usually use for your documents.

Choosing a Label Definition

To choose a label definition, take the following steps:

1. Place the insertion point at the beginning of an empty document, or on a blank page.

2. Choose Fo**r**mat, La**b**els to open the Labels dialog box (see fig. 7.12).

3. In the **L**abels list, move the highlight bar to the definition you want to use, then choose **S**elect. An empty label is displayed on-screen.

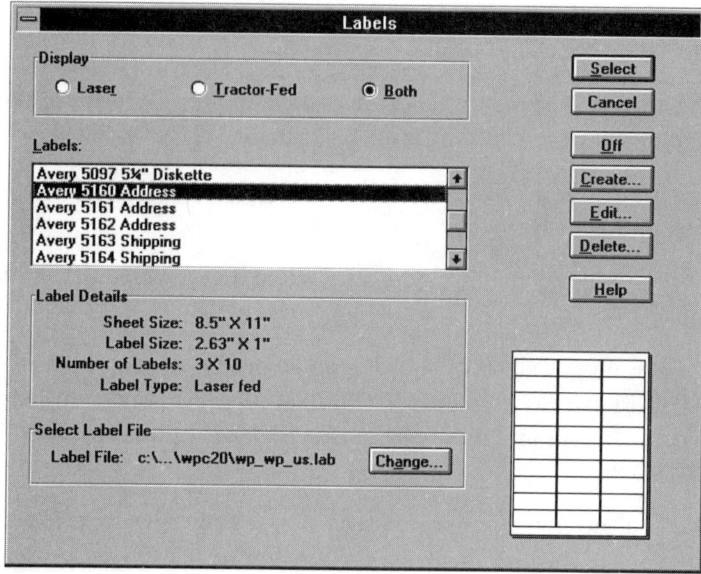

Fig. 7.12
Select the labels you want to print from WordPerfect's list of label types.

Centering Text on Labels

To center the name and address information vertically on each label, so that it doesn't start at the top edge of the label, use WordPerfect's Center Page(s) feature.

To center all names and addresses between the top and bottom of each label, position the insertion point at the beginning of an empty document, or on the first label. Then, choose Fo**r**mat, **P**age, **C**enter. At the Center Page(s) dialog box, choose Current and **S**ubsequent Pages, then choose OK.

Entering Text on Labels

► See "Performing a Merge," p. 227

To understand how the Labels feature works, imagine that each separate label is a page, although there may be many labels on a single sheet of paper. Each label is treated as a logical page, although it may not be a physical page. This means that you can print page headers on each label, you can apply the Center Page(s) feature to all labels, and you can (and need to) create hard page breaks between labels.

1. Type the name and address as you want it to appear on the printed label.

2. At the end of each line, press Enter to move to the next line *only* if there are more lines to be typed for this label. If the line you just typed is the last line for this label, press Ctrl+Enter to create a hard page break.

3. Continue typing names and addresses (or other label text) and inserting hard page breaks after each label, until you have typed all the labels that you want to print. As you add each label, it appears on-screen exactly as it will print. Be careful not to press Enter after you type the last line of each label; this adds an unnecessary blank line and distorts the vertical centering. After you add several names and addresses, your screen may look like figure 7.13.

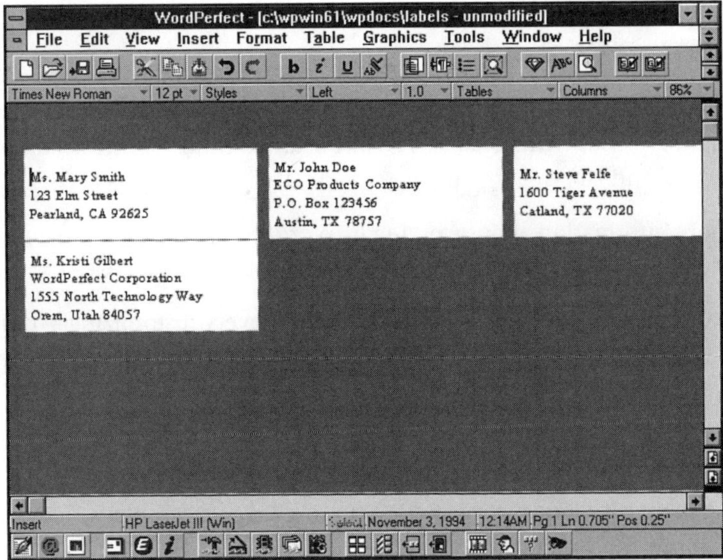

Fig. 7.13
See your labels on-screen just as they will print. Labels are separated by hard page breaks. Center Page(s) centers text vertically on each label.

Troubleshooting

I have several lines of text that overflow to the second page of my document, and I'd like them to be on the first page.

Choose Fo**r**mat, Make **I**t Fit Expert. At the Make It Fit Expert dialog box, pick the options that you want adjusted and choose **M**ake It Fit.

◄ See "Making it Fit," p. 123

After I typed a letter, I told WordPerfect to create an envelope, but the inside address didn't appear in the mailing address area.

If your letter isn't in a standard business format, WordPerfect may not be able to find it and copy it to the mailing address. If this happens, close the Envelope dialog box, select the inside address, and access the Envelope dialog box again. When you select a name and address before using the Envelope feature, the selected information appears automatically in the mailing address on the envelope.

(continues)

(continued)

My names and addresses are jammed up against the top edge of my labels.

Position the insertion point in the first label and choose Fo**r**mat, **P**age, **C**enter, Current and **S**ubsequent Pages, OK.

From Here...

In this chapter you learned to use writing tools to proofread your documents and improve your writing skills. You also learned how to print documents, envelopes, and labels.

For more information about working in WordPerfect, see the following chapters:

- Chapter 8, "Customizing WordPerfect," covers customizing WordPerfect to suit the way you work. You will learn to change Display preferences, Environment preferences, File preferences, Summary preferences, and other preferences. In addition, you will learn to customize the default settings for new documents.

- Chapter 9, "Organizing and Formatting Large Documents," covers outlining and formatting with styles.

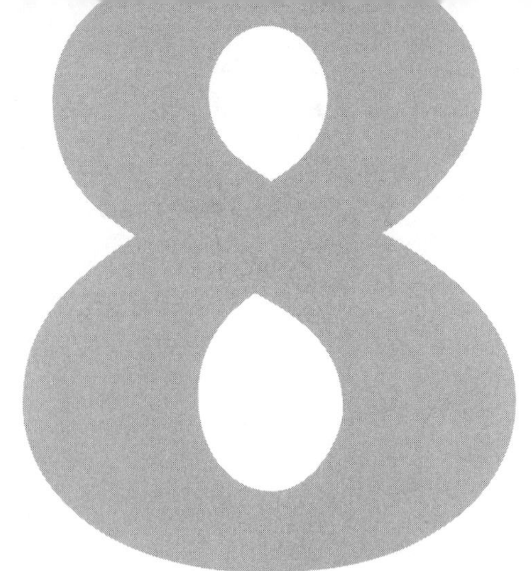

Chapter 8

Customizing WordPerfect

by Judy Felfe

There are many ways that you can customize WordPerfect to suit your working habits and preferences; WordPerfect is very flexible. *Customizing* the program means changing any of its default settings. When you change default settings, your new settings stay in effect until you change them again.

Many types of settings are customized through Preferences. To customize the screen display, for example, you first access Preferences. Other settings are customized through the features that are being customized. When you choose a default initial font for the selected printer, you choose it through the Document Initial Font feature. When you customize the writing style that Grammatik uses to evaluate your writing, you customize it through the Grammatik feature.

◄ See "Changing the Checking Style," p. 144

◄ See "Using the Font Dialog Box," p. 109

In this chapter, you learn to

- Customize the screen display
- Customize the environment (such as the User information and QuickMark options)
- Customize the location of files, default file extensions, and automatic file backups
- Customize document summaries and display descriptive filenames
- Customize the default settings for new documents

This chapter introduces you to some of the ways that you can customize WordPerfect and tailor it to your own personal working habits.

Using the Preferences Dialog Box

Because many of the features you will learn how to customize are accessed from one starting point, the Preferences dialog box, let's begin by looking at this dialog box. Choose **E**dit, Pr**e**ferences. You'll see the dialog box shown in figure 8.1.

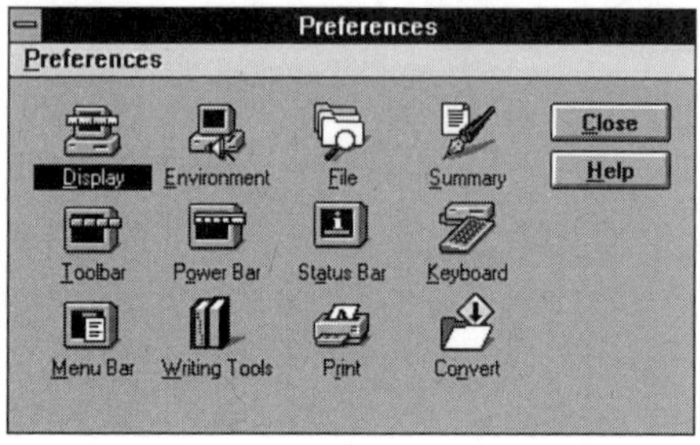

Fig. 8.1
Customize WordPerfect to suit your taste by using the Preferences dialog box.

◀ See "Understanding Views," p. 104

Starting from the Preferences dialog box, you can customize Display preferences, Environment preferences, File preferences, and Summary preferences. These subjects are covered in detail in the sections that follow. Customization of toolbars, the Power Bar, the status bar, the keyboard, the menu bar, writing tools, printing, and file conversions is summarized under "Customizing Other Preferences," later in this chapter.

Customizing Display Preferences

Tip
Right-click the toolbar, Power Bar, ruler bar, status bar, or either scroll bar and choose **P**references from the QuickMenu—you'll go directly to the Preferences for that screen element.

Use Display Preferences to customize the way various screen elements are displayed on-screen. Choose **D**isplay in the Preferences dialog box to open the Display Preferences dialog box. Figure 8.2 illustrates the Display Preferences dialog box with the **D**ocument option selected. The selected option *type* (**D**ocument, **S**how, View/**Z**oom, and so on) determines the options that are available in the lower portion of the dialog box. When you select View/**Z**oom, for example, the available options have to do with the default View mode and the default Zoom percentage. Figure 8.3 illustrates the Display Preferences dialog box with the View/**Z**oom option selected.

Some of the options that you can change through Display Preferences will speed up your work. As you increase the graphics display on-screen, you slow down the screen refresh rate; whatever you do to reduce graphical display will make your work go faster.

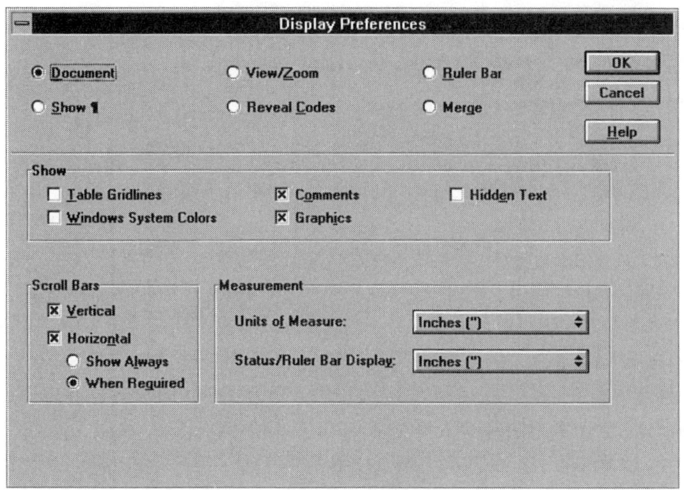

Fig. 8.2 Document options are displayed in the Display Preferences dialog box. Deselect the Horizontal check box at Document display preferences if you don't want to display the horizontal scroll bar on-screen.

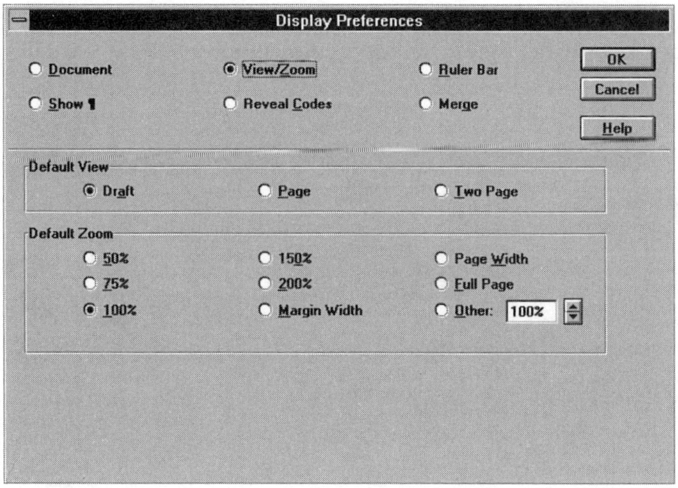

Fig. 8.3 View/Zoom options are displayed in the Display Preferences dialog box. Set the default view to Draft view to hide the display of the top and bottom margins, along with any footers, headers, or footnotes, and page borders.

Display settings you can make to speed up your work include:

▶ See "Changing Borders, Lines, and Shading in a Table," p. 199

- Choose Draft view rather than Page or Two Page view (View/**Z**oom Display Preferences).
- Show **T**able Gridlines rather than table lines and table fill (**D**ocument Display Preferences).
- Deselect Show Graph**i**cs to suppress the display of graphics in the editing window (**D**ocument Display Preferences); when Show Graph**i**cs is deselected, the position of graphics is still indicated in the document window.

All of the settings in this list can be changed on a temporary basis from the View menu. If you've told WordPerfect to work in Draft view by default, you can always use the View menu to switch to Page view when you want to see headers, footers, and page borders. If you've told WordPerfect to show table gridlines in your Display Preferences, you can use the View menu to see lines and fill styles in a table. And, when speed is not all-important, you can use the View menu to display graphics.

◀ See "Typing Text," p. 89

Show ¶ options can help by showing you what keys you've pressed (you won't have to look in Reveal Codes). Although showing nonprinting characters as symbols (spaces, hard returns, tabs, and so on) adds clutter to the screen, many of us can benefit from seeing these symbols. For example, if you can't tell by looking whether you pressed the spacebar once or twice, you'd know for sure by the number of dot symbols that represent spaces. Then, you can easily position the insertion point in the correct location and delete an unneeded symbol. Not only can you instruct WordPerfect to display nonprinting characters as symbols, but you can also choose which characters to display as symbols. See Figure 8.4 for an illustration of Show ¶ display preferences.

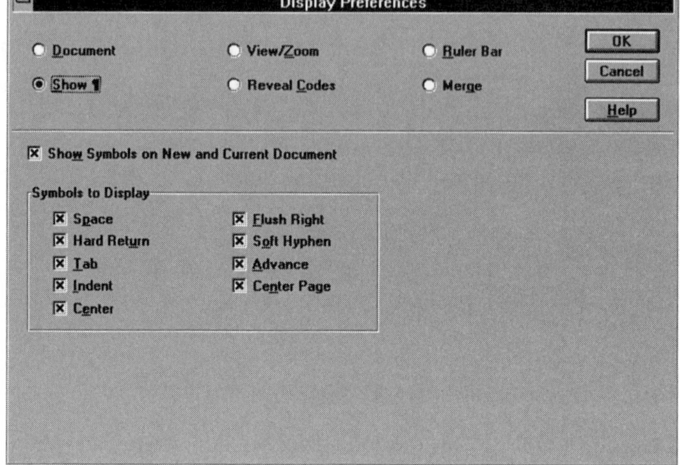

Fig. 8.4
Tell WordPerfect that you want to display nonprinting characters and choose which characters you want to display as symbols.

You can use the View menu to instruct WordPerfect to hide or display nonprinting characters temporarily. When you display nonprinting characters, the characters that are displayed as symbols are the ones that are selected through Display Preferences.

You can determine what suits you best only when you know what options are available. Once you know what your options are, you can think about how the various choices affect your work. Explore the other types of display preferences to see how flexible WordPerfect really is; you probably never guessed how much you could personalize your working environment.

Troubleshooting

I changed my Preferences to display table gridlines and now when I format my table with table lines, they're not there.

Your table lines are there; you'll see them when you choose **V**iew, Table Grid**l**ines (to turn *off* the gridlines and display any defined table lines), or when you print the document.

I'd like to have my Ruler Bar on-screen all the time without having to ask for it.

Under Display Preferences, choose **R**uler Bar, then select the Sho**w** Ruler Bar on the New and Current Document checkbox.

Customizing Environment Preferences

The first time that you access Environment Preferences, you should see the name you entered during installation in the **N**ame text box. Enter your correct name, if it's not already entered correctly, your correct initials, and select a personal color. What you enter in the User Info for Comments and Summary area will be applied in document comments or summaries.

If you have purchased another language version of WordPerfect and you want to use that language's formatting conventions, select the appropriate language from the drop-down list for the Inte**r**face option.

◄ See "Formatting the Page," p. 122

You can specify conditions under which WordPerfect beeps at you with the Beep On options. For example, if you want to be beeped when a find operation is unsuccessful, select the **F**ind Failure option.

The Save Workspace options can be especially handy if you frequently want to work on the same document(s) that you were working on during your last work session in WordPerfect. You can, for example, exit WordPerfect while a particular document is still open, then start WordPerfect and automatically open the same document all at once.

Menu options are all selected by default. If, for simplicity's sake, you'd rather not display any of the items listed in the Menu options area, then deselect the item(s) that you don't want to display.

In the Formatting area of the Environment Preferences dialog box, you can tell WordPerfect how you want to be prompted for hyphenation. You can also specify whether you want to confirm the deletion of formatting codes and to note the position of these codes. Leave Confirm Deletion of Ta**b**le Formulas selected to help you guard against the accidental deletion of table formulas.

When Automatically **S**elect Words is selected, entire words are selected automatically as you drag through text with the mouse (you can still hold down the Shift key and press an arrow key to adjust the selection on a character-by-character basis).

If you work with long documents, by all means select the Set **Q**uickMark on Save option (Environment Preferences). A QuickMark makes it easy to return instantly to the place where you were last working. When Set **Q**uickMark on Save is selected, a QuickMark is created at the insertion point whenever a document is saved. The QuickMark is a temporary placeholder; there is only one QuickMark in a document. When you press Ctrl+Q, you jump to the QuickMark.

When the Ac**t**ivate Hypertext option is enabled, all hypertext links in your documents are automatically activated (although Hypertext can be activated on an as-needed basis). Hypertext links allow you to jump to another location in the same document or a different document, or to execute a macro.

An example of a personalized Environment Preferences dialog box is shown in figure 8.5. User initials have been added and a user color has been selected. Set **Q**uickMark on Save has been selected. Ac**t**ivate Hypertext has been deselected.

Fig. 8.5
Customize User Info, Language options, Beep On options, and other environment options through Environment Preferences.

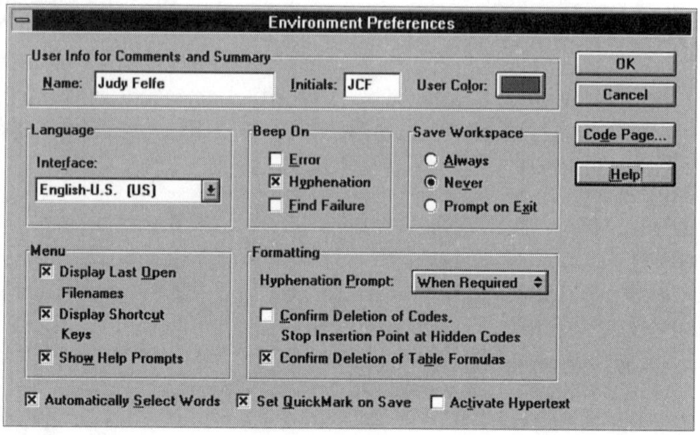

Customizing File Preferences

File Preferences include options about where you save or access various types of files. File Preferences also include choices on the default extension for new documents, and on automatic backup options. The Update **Q**uickList with Changes option tells WordPerfect whether or not to update the QuickList of directory names in directory dialog boxes.

When you install WordPerfect on your computer, the location of files is defined for you by default (you can, however, specify your own locations during installation by using Custom Install rather than Express Install). Documents are stored in one location, templates in another location, and graphics in another location. Normally, this works exactly the way you want, so you probably wouldn't want to change these preferences, although you can change them if desired. When you're working with File Preferences, you can see where a particular type of file is stored by selecting that file type (**D**ocuments/Backup, **T**emplates, **S**preadsheets, and so on), or you can see all of the default storage locations at once by choosing **V**iew All. Figure 8.6 shows the File Preferences dialog box with **D**ocuments/Backup as the selected file type. Use Default E**x**tension on Open and Save has been deselected.

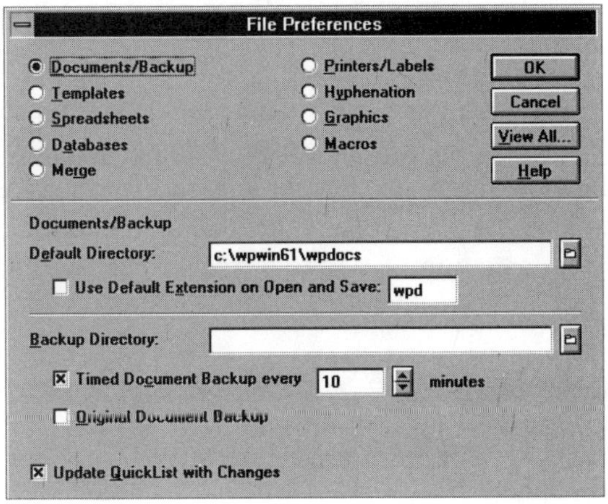

Fig. 8.6
Tell WordPerfect where you want to save and access files using the File Preferences dialog box.

WordPerfect expects to back up any open documents every 10 minutes; you can adjust the interval, but it's not a good idea to deselect the option for automatic timed backup. If your system freezes and you haven't saved changes, the timed backup can spare you a lot of grief.

◀ See "Saving a Document," p. 97

Note

Just because WordPerfect backs up open documents for you doesn't mean that you should wait to save a document until you finish working on it. Save your work at regular intervals—every 10 minutes, for example. Automatic backup is a disaster recovery feature; it is not a substitute for regular file save operations.

◄ See "Opening a Document," p. 98

Just as with Display Preferences and Environment Preferences, you can easily customize your File Preferences to suit the way you work. Through File Preferences, you can specify whether or not to use automatic filename extensions for documents (and for merge files). You can change default storage locations, and you can customize backup options.

Customizing Document Summaries

Tip

Choose the **C**onfigure option in the Document Summary dialog box to specify which fields to use in summaries and the order in which the fields appear.

Would you like to see a description of a file's contents alongside a filename when you access the Open File dialog box? Would you like to include a general overview of a document with the document, or other reference information such as keywords that are used in the file? If the answer to either one of these questions is yes, then customize WordPerfect's document summary preferences.

Even if you don't customize summary preferences, you can include summary information with individual documents through the file menu. Choose **F**ile, Document Summar**y** to enter (or change) summary information for an individual document. The Document Summary dialog box appears, as seen in figure 8.7. Any summary information that you enter is saved with the document when you save the document.

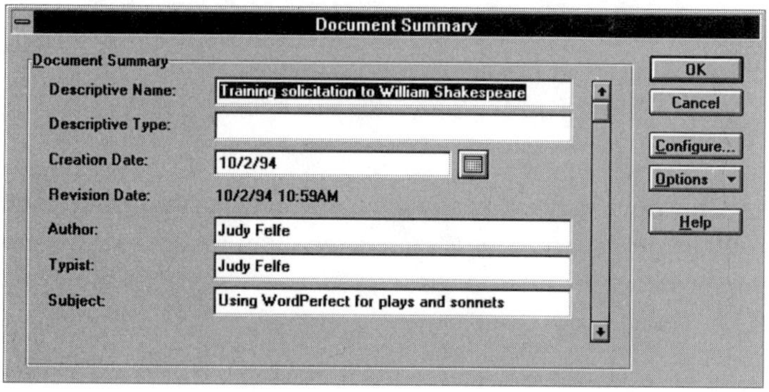

Fig. 8.7
Enter or change summary information for a document, or change the configuration for summaries, in the Document Summary dialog box. Scroll to see other summary fields.

You can see the descriptive name for any file that has a descriptive name even if you don't customize summary preferences. In the Open File dialog box, or in any other directory dialog box, the description for the currently selected filename is displayed below the file list (see fig. 8.8).

◀ See "Opening a Document," p. 98

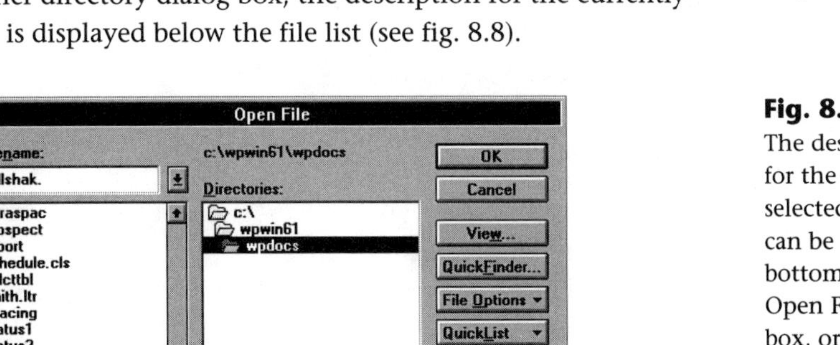

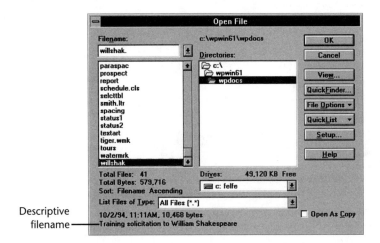

Fig. 8.8
The description for the currently selected filename can be seen at the bottom of the Open File dialog box, or at the bottom of other directory dialog boxes.

To customize your Summary preferences, choose **E**dit, Pr**e**ferences, **S**ummary. The Document Summary Preferences dialog box appears (see fig. 8.9). By default, both checkbox options are deselected; in this example, summary preferences have been customized so that both options are selected. You can use the **S**ubject Search Text option to tell WordPerfect how to identify a document subject. For example, when RE: is the specified subject search text, any text following RE: is automatically inserted in the Subject field in the document summary.

▶ See "Playing a Macro," p. 218

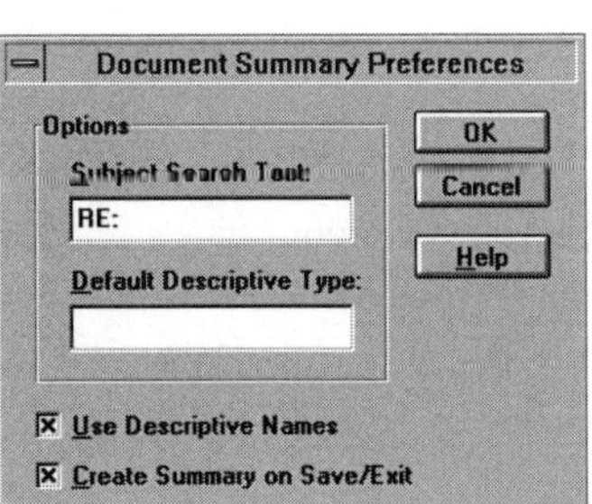

Fig. 8.9
Include descriptive filenames in filename lists and create summary information by default by customizing your Summary preferences.

Using Descriptive Names

Customize your Summary preferences to display descriptive names if you want your directory dialog boxes to look like the one shown in figure 8.10. Descriptive names are listed on the left of the File**n**ame list, and actual filenames on the right. By default, the list is sorted by actual filename; you can change the sort order, if desired, by clicking the **S**etup button in any directory dialog box.

When you specify that you want to use descriptive names, the descriptive name—rather than the actual filename—appears in the title bar of the document window, and in the QuickList of filenames at the bottom of the File menu.

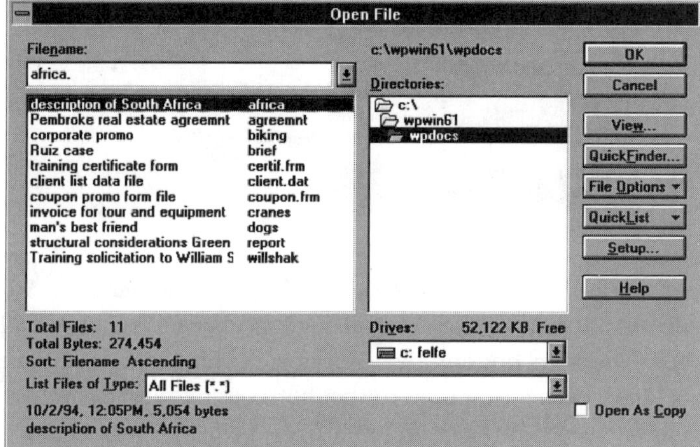

Fig. 8.10
Descriptive filenames help you identify file contents.

Creating Summaries on Save/Exit

When you specify that you want to create summaries on save/exit, WordPerfect automatically asks for summary information when you save a document for the first time. Although this might seem like a nuisance when you don't want to enter summary information, it only takes a single click (OK) or keystroke (Enter) to get past the request. If your only interest in summary information is in seeing descriptive filenames, and you don't want to enter a descriptive name for *every* file, you may still want to select the option to create summaries on save/exit.

Tip
You can change summary information, including the descriptive filename, for the file in the active window after choosing **F**ile, Document Summar**y**. Remember to save the document if you want to save the summary information.

Troubleshooting

I changed my summary preferences and I've been entering descriptive names for new documents, but I'd also like to enter descriptive names for some of my old documents.

Open a document for which you'd like a descriptive name. Choose **F**ile, Document Summar**y**, and enter the descriptive name. Don't forget to save the document after you enter the summary information.

I want to include a document number in my summaries, but there isn't a place to do it.

In the Document Summary dialog box, you can customize document summary fields after choosing **C**onfigure. Document number is one predefined field that you can select. You can remove a field by dragging it off of the **S**elected Fields list, and you can drag a field to a new position in the list of selected fields.

I'd like to print the document summary for my document.

Choose Document Summ**a**ry in the Print dialog box.

Customizing Other Preferences

You can customize Display preferences, Environment preferences, File preferences, and Summary preferences; you can also customize preferences for toolbars, the Power Bar, the status bar, the keyboard, the menu bar, writing tools, printing, and file conversions.

This section summarizes some of the changes you can make for each of these *other* types of preferences. For more information on customizing toolbars, the Power Bar, and menus, see Chapter 37, "Customizing Toolbars, Menus, and Preferences."

▶ See "Adding a Macro to a Toolbar," p. 222

The following list summarizes some of the changes you can make for preferences that are not previously covered in this chapter.

- *Toolbar.* Use **O**ptions to customize the appearance or location of toolbars; you can display text on toolbar buttons, a picture, or both. You can also specify the maximum number of rows to be used for displaying a toolbar (displaying two rows takes more screen space but lets you display more buttons at once). You can also edit the toolbar to add, remove, or rearrange buttons.

- *Power Bar.* Adjust the appearance to display text only, a picture only, or both. You can add, remove, or rearrange buttons.

- *Status Bar.* Add items to the status bar, rearrange items, resize items.

- *Keyboard.* Display, create, or manage another keyboard, including any customized keyboard that you have created for special-purpose work.

Tip
Double-click any of the status bar items to either toggle the action or open its related dialog box. Double-clicking the date or time item will add the date or time text to your document.

- *Menu Bar*. Display, create, or manage another predefined menu bar, including any that you have created.
- *Writing Tools*. Specify or rearrange which items to display on the Tools menu (Spell Checker, Thesaurus, Grammatik).
- *Print*. Specify default size attribute ratio (the percentage of increase in size for relative size adjustments such as fine, small, or large). Also, specify whether to reformat documents for the currently selected printer on Open.
- *Convert*. Specify default delimiters, encapsulation characters, and characters to strip for ASCII text files (options that are most commonly used or referenced when merging with database data files). Specify Code Page options (options that are used when importing or exporting files from or to another language).

Troubleshooting

Help! I experimented with customizing the status bar and now I'd like to put it back the way it was.

In the preferences dialog box for the Status Bar, choose **D**efault.

I frequently import database files in an ASCII-delimited format, and I'd like to have quotation marks stripped when the file is imported.

In the Convert preferences dialog box, specify quotations marks as characters to be stripped.

Customizing the Default Settings for New Documents

Whenever you open a new, empty document, you accept default settings that are associated with the standard template. Many formatting defaults are included in these settings, including margin settings, the justification setting, and tab settings. If you prefer to work with settings that are not the same as these defaults, you can change the defaults for new documents through the Document Initial Codes Style. This section shows you how to change the default settings for new documents based on the standard template.

▶ See "Using Styles," p. 177

To change the default settings for new documents based on the standard template, take the following steps:

1. Choose Format, Document, Initial Codes Style. The Styles Editor appears, with the Document Initial Style as the style to be edited.

2. In the style Contents area, insert any format settings that you want as defaults for all new documents based on the standard template. For example, if you prefer to work with Full justification rather than Left justification, insert a formatting code for Full justification.

3. Select the Use as Default checkbox option.

4. Click OK.

After you customize the Initial Codes Style and specify that the formatting should be used as a default, all new documents based on the standard template will use the customized settings. An illustration of the Initial Codes Style with customized settings is shown in figure 8.11. The **U**se as Default checkbox option has been selected.

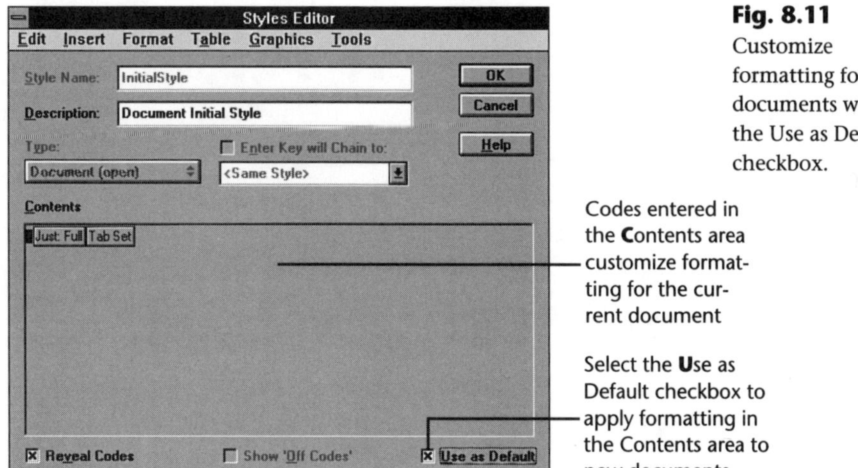

Fig. 8.11
Customize formatting for new documents with the Use as Default checkbox.

From Here...

In this chapter, you learned to customize some of WordPerfect's preferences to suit the way you work. You learned to customize the screen display, the environment, file preferences, and document summaries. In addition, you learned to customize the default settings for new documents.

As you use WordPerfect more and more, you'll be interested in fine-tuning the way WordPerfect works even more than you are now, and you'll explore customization options in more detail.

For more information about working in WordPerfect, see the following chapters:

- Chapter 9, "Organizing and Formatting Large Documents," shows you how to organize simple lists with bullets and numbers, how to organize a document with the Outline feature, and how to use Styles to apply formatting easily and consistently.

- Chapter 10, "Working with Tables and Graphics," shows you how to create, edit, and format tables to format information. Chapter 10 also shows you how to add graphics elements such as lines, borders, boxes containing graphics images, and watermarks to your documents.

Chapter 9

Organizing and Formatting Large Documents

by Judy Felfe

II

Using WordPerfect

When you produce a document with many pages—from ten or fifteen pages to hundreds of pages—you need special organizational and managerial techniques. WordPerfect provides a number of features that help you manage long documents. You can use these features for short documents as well.

Tip

Use the QuickMark to quickly find your place in a long document. You can program WordPerfect to create a QuickMark at the insertion point every time you save a document. Then, when you open the document, press Ctrl+Q to jump to the QuickMark.

In this chapter, you learn to

- Organize a simple list with bullets or numbers
- Create a multi-level outline using WordPerfect's outline feature
- Collapse and expand an outline to display only the portion in which you want to work
- Edit an outline by rearranging outline items
- Use WordPerfect's built-in styles to format a document
- Create and edit your own styles

One organizational feature you can use in a large document is *outlining*. An outline gives you an overview of a document by organizing topics into a list that can have as many as eight different levels. The outline helps you determine what topics you want to cover and in what order the topics should be presented.

◄ See "Customizing Environment Preferences," p. 157

WordPerfect's *Styles* feature helps you format long documents consistently and easily. With a single operation, you can apply a style that includes preformatted fonts, attributes, and even text.

This chapter introduces you to Bullets & Numbers, to Outlines, and to Styles.

Organizing a Simple List with Bullets and Numbers

WordPerfect's Bullets & Numbers feature gives you a quick and easy way to create an outline in a simplified format. Use the Bullets & Numbers feature to create lists like the ones shown in figure 9.1. A bullet or number appears at the left margin, followed by (except for the Paragraph Numbers style) an indent. Numbers increase automatically from paragraph to paragraph.

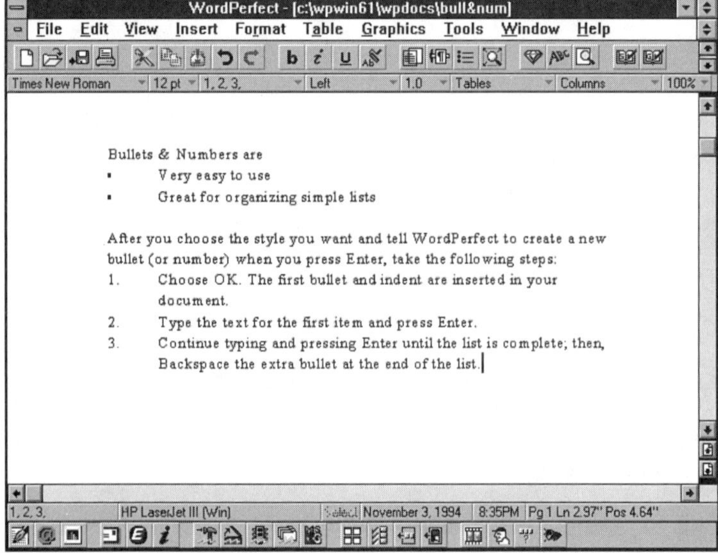

Fig. 9.1
Create bulleted and numbered lists easily with Bullets & Numbers.

WordPerfect gives you a choice of six types of bullet styles and six types of number styles with its Bullets & Numbers feature (see fig. 9.2). You can customize any of the predefined styles. You can, for example, use a different WordPerfect character as a bullet by editing one of the predefined styles and replacing the bullet character with the character of your choice.

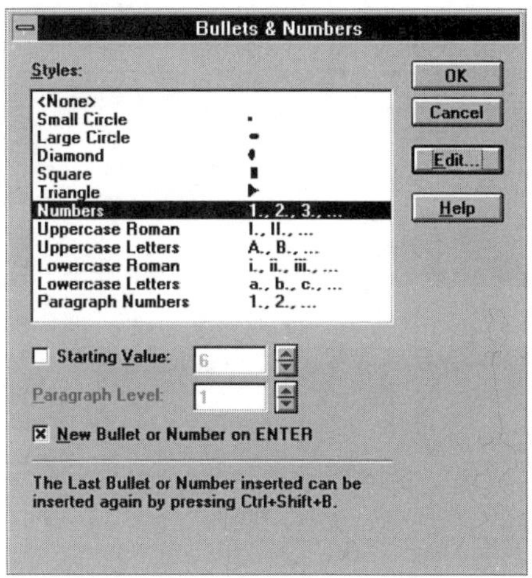

Fig. 9.2
One or two clicks at the Bullets & Numbers dialog box produces a number with an indent.

Take the following steps to create a simple list:

1. Position the insertion point at the left margin of the first line in the list.
2. Choose **I**nsert, Bullets & Numbers. The Bullets & Numbers dialog box appears (refer to fig. 9.2).

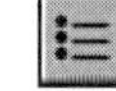

3. Select the style that you want for your list.
4. If you want another bullet or number to appear when you press Enter, make sure that the **N**ew Bullet or Number on ENTER box is checked. If you want blank lines between items in the list, leave the checkbox empty.
5. Click OK. WordPerfect inserts the first bullet (or number) followed by an indent into your document.

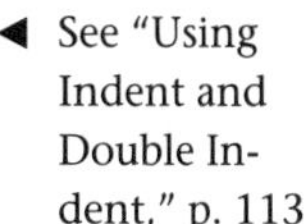
◄ See "Using Indent and Double Indent," p. 113

6. Type your text and press Enter.
7. If you told WordPerfect to create a new bullet or number on ENTER, you already have the next bullet or number. Continue typing text and pressing Enter until you finish typing the list. Use the Backspace key to remove the extra bullet or number at the end of the list and to stop the sequence.
8. If you left the **N**ew Bullet or Number on ENTER checkbox empty, you can add a blank line if desired. When you're ready to create another bullet or number, click the Insert Bullet button; or, press Ctrl+Shift+B.

Tip
Use the Insert Bullet button to quickly create another bullet or number in the current style (you can change the current style at the Bullets & Numbers dialog box).

Troubleshooting

I created a numbered list and now I'd rather have a bulleted list.

Select the entire list and choose a bullet style from the Insert Bullets & Numbers dialog box.

I created a numbered list and I want to add another item to the list.

Insert the item, using the Bullet button to create a number at the beginning of the item. Numbers should resequence automatically.

I typed a list of items without bullets and now I'd like to add bullets at the beginning of each item.

Select the entire list and choose a bullet style from the Bullets & Numbers dialog box.

Outlining a Document

An outline is more than Roman numerals that are typed in at the beginning of each new topic. Once you start an outline, the numerals, if there are any, are created and sequenced automatically. You have a choice of several outline styles (see fig. 9.3 for a few examples), or you can create your own style.

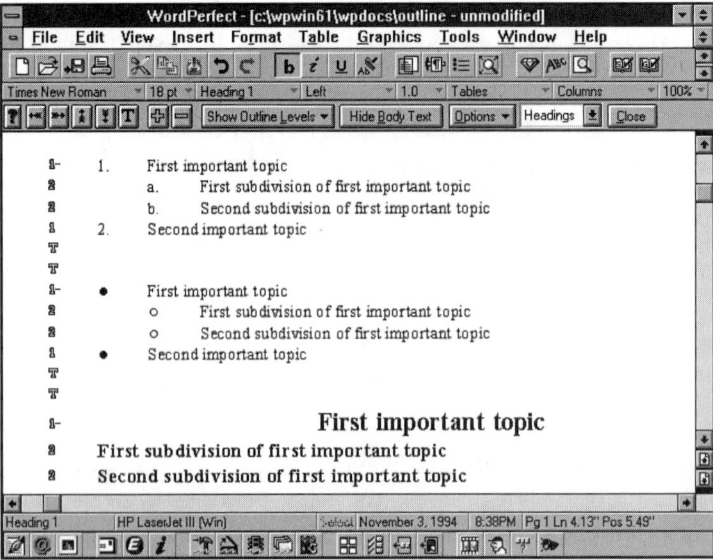

Fig. 9.3
Three different outline styles are applied to the same text.

When you change your mind about the order of topics in your outline, you can easily rearrange topics. The rest of the topics resequence automatically when you rearrange topics—or when you add or delete topics. If you change your mind about the *style* of the outline, place the insertion point anywhere in the outline and choose a different style. To see only the most important topics in your outline, collapse the outline down to the first level.

Before you work with outlines, it helps to familiarize yourself with outline concepts and terminology and with the Outline Feature Bar.

Understanding Outline Concepts and Terminology

The following concepts and terminology will help you work with outlines:

- An outline is a series of paragraphs, called outline items, in which each paragraph has an optional *number* and a hierarchical level. The level number generally corresponds to the number of tabs or indents that separate the beginning of the topic from the left margin.

◄ See "Setting and Using Tabs," p. 114

- An outline can include body text. Body text does not have a number and may not have the same level of indentation as the portions of the outline that surround it.
- An outline *family* is a group of related material consisting of all the numbered paragraphs and body text that are directly underneath the first item in the group.
- An outline *style* is a formatting style that uniquely defines the appearance of the number and text for each level of an outline.

Understanding the Outline Feature Bar

The Outline Feature Bar (see fig. 9.4) is your gateway to the commands that you use when you work with outlines. This section introduces you to the Outline Feature Bar. Table 9.1 describes individual buttons on the feature bar.

Fig. 9.4
The Outline Feature Bar provides one-button access to Outline's capabilities.

Table 9.1 Buttons on the Outline Feature Bar

Button	Function
?	Provides menu access to Outline Feature Bar functionality, and provides outline help
←«	Decreases an outline item's level by 1; This is the equivalent of pressing Shift+Tab
»→	Increases an outline item's level by one; This is the equivalent of pressing Tab
↑	Moves the outline item or selection up one item without changing its level
↓	Moves the outline item or selection down one item without changing its level
T	Changes an item to body text or vice versa
+	Shows/redisplays the collapsed family under the current item
−	Hides/collapses the family under the current outline item
Show Outline Levels	Choose the outline display level
Hide Body Text	Turn the display of body text on or off
Options	Choose outline options: end an outline, display/hide level icons in the left margin, define/edit an outline style, and so on
Headings	Select an outline style (use this to change the current style)
Close	Close the feature bar

Creating an Outline

The general steps for creating an outline are as follows:

1. Position the insertion point at the left margin of the line that will be the first line in the outline.

2. If the Outline Feature Bar is not already visible, choose **T**ools, **O**utline. The feature bar appears, a level 1 outline item is created in the document, and the insertion point is placed so you can enter your text.

   If the style of the inserted outline item is not the one you want, use the Style Definition button to pull down a style list, then select another style.

3. Type the text, and then press Enter. The insertion point is automatically positioned at the same level to enter the text for the next item.

◀ See "Entering Text," p. 88

4. To change the level of the next item before you enter text, press Tab (increase level) or Shift+Tab (decrease level).

◀ See "Formatting Characters," p. 107

5. To add body text to the outline, press Ctrl+H. You can press Indent (F7) to align the text with the associated outline item.

6. After entering the last item's text, choose **O**ptions, **E**nd Outline.

Tip
To insert a blank line between outline items, press Enter twice after entering the text for an item.

> **Note**
>
> If you accidentally delete an outline number, either Undo the action, or Backspace to the end of the previous item and press Enter.

Collapsing and Expanding Portions of an Outline

WordPerfect makes it easy to work with a portion of your outline by letting you display only the portion in which you're currently interested. Using the Outline Feature Bar, you have the following methods to control what portion of an outline is displayed:

- Hide/collapse individual families under their first outline item.
- Hide all outline items of a specified level and their families.
- Hide the entire outline excluding body text.
- Hide only body text.

Once you're displaying just the portion that you want to work with, it's easy to edit (or reorganize) outline items. Because outline items are just normal text with an outline style applied to them, you edit text in outline items just as you do any other text.

Figure 9.5 is an example for the hiding and showing techniques that follow.

Fig. 9.5
The complete outline used in the hiding and showing examples. A minus sign by the level number icon indicates that the family can be collapsed (hidden).

1. First Level 1 text
First body text
a. First Level 2 text (in "First Level 1 text" family)
i. First Level 3 text (in "First Level 1 text" and "First Level 2 text" families)
b. Second Level 2 text (in "First Level 1 text" family)

2. Second Level 1 text
Second body text (preceded by an Indent (F7))
a. Third Level 2 text (in "Second Level 1 text" family)
i. Second Level 3 text (in "Second Level 1 text" and "Third Level 2 text" families)

Hiding/Showing an Outline Family

To hide an outline family—that is, to collapse the family so only its first level item is visible—place the insertion point in the first level of the family and click the Hide Family button. Alternatively, place the mouse pointer to the left of the first level of the family, so that the pointer becomes a vertical, double-headed arrow; then, double-click.

Figure 9.6 shows the result of collapsing the first Level 1 family.

Fig. 9.6
A plus sign by the Level 1 number in the margin indicates that this family can be expanded.

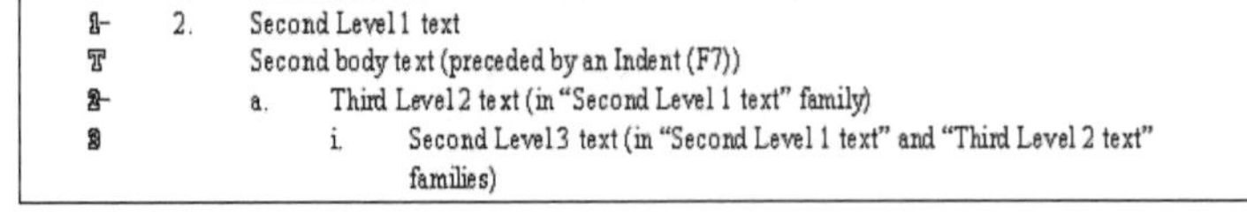

1. First Level 1 text
2. Second Level 1 text
Second body text (preceded by an Indent (F7))
a. Third Level 2 text (in "Second Level 1 text" family)
i. Second Level 3 text (in "Second Level 1 text" and "Third Level 2 text" families)

To show/redisplay a collapsed outline family, place the insertion point in the visible outline item and click the Show Family button. Alternatively, place the mouse pointer to the left of the visible outline item so that the pointer becomes a vertical, double-headed arrow, and then double-click.

Hiding/Showing All Outline Families under a Specified Level

To hide all the outline families under a specified level for the entire outline, place the insertion point in the outline. Then, choose the lowest number that you still want shown from the Show Outline **L**evels button's drop-down list.

Figure 9.7 shows the result of choosing **1** from the Show Outline **L**evels button's drop-down list (body text is also hidden).

To show/redisplay hidden levels, place the insertion point in the outline and choose the lowest level from the Show Outline **L**evels button's drop-down list.

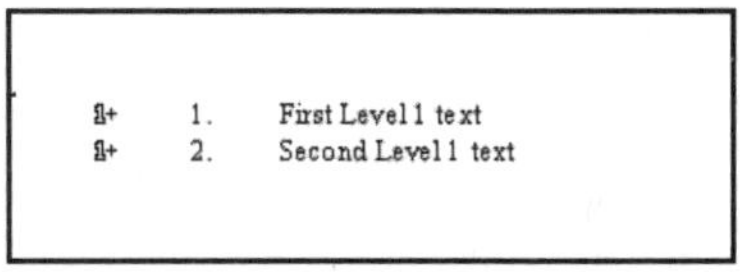

1. First Level 1 text
2. Second Level 1 text

Fig. 9.7
The outline shown in fig. 9.5 collapsed to level 1 and with body text hidden.

Hiding Body Text, Displaying Hidden Body Text

To hide an outline's body text, as in figure 9.8, place the insertion point in the outline and choose the Hide **B**ody Text button. Body text is hidden and the button changes to a Show **B**ody Text button.

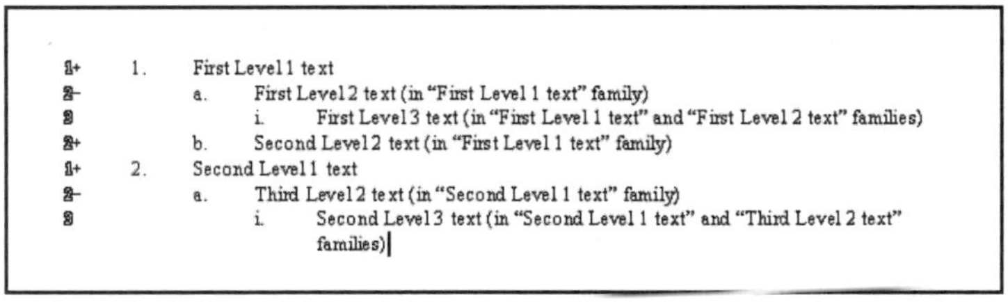

1. First Level 1 text
   a. First Level 2 text (in "First Level 1 text" family)
      i. First Level 3 text (in "First Level 1 text" and "First Level 2 text" families)
   b. Second Level 2 text (in "First Level 1 text" family)
2. Second Level 1 text
   a. Third Level 2 text (in "Second Level 1 text" family)
      i. Second Level 3 text (in "Second Level 1 text" and "Third Level 2 text" families)

Fig. 9.8
The completely expanded outline (shown in fig. 9.5) with body text hidden.

To redisplay body text, place the insertion point in the outline and click the Show **B**ody Text button.

Modifying an Outline's Structure

You can modify an outline's structure by rearranging items and families, by inserting new families, or by deleting families. When the level icons are displayed (in the left margin), it's easy to select families for cutting, copying, and deleting. Another kind of change you can make is to switch an outline item to body text or vice versa. WordPerfect automatically adjusts the numbering of the outline.

Adjusting Levels

To increase the level of an outline item, position the insertion point anywhere in the item and choose the Next Level button. Alternatively, position the insertion point at the beginning of the text in the item and press Tab.

To decrease the level of an outline item, position the insertion point anywhere in the item and click the Previous Level button. Alternatively, position the insertion point at the beginning of the text in the item and press Shift+Tab.

To increase or decrease several levels at once, position the insertion point anywhere in the outline item and choose **O**ptions, **C**hange Level, and then specify a level number.

Changing to and from Body Text

To change an outline item to body text, position the insertion point in the item and click the Show **B**ody Text button; or, press Ctrl+H. The text is placed at the left margin. You may want to adjust its indentation with Tab or Indent (F7).

To change body text to an outline item, place the insertion point anywhere in the body text and click the Hide **B**ody Text button; or, press Ctrl+H. The text becomes an outline item (you may want to adjust the level number).

Moving, Copying, Cutting, Deleting, and Pasting Families

Tip
If you delete something accidentally, or paste in the wrong location, click the Undo button.

Tip
For the most efficient and easiest rearranging of topics, collapse the outline to the level to be moved.

To cut, copy, or delete an outline family, select the family and then use normal WordPerfect techniques to perform the cut, copy, or delete. Selecting a family is easiest if the show level icons are visible (see steps 1 and 2 which follow).

To move a family within an outline, take the following steps:

1. Display the Outline Feature Bar if it is not already displayed by choosing **T**ool, **O**utline. Display the level icons, if they are not already displayed, by choosing **O**ptions, Show Level **I**cons.

2. With the Outline Feature Bar and the level icons displayed, position the mouse pointer to the left of the top item in the family you want to select, so that the pointer becomes a vertical, double-headed arrow. Hold down the left mouse button to select the entire family.

3. While continuing to hold down the left mouse button, move the pointer in the direction in which you want to move the family. A thin, horizontal line appears. When the horizontal line is where you want to place the family (see fig. 9.9), release the mouse button.

To move just one item in a family, select only the paragraph that is the outline item (you can double-click in the margin to select the item). Then, perform a normal cut and paste operation. You may need to turn on Reveal Codes to make sure that your selection includes appropriate codes.

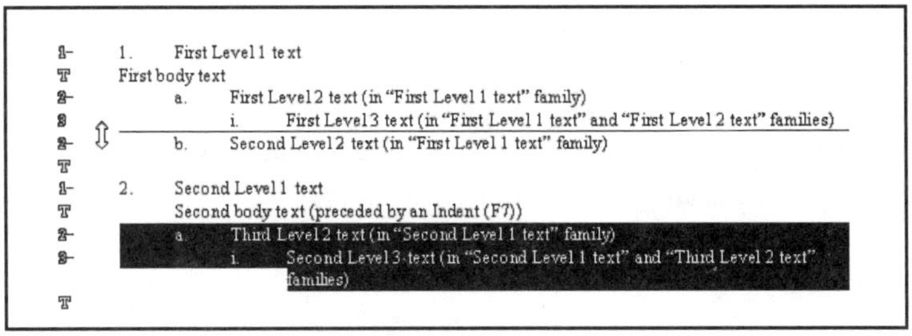

1. First Level 1 text
First body text
a. First Level 2 text (in "First Level 1 text" family)
i. First Level 3 text (in "First Level 1 text" and "First Level 2 text" families)
b. Second Level 2 text (in "First Level 1 text" family)
2. Second Level 1 text
Second body text (preceded by an Indent (F7))
a. Third Level 2 text (in "Second Level 1 text" family)
i. Second Level 3 text (in "Second Level 1 text" and "Third Level 2 text" families)

Fig. 9.9
Ready to move the highlighted outline family to the position of the horizontal line by dragging it with the mouse.

Changing an Outline's Style

To change an outline's style, take the following steps:

◀ See "Deleting and Moving Text," p. 94

◀ See "Copying Text," p. 94

◀ See "Working with Formatting Codes," p. 129

1. Position the insertion point anywhere in the outline.
2. If the Outline Feature Bar is not visible, choose **T**ools, **O**utline.
3. Pull down the outline styles list from the Outline Definition button and select the new style. The outline is formatted with the new style.

Troubleshooting

I want to print only the Level 1 items in my outline.

WordPerfect prints only what is displayed on-screen. Collapse the outline to Level 1 (and hide body text if you wish), then print your document.

I performed several cut and paste operations and now my outline is a mess. I wish I could put it back the way it was.

Choose **E**dit, Undo/Redo **H**istory. Select the last item that you want to undo (the lowest item that you want to undo in the U**n**do list). You can undo as many items as are on the list.

Using Styles

Use styles to format your documents and templates easily and quickly, and to give them a consistent and professional look. Styles are an extraordinarily powerful formatting tool. Instead of applying several separate formatting changes to a subtitle in a long document, you can apply them all at once with a style. You can apply the same style over and over again to every subtitle in the document. If you change your mind about any of the formatting, you have only one change to make—to the style itself. Styles are readily available for use in other documents (see "Sharing Styles between Documents," later in this chapter).

Because styles can incorporate nearly any WordPerfect formatting feature—as well as text, graphics, and even other styles—their potential is nearly unlimited. You can save a great deal of time and work by learning to use styles, especially when you work with long documents.

This section introduces you to styles, shows you how to use WordPerfect's built-in styles, and introduces you to creating and using your own styles.

Considering Types of Styles

One way to classify styles is by their location. Styles can be built into the current document, saved in a style file, or built into a template. Styles are also part of the WordPerfect program. Styles that are part of the WordPerfect program are called *system* styles. When you first access the styles list in a new document (see fig. 9.10), you see a list of built-in styles. When you create a new style, it is added to the list. The styles that you create are called *user* styles.

A style is categorized as one of four types:

- *Character (paired).* The formatting in a Character style takes effect at a specified position and it ends at a specified position. A Character style is suitable for formatting several words in sequence (a company name, for example).

- *Paragraph (paired).* The formatting in a Paragraph style affects the current paragraph (or a series of selected paragraphs). A Paragraph style is ideal for formatting one-line titles and headings.

- *Paragraph (paired-auto).* This type of style is like the Paragraph (paired) style, except that formatting in the style is automatically updated when you change any paragraph that is formatted with the style.

- *Document (open).* When a Document style is applied, the formatting it contains stays in effect for the rest of the document (or, until there's another change for the same type of formatting).

Using WordPerfect's Built-in Styles

You can easily format a document with built-in styles. You can even make a global adjustment to the effects of a style simply by changing the formatting of one paragraph where the style is applied when the style type is Paragraph (paired-auto). In this section, you will learn to format a document with built-in styles and to make an adjustment that affects all paragraphs that are formatted with a style.

To display the Style List dialog box in any document based on the standard template (as shown in fig. 9.10), start a new, empty document. Then, choose Fo**r**mat, **S**tyles, or double-click the Styles List button (a single-click displays only a list of style names; a double-click displays the Style List dialog box).

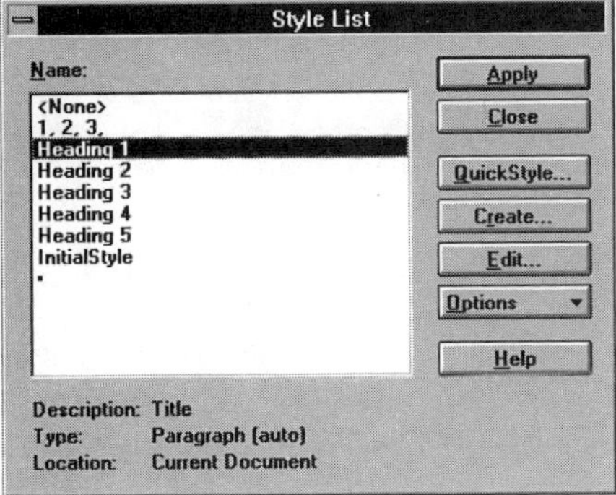

Fig. 9.10
The Style List dialog box in a new empty document based on the standard template.

At the Style List dialog box, you can move the highlight from one style name to the next and see the description and other information about that style below the list.

You can apply a style from the Style List dialog box; or, more easily, from the Select Style button on the Power Bar.

The Initial Style style sets formatting defaults that affect the entire document. The Heading styles are designed to format the title and various levels of headings in a document; these styles contain font changes, centering, and Table of Contents markings. The number and bullet styles (if present) contain formatting for Bullets & Numbers styles.

Suppose that you have a document on-screen that is based on the standard template. The document has a title and headings (see fig. 9.11).

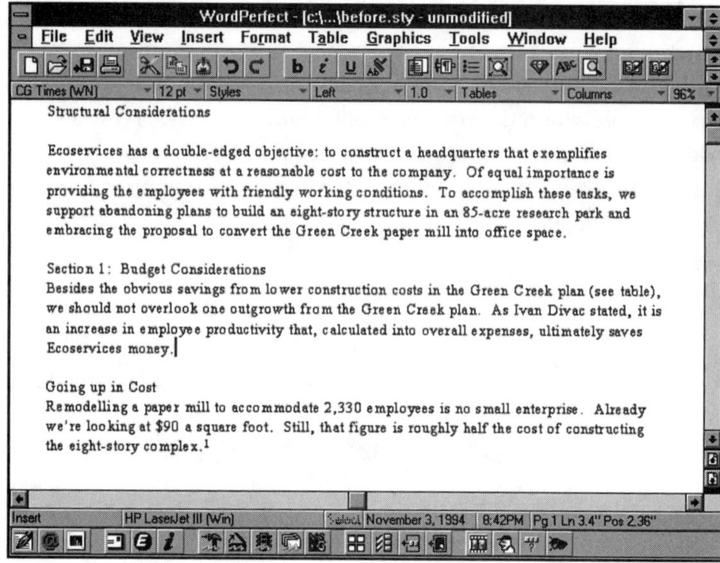

Fig. 9.11
A document before formatting with built-in styles.

To apply and adjust built-in styles, take the following steps:

1. *Format the title with the Heading 1 style.* Position the insertion point anywhere in the title. Pull down the style list from the Select Style button. Select the Heading 1 style. Formatting in the Heading 1 style is now applied to the entire paragraph (which is the entire title). Notice that the title is centered, bold, and very large.

2. *Format the main headings with the Heading 2 style.* Position the insertion point anywhere in the first main heading (in fig. 9.11, "Section 1: Budget Considerations.") Pull down the style list from the Styles button and select the Heading 2 style. Formatting in the Heading 2 style now affects the entire paragraph. Repeat this step for every main heading in the document. When you finish, all main headings are formatted with a consistent appearance.

3. *Format lower-level headings with the Heading 3 style.* Position the insertion point anywhere in the first lower-level heading (in fig. 9.11, "Going up in Cost.") Pull down the style list from the Styles button and select the Heading 3 style. Repeat this step for every lower-level heading in the document (in fig. 9.11, the Heading 3 style should also be applied to "High Rise vs. Low Rise.") All lower-level headings now have a uniform appearance. The example used in figure 9.11 would now appear as shown in figure 9.12.

4. *Make an adjustment that affects all paragraphs formatted with the Heading 3 style.* Suppose you decide that your lower-level headings would look

better in italics. Select any paragraph formatted with the Heading 3 style and click the Italic button. Because Heading 3 is a Paragraph (paired-auto) type style, the change you made now affects all paragraphs formatted with the style (see fig. 9.13).

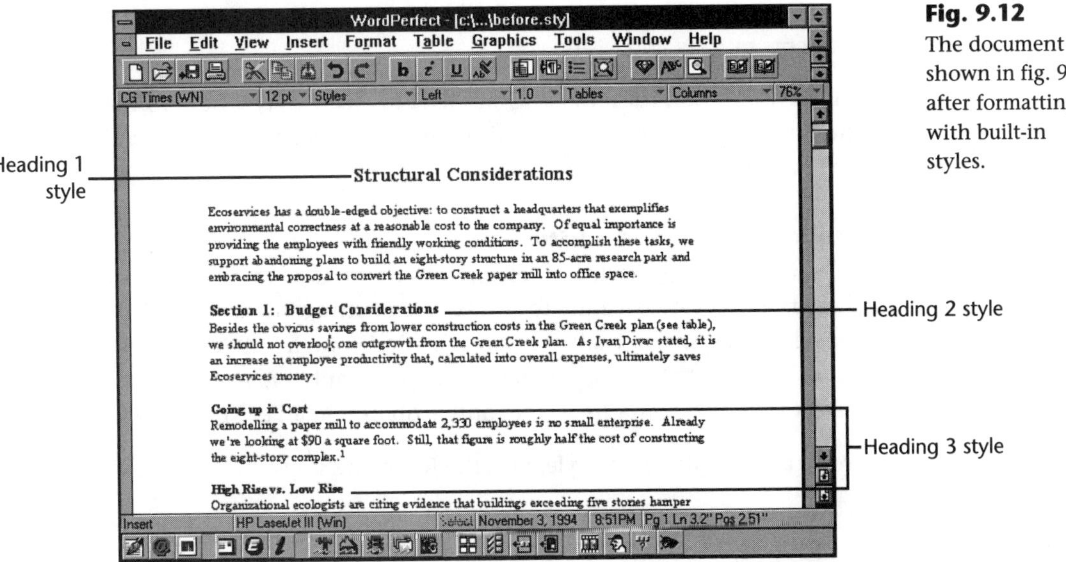

Fig. 9.12
The document shown in fig. 9.11 after formatting with built-in styles.

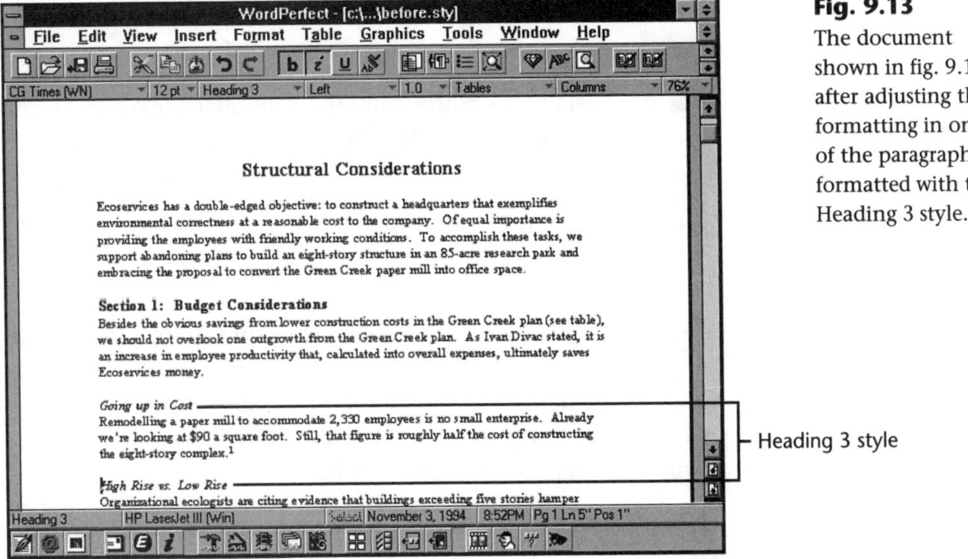

Fig. 9.13
The document shown in fig. 9.12 after adjusting the formatting in one of the paragraphs formatted with the Heading 3 style.

Creating and Using Your Own Styles

Tip

To learn more about styles, explore WordPerfect's templates. Create a document based on a template, then access the styles list for the template and edit the styles to see what they contain.

Once you see and feel the power of styles, you'll be willing to put in some extra time and work learning how to create your own styles. Although the use of styles adds a level of complexity to your work, the results are well worth it. You'll save time formatting, your documents will have a professional, consistent appearance and you'll be able to make global formatting adjustments quickly and easily.

In this section, you'll learn to use QuickStyle to create a style from formatting in effect at the insertion point. Then, you'll learn to create a style from scratch in the Styles Editor window.

Creating a Style with QuickStyle

An easy way to create a style is to format some text as you want it to look and then use the QuickStyle feature to copy the formatting into a style. With QuickStyle, you can create a Paragraph style that contains all of the formatting codes and font attributes in an existing paragraph; or, you can create a Character style that contains all the font attributes on an existing character.

To create a style with QuickStyle, take the following steps:

1. Format a section of text or a paragraph with the features that you want included in the style.
2. Position the insertion point anywhere in the formatted paragraph (to create a Paragraph style), or select the formatted text (to create a Character style).
3. Click the Select Styles button, and then choose QuickStyle; or, choose Fo**r**mat, **S**tyles, **Q**uickStyle. The QuickStyle dialog box is displayed (see fig. 9.14).
4. Enter a name for the style.
5. Enter a description for the style.
6. Select **P**aragraph as the style type if you want the style to affect an entire paragraph (a paragraph style is ideal for formatting headings); select **C**haracter as the style type if you want the style to affect a passage of text of any length (a character style is ideal for formatting a series of words—for example, the company name).
7. Click OK. The style is created and you are returned to the document window.

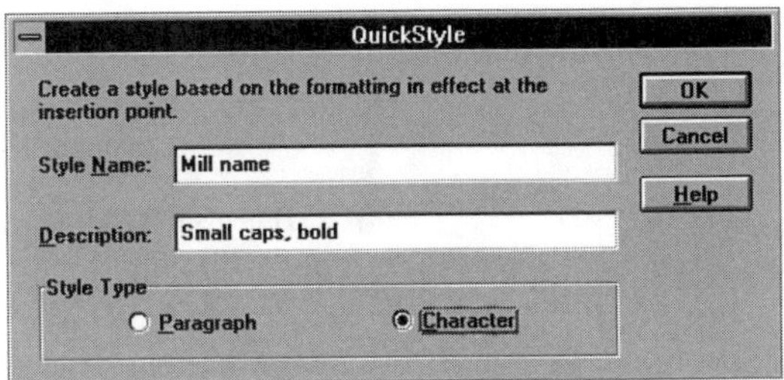

Fig. 9.14
Format text as you want it to look, then use QuickStyle to copy the formatting into a style.

Creating a Style from Scratch

Maximize the power of styles by creating your own styles with just the formatting (and text, and graphics, and even other styles) that suits your work.

◄ See "Working with Formatting Codes," p. 129

To create a style from scratch, you need to enter formatting codes (and any other contents for the style) in the Styles Editor window. Follow these steps to create a style from scratch:

1. Double-click the Select Style button (on the Power Bar), or choose Fo**r**mat, **S**tyles; or, press Alt+F8. The Style List dialog box is displayed (refer to fig. 9.10).

2. Choose C**r**eate. The Styles Editor window is displayed (the Styles Editor window is shown in figs. 9.15 and 9.17).

3. Enter a name for the style.

4. Enter a description for the style. It's helpful to describe the formatting used in the style.

5. Change the type, if desired, by choosing a type from the T**y**pe drop-down list.

6. For a Paragraph or Character style, program the Enter key, if desired, from the E**n**ter Key will Chain to list of options. When you apply the style to existing text, it doesn't matter how the Enter key is programmed. It does make a difference when you apply the style before typing text. The E**n**ter Key Will Chain to options are described in the following list:

   - *None*. The Enter key simply turns off the style.

   - *Same Style*. The Enter key turns off the style and then immediately turns it on again (useful for bulleted lists).

   - *Style name*. The Enter key turns off the current style and turns on the Style name style (useful for linking Question & Answer styles).

Tip
Formatting in a paired style turns off automatically when the style is turned off; *you* don't have to turn off font attributes, or line-spacing changes, or other formatting that is turned on by the style.

7. Click in the **C**ontents area and enter formatting codes (and any other contents) for the style.

8. If the style type is Paragraph or Character, you can specify formatting that takes effect after the text in the paragraph. For example, you might want to insert a graphics line after a heading that is formatted with the style (fig. 9.15 shows a style with "OFF" codes and fig. 9.17 shows text formatted with that style). To specify formatting that takes effect after text in the paragraph, you must first select the Show '**O**ff Codes' check-box option. A comment separates the "ON" and "OFF" areas in the style **C**ontents area.

9. Click OK, and then click **C**lose to return to the document window.

Figure 9.15 illustrates a Paragraph style. Figure 9.16 illustrates a Character style. Figure 9.17 illustrates text that is formatted with both styles.

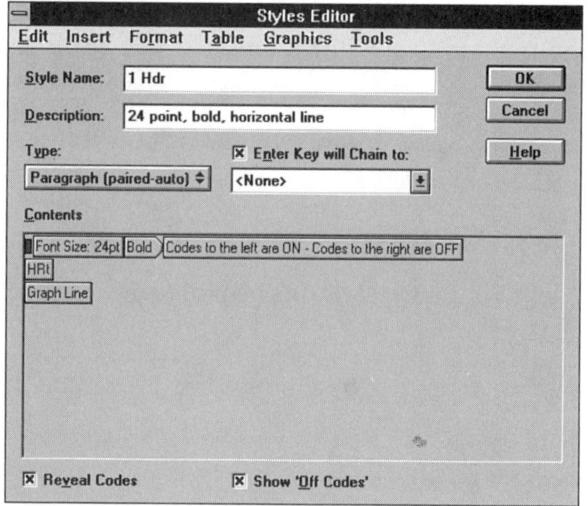

Fig. 9.15
A paragraph style named 1 Hdr that will be used to format headings.

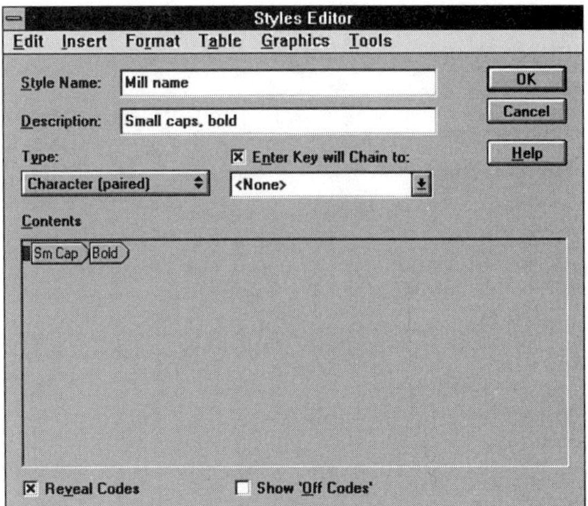

Fig. 9.16
A character style named Mill name with font attributes that will be used to format the mill name.

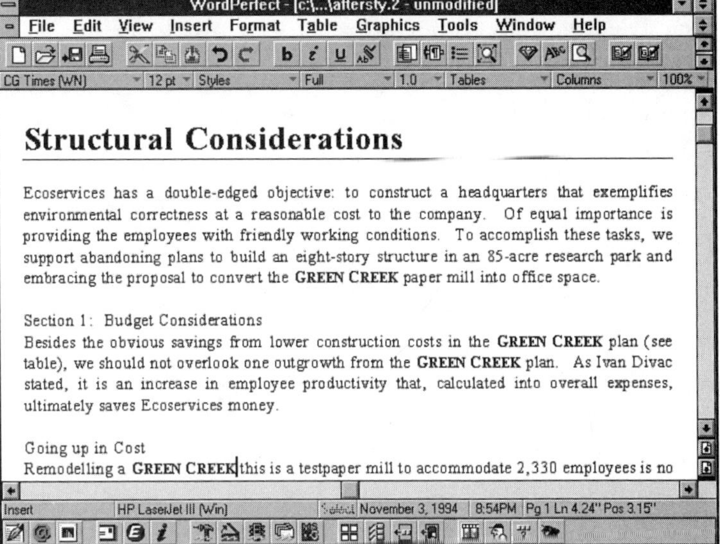

Fig. 9.17
The document after formatting with the 1 Hdr style and the Mill name style.

Applying a Style

You can apply a style either before or after you type text.

> **Tip**
> If the style type is Paragraph (paired-auto), you don't have to edit a style with the Styles Editor. When you change any paragraph that is formatted with the style, the changes are automatically reflected in the style.

To apply a style before you type text, take the following steps:

1. Position the insertion point where you want the effects of the style to begin.
2. Click the Select Style button to display the style list.
3. Select the style that you want to apply.
4. If the style being applied is a Document type or a Paragraph type, you have finished applying the style.

   If the style being applied is a Character style, type the text that is to be affected by the style, then pull down the style list again and select the style. This turns off the style.

To apply a style to existing text, take the following steps:

1. If the style being applied is a Document style, position the insertion point where you want its effects to begin.

   If the style being applied is a Paragraph style, position the insertion point in the paragraph to be affected, or select the paragraphs to be affected.

   If the style being applied is a Character style, select the text to be affected.
2. Click the Select Style button and select the style.

Editing a Style

Once you create and apply a style, you may change your mind about formatting in the style. Styles are very flexible; as soon as you change the style, the changes take effect wherever that style is applied.

◄ See "Using the Font Dialog Box," p. 109

◄ See "Working with Formatting Codes," p. 129

To make any changes that should apply to the document as a whole (except for the Document Initial Font), edit the Initial Style style. Every document contains the Initial Style style code at the beginning of its text (you can't remove the code). When you edit the Initial Style, therefore, your formatting takes effect at the beginning of the document. Because the Initial Style style is a Document (open) style, its formatting stays in effect for the rest of the document, or until it is overridden by other formatting of the same type. You might, for example, insert justification and margin codes in the Initial Style style.

Note

Formatting codes that appear in the body of a document, or in other styles that are applied in the document, override similar formatting in the Document Initial Style.

To edit a style, double-click the Select Style button to open the Style List dialog box. Next, highlight the style you wish to edit and choose **E**dit. The Styles Editor window appears (refer to figs. 9.15 and 9.17). Make any desired changes, then click OK and **C**lose.

Sharing Styles between Documents

Styles are automatically saved with the document containing them. You can save the styles in a document as a separate style file (so you don't have to keep the document that originally contained them) and then retrieve the style file into the style list of another document. If you want customized styles to be available in all new documents based on a particular template, copy the styles to the template, or create the styles while you edit the template.

◄ See "Making Basic Editing Changes to a Template," p. 137

To save styles in the current document to a separate style file, access the Style List dialog box, choose **O**ptions, Save **A**s, and then type a name for the style file and click OK.

To save a style in the current document to the current template, display the Style List dialog box, highlight the style name, choose **O**ptions, **C**opy, **T**emplate, and then click OK.

To retrieve styles from a style file (or from another document), display the Style List dialog box, choose **O**ptions, R**e**trieve, and then enter a (path and) filename and choose OK. You will be asked whether you want to overwrite current styles (with incoming styles that have the same names). Answer Yes or No to complete the retrieve operation.

Troubleshooting

I created a style to format the company name but when I apply it, it formats the entire paragraph.

Change the style type from Paragraph to Character.

I want to use the styles I created in my Report file in a new document.

With the new document on screen, access the Style List dialog box. Choose **O**ptions, R**e**trieve, and then enter the (path and) filename of your Report file and choose OK. When asked whether you want to overwrite current styles, answer **Y**es. The retrieve operation will then be completed.

I want to add Table of Contents markings to a style but I can't figure out how to do it.

You can add Table of Contents markings to any paired style. At the Styles Editor window, select the Show '**O**ff Codes' checkbox option. Select *only* the comment code ([Codes to the left...]). Choose **T**ools, Table of **C**ontents. Choose the level you want by choosing one of the Mark buttons on the Table of Contents feature bar that appears at the bottom of the screen. [Mrk Txt ToC] codes now surround the comment, and will surround any text that is formatted with the style.

From Here...

In this chapter you learned to organize and format large documents. You learned how to organize lists quickly and easily with the Bullets & Numbers feature, you learned how to create and work with outlines, and you learned how to work with styles.

For more information about working in WordPerfect, see the following chapters:

- Chapter 10, "Working with Tables and Graphics," covers creating, editing, and formatting tables, and how to enter basic calculations in a table. Chapter 10 also covers working with graphics lines, creating paragraph and page borders, creating Drop Caps, creating graphics boxes for figures and text, creating special text effects with Text Art, and creating Watermarks.

- Chapter 11, "Automating with Macros and Merge," covers how to create and use a simple macro, how to play macros, and how to assign a macro to a toolbar. Chapter 11 also covers how to set up and perform a mail merge and how to set up and perform a keyboard merge (a keyboard merge is used to fill in a form).

Chapter 10

Working with Tables and Graphics

by Judy Felfe

WordPerfect's Tables feature offers many practical uses. Tables can illustrate, define, and explain text; they can enhance your documents and make them more effective.

WordPerfect provides graphics elements—lines, borders, and boxes containing pictures or text, for example—that can also be used to enhance your documents.

In this chapter, you learn to

- Create a table
- Change column width and insert and delete rows
- Format the table, adjust table lines, and add shading
- Create graphics lines and add borders to paragraphs, columns, and pages
- Create and edit graphics boxes that contain pictures or text
- Use a Drop Cap at the beginning of a paragraph
- Create a watermark

Working with Tables

Tip
Several WordPerfect templates, including the expense report, invoice, and calendar templates, are forms that are based on tables.

A table gives you a convenient way to organize text. Use a table to organize columns of numbers, produce forms, or add spreadsheets to your documents. There are many formatting options you can apply to a table to make it visually appealing. WordPerfect even provides a Table Expert to let you preview and apply a table style (a set of formats) to your table all at once.

A table consists of columns and rows that form a grid of *cells*. You can fill cells with text and/or graphics. When you type text into a cell, the text wraps automatically from one line to the next, and the cell expands vertically to accommodate your text.

Two examples of WordPerfect tables are shown in figures 10.1 and 10.2.

Client	Account Rep	Current Status
ECO Services	Mary Franklin	Met with the prospect on Monday to discuss the benefits of using our accounting services. She'll get back to me on Friday.
Computer Books	Steve Sharp	This company publishes books on popular software programs. They're looking for someone who can provide the accounting services for their business.
Flash Messengers	Joe Martin	A current client. Met with Joe on Tuesday to discuss taxes for last year.

Fig. 10.1
Enter columns of text with automatic word wrap by placing the text in a WordPerfect table.

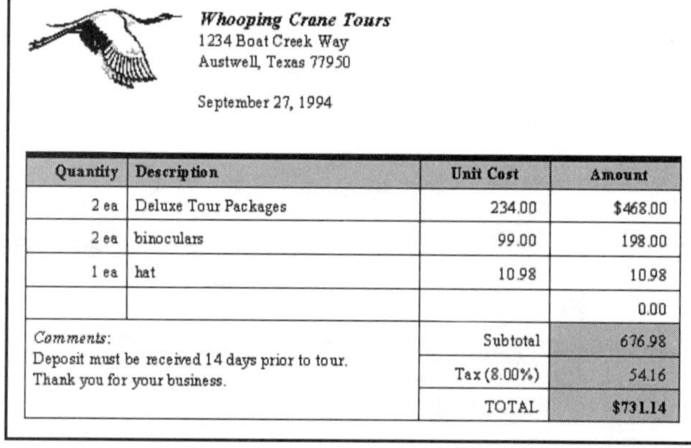

Whooping Crane Tours
1234 Boat Creek Way
Austwell, Texas 77950

September 27, 1994

Quantity	Description	Unit Cost	Amount
2 ea	Deluxe Tour Packages	234.00	$468.00
2 ea	binoculars	99.00	198.00
1 ea	hat	10.98	10.98
			0.00
Comments: Deposit must be received 14 days prior to tour. Thank you for your business.		Subtotal	676.98
		Tax (8.00%)	54.16
		TOTAL	**$731.14**

Fig. 10.2
Columns of text and numbers organized in a WordPerfect table.

Creating a Table

Note

The quickest way to create a table is by pulling down a grid from the Table QuickCreate button on the Power Bar, and dragging through the number of columns and rows that you want for your table. The size of the grid doesn't limit the size of your table; the grid expands as you drag past its edge.

A table can be inserted at any point in a document. You can create a table either with the Table menu or with the Table QuickCreate button on the Power Bar.

To create a table with the Table menu, take the following steps:

1. Position the insertion point where you want the table to begin.
2. Choose T**a**ble, **C**reate. The Create Table dialog box is displayed, as shown in figure 10.3.

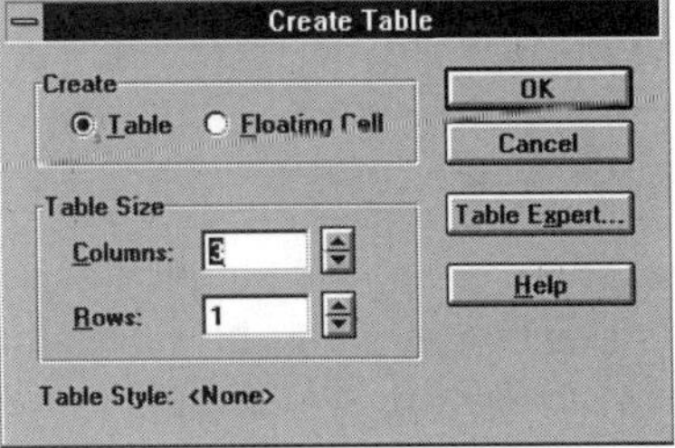

Fig. 10.3
Specify the number of columns and rows when you create a table.

3. Enter the number of columns and rows that you want.
4. Choose a style for your table, if desired, with the Table E**x**pert button. For information on using the Table Expert, see "Using the Table Expert To Enhance a Table," later in this chapter.

Note

It's easy to add rows to a table after you create it. See "Inserting and Deleting Columns and Rows," later in this chapter.

5. Choose OK. A table with the specified number of columns and rows (and predefined style, if any) is inserted in your document. The table spans the width between the left and right margins. All columns have the same width.

Moving Within a Table

Note

A table cell is identified by its column and row. The first cell in the first column, for example, is cell A1 (column A, row 1), and the first cell in the second row is cell A2 (column A, row 2). When the insertion point is in a table cell, the status bar identifies the current table and table cell. When the mouse pointer is over a table cell, the title bar identifies that cell.

Tip
When the insertion point is positioned in a table, WordPerfect automatically displays the Tables toolbar for you.

When you first create a table, WordPerfect positions the insertion point in the upper left corner of the table, in cell A1. To move the insertion point one cell to the next cell, press the Tab key. To move the insertion point to the previous cell, press Shift+Tab. When you're typing text into cells, the most efficient way to move from one cell to the next is with the Tab key (the arrow keys also work, as does the mouse).

Entering Text in a Table

◄ See "Typing Text," p. 89

When you enter text into your table, consider each cell a miniature document with its own margins and formatting. As you enter text, words wrap automatically to a new line and the row increases in depth (fig. 10.1 illustrates table data with automatic word wrap). Press Enter only when you need to force words to wrap to the next line.

Tip
If a table expands past the edge of the screen, click the Zoom button (Power Bar) and zoom to the Margin Width setting.

By default, the text you enter is aligned at the left edge of a cell. You can change the alignment of text within cells. It's normally best to use a table operation to perform any formatting. For example, select a cell (or cells) and use the Table Format button (Tables toolbar) to change the justification to full justification, rather than making the change by positioning the insertion point in the cell and pressing Ctrl+F. See "Formatting Table Cells" later in this chapter for more information.

Editing Table Design

A table has a very flexible structure. When you first create a table, it has a specified number of columns and rows, and every column has the same width. While you work with the table, you can adjust the column width to suit your taste, and you can add or delete columns and rows. You can even join cells to create a single cell, or you can split a cell into rows or columns.

In this section, you learn how to edit the table design.

Changing Column Width

To change the column width in a table, you can drag the column border to the desired position or you can ask for a "best fit" with the Size Column to Fit button (Tables toolbar). Alternatively, you can set a *precise* width for a column. Position the insertion point in the column (or select the column), click the Table Format button, choose Co**l**umn, then Wid**t**h, and specify the width that you want.

To adjust column width by dragging a column border, take the following steps:

1. Position the mouse pointer against the right edge of the column you want to adjust, so that the pointer becomes a cross with horizontal arrowheads. It's a good idea to start with the leftmost column that you're going to adjust and work your way to the right.
2. Drag the border to a new position. As you drag, a dotted vertical line appears and the exact position is indicated on the status bar (see fig. 10.4).

   Alternatively, you can drag the Column Break icon on the Ruler Bar to adjust table column width.

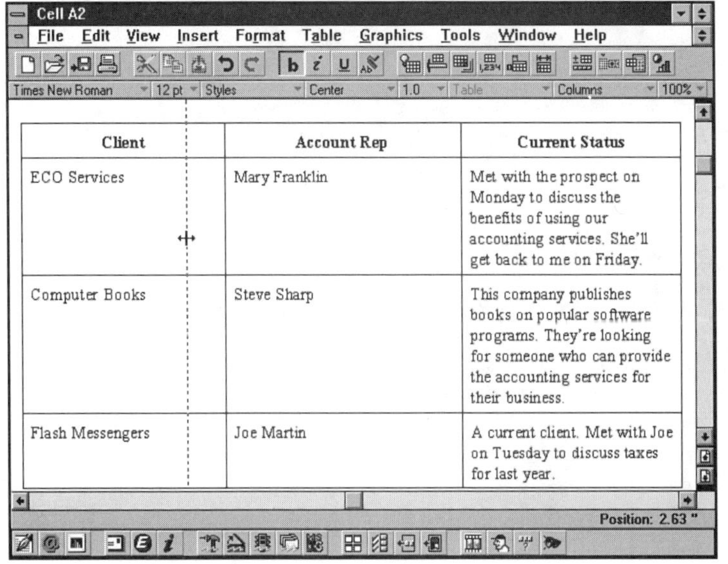

Fig. 10.4
Drag a column border to adjust column width.

When you want to adjust column width so that it's just wide enough for its widest entry, let WordPerfect do the job for you. Just place the insertion point in the column and click the Size Column to Fit button (Tables toolbar).

Inserting and Deleting Columns and Rows

What if you enter several rows of information in your table and you realize that you need a new row in the middle of the table? No problem. You can insert a row (or column) anywhere in the table without disturbing what's already there.

Tip
Insert a row just above the current row by pressing Alt+Insert.

To insert new rows (or columns) in a table, take the following steps:

1. Position the insertion point in the row (or column) next to where you want a new row or column.

2. Choose T**a**ble, **I**nsert; or choose **I**nsert from the QuickMenu. The Insert Columns/Rows dialog box is displayed (see fig. 10.5).

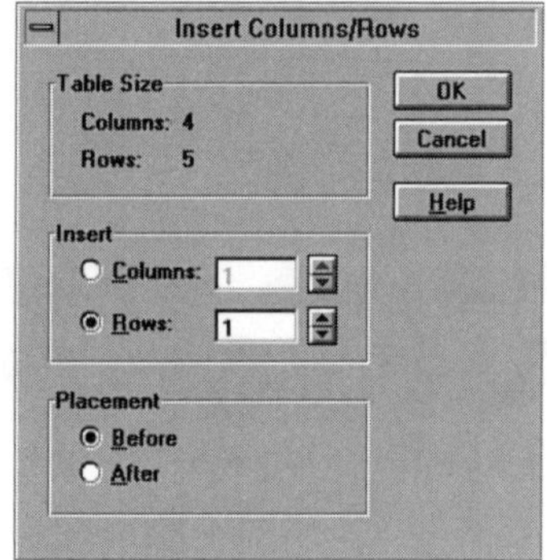

Fig. 10.5
Tell WordPerfect how many rows or columns to insert before the current column or row.

3. Choose **C**olumns or **R**ows, then specify how many to insert.

4. If desired, adjust the Placement from **B**efore to **A**fter.

5. Choose OK.

   New rows (or columns) will contain the same formatting as the current row (or column).

You can add a new row at the bottom of a table with the Tab key. Position the insertion point in the last cell of the table and press Tab to create a new row. If you're entering a list of names and addresses into your table, you can press Tab to add a new row just before you add the next name and address.

Just as you can easily insert new rows or columns, you can easily delete rows or columns.

To delete rows (or columns) in a table, take the following steps:

Tip
Delete the current row by pressing Alt+Del.

1. Position the insertion point in the row or column that you want to delete, or select the rows or columns that you want to delete (see "Selecting Table Cells," later in this chapter).

2. Choose T**a**ble, **D**elete; or choose **D**elete from the QuickMenu. The Delete dialog box is displayed (see fig. 10.6).

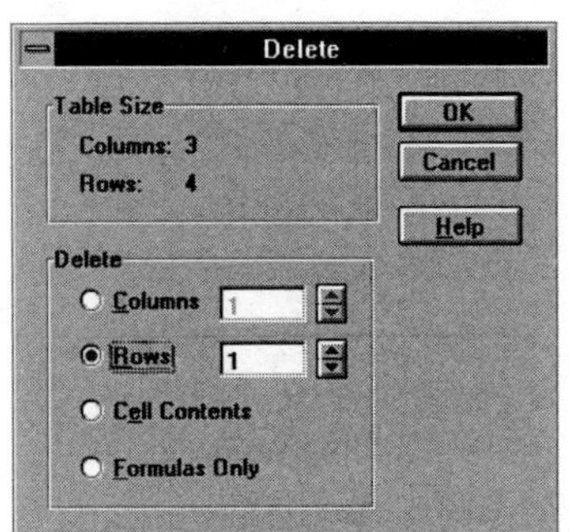

Fig. 10.6
Delete the selected row(s) in the Delete dialog box.

3. Choose **C**olumns or **R**ows. If you selected rows or columns before accessing the Delete dialog box, choose OK. If you positioned the insertion point before accessing the Delete dialog box, you can specify how many rows or columns to delete, then choose OK.

Joining Cells

What do you do when you want a title centered between the left and right edges of your table? You join table cells. When you first create a table, it has the same number of cells in every row and in every column. It doesn't have to stay that way; you can select the cells that you want to join and tell WordPerfect to join them. The lower left corner of the table shown in figure 10.2 has a single cell that was created by joining other cells.

To join table cells, take the following steps:

1. Select the cells that you want to join.

2. Choose T**a**ble, **J**oin, **C**ell; or, from the QuickMenu, choose **J**oin Cells.

Formatting a Table

Use Table Format options to specify justification, text attributes, column margins, and so on for table cells. You can specify formatting either before or after you enter text in cells; in either case, the text is formatted according to the cell format.

> **Note**
>
> A table format is overridden by a column format; a column format is overridden by a cell format. You could, for example, format an entire column for decimal alignment and the cell at the top of the column for center alignment.

Selecting Table Cells

Usually you'll want to select table cells (or columns, or rows) before you apply formatting. Although you can select a *portion* of the text in a cell rather than the *entire cell*, you should select a portion of text *only* when you want mixed formatting within the same cell. This section shows you how to select table cells.

Follow these guidelines for selecting table cells:

- Turn on row/column indicators with the Row/Column Indicators button (Tables toolbar).
- To select a single cell, position the mouse pointer against any edge of the cell, so that it becomes a hollow arrow (see fig. 10.7), then click the mouse button. The entire cell should be highlighted.
- To select several cells, position the mouse pointer in the cell that is in the upper-left corner of all the cells that you want to select. Then, position the mouse pointer against any edge of the cell, so that the pointer becomes a hollow arrow. Drag through the cells that you want to select. The cells should be entirely highlighted.
- To select columns or rows, click or drag in the row/column indicators. The columns or rows in your selection should be entirely highlighted.

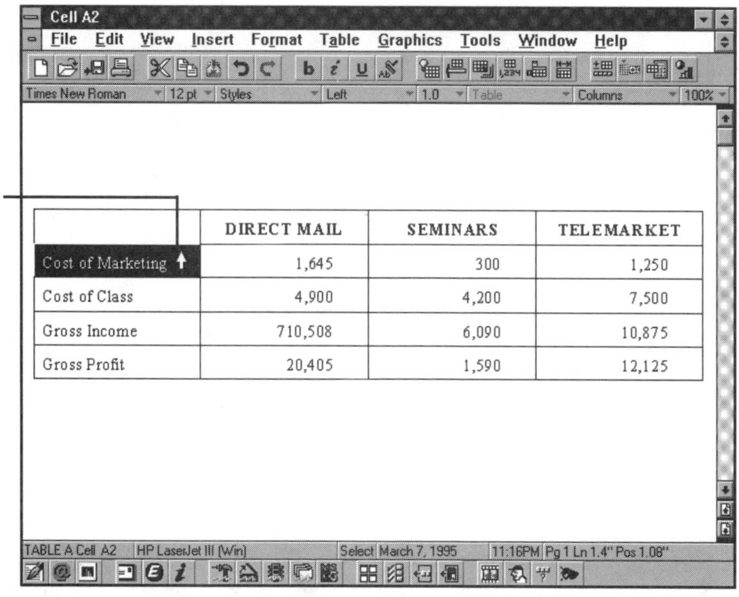

Fig. 10.7
Position the mouse pointer against the edge of a cell so that it becomes a hollow arrow, then click to select the cell.

Figure 10.8 illustrates a table after column A has been selected. Row/column indicators have been turned on (from the Tables toolbar) to make selection easier.

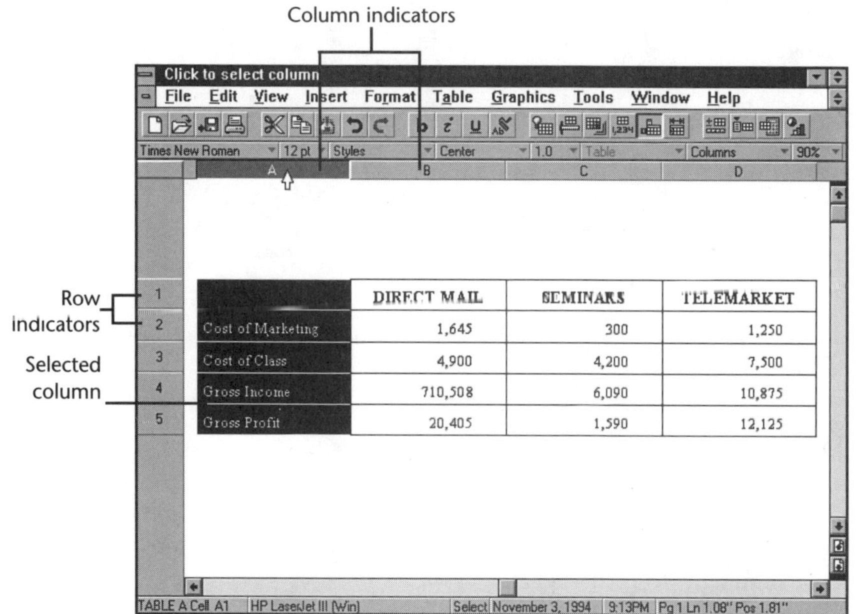

Fig. 10.8
Select table cells before formatting.

Formatting Table Cells

Formatting cells could be a matter of changing the alignment in the cells, or of applying attributes such as bold or underline to text in cells, or of specifying header rows within the table. In this section, "Formatting Table Cells" is used to mean formatting that is applied to any table element, whether that element is cells, columns, rows, or the entire table. To format table cells, follow these steps:

1. Select the cell(s) or column(s) that you want to format.
2. Open the Format dialog box by clicking the Table Format button (Tables toolbar); by using the Tables QuickMenu; or by choosing T**a**ble, F**o**rmat. Figure 10.9 illustrates the Format dialog box with T**a**ble format options displayed (types of format options are C**e**ll, Co**l**umn, R**o**w, and T**a**ble).

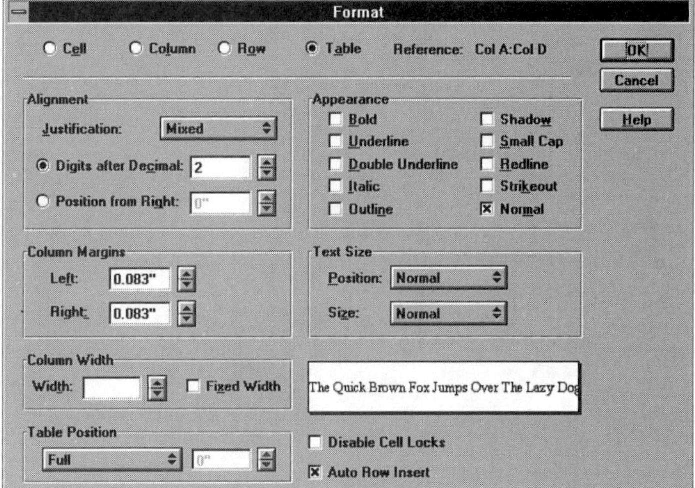

Fig. 10.9
The Format dialog box with Table format options displayed.

3. Choose the option type that you want to format: C**e**ll, Co**l**umn, R**o**w, or T**a**ble.
4. Make the desired formatting changes. Your changes might include items in the following list:
   - When you format Cells or Columns, you can adjust the alignment with the **J**ustification option. Cells containing numbers should be decimal-aligned.

- When you format C**e**lls, you can *lock* cells to keep the insertion point from moving into the cells.
- When you format C**e**lls, you can specify that cell contents will be ignored in calculations (you might have to do this if you're adding a column that has a number in its column header).
- When you format the T**a**ble, you can adjust the Table Position relative to the page margins.
- When you format R**o**ws, you can designate a number of rows as header rows, if desired (format R**o**ws). When a table spans a page break, header rows print at the top of the next page.
- When you format R**o**ws, you can specify a fixed row height. This feature is useful when you create a table with "boxes" (cells) that should have a fixed height, regardless of any text they contain; for example, when you create a calendar. Unless you specify a fixed row height, the row height is a function of the number of text lines in the row.

5. Click OK to exit the Format dialog box and apply the specified changes to your table.

Changing Borders, Lines, and Shading in a Table

Give your tables visual appeal by changing table borders and lines and adding shading to cells. Your "desktop publishing" efforts can make the table more attractive *and* easier to read. When, for example, you shade every other row in a table, it's easy to read across a row.

The four outer lines around a table are called its *border* (by default, a table has no border lines). Lines inside the table are called *lines* (by default, table cells have single lines on their top and left edges). Borders and lines are formatted separately. You can choose from a variety of border/line styles.

In addition to formatting table borders and lines, you can apply a fill style to table cells. Fill styles range all the way from standard gray shading to gradient patterns with blended colors.

You can use the Table Expert to apply a set of changes for you, or you can make your own changes to table borders and lines and shading. This section shows you how to use the Table Expert and how to make each type of change.

Tip
You can Undo the effects after you apply a table style with the Table Expert.

Using the Table Expert to Enhance a Table

The fastest and easiest way to make changes to borders, lines, and shading in a table is to apply a table style (a set of changes) all at once with the Table Expert.

To use the Table Expert, take the following steps:

1. Position the insertion point anywhere in the table.

2. Click the Table Expert button (Tables toolbar); or, choose T**a**ble, E**x**pert. The Table Expert dialog box appears (see fig. 10.10).

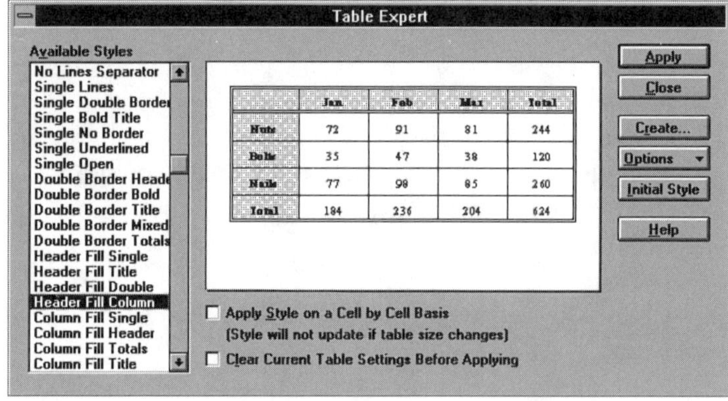

Fig. 10.10
Apply a set of formats to your table with the Table Expert.

Tip
To set the current table style as a default style for all new tables, access the Table Expert dialog box, choose **I**nitial Style, then select **Y**es.

3. Examine the available styles, if desired, by highlighting a style and looking at the preview area.

4. Highlight the style you wish to apply.

5. If you have already applied changes to borders, lines, or shading, you may want to check the C**l**ear Current Table Settings Before Applying checkbox.

6. When you finish making selections in the Table Expert dialog box, choose **A**pply.

Tip
To quickly remove all table lines, choose the T**a**ble radio button, then choose <None> from the drop-down list of **L**ine Style names.

Making Your Own Table Enhancements

To make your own changes to table borders and lines, or to add shading, take the following steps:

1. Position the insertion point in the table, or select the cells for which you want to change borders or lines or add shading (see "Selecting Table Cells," earlier in this chapter).

2. Click the Lines/Fill button (Tables toolbar); or, choose T**a**ble, **L**ines/Fill. The Table Lines/Fill dialog box is displayed.

3. To affect the entire table, select the T**a**ble radio button at the top of the dialog box. Figure 10.11 illustrates the Table Lines/Fill dialog box with T**a**ble options displayed.

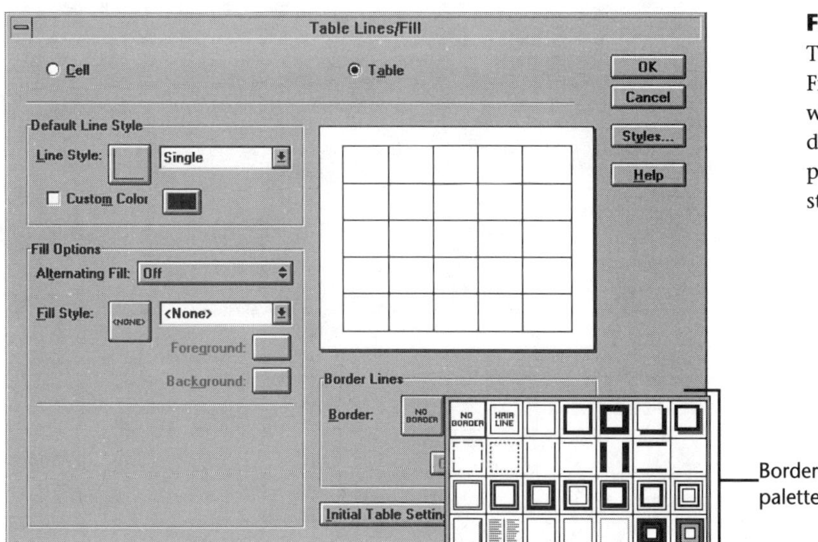

Fig. 10.11
The Table Lines/Fill dialog box with Table options displayed. The palette of border styles is displayed.

4. If the Table radio button is selected, you can select or change the border for the table by displaying either the **B**order palette of border styles or the list of **B**order style names. To add a table border, choose any border style other than <None>.

5. To format lines or shading for selected cells, make sure that Sele**c**tion is the selected option type. Options in the dialog box now apply to the current selection (see fig. 10.12).

6. With **C**ell options selected, change the line style for the sides you want to change (left, right, top, bottom, or outside). You can pull down a palette of line styles or a list of line style names.

7. With either T**a**ble options or **C**ell options selected, you can display a palette of fill styles or a list of fill style names and select a style. If the selected fill style has only one color, select a Fore**g**round color, if desired. If the selected fill style has two colors, you can choose Fore**g**round and Bac**k**ground colors.

8. Choose OK to return to the table.

Tip
To open the palette of border styles, click the button that appears immediately to the left of the pull-down style names.

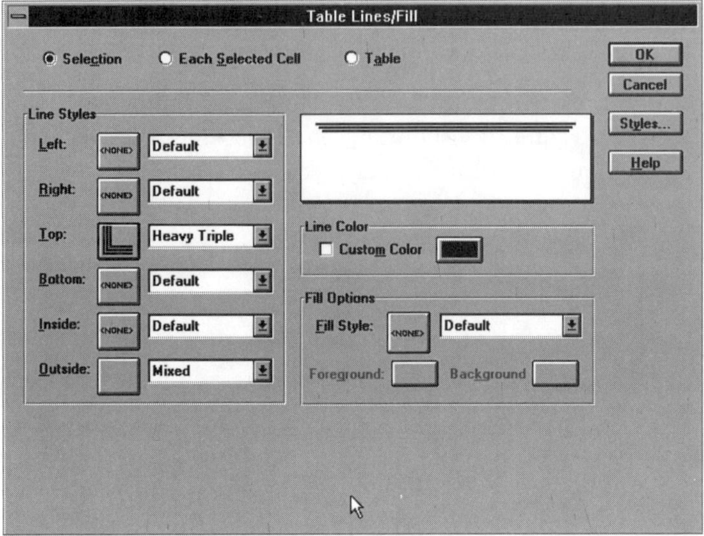

Fig. 10.12
The Table Lines/Fill dialog box with Selection options displayed.

Troubleshooting

My table has cells with paragraphs of text in them. One row has an extra blank line at the bottom and I don't know how to get rid of it.

Turn on the display of nonprinting characters by choosing **V**iew, **S**how ¶. Look for a ¶ somewhere in the row and delete it.

I inserted several rows in the wrong place.

Click the Undo button to remove the unwanted rows. Then position the insertion point in a row right next to where you want a new row or rows. Choose T**a**ble, **I**nsert. Specify how many rows you want and make sure that you choose the correct placement (before or after the current row).

I removed all of the lines in my table and now it's hard to tell which part of the table I'm working in.

Choose **V**iew, Table Grid**l**ines to display dotted gridlines at the edges of cells. When table gridlines are displayed, you see gridlines at the edges of cells, whether or not any lines are defined for the cells. To view the table again as it will print (*without* the gridlines but *with* any defined lines or shading), choose **V**iew, Table Grid**l**ines.

Working with Graphics

Take advantage of WordPerfect's graphics features to add visual pizzazz to your documents. You can add lines, borders, shading, and pictures. Use graphics to call attention to your document, break the monotony of straight text, emphasize text, and pique the reader's interest.

You can add a line above (or below) headings to make them stand out or to help divide information on the page. Create a box with a border and enter text in the box, or add clip art to make a document more interesting. Use the Drop Cap feature to enlarge and emphasize the first letter in a paragraph. Use the Watermark feature to add a logo or clip art image or text behind the printed document text. This section introduces you to adding graphics to your documents.

Working with Graphics Lines

WordPerfect enables you to add horizontal or vertical graphics lines through the Graphics menu and through buttons on the Graphics toolbar. To display the Graphics toolbar, right-click the toolbar and select Graphics.

The default graphics lines are thin lines that extend from margin to margin (left to right or top to bottom). You can tell WordPerfect how thick to make the line, or what the color should be, or how long it should be, or exactly where it should be on the page. Alternatively, you can use the mouse to adjust the thickness, length, and position of the line.

Figure 10.13 illustrates the use of a default horizontal graphics line to separate headings in a memo from the body of the memo.

Creating Instant Lines

You can instantly create a horizontal graphics line by clicking the Horizontal Line button (Graphics toolbar), by choosing **G**raphics, **H**orizontal Line, or by pressing Ctrl+F11. The result is a thin line that extends from margin to margin at the baseline of text on the current line.

Correspondingly, you can instantly create a vertical graphics line by clicking the Vertical Line button (Graphics toolbar), or by choosing **G**raphics, **V**ertical Line. The result is a thin vertical line that is placed at the left margin and extends from the top margin to the bottom margin.

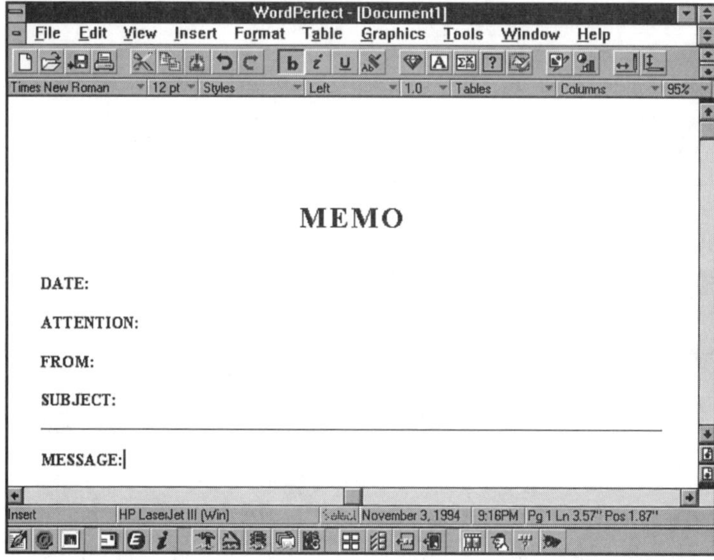

Fig. 10.13 Click the Horizontal Line button to create a horizontal graphics line that effectively separates the headings in a memo from the body of the memo.

Creating a Custom Line

To create a custom line, take the following steps:

1. If the line is to be a horizontal line, position the insertion point where you want the horizontal line. If you want the line to be placed slightly below a line of text, insert a hard return between the text and the horizontal line.

2. Click the Custom Line button, or choose **G**raphics, Custom **L**ine. The Create Graphics Line dialog box is displayed, as shown in figure 10.14.

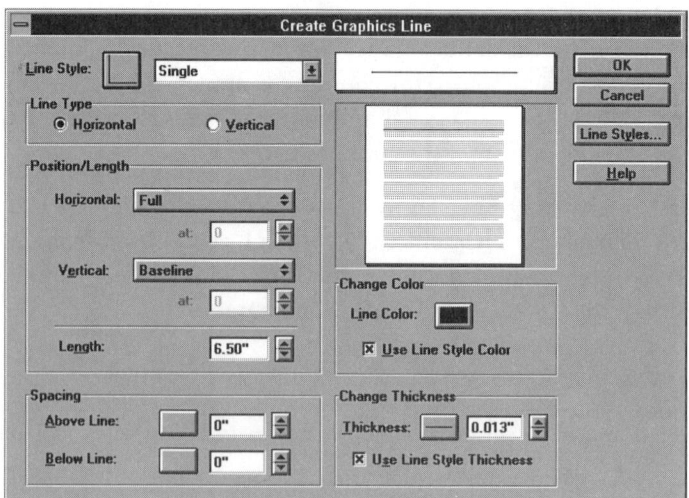

Fig. 10.14 Customize a graphics line in the Create Graphics Line dialog box (or in the Edit Graphics Line dialog box).

3. Adjust settings for the line as desired. For example, use the Ho**r**izontal Position option to specify a position other than **F**ull, then adjust the length of the line. When you finish adjusting settings, choose OK.

4. If the line you created is a horizontal line, you probably want to insert a hard return after the line.

> **Note**
>
> The Create Graphics Line dialog box becomes the Edit Graphics Line dialog box when you edit a line.

Editing a Graphics Line

Edit a graphics line either with the mouse or through the Edit Graphics Line dialog box. Using the mouse is quick and easy, although it's not as precise as using the dialog box.

To edit a graphics line with the Edit Graphics Line dialog box, take the following steps:

1. Click the line to select it.

2. Choose **G**raphics, Edit Li**n**e, or right-click the line and choose Edit **E**dit Horizontal (or Vertical) Line from the QuickMenu. The Edit Graphics Line dialog box appears (it looks like the Create Graphics Line dialog box shown in figure 10.14).

3. Change any settings as desired and choose OK.

To edit a line with the mouse, select the line first. To move the line, place the mouse pointer against the line so that the pointer becomes a four-headed hollow arrow. Then drag the line to a new position. To adjust the thickness or length of the line, position the mouse pointer against a selection handle so that the mouse pointer becomes a two-headed hollow arrow. Then drag the handle to adjust the thickness or length.

Creating Borders

A graphics *border* is a box that surrounds text, emphasizes your message, separates text, or adds pizzazz to the page. You can use a paragraph border to call attention to one particular paragraph of text in a letter, for example; or you can add a page border to each page of a report to guide the reader and to create consistency within the report. Figure 10.15 illustrates a newsletter with a paragraph border, a page border, and a column border.

Tip

You can use a variety of line styles and thicknesses with page and paragraph borders.

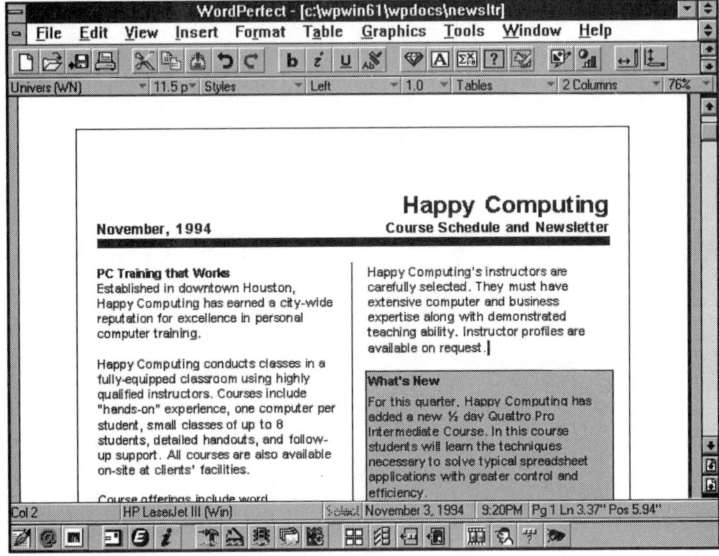

Fig. 10.15
The page border dresses up the page. The paragraph border emphasizes the announcement about "What's New."

Creating Paragraph Borders

A paragraph border is a frame that surrounds an individual paragraph or selected paragraphs. The border can include a fill style. WordPerfect gives you a choice of many border styles and fill styles.

To add a paragraph border to your document, take the following steps:

1. Place the insertion point in the paragraph to which you want to apply a border, or select the paragraphs to which you want to apply a border.

2. Choose Fo**r**mat, P**a**ragraph, **B**order/Fill. The Paragraph Border dialog box appears (see fig. 10.16).

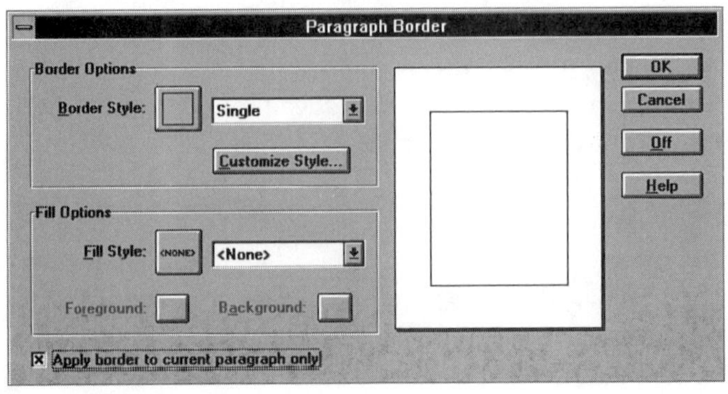

Fig. 10.16
A paragraph border (and a fill, if desired) calls attention to specific text.

3. In the Border Options area, choose the palette button beside **B**order Style or choose the drop-down list to select the border by name. Select a style.

4. To frame the current paragraph and all subsequent paragraphs, deselect the A**p**ply Border to Current Paragraph Only checkbox.

5. To add a fill to your border, choose the palette button beside **F**ill Style or choose the drop-down list to select the fill style by name. Select a style.

6. Choose OK.

Tip
Use Page view to see page borders on-screen; you can't see them in Draft view.

Creating Page Borders

Note

WordPerfect supplies a number of graphics images that can be used as page borders. You can place one of these images in a graphics box that is sized to the full page. Set the text wrap to N**o** Wrap (through). Images files that are designed to be used as page borders have names that begin with "BORD," for example, **BORD01P.WPG**. You can view these borders using the View button that appears in any directory list box. See "Creating a Graphics Box," later in this chapter.

A page border can add pizzazz to any document. Usually, you repeat the page border on all pages of a document, but you can choose to apply it to the current page only (see fig. 10.17).

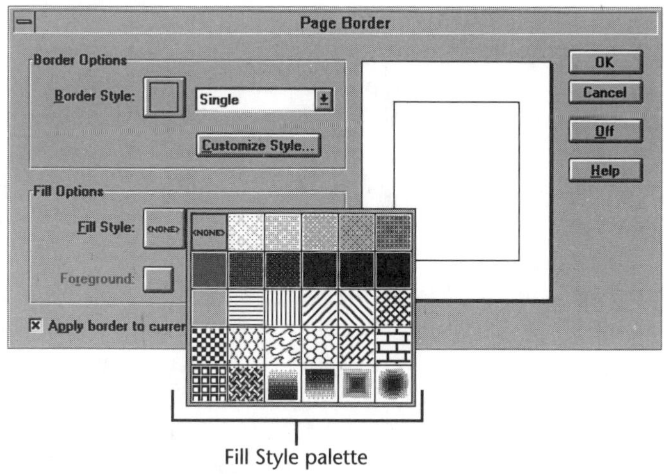

Fig. 10.17
To apply your page border to the current page only, click the box in the lower left corner of the Page Border dialog box. To remove the border from the current page, click the **O**ff button.

To add a page border to your document, take the following steps:

1. Position the insertion point on the first page where you want to apply a page border.
2. Choose Fo**r**mat, **P**age, **B**order/Fill. The Page Border dialog box is displayed (refer to fig. 10.17).
3. In the Border Options area, select a border style.
4. If desired, in the Fill Options area, choose a fill style.
5. Choose OK.

Tip
Be careful to choose a fill style that enables you to read the text easily.

Note

To remove a page border, place the insertion point on the page where the page border begins. Access the Page Border dialog box and choose a border style of <None> (or delete the page border code through Reveal Codes). When you remove the border, you remove any fill that it contains.

Creating Graphics Boxes

A *graphics box* is a box that holds an image or text. For example, a graphics box can hold clip art, a drawing, a callout, a text file, an equation, or a table. The contents of the document are adjusted to make room for the box. The box can be selected and moved or resized. A graphics box has its own contents and its own border; a paragraph or page border, on the other hand, is simply an ornamental frame surrounding text that is already in your document.

Adding graphics boxes to your documents illustrates the text, draws attention to the message, and adds interest to the document. Images, for example, help the reader understand the text, while text callouts attract the reader's attention to the text and break up "gray space" on the page. WordPerfect enables you to add several types of graphics boxes to your documents, each with a style and purpose of its own.

Understanding Graphics Box Styles

Each of WordPerfect's graphics box styles is designed to work best with one particular type of image or text. For example, the Image, Figure, and User styles work well with graphics images, and the Text Box and User styles work well with text. Any box, however, can hold any type of image, text, table, equation, and so on. The box style is simply a suggestion for the box's use.

One aspect of the box style is its line style (width and type of border line). Other aspects of the box style include its placement (how it is attached or anchored to the document), its caption style, and the amount of space allowed both outside and inside the box. When you choose a box style, you choose the default settings for that box style. The style of an individual box, however, can be customized.

The following list describes each graphics box style and its default settings:

- *Image*. No border or fill, anchored to the page, suitable for graphics images.
- *Figure*. Single line border, anchored to the paragraph, suitable for graphics images.
- *Text Box*. Thick line on top and bottom, no fill, anchored to a paragraph, suitable for text.
- *Equation*. No border or fill, anchored to a paragraph, suitable for equations.
- *Table*. Thick line on top and bottom, anchored to a paragraph, suitable for a table or text.
- *User*. No border or fill, anchored to a paragraph, suitable for graphics images.
- *Button*. Button border with Button Fill, no outside border space, anchored to a character, suitable for text or images.
- *Watermark*. No border or fill, anchored to the page, contains images or text that is screened at 75% brightness so that it creates a background for text on the page.
- *Inline Equation*. No border or fill, anchored to a character, suitable for equations
- *OLE 2.0 Box*. No border or fill, anchored to a page, used for data that is linked and embedded in a document.

Examples of a graphics box containing an image and a graphics box containing text are shown in figure 10.18.

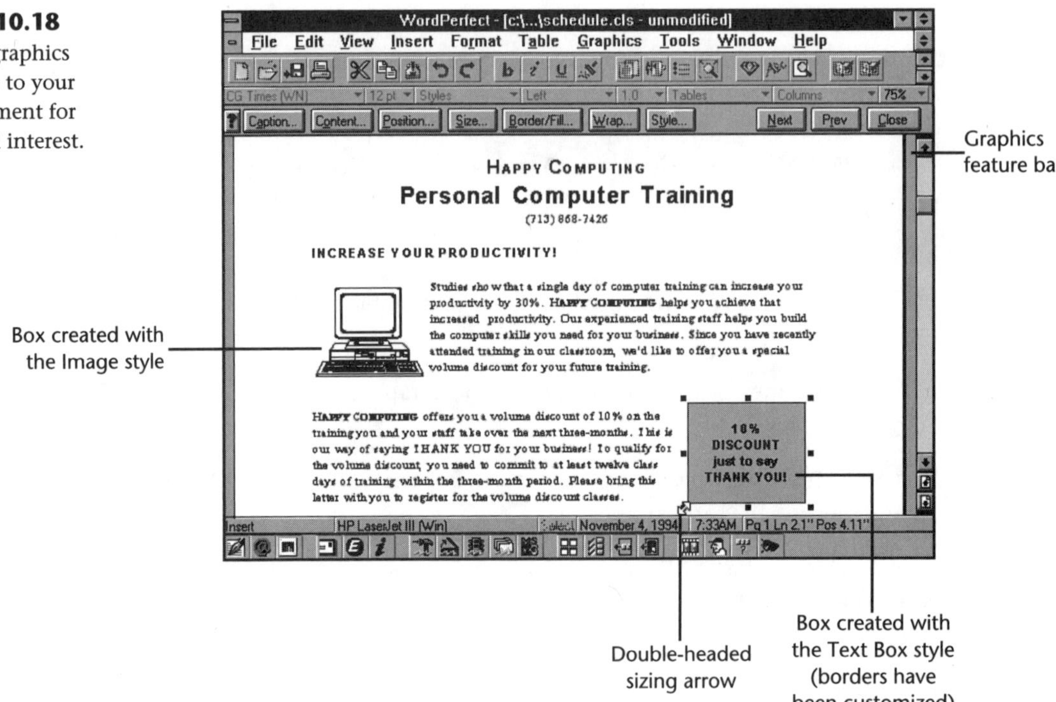

Fig. 10.18
Add graphics boxes to your document for visual interest.

Table 10.1 describes how each type of placement works and for what it is suited:

Table 10.1 Graphics Placement

Placement (anchor type)	How it works	Suitable for
Paragraph	The box stays with the paragraph that contains it	Boxes that are associated with text in the same area
Character	The box is treated like a single character on a line of text	Very small boxes that are associated with a particular line of text
Page	The box stays in a fixed position on the page, regardless of editing changes to the text	Boxes that are meant to stay in the same place on the page, such as a masthead at the top of a newsletter page

Creating a Graphics Box

You can create an instant graphics box with the Image button (WordPerfect and Graphics feature bars), with the Text Box button (Graphics feature bar), or through the **G**raphics menu.

To create a graphics box, take the following steps:

1. To tell WordPerfect that you want to position and size the box with the mouse when you create it, choose **G**raphics, Drag t**o** Create.

   The purpose here is to make sure that the Drag t**o** Create option is selected; if it already has a checkmark by it, cancel the menu so that is stays selected.

2. Click the Image button (to create a box containing an image) or the Text Box button (to create a box containing text).

3. Show WordPerfect where to place the box by dragging from the upper left corner of the box to the lower right corner of the box. You can do this only if Drag t**o** Create (Graphics menu) is selected.

4. If you chose to create a box in the Text Box style, you are placed in the Text Box Editor, where you can enter and format text. When you finish working in the Text Box Editor, choose **C**lose (to return to the document). The Graphics feature bar is displayed beneath the Power Bar (refer to fig. 10.17), for your convenience in case you want to edit the box.

Tip
To contour text around the image in a box, click the **W**rap button on the feature bar. Choose **C**ontour, then OK.

5. If you chose to create a box in the Image style, you are taken to the Insert Image dialog box, where you can choose an image to insert in the box. You can preview the selected image by clicking the Vie**w** button. Select the image you want and choose OK to return to the document. The Graphics feature bar is displayed above the text area on-screen. The box that you just created is selected.

6. To adjust the size or position of the box with the mouse, select the box and use the two-headed sizing pointer or the four-headed moving pointer.

7. To customize the box through the feature bar, select the box first, then choose the appropriate button on the feature bar; or right-click the box and choose a menu option.

8. When you finish working with the graphics box, deselect it by clicking outside of the box.

> **Note**
>
> To remove a graphics box, select it and press the Delete key.
>
> To edit a graphics box, right-click the box and choose **F**eature Bar, or choose another option from the lower portion of the QuickMenu. Alternatively, after you select the box, choose **G**raphics, **E**dit Box. The graphics feature bar is then displayed. Use the feature bar buttons to edit the box.

> **Note**
>
> Choose **G**raphics, **C**ustom Box to select a style for a box before you create the box. The box is created using default formatting options for your selected style.

Tip
To quickly edit the text or the actual image in a graphics box, double-click the box.

Creating Drop Caps

One of WordPerfect's ways of putting desktop publishing within the reach of everyone is its Drop Caps feature. Now it's easy to add visual interest to your text by creating an oversized character at the beginning of a paragraph (see fig. 10.19).

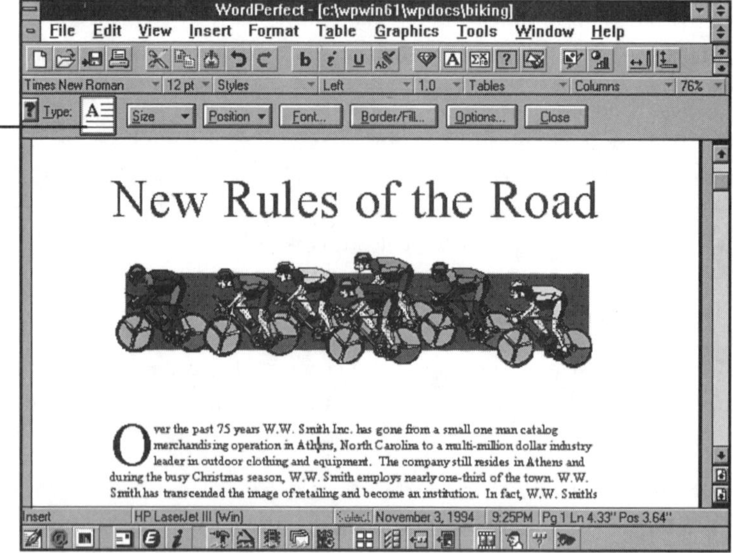

Fig. 10.19
Drop Caps add interest and visual appeal to text.

To create a drop cap, take the following steps:

1. Position the insertion point in the paragraph in which you want a drop cap.
2. Choose Fo**r**mat, D**r**op Cap. WordPerfect creates a drop cap three lines deep using the first character in the paragraph and displays the Drop Cap feature bar above the text area on-screen.
3. Adjust the drop cap, if desired, by using buttons on the feature bar. For example, if you want the drop cap to drop down through four lines of text instead of three, click the **S**ize button, then select **4** Lines High.

Creating Watermarks

A watermark is a special type of graphics box that contains either text or graphics but prints in the background. The contents of the watermark box screens lightly so that the text you enter in the foreground is readable.

Tip
To see your watermark on-screen, choose **V**iew, **P**age; or press Alt+F5. Watermarks are not visible in Draft view.

There are many uses for watermarks. You can dress up a letter to a client with your company logo, you can add text ("Draft") to the background of reports, and so on. You can use any of WordPerfect's watermark files, create your own images or text to use as watermarks, or use images and text from other applications.

Using a Text Watermark

Most of WordPerfect's watermark files (CLASSIFI.WPG, DRAFT.WPG, DUPLICAT.WPG, OVERDUE.WPG, and so on), consist of text that has been saved as a graphics image. You can use WordPerfect's watermark text or you can create your own text (it doesn't have to be saved as a graphics image). Figure 10.20 illustrates one of WordPerfect's watermarks (DRAFT.WPG) in a draft copy of a report.

Using Images as Watermarks

You can use images created in other applications, or you can use any of the WPG images in WordPerfect's GRAPHICS directory as a watermark image. The image you use doesn't have to be designed specifically as a watermark image. Figure 10.21 illustrates one of WordPerfect's image files—TIGER_J.WPG—used as a watermark in an advertisement.

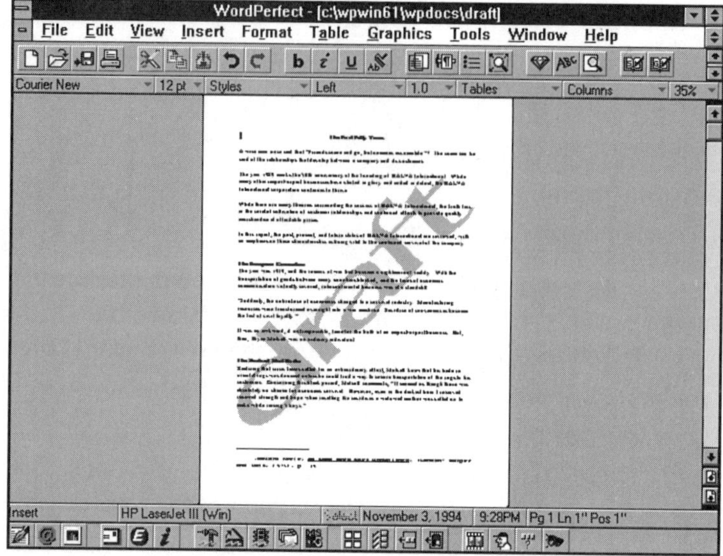

Fig. 10.20
Use the Watermark feature to print background text (or to print text that has been saved as an image) behind the document text.

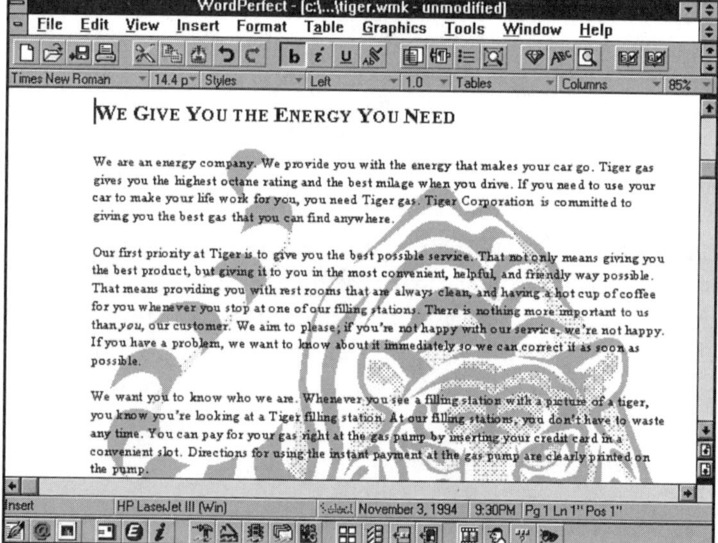

Fig. 10.21
You can use clip art, scanned art, drawings from other programs, or text in a watermark graphics box.

Creating a Watermark

Before creating a watermark, enter and format all document text. When the watermark appears on-screen, text editing slows considerably. To add a watermark to a document, take the following steps:

1. Position the insertion point on the first page that is to have a watermark (the watermark will appear on that page and on every subsequent page).

2. Choose Fo**r**mat, **W**atermark. In the Watermark dialog box, choose **C**reate. You are placed in the Watermark A editing screen. The Watermark feature bar appears above the text area at the top of the screen.

3. If you're going to create a watermark from text, you'll probably want an extremely large font size. Double-click the Font Size button (Power Bar). At the Font dialog box, double-click in the Font **S**ize text box and type the size that you want (for example, type 150). Choose OK. Type (and format) the text that you want as a watermark. Then click the **C**lose button on the Watermark feature bar to return to your document.

4. To create a watermark that contains an image, click the I**m**age button on the Watermark feature bar and choose an image. The image you choose is automatically sized to fill the entire page. Just after you create the image, it is selected and the Graphics feature bar overlays the Watermark feature bar above the text area at the top of the screen. Use the feature bar, if desired, to make any adjustments. Click the **C**lose button on the Graphics feature bar, and then click the **C**lose button on the Watermark feature bar to return to your document.

Troubleshooting

I keep on creating a page border but no matter what I do I can't see it on-screen.

Change the view from Draft view to Page view by choosing **V**iew, **P**age, or by pressing Alt+F5.

My page border only prints on the first page, and I have to specify it again and again on every page.

When you create the page border on the first page, be sure that the **A**pply Border to Current Page checkbox is not selected.

My watermark is too dark.

Edit your watermark by choosing Fo**r**mat, **W**atermark, **E**dit. Right-click the image and choose **I**mage Tools from the QuickMenu. A palette of image-editing buttons appears. Click the brightness level button (it looks like a sun), and then select a lighter image for your watermark. Finally, click the **C**lose button on the Watermark feature bar.

(continues)

(continued)

I created a box and placed an image in it and now I'd like to change the border lines.

Right-click your graphic and choose Border/Fill from the QuickMenu, or choose Border/Fill from the Graphics feature bar, if shown. Make whatever changes you want at the Box Border/Fill Styles dialog box, and choose OK. Click outside of the box to deselect it.

From Here...

In this chapter, you learned how to use tables and graphics to add pizzazz to your document and to make them more effective. You found out how to create, restructure, and format tables. You were introduced to graphics boxes, and you also learned how to create a Drop Cap (an oversized letter) at the beginning of a paragraph. Lastly, you learned how to add a watermark to your document.

For more information about working in WordPerfect, see the following chapters:

- Chapter 8, "Customizing WordPerfect," tells you how to customize WordPerfect to suit your working habits and preferences.
- Chapter 11, "Automating with Macros and Merge," covers how to create and use a simple macro, and how to assign a macro to a toolbar. Chapter 11 also shows you how to set up and perform merge operations—both mail merge and keyboard merge.

Chapter 11

Automating with Macros and Merge

by Judy Felfe

WordPerfect supplies many features that enable you to complete your work quickly and efficiently. Two of these features are macros and merge. Both of these features save you time by automating your work.

You can automate your work with *macros*, or mini-programs, by recording your keystrokes and commands, saving the recording, and then playing back the recording any time you need to repeat the same keystrokes and commands.

WordPerfect's merge feature also saves you time and work. If you ever have to send the same letter to a number of people, you know how much work this can entail. WordPerfect enables you to merge (combine) fixed information (the text in the letter) with variable information (the names and addresses). The form letters are produced all at once in a single merge operation.

In this chapter, you learn to

- Play a macro
- Create your own macros by recording keystrokes and commands
- Make simple editing changes to a macro
- Assign a macro to a button on a toolbar
- Create a data file—address list or database—that you merge with a form letter or other document
- Create and edit a form letter that you merge with a data file

- Create merged letters and envelopes
- Create a form file for a keyboard merge and perform the merge

Using Macros

Tip
To see a description of the macros that are included with WordPerfect, choose **H**elp, **M**acros, Additional Help, WordPerfect Macros.

Macros can save you time by performing repetitive tasks automatically. You can, for example, record a macro that types a closure to a letter. You can use macros to speed everyday formatting and editing, to automate an elaborate set of tasks, or to combine several commands into one (the one that plays the macro).

In addition to using the macros that you create yourself, you can use macros that WordPerfect provides for you. Among the macros that WordPerfect provides (PAGEXOFY.WCM) that places "Page x of y" on every page in a document, a macro (PGBORDER.WCM) that uses graphics to create decorative page borders, and a macro (FILESTMP.WCM) that places the filename and path of the current document in a header or footer.

◄ See "Creating Page Borders," p. 205

You can make a macro easy to use by assigning it to a button on a toolbar. Another way to make a macro easy to use is by naming it with the Ctrl+key method. See the "Creating a Macro" section on the following page.

This section introduces you to playing macros, recording macros, and making simple editing changes to macros. It also shows you how to make a macro easy to use by assigning it to a button on a toolbar.

Playing a Macro

Tip
If you name a macro with the Ctrl+key method, you can play it back instantly by pressing the keys that you used to name the macro.

When you play a macro, you execute the keystrokes and commands that are saved in the macro. The macro may type in text. It may perform formatting functions. It may even ask for your input and then perform certain steps depending upon your input.

To play a macro, take the following steps:

1. Choose **T**ools, **M**acro, **P**lay; or, press Alt+F10. The Play Macro dialog box appears (see fig. 11.1).

   WordPerfect automatically lists macros in the default directory specified for macros through File Preferences.

2. Select a macro name, or enter a (path and) filename in the File**n**ame text box.

3. Choose **P**lay. If this is the first time that you have played the macro, it compiles before it plays, and it takes a little extra time to get going.

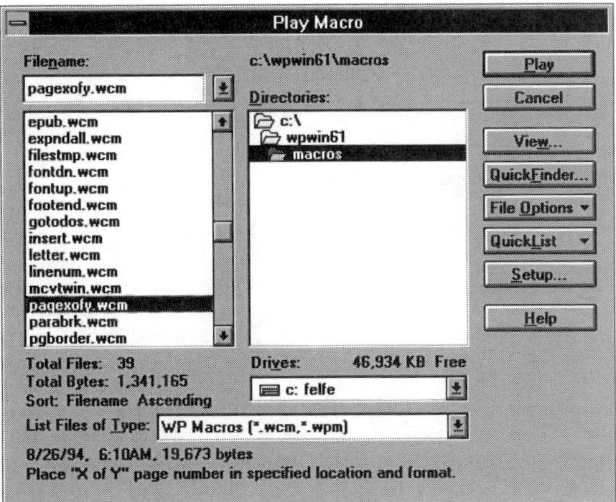

Fig. 11.1
Select a macro to play in the Play Macro dialog box. A description of the selected macro appears at the bottom of the dialog box.

Stopping a Macro

When you're testing a macro, it's a good idea to save any open documents before you play the macro. If something goes wrong during playback (for instance, if the macro adds text to the wrong part of your document), you'll want to cancel macro execution. You can usually stop a macro during playback by pressing the Esc key; however, the Esc key could be disabled or assigned to a specific function by the macro. After you cancel macro execution, you can always close all open documents without saving and then reopen them.

Tip
To play the most recently played macro, choose **T**ools, **M**acro, then press **1** (recently played macros are listed at the bottom of the Macro menu).

Creating a Macro

Creating a macro is simply a matter of starting the macro recorder, performing the actions that you want recorded, and ending the recording session.

To record a macro, take the following steps:

1. Choose **T**ools, **M**acro, **R**ecord; or, press Ctrl+F10. The Record Macro dialog box appears (see fig. 11.2).

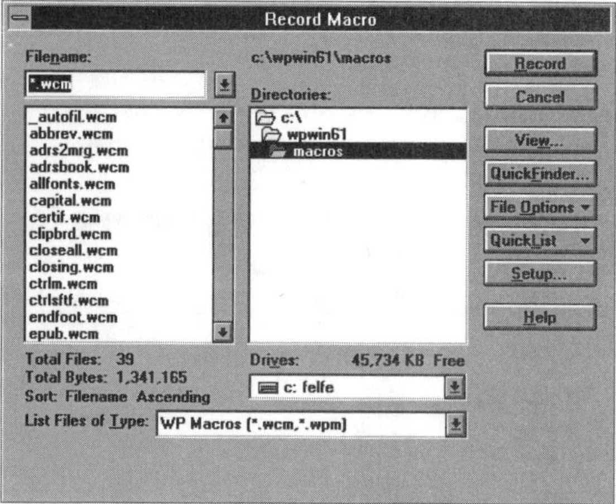

Fig. 11.2
Enter a name for your macro in the Record Macro dialog box.

2. Enter a name for your macro. The name can be up to eight characters in length. WordPerfect assigns a WCM extension to the name.

> **Note**
>
> If you are creating a macro that you will use fairly often, you might want to name it with the Ctrl+key method. In the Record Macro dialog box, press and hold the Ctrl key and the Shift key, press a letter key, and then release the Ctrl key and the Shift key. WordPerfect automatically inserts the name CtrlSft*X*, where *X* is a letter from A to Z. To play a Ctrl key macro, just press the keys that you named it with.

3. Choose **R**ecord. The macro recorder is activated, the Macro feature bar is displayed at the top of the screen, and Macro Record is displayed on the status bar.

4. Perform the actions that you want the macro to record. You can enter text from the keyboard, and you can choose commands from menus (with the keyboard or the mouse). You cannot use the mouse to move the insertion point or to select text while the macro recorder is active.

5. To finish recording, click the Stop Record button on the Macro feature bar; choose **T**ools, **M**acro, **R**ecord; or, press Ctrl+F10. The Macro Record message disappears from the status bar and the macro is saved to disk. You can close the document window *without saving changes* after you end recording, because the macro was saved when you ended recording.

Making Simple Editing Changes to a Macro

Don't be afraid to make simple editing changes to a macro. If you decide, for example, that you want to add a middle initial to a closure that is typed by a macro, you can add the text without having to learn macro syntax and commands.

Take the following steps to make simple editing changes to a macro:

1. Choose **T**ools, **M**acro, **E**dit. The Edit Macro dialog box appears (it looks similar to the Record Macro dialog box).

2. Select the macro that you want to edit, then choose **E**dit. The macro file is opened into an editing window and the Macro feature bar appears just above the text window. An example of what a macro does when you play it is shown in figure 11.3. Figure 11.4 illustrates what the same macro looks like when you edit it.

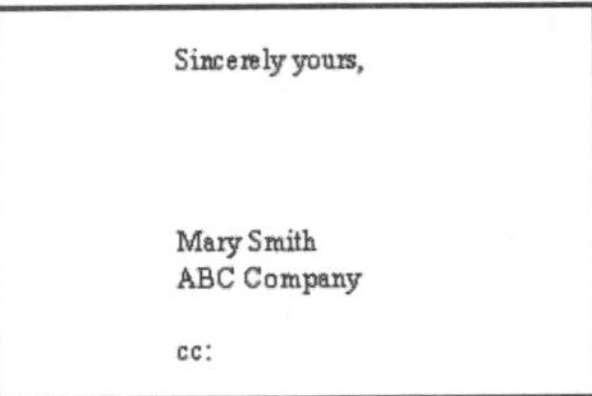

Fig. 11.3
The CLOSE.WCM macro types text as shown in this illustration.

3. Use normal editing techniques to make simple editing changes. For example, to add a middle initial to the signature in the CLOSE.WCM macro (refer to fig. 11.4), insert the middle initial in the appropriate place in the Type command. To remove one of the blank lines before the signature line, select a HardReturn() command and press Delete. To add a blank line above the signature line, type the command HardReturn(), or copy and paste a HardReturn() command. While you're editing the macro, you can press Enter (or Tab, or the spacebar) to separate commands; this formats the macro so that it's easier to read, but it doesn't affect what happens when you play the macro. Be careful, however, not to press Enter when the insertion point is positioned in the middle of a command; the Enter key signals the end of a macro command.

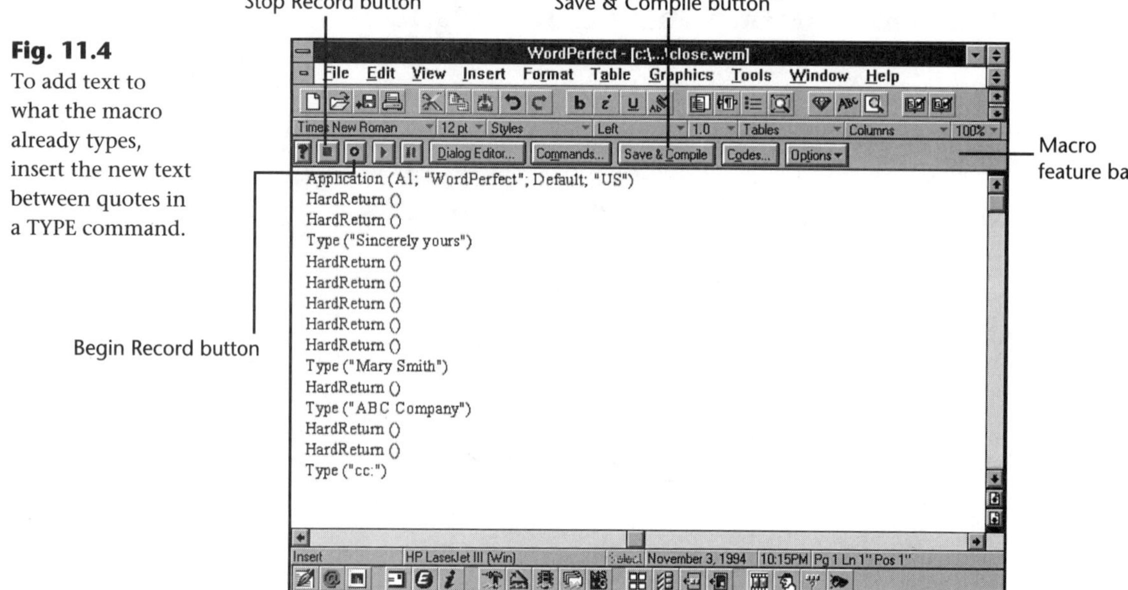

Fig. 11.4
To add text to what the macro already types, insert the new text between quotes in a TYPE command.

4. When you finish editing the macro, click the Save & **C**ompile button on the Macro feature bar. The save and compile process begins; if there are no errors, the process is completed and the macro remains on-screen. If WordPerfect detects errors during compilation, a dialog box appears, describing the error and its location. You can then cancel compilation, correct the error, and try the save and compile operation again.

5. Once the macro successfully saves and compiles, choose **F**ile, **C**lose to close the document window.

> **Note**
>
> WordPerfect provides extensive on-screen help information about macros. For help with a specific macro command, choose **H**elp, **M**acros, then access the index of macro commands. You must then choose between Product and Programming commands, or system variables.

Adding a Macro to a Toolbar

For one-button access to a favorite macro, create a toolbar button that plays the macro. You can then play back all of the keystrokes and commands in the macro by clicking this button.

To add a macro to a toolbar, take the following steps:

1. Access the Toolbar Preferences dialog box by right-clicking the toolbar and choosing Preferences. The Toolbar Preferences dialog box is displayed, as shown in figure 11.5.

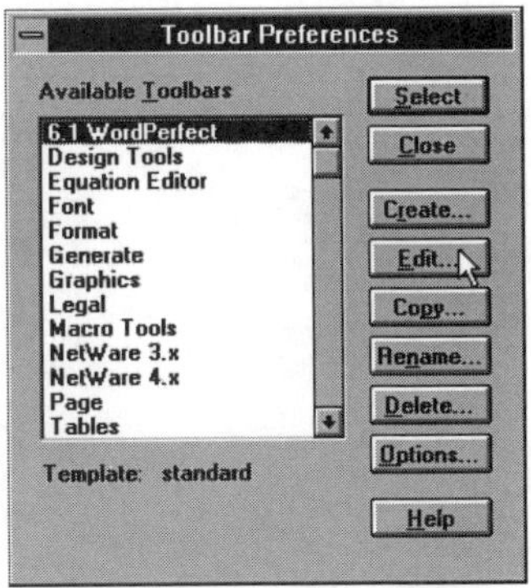

Fig. 11.5
Begin the process of adding a macro button to a toolbar by selecting the toolbar that you want to edit and choosing Edit.

2. Select the toolbar that you want to edit and choose **E**dit. The Toolbar Editor dialog box appears.

3. In the Add a Button To section, select Play a **M**acro. The Toolbar Editor dialog box now looks like figure 11.6.

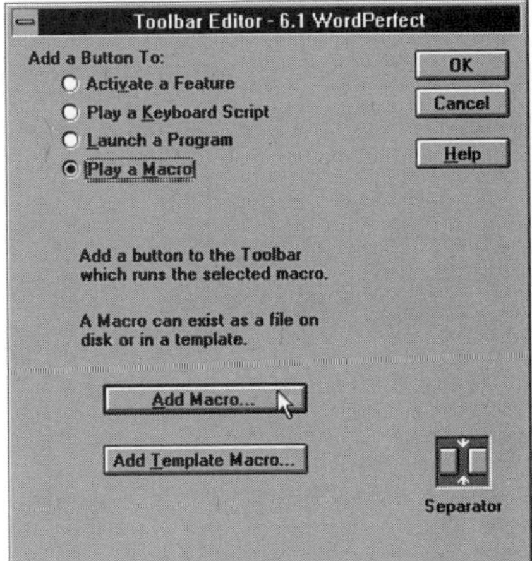

Fig. 11.6
Choose Play a Macro in the Toolbar Editor dialog box, then choose Add Macro.

4. Choose Play a **M**acro, then choose **A**dd Macro. The Select Macro dialog box is displayed (it looks like the Play Macro, Record Macro, and Edit Macro dialog boxes).

5. Select the macro for which you want to create a button, and then choose **S**elect. You are prompted with the `Save macro with full path?` message. Answer **Y**es. A Macro button is added to the toolbar and you are returned to the Toolbar Editor dialog box (see fig. 11.7).

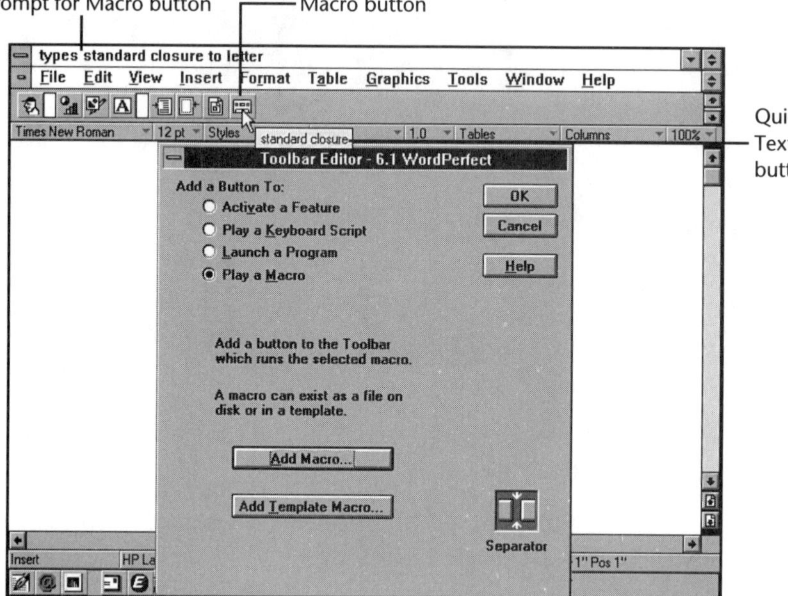

Fig. 11.7
Double-click a button to edit its appearance.

6. If you want to change the Quick Tip/Button Text or the Help **P**rompt for the button, double-click it. The Customize Button dialog box is displayed (see fig. 11.8).

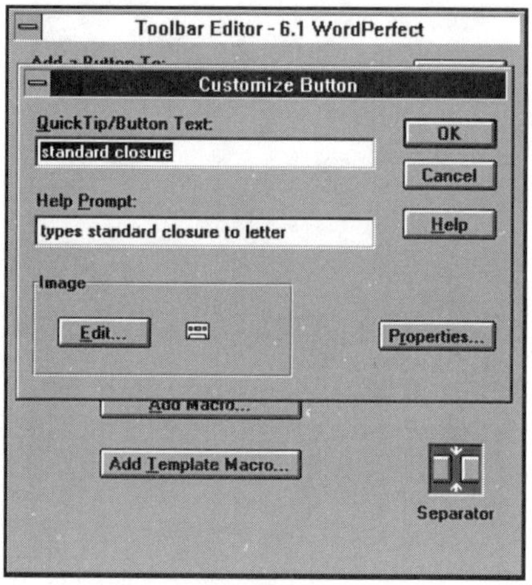

Fig. 11.8
Change a button's name, Help **P**rompt, or icon in the Customize Button dialog box.

Note

You only see button text if you have set Toolbar preferences so that button text is displayed. By default, only a picture is displayed; you can ask for either or both. For information on changing Toolbar preferences, see Chapter 8, "Customizing WordPerfect."

7. In the Customize Button dialog box, you can type a new Quick Tip/ Button Text for the button or a new Help **P**rompt. Unless you change the button text or prompt, they are both assigned the macro name you gave the macro when you created it. When you finish customizing the button, choose OK. The customized button is displayed on the toolbar and you are returned to the Toolbar Editor.

8. Choose OK to return to the Toolbar Preferences dialog box, and then choose **C**lose to return to the document window.

Troubleshooting

I'm recording a macro to move the insertion point and select text; however, I can't use the mouse to move the cursor within the text.

The macro recorder cannot record mouse actions within document text, such as moving the insertion point and selecting text. Use the keyboard to record these actions.

I'd like to type some commands into my macro when I'm editing it, but I don't know the syntax.

While you're editing a macro, you can click the Begin Record button on the Macro feature bar and record commands (this is easier than looking up the syntax and typing in the command). When you turn on the macro recorder, you access a new document window where you can choose the commands you want to record in the macro, either through the menu, the toolbar, or the Power Bar. When you finish recording, click the Stop Record button on the Macro feature bar; choose **T**ools, **M**acro, **R**ecord; or press Ctrl+F10 to return to the editing window for the macro. The steps you performed while recording are added to the macro at the insertion point.

I added a macro to the toolbar, but I can't tell what the macro does by looking at the button.

Remember that when you position the mouse pointer on the button, you see the Quick Tip (just under the button) and the Help text (in the Title bar). To enhance the Quick Tip or the Help text, edit the toolbar and double-click the button you want to edit in the Toolbar Editor dialog box. In the Customize Button dialog box, you can modify the button text and the Help Prompt.

Using Merge

Using WordPerfect's Merge feature, you can mass-produce letters, envelopes, mailing labels, and other documents. When you merge a form letter with a list of names and addresses, each resulting document contains a different name, address, and company name. The process of merging a form letter with names and addresses is sometimes referred to as a mail merge. Because the names and addresses are saved in a separate file (the data file), you only have to enter them once—when you create the data file. You can use that same data file over and over again when you perform a merge.

Not only can you perform a merge in WordPerfect using a data file, but you can also perform a keyboard merge. A keyboard merge merges a form file with input from the keyboard rather than from a data file. The result of a keyboard merge is a single, filled-in form document.

In this section, you learn to create the data file and form file that are used in a merge and to perform a merge. You also learn to create the form file for a keyboard merge and to perform a keyboard merge.

What Is a Merge?

A *merge* is the process of combining fixed information and variable information. The fixed information—a form letter, for example—is in a file referred to as a *form* file. Every merge has a form file. The variable information can come from another file (referred to as a *data* file) or it can come from user input at the keyboard. A data file could be a WordPerfect data file or it could be a file from a database program such as Paradox, dBASE, or Access.

To create a merge data file or form file, or to perform a merge, access the Merge dialog box. Choose **T**ools, M**e**rge; or, press Shift+F9. Figure 11.9 illustrates the Merge dialog box.

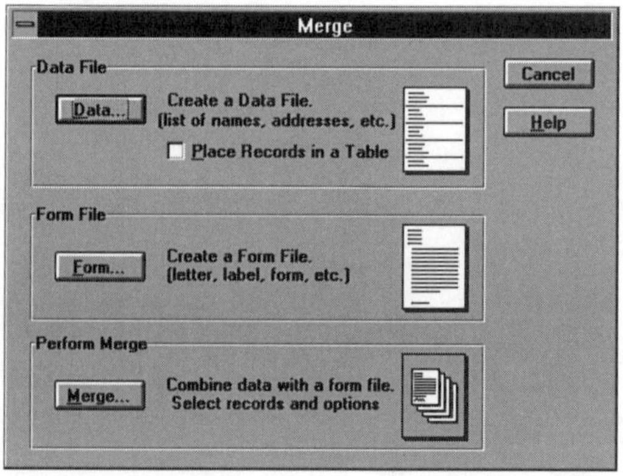

Fig. 11.9
Create a merge file or perform a merge in the Merge dialog box.

Merge

Data File

Data...

Create a Data File.
(list of names, addresses, etc.)

Place Records in a Table

Cancel

Help

Form File

Form...

Create a Form File.
(letter, label, form, etc.)

Perform Merge

Merge...

Combine data with a form file.
Select records and options

Performing a Merge

Performing a simple merge is a matter of creating a data file with variable information, creating a form file that asks for information from the data file, and performing the merge.

Creating a Data File

When you create a data file through the Merge dialog box, WordPerfect guides you through the process of creating the file.

A WordPerfect data file can take one of two forms—a text file or a table. In either form, the data file is organized into fields and records. A *field* is one category of information—for example, a field is a name or a phone number. A *record* contains all of the information about one person; a record is comprised of a complete set of fields.

Tip
If you already have a table that is formatted as a list, you can use the table as a data file.

To create a data file, take the following steps:

◄ See "Working with Tables," p. 190

1. In an empty document window, choose **T**ools, M**e**rge; or, press Shift+F9. The Merge dialog box appears (refer to fig. 11.9). If you want your data records placed in a table, select the **P**lace Records in a Table checkbox.

Note

If you have text in the active document window when you choose **D**ata, WordPerfect displays a Create Merge File dialog box that asks if you want to use the file in the active window or open a new document window to create the data file. Choose New Document Window if you want to create the data file from scratch.

2. Choose **D**ata. Once WordPerfect knows that you want to create a data file, the Create Data File dialog box appears.

3. At the Create Data File dialog box, create a field name list by typing each field name and pressing Enter to add the name to the list. Figure 11.10 illustrates the Create Data File dialog box after field names have been defined.

4. When you finish creating the field name list, choose OK to close the Create Data File dialog box and open the Quick Data Entry dialog box.

Note

A field can have more than one line. An address field, for example, could have one or more lines for the street address and a line for the city, state, and ZIP code. In general, though, it's easier to sort and select records when fields are broken down into small categories. If you do want to enter more than one line of data in a field, press Ctrl+Enter before each subsequent line. Scroll arrows at the right end of the field box let you see different lines in the field.

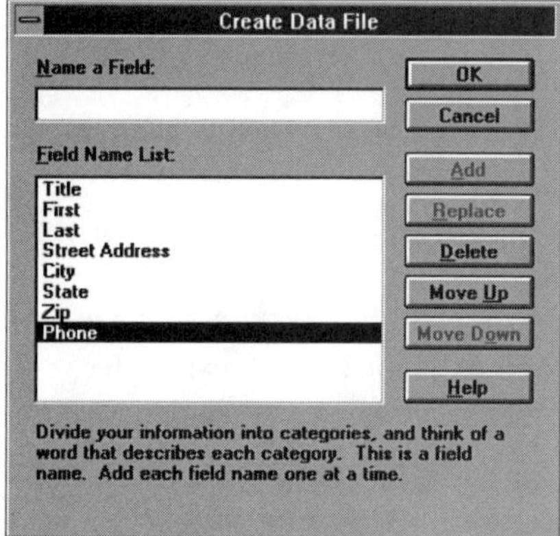

Fig. 11.10
Define field names in the Create Data File dialog box.

5. At the Quick Data Entry dialog box, enter the data for each record, pressing Enter between each field and record. Figure 11.11 illustrates the Quick Data Entry dialog box with a filled-in record.

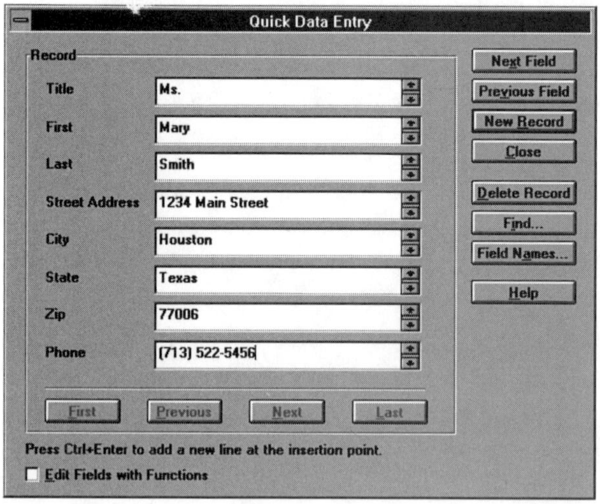

Fig. 11.11
Enter a data record at the Quick Data Entry dialog box.

6. Choose **C**lose when you finish entering records. WordPerfect then prompts you to save the data file. You don't have to type an extension for the filename unless you want to. If you omit the filename extension, WordPerfect automatically supplies a DAT extension.

7. Choose **Y**es to save the data file. Then specify a filename and click OK. If your data file is in a text format (rather than a table format), you see something like the illustration shown in figure 11.12. At the top of the data file are the field names, followed by a page break. The end of each field is marked with an ENDFIELD code—even if the field is empty (the phone field in the second record is empty). The end of each record is marked with an ENDRECORD code and a hard page break. The Merge feature bar is displayed at the top of the screen.

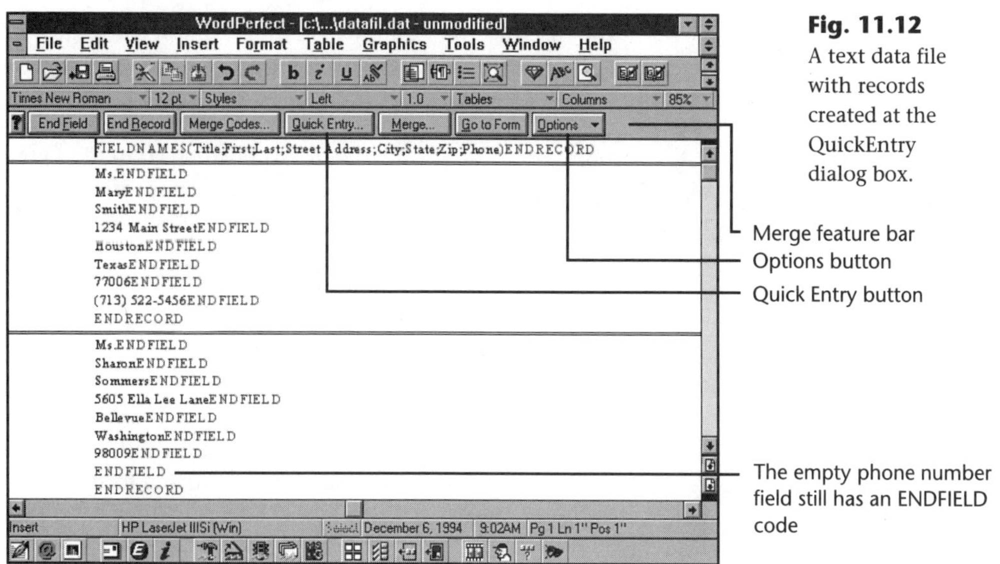

Fig. 11.12
A text data file with records created at the QuickEntry dialog box.

Editing and Printing a Data File

You can edit your data file after creating it to add more records or to change existing data. You may want to print the data for verification. To edit a data file if it's not already in the active window, open it like any other file. When WordPerfect opens the file, it recognizes it as a data file and displays the Merge feature bar at the top of the screen.

Tip
It's easier to read the data on-screen if you choose **O**ptions (on the feature bar), and then select the **H**ide Codes option.

Adding Records. When you don't have time to enter all of your data file records at once, or you don't have all of the information when you create the data file, you'll want to reopen the file later and add records.

To add more records to the data file in the active window, follow these steps:

1. Choose **Q**uickEntry (on the feature bar).
2. In the QuickEntry dialog box, choose New **R**ecord. An empty record form appears.
3. Enter new records until you're finished, and then choose **C**lose.
4. When WordPerfect prompts you to save your file, answer **Y**es and then save it to its existing name.

Editing Records. When you need to update the information in your data file—for example, when someone's address changes—reopen the data file and take the following steps:

1. Position the insertion point anywhere in the first record that you want to change, then choose **Q**uickEntry, or position the insertion point at the *beginning* of the document and choose **Q**uickEntry.
2. If the record that you want to change isn't displayed in the QuickEntry dialog box, choose **F**ind. A Find Text dialog box appears. Enter the text that you want to find and choose **F**ind Next. The first record that contains matching text is displayed in the QuickEntry data form (you may have to perform more than one find operation).
3. When the record you want to edit appears in the data form, make the desired changes and choose **C**lose.

Printing the Data File. It's often helpful to have a printout of your data file. WordPerfect makes it easy to print your data in a readable format. To print your data, follow these steps:

1. With the data file that you want to print on-screen, choose **O**ptions. To suppress the display of codes in the printout, make sure that **H**ide Codes is selected.
2. Then, from the **O**ptions menu, choose **P**rint. WordPerfect asks you to confirm that you want to print with no page breaks between records.
3. Click OK; the printout then takes place.

Creating a Form File

Every merge has to have a form file; the form file controls the merge. The form file contains merge codes that ask for information from another source; it should also contain any text, formatting, and graphics that you want in the final merged documents. When the merge is executed, the text, formatting, and graphics, if any, in the form file appear in every merged document. Merge codes in the form file are replaced by information from the data file or from the keyboard.

To create a form file, take the following steps:

1. If you already have a document with the fixed information for your form file, place the document in the active window.

2. Choose **T**ools, M**e**rge. The Merge dialog box appears (refer to fig. 11.9).

3. Choose **F**orm. WordPerfect asks you whether you want to use the current document window for your form file, or whether you want to create the form file in a new, empty window. Make the appropriate choice.

4. WordPerfect then prompts you for the name of the data file to associate with your form file (see fig. 11.13). The associated data file is the file that is merged with the form file.

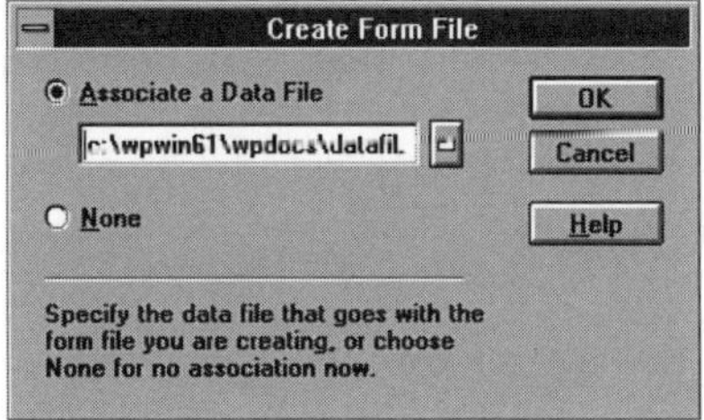

Fig. 11.13
Associate a data file with your form file in the Create Form File dialog box.

5. Enter a name for the data file; or select it after clicking the list button to the right of the text box. Choose OK. The Merge feature bar appears at the top of the screen.

6. Type, edit, and format any fixed (boilerplate) text that is to be in your form file. If the fixed text is already there, proceed to the next step.

7. Position the insertion point where you want to insert the first merge code. If the form file is a form letter, for example, you might want to merge in the computer date at the top of the letter.

8. To insert a DATE merge code, choose the **D**ate button.

9. To insert a FIELD merge code, choose the **I**nsert Field button. The Insert Field Name or Number dialog box appears, displaying a list of field names from the associated data file. Select the desired field name and choose **I**nsert. The field merge code is inserted in the document

◄ See "Editing Text," p. 93

◄ See "Formatting Characters," p.107

◄ See "Formatting Lines and Paragraphs," p. 110

◄ See "Formatting the Page," p. 122

Tip
If the Insert Field Name or Number dialog box obscures your view of the form file, drag it to a new position.

and the dialog box is still on-screen. Figure 11.14 shows a form file just after inserting a date merge code and the first field merge code.

10. Position the insertion point where you want another merge code; or type, edit, and format text until the insertion point is where you want to insert the next merge code. Place commas and spaces between merge codes on the same line as appropriate. For example, if you have just inserted a FIELD code for the City in the inside address of a form letter, press the comma key and then the spacebar.

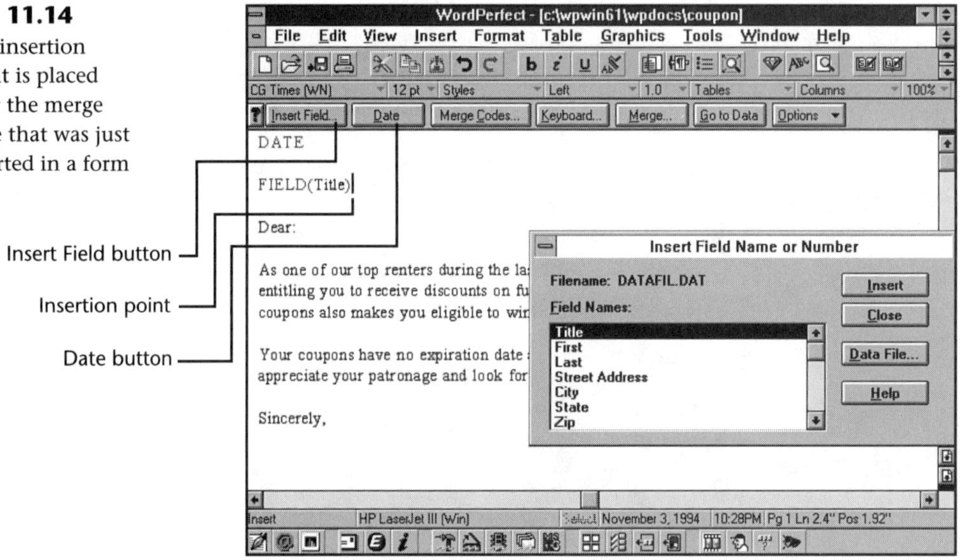

Fig. 11.14
The insertion point is placed after the merge code that was just inserted in a form file.

11. When the insertion point is positioned where you want another merge code, select it from the list and choose **I**nsert.

12. Repeat steps 10 and 11 until you have entered all of the merge codes that you want to enter. When you finish, close the Insert Field Name or Number dialog box. The finished result may appear as illustrated in figure 11.15.

13. Save and close the form file as you would any document. You don't have to type a filename extension; WordPerfect automatically adds an FRM extension to the filename.

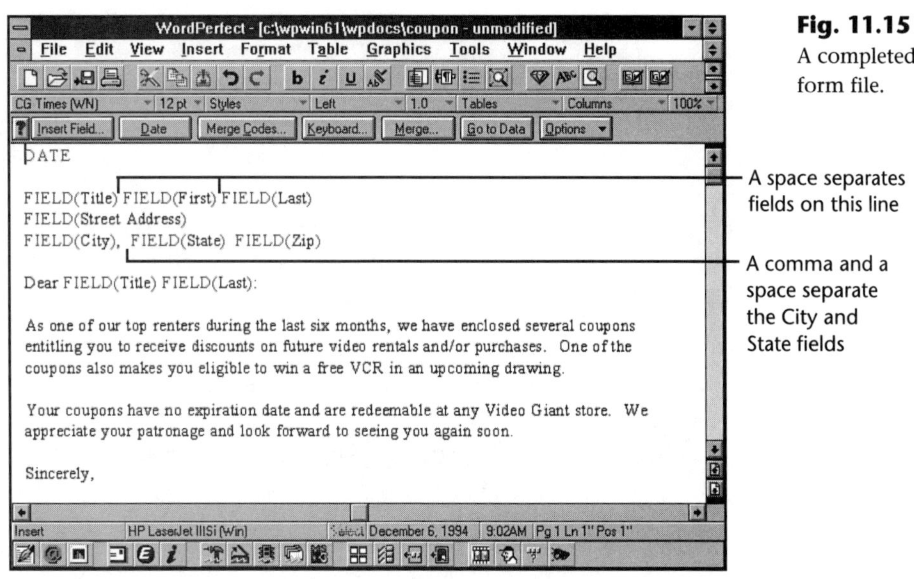

Fig. 11.15
A completed form file.

Performing the Merge

When you have a form file and a data file, you have the ingredients for a merge. To perform a merge, take the following steps:

1. Choose **T**ools, M**e**rge; or, press Shift+F9. The Merge dialog box appears (refer to fig. 11.9).

2. Choose **M**erge. The Perform Merge dialog box appears.

3. Enter the names of your form file and data file, or use the list button for each option to select the name from a list. The dialog box should look like the illustration in figure 11.16.

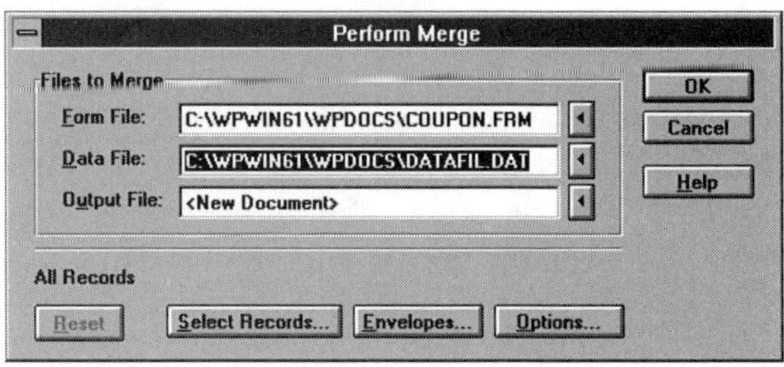

Fig. 11.16
Tell WordPerfect the names of your form file and data file and choose OK to perform a merge.

II

Using WordPerfect

> **Note**
>
> To create merged envelopes at the same time that you create merged form letters, see the next section, "Creating Envelopes."

4. Choose OK to perform the merge. When the merge has completed, the insertion point is positioned at the end of the last merged document. Page breaks separate each document.

5. Scroll through the merged documents to verify the success of the merge. If there are any problems, close the window containing the merged documents (don't save), edit the file that is causing the problem (either the form file or the data file), re-save the corrected file, and perform the merge again.

6. When the merge has completed without problems, you can save the results, if desired, and print the merged documents all at once.

Creating Envelopes

WordPerfect simplifies a merge by making it possible to create merged letters and envelopes all at once. When the merge is completed, both the form letters and the envelopes are in the active document window, ready to print.

To create merged envelopes and form letters in a single merge operation, take the following steps:

1. Enter the names of the form file and data file in the Perform Merge dialog box (see the previous section).

2. Choose **E**nvelopes. The Envelope dialog box is displayed.

3. In the Envelope dialog box, specify fields for mailing addresses (completed information for mailing addresses is illustrated in fig. 11.17). To specify a field, position the insertion point and access the list of field names by choosing F**i**eld. Select the field you want to insert and choose **I**nsert. To position the insertion point for the next field, you can press the spacebar or the comma key, or you can press Enter.

4. You can add a bar code, if desired, through the **O**ptions button.

5. You can specify a return address, if desired.

6. When you finish working in the Envelope dialog box, choose O**K** to return to the Perform Merge dialog box.

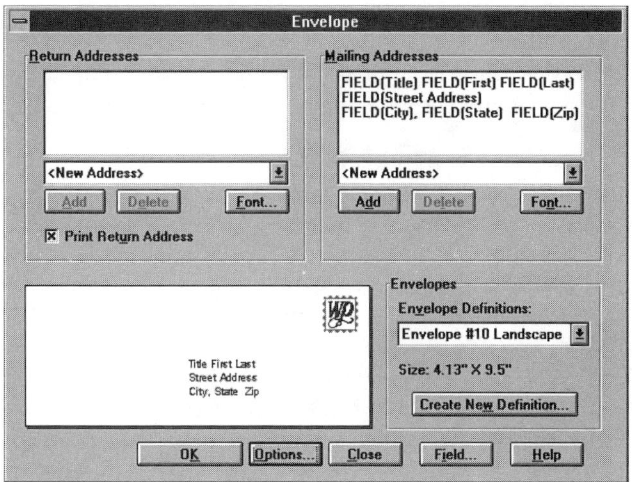

Fig. 11.17
To create merged envelopes, enter field merge codes in the mailing address area.

7. Choose OK to perform the merge. Merged letters and envelopes are created in the designated output file (usually the current document). The insertion point is positioned at the end of the last letter; the envelopes are below the letters.

8. As with any merge, check the results before printing or saving. If there are problems, close the current window (don't save), edit and re-save the problem file (it could be either the form file or the data file), and perform the merge again.

9. When the results are successful, you can save the output file, if desired, and print it all at once.

Filling in a Form with a Keyboard Merge

When you set up a standard form as a keyboard merge file, it becomes easy to fill in the blanks. All you have to do is start a merge and enter information as prompted. You don't have to move the insertion point to the next place that needs input; WordPerfect does it for you. You even get help on what to input (from the prompt that is associated with each KEYBOARD merge code).

Tip
Many of WordPerfect's templates are automated merge forms. The fax templates, for example, prompt you for keyboard input and then place your input in appropriate places on a fax form.

Creating a Form File for a Keyboard Merge

When you create a form file for a keyboard merge, it's usually easier to create the document text first and add the merge codes later. You can, however, add the merge codes while you create the text.

◄ See "Using Templates," p. 134

Take the following steps to create a form file for a keyboard merge:

1. Create a boilerplate document containing all of the fixed information and formatting that should appear in every merged document.

2. Choose **T**ools, M**e**rge. In the Merge dialog box, choose **F**orm. In the Create Merge File dialog box, choose **U**se File in Active Window. Choose OK.

3. At the Create Form File dialog box, choose **N**one (to indicate that there is no associated data file), then choose OK.

4. In your form file, position the insertion point where you want input from the keyboard. Choose **K**eyboard. The Insert Merge Code dialog box appears (this dialog box appears whenever you insert a merge code that requires additional information, such as a prompt).

5. Enter a prompt for the user to see when he inputs information at this specific place on the form. An example of the Insert Merge Code dialog box with a filled-in prompt is shown in figure 11.18. When you finish entering the prompt, choose OK.

> **Note**
>
> It's helpful to tell the user which keystrokes to press to continue the merge after filling in data at the current location. For example, include the prompt "Type recipient's name, then press Alt+Enter to continue."

Fig. 11.18
Remind the user what he should do while filling in variable information from the keyboard.

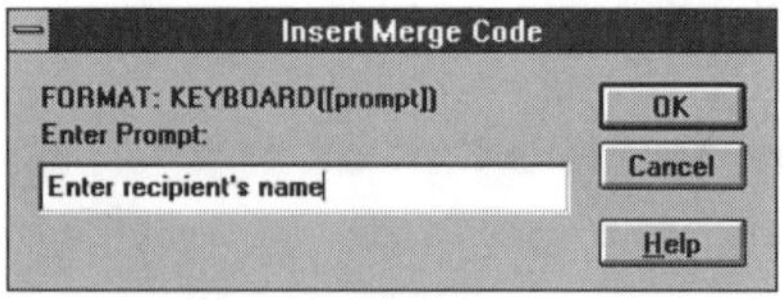

6. Continue to enter keyboard merge codes wherever you want input from the keyboard. A completed fax form might look like the illustration shown in figure 11.19.

7. Save and replace the completed form file.

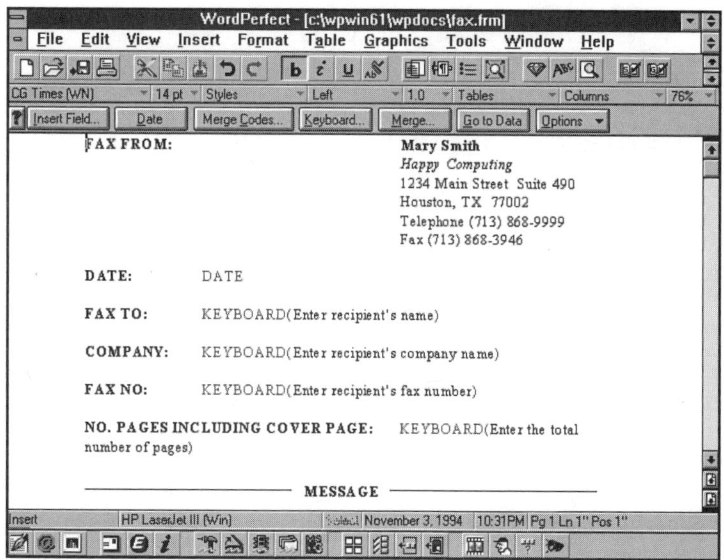

Fig. 11.19
A completed form file for a keyboard merge.

Performing a Keyboard Merge

When you perform a keyboard merge, you fill in the blanks in your form file from the keyboard while the merge occurs. The result is a single merged document. Once the form is filled in, you can print the results and save them.

To perform a keyboard merge, take the following steps:

1. In an empty document window, choose **T**ools, M**e**rge. In the Merge dialog box, choose **M**erge. In the Perform Merge dialog box, specify a form file, then make sure that the **D**ata File text box is empty. Choose OK to begin the merge.

2. A merge feature bar appears at the top of the screen. When the merge pauses at the first KEYBOARD merge code (see fig. 11.20), the prompt that is associated with that particular keyboard code appears in the center of the screen. Type the appropriate information. When you finish typing, press Alt+Enter or choose **C**ontinue from the feature bar. This tells WordPerfect that you have finished entering information here and that you are ready for the merge to move on.

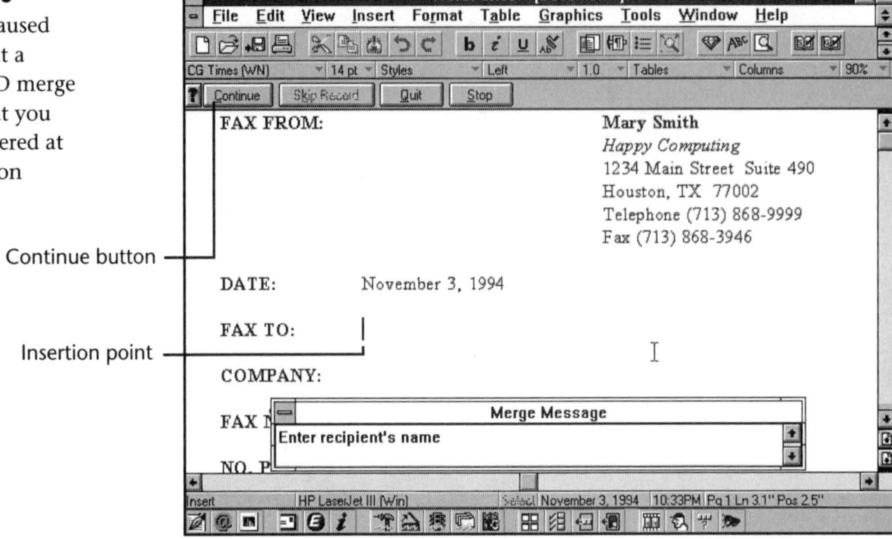

Fig. 11.20
A merge paused for input at a KEYBOARD merge code. What you type is entered at the insertion point.

Tip
You can type as many lines as necessary when stopped at a keyboard prompt. You can also add or correct any formatting on previous entries.

3. The merge moves to the next KEYBOARD code, if there is one, and prompts you for input. As long as you are being prompted for input, the merge is in process. You *must* tell WordPerfect to move on from each KEYBOARD merge code, whether or not you type input at that code.

4. When the merge is complete, you can print the document on-screen and save it, if desired.

Troubleshooting

I created a data file and a form file and then I performed a mail merge, but the city, state, and ZIP code are all jammed together in the inside address.

In a normal letter, you have a comma and a space separating the city and the state
in an inside address. In a form file, you need the same text (a comma and a space) between the FIELD code for the city and the FIELD code for the state. Correspondingly, you need spaces between the state and ZIP code fields.

I performed a merge and asked for envelopes, but they're not there.

When a merge completes, the insertion point is beneath the last form letter, but above the envelopes. Scroll downward to see the envelopes after you perform the merge.

I created a keyboard merge form file but when I performed a merge, I pressed Enter and the merge didn't move on to the next place that needed keyboard input. Then I didn't know what to do.

When you get into a mess like this the best solution is to cancel the merge (press Esc), close the document window without saving, and start again. The only way you will move on from the current KEYBOARD merge code during a merge is by choosing **C**ontinue or by pressing Alt+Enter. You must repeat this action for every KEYBOARD merge code in the form file in order for the merge operation to come to a normal termination.

From Here...

Learning to use macros and merge can save you time and energy. You can automate your work with macros by recording keystrokes and commands, saving the recording, and then playing it back any time you want to perform those same keystrokes and commands. You can save time with merge by creating a data file of names and addresses and merging it into a form letter to create as many personalized letters (and, optionally, envelopes) as you have names and addresses. You can automate the process of filling in the blanks on a standard form by setting it up as a form file for a keyboard merge.

Now that you are familiar with working with WordPerfect, you are ready to use WordPerfect with some of the other Novell PerfectOffice applications. To learn more about using WordPerfect with other Novell PerfectOffice applications, refer to the following chapters:

- Chapters 32 through 35 in Part VII, "Integrating and Customizing PerfectOffice," provide real-life business scenarios that illustrate how to use the Novell PerfectOffice programs together to accomplish various business tasks.

- Chapter 36, "Customizing Toolbars, DAD Bars, and Menus," shows how to customize toolbars and menus.

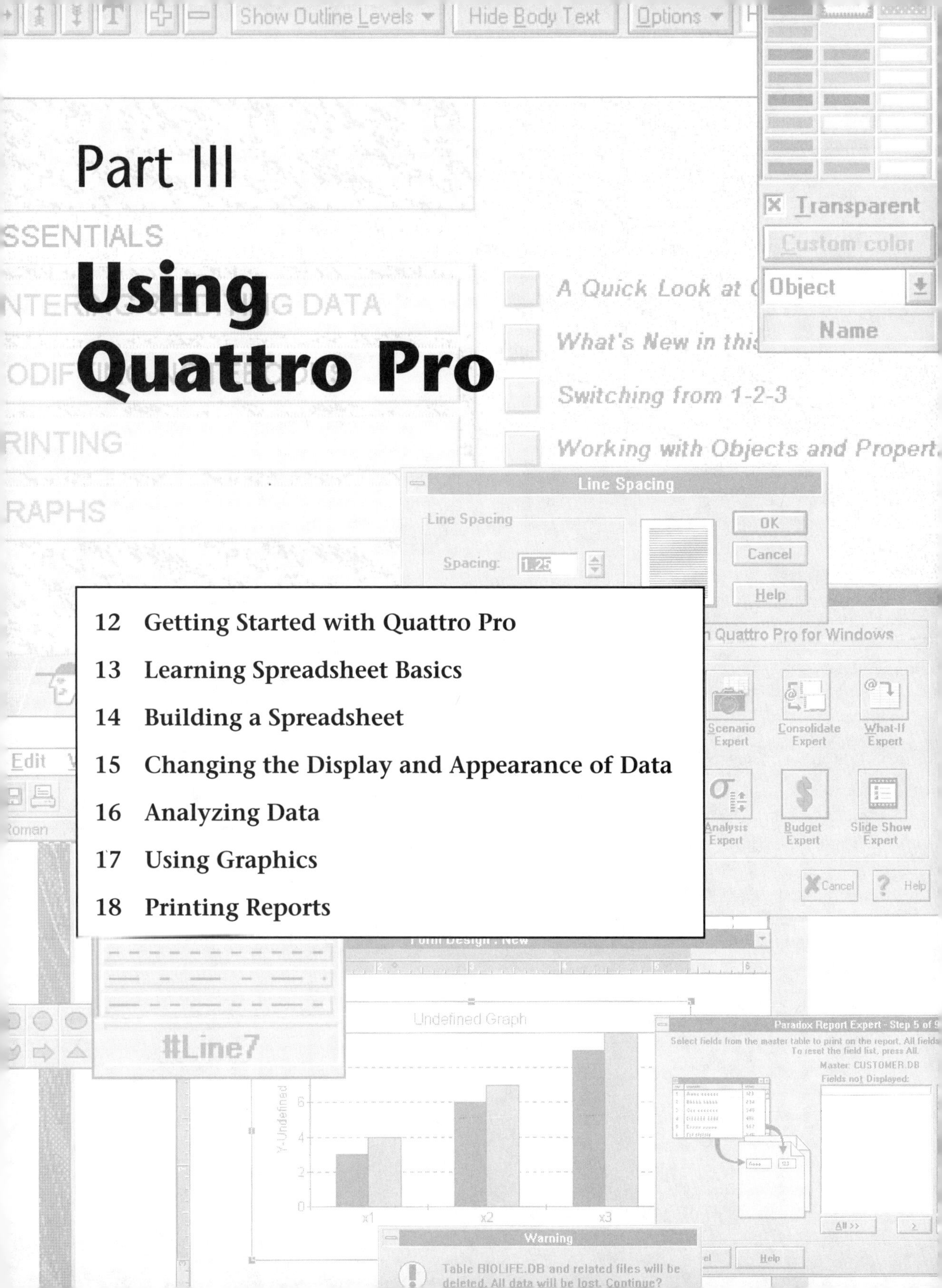

Part III

Using Quattro Pro

Show Outline Levels
Hide Body Text
Options
Object
Name
ESSENTIALS
ENTERING & EDITING DATA
PRINTING
GRAPHS
Switching from 1-2-3
Line Spacing
Line Spacing
Spacing:
1.25
OK
Cancel
Help
Coaches
Quit
WP Presentations - [d:\...\24fig13.shw]
File
Edit
View
Insert
Format
Slide
Graphics
Tools
Slide 2 of 7
Line
#Line7
Graph Expert
Scenario Expert
Consolidate Expert
Performance Expert
Analysis Expert
Budget Expert
Cancel
Form Design : New *
Undefined Graph
Y-Undefined
0
2
4
6
x1
x2
x3
Warning
Table BIOLIFE.DB and related files will be deleted. All data will be lost. Continue?
All >>
Help

Chapter 12

Getting Started with Quattro Pro

by Brian Underdahl

Quattro Pro is the spreadsheet component of the PerfectOffice. This chapter introduces Quattro Pro, and prepares you to quickly begin using this powerful tool to analyze data, prepare reports, and graph results. Once you've learned the basics, you'll be ready to apply your skills to creating your own Quattro Pro spreadsheets.

In this chapter, you learn

- What Quattro Pro adds to your PerfectOffice toolbox
- How to access the correct commands
- Important shortcuts
- How to get expert help from Quattro Pro itself

Understanding Quattro Pro

Quattro Pro is a *spreadsheet* program. You might like to think of a spreadsheet program as an electronic notebook, one which can quickly calculate the results of any formulas you enter. Quattro Pro is a very capable electronic notebook, with hundreds of built-in features designed to make creating your spreadsheets as easy as possible.

What Can You Do with Quattro Pro?

Even the most powerful tool is useless if you don't know what it can do and how to use it. Fortunately, even though Quattro Pro is one of the most advanced spreadsheet programs available, it is also very easy to understand and use. You don't have to be an accountant or a computer whiz to use Quattro Pro. In only a short time you'll be able to create Quattro Pro notebooks that solve some of your problems with ease.

A typical, traditional use for a spreadsheet is to prepare accounting reports. By automatically performing all of a report's calculations with complete accuracy, a spreadsheet makes quick work of the task. If you run a small business, you probably perform many different calculations on a daily basis. You might, for example, want to keep track of the receipts for a video rental business you've recently begun. To know whether the new business is worthwhile, you'd probably want to know whether you're making a profit after paying for the new movies, plus your utilities, and maybe even the cost of hiring someone to help keep the store open evenings.

Even if you don't consider these calculations to be standard accounting reports, wouldn't it be nice to have the calculations done quickly and accurately—the way Quattro Pro can? How about calculating the cost of refinancing your mortgage and determining how long it will take to make up for the fees your lender may charge? Would it be useful to know which products you sell bring the highest profits, and when those products are most likely to be sold? Finally, suppose you needed to calculate the cost of building permits which were based on many different combinations of features for each property. Wouldn't it be nice to just enter the proposed building's size, type, and quantity of fixtures and have an accurate bill printed instantly?

All of these are but a small sample of the things you can do with Quattro Pro. Spreadsheets aren't just for accountants, they also do real work for real people.

Starting Quattro Pro

When you start Quattro Pro, a new, blank notebook named NOTEBK1.WB2 appears (see fig. 12.1). This new notebook is your starting point for creating your own applications. You can use a more descriptive name when you save your notebook in a file on disk.

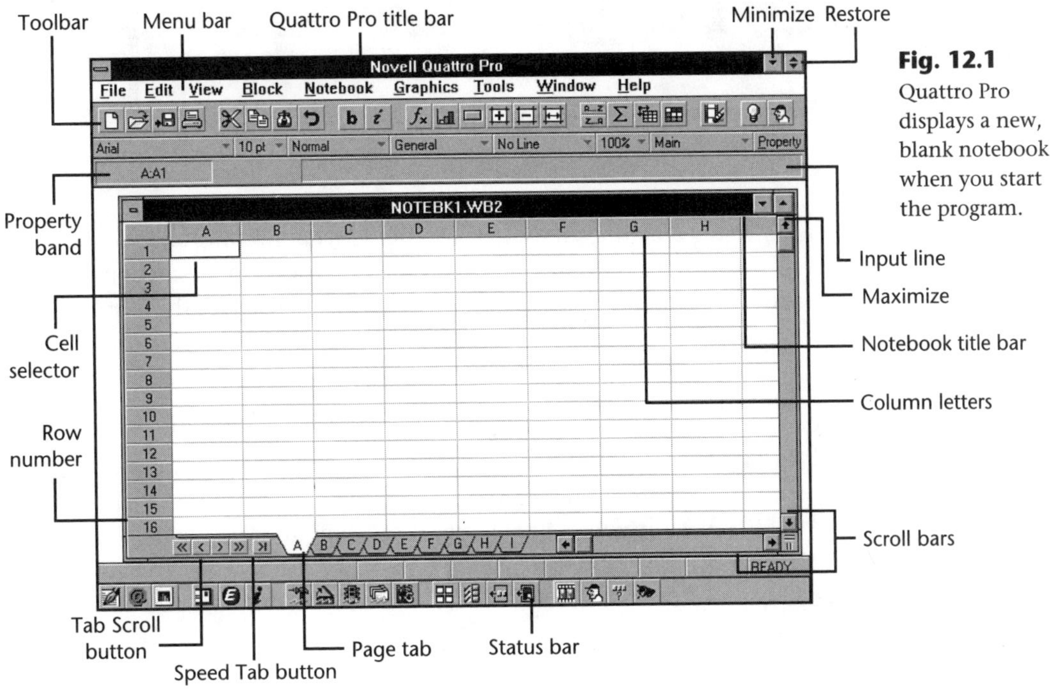

Fig. 12.1
Quattro Pro displays a new, blank notebook when you start the program.

Troubleshooting

My screen shows NOTEBK2.WB2 instead of NOTEBK1.WB2.

Quattro Pro starts new notebooks using sequential numbers. If you create a new notebook, it automatically is named NOTEBK*xx*.WB2, with *xx* replaced by the next higher number. When you save the notebook, you'll be prompted for a new name, so the default name really doesn't matter.

Each Quattro Pro notebook provides a very large workspace—much larger than you can see on the screen at one time. Each notebook has 256 pages (indicated by the page tabs below each page), 256 columns on each page (indicated by the column letters along the top edge of each notebook page), and 8192 rows on each page (indicated by the row numbers along the left edge of each notebook page). The intersection of each row and column on each page is called a *cell*, the place where you store data, formulas, or labels. A Quattro Pro notebook has an incredible 536,870,912 cells—many more than you're ever going to need no matter how complex a report you want to produce.

Note

A single Quattro Pro notebook automatically contains all 256 spreadsheet pages and the Objects page. When you save a Quattro Pro notebook, all of the pages are saved together.

Cells are identified by the page letter, column letter, and row number. The cell in the first row of the first column on the first page of a notebook is designated by the cell address A:A1. If you're referring to a cell on the current page, you don't have to include the page letter, but can instead refer to this same cell address as simply A1.

The location of the current or *active* cell is indicated by the *cell selector*—a darker outline around the cell. In figure 12.1, the cell selector is in cell A:A1, making this the active cell. You can only place data, formulas, or labels in the active cell. To place anything in a different cell, you must first make the new cell the active cell. In addition to locating the cell selector, you can also see the address of the active cell in the cell indicator box at the left end of the input line near the top of the screen.

Moving Around in a Notebook

To do anything effective in a Quattro Pro notebook, you must be able to move the cell selector. When you want to enter data, formulas, or labels in a different cell, you must first move to that cell. There are several methods you can use to move around in a notebook, and the best method often depends on your destination.

You can use the *direction keys*—the up-, down-, left-, and right-arrow keys, or the Pg Up (or Page Up), Pg Dn (or Page Down), and Home keys—to move the cell selector between cells. These direction keys work just about the way you would expect—if you press the down-arrow key, the cell selector moves down to a lower row. Table 12.1 describes the functions of the direction keys.

Table 12.1 The Direction Keys

Key(s)	Action(s)
→ or ←	Moves right or left one column
↑ or ↓	Moves up or down one row
Ctrl+← or Shift+Tab	Moves left one screen

Key(s)	Action(s)
Ctrl+→ or Tab	Moves right one screen
Ctrl+End+Home	Moves to the lower right corner of the active area on the last active page
Ctrl+F6	Makes the next open notebook window active
Ctrl+Home	Moves to cell A1 on the first notebook page
Ctrl+PgDn	Moves to the notebook page immediately below the current page (for example, from page A to page B)
Ctrl+PgUp	Moves to the notebook page immediately above the current page
End+→ or End+←	Moves right or left to a cell that contains data and is next to a blank cell
End+↑ or End+↓	Moves up or down to a cell that contains data and is next to a blank cell
End+Home	Moves to the lower right corner of the active area on the current page
F5 (Go to)	Moves to the cell you specify
Home	Moves to cell A1 on the current notebook page
PgUp or PgDn	Moves up or down one screen on the current notebook page

Because Quattro Pro is a true Windows program, it is often quicker and easier to perform tasks such as moving the cell selector using the mouse instead of the direction keys. For example, to move from cell A:A1 to cell A:C4, you could press the right-arrow key twice and then the down-arrow key three times, or you could simply point to cell A:C4 and click the left mouse button. Of course, if you hold down an arrow key instead of quickly pressing and releasing it, the cell selector will move several rows or columns instead of just one. Even so, a single mouse click is often much faster than the equivalent keystrokes. Moving between pages with the mouse is even faster—just click the appropriate page tab. Use the tab scroll controls to display different page tabs if necessary.

You can also use the scroll bars at the right edge or bottom edge of a notebook to view other parts of the current notebook page. Click the scroll bar or *drag*—hold down the left mouse button as you move an object—the box on the scroll bar to bring a different part of the page into view.

Troubleshooting

The cell selector disappears when I use the scroll bars.

The scroll bars only change the portion of the page that is visible. To move the cell selector, first use the scroll bars to display the destination cell, then click the destination cell to make it the current cell.

Using the Menus

Many tasks you perform in Quattro Pro require use of a command. Commands help you analyze and organize data effectively, copy and move data, graph and format data, sort and manipulate databases, open and close spreadsheet notebooks, and use colors and fonts to customize spreadsheets.

Tip
Learn Quattro Pro's commands by moving the menu pointer through the menus with the direction keys. A description of the command appears in the Quattro Pro title bar.

The Quattro Pro menu appears on the menu bar near the top of the screen. To access a command on the menu bar with the keyboard, you must first activate the menu by pressing the Alt key. A reverse video highlight, the *menu pointer*, appears in the menu bar. You can choose a command by highlighting it with the direction keys and pressing Enter or by simply typing the underlined letter—usually the first letter—of the command name. If you use the mouse to select commands, just click the command you want to use.

Quattro Pro has several different menus. The menus change depending on the type of task you're working on. For example, when you're working with normal data in a notebook, the main menu appears. If you're creating or modifying a graph, the menu changes to include commands appropriate to graphs. Most of the time, however, you'll see the main menu.

Learning the Shortcuts

In any field, the experts are usually the people who know the fastest way to get things done—the shortcuts. Quattro Pro provides many different shortcuts you can learn and use to get things done more quickly. You don't have to learn all of them, but you will find some that you'll use quite often.

Some Important Shortcut Keys

Many shortcut keys are actually key combinations, which means you must press two or more keys at the same time. Although this may seem complicated, key combinations in Quattro Pro always use the Shift, Ctrl, or Alt key as one of the keys you press. A good way to remember this is to consider Ctrl and Alt to be special types of Shift keys. Just as holding down the Shift key as you press a letter modifies the letter (by producing an uppercase letter in place of a lower-case letter), holding down the Ctrl or Alt key when you press many of the shortcut keys modifies the function of the shortcut key.

Table 12.2 describes many of the more useful Quattro Pro shortcut keys. To learn about even more shortcut keys, see the topic "key shortcuts" in the Quattro Pro on-line help system.

Table 12.2 Some Important Shortcut Keys

Key(s)	Action(s)
F1	Displays a Help topic
F2	Places Quattro Pro 6 for Windows in EDIT mode so that you can edit an entry
Alt+F2	Displays the Play Macro dialog box
F3	Displays block names in EDIT mode in a formula
Alt+F3	Displays a list of functions
F4	Toggles formulas from relative to absolute and vice versa
Alt+F4	Closes Quattro Pro 6 for Windows or a dialog box
F5	Moves the cell selector to a cell, spreadsheet, or active file
F6	Moves the cell selector between panes
Ctrl+F6	Displays the next open window
F9	In READY mode, recalculates formulas; in EDIT or VALUE mode, converts a formula to its current value
F10	Activates the menu bar
F11	Displays the current graph
F12	Displays Object Inspector for the selected object
Alt+F12	Displays application Object Inspector
Shift+F12	Displays active window Object Inspector
Ctrl+letter	Same as **T**ools **M**acro **P**lay; executes a macro in Quattro Pro (the replacement for Alt+letter in earlier DOS releases)
Ctrl+Break	Exits from a menu or macro and returns to Ready mode
Ctrl+Esc	Displays the Task List that enables you to switch from one Windows application to another

Troubleshooting

Some Ctrl+letter shortcut keys don't perform the proper shortcut procedure.

If you create macros that use the Ctrl+*letter* naming convention, Quattro Pro runs the macro instead of using the key combination to run the shortcut. If the shortcut is one you use often, consider renaming the macro to restore the shortcut.

Using the Right Mouse Button Menus

In Quattro Pro, almost everything you see is an *object*—something that has properties you can affect. But instead of requiring you to search through Quattro Pro's menus to find the commands necessary to change an object's properties, Quattro Pro gives you another choice. When you point to an object with the mouse pointer and click the right mouse button, you will see either an *Object Inspector* or a *QuickMenu* associated with the object. Object Inspectors are dialog boxes that contain all of the property settings for the object. QuickMenus are short command menus containing only those commands most appropriate for the selected object. QuickMenus always include a selection at the very top of the menu that displays the Object Inspector dialog box for the selected object.

Although QuickMenus and Object Inspectors may sound a little confusing at first, once you begin using them you'll find them to be very helpful. Figure 12.2 shows the QuickMenu that appears when you point to a notebook cell and click the right mouse button. The commands on this menu are also available if you search through several of Quattro Pro's standard menus, but the QuickMenu has gathered several of the commands you might want to apply to a cell in one convenient place.

Notice the top item on the QuickMenu, `Block Properties`. If you select this item, the Active Block Object Inspector dialog box is displayed (see fig. 12.3). You can also use the F12 shortcut key to display the Active Block Object Inspector dialog box directly. This dialog box contains every possible setting for a cell (or block of cells). In figure 12.3, the item labeled Numeric Format is selected, so the right side, or *pane*, of the dialog box displays all possible numeric format settings. As you select different options, such as a different numeric format, or a different property, such as Alignment, the settings pane of the dialog box changes and displays the available options.

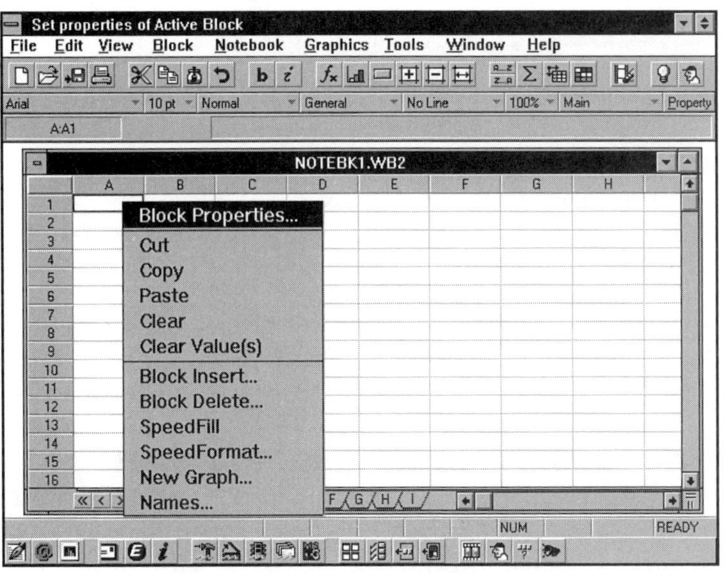

Fig. 12.2
QuickMenus gather commands from several menus into one convenient menu.

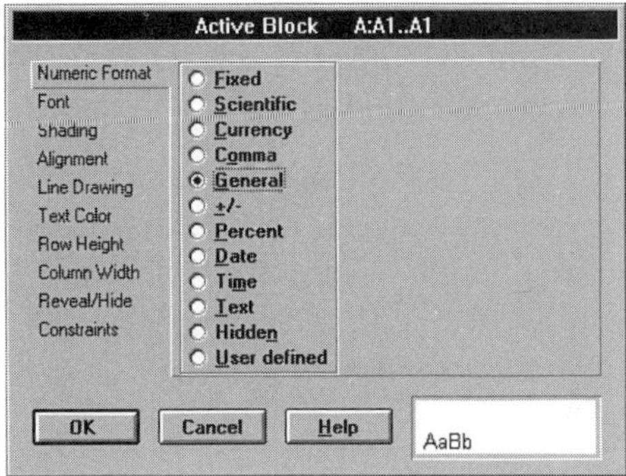

Fig. 12.3
Object Inspector dialog boxes enable you to adjust object properties.

If you change a property setting, such as changing from **G**eneral to **D**ate format for displaying values, the name of the property will be displayed in blue letters instead of black. You can adjust more than one property while the dialog box is active. Simply select OK when you've made all of your changes, or select Cancel if you decide you don't want to apply the changes.

Some of the Quattro Pro objects that you can inspect and adjust by pointing and clicking the right mouse button include cells and blocks; notebook pages (right-click the page tab); a notebook (right-click the notebook title bar); the Toolbar (right-click the Toolbar); graph objects including drawn objects, titles, data series, and the graph background objects (right-click the object); and Quattro Pro itself (right-click the Quattro Pro title bar).

Tip
To find out more about different Quattro Pro objects, point to the object, hold down the Ctrl key, and click the right mouse button.

Using Coaches and Experts

Sometimes it's nice to get a little extra help. It would be very difficult, if not downright impossible, for any one PC user to know how to perform every task on his or her computer. When you're dealing with such a powerful and adaptable program as Quattro Pro, it's even more difficult to know or remember exactly the correct sequence of steps that may be necessary, especially for those tasks you rarely perform.

Fortunately, Quattro Pro includes two specialized tools—*Coaches* and *Experts*—that can ease your way through learning Quattro Pro and executing difficult tasks. The following section includes a quick look at the two tools.

Learning Techniques Through the Coaches

Computer-based training isn't new; programs have included tutorials for years. But most tutorials aren't really very useful because they follow a preprogrammed path and use carefully determined sets of data. If you want to learn how to perform a task, these types of tutorials may not be very useful, because you can't see how the tutorial applies to your problem. Sure, you can go through the tutorial and try to remember all of the steps, but it may take several tries before you're really comfortable.

Quattro Pro's Coaches use a different approach to teaching you tasks. Instead of using a carefully preselected data set, the Coaches enable you to use your own data. Not only that, but the Coaches also enable you to save your work in a real Quattro Pro notebook. When you complete a task, the notebook contains your data, and you've learned a useful skill.

To use the Coaches, choose **H**elp, C**o**aches, or click the Coaches button on the Toolbar. The Coaches dialog box has several main topics, each with a number of individual items you can select (see fig. 12.4). As you complete each item, the box in front of the item is filled with a check to show the items you've already viewed. You can repeat items even if they are checked, so don't worry if you don't fully understand everything the first time through.

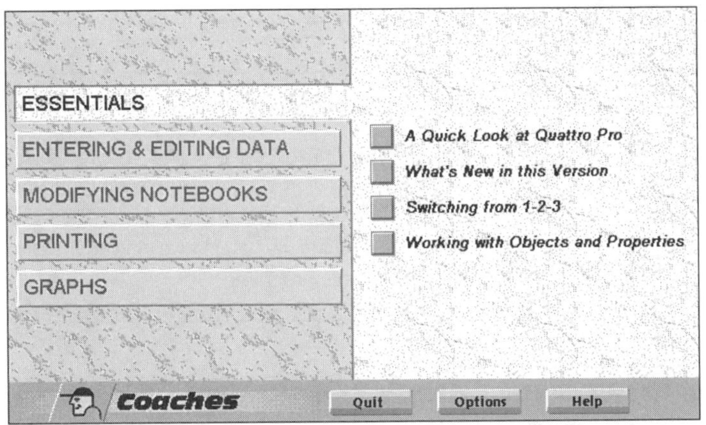

Fig. 12.4
Use the Coaches to learn more about Quattro Pro.

For example, suppose you want to learn more about applying different formats to your data. The Formatting Data item in the Modifying Notebooks section of the Coaches dialog box takes you through the process one step at a time (see fig. 12.5). Just follow the screen prompts as you learn the necessary steps.

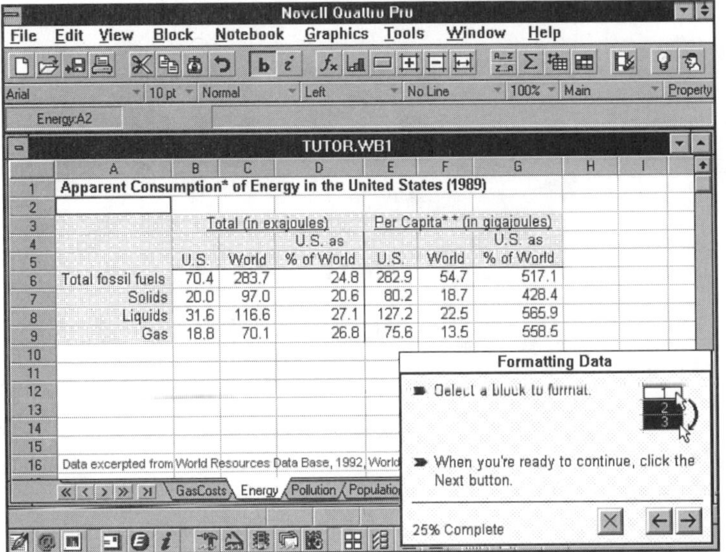

Fig. 12.5
Follow through each step as the Coaches teach you Quattro Pro tasks.

Troubleshooting

When the Coaches are active, I can't switch to another Windows program.

Because the Coaches must remain visible, they use a special property called "Always on top" to stay above Quattro Pro. If you click on the Quattro Pro window, you can then use Ctrl+Esc to display the Task List and select another program. The Coaches will remain on top of all other windows, though, so you may want to quit using the Coaches first if you really need to use another program.

Using Experts for Complex Tasks

Although the Coaches are useful when you want to learn the basics of Quattro Pro, some tasks are just too complex, or are simply too much trouble to learn if you don't need to perform them very often. Quattro Pro offers a group of very powerful Experts to help you on such occasions.

Experts provide the expertise to solve complex problems, while you provide the data. These Experts cover a broad range of topics, which are only hinted at by the Experts dialog box (see fig. 12.6). Table 12.3 provides a brief description of Quattro Pro's Experts.

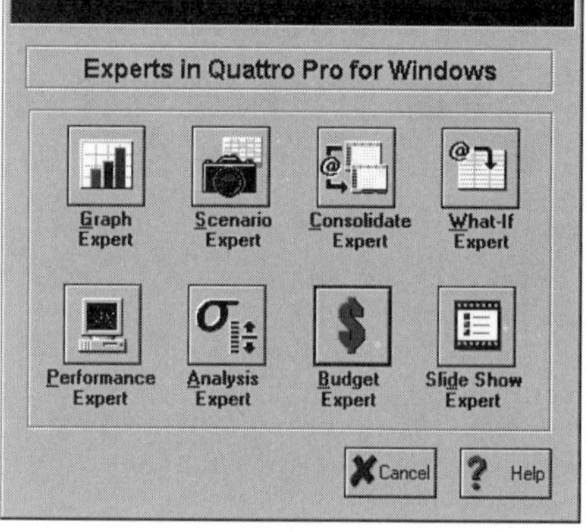

Fig. 12.6
Use the Experts to solve complex problems easily.

Table 12.3 Quattro Pro's Experts

Expert	Description
Graph Expert	Helps you create graphs
Scenario Expert	Helps you create and manage scenarios—multiple groups of related data that enable easy what-if analysis
Consolidate Expert	Helps you combine data from different sources
What-If Expert	Helps you generate what-if scenarios
Performance Expert	Helps you maximize the performance of notebook applications
Analysis Expert	Helps you use the Analysis Tools
Budget Expert	Helps you create and manage home and small business budgets
Sli**d**e Show Expert	Helps you create professional-looking slide shows

For example, the Graph Expert leads you through the steps necessary to create powerful business graphics that present your data in a highly effective visual manner. You don't have to be a graphics expert yourself; all you need to do is answer some questions and make a few selections along the way. The Budget Expert is another tool you'll probably find quite useful. Everyone knows they should have a budget, especially if they're running a small business. The Budget Expert helps you prepare a Quattro Pro notebook containing an individualized budget specific to your needs.

From Here...

In this chapter you learned some of the basics of Quattro Pro, including how to use some shortcuts that will speed up your use of the program. For more information about using Quattro Pro, see the following chapters:

- Chapter 13, "Learning Spreadsheet Basics," shows you how to use Quattro Pro notebook files, how to enter and edit data, and how to save your work.
- Chapter 14, "Building a Spreadsheet," presents the basic commands, shows you how to use blocks of cells, how to copy and move data, and how to include the built-in functions in your notebooks.

- Chapter 15, "Changing the Display and Appearance of Data," provides you the information you need to make your notebooks look more professional.
- Chapter 16, "Analyzing Data," introduces some of the powerful data analysis tools included in Quattro Pro.
- Chapter 17, "Using Graphics," shows you how to graph your data, making it easier to understand.
- Chapter 18, "Printing Reports," shows you how to produce printed reports from your notebooks.

Chapter 13

Learning Spreadsheet Basics

by Brian Underdahl

This chapter presents information you need to use Quattro Pro notebooks. If you are new to electronic spreadsheets, this chapter helps you learn to use a spreadsheet for basic data analysis. If you have used other spreadsheet programs, this chapter is valuable for learning the conventions and features of Quattro Pro.

This chapter shows you how to perform the following tasks:

- Work with single and multiple notebook pages
- Link notebooks
- Enter and edit data
- Document formulas, numbers, and data by adding descriptive notes to cells
- Add labels and headings to make notebooks more understandable
- Use the Undo feature

Understanding Notebooks and Files

In Quattro Pro, a single spreadsheet is called a *page*—a two-dimensional grid of columns and rows. A file that contains 256 spreadsheet pages and an Objects page in a three-dimensional arrangement is called a *notebook*. Besides working with a single notebook, you also can work with several notebooks at the same time, and you can link notebooks by writing formulas that refer to cells in another notebook.

Using 3D Notebooks

Most of the time, you need only a single page to analyze and store data. You can organize simple reports effectively on a single page without the added complication of including page references in your formulas. Page references are necessary for accessing data that spreads across several pages.

Some situations, however, are well-suited to multiple notebook pages. Reports that consolidate data from several departments often work well as multiple-page reports—especially if one person produces the entire report. You can put a formula on one page that refers to cells on other pages.

You also can use multiple pages effectively to separate different kinds of data. You might place data input areas on one page, macros on another, constants on another, and the finished report on yet another page. This technique can provide some assurance that a spreadsheet isn't damaged by an inadvertent error. For example, a data entry error can write over formulas, or the insertion or deletion of a row or column can destroy macros or data tables contained on the same page. Building your notebook by using several pages provides some protection against these all too common problems.

Spreadsheets that use multiple pages are called *3D spreadsheets*—all Quattro Pro notebooks are automatically 3D notebooks whether you have data on one page or multiple pages. You don't have to add pages manually to a Quattro Pro notebook as you do with most other spreadsheet programs.

Naming Notebook Pages

One way to utilize multiple notebook pages is to place each month's data on a separate page and use a 13th page for the yearly totals. Because Quattro Pro enables you to name individual notebook pages, you can name each page for one month so that you easily can locate the correct page when necessary. Figure 13.1 shows a notebook that uses named pages to hold each month's sales data separately.

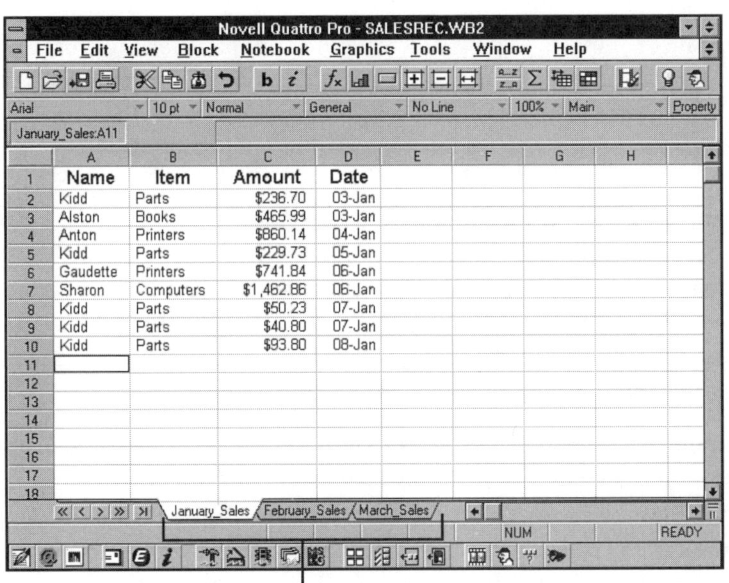

Fig. 13.1
Name notebook pages to indicate their purpose.

You can name a notebook page by pointing to the page tab and double-clicking the left mouse button, or by displaying the Active Page Object Inspector dialog box and selecting the Name pane. If you double-click the page tab, simply type the new name directly on the tab after you double-click the tab.

To display the Active Page Object Inspector dialog box, you can either point to the page tab and click the right mouse button, or select Property on the Property band and then select Active Page to display this dialog box. Either way, you next select Name to display the Page **N**ame pane (see fig. 13.2). Type the new name for the page in the text box, or select **R**eset to restore the original page letter.

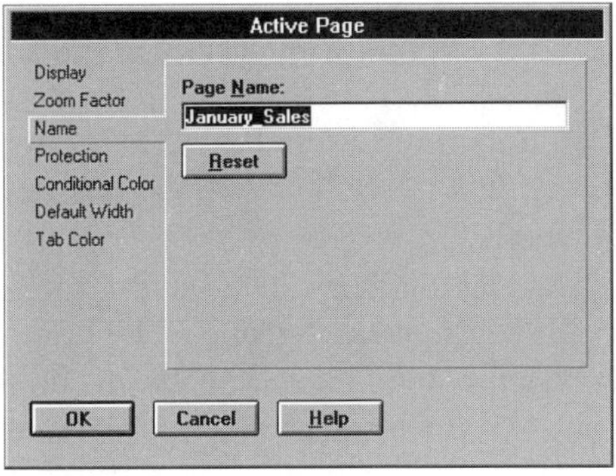

Fig. 13.2
You can use the Active Page Object Inspector dialog box to name a notebook page.

Page names can be up to 63 characters in length, but the longer page names enable fewer page tabs to appear on-screen. You can use both letters and numbers in page names, but you cannot include spaces. To separate words in a page name, use the underscore (_).

Moving Between Pages

Multiple notebook pages wouldn't be of much value if there wasn't a quick way to move between pages. You've already learned that the key combinations of Ctrl+PgDn and Ctrl+PgUp enable you to move through the notebook one page at a time. In addition, you can point to a page tab and click the left mouse button to move to another page.

Sometimes, though, you may want to move to a page were the tab isn't currently visible, such as a page far removed from the current page. The best method for moving to a distant notebook page is to use the **E**dit, **G**o to command (or press the shortcut key, F5) to display the Go to dialog box (see fig. 13.3). Select the page in the **P**ages list box, and press Enter or click OK.

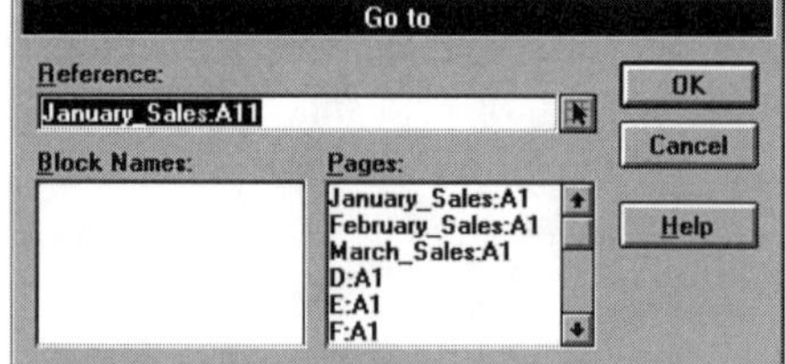

Fig. 13.3 Use the Go to dialog box to move to a different notebook page.

Note

Selecting a page by using the **Edit**, **G**o to command always moves the cell selector to cell A1 on the selected page.

► See "Naming Blocks," p. 285

Create a block name and select the named block in the **B**lock Names list box as the destination. The cell selector will then move to the upper left corner of the named block.

Linking Notebooks

A single notebook, whether it uses multiple pages or is contained on a single page, is not always the best solution. Linking multiple notebook files with formulas is often a better solution than using a single notebook. Consolidating data from several departments or company locations may be easier when using multiple notebooks, especially if several people are producing the individual reports. The person producing the consolidated report can create a notebook that uses formula links to consolidate the data from each notebook.

When you work with data from several notebook files, you enter a formula in one notebook cell that refers to cells in another notebook. This technique is called *linking*. With this capability, you easily can consolidate data from separate notebook files. You may, for example, receive data in notebooks from several departments or locations. A consolidation notebook can use formulas to combine the data from each notebook.

Figure 13.4 shows the notebook CONSRPT.WB2 which is used to consolidate data from three other notebooks: CARSRPT.WB2, SPARRPT.WB2, and RENORPT.WB2. Formulas link the notebooks. The formula in cell A:B5 of CONSRPT.WB2, for example, is:

+[CARSRPT]A:B5+[RENORPT]A:B5+[SPARRPT]A:B5

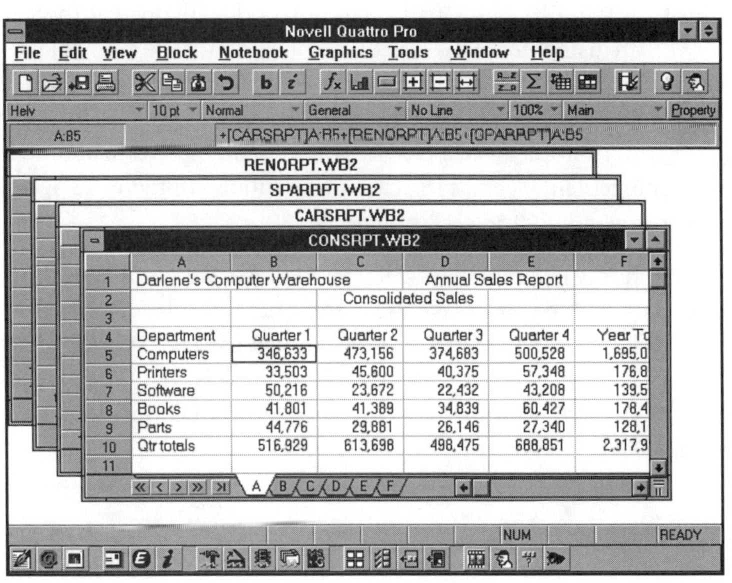

Fig. 13.4
You can use formulas to link to data in other notebooks.

This formula tells Quattro Pro to add together the values in cell A:B5 of CARSRPT.WB2, cell A:B5 of RENORPT.WB2, and cell A:B5 of SPARRPT.WB2. In this case, the same cell in each notebook supplies the data for the formula, but that is not a requirement. You could, for example, create a linking formula which added values from cell A:A1 in one notebook, and cell D:AA216 in another notebook. In most cases, you will find it less confusing if each linked notebook uses a similar structure.

Linking formulas can refer to notebooks which are open or closed. Quattro Pro maintains the formula links even after the supporting notebooks are closed, but must be able to locate the supporting notebooks when the notebook containing the formula links is opened. If the supporting notebooks are not available, Quattro Pro will not be able to determine a value for the linking formulas, and will display NA (Not Available) instead of a value in the notebook.

Tip
If you don't need to see the values of linking formulas, select **N**one when you open notebooks containing linking formulas. The linked notebook will open much faster.

When you open a notebook containing formula links to closed notebooks, Quattro Pro offers three options: **O**pen Supporting, **U**pdate References, or **N**one. If you select **N**one, Quattro Pro changes the linking formula values to NA, but you can use the **N**otebook, **U**pdate Links, **O**pen Links or **N**otebook, **U**pdate Links, **R**efresh Links commands to later update your linking formulas. See the section "Entering Formulas" later in this chapter for more information on creating formulas to link notebooks.

Using Workspaces

In figure 13.4, four different Quattro Pro notebooks are open at the same time. If you are using notebooks that are linked, it may be convenient to open all of the linked notebooks, especially if you have a need to create additional formula links or enter data in more than one of the notebooks. When you work with multiple notebooks, it is often handy to create a standard window arrangement, such as the cascaded windows in figure 13.4, so you always know where to find each notebook.

Quattro Pro has two commands—**F**ile, **W**orkspace, **S**ave and **F**ile, **W**orkspace, **R**estore—that enable you to save the current notebook layout and then restore that same layout at a later time. When you use **F**ile, **W**orkspace, **S**ave, Quattro Pro saves the current screen layout in a file with a WBS extension. Use **F**ile, **W**orkspace, **R**estore to open the same group of notebook files and restore their screen layout in a single command.

Caution

File, **W**orkspace, **S**ave does not save the notebook files, only their current screen layout. You must also save the individual notebook files to save any changes they may contain.

Entering Data

A notebook isn't of much use until you enter data, whether that data consists of labels, values, or formulas. In this section you'll learn how to enter data in Quattro Pro notebooks.

You can only enter data in the currently active cell, so to begin entering data you must first move the cell selector to the appropriate cell. Next, type the data and press Enter. As you type, the data appears in the input line and also in the current cell. If you enter data in a cell that already contains an entry, the new data replaces the existing entry.

If you are entering a column of data, you can move the cell selector down one row in the same column when you press Enter by selecting **M**ove Cell Selector on Enter Key in the Application Object Inspector dialog box General pane. Right-click the Quattro Pro title bar, or press Alt+F12, to display this dialog box. This setting makes entering columnar data much faster and easier.

If you plan to enter labels or values in more than one cell, you do not need to press Enter after each entry. Instead, you can enter the data, and then move the cell selector to the new cell with a direction key to complete the entry and move the cell selector in a single step. This technique does not work if you are entering formulas.

You can create two kinds of cell entries: labels or values. A *label* (or string) is a text entry, and a *value* is a number or formula. Quattro Pro usually determines the kind of entry from the first character you type. The program always treats the entry as a value (a number or a formula) if you begin with one of the following characters:

+ – (@ # . $

If you begin an entry with a number, Quattro Pro assumes you are entering a value unless you include any non-numeric character other than a single period. If you begin by typing any other character, Quattro Pro treats the entry as a label.

Entering Labels

Labels make the numbers and formulas in a notebook understandable. In figure 13.4, labels identify the departments and the time periods that generated the displayed results. Without labels, the numbers are meaningless.

In Quattro Pro, you can place up to 1,022 characters in a single cell. Although this enables you to create very long labels, remember that you will probably not be able to display nearly that many characters on-screen nor in a single line of a report.

When you enter a label, Quattro Pro adds a *label prefix*—a punctuation mark that controls the label's alignment in the cell—to the cell entry. The label prefix is not displayed in the spreadsheet, but does appear in the input line. By default, Quattro Pro adds the label prefix for a left-aligned label, an apostrophe ('). You can change the way a label is aligned using one of the following label prefixes:

' Left-aligned (default)

" Right-aligned

^ Centered

\ Repeating

| Nonprinting (if the label is in the leftmost column of the print block)

Note

Unlike older spreadsheet programs, Quattro Pro enables you to enter labels that begin with numbers. If you use another spreadsheet program, you usually must begin label entries with a label prefix if the first character is a number.

Regardless of the label prefix you enter, any label longer than the column width is displayed as a left-aligned label. If a label is longer than the cell width, the label appears across empty cells to the right. Even a label too long to display on-screen can appear in its entirety in the edit box. When the cell selector rests on the cell that contains the long entry, press F2 (Edit) or double-click the cell with the left mouse button.

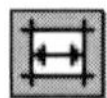

If the cells to the right are not blank, Quattro Pro cuts off the display of an overlapping label at the nonblank cell border. The complete entry still is stored, however. To display more of the label in the spreadsheet, you can insert new columns to the right of the cell that contains the long label, or you can widen the column (move the cell selector to the cell that contains the long label and click the Fit button on the Toolbar).

Entering Numbers

Most calculations involve numbers, so numbers will represent a large portion of the data you'll enter in your Quattro Pro notebooks. To enter a number, type any of the ten numeric characters (0 through 9) and certain other characters, according to the following rules:

- A number can start with a plus sign (+), but the plus sign is not stored when you press Enter. For example, **+302** is stored and displayed as `302`.
- If you start a number with a minus sign (–), the number is stored as a negative number. Negative numbers are usually displayed with the minus sign, but some numeric formats display negative numbers in parentheses. **–302** may be displayed as `-302` or `(302)`.
- Numbers can include only one decimal point, no spaces, and no commas.
- If you end a number with a percent sign (%), the number is divided by 100, and the percent sign is dropped (unless the cell is formatted as Percent).
- Numbers are stored with up to 15 significant digits. If you enter a number with more significant digits, the number is rounded and stored in scientific notation.

The appearance of a number in the notebook depends on the cell's format, font, and column width. If the number is too long to fit in the cell, Quattro Pro tries to show as much of the number as possible. If the cell uses the default General format and the integer portion of the number does not fit in the cell, Quattro Pro displays the number in scientific notation.

Troubleshooting

Quattro Pro displays asterisks instead of the number entered in a cell.

If the cell uses a format other than General or Scientific, or if the cell width is too narrow to display in scientific notation and the number cannot fit in the cell width, Quattro Pro displays asterisks instead of the number. Use the Fit button on the Toolbar to change the column width, select a different numeric format, or change the font to a smaller size.

Entering Formulas

Formulas are the real power of a spreadsheet program like Quattro Pro. Formulas enable the program to calculate results and analyze data. As you change or add new data to a spreadsheet, Quattro Pro recalculates the new results.

Formulas operate on numbers, labels, or the results of other formulas. A formula can contain up to 1,022 characters, and can include numbers, text, operators, cell and block addresses, block names, and functions. A formula cannot contain spaces except in a block name, a quoted text string, or a note (see the section "Adding Reference Notes," later in this chapter).

You can use Quattro Pro as a calculator by typing numbers directly into a formula, as in **123+456**, but doing so disregards the real power of Quattro Pro formulas. A more useful formula uses cell references or block names in the calculation. Figure 13.5 demonstrates this capability.

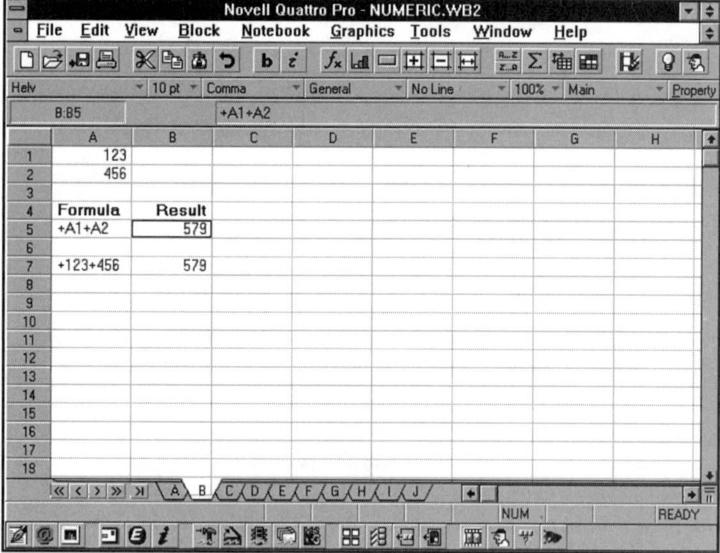

Fig. 13.5
Use cell references instead of the numbers in formulas.

In figure 13.5, the values 123 and 456 are placed in cells A1 and A2, respectively. The formula +A1+A2, which refers to these two cells, produces the same result as the formula 123+456—the value 579 (notice that the formula in cell B5 begins with a plus sign—if the formula begins with a letter, not a plus sign, Quattro Pro assumes that you are entering a label and performs no calculations). Suppose, however, that the data changes and you discover the first value should be 124, not 123. If you used the cell reference formula, you just type **124** in cell A1 and the formula recalculates the new value of 580. If you used the formula with numeric values rather than the cell reference formula, you must edit or retype the formula to change the data and obtain the new result.

Quattro Pro uses four kinds of formulas: numeric, string, logical, and function. The following sections briefly describe each type of formula.

Using Numeric Formulas

Numeric formulas are instructions to Quattro Pro to perform mathematical calculations. You use *operators* to specify the calculations and the order to perform the calculations. Use operators for addition, subtraction, multiplication, division, and exponentiation (raising a number to a power).

Quattro Pro evaluates formulas according to a set of defined operator preferences. That is, exponentiation is performed before multiplication or division, and all three are performed before any addition or subtraction. If the formula includes two operators of the same precedence, this portion of the equation is evaluated left to right. You can control a formula's evaluation order by placing portions of a formula within parentheses, because Quattro Pro always evaluates items within a set of parentheses first.

For example, the formula 5+3*2 results in a value of 11, while the formula (5+3)*2 results in a value of 16. In the first formula, Quattro Pro multiplies 3 times 2 and adds the result, 6, to 5. In the second formula, Quattro Pro adds 5 and 3, and multiplies the result, 8, by 2. As you can see, a slight change in the formula produces quite different results.

Note

Because Quattro Pro attempts to evaluate simple numeric formulas that use division, such as 6/26, as a date entry, you must begin such formulas with a plus sign (+6/26). This tells Quattro Pro you want to perform a calculation rather than trying to use the entry as a date.

Using String Formulas

A *string* is a label or the result of a string formula. A string is text rather than numbers.

Only two string formula operators exist: the plus sign (+), which repeats a string, and the ampersand (&), which *concatenates* (joins) two or more strings. String formulas use different rules than numeric formulas. String formulas always begin with the plus sign but cannot include more than one plus sign. To add two strings, you concatenate them using the ampersand.

Figure 13.6 shows several examples of string formulas. In the figure, cell C10 shows how the plus sign is used to repeat a string value. The formula is the same to repeat a string or a numeric value. C11 shows the result of concatenating two strings. Notice that no spaces exist between the two concatenated values. C12 and C13 demonstrate how to include spaces and commas in quoted strings to produce more attractive results.

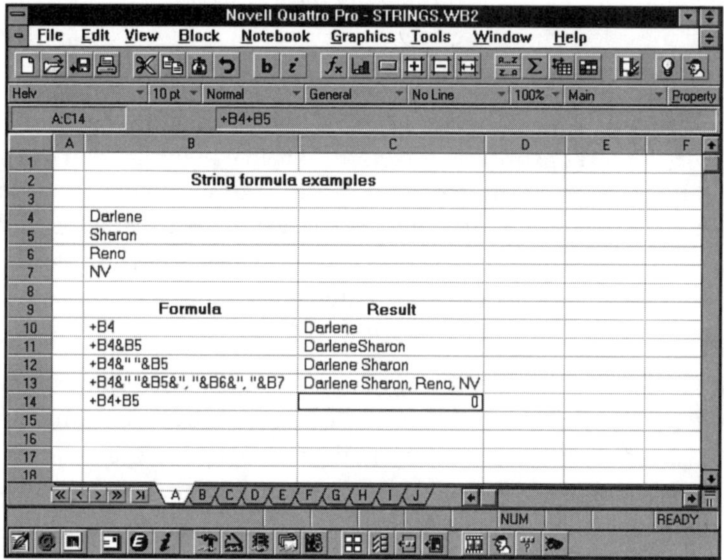

Fig. 13.6 Using string formulas.

If you attempt to add two strings using the plus sign rather than the ampersand, Quattro Pro treats the formula as a numeric formula rather than a string formula. A cell that contains a label has a numeric value of 0 (zero), so the formula +B4+B5 in C14 returns a value of 0. You can use the ampersand only in string formulas. Also, if you use any numeric operators (after the plus sign at the beginning) in a formula that contains an ampersand, the formula results in ERR.

Using Logical Formulas

Logical formulas are true/false tests. A logical formula returns a value of 1 if the test is true and a value of 0 if the test is false. Logical formulas often are used in database criteria tables and also to construct the tests used with the @IF function, which is discussed in the next section, "Using Function Formulas."

Logical formulas provide a shortcut method of performing conditional calculations. Suppose that you want to include the value contained in cell A1 only if this value is greater than 100. The logical formula +A1*(A1>100) returns the result you want. In this formula, the logical test, A1>100, evaluates as 0 unless the value in A1 is greater than 100. If A1 contains a value over 100, the logical test evaluates to 1. Because any value multiplied by 0 equals 0, and any value multiplied by 1 is the original value, the logical formula returns the result you want.

Using Function Formulas

Although you can build many formulas using the numeric, string, or logical operators, some calculations are simply too complex to create with these simple operators. For example, if you want to calculate the interest due on a loan payment, you can simply multiply the beginning balance by the periodic interest rate. It's much more difficult, however, to calculate the actual payment amount necessary to pay off a loan in a series of equal payments.

Fortunately, Quattro Pro provides a large number of built-in *functions*—preconstructed formulas that handle a broad range of calculations. These functions enable you to perform many different types of calculations by simply supplying the raw data. For example, to determine the payments on a loan, you can use the @PAYMT function. You supply the necessary data—the interest rate, number of payments, and the loan amount, and Quattro Pro solves the problem.

Quattro Pro includes well over 350 powerful built-in functions you can use in your formulas. Figure 13.7 shows an example of how the @PAYMT function calculates the loan payment on a slightly more complex loan, one with a balloon payment due at the end of the loan. In this case, a borrower wants to know the monthly payments on a loan with the following terms:

Principal	$100,000
Annual rate	9%
Term	15 years
Balance due at end of loan (balloon)	$10,000

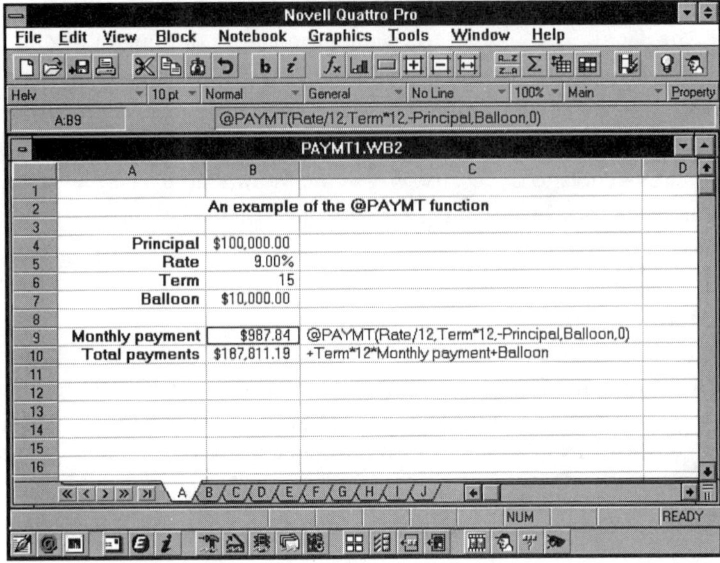

Fig. 13.7
Function formulas quickly perform complex calculations using your data.

In this case, because the payments are made monthly, but the interest rate and term are stated in yearly amounts, the term must be multiplied by 12, and the rate must be divided by 12 to obtain the term in months, and the monthly interest rate. The monthly loan payment, $987.84, is automatically adjusted if any of the raw data in cells B4..B7 is changed.

► See "Using Functions," p. 304

When you create formulas in a Quattro Pro notebook, you can often combine functions with numeric, logical, and string formulas to produce the results you need.

Creating Formulas by Pointing to Cells

Most formulas you create will contain operators and cell references. As you enter a cell reference in a formula, type the cell address or point to the cell by moving the cell selector with the direction keys or the mouse. When you move the cell selector as you are entering a formula, the mode indicator at the right edge of the status line changes from VALUE to POINT, and the address of the cell selector appears in the input line.

If the formula requires additional entries, type the next operator and continue entering arguments until you finish. Press Enter or click the Confirm button (the green check mark at the left of the input line) to place the formula in the notebook. You can combine pointing and typing cell addresses—the result is the same.

To refer to a cell on another notebook page, include the page letter or name, followed by a colon and the cell address. To include the value of cell A13 from a page named EXPENSES, for example, type **+EXPENSES:A13**. To point to a cell on another page, type +, and then use the direction keys, including Ctrl+PgDn and Ctrl+PgUp, to move the cell selector to other pages. You also can click the page tab with the mouse, and then point to the cell.

Finding Formula Errors

Sometimes you may find your formulas display ERR or NA instead of the value you expected. ERR means the formula contains an erroneous calculation, such as dividing by zero, and can result from missing data or even from an error in entering a cell address. NA means some of the necessary information is currently not available, and can result from including a reference to a cell containing the @NA function, or from linking formulas that were not updated when the notebook was opened. Finding the source of such errors can prove difficult, especially in a complex formula.

To quickly find the source of an ERR or NA value, use the Go to feature. First move the cell selector to the cell displaying ERR or NA, and then press F5 (Go to) or select **E**dit, **G**o to. Do not select a destination, but simply press Enter or click OK, the cell selector will move to the cell which is the source of the error.

Adding Reference Notes

Documentation is always important, and it is even more important when you create complex formulas that may be difficult to understand. It's pretty easy to forget why you built a formula exactly as you did, but even a brief note is often all you need to remind yourself. Quattro Pro makes documenting formulas and values easy by enabling you to add notes to cell entries.

These reference notes don't appear when you print a report, but as figure 13.8 shows, the notes can appear on-screen in the edit box. Move the cell selector to a cell that contains a note and press F2 (Edit) or double-click the cell.

Fig. 13.8
Add notes to formulas to provide valuable documentation.

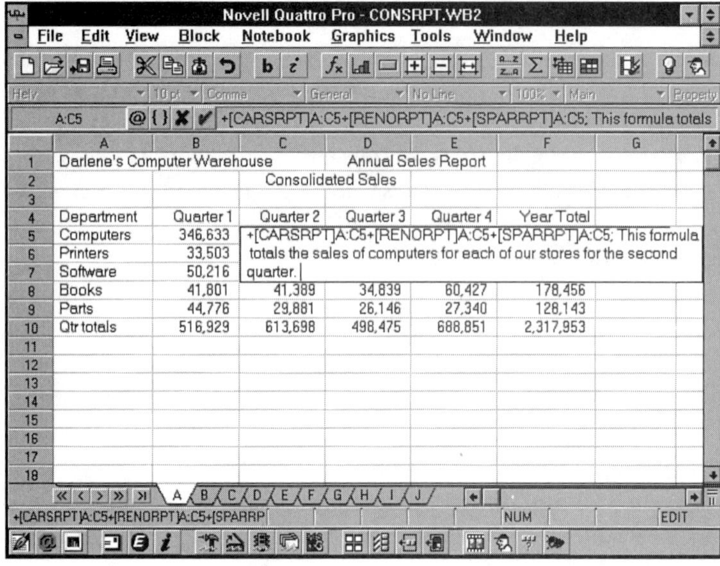

The note attached to the formula in cell C5 in figure 13.8 clearly states the purpose of the formula—to show the combined total of sales of computers in each store during the second quarter.

Tip
Print the notes attached to formulas by using the **F**ile, **P**rint, Sh**e**et Options, **C**ell Formulas command.

To attach a note, type a semicolon immediately following the formula or value—don't leave any spaces before the semicolon, then type the note. You can include up to 1,022 characters in a cell, including the length of the formula or value and the note. Because these notes won't have any effect on your printed reports, they are a good method of creating internal documentation that will always remain with the notebook.

Editing Cell Entries

Sometimes you need to change an entry you have made in a Quattro Pro notebook. You can edit cell entries several different ways. If you want to completely replace a cell entry, simply retype the entire entry (first make certain the cell selector is around the correct cell). When you press Enter or move the cell selector to another cell, your new entry replaces the existing entry. To cancel the new entry, press Esc before you press Enter or move the cell selector.

To replace part of a cell's current contents, press F2 (Edit) or double-click the cell with the left mouse button. You can then use the mouse pointer or the direction keys to place the insertion point at the characters you want to replace. Press Enter or click another cell to confirm your edits. Press Esc to cancel any edits.

Correcting Errors with Undo

When you type an entry, edit a cell, or issue a command, you make changes in the notebook. If you make a change in error, you can usually choose the **E**dit, **U**ndo command (or press Ctrl+Z) to reverse the previous change. If you type over an entry in error, you can undo the new entry to restore the previous entry. The Undo feature undoes only the last action performed, whether you were entering data, using a command, running a macro, or using Undo.

◄ See "Some Important Shortcut Keys," p. 248

The Undo feature is powerful and using it can be a little tricky. To use Undo properly, you must first understand what Quattro Pro considers to be a change that can be undone. A change occurs between the time Quattro Pro is in READY mode and when the program returns to READY mode. If you press F2 (Edit), Quattro Pro enters EDIT mode. After you press Enter to confirm the edits, Quattro Pro returns to READY mode. If you choose **E**dit, **U**ndo, Quattro Pro restores the cell contents that existed before you pressed F2 (Edit). To restore the last change, choose **E**dit, **R**edo (which replaces **E**dit, **U**ndo until you make another change that can be undone). If a single command makes the change, the Undo feature can undo changes made to an entire block of cells or even a complete notebook.

Note

The **E**dit, **U**ndo and **E**dit, **R**edo commands inform you of the action which can be undone or redone by including a one word description following the command. If you make an entry in a cell, for example, the command appears as `Edit, Undo Entry`. If you use the **E**dit, **U**ndo Entry command, the command then changes to `Edit, Redo Entry`.

Quattro Pro cannot undo some commands. Moving the cell selector, saving a notebook, and the effects of recalculating formulas are examples of commands that cannot be undone. Before you make a serious change to an important file, always save the work to protect against errors that Undo may not reverse.

Quattro Pro has two levels of Undo command functionality. To ensure that the full Undo feature is available, make sure that the **U**ndo Enabled check box in the General section of the Application Object Inspector dialog box is selected (see fig. 13.9). To access this dialog box, right-click the Quattro Pro title bar or press Alt+F12. If you don't enable the full Undo command, you will still be able to undo certain actions, such as entering data into a cell or changing a graph type or a graph title.

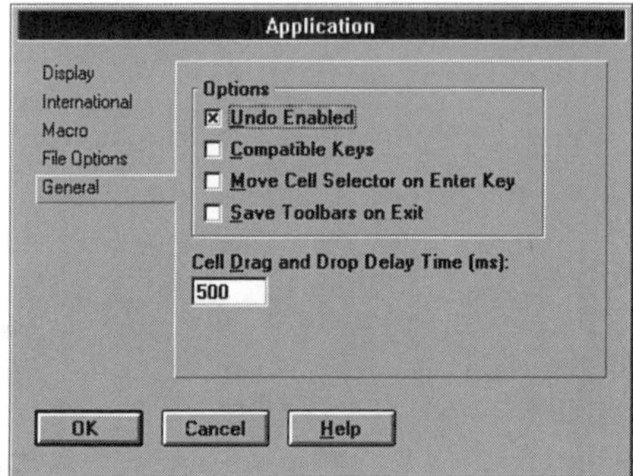

Fig. 13.9
Select **U**ndo Enabled to ensure that the full Undo feature is available.

Saving Your Work

When you create a Quattro Pro notebook, it first exists only in your computer's volatile memory—RAM. To make the notebook available for future use, save the notebook in a file on disk. If you don't save new notebooks or changes before you quit Quattro Pro, you lose your work. Also save a notebook in a disk file if you want to share the notebook with other people. The notebook file remains on disk after you quit Quattro Pro or turn off the computer.

Saving Notebook Files

To save your work, use **F**ile, **S**ave or **F**ile, Save **A**s. If you have not yet saved the notebook, Quattro Pro suggests a default name—NOTEBK1.WB2. When you use **F**ile, **N**ew to open new blank notebooks, Quattro Pro increases the numerical portion of the file name. The second new notebook is NOTEBK2.WB2, and so on.

If you already have saved the active notebook and assigned a name, **F**ile, **S**ave saves the active notebook to disk using the assigned name. If you choose **F**ile, Save **A**s, Quattro Pro saves the active notebook using a name you specify in the Save File dialog box (see fig. 13.10).

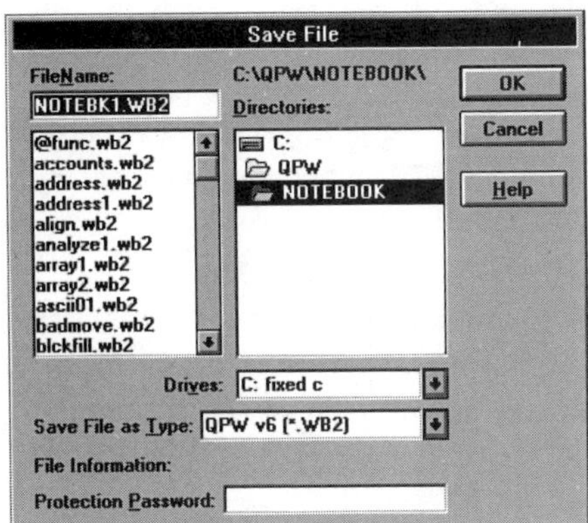

Fig. 13.10
Use the Save File dialog box to name your notebook files.

In current versions of DOS, a file name can be up to eight characters long and can have an optional extension of up to three characters. The name can contain any combination of letters, numbers, and the following characters:

– ^ $ ~ ! # % & { } ( ) @ _ '

Don't use any other special characters, such as spaces, commas, backslashes, or periods, except for a single period between the file name and the extension. Also, don't use any of the following names, which are reserved by DOS for its own use:

CLOCK$	LPT1	COM1
CON	LPT2	COM2
AUX	LPT3	COM3
NUL	LPT4	COM4
PRN		

The standard extension for Quattro Pro notebooks is WB2. The standard extension for Quattro Pro workspace files is WBS. When you type a notebook or workspace name to be saved, type only the descriptive part of the name. Quattro Pro adds the appropriate file extension for you.

◄ See "Saving, Opening, and Closing Files," p. 59

Protecting Files with Passwords

When you save a Quattro Pro notebook in a disk file, anyone with access to your computer can open the file. While this isn't a problem in most instances, you may have some files that should remain confidential and restricted. To prevent unauthorized access to certain notebook files, you can apply a password when you save them. When a notebook is protected by a password, you must know the correct password before Quattro Pro permits you to retrieve or open the notebook.

To apply a password to a notebook file you are saving, select the Protection **P**assword text box in the Save File dialog box, and enter up to 15 characters. As you enter characters, Quattro Pro displays graphics blocks rather than the password. After you choose OK to confirm the dialog box, Quattro Pro displays the Verify Password dialog box. Retype the password using the same combination of uppercase and lowercase characters—passwords are case-sensitive. Choose OK to confirm the dialog box.

Troubleshooting

Quattro Pro reports that I used the wrong password when I attempt to open a password protected notebook file.

Passwords are case-sensitive, and can be very tricky to use. *BRIAN* is not the same as *brian*. Try entering the password again with the case reversed—press the Caps Lock key before entering the password.

An employee who recently left our company used passwords to protect her files, but we don't know the passwords and can't open the files.

There is no method you can use to open password-protected Quattro Pro files without the password. Consider this a strong lesson in the value of making certain a responsible person keeps a list of all passwords.

Saving Files in Other Formats

Quattro Pro can read and save files in the following popular formats: Lotus 1-2-3 for DOS Releases 2.x and 3.x, Lotus 1-2-3 for Windows, Quattro Pro for DOS, Excel, Paradox, dBASE, and text. If you want to save a Quattro Pro notebook in another format, select the correct file extension in the Save File as **T**ype drop-down list box in the Save File dialog box. To save a notebook as a Lotus 1-2-3 for Windows file, for example, change the extension to WK3.

Tip
Unless you need to share a notebook file with someone who does not have Quattro Pro, always save notebooks using the default WB2 extension.

If you save a notebook in any type other than the default "QPW v6 WB2" format, any features unique to the newest version of Quattro Pro will be lost. For example, because Lotus 1-2-3 Release 2.x spreadsheets cannot have multiple pages, only the first notebook page is saved if you use the WK1 file type.

Making Space on Your Disk

Each time you create a file, you use space on a disk—usually your hard disk. Eventually, you'll run out of disk space if you don't occasionally erase old, unneeded files from the disk. Even if you have disk space left, too many files make searching through the file list to find a specific file difficult.

Before you erase old files, consider saving them to a floppy disk in case you need them again. Quattro Pro notebook files are quite space efficient, and you can store a large number of files on a single floppy disk. Quattro Pro doesn't have a command for erasing files. You can use the Windows File Manager or DOS to erase old, unneeded files.

Using Automatic Backups

Many different types of problems can cause you to lose the results of your work. If there is a power failure, for example, any Quattro Pro notebook which hasn't been saved to disk will be lost. If a program crashes and locks up your system, the same thing may occur. Of course, there's always the problem of the overconfident user, too. Have you ever lost work because you thought you had already saved your work, but hadn't because you were distracted? These are only a few of the many problems that present a danger to your notebooks and your data.

Saving your work frequently is the best insurance against losing a notebook or data. Unfortunately, it's pretty easy to forget to save your work often enough. When you're under deadline pressure, who remembers to select **F**ile, **S**ave?

Fortunately, Quattro Pro can quickly save your notebooks automatically at intervals you specify. That way, if a problem occurs, your notebook file on disk won't be too far behind, and you won't lose too much work.

To activate the automatic backup feature, right-click the Quattro Pro title bar, or press Alt+F12, to display the Application Object Inspector dialog box. Select the File Options pane (see fig. 13.11). Use the Auto-**b**ackup time spin control to specify how often you want Quattro Pro to automatically back up your notebook files. Select the Ac**t**ivate check box to enable the automatic backup feature. Press Enter or select OK to close the dialog box.

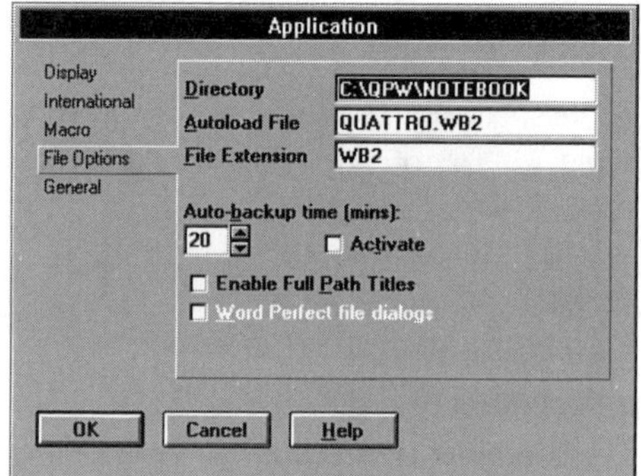

Fig. 13.11
Use the automatic backup feature to automatically save your notebook files at specified intervals.

How often should you have Quattro Pro save your files? The best answer to that is another question; how much work are you willing to do over? Most notebook files can be saved quite quickly, so you won't notice much of a delay as they're being saved. A setting of 10 minutes between backups would probably be a good compromise, but you'll want to adjust the setting to one that suits your work style.

From Here...

In this chapter, you learned that Quattro Pro uses a 3D model for its notebooks to provide you with an extremely flexible spreadsheet work environment. You also learned the basic skills you need to enter data in a notebook, and how to protect your work by saving it on disk. For more information on working with Quattro Pro notebooks, see the following chapters:

- Chapter 14, "Building a Spreadsheet," builds upon the skills you learned in this chapter by presenting basic commands, showing you how to use blocks of cells, showing you how to copy and move data, and expanding on the use of functions in your notebooks.

- Chapter 15, "Changing the Display and Appearance of Data," shows you how to make your notebooks look more professional.

Chapter 14

Building a Spreadsheet

by Brian Underdahl

Building a Quattro Pro spreadsheet can be fun. When you create a spreadsheet model, your computer does your bidding, actually performing actions you specify. If you tell Quattro Pro to use your business' past performance to predict future business, it will do just that. If you tell Quattro Pro to analyze your investments, showing the poorest ones that you might want to reconsider, you can bet that's what Quattro Pro will show you, too. Regardless of whether your uses for Quattro Pro are these or perhaps something a little more ordinary, you must begin by building a spreadsheet, the subject of this chapter.

If you're new to Quattro Pro, you may think that building a spreadsheet model sounds like quite a task. It's true that some complex models can be pretty complicated, but most of the time you'll find it's really pretty simple. Remember, you don't have to build a complete, complex masterpiece all at once. You don't even have to start with complicated models, either. The best way to learn to build Quattro Pro spreadsheet models is to start small, and then work your way up.

This chapter covers some of the basic subjects that will help you begin building your models (don't be confused if you see the terms "spreadsheet," "model," "worksheet," and "notebook" used interchangeably, they all refer to the same thing in most cases). In this chapter, you learn:

- Where to find and how to use basic Quattro Pro commands
- How to use blocks of cells as a unit
- How to copy and move data
- Methods for automatically filling blocks of cells with useful data
- How to use built-in functions to leverage the power of Quattro Pro in your notebooks

Choosing Commands from Menus

Commands are used for almost everything you do in Quattro Pro. Commands tell Quattro Pro to perform a task, change the basic operation, or operate on a notebook, a notebook page, a block of cells, or individual cells. Some commands are used every time you run Quattro Pro; other commands you rarely, if ever, use. Some commands are general enough to apply to all notebooks; other commands are specialized and apply to individual objects such as blocks or cells.

The Quattro Pro main menu includes nine options. Each option leads to a *drop-down menu* similar to the **F**ile menu (see fig. 14.1).

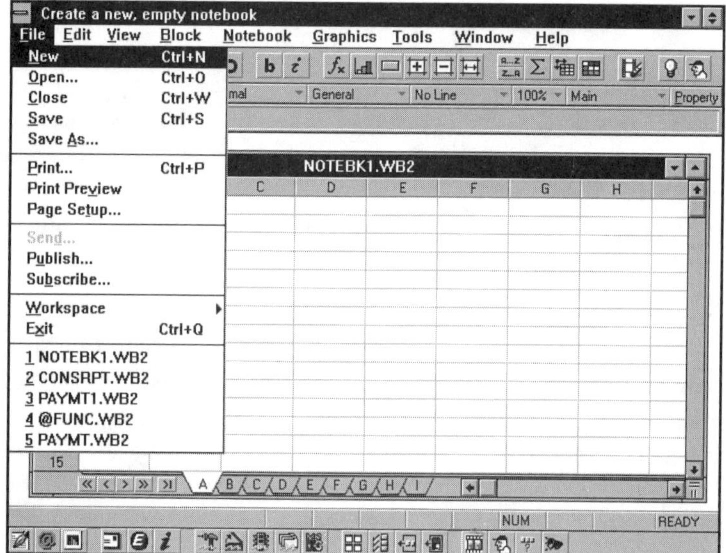

Fig. 14.1
The **F**ile menu on the Quattro Pro main menu.

Each drop-down menu provides a series of commands you use to accomplish specific types of tasks. You'll save quite a bit of time if you understand the basic purpose of each main menu selection, because you won't spend as much time hunting for the correct command. The following is a summary of the main menu options.

- The **F**ile commands enable you to save and open notebooks, print reports, set up your printer, and quit Quattro Pro.

- The **E**dit commands enable you to undo commands; use the Windows Clipboard to copy, cut, and paste information; create links to other Windows applications; move the cell selector; search and replace; and insert page breaks.

- The **V**iew commands enable you to move between the notebook pages and the Objects page, group pages, split the notebook into horizontal or vertical panes, lock rows or columns on screen, zoom in or out, and control the display of screen elements.
- The **B**lock commands enable you to copy, move, and fill blocks; insert and delete rows, columns, and pages; name blocks of cells; transpose data; convert formulas to unchanging values; reformat text; and restrict input to specified cells in a block.
- The **N**otebook commands enable you to create and modify styles and customized fill series; create, modify, and move groups of pages; extract and insert portions of notebooks; import and parse text files; and control formula links with other notebooks.
- The **G**raphics commands enable you to create, view, and modify graphs; insert graph objects on notebook pages; and create on-screen slide shows.
- The **T**ools commands enable you to create, run, and debug macros; create formulas using the Formula Composer; check spelling; use Scenario Manager and Consolidator; change the order of floating objects; use the Database Desktop and Data Modeling Desktop utilities; query and sort databases; perform what-if analyses; perform data regression and matrix manipulation; use the Optimizer and Solve For utilities; create your own dialog boxes and Toolbars; use the Analysis Tools utilities; and use the Object Exchange to share data.
- The **W**indow commands enable you to create additional views of your notebooks, control the display of open windows, and select a window.
- The **H**elp commands enable you to access the Quattro Pro Help system, use the Experts and Coaches, and determine available memory.

For more detailed information on Quattro Pro's menus, you can use the **H**elp **C**ontents command. Select Additional Help, and then Menu Commands to display a description of each item on the main menu. For more details on a specific command, select the appropriate main menu item to display the individual commands. If you want even more information, select a specific command to see a detailed help screen. Press Esc or select close to return to Quattro Pro.

Tip
Watch the Quattro Pro title bar for a description of the highlighted menu option.

> **Troubleshooting**
>
> *Sometimes it's difficult to determine where to find the command necessary to perform a task.*
>
> Try **H**elp **S**earch or **H**elp **C**ontents How Do I to find a help screen relating to the task. If the steps described in the help screens seem too complicated to remember, select **P**rint to make a printed copy for future reference.
>
> *I want to use my old, familiar Quattro Pro for DOS command menus.*
>
> Select the Quattro Pro–DOS option in the **S**lash Key list box of the Macro pane of the Application Object Inspector dialog box (press Alt+F12 or right-click the Quattro Pro title bar).

Using Blocks

Tip
Blocks are called *ranges* in Lotus 1-2-3 and Excel.

A *block* is usually a rectangular group of cells in a notebook. In Quattro Pro, a block also can contain several groups of cells, defined by collections of rectangular blocks. That is, a single named block does not have to be rectangular, but can contain several smaller rectangular blocks. Figure 14.2, for example, shows one rectangular block in cells A1..B3; a nonrectangular block including B5..B6, B7..D9, and E7..F7; and a noncontiguous block that includes C14..D15 and E17..F18 (the blocks are shaded gray to make them easier to see).

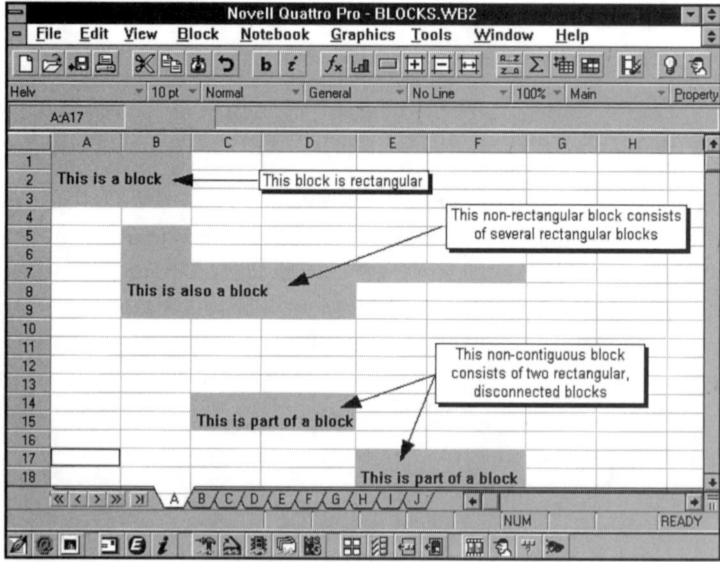

Fig. 14.2
Several different Quattro Pro blocks on one page.

Specify a block address by using cell addresses of any two diagonally opposite corners of the block. You separate the cell addresses with one or two periods and separate each rectangular block with commas. You can specify the nonrectangular block shown in figure 14.2 by typing **B5..B6, B7..D9, E7..F7**, for example. You also can specify this block in several other ways, as long as you separate each rectangular block with commas.

A block also can be *three-dimensional*, spanning two or more notebook pages. A three-dimensional block includes the same cells on each page. When you use a three-dimensional block, you must include the page letter or page name with the cell addresses.

Selecting Blocks

Many commands act on blocks. The **B**lock, **C**opy command, for example, displays a dialog box asking for a **F**rom and a **T**o block. To enter a block, you can type the address of the block, highlight the block with the keyboard or the mouse before or after you choose the command, or type the block name (if you have created a name).

Typing the Block Addresses

If you want to type a block address, type the addresses of cells diagonally opposite in a rectangular block, separating each cell with a period. If the block is nonrectangular, you must specify each rectangular block and separate each block with a comma. To specify the block A1..C4, for example, you type **A1..C4**, **A1.C4**, **A4..C1**, or **A4.C1**. Quattro Pro regards each of these addresses the same as A1..C4.

Selecting Blocks by Highlighting

The easiest method of specifying a block's cell addresses is usually highlighting the block by pointing with the keyboard or the mouse. You can highlight a block before or after you issue a command. In a formula, however, you must highlight the block after you begin typing the formula. If you select a block before you issue a command, the block remains highlighted, allowing you to use the same block with more than one command without reselecting the block.

If you use the keyboard to highlight a block, you can use the Shift+F7 keyboard shortcut as a method of anchoring a block selection. You also can anchor a block selection by pressing and holding down the Shift key while you move the cell selector. If you use the mouse to highlight a block, simply hold down the left mouse button as you drag the highlight across the block.

When you preselect a block, the address automatically appears in the text boxes of any command dialog boxes. Some dialog boxes, however, require you to specify more than one block. For example, if you use the **B**lock, **C**opy command, you must specify both a **F**rom (source) and a **T**o (destination) block. If you have selected a block before you issue the command, both the **F**rom and **T**o text boxes will show the same block—the selected block. You can press Tab and Shift+Tab or use the mouse to move the highlight between the text boxes; then enter the second block by typing its address or block name or by pointing.

Specifying a Block with a Name

You also can specify a block in a dialog box using a name you assign to the block (see "Naming Blocks," later in this chapter). You can use up to 64 characters to name a block, and can use block names in formulas, functions, commands, and macros.

Whenever Quattro Pro expects the address of a cell or a block, you specify a block name. You can enter a block name in the Go to dialog box, for example, and Quattro Pro moves the cell selector to the upper left corner of the named block.

You gain a number of advantages by using block names. First, block names are easier to remember than block addresses—especially if a block is noncontiguous. Second, typing a block name usually is easier than pointing to a block in another part of the notebook. Third, macros that use block names rather than cell addresses automatically adjust after you move a block. Finally, block names also make formulas easier to understand. The formula +QTR_1_TOTAL is easier to understand than the formula +B10.

Extending Block Selections

Extending a block selection to include a three-dimensional block or a group of blocks allows you to include more than a single two-dimensional block in a command or a block name. These extended blocks make some operations easier and faster because one command can replace a series of commands.

Selecting noncontiguous blocks by using the mouse is much easier than selecting noncontiguous blocks by using the keyboard. You can select noncontiguous blocks using the mouse before or after you choose a command, but to select noncontiguous blocks using the keyboard, you must select the block after choosing a command.

If you use the mouse to extend a block selection that includes noncontiguous blocks, you can select the blocks before or after you choose a command. Use the following procedure:

1. Press and hold down the Ctrl key.
2. Select the first rectangular block.
3. Select each additional rectangular block.
4. Release the Ctrl key.

To use the keyboard to extend a block selection that includes noncontiguous blocks, perform the following steps:

1. Choose the command in which you want to use the noncontiguous blocks.
2. Select the appropriate block text box by pressing the Tab key or, if the text box has an underlined letter, by pressing Alt plus the underlined letter.
3. Enter the block addresses by typing the addresses of rectangular blocks and separating each block with a comma. You also can point to the first cell of each rectangular block, press the period key to anchor the highlight, and use the direction keys to highlight the block. Enter a comma and continue selecting rectangular blocks until you have selected each block.

Naming Blocks

Block addresses can be difficult to remember, and it's pretty easy to type the wrong set of cell addresses when specifying a block. Quattro Pro provides a solution to this problem—*block names*. If you name blocks, you can always substitute the block name for the block's cell addresses in commands and formulas, ensuring the correct block will be affected by the command or formula. Block names also make formulas much easier to read and understand, because Quattro Pro will always substitute block names where appropriate in formulas—even if you didn't use block names when you created the formula.

Quattro Pro does not distinguish between uppercase and lowercase letters; Block_1, block_1, and BLOCK_1 are equivalent block names.

You should follow certain rules and cautions when creating block names:

- Don't use the following characters in block names:

  + – * / & > < @ #

- Although block names that start with numbers are valid, avoid starting block names with numbers because they may cause problems in formulas.

- Don't create block names that are also cell addresses, column letters, or row numbers (such as A1, AA, or 199), names of keys (such as Edit), function names (such as @AVG), or advanced macro commands (such as WRITE).

- Use descriptive block names. This will make it easier to select the correct block names when you later use them in formulas or when specifying blocks to print.

- Join parts of block names with the underscore (such as QTR_1_TOTALS) rather than spaces.

- If you share spreadsheet files with users of other spreadsheet programs (such as Microsoft Excel, Lotus 1-2-3, or even older versions of Quattro Pro), limit block names to 15 characters.

Quattro Pro provides several methods of creating block names. Each method uses the **B**lock, **N**ames command (Ctrl+F3) to first display the Block Names dialog box (see fig. 14.3). The following sections describe the block naming options available through this dialog box.

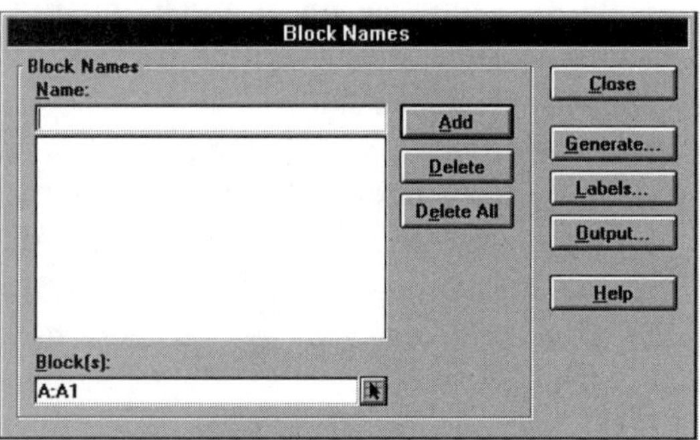

Fig. 14.3
The Block Names dialog box provides several block naming options.

Creating Block Names with Block Names Add

You can use the **B**lock, **N**ames, **A**dd command to assign a name to a cell or a block. To create a block name using this command, follow these steps:

1. Select the cell or block you want to name.
2. Choose **B**lock, **N**ames (or press Ctrl+F3). The Block Names dialog box shown in figure 14.3 appears.
3. Type the block name in the **N**ame text box.
4. Select **A**dd (or press Enter).
5. Select **C**lose.

If you want to add more than one block name, repeat steps 3 and 4 as necessary.

Creating Block Names with Block Names Generate

You also can create block names automatically using the **B**lock, **N**ames, **G**enerate command. This command can generate block names for a row, a column, or for every cell in a selected block, using labels in the block. To create block names using this command, follow these steps:

1. Select the cell or block you want to name.
2. Choose **B**lock, **N**ames (or press Ctrl+F3).
3. Select **G**enerate to display the Generate Block Names dialog box (see fig. 14.4).

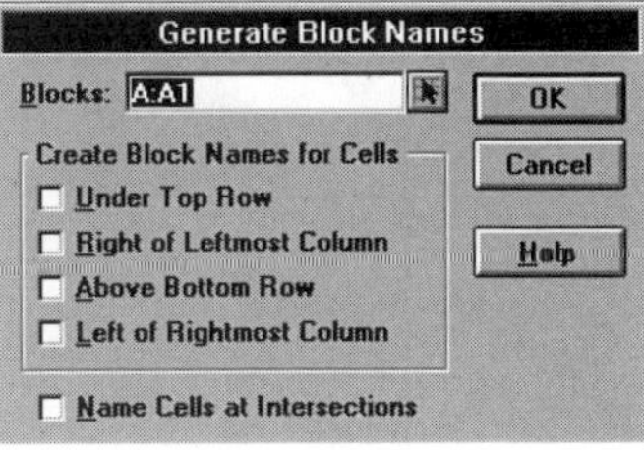

Fig. 14.4
Use the Generate Block Names dialog box to automatically create block names from row and column labels.

4. The check boxes in this dialog box determine which cells the labels identify. Choose **U**nder Top Row, **R**ight of Leftmost Column, **A**bove Bottom Row, or **L**eft of Rightmost Column.

5. To name all cells in the block using the label cells in combination, select **N**ame Cells at Intersections.

6. Select OK to return to the Block Names dialog box.

The **N**ame Cells at Intersections option creates block names by concatenating (joining) the column label, an underscore, and the row label. For example, if the column label is "Year Total" and the row label is "Software," the name generated for the intersecting cell is Year Total_Software.

Creating Block Names with Block Names Labels

You also can use the **B**lock, **N**ames, **L**abels command to create block names. With this command, you use labels already typed on a notebook page as block names for adjacent cells. To create block names using this command, follow these steps:

1. Select the cell or block you want to name.

2. Choose **B**lock, **N**ames (or press Ctrl+F3).

3. Select **L**abels to display the Create Names From Labels dialog box (see fig. 14.5).

4. The Directions choices determine which cells are named using the labels. Select the appropriate direction, **R**ight, **L**eft, **U**p, or **D**own.

5. Select OK to return to the Block Names dialog box.

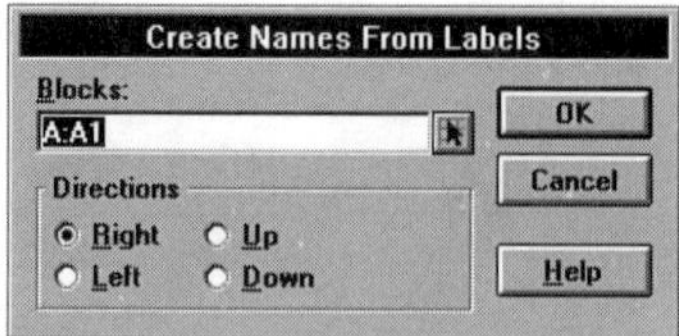

Fig. 14.5
Use the Create Names From Labels dialog box to create single-cell block names from labels.

The **B**lock, **N**ames, **L**abels command ignores blank cells in the label block as it creates single-cell blocks. If you need to create multiple-cell blocks, you must use the **B**lock, **N**ames, **A**dd command.

Listing Block Names

A table of block names serves as important notebook documentation. Quattro Pro creates a two-column table of block names and addresses using the **B**lock, **N**ames, **O**utput command. When you choose the **B**lock, **N**ames, **O**utput command, select an area with enough room for the block name table, because the table overwrites any existing data without warning. You may want to place the block name table on a separate notebook page to prevent data from being overwritten.

Troubleshooting

The block name table doesn't seem to show the correct addresses for some blocks.

If you change the definition of a block name, or add or delete block names, the block name table is not updated automatically. You must issue the **B**lock, **N**ames, **O**utput command again to update the table.

Some formulas don't show the correct results even though they appear to contain correct block names.

Make certain your block names don't contain any mathematical operators, such as a minus or plus sign. Quattro Pro may be confused if you include blocks with such symbols in your formulas.

Deleting Block Names

There's little reason to remove block names from a Quattro Pro notebook. Block names don't use much memory, and the documentation they provide can be very valuable. Still, if you want to delete block names, Quattro Pro has two commands that delete block names from the notebook. Use the **B**lock, **N**ames, **D**elete command to delete a single block name. You delete all block names at one time using the **B**lock, **N**ames, D**e**lete All command.

Copying and Moving Data

Few Quattro Pro notebooks are masterpieces when first created. Most often, it's useful to copy or move data from one place to another. You might, for example, want to duplicate the appearance of an existing report, or you may simply find it's awkward to enter data correctly in the notebook's initial layout. Whatever your reason, you'll find Quattro Pro offers several different methods of copying and moving data.

The three primary methods of moving and copying data in Quattro Pro are the **E**dit commands, which use the Windows Clipboard, the **B**lock commands, which do not use the Clipboard, and the mouse. In the following sections, you'll learn the advantages and disadvantages of each, and why each method is important to you.

It is important to understand how moving data and formulas in Quattro Pro differs from copying data and formulas. When you move data, any formulas that refer to the moved data automatically update to refer to the same data in its new location. When you copy data, formulas referring to the original data location continue to refer to the same location. When you move formulas, the formulas do not change. When you copy formulas, the formulas may or may not change, depending on the types of references the formulas contain.

Copying and Moving Using the Clipboard

The Windows Clipboard is a feature shared by most Windows applications. Data stored on the Clipboard is available to any Windows program that is able to use the data. Once you place data on the Clipboard, it remains there until new data replaces it, or until you exit from Windows. This permits you to make multiple copies of the same data without having to add the data to the Clipboard each time—as long as you don't use another command that places new data on the Clipboard.

Quattro Pro follows the Windows convention of placing the commands that use the Clipboard on the **E**dit menu. These commands include **E**dit, Cu**t**; **E**dit, **C**opy; **E**dit, **P**aste; and **E**dit, Paste Spec**i**al. You will probably use the first three of these commands most often; **E**dit, Paste Spec**i**al is more specialized. Most Windows programs have similar options on their **E**dit menus.

You'll notice that there isn't a Move command on the **E**dit menu. Such a command really isn't necessary, though, because you can accomplish this task using the other **E**dit commands.

Using Edit, Cut

Caution

The **E**dit, Cu**t** command replaces any existing Clipboard data with new data. You cannot recover the old data, so be sure to use **E**dit, **P**aste to save the data if you will need it in the future.

The **E**dit, Cu**t** command removes—or *cuts*—data from the notebook and places the data on the Clipboard. Any existing Clipboard data is lost unless it has been saved elsewhere. Once you place data on the Clipboard, you can make as many copies of the data as you want.

You can place any selectable object on the Clipboard. If you select a single cell, the **E**dit, Cu**t** command removes the data from the selected cell and places the data on the Clipboard. If you select a block of cells, the entire block is removed from the notebook and placed on the Clipboard. You also can use **E**dit, Cu**t** to place other types of objects, such as graphs or drawn objects, on the Clipboard. Any object placed on the Clipboard using Quattro Pro's **E**dit, Cu**t** command can later be returned to the notebook using **E**dit, **P**aste; but other Windows applications may not be able to accept all types of Quattro Pro objects, such as macro buttons.

To use **E**dit, Cu**t**, first select the object you want to cut, and then select **E**dit, Cu**t** (Ctrl+X) or click the Cut button on the Toolbar. The selected object will disappear from the Quattro Pro notebook. If you cut an object in error, immediately select **E**dit, **U**ndo before selecting any other commands.

Edit, Cu**t** places any numeric formatting, alignment, or other object properties on the Clipboard along with the data. If you've used the Object Inspectors to modify any of the properties for the selected object, those properties will be removed from the notebook along with the object, and placed on the Clipboard for possible use later.

Using Edit, Copy

The **E**dit, **C**opy command works much like the **E**dit, Cu**t** command, but there is one important difference between these two commands. When you use **E**dit, **C**opy, the selected object remains in your Quattro Pro notebook, and an exact duplicate is created on the Clipboard. This duplicate shares all of the original object's properties, including any numeric formatting, alignment, and so on. Once the duplicate is placed on the Clipboard, however, the two objects (the original and the duplicate) are totally independent of each other. That is, any changes you make to the original object in your notebook are not reflected in the duplicate on the Clipboard. If you want the duplicate to match the changed original, use **E**dit, **C**opy to create an updated duplicate.

It's easy to become confused by the title of the **E**dit, **C**opy command. Although you might expect this command to make a copy of an object, the copy it produces isn't visible to you. The copy of the selected object only exists on the Windows Clipboard, ready to be pasted into another location in your Quattro Pro notebook, or into another document created in another Windows application.

To use **E**dit, **C**opy, first select the object you want to copy, and then select **E**dit, **C**opy (Ctrl+C) or click the Copy button on the Toolbar. You won't see any change in the notebook, but the Clipboard will now contain an exact duplicate of the selected object.

Note

Objects placed on the Windows Clipboard are stored in your computer's memory until you use **E**dit, Cu**t** or **E**dit, **C**opy to replace them with another object, or until you exit from Windows. Very large objects, such as bitmaps or sound files, can use a large portion of your system's memory, making your system operate at an unusually slow pace. If you have copied a very large object to the Clipboard, but no longer need to store the object there, copy a single notebook cell to the Clipboard to free the memory for other uses.

Using Edit, Paste

The **E**dit, **P**aste command places a copy of data contained on the Clipboard into your Quattro Pro notebook. The object on the Clipboard is unaffected by this command, and can be pasted into more than one location using additional **E**dit, **P**aste commands.

Quattro Pro notebooks can contain most types of objects that can be placed on the Clipboard. Quattro Pro fully supports OLE 2.0 (Object Linking and Embedding), including *in-place editing*. If you place an object on the Clipboard using an application that supports OLE 2.0, the object can be edited directly in another OLE 2.0 compliant application. Documents created using objects from more than one Windows application are called *compound documents*.

To use the **E**dit, **P**aste command, first use **E**dit, **C**opy or **E**dit, Cu**t** to place the object on the Clipboard. Next, position the cell selector at the location where you want to place a copy of the data, and select **E**dit, **P**aste (Ctrl+V) or click the Paste button on the Toolbar.

The following guidelines enable you to determine the number and type of copies that will be created:

- If the data moved to the Clipboard with the **E**dit, **C**opy or **E**dit, Cu**t** command was from a single cell, one copy of the data will be added to each highlighted cell after you choose **E**dit, **P**aste.

- If the data moved to the Clipboard with the **E**dit, **C**opy or **E**dit, Cu**t** command was from several rows in a single column, one copy of the data will be added to each highlighted column after you choose **E**dit, **P**aste.
- If the data moved to the Clipboard with the **E**dit, **C**opy or **E**dit, Cu**t** command was from several columns in a single row, one copy of the data will be added to each highlighted row after you choose **E**dit, **P**aste.
- If the data moved to the Clipboard with the **E**dit, **C**opy or **E**dit, Cu**t** command was from several rows and several columns, one copy of the data will be added to the spreadsheet page starting at the highlighted cell after you choose **E**dit, **P**aste.

Three-dimensional data always creates a three-dimensional copy. If the source or destination data block includes more than one page, the same rules that apply to rows and columns also apply to the page dimension.

If you want additional copies of the same data, just reposition the cell selector and select **E**dit, **P**aste. Don't use any additional **E**dit, Cu**t** or **E**dit, **C**opy commands if you want additional copies of the same data, because the Clipboard holds only the most recent **E**dit, Cu**t** or **E**dit, **C**opy contents.

If you paste data to a block that already contains data, Quattro Pro replaces the existing data with the new data. Use care when pasting data to avoid pasting data into cells that contain formulas or other data you don't want to lose.

Copying and Moving Using Block Commands

Quattro Pro includes a second set of commands you can use to copy or move data from one place in the notebook to another. **B**lock, **M**ove and **B**lock, **C**opy move and copy data directly within the notebook without using the Clipboard.

Because these commands don't use the Clipboard, any objects you've already placed on the Clipboard aren't affected by the **B**lock, **M**ove and **B**lock, **C**opy commands. You can still use **E**dit, **P**aste to make copies of the unchanged Clipboard contents even after you use **B**lock, **M**ove or **B**lock, **C**opy. This characteristic makes **B**lock, **M**ove and **B**lock, **C**opy good complements to the **E**dit commands.

Using Block, Move

When you use the **B**lock, **M**ove command, the moved data includes the same formulas and values, as well as the same alignment, fonts, and numeric formats. Column widths and row heights do not move, however. The source cells still exist after the move, but they are empty.

To move data and formulas with the **B**lock, **M**ove command, follow these steps:

1. Select the cell or block you want to move.
2. Choose the **B**lock, **M**ove command. The Block Move dialog box shown in figure 14.6 appears.
3. Press Tab or use the mouse to move the highlight to the **T**o text box. Use the direction keys or the mouse to select the destination for the data, or type the destination address in the text box.
4. Press Enter or click OK to confirm the dialog box and move the data.

To specify the **F**rom and **T**o blocks, type the cell addresses, highlight the blocks, or enter block names. After you preselect a block, as you just did in step 1, the address appears in both the **F**rom and **T**o text boxes. You can use the preselected block as the source or destination of the move.

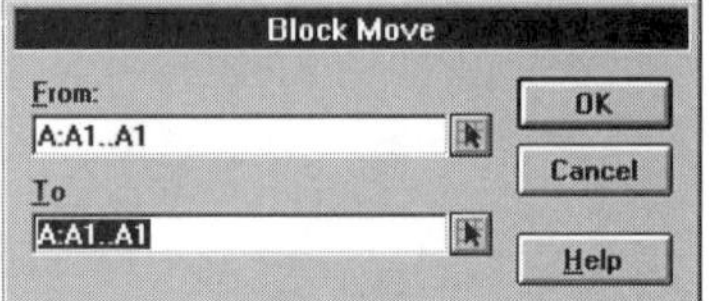

Fig. 14.6 Use the Block Move dialog box to specify the source and destination of data you want to move.

Using Block, Copy

When you copy data, the copy contains the same labels, values, formatting, and style properties as the original data. The data in the original location remains unchanged.

You can copy a single cell or a block to another part of the same notebook page, to another notebook page, or to another open notebook. You can make a single copy or multiple copies at the same time. To copy data with the **B**lock, **C**opy command, follow these steps:

1. Highlight the cell or block you want to copy. If you preselect a block, it appears in both the **F**rom and **T**o text boxes.

2. Choose the **B**lock, **C**opy command. The Block Copy dialog box shown in figure 14.7 appears.

3. Press Tab to highlight the **T**o text box.

4. Type the destination address, or use the direction keys or the mouse to highlight the destination block.

5. Choose OK to confirm the dialog box and copy the block.

Quattro Pro copies the data, overwriting existing data in the destination block.

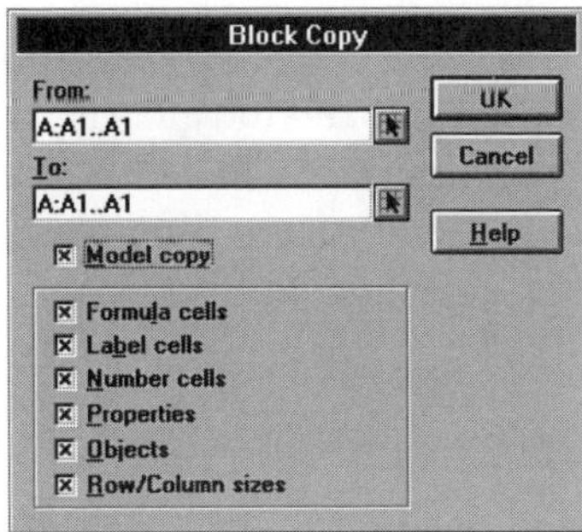

Fig. 14.7
Use the Block Copy dialog box to specify the source and destination of data you want to copy.

You can use the **M**odel copy option to make a copy that uses the **F**rom block as a model for the **T**o block. If you select **M**odel copy, formula references—even absolute references—adjust to fit the **T**o block (see the section "Copying Formulas" later in this chapter for more information on formula references). In addition, if you select **M**odel copy, you can specify whether to copy For**mu**la cells, La**b**el cells, **N**umber cells, **P**roperties, **O**bjects, or **R**ow/Column sizes.

Copying and Moving Using the Mouse

Quattro Pro offers yet another method of moving or copying data—one that takes advantage of the graphical nature of the Windows environment. This method, called *drag-and-drop*, uses the mouse and is by far the easiest method of moving data short distances within a Quattro Pro notebook.

To move data using the drag-and-drop method, perform the following steps:

1. Select the block of data you want to move. The block can be any size, including a single cell.

2. Point at the selected block and hold down the left mouse button until the mouse pointer changes to a hand.

3. Move the mouse pointer to the upper left corner of the destination block. As you move the mouse pointer, Quattro Pro displays an outline the size of the selected block.

4. Release the mouse button to drop the block of data in the new location.

To copy—rather than move—the selected block of data, hold down the Ctrl key when you point to the block in step 2.

If the mouse pointer changes to a hand too quickly when you are selecting a block, adjust the Application General Cell **D**rag and Drop Delay Time property. Right-click the Quattro Pro title bar or press Alt+F12 to display the Application Object Inspector dialog box. Select the General pane (see fig. 14.8). The default delay time is 500 ms—one-half second. Try a slightly higher setting, such as 750 ms.

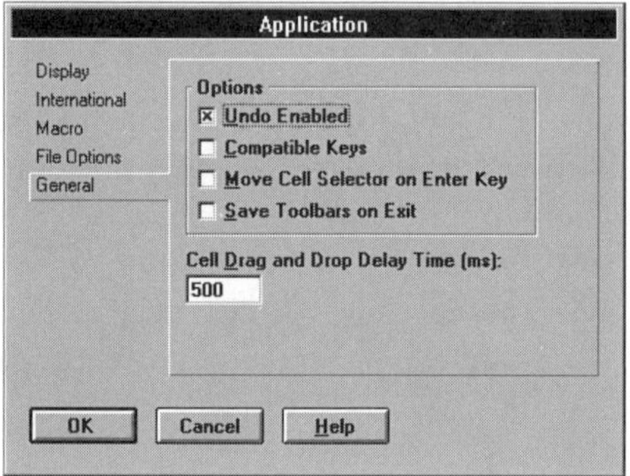

Fig. 14.8
Select a longer delay time in the Application Object Inspector dialog box to provide more time to select blocks.

Copying Formulas

Copying formulas in Quattro Pro is more complex than copying data because of the way the program stores addresses in formulas. Addresses may be *relative*, referring to column, row, and page offsets from the formula cell; *absolute*, always referring to a specific cell; or *mixed*, a combination of relative and absolute.

If you enter the formula **+B2** in cell C5, Quattro Pro does not store the formula quite the way you may expect. The formula tells Quattro Pro to add the value of the cell one column to the left and three rows above C5. When you copy this formula from C5 to D6, Quattro Pro uses the same relative formula but displays the formula as +C3. This method of storing cell references is called *relative addressing*. After you copy a formula that uses relative addressing, Quattro Pro automatically adjusts the new formula so its cell references are in the same relative location as they were in the original location.

Sometimes you do not want a formula to address new locations after you copy the formula. You may, for example, create a formula that refers to data in a single cell, such as an interest rate or a growth factor percentage. Formulas that always refer to the same cell address, regardless of where you copy the formula, use *absolute addressing*.

To specify an absolute address, type a dollar sign ($) before each part of the address you want to remain absolutely the same. The formula +$B:$C$10, for example, always refers to cell C10 on notebook page B regardless of where you copy the formula.

You also can create formulas that use *mixed addressing*, in which some elements of the cell addresses are absolute and other elements are relative. You can create a formula, for example, that always refers to the same row but adjusts its column reference as you copy the formula to another column. To create a mixed address, use a dollar sign to indicate the absolute address portions of the formula, leaving off the dollar sign for relative addresses. The formula +$B1, for example, always refers to column B on the current notebook page, but adjusts the row reference relative to the current row.

Filling Blocks

Creating Quattro Pro notebooks can seem like quite a task, especially if the model you want to build requires you to enter a series of data in a large number of consecutive cells. For example, a notebook based on an incrementing time series, such as a loan amortization schedule, may require you to include dates in monthly intervals. A notebook tracking results from each of your company's locations may require you to enter the location names, possibly in several different places. Entering the same data quite a number of times seems like a lot of work, doesn't it? Wouldn't it be nice if you could get someone else to do that for you?

Fortunately, there is one thing computers are very good at—doing repetitive work. Quattro Pro takes this concept a step further by providing easy-to-use methods of filling blocks automatically with either a number series, or groups of related labels. In the following sections, you'll learn how to use both types of block filling options.

Using Block, Fill

You use the **B**lock, **F**ill command to fill a block with numeric values. This command offers a very large range of options, suitable for almost any instance needing an incrementing number series, such as a series of interest rates or budget percentages.

To use the **B**lock, **F**ill command, follow these steps:

1. Highlight the block you want to fill.

2. Choose **B**lock, **F**ill. The Block Fill dialog box appears (see fig. 14.9).

3. Enter the St**a**rt, St**e**p (or increment), and **S**top values in the appropriate text boxes.

4. If the block spans multiple rows and multiple columns, choose **C**olumn to begin filling the block in the first column, then the second column, and so on; choose **R**ow to fill the first row, then the second row, and so on.

5. In the Series field, choose the type of fill. Table 14.1 summarizes the fill options.

6. Choose OK to confirm the dialog box and fill the block.

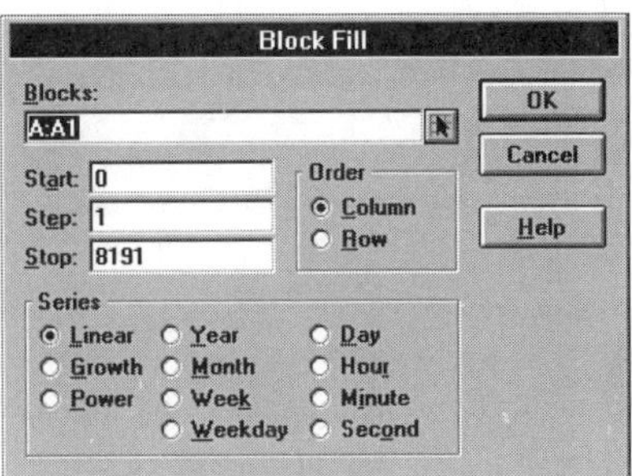

Fig. 14.9
Use the Block Fill dialog box to specify how to fill a block.

Table 14.1 Block Fill Types

Series	Type of Fill
Linear	Step value is added to start value.
Growth	Step value is used as a multiplier.
Power	Step value is used as an exponent.
Year	Step value is in years and is added to start value.
Month	Step value is in months and is added to start value.
Week	Step value is in weeks and is added to start value.
Weekday	Step value is in days with weekend days skipped and is added to start value.
Day	Step value is in days and is added to start value.
Hour	Step value is in hours and is added to start value.
Minute	Step value is in minutes and is added to start value.
Second	Step value is in seconds and is added to start value.

By default, Quattro Pro uses 0 for the start number, 1 for the step (or increment), and 8191 as the stop number. Be sure to adjust these values to fit your needs. When filling a block, Quattro Pro stops entering additional values when the specified block is filled or the stop number is reached. If you specify a start value larger than the stop value, no values enter the block.

If you want to fill a block with a sequence of dates, it's important to understand how Quattro Pro enters date values. Quattro Pro uses *date serial numbers* to determine dates. Date serial numbers increment by one for each day, starting with 1 for December 31, 1899.

Note

For compatibility with Lotus 1-2-3 and Microsoft Excel, Quattro Pro uses the value 61 for March 1, 1900, even though the year 1900 was not a leap year. Dates prior to March 1, 1900, are incorrect in Lotus 1-2-3 and Microsoft Excel. Dates prior to January 1, 1900, and dates after December 31, 2099, are not allowed in Lotus 1-2-3. Dates prior to January 1, 1900, and dates after December 31, 2078, are not allowed in Excel. Quattro Pro correctly determines dates in the entire range of January 1, 1600, through December 31, 3199, using negative date serial numbers for dates prior to December 30, 1899.

Because date serial numbers increment by one each day, the default **S**top value is too small for most useful dates. For example, you cannot use **B**lock, **F**ill to enter a date such as June 26, 1995, which has a serial number of 34876, unless you remember to increase the stop value to a number at least as high as the serial number of the ending date you want.

Using SpeedFill

Tip
You also can use SpeedFill to name a series of pages. Right-click an empty cell, select SpeedFill, select a **S**eries Name, and choose **T**abs.

Quattro Pro has another option for filling blocks—*SpeedFill*. Unlike **B**lock, **F**ill, SpeedFill can fill a selected block with a set of labels, such as month names or store locations. SpeedFill also differs from the **B**lock, **F**ill command in another important way—you must activate SpeedFill using the mouse, because there is no SpeedFill menu command.

The SpeedFill option functions in two different ways, depending on whether the block you select already has sample values. If the block has sample values, those values are used as a *seed value*, or pattern for filling the block. If the block is empty, SpeedFill presents a list of predefined fill series for selection.

Filling a Block Using Sample Values

To fill a block based on sample values you enter in the block (such as Jan, Feb, Mar, or Qtr 1, Qtr 2, Qtr 3), follow these steps:

1. First, enter some sample values in the top left corner of the block. If the first sample value is enough to define the series, you only have to enter one value. If you want to use an increment other than 1, you must enter at least two sample values.

2. Select the block you want to fill.

3. Click the SpeedFill button.

Filling a Block Using a SpeedFill Series

You also can use a predefined series to fill a block. To fill a block based on a predefined series, follow these steps:

1. Select the block you want to fill. The block should not contain any sample values.
2. Click the SpeedFill button to display the SpeedFill dialog box (see fig. 14.10).
3. Select the series you want in the **S**eries Name list box.
4. If necessary, select Co**l**umns, **R**ows, or **T**abs.
5. Press Enter or click OK.

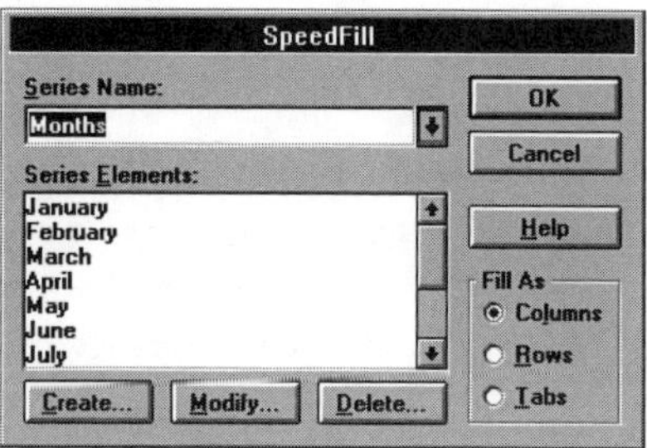

Fig. 14.10
Select customized fill series in the SpeedFill dialog box.

Troubleshooting

The Tabs option doesn't appear in the SpeedFill dialog box, preventing use of SpeedFill to name page tabs.

The **T**abs option will only appear if an empty, single-cell block is selected when you click the SpeedFill button. The Co**l**umns and **R**ows options only appear if an empty, single-cell block, or an empty, multiple-row and multiple-column block is selected. If the selected block consists of multiple cells in a single row or a single column, none of these options are available.

The SpeedFill dialog box does not appear when I click the SpeedFill button.

Make certain the upper left cell of the selected block is empty, otherwise Quattro Pro uses the value in that cell to determine how to fill the block.

Creating a Custom SpeedFill Series

Quattro Pro includes several predefined SpeedFill series for entering months, quarters, and days, but this limited set of options is really only a sampling of what you can do with SpeedFill. This tool can really make the task of creating a Quattro Pro notebook much easier by automatically entering any series of labels you want.

Imagine, for example, that you work for a company with twenty stores, and that you're often asked to create new analyses of sales data, advertising costs, or any other the other factors that affect your business' bottom line. Each time you create a new notebook, you have to enter each of the store's names, the sales representative's names, or even the region names associated with store groupings. Sounds like quite a job, doesn't it? Fortunately, by creating a custom SpeedFill series, you can do the job once, and except for occasional modifications, simply use SpeedFill to automatically enter the same series into any new notebooks.

Creating a custom SpeedFill series is pretty easy. You can enter the series as a set of labels in a dialog box, or you can even use a series of labels you've already entered in a notebook block. Modifying or deleting an existing series is just as easy. To create, modify, or delete a custom series, follow these steps:

1. Select **N**otebook, Define Se**r**ies to display the Define Series dialog box (see fig. 14.11).

2. Select the **C**reate, **M**odify, or **D**elete button to display the Create Series, Modify Series, or Delete Series dialog box. Figure 14.12 shows the Create Series dialog box.

3. Use the options in the Create Series, Modify Series, or Delete Series dialog boxes to customize the fill series to suit your needs. For example, to create a custom series that automatically fills in the locations of your company's stores, enter each location in the **V**alue text box and then select **A**dd. Continue until you have completed the series. Be sure to use a descriptive Series **N**ame.

4. Select OK to confirm the dialog box.

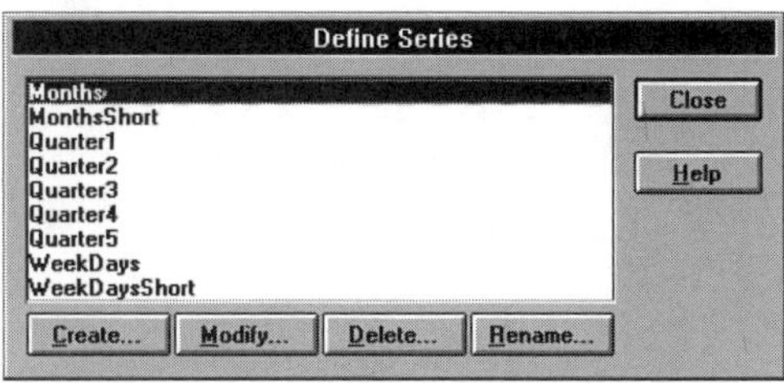

Fig. 14.11
Select a fill series in the Define Series dialog box.

Fig. 14.12
Create a new fill series in the Create Series dialog box.

Note

If the cell selector is highlighting an empty block, you can also access the Create Series, Modify Series, or Delete Series dialog boxes using the **C**reate, **M**odify, or **D**elete buttons in the SpeedFill dialog box. If you use this method to access the Create Series, Modify Series, or Delete Series dialog boxes, you can immediately use the new or modified series when you return to the SpeedFill dialog box following step 4.

To use an existing series of labels, select **E**xtract in step 3 and then specify the notebook block containing the labels you want to save as a custom SpeedFill series. For example, if you already have the set of store names in cells A1..A20, select **N**otebook, Define Se**r**ies, **C**reate, **E**xtract and specify **A1..A20** as the block to use. Complete steps 3 and 4.

Use custom SpeedFill series to make repetitive notebooks entries, even if the fill series is not an incrementing series. When you create a custom SpeedFill series, it will then be available for use in all of your Quattro Pro notebooks. You don't have to save the custom SpeedFill series—it is automatically saved for you.

Using Functions

As you learned in chapter 13, the real power of a Quattro Pro notebook is its ability to perform calculations. You can create many different types of formulas, and perform many different types of calculations quickly and easily in Quattro Pro. Using the built-in functions can make your formulas even more powerful, permitting you to perform calculations far too complex to build using simple arithmetic operators.

Understanding Functions

When electronic spreadsheets were first introduced in the late 1970s, the programs included a few limited, built-in functions. The calculations you could perform using these functions were fairly simple, but they provided a glimpse of what might be possible. When Lotus 1-2-3 made spreadsheets a standard business tool in the early 1980s, the program offered nearly 100 different functions covering a wide range of calculations. Still, there were gaps in what the built-in functions offered, and PC users with specialized needs often had to resort to complex contortions, or had to turn to third-party developers to solve demanding equations.

Quattro Pro sets a new standard in spreadsheets by offering over 370 built-in functions, covering the bases with specialized functions for many unique types of calculations. Some of these functions perform sophisticated financial calculations, while others perform engineering calculations, perform many different statistical analyses, or analyze database records. The following sections briefly summarize the function categories included in Quattro Pro.

Understanding Database Functions

You use database functions to perform statistical calculations and queries on a database. Each database function has an equivalent statistical function. Database functions differ from statistical functions in a very important way—database functions calculate values that meet criteria you specify, while statistical functions calculate all values in a block.

For example, @DAVG finds the average value in a field in a database, but only for records that meet specified criteria. @AVG finds the average value of all cells in a block.

Understanding Date and Time Functions

You use the date and time functions to perform date and time arithmetic. These functions enable you to easily calculate differences between dates or times, sort by dates or times, and compare a range of dates or times. Date and time arithmetic uses date/time serial numbers.

For example, to convert a date into a date/time serial number, you can use the @DATE function to convert a date given as a year, month, and day into a date/time serial number. You can then use this serial number in additional calculations. To find the number of business days between two dates, you can use the @BDAYS function.

Understanding Engineering Functions

You use the engineering functions to perform calculations for solving complex engineering problems; perform binary, octal, decimal, and hexadecimal number manipulations; work with imaginary numbers; convert between numbering systems; and test results. The engineering functions return modified Bessel functions; join, compare, and shift values at the bit level; convert or modify a complex number (a number whose square is a negative real number); and return error functions or test the relationship of two numeric values.

For example, you use the @BASE function to convert a decimal number to another numbering system. You can use the @CONVERT function to convert between different systems of measurement, such as from miles to kilometers.

Understanding Financial Functions

You use the financial functions to discount cash flow, calculate depreciation, and analyze the return on an investment. These functions greatly ease the burden of complex financial and accounting calculations. They also provide tools allowing the average user to perform less complex, everyday financial computations.

For example, you can use the @AMPMTI function to calculate the interest portion of the *n*th periodic payment of an amortized loan. You can use the @PRICEDISC function to calculate the price per $100 face value of a security that pays periodic interest.

Understanding Logical Functions

You use the logical functions to add standard true/false logic to the spreadsheet. The logical functions evaluate Boolean expressions, which are either true (returning a value of 1) or false (returning a value of 0). These functions can help to prevent errors that may occur if a cell used in a formula contains the wrong data, to test for the values ERR (error) or NA (not available), or to determine whether a specified file exists. These functions are important for decision making when conditions elsewhere in the spreadsheet lead to different answers in the function results. Logical functions also control the operations of advanced macro programs.

For example, you can use the @IF function to select between different results based upon evaluation of an expression, such as including a value only if it is positive.

Understanding Mathematical Functions

You use the mathematical functions, which include transcendental (logarithmic) and trigonometric operations, to perform a variety of standard arithmetic operations, such as adding and rounding values or calculating square roots.

For example, you can use the @CEILING function to round a number up to the nearest integer, @RANDBETWEEN to generate a random number between two values, and @LN to calculate the natural logarithm of a number.

Understanding Miscellaneous Functions

You use the miscellaneous functions to determine information about notebooks and cell attributes, current command settings, system memory, object properties, and Quattro Pro's version number. You also use the miscellaneous functions to perform table lookups.

For example, you can use @CELL to determine whether a given cell is blank, contains a label, or contains a numeric value. You can determine the value contained in a given cell in a block using @INDEX. A single @ARRAY function can perform a series of calculations, producing many different results from a single formula.

Understanding Statistical Functions

You use the statistical functions to perform all standard statistical calculations on your notebook data, such as aggregation, counting, and analysis operations on a group of values. The statistical functions are separated into two subcategories, descriptive and inferential.

For example, you can use the @AVG function to determine the average of all numeric values in a list, and @COUNT to determine the number of nonblank cells in the list. You can use @CONFIDENCE to compute the confidence interval around the mean for a given sample size, using the normal distribution function.

Understanding String Functions

You use the string functions to manipulate text. You can use string functions to repeat text characters, convert letters in a string to upper- or lowercase, change strings to numbers, and change numbers to strings. You also can use string functions to locate, extract, or replace characters. String functions can be important also when you need to convert data for use by other programs. They are invaluable when you need to read or write directly to ASCII text files.

@PROPER, for example, converts to uppercase the first letter of each word in a string and converts the rest to lowercase. @REPLACE changes specified characters in a string to different characters. @STRING changes a numeric value into a string, making it possible to use the value in a string formula.

Using the Formula Composer

If these short descriptions of Quattro Pro's function categories have whetted your interest in using functions, you're probably wondering how you can ever build your own function formulas, especially with over 370 functions to select from. After all, a comprehensive description of each function, especially one with examples, would fill a complete book all by itself. How can you possibly get started, and how can you use the functions effectively in your formulas?

One answer to learning and using Quattro Pro's many functions is to turn to the new *Formula Composer*—a calculator-like tool that helps you include functions in your formulas. Using this tool, you build formulas one step at a time, adding functions and supplying arguments as necessary. As you build a formula, you can even see an outline of the formula, so you can make certain you're creating exactly what you need to solve a problem.

To use the Formula Composer, select **T**ools, **F**ormula Composer (Ctrl+F2) or click the Formula Composer button on the Toolbar. This displays the Formula Expert dialog box (see fig. 14.13). You use this dialog box to build your formula with the Formula Composer.

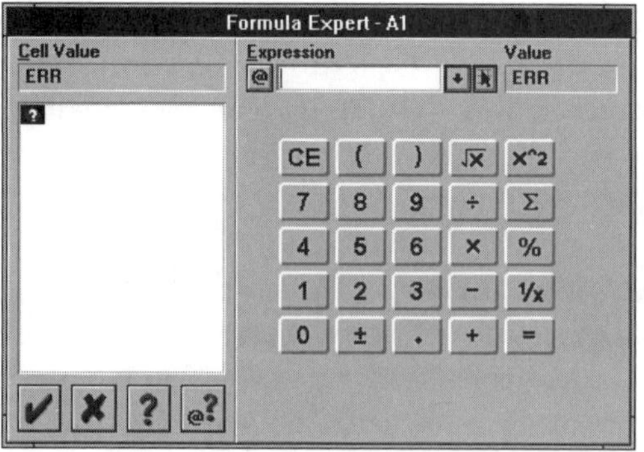

Fig. 14.13 Use the Formula Expert dialog box to enter and edit formulas.

The Formula Composer functions like a very sophisticated scientific calculator, but has capabilities far beyond any calculator you can buy. If you want to use one of the Quattro Pro built-in functions, simply click the @ button in the right-side pane of the Formula Expert dialog box. Select the function you want to use, and the Formula Composer adds it to the formula. When you select a function, the right-side pane of the Formula Expert dialog box changes from a calculator to the function pane, and describes the selected function as well as any arguments.

For example, suppose you want to enter a formula in cell A1 that calculates the number of business days between June 26, 1995 and December 25, 1995. To make your formula flexible, allowing you to use the same formula to determine the number of business days between any other two dates, you place the two dates in cells A2 and A3. This enables you to replace the dates in these two cells and instantly calculate new formula results. To begin building your formula, follow these steps:

1. Select **T**ools, **F**ormula Composer (Ctrl+F2) or click the Formula Composer button on the Toolbar.

2. Click the @ button in the right-side pane of the Formula Expert dialog box.

3. In the Functions dialog box, select Date in the Function **C**ategory list box, and then BDAYS in the **F**unction list box. As you select a function, the description pane at the bottom of the dialog box describes the selected function (see fig. 14.14).

4. Press Enter or click OK to return to the Formula Expert dialog box. The dialog box changes to display the function pane, and describes the selected function as well as its arguments (see fig. 14.15).

5. Fill in each argument by selecting the argument's text box, and then pointing to the notebook cell containing the argument. When you have entered the minimum required set of arguments, the dialog box displays the results of the calculation (see fig. 14.16). In this case, **H**olidays is an optional argument, and does not require an entry.

6. Click the Confirm button (the checkmark) to return to the notebook and enter the formula in the cell.

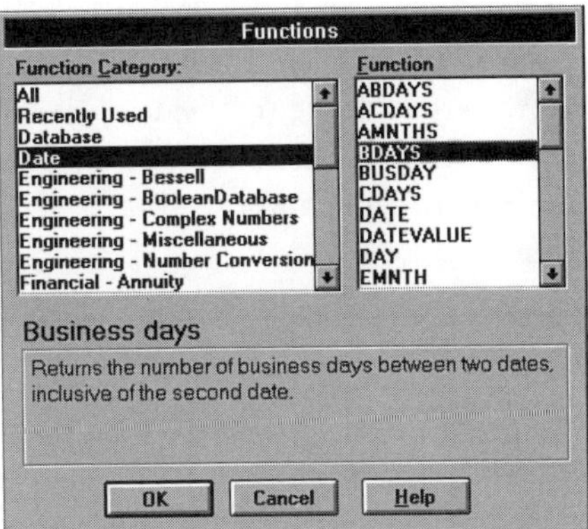

Fig. 14.14
Select a function in the Functions dialog box.

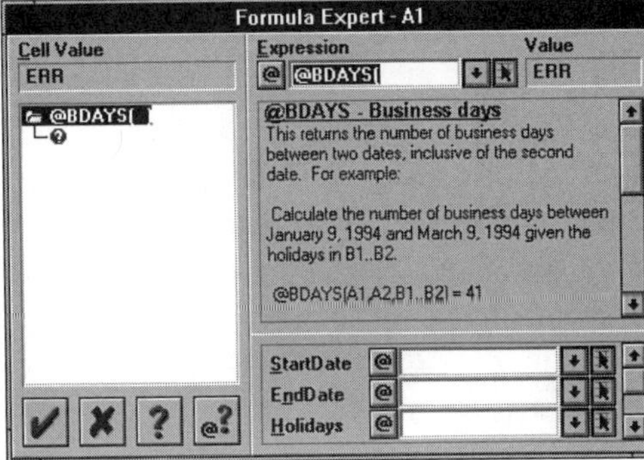

Fig. 14.15
After you select a function, the Formula Expert dialog box displays the function pane.

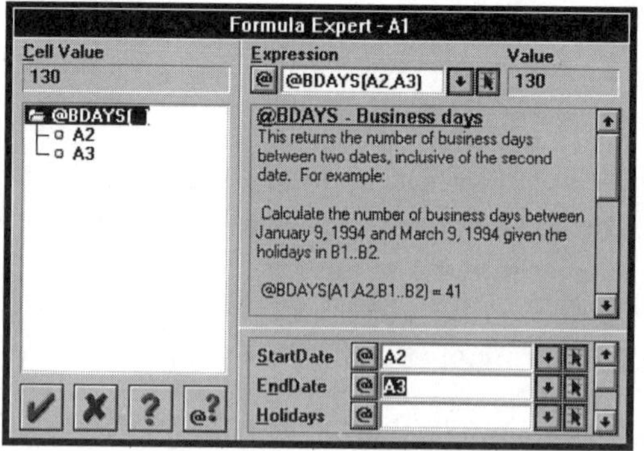

Fig. 14.16
After you specify all required arguments, the Formula Expert dialog box displays the result.

To enter any of the required or optional arguments in step 5, you can point to the cell containing the argument, select from the block names in the notebook by clicking the down-arrow at the right side of the argument's text box, or you can type an address or block name. If you want to use another function to specify the value for an argument, click the @ button at the left side of the argument's text box.

Troubleshooting

It's often difficult to remember which cells hold each of the function arguments.

Enter labels in the notebook to identify the arguments, and then use the **B**lock, **N**ames, **L**abels command to name the cells. You can then use the block names instead of cell addresses in your formulas, making the formulas much easier to understand.

Functions really unlock the power of Quattro Pro. The brief descriptions provided in these sections on using functions have only touched the surface of how powerful Quattro Pro's set of built-in functions really are. For more detailed information on using functions, you can use the Quattro Pro **H**elp, **C**ontents @Functions command. You may also want to consider Using Quattro Pro 6 for Windows, Special Edition, for an in-depth look at Quattro Pro.

From Here...

In this chapter, you learned how to create your own Quattro Pro spreadsheets, use named blocks, copy and move data, and fill blocks. You also learned a little about the types of functions that are built into Quattro Pro, making it possible for you to perform many different types of analysis of your data. For more information on using Quattro Pro notebooks, see the following chapters:

- Chapter 15, "Changing the Display and Appearance of Data," shows you how to make your Quattro Pro notebooks look as good as they should.
- Chapter 16, "Analyzing Data," provides a look at some additional analysis tools that are a part of Quattro Pro.

Chapter 15

Changing the Display and Appearance of Data

by Brian Underdahl

Quattro Pro provides you with a *WYSIWYG*—what you see is what you get—view of your data. If you change the on-screen appearance of a Quattro Pro notebook, those changes are also reflected in any printed reports you produce. In this chapter, you learn to use the commands that control the appearance of data—both on-screen and in printed reports.

Producing clearly understandable information from raw data can be as important as calculating correct answers. To make data understandable, you can control the *format*, *style*, and *alignment* of data. These commands change only the way data appears, not the value of the data when you customize its format.

This chapter shows you how to perform the following tasks:

- Adjust the display using column width and row height adjustments
- Remove columns, rows, or pages from the notebook
- Lock data on-screen
- Apply the available formats to change the appearance of data
- Enhance the appearance of data using fonts, label alignment options, lines, colors, and shading

Changing the Display

The Quattro Pro display is extremely flexible, enabling you to select exactly how the screen appears. For example, you can zoom in to enlarge the on-screen appearance of a notebook on small screens. You can also control whether screen elements such as the Toolbar, the Property band, or the Status line are displayed. These options exist for your convenience, but they don't really have much effect on the display of data or reports.

Some other options, such as the width of each column or the ability to lock rows or columns on-screen as you scroll, directly affect your notebooks. Column widths, for example, determine whether numbers are displayed properly. Locked titles enable you to scroll the display to different locations in the notebook without losing track of which data should be entered in the individual cells. These options, which most directly affect the use of your Quattro Pro notebooks, are covered in the following sections.

Adjusting Column Widths and Row Heights

When you start a new notebook, all the columns on each spreadsheet page are set to the default column width of approximately nine characters. All the row heights are set to a default height of twelve points (one-sixth of an inch).

Note

Column widths are stated in characters, but are only valid for non-proportional (or *fixed-pitch*) fonts. Most Windows fonts are *proportional* fonts, allowing each character to have a different width, which is based on the actual space necessary to display a character. For example, the letter *m* requires more space than the letter *i*. In a proportional font, several *i*'s will fit in the space required for a single *m*.

If columns are too narrow to display numeric data, asterisks appear rather than the numbers. If columns are too narrow for the length of labels and the cell to the right contains data, the labels are truncated. If columns are too wide, you may not see all the columns necessary to view the complete data, and you may not be able to print reports on the number of pages you want.

Quattro Pro automatically adjusts row heights to fit different fonts and point sizes, vertical orientation, and word wrap; but you can override the default to create special effects or to add emphasis. You can also adjust row heights in Quattro Pro to make notebook entries easier to understand and more attractive.

Figure 15.1 shows why you must sometimes adjust column widths or row heights. Cells A1 and B4 contain the same number, 1234567890. Both cells are formatted to display the number using the comma numeric format with two decimals. Because column A is set to the default width, asterisks appear in place of the number in cell A1. The width of column B was adjusted to correctly display the number.

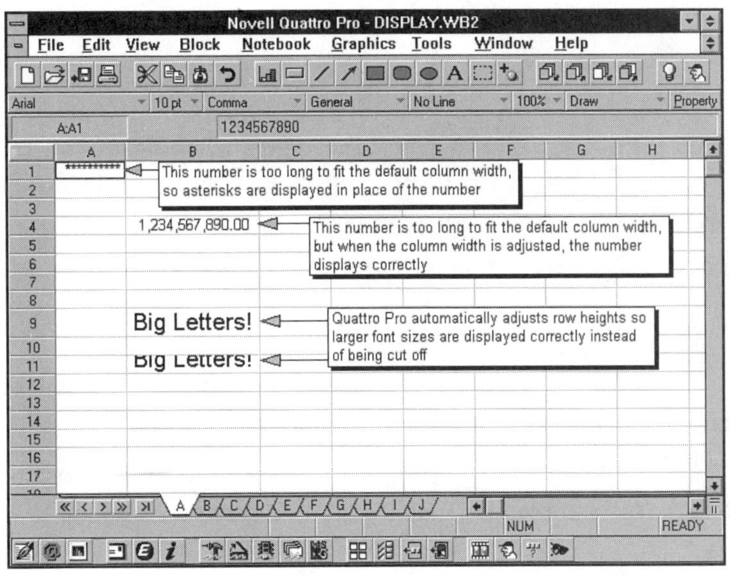

Fig. 15.1
Sometimes you must adjust column widths or row heights.

Even though Quattro Pro automatically adjusts row heights to fit different fonts and point sizes, as shown in row nine of figure 15.1, you can make manual adjustments, too. In the figure, the height of row eleven was adjusted to show how Quattro Pro cuts off the tops of characters if a row is too short.

Setting Column Widths

Whether a number fits in a cell depends on the column width, numeric format, font type, and font size. If a number appears as a series of asterisks, you need to change the column width, numeric format, font type, font size, or some combination of these factors.

Tip
Column widths you set manually do not change if you later change the default column width for the page.

You can change the width of a single column or a group of columns. When you are adjusting the column width, Quattro Pro displays a dashed line to indicate the position of the new column border. If you move the right column border to the left of the left border, you hide the column. Hidden columns can still be used in formulas, but they do not appear on-screen or in printed reports.

There are several methods you can use to set column widths. You can drag a column width using the mouse, use the Active Block Object Inspector, or use the Fit button. Each method can be useful, depending on your needs.

To change column widths by dragging the mouse, follow these steps:

1. If you want to adjust more than one column at a time, highlight the columns you want to adjust by pointing to the column letter in the notebook frame and clicking the left mouse button (drag the mouse pointer to select adjacent columns). If the columns are not adjacent, hold down the Ctrl key as you select the columns.

2. With the mouse, point to the column border to the right of the column letter (in the spreadsheet frame). The mouse pointer changes to a horizontal double arrow.

3. Press and hold the left mouse button.

4. Drag the column border left or right until the column is the width you want. Release the mouse button.

To change column widths using the Active Block Object Inspector, perform the following steps:

1. Select a block containing each column whose width you want to adjust. You can use the keyboard or the mouse to select adjacent columns, but you can only select non-adjacent columns using the mouse.

2. Press the right mouse button to activate the Active Block QuickMenu, and then select Block Properties to display the Active Block Object Inspector dialog box. You can also press F12 to activate the Active Block Object Inspector dialog box, or select Current Object from the Property section of the Property band.

3. Select Column Width.

4. If you want to enter the column width in inches or centimeters, choose the appropriate check box under Unit.

5. If you want to reset the column width, select **R**eset Width to return the selected columns to the page default column width.

6. If you want to set the column width automatically based on the length of data, select **A**uto Width. If you select Auto Width, you can specify (in the **E**xtra Characters text box) that the column should be 0 to 40 characters wider than the data.

7. If you want to specify the column width, type the value in the Column **W**idth text box.

8. Choose OK to confirm the dialog box.

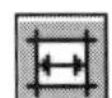

You also can click the Fit button on the Toolbar to adjust the widths of columns automatically. The width of columns set using the Fit button (or the **A**uto Width setting in the Active Block Object Inspector dialog box) depends on the number of rows that are selected when you adjust the width. If you select a single row, the column width adjusts to fit the longest data below the cell selector in the entire column. If you select more than one row, the column width adjusts to fit the cell with the longest data below the cell selector in the same column.

Setting the Default Column Width for a Page

If you find yourself setting the column widths for most columns on a page, you can change the default column width for the entire notebook page. To select a new default column width for a page, follow these steps:

1. With the mouse, point to the page tab and click the right mouse button; or select Active Page from the Property section of the Property band. This displays the Active Page Properties dialog box.

2. Select Default Width and enter the new default width in characters, inches, or centimeters—depending upon which Unit field option button you choose.

3. Choose OK to confirm the dialog box.

Each page in a notebook has its own default column width setting. You set each page individually.

Troubleshooting

Some columns don't adjust when a new default column width is set for a notebook page.

Column widths you set using the Fit button (or the **A**uto Width setting) remain at the current setting even when the length of data in the column changes. If you want the column width adjusted to fit new data, you must select the **A**uto Width setting or the Fit button again.

Some data does not fit in a cell even though the number of characters in the data are fewer than the column width setting listed in the Active Block Object Inspector dialog box.

You may be using a proportional font, or one which is larger than 10 points. The column width setting is only accurate for fixed pitch, 10 point type.

Setting Row Heights

You can adjust row heights in Quattro Pro to make notebook entries easier to understand and more attractive. As you change fonts and point sizes, or apply vertical orientation or word wrap, Quattro Pro automatically adjusts row heights to fit; but you can override the default to create special effects or to add emphasis.

You can set the row height for an individual row or a group of rows at one time. You also can hide rows by setting their height to zero. You can set row heights by dragging the row height using the mouse, or by using the Active Block Object Inspector dialog box. Because Quattro Pro automatically adjusts row heights to fit, there is no equivalent to the Fit button for row heights.

To adjust the height of rows by dragging with the mouse, follow these steps:

1. Highlight the rows you want to adjust. If the rows are not adjacent, hold down the Ctrl key as you select the rows.

2. With the mouse, point to the row border just below the row number (in the spreadsheet frame). The mouse pointer changes to a vertical double arrow.

3. Press and hold down the left mouse button.

4. Drag the row border up or down until the row is the height you want. Release the mouse button. When you are adjusting the row height, Quattro Pro displays a dashed line to indicate the position of the new row border. If you move the lower row border above the top border, you hide the row.

To change the height of rows by using the Active Block Object Inspector dialog box, follow these steps:

1. Highlight the rows you want to adjust. If the rows are not adjacent, hold down the Ctrl key as you select the rows using the mouse. If you want to adjust the height of adjacent rows, place the cell selector in the first row you want to adjust, hold down the Shift key, and move the cell selector to highlight each of the rows you want to adjust.

2. Press the right mouse button to activate the Active Block QuickMenu, and select Block Properties to activate the Active Block Object Inspector

dialog box. You can also press F12 to activate the Active Block Object Inspector dialog box, or select Current Object from the Property section of the Property band.

3. Select Row Height.

4. If you want to enter the row height in inches or centimeters, select the appropriate check box under Unit.

5. If you want to reset the row height, choose **R**eset Height to return the selected rows to automatic.

6. If you want to specify the row height, type the value in the Row **H**eight text box.

7. Press Enter or click OK to confirm the dialog box.

Removing Columns, Rows, or Pages

Sometimes you may want to delete sections from a notebook. Perhaps you made extra copies of some data while you were creating the notebook, or maybe you simply rearranged a notebook and have some unsightly gaps you'd like to eliminate.

Tip
Don't forget to use **E**dit, **U**ndo immediately if you delete the wrong block in error.

You can remove part or all of a notebook in several ways. Any data that you remove is cleared from the notebook in memory, but does not affect the notebook file on disk until you save the notebook file. **E**dit, **U**ndo can restore the data if you use the command before making any other changes.

Some Quattro Pro commands, such as **E**dit, Cu**t**; **E**dit, Cl**e**ar; or **E**dit, Clear **V**alues, erase cell contents but leave behind blank cells. In contrast, after you delete a row, column, or page, Quattro Pro deletes the row, column, or notebook page and moves remaining data to fill the gap created by the deletion. Cell addresses in formulas are also updated when you delete a row, column, or page.

To delete a row, column, or page, follow these steps:

1. Select the **B**lock, **D**elete command. Quattro Pro displays the Delete dialog box (see fig. 15.2).

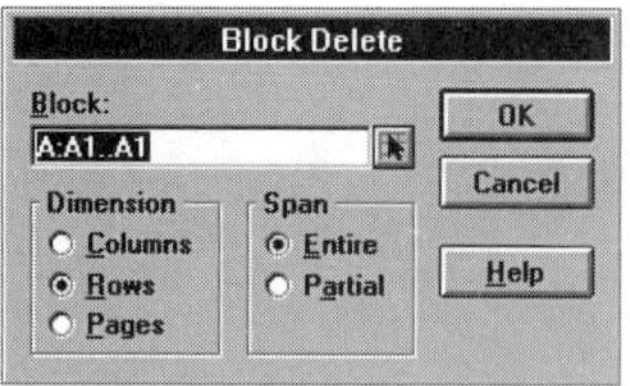

Fig. 15.2
Use the Block Delete dialog box to select the block dimension you want to delete.

2. In the **B**lock text box, specify the block you want to delete. You can type the address, highlight cells, or preselect the block.
3. Select the **C**olumns, **R**ows, or **P**ages radio button.
4. Select the **E**ntire or P**a**rtial radio button. (The P**a**rtial radio button is discussed in detail later in this section.)
5. Click OK to confirm the dialog box and delete the block.

Note

Deleting a column, row, or page does not reduce the number of columns, rows, or pages in the notebook. Quattro Pro replaces the deleted columns, rows, or pages at the end of the page or the notebook; therefore each page continues to have 256 columns and 8192 rows, and each notebook has 256 spreadsheet pages.

When you delete an area, Quattro Pro moves data to fill the gap created by the deletion. If you delete a row, data below the deletion moves up on the current page. If you delete a column, data to the right of the deleted column moves to the left. If you delete a page, data on following pages moves forward in the notebook.

Formula references adjust to reflect the new addresses of the data. If you delete rows 5 and 6, for example, the formula @SUM(A1..A10) becomes @SUM(A1..A8). If a formula refers specifically to a deleted cell, however, the formula returns ERR.

If you delete rows, columns, or pages that are part of a named block, the block becomes smaller. If you delete a row, column, or page that contains one of the block borders, the block becomes undefined and any references to the block return ERR.

You don't have to delete an entire row, column, or page; you may want to delete only part of a row, column, or page, and move remaining data to fill the gap. To accomplish this task, you choose the P**a**rtial radio button. When you specify P**a**rtial as the span, Quattro Pro does not remove data from surrounding rows, columns, or pages.

Inserting Columns, Rows, or Pages

You also can insert rows, columns, or pages anywhere in the notebook. After you insert a row, column, or page, all existing data below, to the right, or on subsequent notebook pages moves to create room for the new data. Cell references in formulas and block names adjust automatically, but explicit cell addresses in macros do not adjust. If you make an insertion in the middle of a block, the block expands to include the new rows, columns, or pages. Formulas referring to that block automatically include the added cells.

Note

Inserting a column, row, or page does not increase the number of columns, rows, or pages in the notebook. Each page continues to have 256 columns and 8192 rows, and each notebook has 256 spreadsheet pages. If Quattro Pro cannot delete the columns, rows, or pages at the end of the page or the notebook because data would be lost, an error message is displayed and the insertion fails.

To insert a row, column, or page, perform the following steps:

1. Move the cell selector to the cell where you want to begin inserting.
2. Highlight the number of rows, columns, or pages you want to insert.
3. Choose the **B**lock, **I**nsert command and choose **R**ows, **C**olumns, or **P**ages.
4. To insert a partial row, column, or page, select the P**a**rtial radio button.
5. Choose OK to confirm the dialog box and make the insertion.

Locking Data On-Screen

Notebook pages often are too large to display at one time. As you move the cell selector to display different areas of the page, data scrolls off the opposite edge of the display. This can make it difficult to understand data, because you can't see the labels describing the data. To prevent titles from scrolling off the screen, you can lock a number of rows, columns, or both rows and columns so they remain on-screen as you move the cell selector.

Before you lock rows or columns to keep them on-screen, you need to position the cell selector to tell Quattro Pro which rows or columns you want to remain visible. If you are locking horizontal titles, place the cell selector in the row below the last row you want locked. If you are locking vertical titles, place the cell selector in the column to the right of the last column you want locked. If you are locking both horizontal and vertical titles, place the cell selector in the row just below and the column just right of the intersection of the rows and columns you want to lock.

Once you have positioned the cell selector properly, select **V**iew, **L**ocked Titles to display the Locked Titles dialog box (see fig. 15.3).

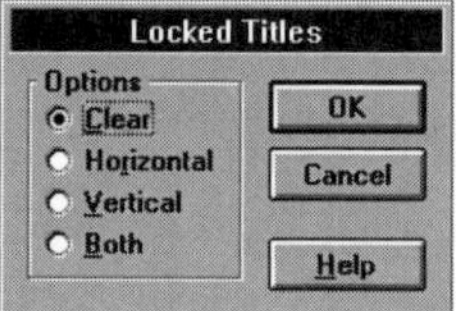

Fig. 15.3
Use the Locked Titles dialog box to keep specified rows or columns visible when you move the cell selector.

You can lock the rows above the cell selector by choosing the **H**orizontal radio button. To lock the columns left of the cell selector, choose the **V**ertical radio button. You can lock both horizontal and vertical titles by choosing the **B**oth radio button. The **C**lear radio button unlocks titles.

Figure 15.4 shows a Quattro Pro notebook containing an address database. In this figure, the cell selector was placed in cell B2 before issuing the **V**iew, **L**ocked Titles command and choosing **B**oth. The cell selector was then moved to cell H25, the last cell in the database. Column A and row 1 remain visible enabling you to more easily understand the data, because you can see both the field names (row 1), and the value contained in the LAST_NAME field (column A).

When rows or columns are locked on-screen, you can't move the cell selector directly into the locked rows or columns. Pressing the Home key moves the cell selector to the position below and to the right of the titles rather than to cell A1. You can't use the mouse or the direction keys to move the cell selector into the locked titles, either.

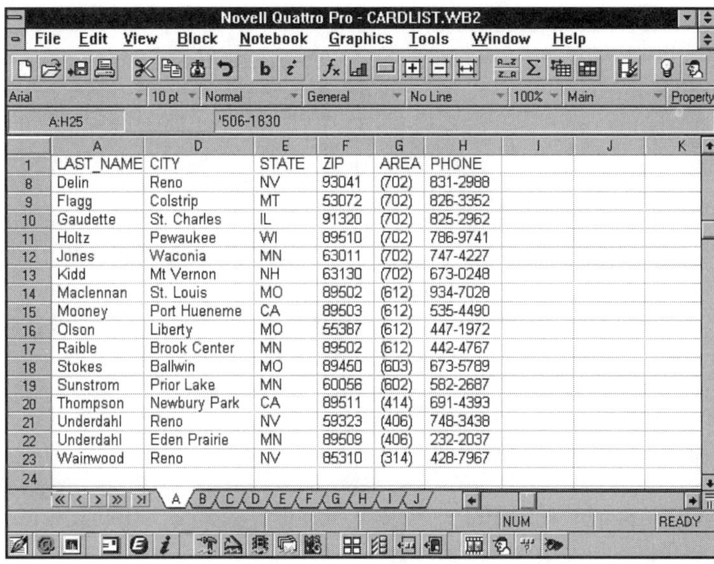

Fig. 15.4
Titles locked on-screen can make data easier to understand.

The only way to move the cell selector into the locked titles is to use the F5 (Go To) key, and specify an address in the locked rows or columns. If you do, you'll see an extra copy of the locked rows or columns. Use the direction keys to move at least one screen right and down to clear the duplicate display.

Changing the Appearance of Data

How your data appears in a notebook or in a report really doesn't affect the data, but it can have a major effect of how well people can understand the data. Appearance can also make quite a difference in how people perceive your business. A well prepared financial statement, for example, might not ensure that you'll be able to obtain a small business loan; but would you feel comfortable presenting your banker something that looked unprofessional and sloppy?

A few simple steps can greatly improve the appearance of data. Simply applying the proper numeric format can change 1234567 into $1,234,567.00—changing raw data into a value anyone can quickly understand. In addition to numeric formats, you can use alignment, different fonts, borders, and shading to turn an ordinary report into something that is much more. The following sections show you some of the options you can use to improve the appearance of your Quattro Pro notebooks.

Using Numeric Formats

You can display data in a cell in a variety of different numeric formats. Quattro Pro offers a wide choice of numeric formats, which you access through the Active Block Object Inspector dialog box. Most formats apply only to numeric data, although Text format can apply to string formulas, and Hidden format can apply to any type of data.

Formatting changes the appearance but not the value of data. The number 7892, for example, can appear in the format 7,892, $7,892.00, or 789200.0%, as well as many other formats. No matter how Quattro Pro displays the number in a cell, the number remains the same.

To change the numeric format of a cell or block, follow these steps:

1. Select the cell or block.

2. With the mouse, point to the cell or block, and click the right mouse button to display the Active Block QuickMenu.

3. Select Block Properties to open the Active Block Object Inspector dialog box (see fig. 15.5). You can also press F12 or select Current Object from the Property section of the Property band to display this dialog box.

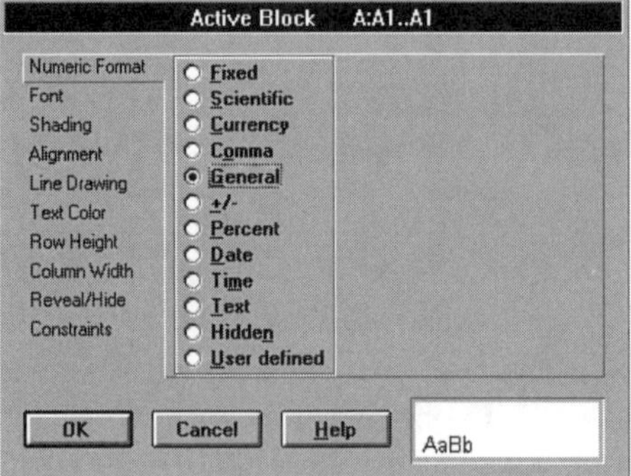

Fig. 15.5 Select a Numeric Format from the Active Block Object Inspector dialog box.

4. The Numeric Format pane is selected by default. If no numeric format has been assigned, the default **G**eneral format is checked, as shown in figure 15.5. Select the desired numeric format.

5. If you choose **F**ixed, **S**cientific, **C**urrency, C**o**mma, or **P**ercent, enter the number of decimal places in the spin control that appears after you choose one of these formats. Quattro Pro suggests a default of 2 decimal places, but you can type another number between 0 and 15.

6. Choose OK to confirm the dialog box and apply the format to the highlighted cell or block.

Troubleshooting

After formatting a block, some cells display asterisks instead of the values.

If you apply a numeric format to a cell, the column width must be wide enough to display the cell's data in the format. Otherwise, asterisks display in the cell rather than the formatted value. You may need to adjust the column width to fit the new format.

The following sections briefly describe Quattro Pro's numeric format options.

Fixed Format

You use the **F**ixed format when you want to display values with a specified, fixed number of decimal points. Quattro Pro displays values with up to 15 decimal places. Negative numbers have a minus sign, and decimal values have a leading zero. No punctuation is used to denote thousands.

Scientific Format

You use the **S**cientific format to display very large or very small numbers. Such numbers usually have a few significant digits and many zeros.

A number in scientific notation has two parts: a *mantissa* and an *exponent.* The mantissa is a number from 1 to 10 that contains the significant digits. The exponent tells you how many places to move the decimal point to get the actual value of the number.

Quattro Pro displays numbers in **S**cientific display format in powers of 10, with 0 to 15 decimal places, and an exponent from -308 to +308. If a number has more significant digits than the cell can display using the specified number of decimal places, the displayed value is rounded but the stored value is used in calculations.

Currency Format

Currency format displays values with a currency symbol, such as a dollar sign ($) or the British pound sign (£), and punctuation to denote thousands, depending on the current international settings. If you specify a currency symbol, the column width needs an extra position to display each character in the currency symbol. Values formatted as **C**urrency can have from 0 to 15 decimal places. Thousands are separated by commas, periods, or spaces according to the current international settings. Negative numbers appear in parentheses.

Comma Format

Like the **C**urrency display format, the C**o**mma format displays data with a fixed number of decimal places and punctuation to denote thousands. The thousands separator and the decimal point depend on the current international settings. Negative numbers appear in parentheses, and positive numbers less than 1000 appear the same as **F**ixed display format.

If a value has more decimal digits than the cell can display using the specified number of decimal places, the displayed value is rounded but the stored value is used in calculations.

General Format

General format is the default format for all new notebooks. Numbers in **G**eneral display format have no thousands separators and no trailing zeros to the right of the decimal point. A minus sign precedes negative numbers. If a number contains decimal digits, it contains a decimal point. If a number contains too many digits to the right of the decimal point to display in the current column width, the decimals are rounded in the display. If a number is too large or too small, it appears in **S**cientific display format.

+/– Format

The +/– format displays numbers as a series of plus signs (+), minus signs (–), or as a period (.). The number of signs equals the integer portion of the value. A positive number appears as a row of plus signs, a negative value appears as a row of minus signs, and a number between -1 and +1 appears as a period.

Percent Format

Percent format is used to display values as percentages with 0 to 15 decimal places. The number appears with its value multiplied by 100, followed by a percent sign (%). The number of decimal places you specify is the number displayed in the percent—not the number of decimal places in the value.

If a value has more decimal digits than the cell can display using the specified number of decimal places, the displayed value is rounded but the stored value is used in calculations.

Date Format

Date formats display date serial numbers as dates rather than numbers. Quattro Pro stores dates as serial numbers starting with January 1, 1600, (which is -109571) and increases the number by one for each whole day. December 31, 1899 is counted as 1. The latest date Quattro Pro can display is December 31, 3199, with a serial number of 474816.

If the number is less than -109571 or greater than 474816, a date format appears as asterisks. Date formats ignore decimal fractions; 34876.55 with a short international date format appears as 6/26/95. The decimal portion of a date serial number represents the time as a fraction of a 24-hour clock.

Quattro Pro gives you a choice of five different **D**ate display formats. Both Long Date Intl. and Short Date Intl. depend on the current international date format set using the **P**roperty **A**pplication Object Inspector dialog box.

Time Format

You use the Ti**m**e formats to display date serial numbers as times. The decimal portion of a date serial number is a *time fraction*. The time fraction represents a fraction of a 24-hour day. For example, the time fraction for 8 a.m. is .33333..., the time fraction for noon is .5, and the time fraction for 3 p.m. is .675. When you use a Ti**m**e format, Quattro Pro displays the fraction as a time.

If a date serial number is greater than 1, the time formats ignore the integer portion. Both .5 and 33781.5 display 12:00:00 PM.

Text Format

You use **T**ext format to display the text of a formula rather than its result. Numbers in cells formatted as **T**ext appear in **G**eneral format. Unlike long labels that appear in blank cells to the right, formulas formatted as **T**ext are truncated if they are too long to display in the column width. Quattro Pro continues to use the value of formulas when you format them as **T**ext.

Hidden Format

A cell or block formatted as Hidde**n** always appears blank. You use Hidde**n** format for intermediate calculations that you don't want to appear in a final report or for sensitive formulas you don't want displayed. The contents of a Hidde**n** cell appear in the input line when you highlight the cell, however, so Hidde**n** format offers little security

User-Defined Format

Quattro Pro enables you to define and apply your own numeric formats. **U**ser-defined formats can include many different elements. For example, you can include text, the names of days or months, or leading zeros. For more information on creating your own numeric formats, see "Defining Custom Numeric Formats" in the Quattro Pro help screens for details on the symbols you can use.

Avoiding Apparent Errors

Some formats display a number in rounded form. Even when the displayed number appears rounded, however, Quattro Pro still stores and uses the exact value in calculations. If you format the value 1.5 as Fixed with zero decimal places, Quattro Pro displays the number as 2 in a cell but uses the actual value of 1.5 in calculations. This can make it seem as though Quattro Pro is making arithmetic errors, such as "2+2=3." In fact, Quattro Pro is correct, because the two values it is adding are 1.5 and 1.5, so the formula is actually "1.5+1.5=3." This apparent error is caused by rounding the display but not rounding the values.

You easily can create apparent rounding errors—especially when you produce cross-tabulated reports. To avoid apparent rounding errors, you need to round the actual value of the numbers used in formulas, not just their appearance or format. To round the values used in a formula, use the @ROUND function to round each value before the value is used in the formula.

Aligning Data

Just as Quattro Pro offers a very broad range of numeric format options, it also provides quite a few choices you can use to align labels and values. By default, labels are aligned to left side of cells, and values are aligned to the right side of cells. These default alignments are easily changed; and you can change alignment for both labels and values.

You can align labels and values to the left side of cells, center them in a cell or across a block, or to the right side of the cell. You can also align them to the top, center, or bottom of the cell. You can orient labels and values horizontally or vertically. Finally, you can wrap text on multiple lines in a single cell.

To change the label alignment for existing labels or values, follow these steps:

1. Select the cell or block.

2. With the mouse, point to the cell or block, and click the right mouse button to display the Active Block QuickMenu.

3. Select Block Properties to open the Active Block Object Inspector dialog box. You can also press F12 or select Current Object from the Property section of the Property band to display this dialog box.

4. Select the Alignment pane in the Active Block Object Inspector dialog box (see fig. 15.6).

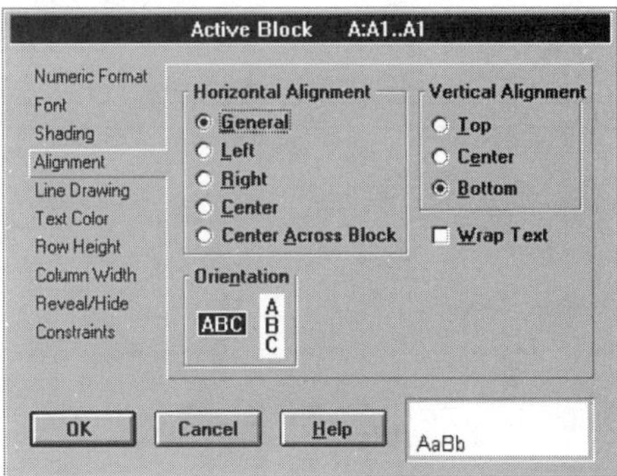

Fig. 15.6
Use the Alignment section of the Active Block Object Inspector dialog box to specify data alignment.

5. In the Horizontal Alignment field, choose **G**eneral to reset the alignment to the page default; or choose **L**eft, **R**ight, **C**enter, or Center **A**cross Block.

6. In the Vertical Alignment field, choose **T**op, C**e**nter, or **B**ottom.

7. In the Orie**n**tation field, choose whether you want horizontal or vertical orientation.

8. Select the **W**rap text check box to wrap labels on multiple lines within a single cell.

9. Select OK to confirm the dialog box and apply the selected alignment options.

Figure 15.7 demonstrates the various horizontal and vertical alignment and orientation options.

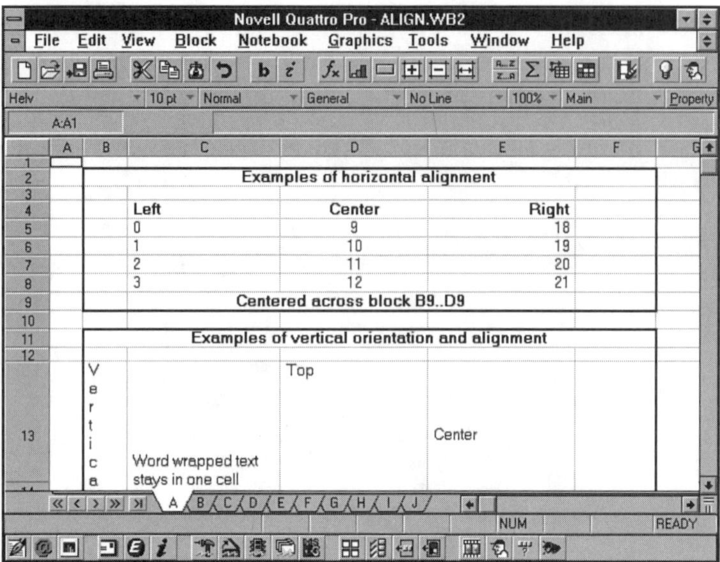

Fig. 15.7
Quattro Pro offers many horizontal and vertical alignment and orientation options.

Changing Fonts

Quattro Pro applies the term *font* to the combination of *typeface*, *point size*, and *attributes* used for the characters displayed in your notebooks. A typeface is a type style, such as Arial, Courier New, or Times New Roman. Typefaces are available in a number of point sizes that represent character height. The standard 10 character-per-inch size usually is considered equivalent to a 12-point type size. Typefaces also have different attributes, such as weight (normal or **bold**) and *italic*.

You can use the Font pane in the Active Block Object Inspector dialog box to choose different fonts. You can also use the Font and Font Size sections on the Property band to make these two selections, and the Bold and Italic buttons on the Toolbar to apply either of these two attributes.

Several factors determine which font options are available. If you have installed additional fonts on your system, you'll be able to select from a larger list of options. Scaleable fonts, such as the TrueType fonts in Windows 3.1, greatly improve the quality of your reports.

If you increase font size, Quattro Pro enlarges the row height to fit the selected fonts. Column widths do not adjust automatically, however; so numeric data may not fit in a cell after you change the font, and the data may display as asterisks. Adjust the column widths as needed to display the data correctly. Figure 15.8 shows how several different typefaces, point sizes, and attributes change the appearance of your data (you probably will have a different selection of fonts installed on your system).

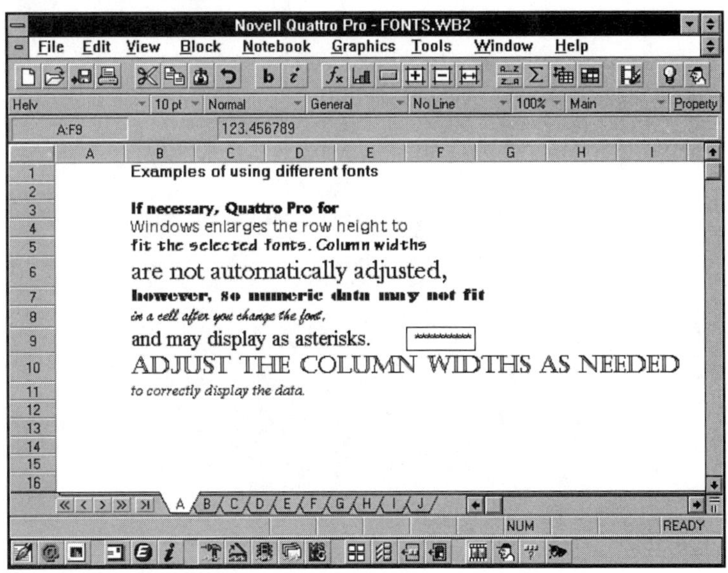

Fig. 15.8
Different fonts change the appearance of data in your notebooks.

Adding Borders and Shading

If you really want to add a professional looking touch to your notebooks, *borders* and *shading* can do the trick. Borders are lines around a cell or block. Shading is a background tint within a cell or block.

You can use borders to effectively isolate groups of data, making it easy to see all related data. You can also use borders as separators between report sections. Shading is most often used for emphasis, or to make certain report data cannot be altered without the alterations being immediately apparent.

Adding Borders to Cells or Blocks

You can use the Line Drawing pane in the Active Block Object Inspector dialog box to draw lines above, below, on the sides, and around cells and blocks. You can also use the Underline section of the Property band to draw lines at the bottom of cells or blocks. Borders can be single lines, double lines, or thick lines.

To draw borders within or around a cell or block, follow these steps:

1. Select the cell or block.

2. Open the Active Block Object Inspector dialog box by clicking the right mouse button inside the cell or block and selecting Block Properties from the QuickMenu; or by pressing F12 or selecting Current Object from the Property section on the Property band.

3. Select the Line Drawing pane (see fig. 15.9).

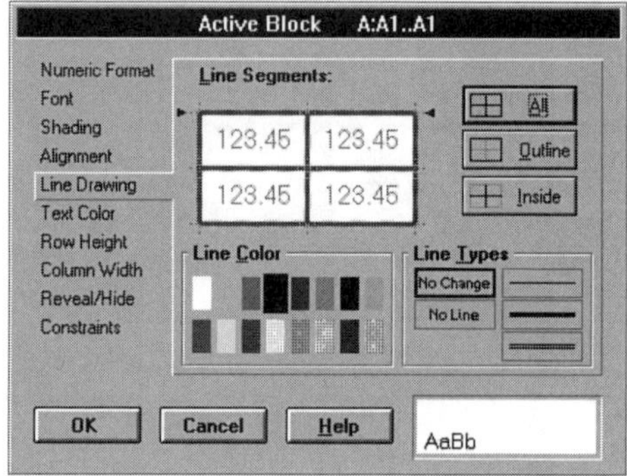

Fig. 15.9
Use the Line Drawing options in the Active Block Object Inspector dialog box to add borders to cells or blocks.

4. Select the placement options you want using the **L**ine Segments, **A**ll, **O**utline, and **I**nside options.

5. Select the Line **T**ypes you want.

6. Select the Line **C**olor you want.

7. Choose OK to confirm the dialog box and add the selected borders.

Adding Shading to Cells or Blocks

You can draw attention to cells or blocks by adding shading, a special effect that changes the background from white to a color. When you select shading, you also can select the blend of two colors.

To add shading, follow these steps:

1. Select the cell or block.

2. Open the Active Block Object Inspector dialog box by clicking the right mouse button inside the cell or block and selecting Block Properties from the QuickMenu; or by pressing F12 or selecting Current Object from the Property section on the Property band.

3. Select the Shading pane (see fig. 15.10).

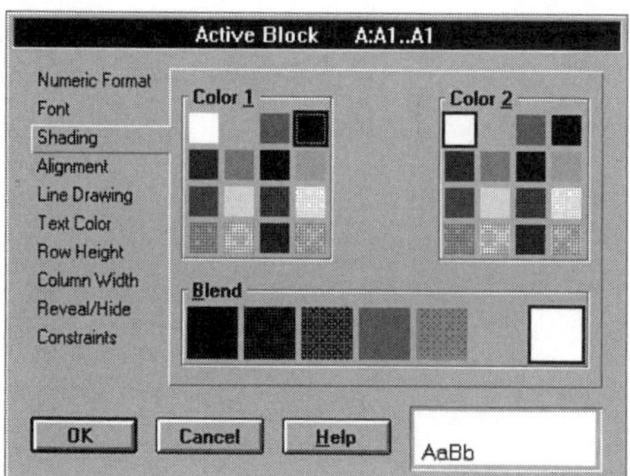

Fig. 15.10
Use the shading options in the Active Block Object Inspector dialog box to add shading to cells or blocks.

4. Select Color **1**, Color **2**, and the **B**lend (shading pattern). Quattro Pro enables you to select from 16 colors for both the background and the foreground, and from 7 different patterns.

5. Click OK to confirm the dialog box and apply the shading.

Tip
Not all printers can properly print text on a shaded background. Test printing shades on your printer.

Any borders or shading you add to cells or blocks print with the labels and values in a report. It's generally best to use light shading in cells or blocks containing values that must be visible in a printed report or one which must be photocopied.

From Here...

In this chapter, you learned how to improve the appearance of your notebooks, and how to make your data more readily understandable. With these options, you can produce professional appearing reports equal to those from dedicated accounting programs. For more information on related subjects, see the following chapters:

- Chapter 17, "Using Graphics," teaches you how to incorporate Quattro Pro graphs in your reports.
- Chapter 18, "Printing Reports," discusses the how-tos of producing printed reports from your Quattro Pro notebooks.

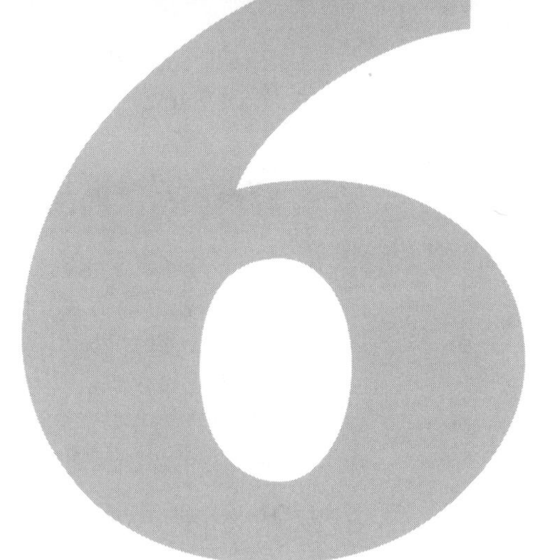

Chapter 16

Analyzing Data

by Brian Underdahl

Raw data is the foundation of every business report, but the most effective reports are those which effectively analyze that data. Quattro Pro provides you with a powerful suite of data analysis tools that enable you to solve complex problems, analyze results, produce cross-tabulation summaries, and work directly with external data. These tools are the subject of this chapter.

The concepts introduced in this chapter give you a glimpse of some of the more complex tools in the Quattro Pro tool bag. Several of the functions provided by some of these tools were formerly only available in specialized and costly stand-alone programs. These programs were not only specialized, but they were complex, were usually difficult to use, and often required advanced training before you could use them effectively. As a part of Quattro Pro, these tools are much easier to learn and use. This ease of learning and use hasn't come at the expense of power, though. The data analysis tools in Quattro Pro provide the same level of powerful functions available in those stand-alone programs, but you don't have to pay extra to use them.

This chapter introduces the following subjects:

- Using the Optimizer and Solve For to find the best answers to problems
- Understanding how to use what-if tables to analyze data
- Viewing the complex relationships in your data with the Data Modeling Desktop
- Accessing external database information using the Database Desktop

Using the Optimizer and Solve For

The Optimizer and Solve For tools are powerful utilities that help you create *what-if* scenarios with notebook data. What-if scenarios are a common way to analyze problems, using many different values for a set of variables to find optimal answers. What-if scenarios can be quite time-consuming, especially if done manually, because even problems with a limited number of variables have many possible solutions.

The Optimizer tool can analyze problems with up to 200 variables and 100 constraints to determine the best answer. The Solve For tool modifies a single variable to find a specified answer to a problem.

Solving Complex Problems Using the Optimizer

You use the Optimizer to determine a series of possible answers to a specific problem, and to select the answer that best fits your criteria. You can use the Optimizer, for example, to find the production mix that produces the highest profit, to analyze investment portfolios, to determine the least costly shipping routes, and to schedule your staff.

Each Optimizer problem must have one or more *adjustable* cells. Adjustable cells contain the variables that the Optimizer changes in search of the optimal answer, and can contain numbers only. Adjustable cells might include production quantities, numbers of employees, or capital invested in a project.

Constraints are conditions that serve as problem limits, such as the range of acceptable values. Constraints are expressed as logical formulas that evaluate to true or false; and all constraints must be met before an answer is considered acceptable. Constraints might include limits on production levels, a requirement to produce a profit, or an obligation that at least one employee be on duty.

A solution cell contains the formula that defines the problem, and is optional. If you do not include a solution cell, the Optimizer finds answers that meet all the defined constraints. Solution cells might include formulas that calculate profits, overall costs, or the amount earned from different activities.

Using a Production Scheduling Notebook

Figure 16.1 shows a sample notebook that represents the costs involved in producing three different products. In this example, it is assumed that the factory can produce 50,000 total parts per month and that the production can be divided among the three parts in the most profitable manner.

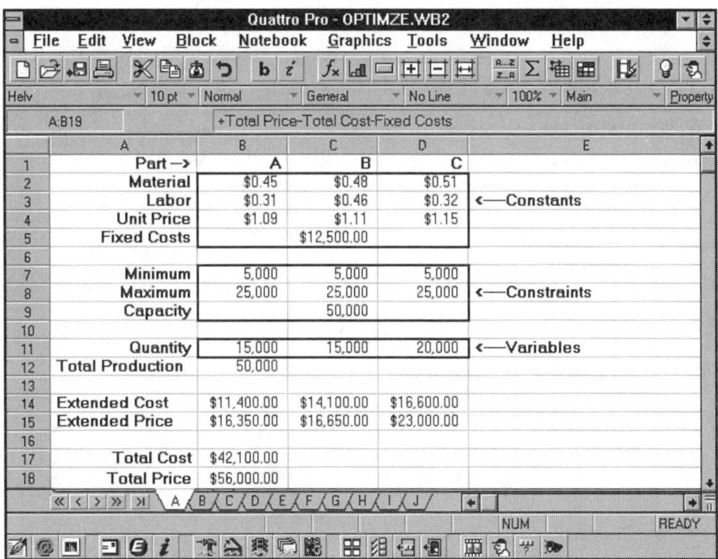

	A	B	C	D	E
1	Part-->	A	B	C	
2	Material	$0.45	$0.48	$0.51	
3	Labor	$0.31	$0.46	$0.32	<—Constants
4	Unit Price	$1.09	$1.11	$1.15	
5	Fixed Costs		$12,500.00		
6					
7	Minimum	5,000	5,000	5,000	
8	Maximum	25,000	25,000	25,000	<—Constraints
9	Capacity		50,000		
10					
11	Quantity	15,000	15,000	20,000	<—Variables
12	Total Production	50,000			
13					
14	Extended Cost	$11,400.00	$14,100.00	$16,600.00	
15	Extended Price	$16,350.00	$16,650.00	$23,000.00	
16					
17	Total Cost	$42,100.00			
18	Total Price	$56,000.00			

Fig. 16.1
You can use a notebook to compute optimal product mix.

Several factors affect the final profit. In figure 16.1, the production manager has scheduled the production run at 15,000 each for parts A and B, and 20,000 for part C. The net profit with this mix is $1,400. Of course, it would be possible to try other sets of values for each product's production quantity. Because each of the three values can vary between 5,000 and 25,000, however, the number of possibilities would be enormous.

To use the Optimizer to find a better solution, follow these steps:

1. Choose **T**ools, **N**umeric Tools, **O**ptimizer to display the Optimizer dialog box.

2. To make the production quantities of the three parts adjustable in the notebook, enter the cell addresses in the **V**ariable cells text box. In this example, you enter **B11..D11**.

3. Next, define the constraints that the Optimizer must satisfy in solving the problem. Select **A**dd to display the Add Constraints dialog box.

4. The quantities of the parts (cells B11..D11) must be equal to or greater than the minimum quantity shown in cells B7..D7. Thus you need to enter **B11..D11** in the **C**ell text box, select the **>=** (greater than or equal to) radio button in the Operator group box, and enter **B7..D7** in the Co**n**stant text box.

5. After you enter the first constraint, select **A**dd Another Constraint to enter additional constraints. The quantities of the parts (cells B11..D11) must be equal to or less than the maximum quantity shown in cells B8..D8. Thus you need to enter **B11..D11** in the **C**ell text box, select the <= (less than or equal to) radio button in the Operator group box, and enter **B8..D8** in the Co**n**stant text box.

6. Select **A**dd Another Constraint to enter the last constraint. Cell B12 (total production) must be less than or equal to the value in C9 (capacity).

7. Select OK when all constraints have been entered.

8. Next, select the **S**olution Cell text box in the Optimizer dialog box and enter **B19**, the address of the formula cell. The dialog box should now look like figure 16.2.

Fig. 16.2
The Optimizer dialog box shows the completed entries.

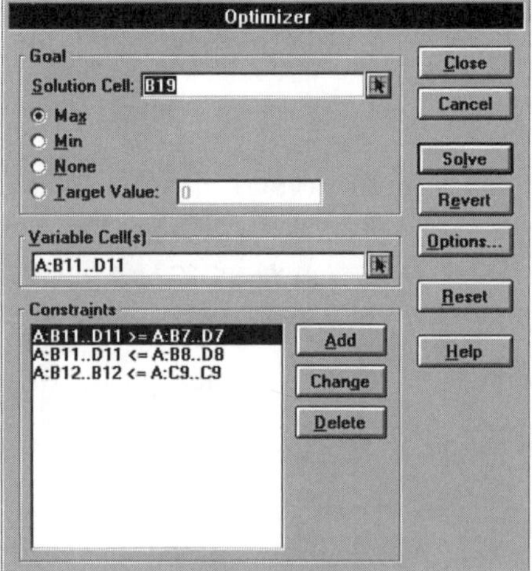

9. Select So**l**ve to instruct the Optimizer to calculate the solution. Figure 16.3 shows the result in the production mix example.

The Optimizer found a much different solution than the one proposed by the production manager. After redistributing production quantities, the total monthly profit jumped from $1,400 to $3,000. Although this example did not take all possible factors into account, it clearly demonstrates the value of applying the Optimizer to a what-if scenario.

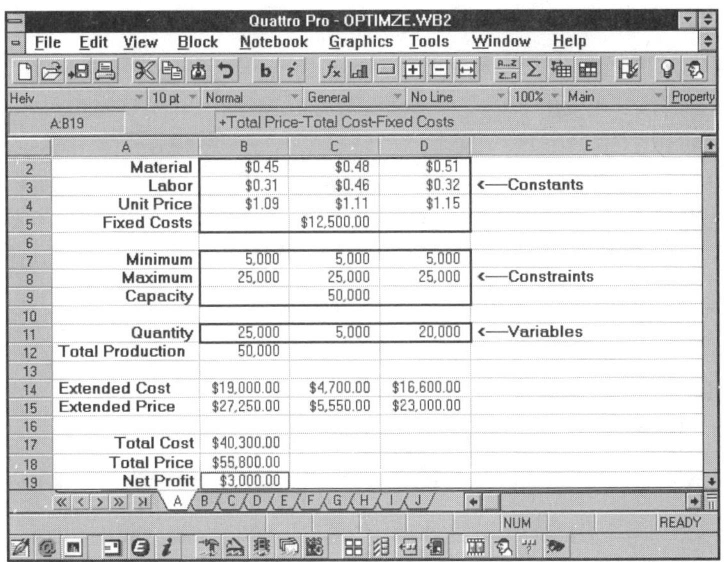

Fig. 16.3
The notebook shows the optimal solution for the product mix example, as determined by the Optimizer.

Troubleshooting

Optimizer is unable to find an optimal solution to a complex problem, or sometimes produces different results when solving the same problem a second time.

Try to supply initial values for the variables that you feel will be somewhat close to its final values. Optimizer usually has better success when it can start with a reasonable solution.

I can't tell whether the Optimizer's solution is the best solution to my problem.

Use the **R**eporting option to create an answer report. This report shows the values Optimizer used to find its solution.

Solving for a Known Answer Using Solve For

Sometimes you know the answer you want, but don't quite know how to get there. The Solve For tool is a Quattro Pro analysis utility that you use to find the value of a variable when you are seeking a specific goal. Rather than calculating an optimum answer by adjusting a block of variables, the Solve For tool adjusts a single variable to produce an answer you specify.

For example, suppose you know you can afford $325 as a monthly payment on an automobile, but don't know how large a loan you can receive for such a payment. The Solve For tool makes it easy to make this type of reverse calculation, where you already know the answer, but don't know the key to finding the answer. To use Solve For to find the loan amount, follow these steps:

1. Create a Quattro Pro notebook that uses the @PMT function to calculate the loan payment on a loan. For this example, use a loan amount of **$10,000** in cell C2, **9%** interest in cell C3, a term of **60** months in cell C4, and the formula, **@PMT(C2,C3/12,C4)** in cell C6.

2. Select **T**ools, **N**umeric Tools, **S**olve For.

3. Specify **C6** in the **F**ormula Cell text box. This is the cell that contains the formula whose value you want to specify.

4. Specify **325** in the **T**arget Value text box. This is the value you want to achieve in the goal cell.

5. Next, specify **C2** as the **V**ariable Cell, the cell whose value Solve For will adjust. Your screen should now appear similar to figure 16.4 (in this figure, block names were added to make the formula easier to understand, and cells were formatted to display numbers correctly).

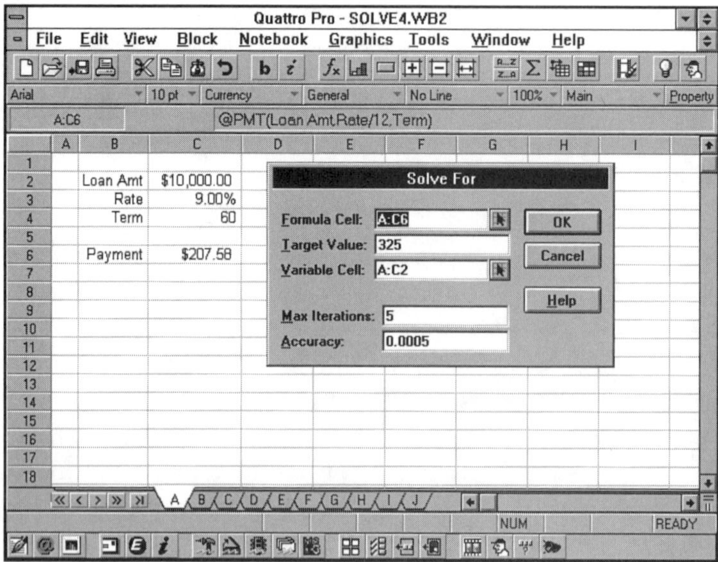

Fig. 16.4
The Solve For dialog box is completed.

6. Select OK to execute the command and return to the notebook. Figure 16.5 shows the notebook with the solution.

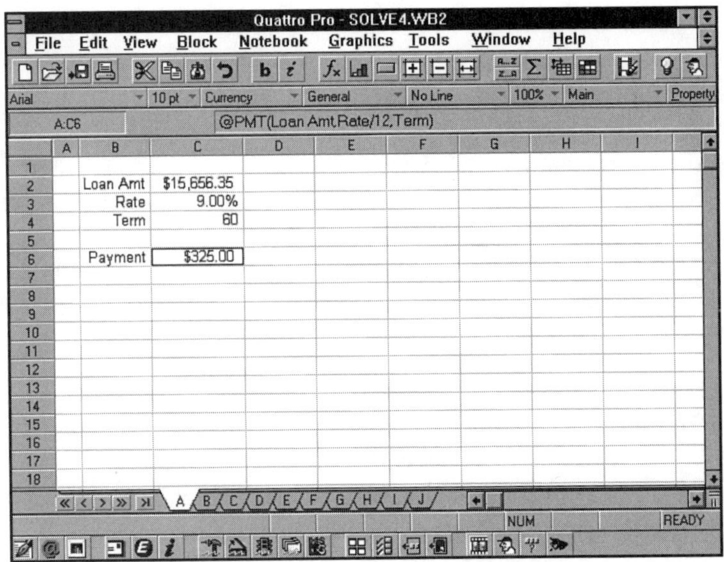

Fig. 16.5
The solved problem shows the answer you seek.

Your $325 monthly budget allows for payments on a loan of $15,656.35. Although you could probably find an answer close to this by trying several different values in cell C2, using Solve For makes the process both simple and fast.

When you use Solve For, the adjustable value is permanently changed in the notebook. You can return to the previous value if you immediately select **E**dit **U**ndo.

Using What-If Tables

In most notebook models, the variables your formulas use are known quantities. What-if tables enable you to work with variables whose values are unknown. Models for financial projections often fall into this category. For example, next year's cash flow projection may depend on prevailing interest rates or other variable costs you cannot predict exactly.

With the **T**ools, **N**umeric Tools, **W**hat-if commands, you can create tables that show the results of changing one variable in a problem or the combined effect of changing two variables simultaneously. Another function of the **T**ools, **N**umeric Tools, **W**hat-if commands is to create *cross-tabulation tables.* A cross-tabulation table provides summary information categorized by unique information in two fields, such as the total amount of sales each sales representative makes to each customer.

Understanding What-If Tables

A *what-if table* is an on-screen view of information in a column format with the field names at the top. A *variable* is a formula component whose value can change. An *input cell* is a notebook cell used by Quattro Pro for temporary storage during calculation of a what-if table. One input cell is required for each variable in the what-if table formula. The cell addresses of the formula variables are the same as the input cells. The formulas used in what-if tables can contain values, strings, cell addresses, and functions; but you should not use logical formulas because this type of formula always evaluates to 0 or 1, which is usually meaningless in a what-if table.

You can build two types of what-if tables in Quattro Pro. They differ in the number of variables, and the number of formulas that can be included. A one free variable what-if table can contain one variable, and can have one or more formulas. A two free variables what-if table can contain two variables, but only one formula. In a one free variable what-if table, you place the formulas in the top row of the table. In a two free variables what-if table, you place the formula at the intersection of the top row and the left column of the table.

A common use for a one free variable what-if table would be to calculate both the interest and principal portions of each payment on a loan. A two free variables what-if table might be used to calculate monthly payments on a given loan amount at different combinations of interest rates and terms.

Figure 16.6 shows a typical two free variables what-if table. This table calculates monthly payments on a given loan amount at different combinations of interest rates and terms.

To create a similar what-if table, follow these steps:

1. Place the loan amount **15000** in cell B1.
2. For documentation purposes, place identifying labels in column A. In this case, use **Loan Amt** in A1, **Interest rate** in A2, and **Term** as in A3.
3. Enter the formula **@PMT(B1,B2/12,B3)** in cell A5.
4. Enter the interest rates in A6..A17. The fastest method of entering these rates is to enter **8%** in A6, **8.5%** in A7, select A6..A17, and click the SpeedFill button. (To improve the appearance of the table, format A6..A17 as **P**ercent, 1 decimal.)
5. Enter the loan terms in B5..G5. Once again, you can use SpeedFill.

6. Highlight the table block A5..G17.
7. Choose **T**ools, **N**umeric Tools, **W**hat-if.
8. Select **T**wo free variables.
9. Enter **B2** as the **C**olumn input cell and enter **B3** as **R**ow input cell.
10. Select **G**enerate to calculate the what-if table values.
11. Click Close or press Enter to confirm the dialog box and return to the notebook.

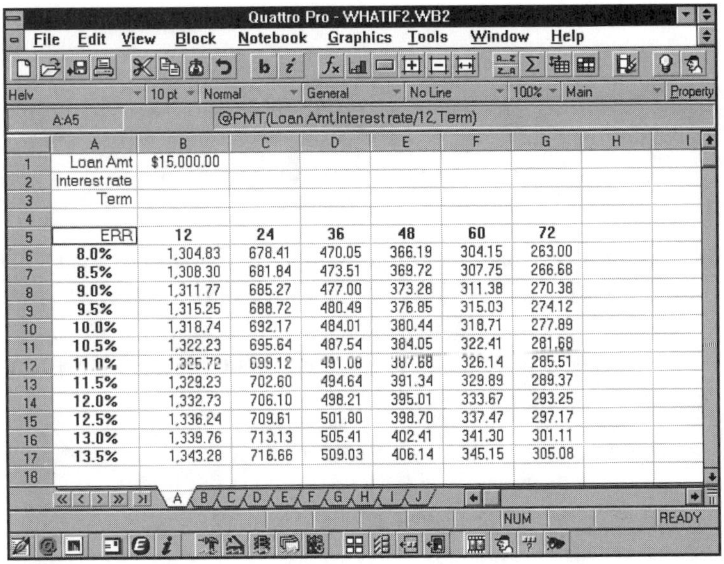

	A	B	C	D	E	F	G
1	Loan Amt	$15,000.00					
2	Interest rate						
3	Term						
4							
5	ERR	12	24	36	48	60	72
6	8.0%	1,304.83	678.41	470.05	366.19	304.15	263.00
7	8.5%	1,308.30	681.84	473.51	369.72	307.75	266.68
8	9.0%	1,311.77	685.27	477.00	373.28	311.38	270.38
9	9.5%	1,315.25	688.72	480.49	376.85	315.03	274.12
10	10.0%	1,318.74	692.17	484.01	380.44	318.71	277.89
11	10.5%	1,322.23	695.64	487.54	384.05	322.41	281.68
12	11.0%	1,325.72	699.12	491.08	387.68	326.14	285.51
13	11.5%	1,329.23	702.60	494.64	391.34	329.89	289.37
14	12.0%	1,332.73	706.10	498.21	395.01	333.67	293.25
15	12.5%	1,336.24	709.61	501.80	398.70	337.47	297.17
16	13.0%	1,339.76	713.13	505.41	402.41	341.30	301.11
17	13.5%	1,343.28	716.66	509.03	406.14	345.15	305.08

Fig. 16.6
The completed two free variables what-if table of loan payment amounts.

Troubleshooting

My what-if tables don't display new values when the formula variables are changed.

What-if tables don't recalculate when values change because the tables don't contain formulas. Choose **T**ools, **N**umeric Tools, **W**hat-if, **G**enerate to recalculate the what-if table values.

Understanding Crosstabs

Crosstabs (or cross-tabulation tables) are tables that summarize the values in a database. For example, an address list showing customers in many different states might include information you could use to determine where you get most of your business, and therefore, where you should plan to spend your advertising dollars. You might also use a crosstab to see a sales summary by each salesperson for each product line. Quattro Pro can even generate a graph to quickly display the results of the analysis.

The structure of a what-if table block for a cross-tabulation analysis is similar to the structure for a what-if analysis. If you are analyzing the effects of one variable, the upper left cell may be empty, the top row contains the formula(s) that are to be evaluated, and the left column contains the sample values. If you are analyzing the effects of two variables, you place the formula in the upper left cell of the table, and the two sets of sample values in the top row and left column of the table. In most cases, the formulas contain one or more database functions.

In addition, you must create one or two input cells, depending on the number of variables in the crosstab. For a crosstab analysis, you must place the input cells directly below cells that contain the corresponding database field names.

You also use the **T**ools, **N**umeric Tools, **W**hat-if command to create a cross-tabulation table. The sample values in the left column, or in the left column and top row, are used to select the values displayed in the crosstab. The sample values for a cross-tabulation analysis are the values or labels that you can use as criteria for the analysis.

After the what-if table has been calculated, each cell in the results block contains the result of the formulas. The formulas have been applied to those database records that meet the crosstab criteria.

Figure 16.7 demonstrates a crosstab analysis of a sales database. In this case, the crosstab is analyzing sales totals for each product line broken down by salesperson. The @DSUM database function is used to perform the analysis. Figure 16.8 shows how Quattro Pro can quickly create a graphical representation of the crosstab analysis.

You use nearly the same steps to create a crosstab with the **T**ools, **N**umeric Tools, **W**hat-if command as you do to create a what-if table. Notice the similarities between the what-if table in figure 16.6 and the crosstab in figure 16.7. In both tables, the formulas are evaluated based upon the values of the variables. The primary difference between the two types of tables is the data source. A what-if table generates new data, while a crosstab evaluates existing database data.

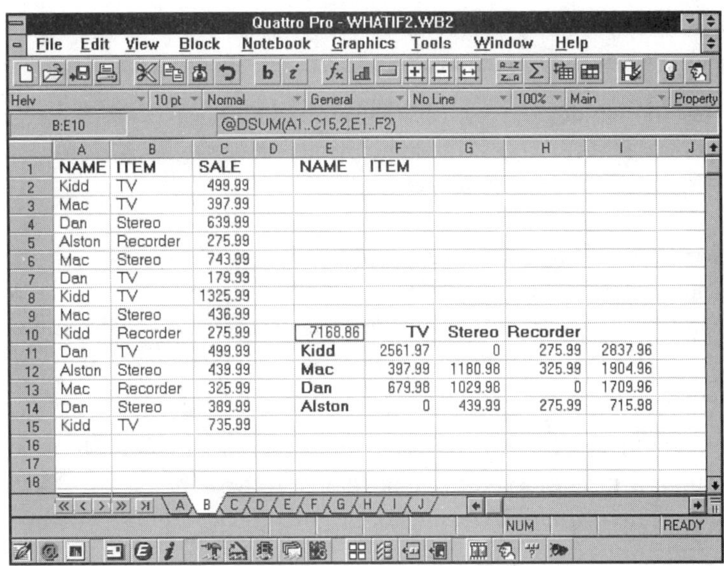

	A	B	C	D	E	F	G	H	I
1	NAME	ITEM	SALE		NAME	ITEM			
2	Kidd	TV	499.99						
3	Mac	TV	397.99						
4	Dan	Stereo	639.99						
5	Alston	Recorder	275.99						
6	Mac	Stereo	743.99						
7	Dan	TV	179.99						
8	Kidd	TV	1325.99						
9	Mac	Stereo	436.99						
10	Kidd	Recorder	275.99		7168.86	TV	Stereo	Recorder	
11	Dan	TV	499.99		Kidd	2561.97	0	275.99	2837.96
12	Alston	Stereo	439.99		Mac	397.99	1180.98	325.99	1904.96
13	Mac	Recorder	325.99		Dan	679.98	1029.98	0	1709.96
14	Dan	Stereo	389.99		Alston	0	439.99	275.99	715.98
15	Kidd	TV	735.99						
16									
17									
18									

Fig. 16.7
A cross-tabulation displays an analysis of data.

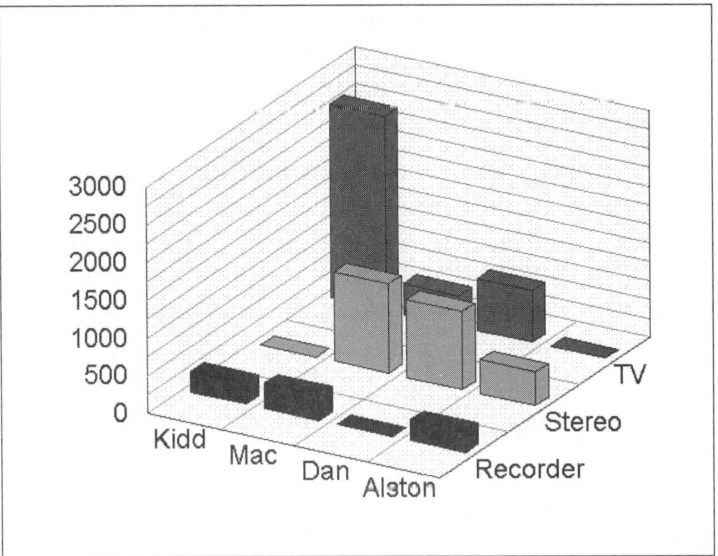

Fig. 16.8
Quattro Pro displays a graph of the cross-tabulation analysis.

Using the Data Modeling Desktop

By now, you can see that crosstabs can be a very effective data analysis tool. A crosstab can often display data relationships you might not otherwise be able to quickly grasp. Unfortunately, creating a crosstab takes some planning and is a lot of work. Not only that, but crosstabs created with the **T**ools,

Numeric Tools, **W**hat-if command aren't too flexible—once you create a crosstab, it's difficult to change so you can see different data relationships.

Quattro Pro includes another very powerful tool, the Data Modeling Desktop, that's a master at the art of creating crosstab data analyses. This tool is much more flexible, and is fun to use, too.

Understanding the Data Modeling Desktop

Until now, whenever you've created a crosstab, the finished crosstab was static and unchanging. You determined the data relationships you wanted to view, and created a crosstab displaying that view. If you wanted to see a different view, you had to go back to the beginning and start over.

The Data Modeling Desktop provides a much different approach to crosstab generation. Instead of a static and unchanging crosstab, the Data Modeling Desktop creates a *dynamic crosstab*—a crosstab you can quickly modify to display additional data relationships.

The Quattro Pro Data Modeling Desktop is quite similar to Lotus Improv and Excel Pivot Tables, but is easier to use because Data Modeling Desktop is an integrated part of Quattro Pro. Creating a data model for use in Data Modeling Desktop is easy because you can use data already contained in a Quattro Pro notebook or from an external database file.

When you first use a dynamic crosstab tool such as the Data Modeling Desktop, you may find the appearance quite similar to a standard spreadsheet, such as Quattro Pro. You'll see the familiar row and column layout, but you'll also see some differences. Rows and columns aren't identified by numbers and letters, and individual cells don't contain formulas. Not only that, but there may be several rows of labels at the top of the Data Modeling Desktop workspace, or several columns of labels along the left side of the workspace. What does this all mean?

Data Modeling Desktop analyzes data by using certain data sets as row or column labels, and a single numerical data set as the data being analyzed. The labels are used as selection criteria to determine which values to include at the intersections of the labels. For example, if your database contained sales information, you might place the names of the salespeople as labels along the left side of the workspace and items along the top. The intersection of the labels "John" and "Computers" would show the total of all computers sold by John.

Simple crosstabs such as this little example really don't show the true power of the Data Modeling Desktop. Adding even one additional piece of data to the picture, though, really complicates matters. Suppose you decided to add time period data to the crosstab. You track sales by date, so you'd like to analyze how well each salesperson did each month, but you want to know how well they did in each product line, too. Now your crosstab is considerably more complicated, and you've only scratched the surface. Imagine that you'd rather change the focus and see how well each product line did each month, rather than each salesperson. Data Modeling Desktop enables you to quickly make such changes in focus, so you can find the hidden relationships in your data.

Creating a Dynamic Crosstab

To analyze data using the Data Modeling Desktop, you must organize the data in a fashion Data Modeling Desktop can use—using a layout identical to a typical Quattro Pro notebook database. Data must be in tabular format, with each record in a single row and field names in the top row.

To send data you want to analyze to the Data Modeling Desktop, follow these steps:

1. Highlight the notebook database block—the block containing the data you want to analyze.

2. Next, choose the **T**ools D**a**ta Modeling Desktop command or click the Data Modeling Desktop button (on the Modeling Toolbar) to open the Send Data to Data Modeling Desktop dialog box (see fig. 16.9).

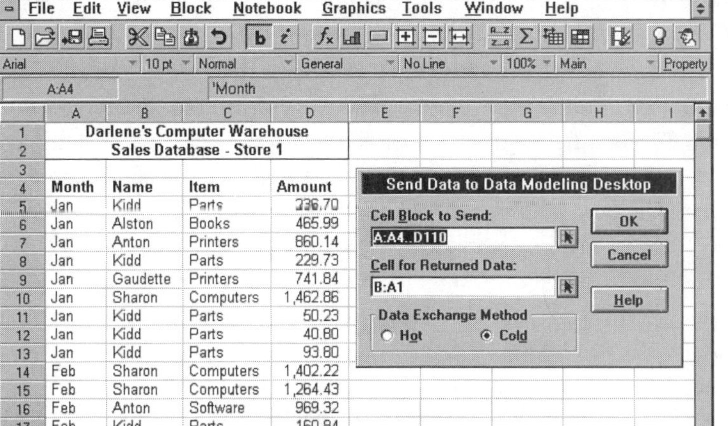

Fig. 16.9
Use the Send Data to Data Modeling Desktop dialog box to specify the data you want to analyze.

3. Press Enter or click OK to display the Data Modeling Desktop window. If necessary, maximize the Data Modeling Desktop window so that you have a larger work area. Your screen should now be similar to figure 16.10.

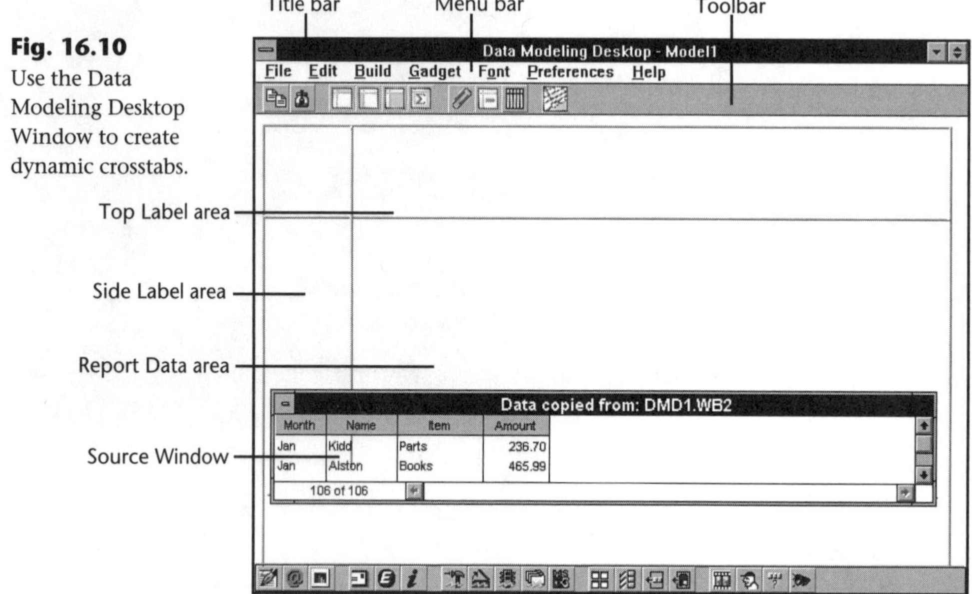

Fig. 16.10
Use the Data Modeling Desktop Window to create dynamic crosstabs.

When you first start the Data Modeling Desktop, the screen looks similar to figure 16.10. Several screen elements are similar to Quattro Pro. The title bar shows the program title and the name of the current model. The menu bar has three familiar menus—**F**ile, **E**dit, and **H**elp—as well as four new menus—**B**uild, **G**adget, F**o**nt, and **P**references. The third line has the Data Modeling Desktop Toolbar. Below the Toolbar is the Report Data area, which has three parts. The Top Label Bar area and the Side Label Bar area are the areas where you place the field names of the data categories you want to tabulate. The Report Data area is the area where you place the data to summarize. The Source Window holds the data you are transferring from Quattro Pro.

Adding Data to the Report

The Side Label Bar and Top Label Bar areas on the Data Modeling Desktop hold the categories of data you want to analyze. Usually, the data categories you add to the Side Label Bar or Top Label Bar areas contain labels or dates, such as a month, item, or sales representative's name. The Report Data area holds the summary data. In this case, you want to summarize the sales for each month, showing which sales representatives sold which items. The data categories you add to the Report Data area should contain numeric data that can be summarized mathematically, such as the sales totals.

To begin building the report, follow these steps:

1. Add the first field to the Side Label Bar by dragging the field to the Side Label Bar area. In this case, select the *Month* field, hold down the left mouse button, and drag it to the Side Label Bar area.

2. Select the next field you want to add and drag the field to the appropriate area. In this case, select the *Item* field and copy it to the top label area by dragging the field to the Top Label Bar area.

3. Select any other fields you want to add to the label bar areas and copy the fields to the appropriate area. In this case, select the *Name* field and copy it to the top label area. The top label area now contains two field labels, with the *Name* field displayed below the *Item* field.

4. Finally, select the field containing the numeric data you want to summarize and copy the field to the report data area. In this case, select the *Amount* field and drag it to the report data area. The basic report now is finished and looks like figure 16.11.

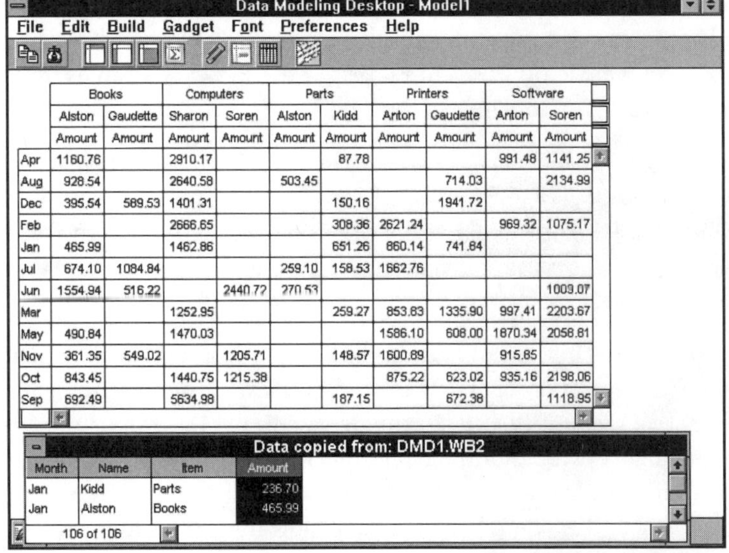

	Books		Computers		Parts		Printers		Software	
	Alston	Gaudette	Sharon	Soren	Alston	Kidd	Anton	Gaudette	Anton	Soren
	Amount	Amount	Amount	Amount	Amount	Amount	Amount	Amount	Amount	Amount
Apr	1160.76		2910.17			87.78			991.48	1141.25
Aug	928.54		2640.58		503.45			714.03		2134.99
Dec	395.54	589.53	1401.31			150.16		1941.72		
Feb			2666.65			308.36	2621.24		969.32	1075.17
Jan	465.99		1462.86			651.26	860.14	741.84		
Jul	674.10	1084.84			259.10	158.53	1662.76			
Jun	1554.94	516.22		2440.72	270.53					1009.07
Mar			1252.95			259.27	853.83	1335.90	997.41	2203.67
May	490.84		1470.03				1586.10	608.00	1870.34	2058.81
Nov	361.35	549.02		1205.71		148.57	1600.89		915.85	
Oct	843.45		1440.75	1215.38			875.22	623.02	935.16	2198.06
Sep	692.49		5634.98			187.15		672.38		1118.95

Month	Name	Item	Amount
Jan	Kidd	Parts	236.70
Jan	Alston	Books	465.99

Fig. 16.11
The finished basic report.

Note

If you want a less cluttered work area, remove the Source Window after all the fields have been copied to the cross-tabulation report. To remove the Source Window, double-click the Source Window control menu. You can redisplay the Source Window at any time by clicking the Source Window button.

Troubleshooting

Some cells in the crosstab say "Multiple Possibilities."

You probably dropped a label field a little too low, making it a data item rather than a top label. Click the handle for the field's label bar and then select **E**dit, Cl**e**ar. Reselect the field in the Source window, and drag it slightly above the top label bar.

Numbers appear in one of the label areas.

Always add numeric data to the report data area, and the identifying data labels to the label areas. If you add numeric data to the label bars, or labels to the report data area, your reports will be meaningless.

Modifying the Report

The real power of the Data Modeling Desktop becomes apparent when you learn how to rearrange the report by moving label bars. As you move the label bars, you change the entire basis of the report and can examine different types of relationships in the data.

You can move the label bars in two ways. You can *pivot* a label bar, changing it from a Side Label Bar to a Top Label Bar or from a Top Label Bar to a Side Label Bar. You also can change the *order* of the label bars in the top or Side Label Bar area. Both types of changes have a profound effect on the cross-tabulation report.

The report created in the earlier example does a good job of summarizing the sales for each type of product, but the report does not summarize each sales representative's sales very well. Fortunately, with the Data Modeling Desktop, you can change the focus of the report quickly and easily. The first step is to pivot the label bar containing the sales representatives' names from the Top Label Bar area to the Side Label Bar area. Follow these steps to pivot the label bar:

1. With the mouse, point to the *handle* for the Top Label Bar containing the sales representatives' names (the handle is the empty box to the right of the names).

2. Hold down the left mouse button and drag the label bar handle to the Side Label Bar area. As you drag the label bar handle, a dotted line shows the label bar pivoting.

3. Release the mouse button when the label bar handle is in the Side Label Bar area. The report changes to reflect the new cross-tabulation summary generated by the new positions of the label bars (see fig. 16.12).

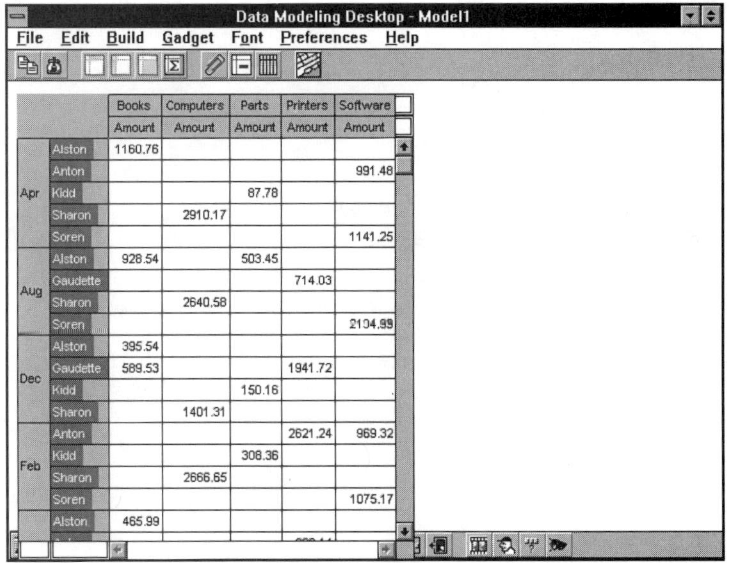

Fig. 16.12
The report changes to reflect the new cross-tabulation summary.

The new report shows the total sales for each sales representative for each month. You easily can see who had sales for each product line and who did not. This entirely new view of the relationships resulted from simply pivoting the label bar containing the names from the Top Label Bar area to the Side Label Bar area.

The report still does not focus on the individual results for each sales representative, but you quickly can move the label bar containing the names to change the cross-tabulation report again. Moving a label bar within the same label bar area changes the *level*, or importance, of the items in the label bars. If you move the names label bar to the left, the items in the names label bar become more important. To move the names label bar to the left, use your mouse to grab the handle for the names label bar and drag it to the left of the months label bar. The report changes to reflect the new cross-tabulation summary generated by the new positions of the label bars (see fig. 16.13).

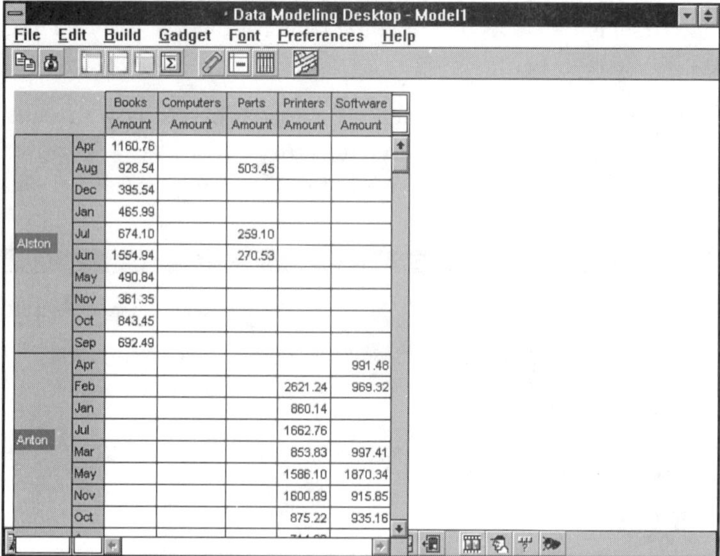

		Books	Computers	Parts	Printers	Software
		Amount	Amount	Amount	Amount	Amount
Alston	Apr	1160.76				
	Aug	928.54		503.45		
	Dec	395.54				
	Jan	465.99				
	Jul	674.10		259.10		
	Jun	1554.94		270.53		
	May	490.84				
	Nov	361.35				
	Oct	843.45				
	Sep	692.49				
Anton	Apr					991.48
	Feb				2621.24	969.32
	Jan				860.14	
	Jul				1662.76	
	Mar				853.83	997.41
	May				1586.10	1870.34
	Nov				1600.89	915.85
	Oct				875.22	935.16

Fig. 16.13
Changing the position of the label bar changes its importance in the report.

Pivoting label bars and moving label bars within the same label bar area completely change the focus of the cross-tabulation. You can try any number of combinations to see the many different relationships contained in your data. The Data Modeling Desktop enables you to examine every possibility easily.

You can explore many more options in Data Modeling Desktop reports. You'll notice, for example, that the months are listed in alphabetical, rather than calendar, order. You can drag individual labels to new positions within the same label bar, so it's easy to rearrange the months into calendar order. You can use the **B**uild, Add T**o**tal Element to add totals to the report; you can use **G**adget, F**o**rmula to use a different type of summary; and you can use **B**uild, **G**roup Elements to combine items (such as combining months into quarters).

After you have created your cross-tabulation report in the Data Modeling Desktop, you copy the report to a Quattro Pro notebook for formatting and printing. The report data copies to cells in the notebook, but any formatting (such as numeric format or lines) does not copy. Use the **E**dit, Copy to

Quattro Pro command or click the Copy to Quattro Pro button to copy the current report to the Quattro Pro notebook. You can then include the crosstab in a Quattro Pro report, or even graph the data.

Using the Database Desktop

By now, you've learned that data is extremely important. You also know that access to data in Quattro Pro provides you many options for analyzing data. Sometimes, though, you may want to use Quattro Pro to analyze data that isn't already in a notebook file. For example, you may want to use data contained in a dBASE or Paradox database file.

Understanding the Database Desktop

Quattro Pro can open many database files directly, treating them as though they were actually Quattro Pro notebook files. This isn't always the best option, though, and if the database file is very large, may not be possible. To use a Quattro Pro notebook, it must be loaded completely into your computer's memory. Database managers, such as Paradox, access database files differently. Instead of loading an entire database into memory, Paradox loads a few records into memory, leaving the rest of the records in the database file on disk. Because only a small portion of the database must fit into memory, disk-based databases can be much larger than databases in a Quattro Pro notebook.

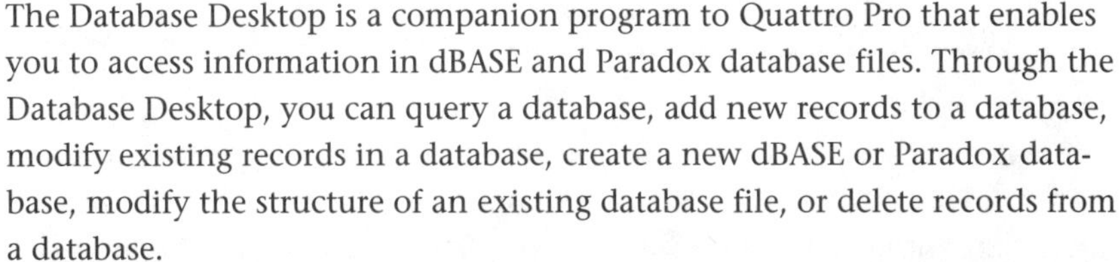

The Database Desktop is a companion program to Quattro Pro that enables you to access information in dBASE and Paradox database files. Through the Database Desktop, you can query a database, add new records to a database, modify existing records in a database, create a new dBASE or Paradox database, modify the structure of an existing database file, or delete records from a database.

> **Note**
>
> The Database Desktop is closely related to Paradox for Windows. The Database Desktop lacks many of the more powerful features of Paradox for Windows such as scripts, forms, reports, and the ObjectPAL programming language. You may find the Database Desktop a little more convenient to use with Quattro Pro, however, because you can access the Database Desktop from the Quattro Pro **T**ools menu, or by simply clicking a Toolbar button.

Using Database Files

To load the Database Desktop into memory, select the **T**ools, **D**atabase Desktop command. Your system briefly displays a message informing you of its progress loading the program, and then displays the Database Desktop (see fig. 16.14). If only the Database Desktop title bar appears, or if the Database Desktop does not fill the screen, click the Maximize button or select Ma**x**imize from the Database Desktop Control menu to provide the largest possible work area.

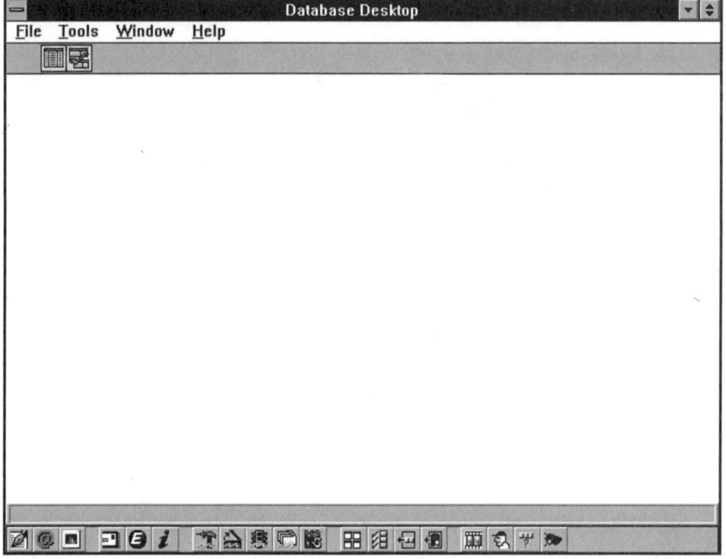

Fig. 16.14
Use the Database Desktop to access disk-based database tables.

Because the Database Desktop is designed to provide easy access to databases from within Quattro Pro, this section will deal specifically with selecting and sharing data with Quattro Pro. Since the Database Desktop is so closely related to Paradox, you will find that much of the information in part four of this book, "Using Paradox," applies to the Database Desktop as well, and will not be repeated here.

Rather than opening a database table and viewing the complete set of records, often you may want to view a subset of those records that you select by using specified criteria. You may want to search for records for a single customer, as an example, for records applying to sales over a specified amount, or for customers in a certain group of states. You use the Query commands in the Database Desktop to select specified records. You can then save the query, and use the saved query with Quattro Pro to add the selected records into a Quattro Pro notebook.

To create a new query, select **F**ile, **N**ew Query and choose the database table whose records you want to view. After you select a database table, the Database Desktop Query Editor appears. The Query Editor uses *Query by Example* (QBE) to build a database query; you place example values in the fields displayed in the Query Editor, and records are selected based on these values.

To build a query, you use symbols, operators, and reserved words. Query Editor *symbols* indicate the fields you want included in the answer table, whether to include duplicate values, and the default sort order. *Operators* select field values based on criteria you specify. The >= operator, for example, selects records that contain a value in the selected field greater than or equal to a specified value. *Reserved words* perform special database operations, such as inserting and deleting records.

Figure 16.15 shows an example of a query that selects books from a database. In this example, the query specifies that only those titles by Aristotle should be selected. The results of running the query appear in the answer table.

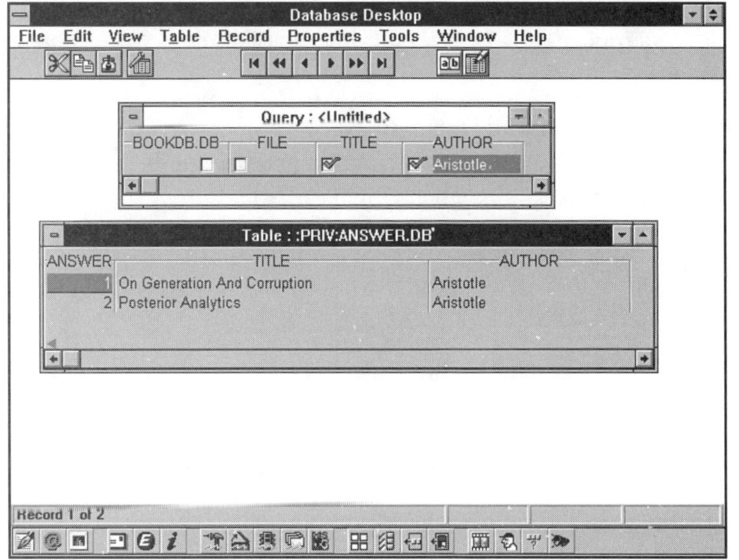

Fig. 16.15
A query selects specific database records.

In this case, the answer table shows that the database contains two titles by Aristotle. By changing the comparison value and rerunning the query, you can produce different sets of answers. To reuse the same query in the future, choose **F**ile, **S**ave or **F**ile, Save **A**s before you close the query or the Database Desktop. Queries you create in either in the Database Desktop or Paradox are saved in text files which use the extension QBE. You can use such saved queries in the Database Desktop, Paradox, or through the Quattro Pro **T**ools, Data**b**ase Tools, **T**able Query command.

Sharing Results with Quattro Pro

The Database Desktop stores the current answer in a temporary file called ANSWER.DB in your working directory. You can import this file into a Quattro Pro notebook; but when you do, the imported information is static and is not updated when the database changes.

A better way to share database information between the Database Desktop and Quattro Pro is use the Database Desktop QBE file along with the Quattro Pro **T**ools, Data**b**ase Tools, **T**able Query command. In this way, the information in your notebook is updated to reflect changes in the database. You can, for example, create and refine a database query, and then execute your fully developed query from within a notebook application.

To run a saved query from within a Quattro Pro notebook, follow these steps:

1. Choose **T**ools, Data**b**ase Tools, **T**able Query to display the Table Query dialog box.

2. Select Query in the **F**ile menu to execute a query in a QBE file, or Query in **B**lock to execute a query that you previously imported into a notebook block (remember, QBE files are text files).

3. If you select Query in **F**ile, specify the name of the QBE file. If you select Query in **B**lock, specify the notebook block that contains the query.

4. Specify the **D**estination—the upper left corner of the notebook block where you want to place the database records.

5. Click OK to confirm the dialog box and execute the query.

Figure 16.16 shows the completed Table Query dialog box and the results of executing the saved query within a Quattro Pro notebook.

The Database Desktop serves as a tool for creating more powerful Quattro Pro applications that feature easy access to dBASE and Paradox database files. You could use a saved query to automatically update the information in a Quattro Pro notebook to include the latest data—especially if you use shared database files on a network and need to make certain your notebooks are up to date.

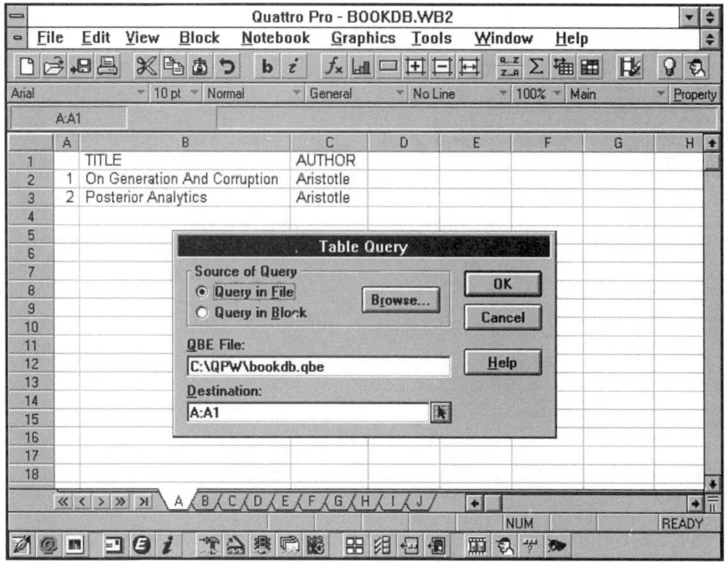

Fig. 16.16
You can run saved queries within a Quattro Pro notebook.

From Here...

This chapter provided a quick look at some of the powerful extras in Quattro Pro—its data analysis tools. For more information on related subjects, see the following chapters:

- Chapter 17, "Using Graphics," discusses how you can give your data real impact using graphs.
- Chapter 20, "Querying Your Data," talks about how to create sophisticated queries that enable you to select just the records you need from a database.

Chapter 17

Using Graphics

by Brian Underdahl

Quattro Pro's presentation graphics features help you present data in an easier-to-understand manner. Instead of trying to understand countless rows and columns of data, a well-executed graph can enable you to see and analyze large amounts of information quickly. The most effective reports are those which clearly analyze that data.

Quattro Pro includes many powerful graphics capabilities. Because these graphics features are built-in, you will find that creating sophisticated graphics within Quattro Pro is quite easy. You don't need to use a separate, dedicated graphics package to produce graphs of your Quattro Pro data.

In this chapter, you learn how to

- Create graphs from data in a notebook
- Select different types of graphs
- Enhance a graph

Creating a Simple Graph

You can create extremely sophisticated, complex, and stunning graphs with Quattro Pro. You can even create on-screen slide shows that automatically change from one graph to the next at specified intervals using such fancy effects as dissolves, fades, wipes, or spirals. Learning all the intricacies of such fancy productions could use up all your time for weeks or even months. For most of us, a relatively simple graph that effectively displays our data is a much more reasonable goal, so that's where we'll start—by learning how to create a simple graph.

Although most of your work in Quattro Pro is done in the spreadsheet, Quattro Pro also provides a Graph window that gives you much more power and control over graphing. The Graph window provides you specialized commands, Toolbars, and a Property band all designed to help you enhance a graph. Before you can access the Graph window, however, you first must create a graph, so let's start there.

Starting a Basic Graph

The data you want to graph must be in a tabular format, similar to a typical Quattro Pro notebook database. The requirements for data you want to graph aren't quite as strict as they are for a database, though, because you can use either rows or columns for similar data. A crosstab table is often a very good choice for the layout of data you want to graph, because a crosstab has labels identifying both the groups and the elements in your data.

Figure 17.1 shows a notebook containing the annual sales report for a fictitious company. We'll use this notebook to demonstrate the steps in creating a Quattro Pro graph.

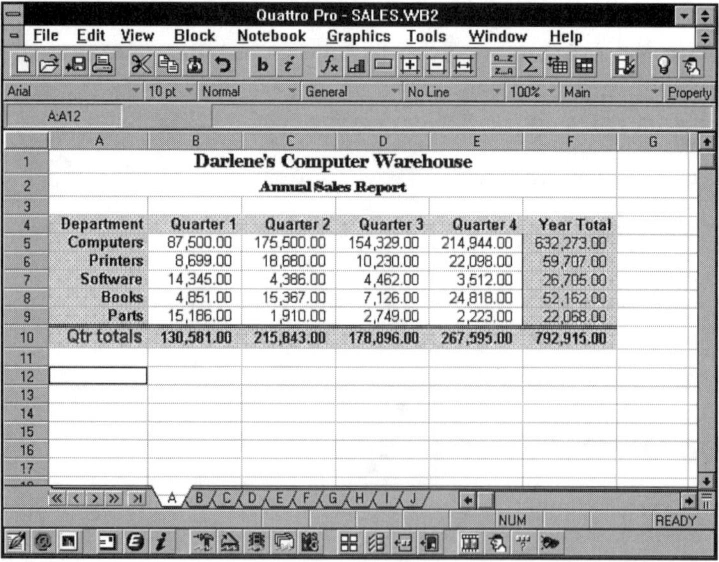

Fig. 17.1
A sample sales data notebook used for creating graphs.

You use the **G**raphics commands to create a graph that is linked to notebook data. With these commands, you can graph data from one notebook. The commands on the **G**raphics menu enable you to create a graph, view a graph, add an existing graph to the notebook, and view a slide show. Before you create a graph in a notebook, most selections in the **G**raphics menu are dimmed. These commands are not available when a Notebook window is the active window and no graph currently exists, but they become available when the Graph window is the active window, or when you have added a graph to a notebook and are editing the graph.

Choose **G**raphics, **N**ew Graph to create a graph. By default, the first graph is named Graph1, the second is Graph2, and so on.

Quattro Pro uses the currently highlighted spreadsheet block as the block to be graphed. If you don't select a block, but the cell selector is located within a block of data, Quattro Pro uses the entire block. If the block you want to graph is contained within a larger block of data, select the block of data to graph before choosing **G**raphics, **N**ew Graph.

Troubleshooting

The new graph includes data I don't want to graph.

Highlight the block you want to graph before you select **G**raphics, **N**ew Graph.

To graph information from the sales data notebook, you need to know which data you want to plot and which data you want to use in labeling the graph. In figure 17.1, time-period labels are listed across row 4. Category identifiers are located in column A. The numeric entries in rows 5 through 9, as well as the formula results in row 10 and column F, are suitable for graphing as data points. For this example, however, the totals in row 10 and column F are not included in the graphed data. The column and row labels can be used to label the points on the graph.

After you have selected a block to graph, choose **G**raphics, **N**ew Graph from the Quattro Pro menu to display the New Graph dialog box (see fig. 17.2). If you want, you can change the default graph name by typing a new name in the **G**raph Name text box. If necessary, adjust the blocks shown in the Series range text boxes.

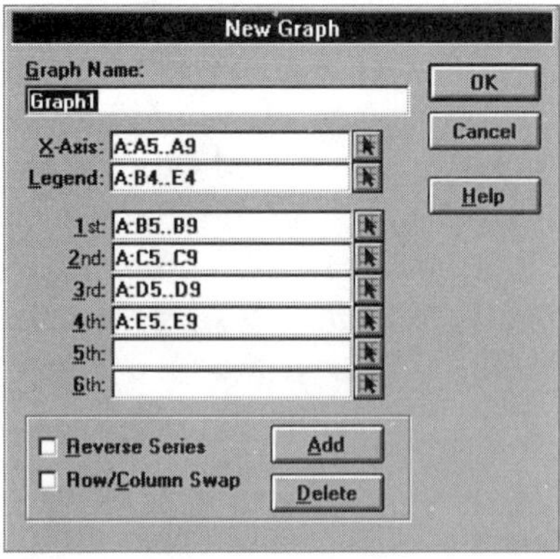

Fig. 17.2
Type the name of the graph in the New Graph dialog box.

Press Enter or click OK to confirm the dialog box. You can change the graph type after the graph appears by using the **G**raphics, T**y**pe command. Figure 17.3 shows the basic graph. Later in this chapter, you will learn how to modify the basic graph to improve its appearance.

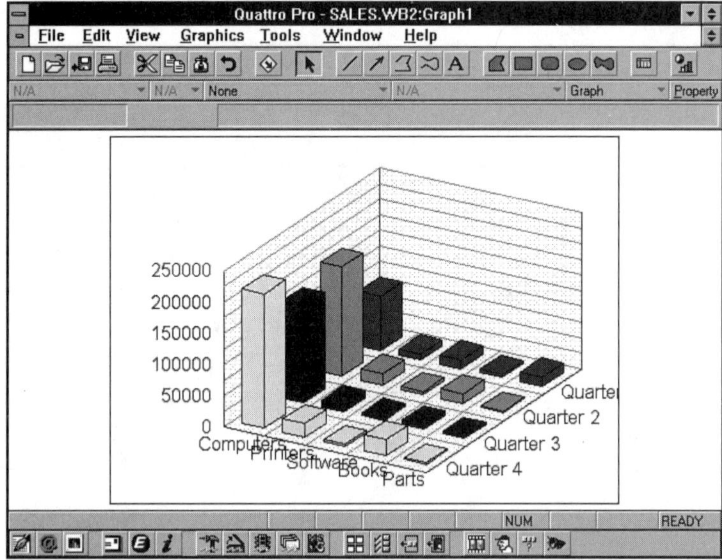

Fig. 17.3
The default graph of the sales data spreadsheet.

Troubleshooting

Most of the data values on a graph can't be determined because the Y-axis goes too high.

Quattro Pro automatically scales the Y-axis to show the largest values in the graph. You may need to select a smaller data block that doesn't include the largest values, or change the graph to a two-dimensional graph and graph the largest values on the second Y-axis. Right-click a data series, select Series Properties, and click the Se**c**ondary Y-axis radio button to graph the data on the second Y-axis.

Understanding the Graph Window

Note in figure 17.3 that the command menu, the Toolbar, and the property band have changed. When you graph data from the notebook, Quattro Pro displays the graph in a separate Graph window and automatically uses the Graph window menu, the Graph window Toolbar, and the Graph window property band. If you press Nex**t** (Ctrl+F6) or select the notebook window from the **W**indow menu, the menu bar changes and displays the Quattro Pro Notebook menu.

The Graph window has several Toolbars that are specially designed for working with graph objects. The Graph Toolbar, for example, provides tools you can use to draw objects on graphs. The Palette Toolbar enables you to select colors and patterns, and the Align Toolbar enables you to group and ungroup graph objects, change positions of graph objects so that they are in front of or behind others, and control object alignment. In addition, the options on the Graphics menu are no longer dimmed as they were when the Notebook window was active, indicating that they now are available.

Understanding Common Graph Terms

Most graphs (except for bullet charts, text charts, pie graphs, and doughnut graphs) have a *y-axis*—a vertical left edge—and an *x-axis*—a horizontal bottom edge (in rotated graphs, the y-axis is the bottom edge, and the x axis is the left edge). Quattro Pro automatically divides each axis with tick marks and scales the numbers on the y-axis, based on the minimum and maximum numbers in the associated data block. The intersection of the y-axis and the x-axis is called the *origin*. The origin is zero unless you specify otherwise.

A graph is made up of one or more *data series*, each of which reflects a category of data. The first category of data is always series 1, the second is series 2, and so on. Some graph types use a limited number of data series; for example, pie and doughnut charts use one data series, and XY graphs use two or more. Other graph types, such as line graphs, can graph multiple data series.

Legends are text placed beside or below a graph that explain the symbols, colors, or fill used to denote each data series. *Titles* are text placed above the graph and along the horizontal and vertical axis that provide information about the overall graph. *Labels* are text entries used to explain specific data items or entries in a graph.

Understanding Graph Types

Quattro Pro automatically selects a graph type when you use the **G**raphics, **N**ew Graph command. To change the type of graph Quattro Pro displays, choose **G**raphics, T**y**pe after you use **G**raphics, **N**ew Graph. When you choose the type of graph you want, Quattro Pro changes the display to reflect your choice. You can also choose the graph type in the Graph Setup and Background dialog box.

Several types of graphs are available in Quattro Pro: **2**-D, **3**-D, **R**otate, **C**ombo, **B**ullet, and B**l**ank. Except for **B**ullet and B**l**ank graphs, each of the graph types also offers several variations.

Selecting a Different Type of Graph

You can change a graph to a different type several different ways, but you can only change a graph's type if the graph is displayed in the Graph window, or if you first select the graph if it is displayed in a notebook.

To select a new type for a graph which is displayed in the Graph window or which has been selected in the notebook, select **G**raphics, T**y**pe to display the Graph Types dialog box (see fig. 17.4). You can also display this dialog box by pointing to an area in the graph outside any graph objects and clicking the right mouse button. Select Type from the QuickMenu. If you select Graph Setup and Background Properties from the QuickMenu, the Graph Setup and Background dialog box includes a Graph Type pane that serves the same function as the Graph Types dialog box.

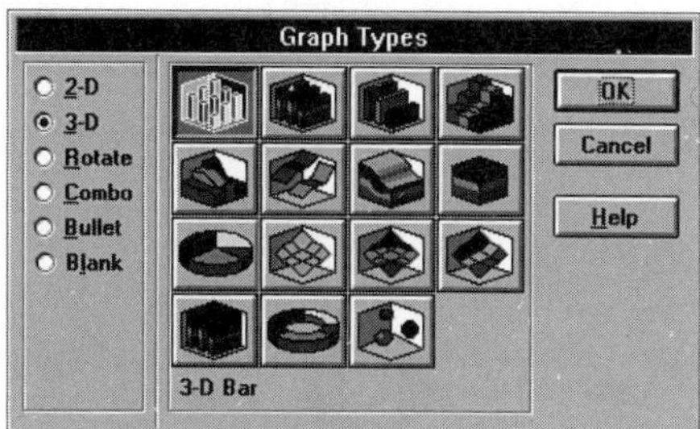

Fig. 17.4
Use the Graph Types dialog box to select a new graph type.

As you select each basic type of graph, **2**-D, **3**-D, **R**otate, **C**ombo, **B**ullet, or B**l**ank, small samples of each of the optional variations are shown in the dialog box. As soon as you select a new graph type and click OK, your graph is changed to the selected type. The following sections briefly describe the basic graph types.

Understanding 2-D Graphs

2-D (two-dimensional) graphs are the most common type of business graphs. In this graph, data is plotted using an x-axis and a y-axis or, in the case of column and pie graphs, using no axis at all.

Tip
If you want to graph some data using the second Y-axis, you must use a 2-D graph.

Bar Graphs

A *bar graph* shows data as a series of bars drawn next to each other. This type of graph is useful for showing how data categories compare over time.

Variance Graphs

A *variance graph* is similar to a bar graph, except that the origin is adjustable to show how data varies from a specified value. Initially, a variance graph has the origin set to 0, and so the graph appears identical to a standard 2-D bar graph. After you create the basic variance graph, adjust the origin by pointing to the graph y-axis and clicking the right mouse button, or by choosing Y Axis from the Property section of the Property band. Select the Zero line at text box in the Scale pane of the Y-Axis dialog box, and enter a new value for the origin.

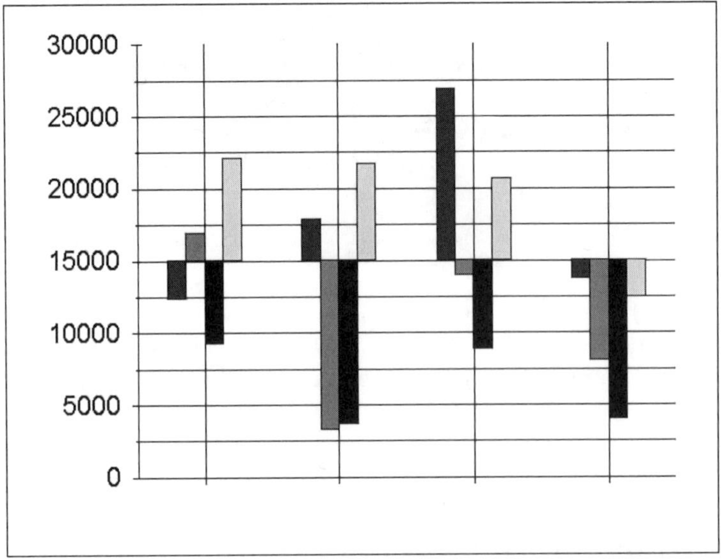

Fig. 17.5
A variance graph uses an origin you specify.

Stacked Bar Graphs

A *stacked bar graph* shows data as a series of bars stacked on top of one another. This type of graph is useful for showing the portion that data categories contribute to a whole, as well as comparing changes in those contributions over time. Stacked bar graphs not only show how each data item varies over time, but also how the total of all data items varies over the same time period.

A *100% stacked bar graph* is a variation of the stacked bar graph; in this type of graph, the bar is always full height, and the individual data items are shown as their percentage of 100 percent.

Comparison graphs and *100% stacked bar comparison graphs* are also variations of stacked bar graphs. For these graph types, the boundaries between the data segments in each bar are connected to the corresponding boundaries between the data segments in the next bar. These connecting lines can help you to spot trends more easily, but they may be difficult to understand if the bars contain too many data segments.

High-Low Graphs

High-low graphs are sometimes called HLCO graphs, which stands for high-low-close-open. A high-low graph is especially useful for graphing data about the price of a stock over time. The high-low-close-open figures represent the stock's highest and lowest price in the given time period, the stock's price at the end of the time period, and the stock's price at the start of the time period (see fig. 17.6).

Each set of data consists of four figures representing high, low, close, and open values. The set of data is typically represented on the graph as a vertical line with tick marks. The line extends from the low value to the high value. The close value is represented by a tick mark extending to the right of the line, and the open value is represented by a tick mark extending to the left. The total number of lines on the graph depends on the number of time periods included.

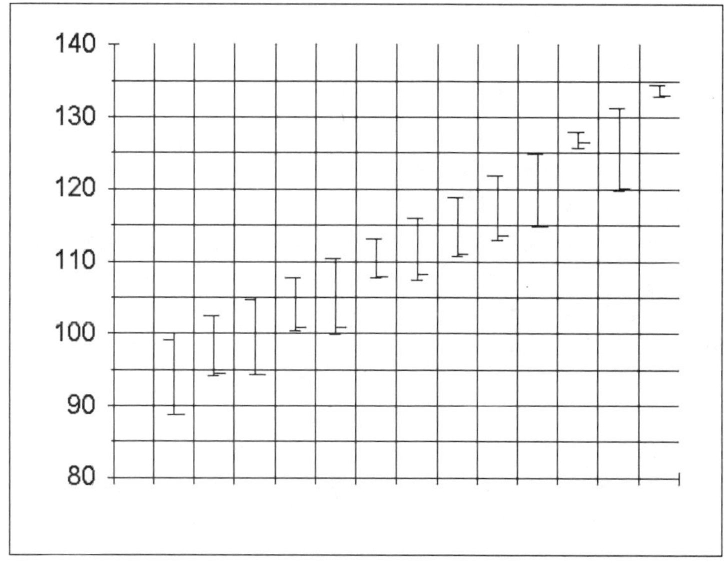

Fig. 17.6
High-low graphs often display stock prices.

Line Graphs

Line graphs are the most common type of graph and one of the easiest to understand. Line graphs plot values using individual lines to connect the data points for each data series.

XY Graphs

The *XY graph*, often called a *scatter graph*, is a variation of a line graph. Like a line graph, an XY graph has values plotted as points in the graph. Unlike a line graph, an XY graph has its x-axis labeled with numeric values instead of labels.

Quattro Pro always plots the independent variable (data you can change or control) on the x-axis, and the dependent variables (data you cannot control or change, and which is dependent on the independent variable) on the y-axis; thus, the independent data should be in the first row or column, and the dependent data should be in the second and succeeding rows or columns.

Area Graphs

An *area graph*, which emphasizes broad trends, is a combination of a line graph (which illustrates a change in data over time) and a stacked-bar graph (which illustrates individual sets of values). Area graphs plot the first data series closest to the x-axis, and stack additional data series above each other. Each data series line represents the total of the data series being plotted plus all lower data series. Area graphs are filled between the origin and the plotted lines.

Column Graphs

A *column graph* compares values in a single set of data that contains only positive numbers. Each value appears as a section of the column and represents a percentage of the total. You can plot only one row or one column of numeric data in a column graph. Column graphs are very similar in function to pie graphs, but column graphs are more effective when you want to plot a large number of data items.

Tip

If you attempt to plot too many data items, the wedges of the pie graph become too small to understand easily. Use column graphs to plot data series with large numbers of individual items.

Pie Graphs

Like a column graph, a *pie graph* compares values in a single set of data that contains only positive numbers. Each value appears as a slice of the pie and represents a percentage of the total. You can plot only one row or one column of numeric data in a pie graph. To explode a pie graph section (make it stand out from the rest of the pie sections), right-click the slice you want to explode, select Pie Graph Properties, and select the E**x**plode check box.

Doughnut Graphs

A *doughnut graph* is a variation of a pie graph; unlike a pie graph, however, a doughnut graph has a center ring cut out (see fig. 17.7). You use a doughnut graph exactly as you use pie graphs.

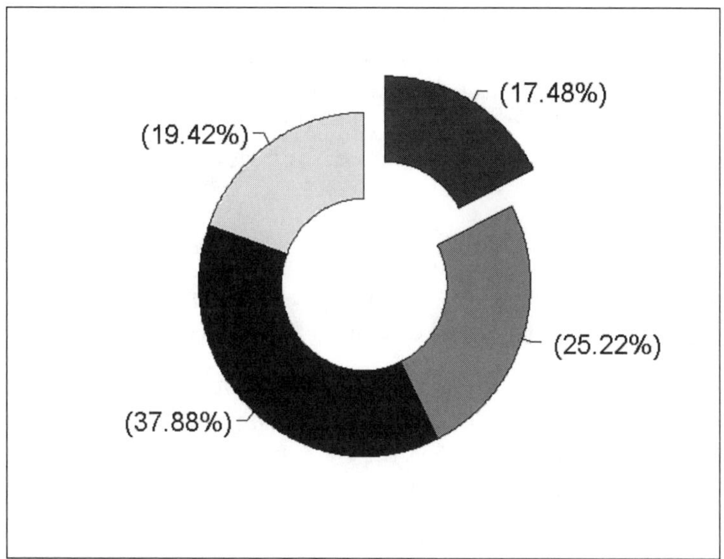

Fig. 17.7
A doughnut graph is a variation of a pie graph.

Radar Graphs

A *radar graph* plots data radiating out from a single center point. X-axis values appear as spokes in a wheel, and y-axis data is plotted on each spoke. Radar graphs may make spotting trends easier, depending on the type of data being graphed.

Understanding 3-D Graphs

A *3-D graph* plots data in three-dimensional perspective. Instead of just using an x-axis and a y-axis, a 3-D graph adds a z-axis. In some cases, 3-D graphs do a better job than 2-D graphs of showing the complex relationships between groups of data items.

3-D Stacked Bar Graphs

Similar to regular stacked bar graphs, *3-D stacked bar graphs* work best with small amounts of data in comparing sets of data over time. A 3-D stacked bar graph shows data as a series of 3-D bars stacked on top of one another. This type of graph is useful for showing the portion that data categories contribute to a whole, as well as comparing changes in those contributions over time. 3-D stacked bar graphs not only show how each data item varies over time, but also how the total of all data items varies over the same time period.

2.5-D Bar Graphs

2.5-D bar graphs show data as a series of deep bars drawn next to each other. A 2.5-D bar graph is not a true 3-D graph, because it does not use depth to portray a z-axis value, but instead, to add a third dimension to the bars. This type of graph is useful for showing how data categories compare over time.

3-D Bar Graphs

3-D bar graphs show data as groups of bars plotted on a three-dimensional grid. Often a 3-D bar graph provides an easier-to-understand display of the relationship between the plotted data series than a 2-D bar graph can.

Tip
A 3-D bar graph may hide smaller values behind large values. Arrange the data series with the largest values first and the smallest values last.

You may also want to experiment with the **E**levation setting in the 3D View section of the Graph Setup and Background dialog box. Using a number higher than the default 30 displays the graph from a higher view point, and may make it easier to see all the data.

Step Graphs

Step graphs are nearly identical to 3-D bar graphs, except that the bars in a step graph touch. Step graphs are most useful for displaying data that changes in regular increments, rather than data that may change abruptly in either direction.

Troubleshooting

It's hard to see the data in 3-D graphs.

Use 3-D ribbon graphs to display data without hiding smaller values behind larger ones.

3-D Unstacked Area Graphs

3-D unstacked area graphs plot values using lines (which are stretched to add depth) to connect the data points for each data series, while filling the area between the lines and the origin. Because larger values in a 3-D unstacked area graph can hide lower values plotted behind them, this type of graph is best suited to displaying sorted data.

Ribbon Graphs

Ribbon graphs are similar to 3-D unstacked area graphs; they plot values using lines (which are stretched to add depth) to connect the data points for each data series. Ribbon graphs, however, do not fill the area between the lines and the origin. Ribbon graphs are better than 3-D unstacked area graphs at displaying unsorted data because larger values are less likely to hide lower values plotted behind them in a ribbon graph (see fig. 17.8).

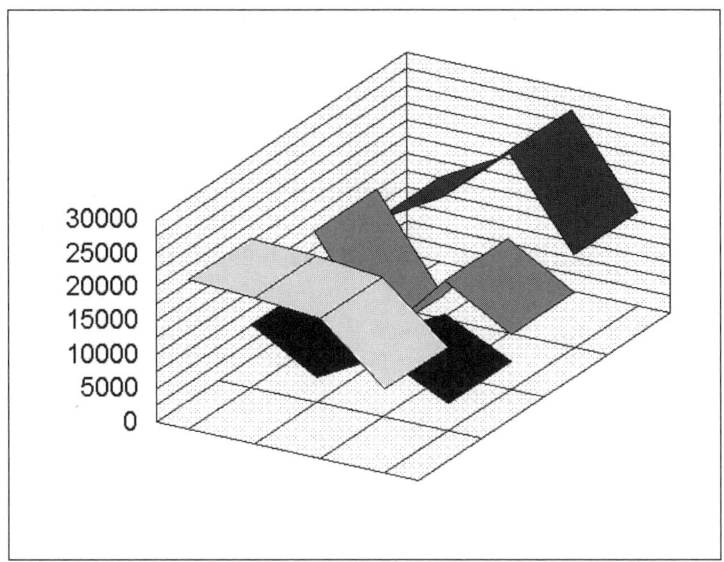

Fig. 17.8
Ribbon graphs display data as floating segments.

3-D Area Graphs

3-D area graphs, which emphasize broad trends, are a combination of a line graph and a 3-D stacked-bar graph. 3-D area graphs plot the first data series closest to the x-axis, and stack additional data series above each other. Each data series line represents the total of the data series being plotted plus all lower data series. 3-D area graphs are filled between the origin and the plotted lines.

3-D Column Graphs

A *3-D column graph* compares values in a single set of data that contains only positive numbers. Each value appears as a section of the column and represents a percentage of the total. You can plot only one row or one column of numeric data in a 3-D column graph. 3-D column graphs are very similar to 2-D column graphs, except that the column is displayed with a third dimension: depth.

3-D Pie and Doughnut Graphs

3-D pie graphs and *3-D doughnut graphs*, like 3-D column graphs, are extensions of the standard 2-D graphs—in this case, the 2-D pie or doughnut graphs. Like a 2-D pie graph, a 3-D pie graph plots a single data series, showing each data item as a percentage of the total. A 3-D doughnut graph also plots a single data series, showing each data item as a percentage of the total. The data series cannot contain negative values.

Surface Graphs

Surface graphs display data as lines connecting the data items for each series. The line for each data series is connected to the line for the next data series, and the area between the lines is filled in with different colors.

Contour Graphs

Contour graphs are very similar to surface graphs, except in the method used to color the surface plot. Instead of coloring the segments between each set of lines with a distinct color, contour graphs apply color to show how far the surface lies above the origin. Contour graphs can be used to show elevations, as in contour maps.

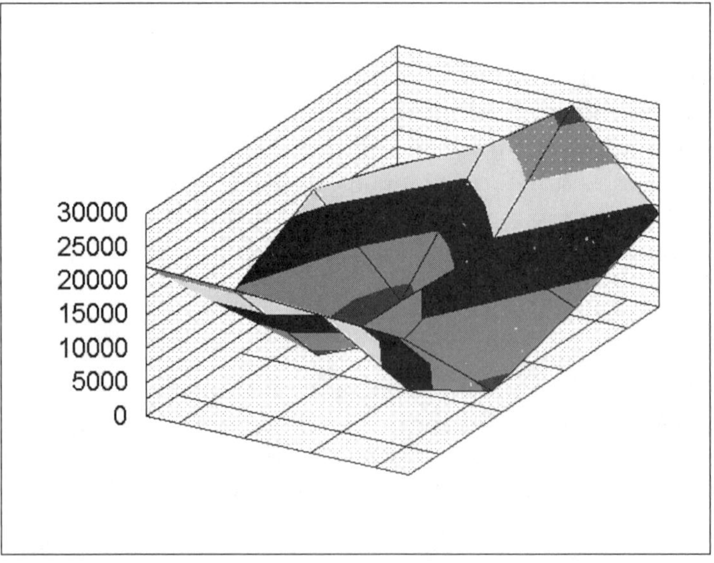

Fig. 17.9
Contour graphs can be used to display elevations contained in topographical data.

Troubleshooting

My contour graphs don't look like topographical maps.

Set the **E**levation property in the 3D View pane of the Graph Setup and Background dialog box to 90. This provides a direct, overhead view.

I need finer increments between values to better show the scale gradients.

Use the **I**ncrement option in the Scale pane of the Y-Axis dialog box to select a smaller increment.

Shaded Surface Graphs

Shaded surface graphs are another variation on surface and contour graphs. The shaded surface graph uses a single color to create the surface, but applies different shading to show the slope of the surface between data points. Shaded surface graphs may reproduce better than surface and contour graphs on black-and-white printers.

Understanding Rotated Graphs

Sometimes you can create a more stunning visual effect by rotating a graph. *Rotated graphs* place the x-data series along the left vertical axis and the y-data series along the horizontal axis. Values are plotted as horizontal distances from the left axis instead of vertical distances from the lower axis.

Quattro Pro enables you to plot eleven of its standard graphs as rotated graphs: 2-D Bar, 3-D Bar, 2.5-D Bar, Area, Line, Stacked Bar, 2-D 100% Stacked Bar, 2-D Comparison, 2-D 100% Comparison, 3-D Stacked Bar, and 3-D 100% Stacked Bar.

Tip

Graphs that combine a bar graph and a line, area, or a high-low graph, are used to display data that is related, but that requires different types of plotting to best show different data series.

Understanding Combo Graphs

Quattro Pro enables you to mix graph types so that you can compare different sets of data. The **G**raphics T**y**pe **C**ombo command enables you to select from several different combinations of graph types. You can combine a bar graph and a line, area, or a high-low graph. You also can display multiple column, 3-D column, pie, 3-D pie, or bar graphs.

Graphs that show multiple columns, pies, or bars show several different data series plotted as individual graphs, but include each individual graph within a single-named graph in the notebook. When you use multiple columns or pies, each column or pie is the same size. You can compare how the data items within each data series relate as a percentage of the total of the data series, but you cannot determine the relative values of data items between series.

Understanding Bullet Graphs

Bullet graphs are a special type of chart often used in presentations. Instead of graphing numerical data, bullet graphs display notebook text in a special format. In a bullet graph, a title line is followed by one or more levels of bulleted text, usually presenting information in an outline style format.

To create a bullet graph, you use a block of text either two or three columns wide in the notebook as the source of graph data. The first column contains the graph title, the second contains the first level of bulleted text, and the third contains an optional second level of bulleted text.

Understanding Blank Graphs

Blank graphs are a special type of Quattro Pro graph. Instead of plotting notebook data, blank graphs enable you to create graphics objects that you can place anywhere you like in a notebook. Blank graphs can contain text, objects you create using the drawing tools available in the Graph window, and imported graphics.

You can also use the tools on the notebook window Draw Toolbar to draw floating objects directly on a notebook page. Floating objects drawn on the notebook page are very similar to the objects you draw in a blank graph, except that floating objects drawn on the notebook page do not have an opaque graph pane to obscure other objects on the page. For example, if you draw an arrow directly on a notebook page, objects under the arrow's path are not covered by a rectangular box as they would be by an arrow drawn in a floating graph and then added to the page.

Enhancing a Graph

Quattro Pro offers several options for improving the appearance of your graphs and producing final-quality output suitable for business presentations. After you have created the basic graph, you use the Graph window menu commands to change the selection of graph blocks, types, and orientation;

data labels and legends; x-, y-, and optional second y-axes; borders and grids; colors; hatch patterns; fonts; and lines.

Changing the Graph Orientation

The initial orientation Quattro Pro selects for the rows and columns of data may not always be the optimal choice. A different graph layout may be more effective in representing your data.

By default, Quattro Pro assumes that the first row or column of your data with labels contains the x-axis labels (the labels along the bottom of the graph that group the data series in comparable sets). To change the orientation of the data series, choose **G**raph, **S**eries, Row/**c**olumn swap. Figure 17.10 shows the graph after the Row/**c**olumn swap check box in the Graph Series dialog box is selected. Compare figure 17.10 to figure 17.3, and you'll quickly see how changing the graph orientation provides quite a different view of the data.

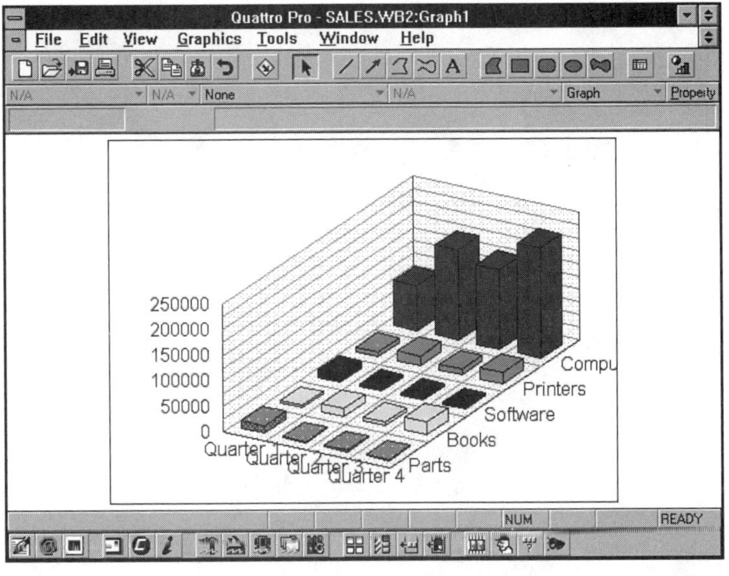

Fig. 17.10
The reoriented graph after Row/**c**olumn swap is selected.

Adding Titles

When you graph data from a notebook, you can specify the titles after you create and view the graph. With the **G**raphics, **T**itles command, you can create a **M**ain Title, a **S**ubtitle, an **X**-Axis Title, a Y**1**-Axis Title, and a Y**2**-Axis Title (see fig. 17.11).

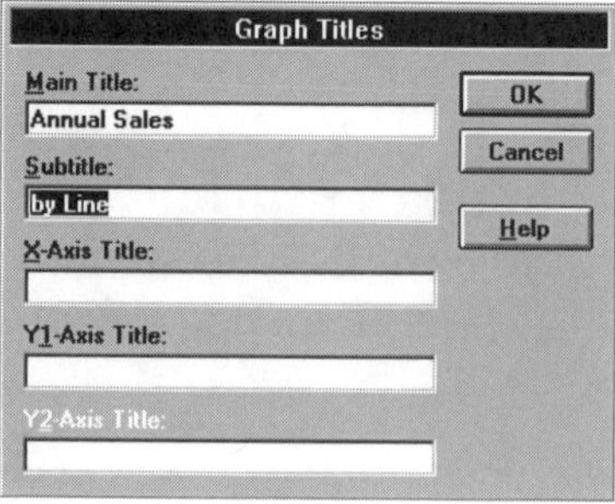

Fig. 17.11
Use the Graph Titles dialog box to add titles to your graphs.

You use the **M**ain Title and **S**ubtitle text boxes to create the first and second titles; they appear centered above the graph, with the first title in larger type above the second title. You use the **X**-Axis Title, Y**1**-Axis Title, and Y**2**-Axis Title text boxes to add titles for the graph axes. You can move the main and subtitles, but you cannot move the x- or y-axis titles. Figure 17.12 shows the graph with main and subtitles added.

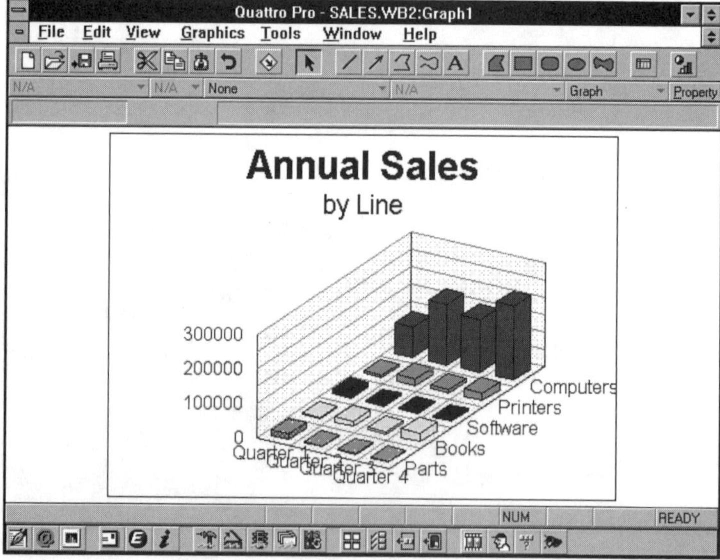

Fig. 17.12
The graph after adding titles.

You can edit the titles and notes by choosing the **G**raphics, **T**itles command and changing or editing the contents of the text boxes. When you have finished entering or editing the titles, click OK or press Enter to confirm the dialog box. You also can edit any single title, as well as control its use of color, font, and text attributes by using the Object Inspectors dialog box (point to the title you want to change and click the right mouse button).

Quattro Pro offers many different options for enhancing graphs. These sections have shown only a few of the possibilities. You'll also want to explore some other options such as changing the viewpoint for a 3-D graph, changing the fonts used to display text objects in a graph, and even using bitmaps (pictures) as backgrounds in your graphs. To see the many possibilities, use the Object Inspectors dialog box to see the properties you can change. Point to an object, such as a data series, the graph background, or a title, and click the right mouse button. You'll find the Object Inspector dialog boxes provide literally thousands of option combinations you can use to fully customize your Quattro Pro graphs.

Displaying Graphs in the Notebook

Quattro Pro can print a graph from the Graph window or as part of a notebook report. In many cases, though, you'll find that by adding a graph directly into a notebook-based report, the report will be much more effective.

You add a graph to a notebook by using the Notebook menu **G**raphics, **I**nsert Graph command. In the **S**elect Graph list box, select the name of the graph. Click OK or press Enter to confirm the dialog box. Then click the Graph Tool button and select the notebook block where you want the graph displayed. Figure 17.13 shows a print preview view of a notebook with a graph added to the notebook. **F**ile, Print Pre**v**iew changes the appearance of the notebook to printer preview mode and displays the notebook as it will appear when printed.

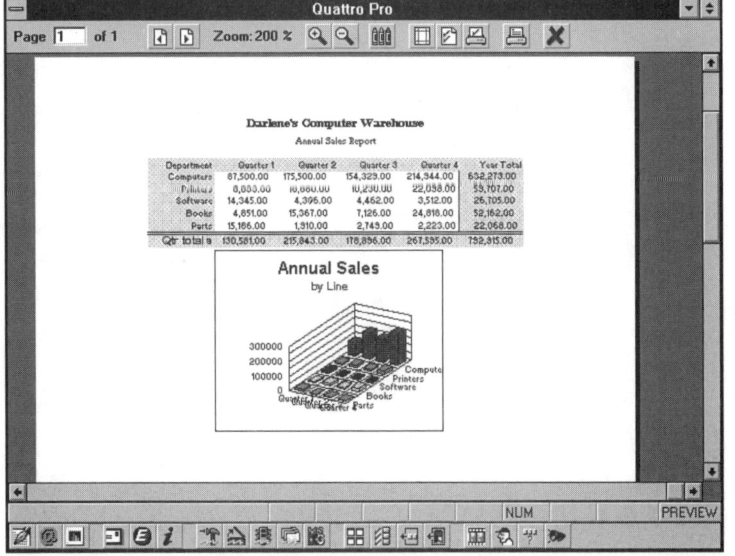

Fig. 17.13
A print preview of a graph added to a notebook block.

Whenever you plan to print a notebook, you should first view it in **F**ile, Print Pre**v**iew mode. You might, for example, find that you need to adjust the size of graphs added to the notebook.

From Here...

In this chapter, you've learned how to create a basic Quattro Pro graph, and how to apply some enhancements to make graphs more effective. For more information on related subjects, see the following chapters:

- Chapter 18, "Printing Reports," shows you how to print your Quattro Pro reports most effectively.
- Chapter 25, "Working with Data Charts," and Chapter 26, "Adding and Enhancing Objects," show you how to use WordPerfect Presentations to produce graphics with even more punch.

Chapter 18

Printing Reports

by Brian Underdahl

The final step in creating a useful Quattro Pro notebook is to produce an effective, printed report. This step enables you to make good use of the data in your notebook and database files by sharing it with other people. This chapter introduces the commands and procedures you use to print Quattro Pro reports.

In this chapter, you learn how to

- Use the Quattro Pro printing commands
- Preview reports before printing
- Enhance reports with headers and footers
- Control print margins
- Select your printer

Setting Up a Report

Setting up a report in Quattro Pro can be quite simple. A very basic report, for example, requires only a few commands or mouse clicks to print. Usually, however, an effective report is one that results from a little more planning and thought. Quattro Pro has many options that enable you to customize your printed reports so they look professional and convey the information properly.

The following sections show you how to print reports quickly and efficiently. Whether your report is a short report of a page or less, or a longer multiple-page report, you'll find the process is quite similar.

Selecting the Print Block

If you don't specify a block to print, Quattro Pro automatically sets the entire *active area* of the current notebook page as the print block, so it's important to understand how Quattro Pro determines the active area of a notebook page. The active area of a page is defined as the rectangular area between cell A1 and the intersection of the last column and the last row which contain entries. Figure 18.1 demonstrates how this works. In this figure, the active area extends from A1 to E14. Cell E14 does not contain any data, but is at the intersection of the last column and the last row used in the notebook. If you print the notebook shown in figure 18.1 but don't specify a print block, Quattro Pro will print the block A1..E14.

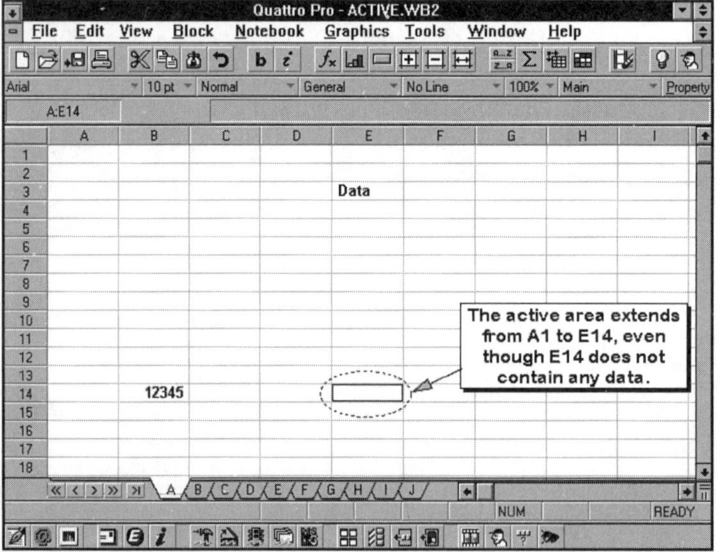

Fig. 18.1
Quattro Pro automatically prints the active area of the current page if you don't specify a block.

Printing a Single Block

If you preselect a block, the selected block becomes the print block. Once a print block has been specified, Quattro Pro remembers the specified block and uses the same block as the print block unless you specify a different block. If you forget to preselect the block to print, you can specify the block in the Print Area text box of the Spreadsheet Print dialog box. You can type the block addresses, or you can highlight the block with the keyboard or the mouse.

To print a specified print block, follow these steps:

1. Highlight the block you want to print.
2. Choose **F**ile, **P**rint to display the Spreadsheet Print dialog box (see fig. 18.2).
3. Click **P**rint.

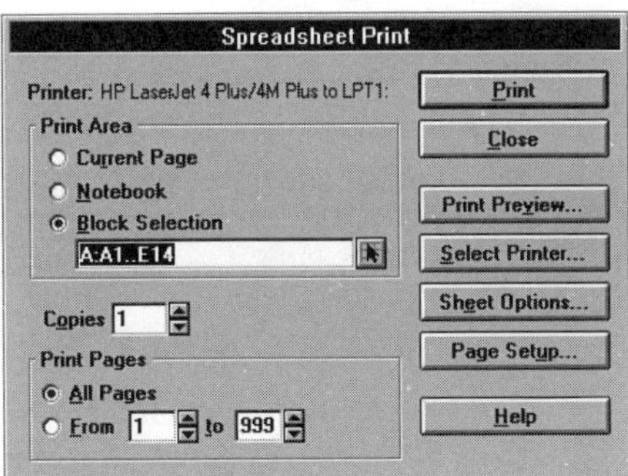

Fig. 18.2
Use the Spreadsheet Print dialog box to specify what you want to print.

Troubleshooting

Even though the correct print block is selected, text is cut off when a report prints.

Long labels can spill over into empty cells to the right. If a label spills over to a cell outside the print block, only the text within the block is printed. Extend the print block to the right to include all the text.

The printed report includes blank pages.

Select the area you want to print before choosing **F**ile, **P**rint. Otherwise, Quattro Pro prints even the blank pages included in the active area of the notebook.

Printing Multiple Blocks

For many reports, a two-dimensional block—a single rectangular area on one notebook page—is all you need to print. Sometimes, though, you may need to print three-dimensional blocks or multiple two-dimensional blocks contained on one or more notebook pages.

A three-dimensional print block includes the same block on two or more notebook pages. You specify a three-dimensional print block by preselecting the block or by entering the block address or block name in the Spreadsheet Print dialog box—the same way you specify a two-dimensional block. After

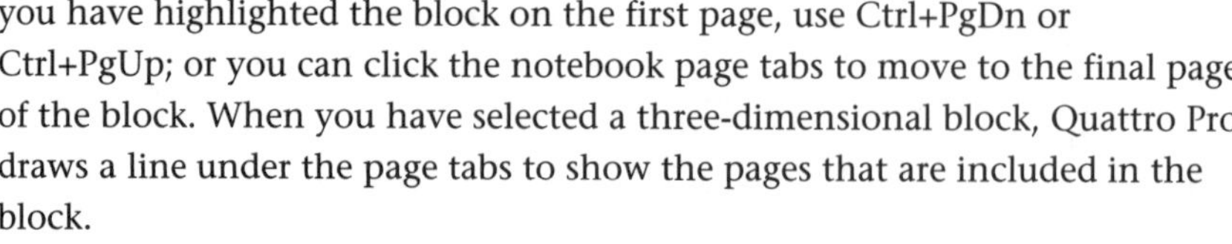

you have highlighted the block on the first page, use Ctrl+PgDn or Ctrl+PgUp; or you can click the notebook page tabs to move to the final page of the block. When you have selected a three-dimensional block, Quattro Pro draws a line under the page tabs to show the pages that are included in the block.

Tip
When you specify multiple print blocks, previewing the printed output is always a good idea, so you may want to choose **F**ile, Print Pre**v**iew, or **F**ile, **P**rint, Print Pre**v**iew.

Multiple print blocks are two or more blocks that may be on the same or different notebook pages. You can use multiple print blocks when you want to print part of the information on a page, but don't want to include certain information that may be between the blocks you do want to print. To specify multiple print blocks, press and hold down the Ctrl key while you are selecting the blocks. To type the names or addresses of multiple print blocks, enter the first block name or address in the Spreadsheet Print dialog box, type a comma, and type the next block.

Figure 18.3 shows a notebook with four print blocks selected, and figure 18.4 shows the result of choosing **F**ile, Print Pre**v**iew to preview the printed output. If you are satisfied with the previewed printed output, click the printer button to print the reports, or press Esc to return to the notebook display.

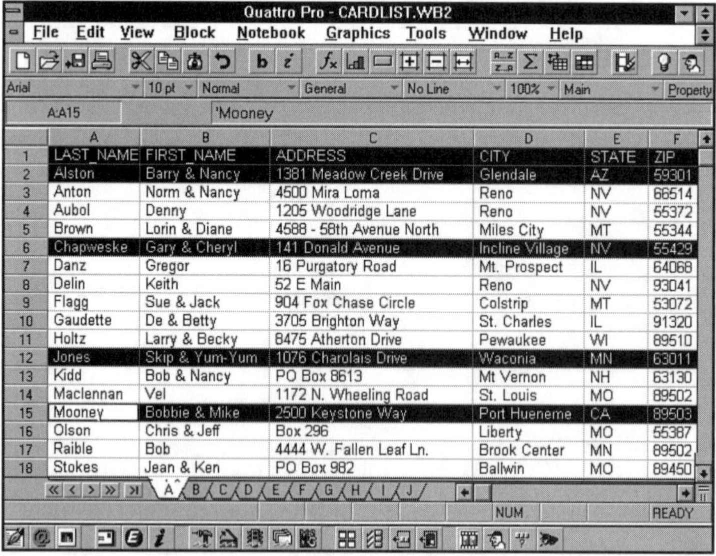

	A	B	C	D	E	F
1	LAST_NAME	FIRST_NAME	ADDRESS	CITY	STATE	ZIP
2	Alston	Barry & Nancy	1381 Meadow Creek Drive	Glendale	AZ	59301
3	Anton	Norm & Nancy	4500 Mira Loma	Reno	NV	66514
4	Aubol	Denny	1205 Woodridge Lane	Reno	NV	55372
5	Brown	Lorin & Diane	4588 - 58th Avenue North	Miles City	MT	55344
6	Chapweske	Gary & Cheryl	141 Donald Avenue	Incline Village	NV	55429
7	Danz	Gregor	16 Purgatory Road	Mt. Prospect	IL	64068
8	Delin	Keith	52 E Main	Reno	NV	93041
9	Flagg	Sue & Jack	904 Fox Chase Circle	Colstrip	MT	53072
10	Gaudette	De & Betty	3705 Brighton Way	St. Charles	IL	91320
11	Holtz	Larry & Becky	8475 Atherton Drive	Pewaukee	WI	89510
12	Jones	Skip & Yum-Yum	1076 Charolais Drive	Waconia	MN	63011
13	Kidd	Bob & Nancy	PO Box 8613	Mt Vernon	NH	63130
14	Maclennan	Vel	1172 N. Wheeling Road	St. Louis	MO	89502
15	Mooney	Bobbie & Mike	2500 Keystone Way	Port Hueneme	CA	89503
16	Olson	Chris & Jeff	Box 296	Liberty	MO	55387
17	Raible	Bob	4444 W. Fallen Leaf Ln.	Brook Center	MN	89502
18	Stokes	Jean & Ken	PO Box 982	Ballwin	MO	89450

Fig. 18.3
Four print blocks are preselected.

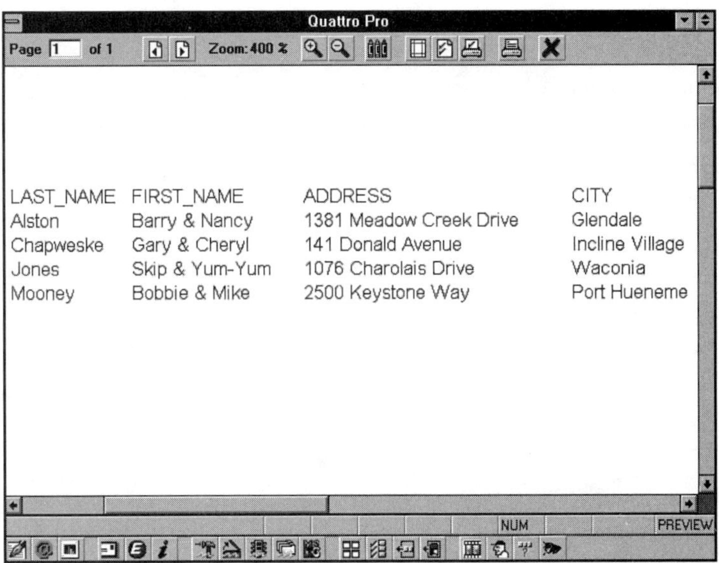

Fig. 18.4
Previewing the printed report containing four print blocks.

You can specify any combination of two- and three-dimensional print blocks. Quattro Pro prints the blocks in the order in which you select the blocks or enter the block names or addresses.

Adding Enhancements to the Report

You can use Quattro Pro's options to enhance your reports in many different ways. You select many printing options through the Spreadsheet Page Setup dialog box, which displays when you select **F**ile Page Se**t**up, or when you select **F**ile **P**rint Page Set**u**p. The Spreadsheet Page Setup dialog box includes options for specifying paper type, a header and footer, margins, print scaling, and for saving the print settings (see fig. 18.5).

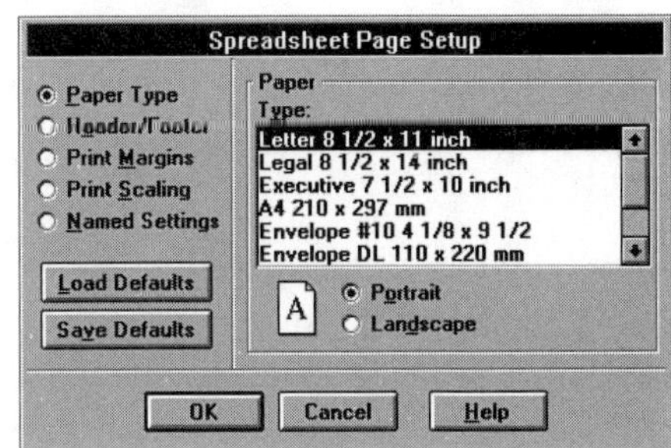

Fig. 18.5
The Spreadsheet Page Setup dialog box **P**aper Type pane.

Selecting the Type of Paper

> **Note**
>
> You may have to change the paper in your printer if you select a different paper size. The T**y**pe list shows the paper sizes your printer can use—not the sizes loaded into your printer.

The **P**aper Type pane of the Spreadsheet Page Setup dialog box shown in figure 18.5 enables you to select the type of paper, and whether the report will print in P**o**rtrait or Lan**d**scape orientation. The T**y**pe list box has a scroll bar you can use to display the paper sizes available to fit your selected printer.

The P**o**rtrait and Lan**d**scape options are radio buttons—meaning you can select one or the other, but not both at the same time. The P**o**rtrait selection prints with the paper tall and narrow, the Lan**d**scape selection prints with the paper short and wide.

Printing a Header or Footer

A *header* is information printed in one or two lines at the top of each page of a report. A *footer* is information printed in one or two lines at the bottom of each page of a report. You specify a header or footer in the Spreadsheet Page Setup dialog box H**e**ader/Footer pane (see fig. 18.6). Choose **F**ile, Page Se**t**up to display the Spreadsheet Page Setup dialog box.

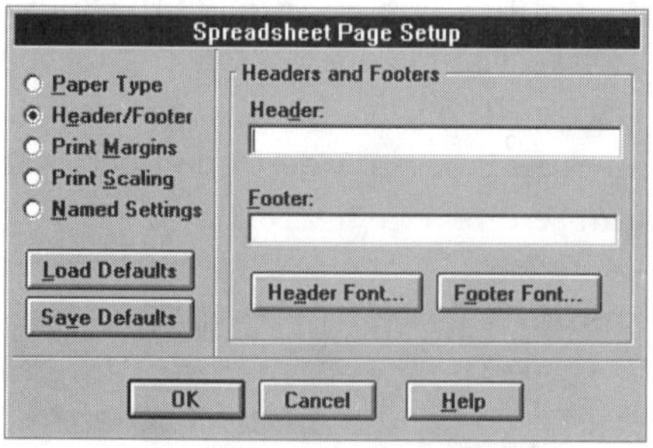

Fig. 18.6
The Spreadsheet Page Setup dialog box H**e**ader/Footer pane.

Each line of a header or footer can have up to three parts: a left-aligned, a centered, and a right-aligned section. When you enter header or footer text, separate the segments with a vertical bar (|). Segments that precede the first vertical bar are left-aligned, segments following the first vertical bar but preceding the second vertical bar are centered, and segments following the second vertical bar are right-aligned. To place the remaining segments of the header or footer on a second line, use **#n** in the header or footer at the point where you want to create the line break.

Table 18.1 describes the symbols you use to display information in headers and footers. You also can instruct Quattro Pro to include the contents of a cell by entering a backslash (\) followed by the cell address or block name.

Table 18.1 Header and Footer Formatting Symbols

Symbol	Description
#	Current page number
#d	Current date in Short International format
#D	Current date in Long International format
#ds	Current date in standard Short format
#Ds	Current date in standard Long format
#f	Notebook name
#F	Notebook name with path
#n	Prints balance of text on new line
#p	Current page number
#P	Total number of pages in printout
#p+*n*	Current page number plus the number *n*
#P+*n*	Total number of pages in printout plus the number *n*
#t	Current time in Short International format
#T	Current time in Long International format
#ts	Current time in standard Short format
#Ts	Current time in standard Long format
@	Current date
|	Left, center, or right aligned text

Setting Print Margins

Print margins are the distance between the edges of the paper and the beginning of the area where Quattro Pro can print. The Spreadsheet Page Setup dialog box Print **M**argins pane enables you to change margins (see fig. 18.7). Choose **F**ile, Page Se**t**up to display the Spreadsheet Page Setup dialog box.

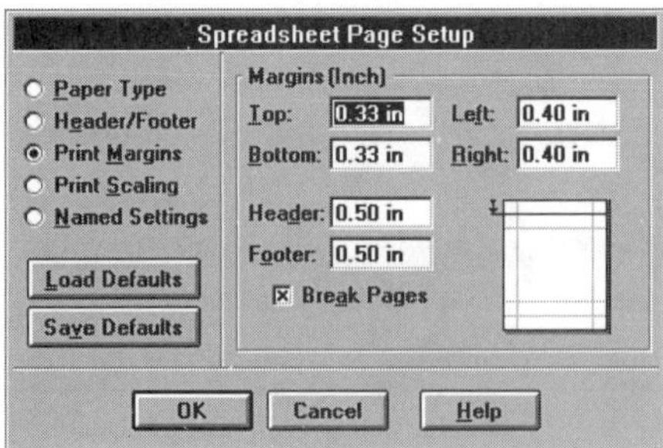

Fig. 18.7
The Spreadsheet Page Setup dialog box Print **M**argins pane.

By default, Quattro Pro reserves a margin of .33 inches at the top and at the bottom of each page, and .4 inches at each side of the page, which is not used for any printing. In addition, another .5 inches are reserved between the top and bottom margins and any data. Any headers or footers you specify are printed in this space.

The Spreadsheet Page Setup dialog box Print **M**argins pane contains six different text boxes you can use to set the page margins. The **T**op and Hea**d**er margins work together, as do the **B**ottom and F**o**oter margins. The **T**op margin, for example, specifies the distance between the top of the page and the beginning of the header text. The Hea**d**er margin specifies the distance between the top margin and the beginning of the report text.

Setting Print Scaling

You can reduce or enlarge the size of a printed report by using *print scaling*. This option enables you to specify an exact percentage, or to have Quattro Pro automatically reduce the size of the print enough to fit the entire report on as few pages as possible. You use the Print **S**caling pane of the Spreadsheet Page Setup dialog box to specify print scaling (see fig. 18.8). Choose **F**ile, Page Se**t**up to display the Spreadsheet Page Setup dialog box.

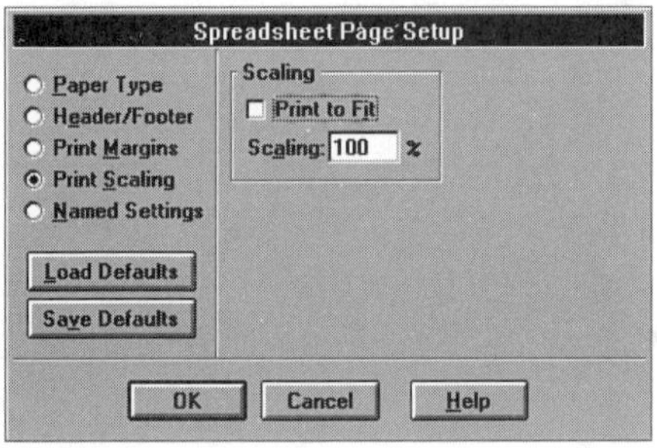

Fig. 18.8
The Spreadsheet Page Setup dialog box Print **S**caling pane.

To fit all the printed output on as few pages as possible, select the Print to Fit check box. Quattro Pro attempts to reduce the size of the print enough to fit the entire report on a single page. If the report still does not fit a single page, Quattro Pro uses the maximum compression on all pages.

To control the exact level of compression, enter a percentage in the Scaling text box, and make certain the Print to Fit check box is not selected. To reduce the size of print by one-half, for example, enter **50** in the Scaling text box. You can expand the print also by entering a number larger than 100. To print the report three times the normal size, enter **300**.

Tip
If you use Print to Fit, choose File, Print Preview before printing to preview the printed report.

Troubleshooting

Reports printed using Print to Fit print much too small, and leave large blank spaces at the right or the bottom of the page.

Be sure to specify the print block. Quattro Pro is probably printing the entire active area of the current notebook page.

Even though the correct print area is specified, the report is still too small to read.

Specify an exact percentage in the Scaling text box rather than using the Print to Fit check box.

Using Named Print Settings

You can save current print settings under a unique name, recall the settings with this name, and reuse the settings without specifying each setting individually. You use the Named Settings pane in the Spreadsheet Page Setup dialog box to create or use named print settings (see fig. 18.9). Choose File, Page Setup to display the Spreadsheet Page Setup dialog box.

Fig. 18.9
The Spreadsheet Page Setup dialog box Named Settings pane.

To assign a name to the current print settings, enter the name in the New Set text box and click Add. To change an existing named print setting, highlight the setting you want to change, and click Update. To remove a named setting, highlight the setting you want to remove, and click Delete. To use an existing named setting, highlight the setting you want to use, and click Use.

Printing Row and Column Headings

Multiple-page reports can be difficult to understand. This is especially true when you can not easily determine the correct column or row for data on pages after the first page. One improvement that often makes multiple-page reports easier to understand is to include row or column headings, so each printed page includes the descriptive text that explains the data being presented. Setting headings in a printout has an effect similar to freezing titles on a notebook page.

Tip
Don't include any rows you designate as a **T**op Heading and any columns you designate as a Le**f**t Heading in the print block—they'll be printed twice.

To include row or column headings, choose **F**ile, **P**rint, and then click the Sh**e**et Options button to display the Spreadsheet Print Options dialog box (see fig. 18.10). For the **T**op Heading, select one or more rows of labels to print above each page of data. For the Le**f**t Heading, select one or more columns of data to print at the left of each page of data.

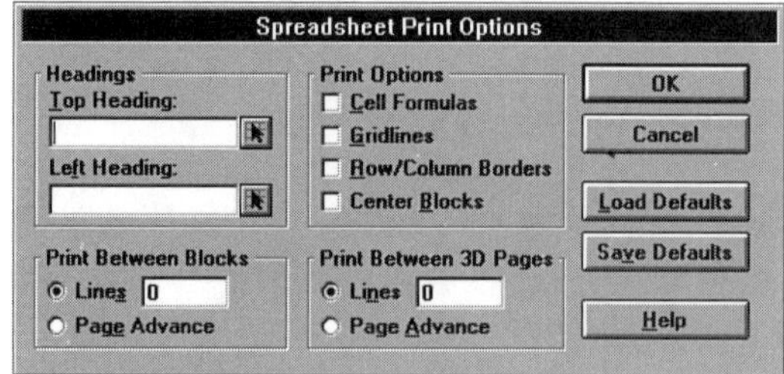

Fig. 18.10
Use the Spreadsheet Print Options dialog box to specify row or column headings.

Using Additional Print Options

The Spreadsheet Print Options dialog box has several additional settings you can use to enhance your printed reports. These include:

- *Cell Formulas.* Prints cell formulas instead of the calculated results. This option is primarily for notebook documentation purposes.
- *Gridlines.* Prints the spreadsheet grid lines. This makes your report look more like the notebook page.
- ***R**ow/Column Borders.* Includes the spreadsheet frame in your printed report. This is useful when you are developing a notebook, because the printouts show the location of data on the notebook page.
- *Center **B**locks.* Prints the report centered between the page margins.

You use the Print Between Blocks and Print Between 3D Pages options to specify the separation you want between multiple or 3-D blocks.

Selecting Your Printer

You use the **F**ile, **P**rint, **S**elect Printer command to select or configure a printer, or to redirect print output to a file (see fig. 18.11). The choices in the Printer Setup dialog box depend on your system configuration.

To configure your printer, select **S**etup. When you make this selection, Windows displays a dialog box specific to your printer. Although each printer type offers different setup options, each Windows Printer Setup dialog box includes a **H**elp option. If you are unsure of the correct setting of any option available for your printer, select **H**elp to display information about the different options.

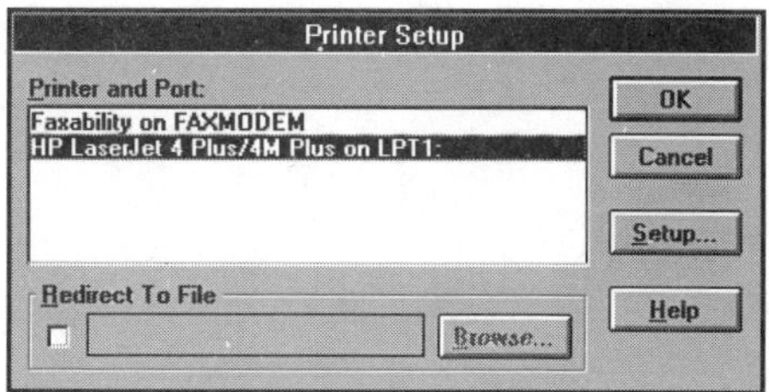

Fig. 18.11
Use the Printer Setup dialog box to select your printer.

If you want to delay printing, perhaps because you want to create a report you'll print on a printer that is temporarily unavailable, select the **R**edirect To File check box and specify a name for the print file. The print file will contain instructions specific to the selected printer, and will probably not print correctly on any other type of printer.

From Here...

This chapter provided the information you need to print effective reports from your Quattro Pro notebooks. For related information, see the following chapters:

- Chapter 15, "Changing the Display and Appearance of Data," to learn how to improve the appearance of your notebooks and reports.
- Chapter 17, "Using Graphics," to learn how to create graphs of your data which you can add to your reports.

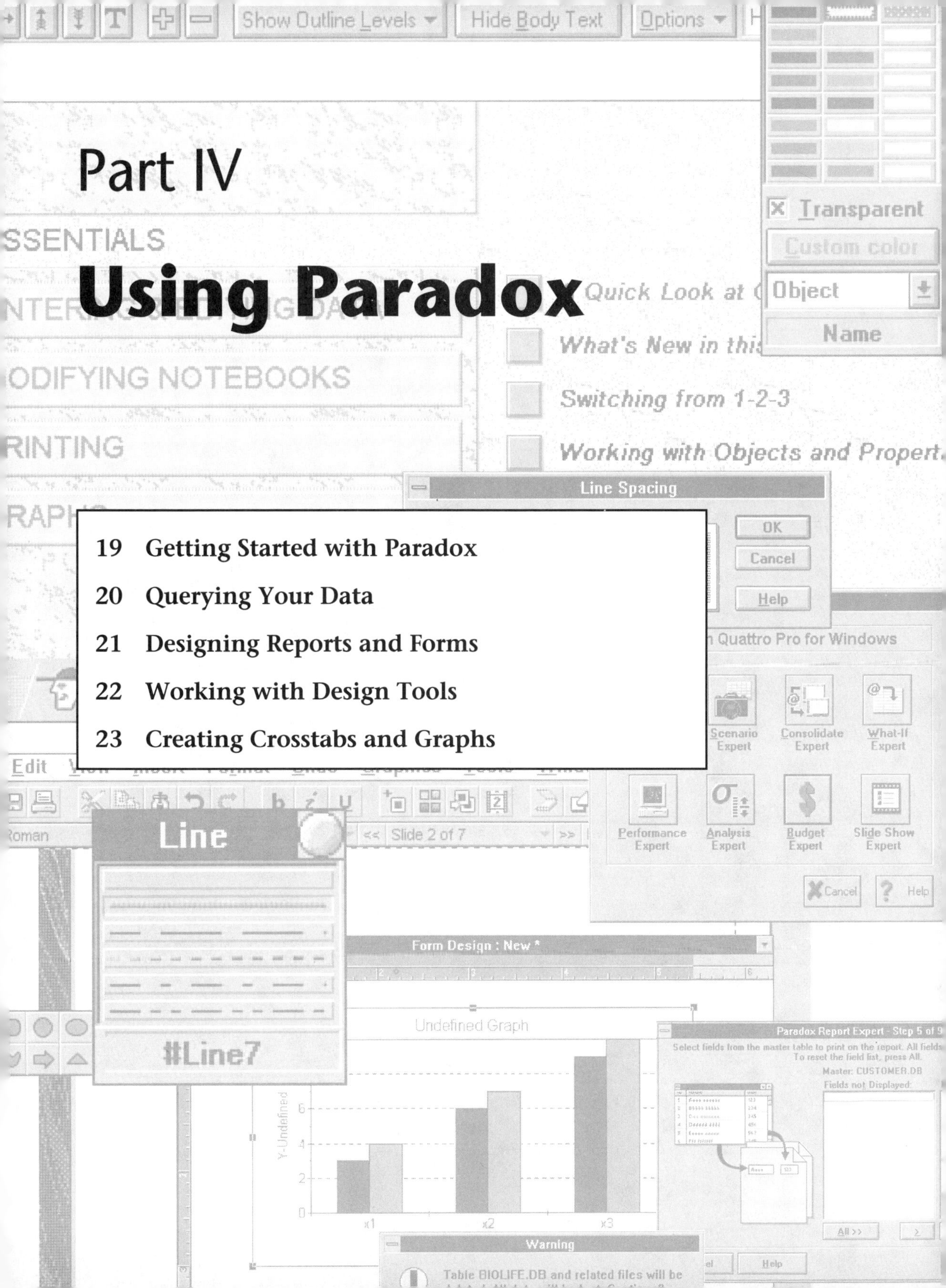

Part IV

Using Paradox

Show Outline Levels
Hide Body Text
Options
Transpar
Custom co
Object
Name
ESSENTIALS
ENTERING & EDITING DATA
ODIFYING NOTEBOOKS
PRINTING
GRAPHS
A Quick Look at
What's New in this
Switching from 1-2-3
Working with Objects and Pro
Line Spacing
Line Spacing
Spacing: 1.25
OK
Cancel
Help
Experts in Quattro Pro for Window
Graph Expert
Scenario Expert
Consolidate Expert
Performance Expert
Analysis Expert
Budget Expert
Cancel
Coaches
Quit
WP Presentations - [d:\...\24fig13.shw]
File Edit View Insert Format Slide Graphics Tools Wind
s New Roman
Slide 2 of 7
Line
#Line7
Form Design : New *
Undefined Graph
Y-Undefined
x1
x2
x3
Paradox Report Expert
Select fields from the master table to print on the re
To reset the field list,
Master: CUSTO
Fields not Disp
All>>
Warning
Table BIOLIFE.DB and related files will be
Help

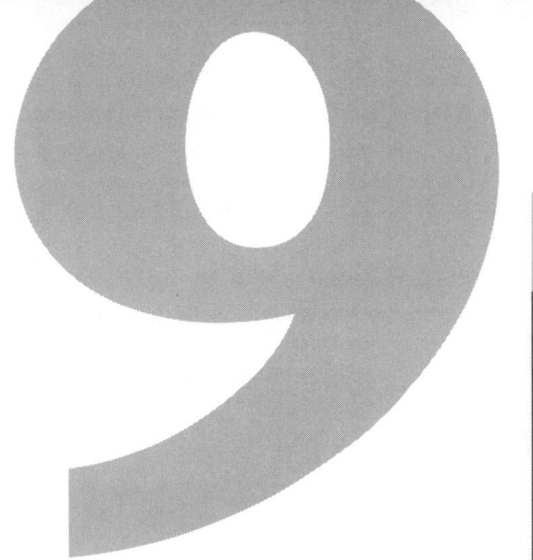

Chapter 19

Getting Started with Paradox

by Patrice-Anne Rutledge

Paradox is the relational database program that is part of the PerfectOffice suite. A database is essentially a collection of data or information. Some common examples of databases in the business world include lists of customers, orders, or products. What makes Paradox a *relational* database is its ability to relate the information in one database, or table, to the data contained in another. For example, you could relate a master customer database to a detailed database containing all orders for 1995.

Of course, you could also list this data in a word processor such as WordPerfect or in a spreadsheet such as Quattro Pro, but if you want to relate one database to another, and create meaningful analyses and calculations based on these relations, then Paradox is the software you need. Paradox also offers sophisticated report and form design tools, graphing tools, and the ability to create crosstabs, which resemble spreadsheets. All of these database components—tables, forms, reports, queries, graphs, and crosstabs—are called *objects*.

Paradox also offers a powerful object-oriented programming language named ObjectPAL, which can create complex database applications. This section of *Using Novell PerfectOffice*, however, will focus on getting you up and running with Paradox and introducing you to its basic features. In this chapter, you learn to

- Use the Project Viewer to locate files
- Create and use aliases

- Create a table
- Define keys and indexes
- Restructure a table
- Edit a table
- Sort a table

Note

For more in-depth coverage of the powerful tools and techniques Paradox has to offer, refer to *Using Paradox 5 for Windows, Special Edition* and *Killer Paradox 5 for Windows,* also published by Que.

Using the Project Viewer to Locate Files

The Project Viewer gives you an immediate visual overview of your Paradox files. It displays all files, or objects, in your *working* and *private* directories. A working directory is the directory in which you're currently working. Its directory path is displayed in the Working Directory box at the top of the Project Viewer. A private directory is your personal directory, where temporary tables that are created by Paradox are stored. If you are using Paradox on a network, this is important; without a private directory your temporary files could be overwritten by another user. In a stand-alone environment, your default private directory is named PRIVATE.

The Project Viewer default is to show all files, but by selecting the icons listed on the left side of the Project Viewer window, you can view only specific files, such as tables, forms, or queries. This feature is useful in directories with numerous files, because it makes finding specific files easier.

By default, the Project Viewer appears in the upper-left corner of your screen when you first open Paradox. Figure 19.1 shows the Project Viewer as it appears on startup.

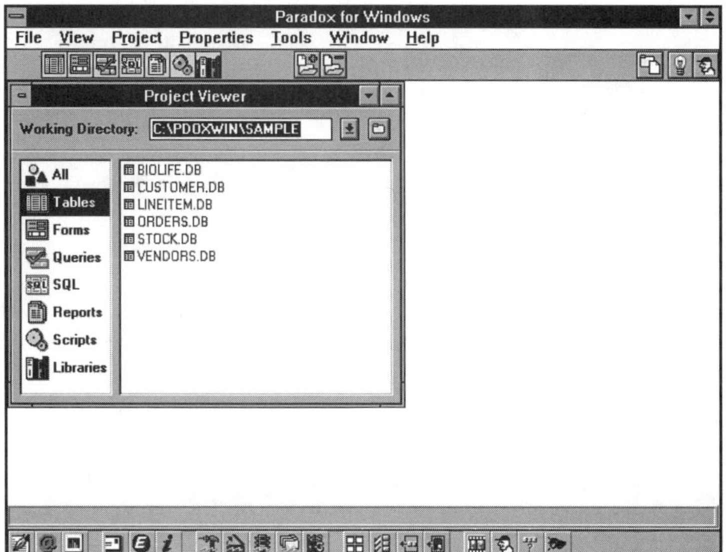

Fig. 19.1
The Project Viewer gives you a visual overview of your files.

Note

Although the default is to open the Project Viewer on startup, you can change this feature if you desire. To not activate the Project Viewer on startup, open the Properties menu and choose Properties to access the Project Viewer dialog box. Click the Open Project View on Startup box to remove the check mark, and then choose OK to save that setting. You can go back at any time to change the setting again. If the Project Viewer isn't currently displayed, you can click the Project Viewer button in the Toolbar to access it.

Locating Files in Other Directories

Although the Project Viewer is useful for viewing the files in your current working directory, you also can use it to locate files in other directories. The Project Viewer displays your current working directory in the Working Directory box. If this isn't where your desired file is located, you can type the complete path or alias of the directory in the Working Directory box. Alternatively, you can click the down arrow to access a list of the last 10 paths or aliases that you have called working directories. You can also click the folder button to access the Directory Browser.

Note

Aliases are defined in the next section.

The Directory Browser is very similar to the Windows File Manager. To locate a file in a different directory, you can scroll the directory list, highlight the file you want, and click the OK button to retrieve it.

From the Project Viewer you also can *inspect* (right-click) the name of any object to access an options menu for that file. Double-clicking a highlighted file automatically performs the first action in the menu. Double-clicking a table or form, for example, enables you to view it; double-clicking a report prints it.

Note

When organizing your data, it's best to use separate subdirectories for specific applications or data groups. All your customer files might be in the subdirectory C:\PDOXWIN\CUSTOMER, for example, and the files pertaining to your budget could be in the subdirectory C:\PDOXWIN\BUDGET. This arrangement makes it easier to find related files when you need them. In addition, you'll never accidentally confuse files that you created with Paradox program files.

Defining Aliases

An *alias* is a name that you give a specific directory to provide faster access to that directory. Paradox's Alias feature enables you to define shortcut names for your directories. These shortcut names can be temporary (referred to as *project aliases*), lasting only until you change working directories, or permanent (referred to as *public aliases*), available from all directories. Even if you define an alias permanently, however, you can remove it at a later time.

To define an alias, follow these steps:

1. Choose **F**ile, A**l**iases to access the Alias Manager dialog box, shown in figure 19.2.

2. Click the New button to enter a new alias name.

3. In the Database Alias box, enter the name you want to assign to your alias.

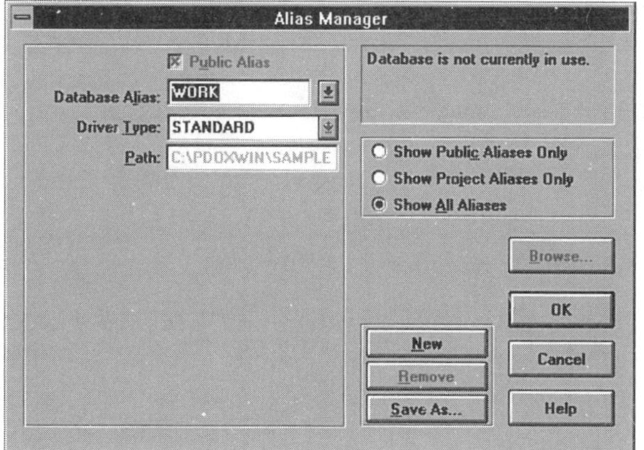

Fig. 19.2
The Alias Manager enables you to create abbreviated path names, which saves you time.

4. Enter the complete directory path name of the subdirectory to which you want to assign the alias.

5. If you want to create a public alias, be sure the Public Alias box is checked. If you want your alias to be temporary, remove the check mark from this box.

6. Select Keep New if you want to create another alias after you have finished the one you are creating now.

7. Select Save As. The Save Configuration File dialog box appears. The New File Name box offers IDAPI as the new name for your configuration file, if you selected a public alias. Choose OK to exit. If you selected a temporary (project) alias, Paradox opens the Save Project Aliases dialog box, prompting you to select PDOXWORK as a new file name. Click OK.

Note

IDAPI refers to the Independent Database Applications Programming Interface. This is the interface that Paradox uses to access your data. When you overwrite the IDAPI.CFG file while creating a new alias, you update this file with your new alias information.

8. A dialog box appears, telling you that the file name already exists and asking whether you want to overwrite that name. Click Yes.

Modifying an Alias

To modify an alias you've defined, follow these steps:

1. Choose **F**ile, A**l**iases to access the Alias Manager dialog box.
2. In the Database Aliases drop-down list, select the alias you want to modify.
3. Change the path of your alias.
4. Choose OK. The dialog box asks you if it is OK to save changes. Click Yes to save.

Removing an Alias

To remove an alias you've defined, follow these steps:

1. Choose **F**ile, A**l**iases to access the Alias Manager dialog box.
2. In the Database Aliases drop-down list, select the alias you want to remove.
3. Click the Remove button.
4. Click OK. A dialog box asks you if it is OK to save changes. Click Yes to save.

Creating a New Table

Tip
Use the Coaches "Planning a Database" and "Creating a Table" for guidance on planning and creating your tables.

◄ See "Coaches and Experts," p. 11

To create a new table, follow these steps:

1. Choose **F**ile, **N**ew, **T**able to access the Table Type dialog box.
2. The drop-down list offers several Paradox and dBASE table types, including the default Paradox 5.0 Windows. Select your desired table type and click OK to open the Create Paradox 5.0 for Windows Table dialog box (assuming you selected the default), illustrated in figure 19.3.
3. In the Field Roster, enter your first field name in the Field Name column, up to a maximum of 25 characters.
4. Tab to the Type column. Right-click (or press the spacebar) to view the list of field types. This list is illustrated in table 19.1. Select your field type.
5. Tab to the size column and enter your desired size, if it is required for that field type.

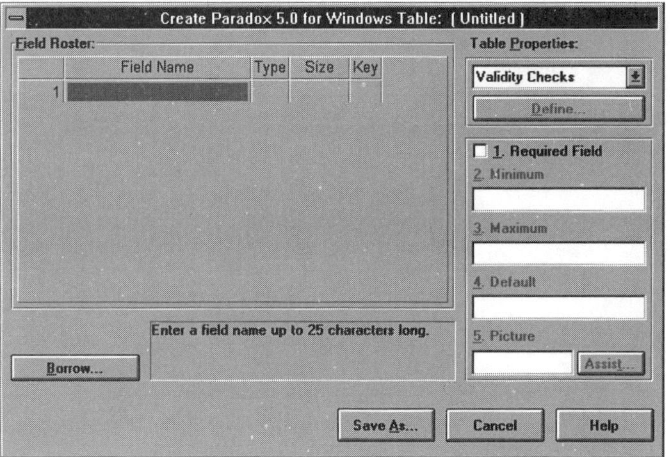

Fig. 19.3
You can create a new table in the Create Table dialog box.

6. Press the down-arrow and continue with steps 3 through 5 until your table is complete.
7. To insert a field between existing fields, select the field below where you want to insert and press the Insert key. To delete a field, select it and press Ctrl+Delete.
8. When you are finished with your table, click Save As.

Note

It's a good idea to write down your table structure on paper before you create it on the screen, particularly if you're new to creating tables. For each table you will need appropriate field names, a field type, and in some cases, field length. If you want to create other tables that you can later relate to this one, be sure you include one common field.

Table 19.1 Table Field Types

Field Type	Symbol	Size Limit	Description
Alpha	A	1-255	Field containing letters, numbers or symbols
Number	N	None	Numeric field; can perform calculations
Money	$	None	Numeric field formatted for currency

(continues)

Table 19.1 Continued

Field Type	Symbol	Size Limit	Description
Short	S	None	Contains a whole number; use Number field unless you have a specific reason to create a Short field type
Long Integer	I	None	Contains a 32-bit signed integer
BCD	#	0-32	Contains numeric data in the BCD format
Date	D	None	Contains a valid date
Time	T	None	Contains a time of day
Timestamp	@	None	Contains a date and time
Memo	M	1-240	Can contain any combination of characters or numbers
Formatted Memo	F	0-240	A memo field you can format with a typeface, style, size, or color
Graphic	G	0-240	Contains a graphic in .BMP, .PCX, .GIF, .EPS, or .TIF format
OLE	O	0-240	Contains object from another application such as Quattro Pro or WordPerfect
Logical	L	None	Allows true or false entries
Auto-increment	+	None	Contains a long integer in a read-only field
Binary	B	0-240	Contains data Paradox can't interpret, such as sound files
Bytes	Y	1-255	Contains data Paradox can't interpret, such as a bar code

Creating Field Names

Paradox has a number of rules you need to keep in mind when creating field names. These are:

- A field name can't exceed 25 characters.
- You can't have two fields with the same name.

- A field can contain a blank space, for example Sales 1995, but it can't begin with a blank space.
- It's best to avoid the following symbols in a field name: [], {}, ->, (), ., _, |, ! and ,. All of these symbols either aren't allowable as field names or can cause conflicts with queries or ObjectPAL.

Borrowing from an Existing Table Structure

If you want to create a table that is similar or identical in structure to a table you previously created, follow these steps:

1. Click the Borrow button in the Create Table dialog box before you create any field names. The Borrow Table Structure dialog box will appear (see fig. 19.4).
2. Select the table whose structure you want to borrow.
3. Select any of the options you want to borrow. These include: Primary Index, Validity Checks, Lookup Table, Secondary Indexes, or Referential Integrity.
4. Click OK to return to the previous dialog box.

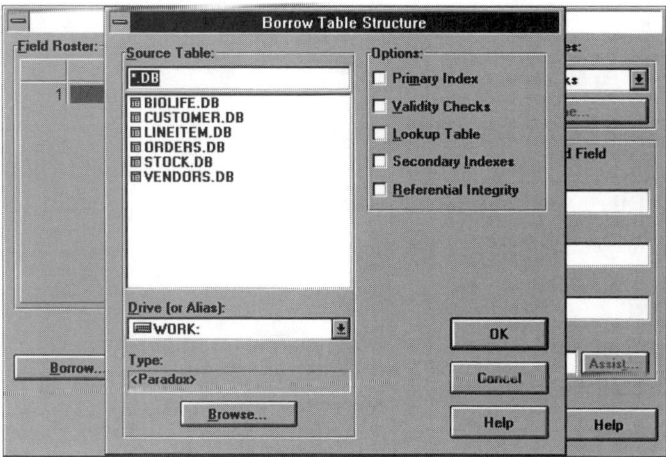

Fig. 19.4
If you want to create an identical or similar table, you can borrow the structure of an existing table.

Defining a Primary Key

A *key* is the primary index in a Paradox table. Keys are not required, but are useful for maintaining data integrity and for creating links. When you select a field as a key, it must have a unique value in each record of the table. For example, if you selected the field *order number* as the key in your ORDERS table, each *order number* should be unique.

> **Caution**
>
> You must have a key field if you are defining a link.

Each Paradox table can only have one key, but it can be made up of one or more field combinations. If you select only one field as your key, it must be the first listed field in the Field Roster. A key with more than one field is called a *composite key*. These fields must also be unique values and you must start with the first field in the Field Roster.

Tip
For additional guidance on creating a key, use the "Adding a Key" Coach.

To add a key to your table, move to the Key column of the field you wish to key. Double-click this column and you will see the * symbol, which indicates a keyed field. To remove the key, double-click again on the Key column and the * will disappear.

> **Caution**
>
> Only certain fields can be keyed. Memo, formatted memo, graphic, OLE, binary, logical, and bytes fields cannot be keyed because you can't logically sort the data they contain.

Defining a Secondary Index

In some cases you may want to define a second index in addition to your primary key. This is useful for later viewing data in a specific order in your table or for linking tables.

To create a secondary index, follow these steps:

1. In the Create Table dialog box, select Secondary Indexes from the Table Properties drop-down list.

2. Click the Define button to open the Define Secondary Index dialog box (see fig. 19.5).

3. Select the field or fields on which you wish to index by double-clicking on their name in the Fields list. You can also use the left arrow button to move your desired fields to the Indexed Fields list.

4. If you change your mind you can remove all indexed fields by clicking the Clear All button. You can also move individual fields by selecting them and clicking the right arrow button.

5. To change the order of your indexed fields click the up and down arrow buttons.

6. Select the Maintained box under Index Options if you want to update your index automatically. This is a preferred option.

7. Select the Case-Sensitive box if you want Paradox to recognize capitalization as it sorts your table.

8. Click OK to save.

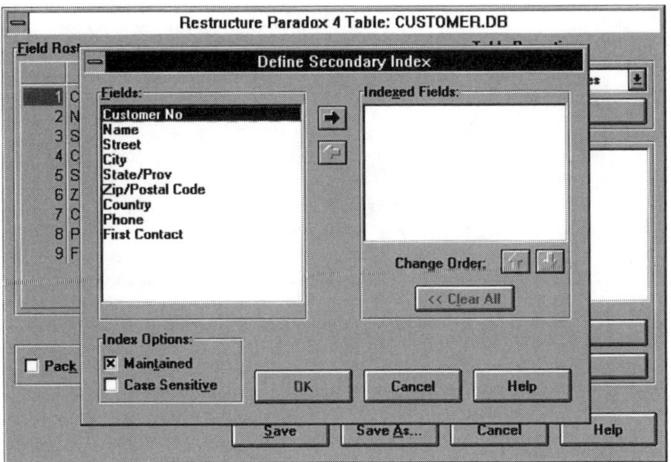

Fig. 19.5
In addition to keying your tables, you can also define secondary indexes in Paradox.

Defining Validity Checks

A validity check is a way to ensure that the data in a specific field meets certain conditions. There are five types of validity checks, detailed in table 19.2.

To define a validity check in the Create Table dialog box, follow these steps:

1. Choose Validity Checks from the Table Properties drop-down list.

2. Select the field on which you want to place the validity check in the Field Roster.

3. Select the Required Field box if you want to make data entry mandatory in this field.

4. Otherwise, enter the appropriate validity check information in the Minimum, Maximum, Default or Picture box. Click the Assist button for more help in defining a picture template.

To remove a validity check, select the appropriate field in the Field Roster, and remove the validity check value from the box where you originally entered it.

Table 19.2 Validity Check Types

Validity Check	Description
Default	Specifies a default entry in that field. You can later overwrite if desired.
Maximum	Specifies a maximum value for the field.
Minimum	Specifies a minimum value for the field.
Picture	Specifies a character string that serves as a template for how the field is formatted. For example, you could enter (###)###-#### to format all phone numbers in this manner.
Required Field	Requires an entry in this field in every record.

Tip
To reuse leftover disk space after deleting records from a table, select the Pack Table box in the Restructure Table dialog box.

Restructuring a Table

After you've created a table, there are often instances when you'll want to restructure it. You may want to add fields, change keys, or adjust field lengths, for example.

To restructure a table, click on the Restructure button on the Toolbar. You can also choose **T**able, **R**estructure Table, or inspect a table in the Project Viewer and select Restructure from the menu. Any of these steps will open the Restructure Table dialog box (see fig. 19.6).

In the Restructure Table dialog box you can make field name, length, and type changes as well as define and remove validity checks and keys, just as you did when you first created your table in the Create Table dialog box.

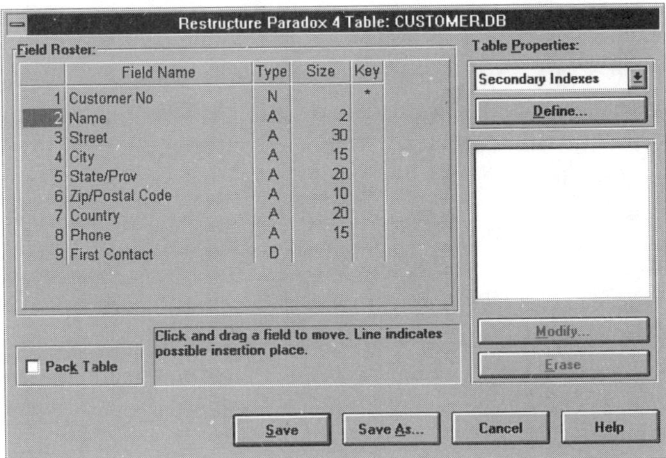

Fig. 19.6
You can restructure your table in the Restructure Table dialog box.

Although restructuring a table can be a simple process, you can also risk losing some of your data if you change field type, field length, or a validity check, for example. When this occurs, Paradox opens the Restructure Warning dialog box when you try to save your restructure. This dialog box asks you what to do with each problem field in your restructure (see fig. 19.7).

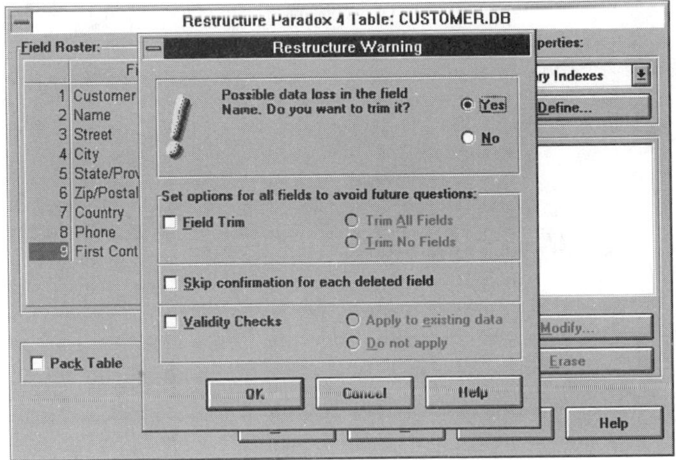

Fig. 19.7
The Restructure Warning dialog box gives you several options for handling field restructuring problems.

There are several things to be aware of when you restructure your table:

- If you add or change a key that violates the rules for setting a key (such as no duplicates), you will get a key violation. All of the records that violate the key will be deleted and moved to a special KEYVIOL table in your private directory. You can then change these records so that they will work with your current key and then add them back into the original table.
- If you confirm changes or don't enable field trimming in the Restructure Warning dialog box, Paradox will delete and move the non-compliant records to a PROBLEMS table in your private directory. Again, you can make changes and add these records back into your original table if desired.
- If you add or change a validity check and enforce the check on your new data in the Restructure Warning dialog box, your non-compliant records will be deleted and moved to a KEYVIOL table. Again, change and add the records back if you wish.

Note

Paradox has the ability to name up to 100 temporary tables such as PROBLEMS or KEYVIOL. A second key violation table, for example, would be named KEYVIOL2. This is useful, because you may create several such temporary tables when you restructure a table.

Working with Tables

Tip
Use the "Viewing a Table" Coach for a hands-on look at viewing tables.

Now that you've created a table structure, you need to enter data to start taking advantage of Paradox's powerful query, report, and form capabilities. Although you can also enter data in a specially-designed data entry form, in this chapter you will focus on simply entering data from a table view.

Opening and Editing a Table

There are three ways to open an existing table. In the Project Viewer, click the Tables icon and then double-click on your desired table. You can choose **F**ile, **O**pen, **T**able; or you can click the Open Table icon on the Toolbar.

In order to start entering data in your table, you must enter Paradox's Edit mode. Otherwise you will only be able to view your data. To enter Edit mode, click the Edit Data button on the Toolbar, press F9, or choose **V**iew, **E**dit Data. To begin editing your data, you can move to a particular field and begin typing in your data. To exit Edit mode, click the Edit Data button on the Toolbar or choose **V**iew, **E**nd Edit.

Moving Around a Paradox Table

Paradox offers several shortcuts for getting around a table and performing simple, repetitive functions. For example, the left and right arrow keys move across columns and the up and down arrow keys move across rows. Some other examples:

Tip
Use the "Inserting and Deleting Records" Coach for help in inserting and deleting records.

Keystrokes	Action
Alt+Backspace	Undoes changes to a field
Ctrl+Backspace	Deletes the selected field contents
Ctrl+D	Duplicates field contents from record above
Ctrl+Delete	Deletes the current record
Ctrl+End	Moves to the last field of the last record
Ctrl+Home	Moves to the first field of the first record
Esc	Undoes a field edit
End	Moves to the last field in the row
Enter	Moves to next field
Home	Moves to the first field in the record
Insert	Inserts a new record above the currently selected record
PgDn	Moves down one screen
PgUp	Moves up one screen
Tab	Moves to next field

The Table Toolbar has many tools that simplify working with tables. These tools are listed in table 19.3.

◀ See "Copying and Moving Using the Clipboard," p. 290

Table 19.3 Table Toolbar

Icon	Function	Description
	Print	Enables you to access the Print File dialog box and print your table
	Cut to Clipboard	Deletes a selected object and moves it to the Clipboard
	Copy to Clipboard	Copies a selected object to the Clipboard
	Paste from Clipboard	Pastes the current Clipboard contents into the document
	Restructure	Opens the Restructure Table dialog box
	Locate Value	Locates a specific field value
	Locate Next Value	Locates the next value in that set
	First Record	Moves to the first record in the table
	Previous Record Set	Moves to previous screen of records
	Previous Record	Moves the previous record in the table
	Next Record	Moves to the next record
	Next Record Set	Moves to the next screen of records
	Last Record	Moves to the last record in the table
	Set Filter	Filters your table for specific data
	Field View	Enters Field View
	Edit Data	Allows you to edit your data
	Quick Form	Creates a form based on the table
	Quick Report	Creates a report based on the table

Icon	Function	Description
	Quick Graph	Creates a graph based on the table
	Quick Crosstab	Creates a crosstab based on the table
	Open Project Viewer	Opens the Project Viewer
	Expert	Opens the Experts Control Panel
	Coaches	Accesses the Coaches feature

► See "Understanding Graphs," p. 480

► See "Understanding Crosstabs," p. 471

◄ See "Using Coaches and Experts," p. 37

Using Field View

So far when you have edited or changed existing data in a table, you have overwritten the entire field contents. In many cases, however, you may want to change only a part of a field's contents. Rather than retyping the entire field contents to make minor changes, Paradox offers a Field View feature which enables you to insert or change text in an existing field. To enter Field View, select the field you wish to edit and then click the Field View button on the Toolbar, press F2, or choose **V**iew, **F**ield View. You can also click twice in a field to place the insertion point where you are clicking. To exit Field View, click the Field View button on the Toolbar, press F2, or choose **V**iew, **F**ield View.

Tip

See the "Editing Records" Coach for more information on Field View.

Viewing the Data in Your Table

If your table is not keyed, the records will appear in the order in which you entered them. If your table is keyed, the sort order will be based on that particular key. There are two ways to sort records, based on what you want to accomplish. If you want to change the physical location of the records in the table, you can sort to a new table (you can't override a key in a current table). If you simply want to look at your records in a different order without changing their physical location, you can filter your data.

Sorting a Table

To sort an unkeyed table, or sort a keyed table to a new table, follow these steps:

1. While viewing your table, choose **T**able, **S**ort to open the Sort Table dialog box, as shown in figure 19.8.

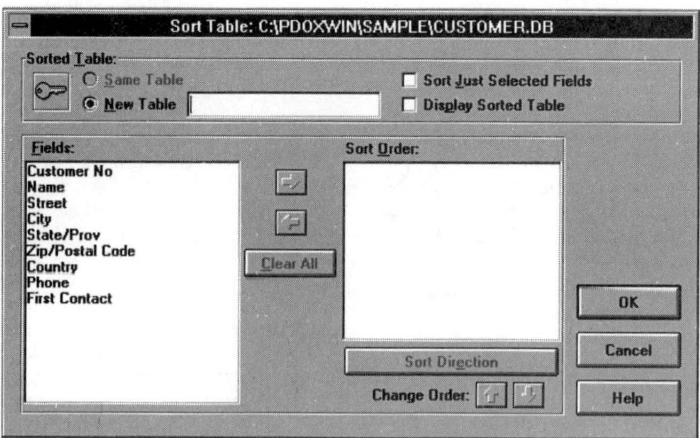

Fig. 19.8
You can sort the order of your records in the Sort Table dialog box.

2. Under Sorted Table you have a choice of Same Table or New Table. If your table is keyed, a key will appear to the left of these two choices and the Same Table option will be dimmed. Enter a name for your new table.

3. Select the first field on which you wish to sort from the Fields list and double-click (or choose the left arrow) to move it to the Sort Order list. Fields that can't be sorted, such as memo, logical, OLE, etc. are dimmed.

4. Continue moving fields in this manner until you have listed all the fields you wish to sort in the Sort Order list.

5. To rearrange the Sort **O**rder list, select the field you wish to move and click on the up or down Change Order arrow.

6. To remove a field from the Sort Order list, select it and click on the right arrow. Select the Clear All button to remove all fields from the list.

7. Fields are sorted in ascending (represented by a +) order by default. To change to descending (represented by a —) order, select the field you wish to change and double-click or click on the Sort Dir**e**ction button.

8. If you want sort only the selected fields, select the Sort **J**ust Selected Fields box. This will sort those fields, but leave the other fields in their original position on the table.

9. If you want to display your sorted table when you are finished, select the Dis**p**lay Sorted Table box.

10. Click OK to perform your sort.

Filtering Your Data

You can also view the data in a keyed table in an order other than the primary key. To do so you must have created a secondary index. To view your table sorted by this secondary index you use the filter feature. To filter your data, follow these steps:

1. Select the Filter button from the Toolbar or choose **T**able, **F**ilter to open the Filter Tables dialog box (see fig. 19.9).

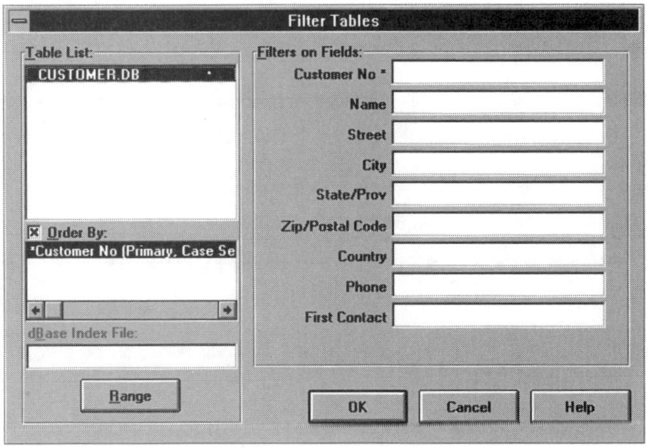

Fig. 19.9
You can sort the order of your records, or set specific filters in the Filter Tables dialog box.

2. Select the Order By check box.
3. Select your secondary index from the list beneath the Order By check box.
4. Click OK.

You can also use the Filter Tables dialog box to set a specific filter on your data. For example, in your CUSTOMER table you only want to view customers in California, listed as CA in the state field. In the Filter Tables dialog box you can enter CA in the State box in the Filters on Fields list and select OK to view.

> **Note**
>
> A quick way to perform a simple filter is to inspect the field on which you want to filter and select Filter... from the menu. This opens the Field Filter dialog box, shown in figure 19.9. Enter your filter information and select OK to filter.

Troubleshooting

I can't enter the data I want in my table.

There are several possible problems:

- The data you are trying to enter isn't in compliance with a validity check you have specified. For example, you may have specified a minimum or maximum numeric range.
- There isn't enough space to enter your desired text. You may have given an alpha field a length that isn't long enough for the text you are trying to enter.
- The field type you originally selected isn't compatible with the data you are trying to enter. For example, you can't enter text data in a numeric field.

To change your table to fit your new data entry needs, click the Restructure button on the Toolbar, or choose T**a**ble, Restructure **T**able.

Transferring Records

Now that you have learned to create and enter data in tables, you will find instances in which you may want to transfer your records to other tables. Paradox has several options for transferring records, including options that append, update, or append and update. It's important to clarify the meaning of each option and its effects on your tables. These are described in table 19.4.

Tip
A fast way to add records to a table is to inspect (right-click) its highlighted file name in the Project Viewer and select Add from the menu.

Table 19.4 Description and Effects of Append, Update, and Append & Update

Option	Description
Append	Adds records without changing any of the table's existing records. In a keyed table, records that violate the key (such as duplicates) are placed in a temporary Keyviol table in the Private directory and aren't added into the destination table. In a table that's not keyed, Append adds in records whether or not those records are duplicates. In an empty table, the Append function simply adds records.

Option	Description
Update	Updates existing records with new information, but doesn't add records that don't match the key field. In a keyed table, records that were changed in the original table after updating are placed in the temporary Changed table in the Private directory. You must use a keyed table to update, and you can't update an empty table.
Append & Update	Updates existing records and adds new ones to the table. In a keyed table, records that were changed in the original table after updating are placed in the temporary changed table in the Private directory. You must use a keyed table to append and update.

To transfer records from one table to another, follow these steps:

1. Choose **T**ools, **U**tilities, **A**dd to access the Add dialog box (see fig. 19.10).

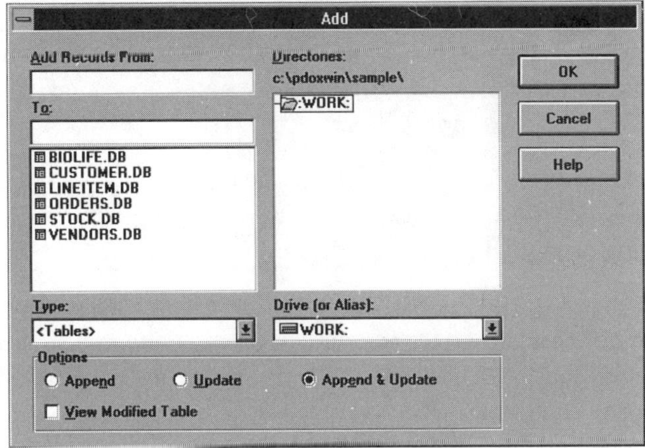

Fig. 19.10
Paradox offers three options for transferring records from one table to another: append, update, or both.

2. With the cursor in the Add Records From box, click your source table.
3. Move the cursor to the To box, and click your destination table.
4. Select one of the following options: Appe**n**d, **U**pdate, or App**e**nd & Update.

5. Select the View Modified Table box if you want to view your destination table immediately.

6. Click OK.

> **Caution**
>
> You cannot transfer records between tables that have incompatible structures. To restructure your tables to match each other, see "Restructuring a Table" in this chapter.

Copying, Renaming, and Deleting Objects

Paradox has several utilities that simplify copying, renaming, and deleting objects such as tables, reports, and queries. There are many reasons why you might want to copy, rename, or delete an object. Before making changes to a table or report, for example, you might want to copy the original to another file, just in case you make a mistake, want to start your modification over again, or don't like the outcome of your changes. You also might need to copy an object over and over if you use it as a template on a regular basis, such as a table used for a monthly or quarterly report.

The rename utility is useful if you later decide that you want to change the name of a particular object or if you want to rename a group of objects in a more uniform way, such as adding a date or number to the file name for easier reference.

Deleting an object is similar to renaming or copying, but you should use this procedure with caution. Deletions in Paradox are permanent, and although you potentially could use a DOS or other utility to recover your deleted files, it's better to be sure before deleting. If you are deleting simply to make more room on your hard disk or to lessen the number of files in a particular directory, you might want to move the object to another directory or to a floppy disk rather than delete it.

Tip
Inspecting (right-clicking) an object in the Project Viewer is a shortcut method of accessing the Copy dialog box.

Copying an Object

To copy an object, follow these steps:

1. Choose **T**ools, **U**tilities, **C**opy to access the Copy dialog box (see fig. 19.11).

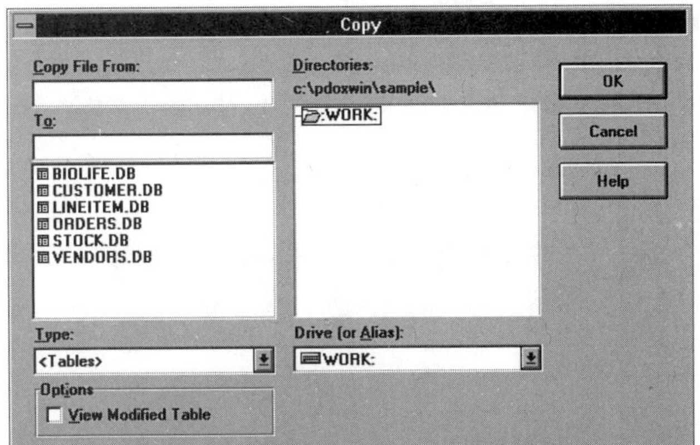

Fig. 19.11
The Copy dialog box enables you to copy Paradox objects and their related files.

2. Click the name of the file you want to copy. The name appears in the Copy File From box.
3. In the To box, enter the name of your new file.
4. If you want to access a different directory or select a specific file type, use the Drive and Type drop-down lists to find the object for which you are looking.
5. If you want to view your new table immediately, select the View Modified Table box; otherwise, leave it deselected.
6. Click OK to copy. The status bar lets you know whether your copy operation was successful.

Caution

Don't use the DOS COPY command or the Windows File Manager to copy an object. Copying objects through Paradox's copy utility ensures that the data, structure, indexes, validity checks, and table properties will be copied correctly.

Tip
To rename a table you're viewing, open the Table menu, and choose Rename to access an abbreviated version of the Rename dialog box.

Renaming an Object

You can use the same basic steps to rename or delete an object. To rename, choose **T**ools, **U**tilities, **R**ename to access the Rename dialog box.

Deleting an Object

Choose **T**ools, **U**tilities, **D**elete to delete an object by using the Delete dialog box. The Warning dialog box appears after you choose OK (see fig. 19.12). This dialog box is a safety feature that enables you to cancel a deletion if you change your mind or discover that you made a mistake.

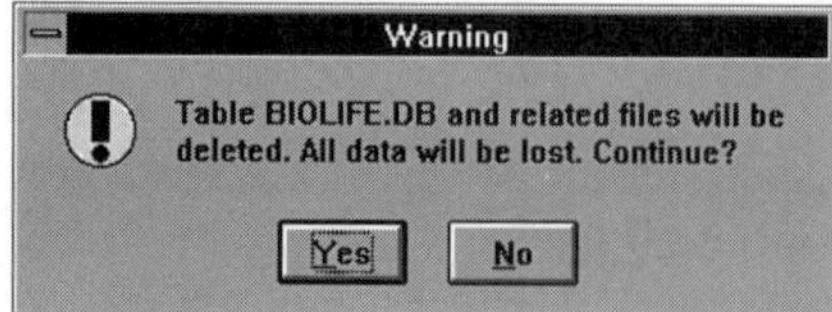

Fig. 19.12
The Warning dialog box is a safety feature that enables you to cancel a deletion.

Emptying a Table

Paradox also has an Empty utility that enables you to empty a table of its data but keep its structure intact. This utility can be useful if you use a particular table as a master or template and add new information on a regular basis. The Empty utility is also handy when you want to create a new table that will have the same basic structure as an existing table. You empty a table in much the same way as you delete one. Choose **T**ools, **U**tilities, **E**mpty. The Empty dialog box appears (see fig. 19.13). Select the table you want to empty and click OK. Click Yes in the Warning dialog box to empty the table.

Empty
Empty Table:
BIOLIFE.DB
CUSTOMER.DB
LINEITEM.DB
ORDERS.DB
STOCK.DB
VENDORS.DB
Directories:
c:\pdoxwin\sample\
:WORK:
OK
Cancel
Help
Type:
<Tables>
Drive (or Alias):
WORK:

Fig. 19.13
You can empty a table from the Empty dialog box.

Troubleshooting

When I try to add records from one table to another, I see the Table Structure Mismatch Warning dialog box.

The two tables you selected do not have compatible structures. You can either follow the prompts in the dialog box, specifying whether to trim the data in each field, or whether to trim the fields globally. If the tables are totally incompatible, you will see an additional error message: `Incompatible record structures`. You can also restructure a table by choosing **T**ools, **U**tilities, Res**t**ructure.

When I try to update a table, I see an error message telling me that my table isn't keyed.

You can update only a keyed table. To set a key (index) for your table, choose **T**ools, **U**tilities, Res**t**ructure, and double-click the Key column of the field you want to key.

I have duplicate records in my table.

You appended to a table that wasn't keyed. To remove the duplicates, choose **T**ools, **U**tilities, Res**t**ructure, and set a key. When you complete your restructuring, your duplicates will appear in the Keyviol table in your private directory.

From Here...

For more details on the information covered in this chapter, refer to the following chapters:

- Chapter 1, "Introducing PerfectOffice," overviews the common user interface between all PerfectOffice applications, and how to share resources across these applications.
- Chapter 2, "Getting Started with PerfectOffice," covers the basics: menus, selecting and editing text, using the clipboard, formatting documents, and using Coaches and Experts.
- Chapter 3, "Using Common PerfectOffice Tools," discusses the use of Toolbars, PowerBars, and feature bars, as well as QuickMenus.
- Chapter 4, "Managing Files," covers working with and finding files and directories.
- Chapter 5, "Getting Started with WordPerfect," covers the basics of the word processing program included with PerfectOffice.
- Chapter 12, "Getting Started with Quattro Pro," covers the basics of the spreadsheet program included with PerfectOffice.

Chapter 20

Querying Your Data

by Patrice-Anne Rutledge

One of the most useful features of a relational database like Paradox is the ability to extract meaningful information from your data. Through its querying function called QBE (Query By Example), Paradox lets you *query*, or ask questions of, your data when you provide an example of what you are looking for. Queries can not only extract pertinent data, but also perform calculations based on that data.

In this chapter, you learn to

- Create a basic query
- Create a live query view
- Create a multi-table query
- Perform calculations in your queries

Understanding Queries

You create a query in a query image. This window resembles a regular table window without data. Under each field there is a box that you can check by clicking it. You can remove a checkmark by clicking it again. Use the scrollbar to move to fields to the right of the screen. *Checkmarks* are the tools that tell Paradox what data you want in your query and what you want to do with it.

The four checkmark types are described in table 20.1.

Table 20.1 Query Checkmark Descriptions

Checkmark	Description
	Check shows all unique values for the checked field in ascending order.
	CheckPlus shows all values, including duplicates, in the order they appear in your table.
	CheckDescending shows all unique values for the checked field in descending order.
	GroupBy specifies a record group used in a Set query, without including the field in the ANSWER table.

The Toolbar in the query window is also unique. The buttons on this Toolbar are described in table 20.2.

Tip
For step-by-step guidance on creating a single-table query, use the "Creating a Query" Coach.

Tip
Click the leftmost box to quickly select all the fields in your table.

Table 20.2 Query Tools

Icon	Function	Description
	Run Query	Run a query.
	Join Tables	Joins two tables.
	Answer Table Properties	Opens the Answer Options dialog box.
	Sort Answer Table	Opens the Sort Answer dialog box.
	Show SQL	Shows the query in an SQL (Structured Query Language) format.
	Add Table	Adds a table.
	Remove Table	Removes a table.
	Field View	Allows you to edit a field.

When you have selected the appropriate fields for your query, you can run it by selecting the Run Query button on the Toolbar. Your query will then create a new ANSWER table with your desired information. This table is located in your Private directory.

Creating a Basic Query

To create a basic one-table query that lists all customers and their cities in the CUSTOMER table, follow these steps:

1. Choose **F**ile, **N**ew, **Q**uery to open the Select File dialog box, seen in figure 20.1.

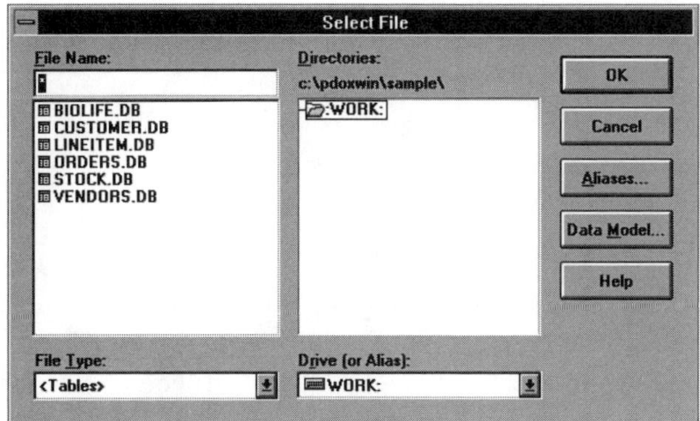

Fig. 20.1
Select the table you want to query in this dialog box.

2. Select the CUSTOMER table, and click OK to open the query image, illustrated in figure 20.2.

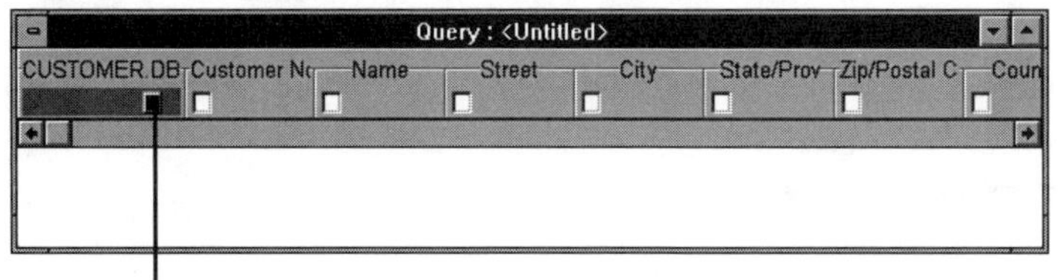

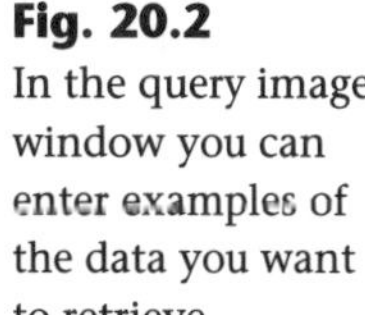

Fig. 20.2
In the query image window you can enter examples of the data you want to retrieve.

3. Select the Customer No and City fields.

4. Click the Run Query button on the Toolbar to run the query.

5. The ANSWER table appears, shown in figure 20.3. Double-click the Control menu box to close this table.

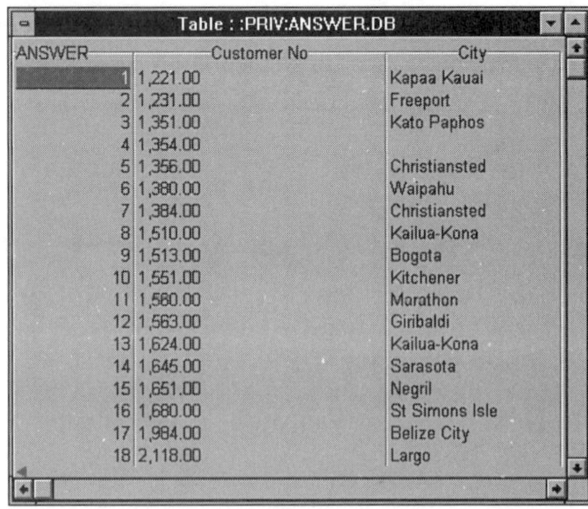

Table : :PRIV:ANSWER.DB

ANSWER	Customer No	City
1	1,221.00	Kapaa Kauai
2	1,231.00	Freeport
3	1,351.00	Kato Paphos
4	1,354.00	
5	1,356.00	Christiansted
6	1,380.00	Waipahu
7	1,384.00	Christiansted
8	1,510.00	Kailua-Kona
9	1,513.00	Bogota
10	1,551.00	Kitchener
11	1,560.00	Marathon
12	1,563.00	Giribaldi
13	1,624.00	Kailua-Kona
14	1,645.00	Sarasota
15	1,651.00	Negril
16	1,680.00	St Simons Isle
17	1,984.00	Belize City
18	2,118.00	Largo

Fig. 20.3
The ANSWER table shows only the Customer No and City fields.

6. Choose **F**ile, **S**ave As to save your query. The Save File As dialog box opens.

7. Enter a name for your query and select OK.

Tip
To rename your ANSWER table, choose **T**ools, **U**tilities, **R**ename to open the Rename dialog box. If you don't rename your ANSWER table, it will be overwritten the next time you perform a query.

Querying for Exact Matches

Although a query is useful for viewing specific fields in a table, its power is much greater than that. You can also view records that contain specific information. To specify an exact match, check the fields you wish to view, and enter the data you wish to match in the text area to the right of the checkbox for that field.

Note

If you want to search for text that contains a comma or another reserved Paradox symbol, enter your text in quotations to search correctly. If the text itself contains quotations, use a backslash (\) instead. For example, "Smith, John" and \"hot" list\ are both valid search entries.

For example, let's say you wanted to locate all customers in California (CA in the State/Prov field) from the CUSTOMER table. This query image is illustrated in figure 20.4. This would result in the ANSWER table seen in figure 20.5, which contains only customers in California.

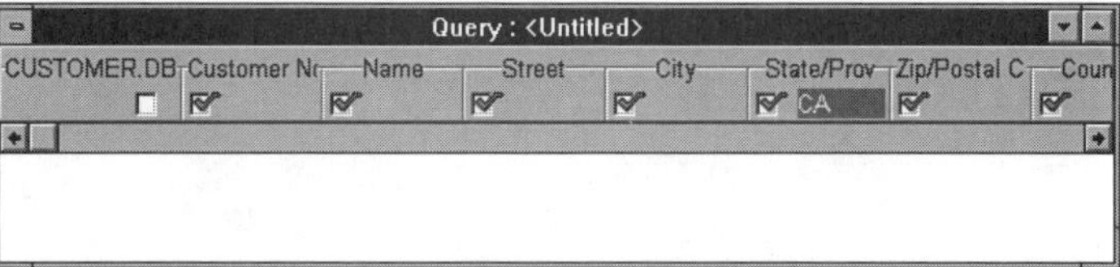

Fig. 20.4
This query will result in a table containing only customers with the State/Prov listed as CA.

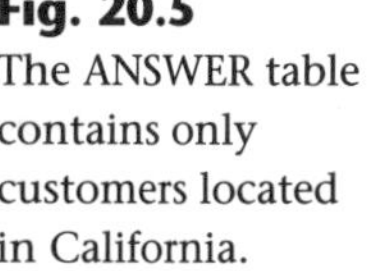

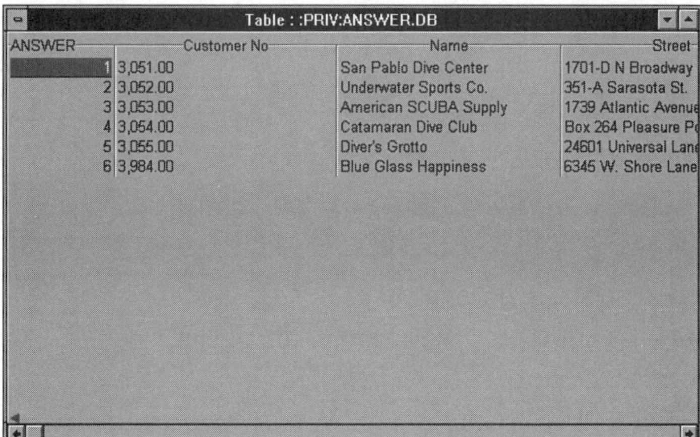

Fig. 20.5
The ANSWER table contains only customers located in California.

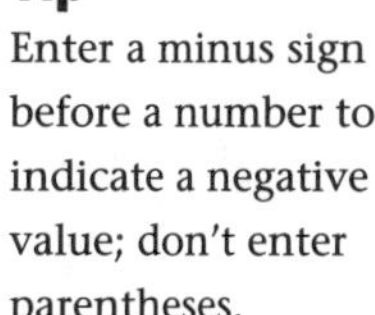

Tip
Enter a minus sign before a number to indicate a negative value; don't enter parentheses.

As an example, let's say you want to find all records for orders shipped on 8/8/88. This query image is seen in figure 20.6 and the resulting ANSWER table in figure 20.7.

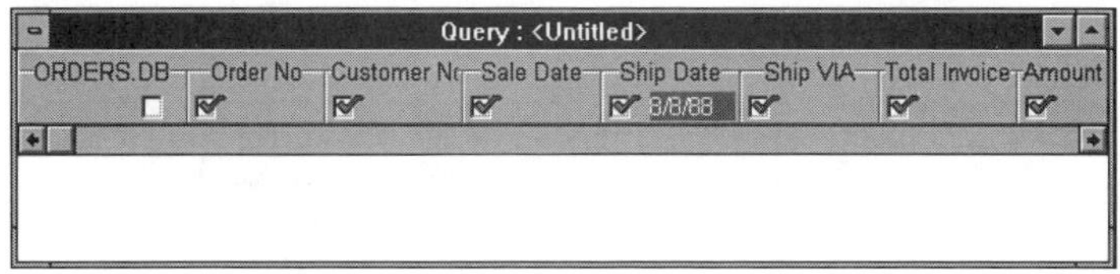

Fig. 20.6
You can specify exact dates in a Paradox query.

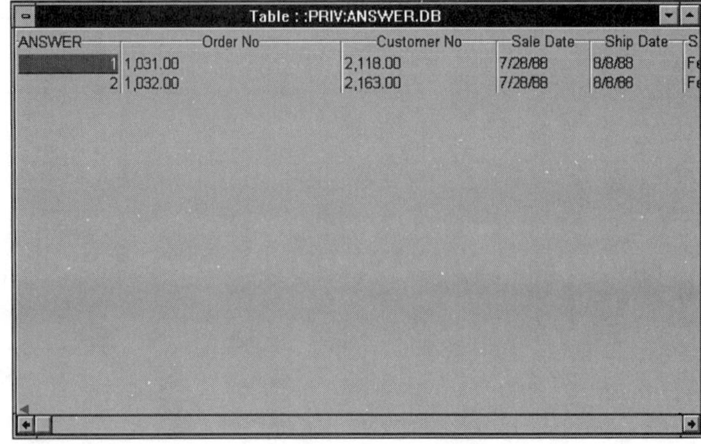

Fig. 20.7
This table lists the results of a query specifying only orders shipped on 8/8/88.

Querying Using Operators

Tip
For more information on query operators, search for this topic in the online help or refer to *Using Paradox 5 for Windows, Special Edition*, also published by Que.

You can also use special operators to search for specific records. Paradox has several kinds of operators: arithmetic, comparison, wildcard, special, summary, and set comparison. The most common of these operators are described in table 20.3.

Table 20.3 Query Operators

Operator	Definition
+	Adds
–	Subtracts
*	Multiplies
/	Divides
=	Equal to
>	Greater than
>=	Greater than or equal to
<	Less than
<=	Less than or equal to
@	A single character wildcard
..	Two or more character wildcards

Operator	Definition
LIKE	Similar to, sounds like
NOT	Doesn't match
BLANK	No entered value
TODAY	Today's date
OR	Or
,	And
AVERAGE	Averages
COUNT	Counts
MAX	Shows maximum
MIN	Shows minimum
SUM	Summarizes

Using the Wildcard Operator

One of the most useful operator groups are the wildcard operators. You can match any single character with the wildcard operator @ or any series of characters with the .. wildcard. For example, let's say you have a table that lists all company employees. If you want to search for someone whose last name is either Smith or Smyth (you can't quite remember how she spells it), you could enter SM@TH in the table's name field to search for both possible conditions. As another example, you can search for a series of dates using the .. wildcard. In figure 20.8, you see a query image that results in all the orders placed in 1988.

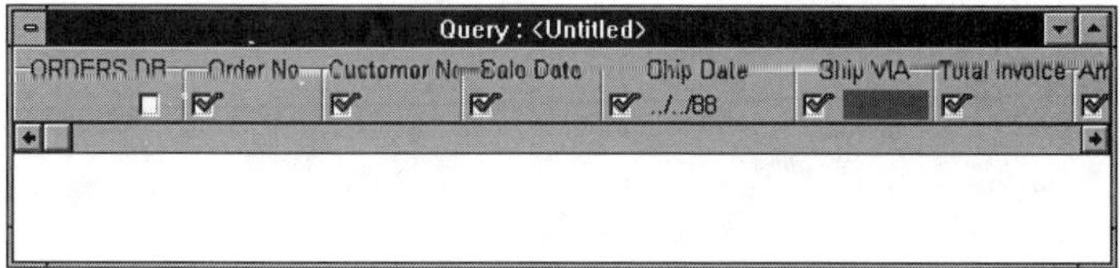

Fig. 20.8
The query resulted in a list of all orders placed in 1988.

Using Special Operators

Paradox offers several special operators—LIKE, NOT, BLANK, TODAY, AND (written as a comma), and OR—which are described on the following page.

- *LIKE*. The LIKE operator is useful when you're not sure of the exact spelling of a particular word you're searching for or think it may be misspelled in your table. You must start with the correct first letter and include as much of the text as possible to successfully come up with a match.
- *NOT*. The NOT operator gives you a way to list records that do not contain a specific value.
- *BLANK*. This operator lets you query for records that contain no data in a specific field.
- *TODAY*. Use this operator to find today's date in date fields.
- *AND (,)*. This operator allows you to specify records that contain all of a series of conditions. It is used in conjunction with other operators =, >, >=, <, or <=.
- *OR*. This operator allows you to specify a set of records meeting either of two or more conditions.

For example, if you wanted to find all records in the ORDERS table for total invoices greater than $1,000 but less than $10,000, you could create the query in figure 20.9.

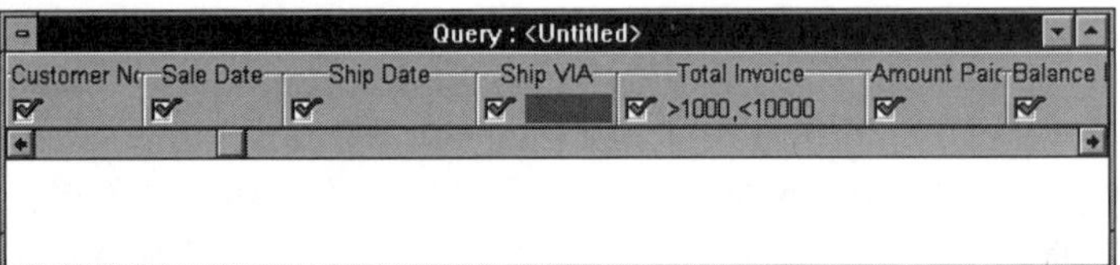

Fig. 20.9
This query would show all records for total invoices between $1,000 and $10,000.

As another example, if you wanted to list all customers *except* those in California, you could create a query like the one in figure 20.10.

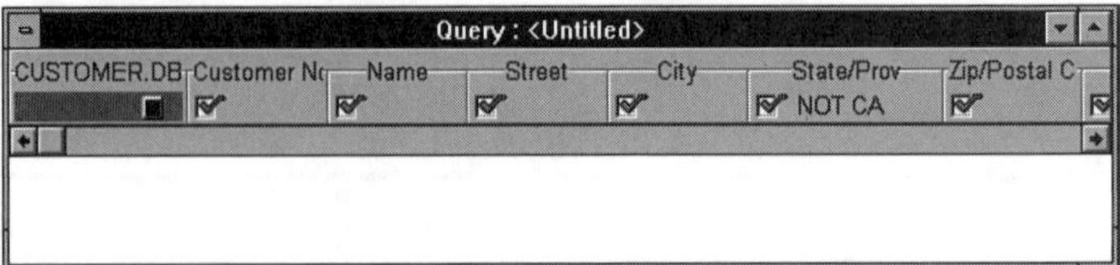

Fig. 20.10
This query would find all customers except those in California.

Troubleshooting

I queried my table using the TODAY operator and didn't receive records with today's date.

Paradox looks at your computer's system date when using the TODAY operator. Check this system date and change it if necessary.

I queried my table using the LIKE operator and didn't get the right records.

Using the LIKE operator, you need to be sure you start with the right first letter and enter enough of the requested text for Paradox to find it. Entering only the first or second letters may not be enough information to perform the query.

Creating a Live Query View

In many cases you may want to create a live query view rather than a traditional query. In a *live query* view you actually view the table you're querying rather than a secondary answer table. Any changes you make to the new queried table will be directly reflected in the original table. You can only create a live query view with a single-table query.

To create a live query view showing only vendors in California, as listed in the VENDORS table, follow these steps:

1. Choose **F**ile, **N**ew, **Q**uery to open the Select File dialog box.

2. Select the VENDORS table, and click OK to open the query image.

3. Place CheckPlus marks in the Vendor Name and State/Prov fields. This query image is illustrated in figure 20.11.

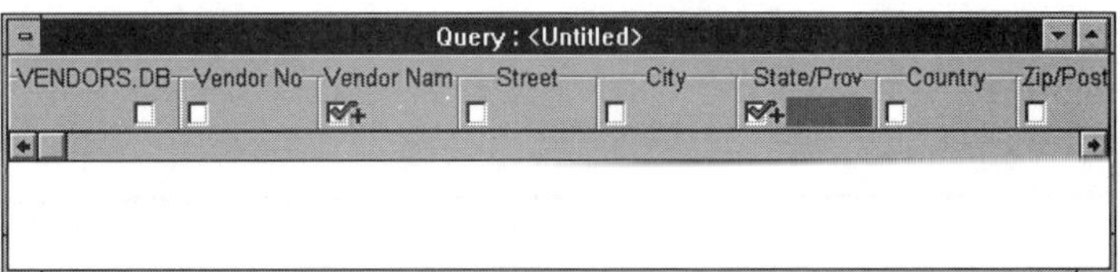

Fig. 20.11
A live query view requires the use of the CheckPlus mark.

4. Choose **P**roperties, Answer Opt**i**ons to open the Answer Options dialog box, seen in figure 20.12. You can also select the Answer Table Options from the Toolbar.

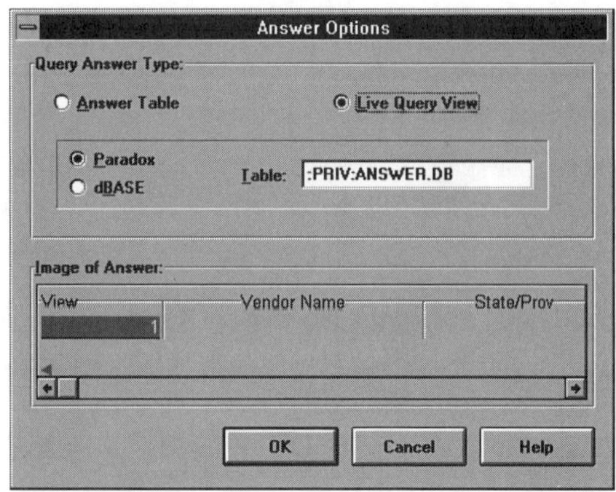

Fig. 20.12
You can set a live query view in the Answer Options dialog box.

5. Select the **L**ive Query View radio button and click OK to close.

6. Click the Run Query button on the Toolbar to run the query.

Tip
To save your live query view as a new table, choose **F**ile, Save **A**s to open the Save File As dialog box.

> **Caution**
>
> Remember that any change you make to the answer of a live query view will be included in the original table. If you don't want to keep these changes, use a traditional query which gives you a separate answer table. You can also make a copy of your original table in case you change your mind about the changes you've made.

> **Troubleshooting**
>
> *I changed the data in my queried table and it didn't appear in my original table.*
>
> Any changes you make to your ANSWER table won't be included in your original table unless you selected a Live Query View. To do so, select the Answer Table Options icon from the Toolbar.

Tip
To add or remove tables in the query window, you can select the Add Table or Remove Table buttons from the Toolbar.

Creating a Multi-Table Query

One of Paradox's powerful query features is the ability to query data in more than one table by linking tables with common keyed fields. To create a multi-table query showing Total Invoice by Stock No., follow these steps:

1. Choose **F**ile, **N**ew, **Q**uery to open the Select File dialog box.

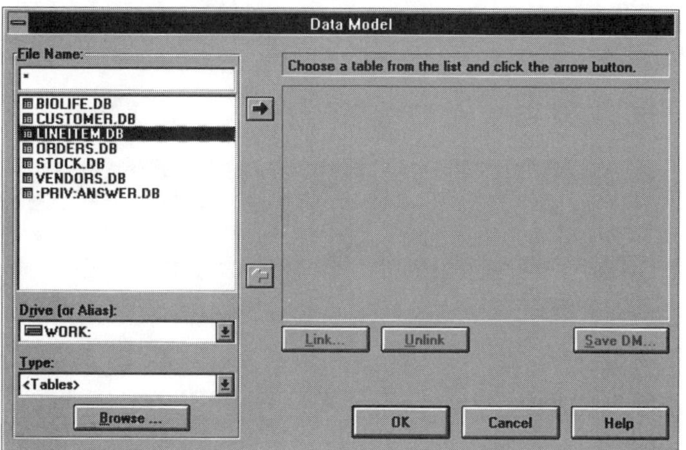

Fig. 20.13
The Data Model dialog box enables you to set links between your tables.

2. Select the Data **M**odel button to open the Data Model dialog box, illustrated in figure 20.13.

3. Double-click the ORDERS table to select it. You can also highlight the table name and click the right arrow to select.

4. Double-click the LINEITEM table to select.

5. To link the two tables, point the pointer to the ORDERS table and click and draw a line to the LINEITEM table.

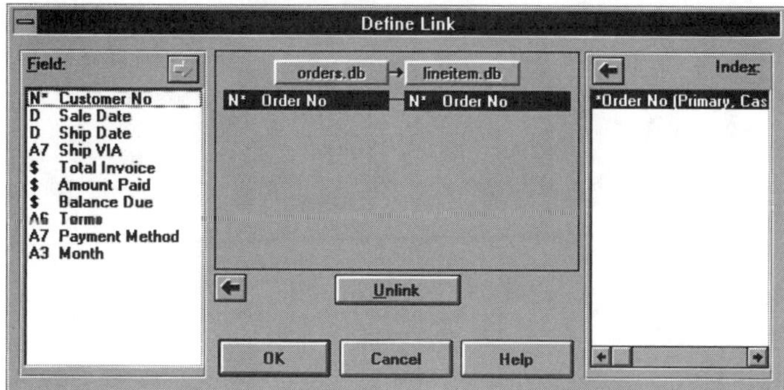

Fig. 20.14
Define how you want to link your tables in the Define Links dialog box.

6. The Define Link dialog box opens, illustrated in figure 20.14. You will accept the linking field suggested by this dialog box.

7. Click OK to return to the Data Model dialog box.

8. Click the Save DM button to save the Data Model. The Save File As dialog box opens.

9. Enter a name for your data model and click OK to open the query image, shown in figure 20.15. The query image shows a separate query line for each table.

Fig. 20.15 In a multi-table query, each table has a separate query line.

10. Place a checkmark in the Stock No. field of the LINEITEM table.

11. Place a checkmark in the Total Invoice field of the ORDERS table.

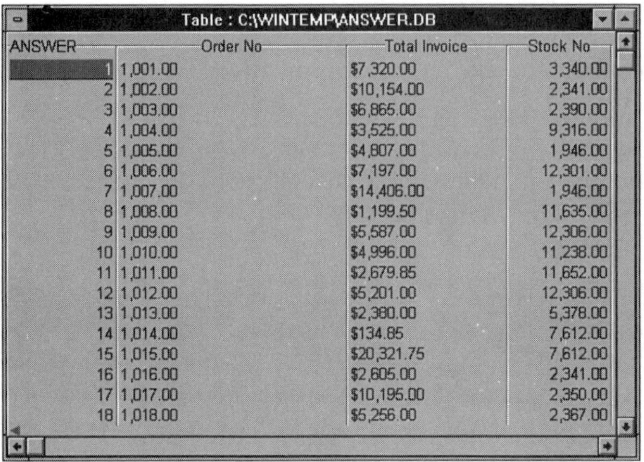
Table : C:\WINTEMP\ANSWER.DB

ANSWER	Order No	Total Invoice	Stock No
1	1,001.00	$7,320.00	3,340.00
2	1,002.00	$10,154.00	2,341.00
3	1,003.00	$6,865.00	2,390.00
4	1,004.00	$3,525.00	9,316.00
5	1,005.00	$4,807.00	1,946.00
6	1,006.00	$7,197.00	12,301.00
7	1,007.00	$14,406.00	1,946.00
8	1,008.00	$1,199.50	11,635.00
9	1,009.00	$5,587.00	12,306.00
10	1,010.00	$4,996.00	11,238.00
11	1,011.00	$2,679.85	11,652.00
12	1,012.00	$5,201.00	12,306.00
13	1,013.00	$2,380.00	5,378.00
14	1,014.00	$134.85	7,612.00
15	1,015.00	$20,321.75	7,612.00
16	1,016.00	$2,605.00	2,341.00
17	1,017.00	$10,195.00	2,350.00
18	1,018.00	$5,256.00	2,367.00

Fig. 20.16 The result of your multi-table query appears in this ANSWER table.

12. Click the Run Query button in the Toolbar. Your ANSWER table appears in figure 20.16.

Creating Queries with Calculated Fields

You also can create calculations in your queries by using the CALC operator. You can do so by using *example elements*. You can place an example element in a query by pressing F5 and entering a name for that example. The example will be highlighted in your query. You can then use these example names in conjunction with arithmetic operators and the CALC operator to perform calculations based on your fields. To multiply the quantity of each stock item by its list price in the STOCK table, follow these steps:

1. Choose **F**ile, **N**ew, **Q**uery to open the Select File dialog box.

2. Select the STOCK table, and click OK to open the query image.

3. Select the Stock No., Qty, and List Price fields to activate them.

4. With the cursor in the Qty field, press F5 to place an example element in it. Enter Qty as your example element.

5. With the cursor in the List Price field, press F5 to place an example element. Enter Lpr as your example.

6. With the cursor still in the List Price field, place a comma after Lpr and enter **CALC Qty * Lpr**. Be sure to enter Qty and Lpr as example elements by selecting F5 first. Your query image is illustrated in figure 20.17.

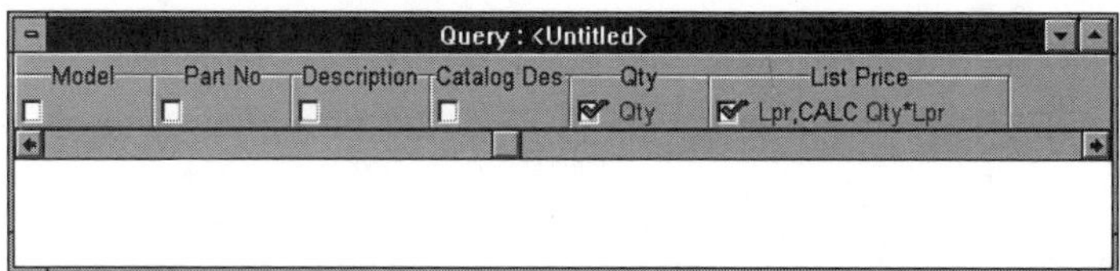

Fig. 20.17
You can perform calculations in your queries with the CALC operator.

7. Click the Run Query button on the Toolbar to run the query.

8. The ANSWER table appears, shown in figure 20.18. Double-click the Control-menu box to close this table.

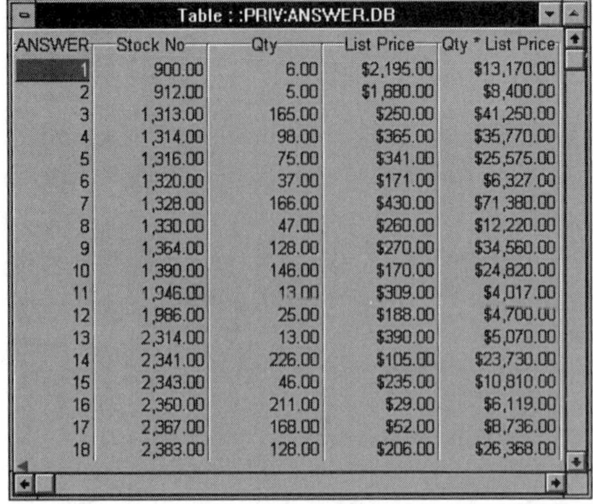

Table : :PRIV:ANSWER.DB

ANSWER	Stock No	Qty	List Price	Qty * List Price
1	900.00	6.00	$2,195.00	$13,170.00
2	912.00	5.00	$1,680.00	$8,400.00
3	1,313.00	165.00	$250.00	$41,250.00
4	1,314.00	98.00	$365.00	$35,770.00
5	1,316.00	75.00	$341.00	$25,575.00
6	1,320.00	37.00	$171.00	$6,327.00
7	1,328.00	166.00	$430.00	$71,380.00
8	1,330.00	47.00	$260.00	$12,220.00
9	1,364.00	128.00	$270.00	$34,560.00
10	1,390.00	146.00	$170.00	$24,820.00
11	1,946.00	13.00	$309.00	$4,017.00
12	1,986.00	25.00	$188.00	$4,700.00
13	2,314.00	13.00	$390.00	$5,070.00
14	2,341.00	226.00	$105.00	$23,730.00
15	2,343.00	46.00	$235.00	$10,810.00
16	2,350.00	211.00	$29.00	$6,119.00
17	2,367.00	168.00	$52.00	$8,736.00
18	2,383.00	128.00	$206.00	$26,368.00

Fig. 20.18
The ANSWER table shows your calculated field.

As another example, let's say you wanted to see what the new list price would be for each stock item if you increased it by 8 percent. This query image appears in figure 20.19.

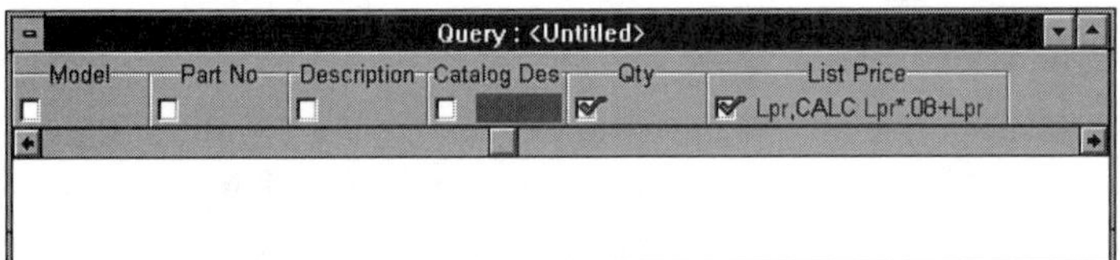

Fig. 20.19
You can perform "what if" calculations in a query.

From Here...

For more details on the information covered in this chapter, refer to the following chapters:

- Chapter 2, "Getting Started with PerfectOffice," shows you how to manipulate objects and use toolbars.
- Chapter 12, "Getting Started with Quattro Pro," covers the basics of working with spreadsheets (if you want to create a spreadsheet based on your query).
- Chapter 24, "Getting Started with Presentations," introduces you to designing charts and graphs in WordPerfect Presentations (a good way to represent your query results graphically).

Chapter 21

Designing Reports and Forms

by Patrice-Anne Rutledge

The ability to create meaningful reports and user-friendly data entry forms is one of the greatest benefits of using a database. Paradox has many powerful reporting features that enable a user to summarize and filter data, to create reports based on one or many tables, and to create aesthetically-pleasing design documents. Although creating a basic form or report is relatively easy, Paradox also offers sophisticated design options in the design window, which are covered in Chapter 22, "Working with Design Tools."

In this chapter, you learn how to

- Create a new report or form
- Work with bands
- Create group bands
- Print and save a report or form

Creating a New Report or Form

In Paradox, there are three ways to create a new report or form:

- Use the Report or Form Expert to guide you step-by-step.
- Use the Data Model dialog box and predetermine your selected fields and basic design layout (this is how Paradox's Coach feature guides you to create a report or form).

Tip
Draw a rough sketch of your design document on paper before you start designing it on-screen.

- Use the Quick Report or Quick Form feature to create a design document that contains all the fields in the table you're currently viewing.

The following sections show you how to create a simple form or report using these three methods. Each method has its own advantages and disadvantages, depending on your level of experience with the software and the type of *design document* (Paradox's term for a form or report) you want to create.

Using Experts to Create Reports and Forms

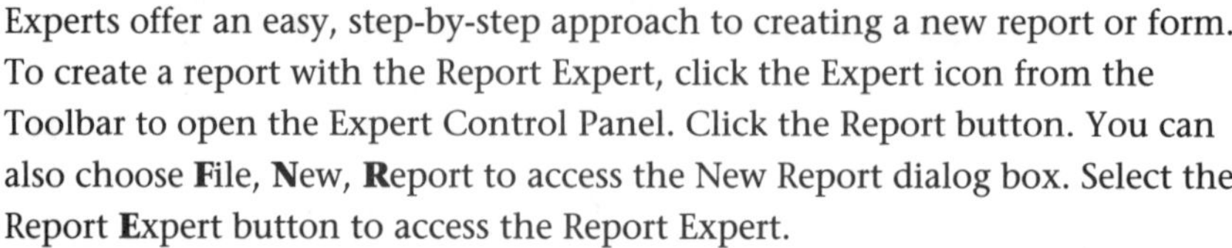

Experts offer an easy, step-by-step approach to creating a new report or form. To create a report with the Report Expert, click the Expert icon from the Toolbar to open the Expert Control Panel. Click the Report button. You can also choose **F**ile, **N**ew, **R**eport to access the New Report dialog box. Select the Report **E**xpert button to access the Report Expert.

Tip
If you make a mistake, the Expert Message dialog box will open and offer guidance on what to do next.

Step 1: Choose a Layout

The Report Expert layout window is illustrated in figure 21.1. The Form Expert is illustrated in figure 21.2.

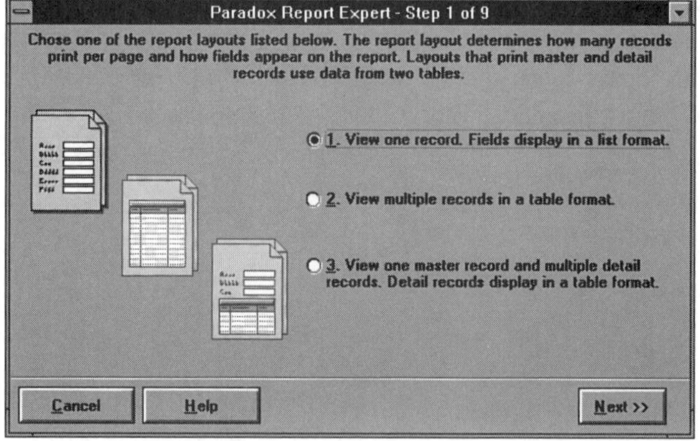

Fig. 21.1
Choose your report layout in Step 1 of the Report Expert.

The Report Expert offers three choices for report layout:

- View one record. Fields display in a list format.
- View multiple records in a table format.
- View one master record and multiple detail records. Detail records display in a table format.

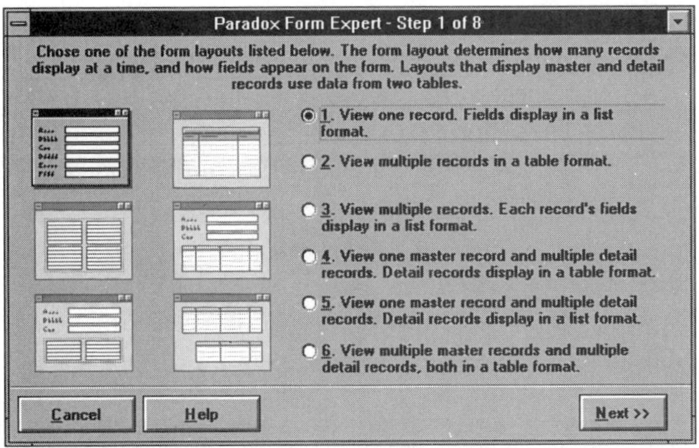

Fig. 21.2
Determine your form layout in the first step of the Form Expert.

The Form Expert offers the above choices plus three additional options:

- View multiple records. Each record's fields display in a list format.
- View one master record and multiple detail records. Detail records display in a list format.
- View multiple master records and multiple detail records, both in a table format.

Choose one of these options and click the **N**ext button to continue to Step 2.

Tip
Click the **P**rev button to go back to previous steps.

Step 2: Select a Master Table

The Step 2 window is the same for the both the Form and Report Expert (see fig. 21.3).

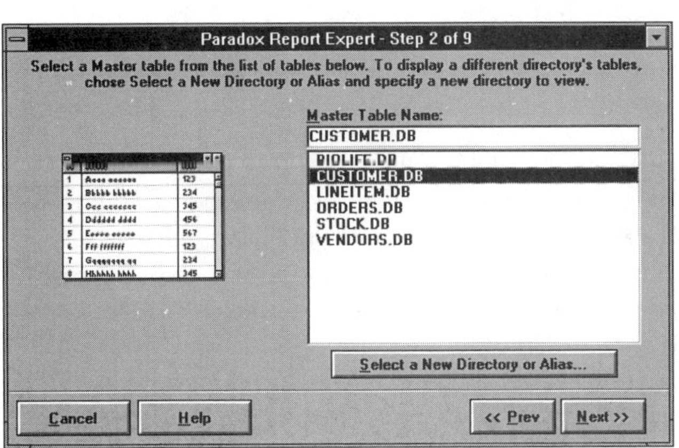

Fig. 21.3
This Report Expert window lets you locate and select a Master table.

◀ See "Managing Directories," p. 67

Select your desired table from the **M**aster Table Name list. This list contains only the tables in your current working directory. To locate tables in other directories, click the **S**elect a New Directory or Alias button to open the Directory Browser dialog box. Highlight your file and click OK to return to the main window of Step 2. When you are ready to continue, click the **N**ext button.

Step 3: Select a Detail Table

Step 3 will only appear if you chose to view both master and detail tables in Step 1 (see fig. 21.4).

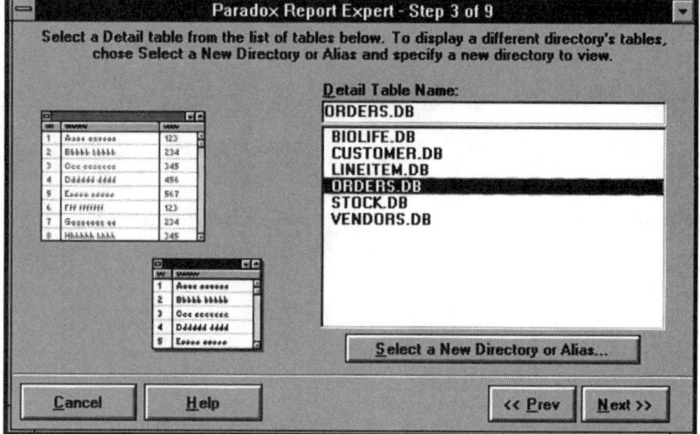

Fig. 21.4
Selecting a Detail table enables you to create a link to the Master table you chose in Step 2.

Select your desired table from the **D**etail Table Name list. Again, this list contains only the tables in your current working directory. When you are ready to continue, click the **N**ext button.

Step 4: Specify How to Link the Tables

Step 4 is only displayed if you chose view one master record and multiple detail records in Step 1 (see fig. 21.5).

Step 4 displays possible fields to link from first the Master table and then the Detail table in the *Linking fields from* lists. To select the optimal linking choice, click **B**est Links. To view all potential links, choose **A**ll Links. If you don't want to link, select N**o** Link. If there is more than one possible link, you can click the P**r**ev Link or N**e**xt Link button to view the other options. When you are finished, click the **N**ext button.

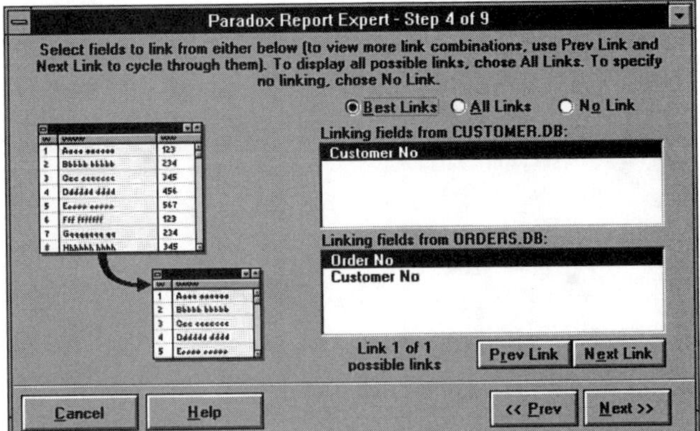

Fig. 21.5
Paradox offers several ways to link your tables.

Step 5: Select Fields from the Master Table to Include in the Report

Select fields from the master table to include in your report or form (see fig. 21.6). All fields are displayed by default in the Fields to Display list. To remove all fields from the report, click **N**one. This will move all fields to the Fields No**t** Displayed list. To move all fields back to the Fields to Display list, click **A**ll. Move fields from one list to another by highlighting the field and clicking > or <. Continue by clicking the **N**ext button.

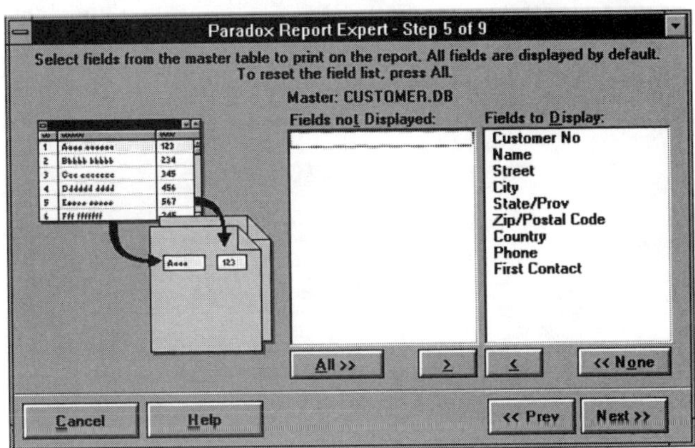

Fig. 21.6
You can include all table fields in a report or form, or only the ones you choose.

Step 6: Select Fields from the Detail Table to Include in the Report

Step 6 only appears if you have selected a Detail table (see fig. 21.7).

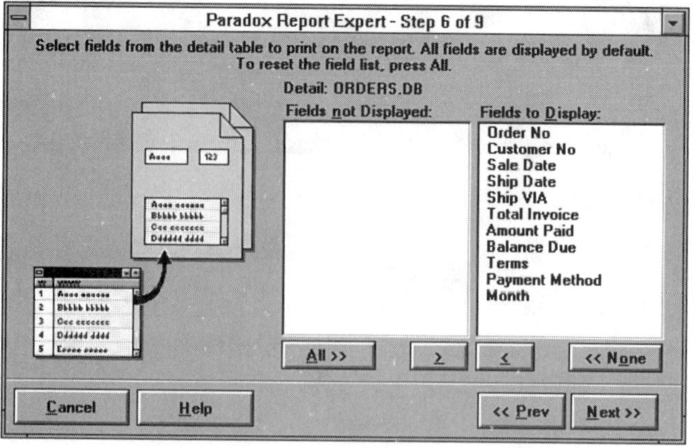

Fig. 21.7
Step 6 enables you to select specific fields from the Detail table to include in your report.

Select fields from the Detail table to print on the report. This step works in much the same way as Step 5. Click **N**ext to continue.

Step 7: Select Your Page Layout and Print Options

Use this dialog box to determine output, page orientation, and printer options (see fig. 21.8).

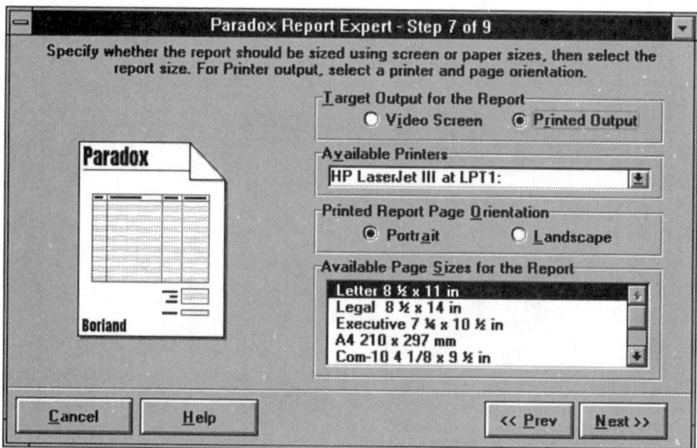

Fig. 21.8
This window enables you to select your printing and page layout options.

1. Select the **T**arget Output for the Report/Form—either V**i**deo Screen or P**r**inted Output.

2. If you are printing your report or form, select your desired printer from the A**v**ailable Printers drop-down list.

3. Choose either Portr**a**it or **L**andscape for your Printed Report/Form Page **O**rientation.

4. Select your page size from the Available Page **S**izes for the Report/Form drop-down list.

5. Click the **N**ext button to proceed.

Step 8: Select Page Title and Date Placement

This step is available only with the Report Expert (see fig. 21.9).

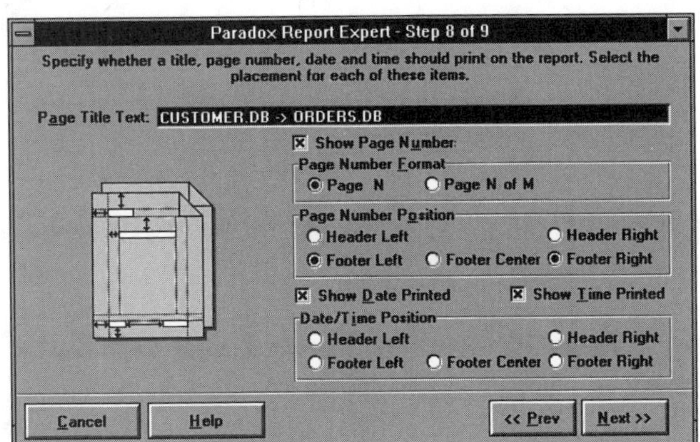

Fig. 21.9
You can choose to place a title, page number, date, or time on your report.

1. Enter the desired title of your report in the P**a**ge Title Text. Your table name will be listed as default.

2. Check the Show Page N**u**mber box if you want a page number to print. If you don't, skip to step 5.

3. Choose your Page Number **F**ormat—either Page N or Page N of M.

4. Select your Page Number P**o**sition. Paradox offers a choice of Header Left, Footer Left, Footer Center, Header Right, or Footer Right.

5. Select Show **D**ate Printed and/or Show **T**ime Printed if desired.

6. If you chose to have a date and/or time printed, select the Date/T**i**me Position. Again, you have choices of Header Left, Footer Left, Footer Center, Header Right, or Footer Right.

7. Select the **N**ext button to proceed.

Step 9: Select a Style Sheet

The Report Expert version is illustrated in figure 21.10. This is Step 8 in the Form Expert.

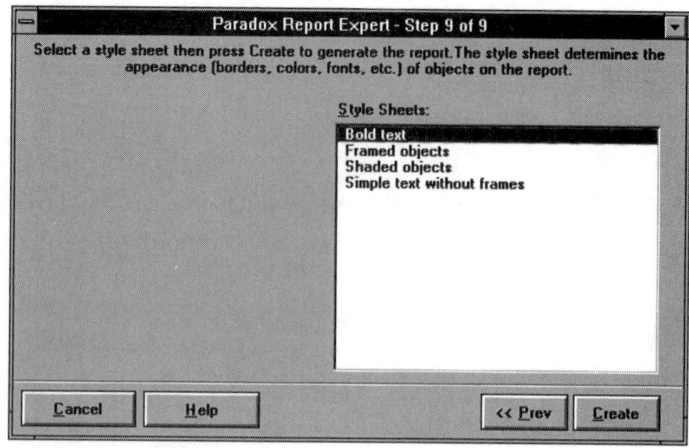

Fig. 21.10
Paradox offers many pre-formatted style sheets for your reports and forms.

Tip
Use the interactive Coach to guide you through these steps. Click the Coach icon on the Toolbar and select either Creating a Standard Report, or Creating a Standard Form.

Choose a style sheet from the **S**tyle Sheets list. Click the **C**reate button to continue to the Design window.

Creating a New Report or Form from the Data Model Dialog Box

A *data model* defines the way tables relate to each other in a design document. Although establishing table relationships isn't necessary to create reports or forms based on a single table, using the Data Model/Design Layout method is still a useful way to create a single-table document.

In this example, you use the Data Model to create a simple report based on the VENDOR table found in the SAMPLE subdirectory.

◀ See "Using Coaches and Experts," p. 252

To create, preview, print, and save this basic report, follow these steps.

1. Choose **F**ile, **N**ew, **R**eport to access the New Report dialog box (see fig. 21.11).

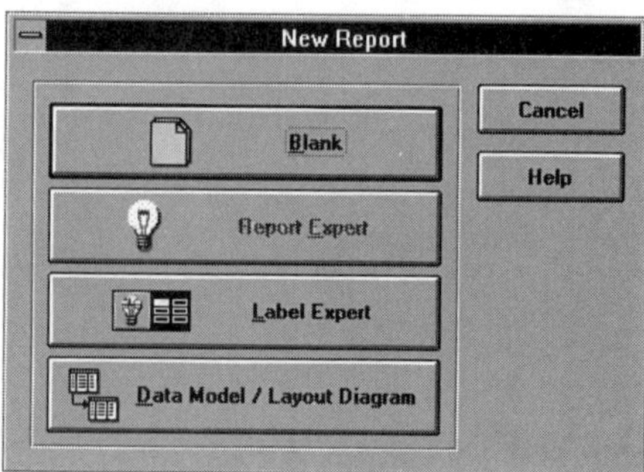

Fig. 21.11
The New Report dialog box offers four options for creating new reports and labels.

2. Click the **D**ata Model/Layout Diagram button. The Data Model dialog box appears (see fig. 21.12).

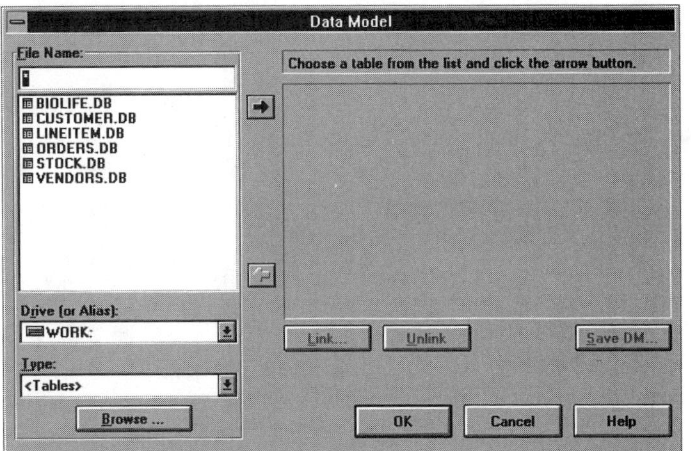

Fig. 21.12
The Data Model dialog box defines table relationships in a design document.

3. Select your desired table, VENDOR.DB, and then click **S**ave DM to save this data model for future use. The Save File As dialog box appears.

4. Enter the name of your desired data model. In this instance, name your data model **VENDOR**. Click OK. The Data Model dialog box appears again. Click OK to continue on to the Design Layout dialog box (see fig. 21.13).

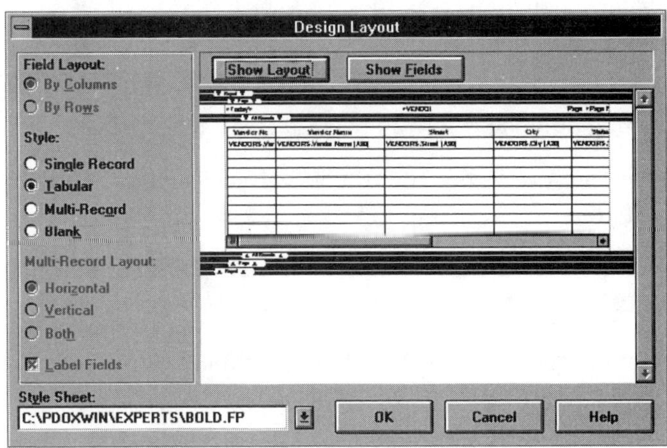

Fig. 21.13
In Design Layout, you can select and order the fields you want in your report as well as choose a report style.

5. The Design Layout box offers you the option to *Show Layo**u**t* or to *Show **F**ields*. When you first access this dialog box you view the layout options, offering you choices for field layout, style, and multi-record layout, as well as the option of choosing a style sheet. Use the defaults in this exercise.

Tip
If you make a mistake, click the R**e**set Fields button to start over again with your default field listing.

6. Select the Show **F**ields box. All the fields in the table are listed in the **S**elected Fields list as default, as illustrated in figure 21.14.

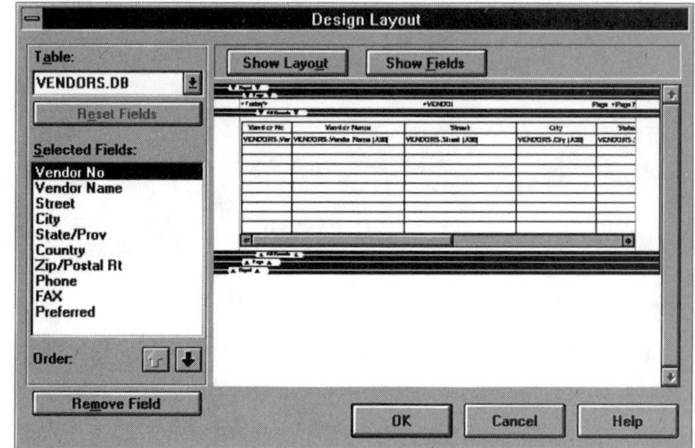

Fig. 21.14
Design Layout also gives you options for selecting fields for your report.

Tip
To remove more than one field at a time, press Control and click all the fields you want to remove. Then choose the Re**m**ove Field button.

7. In this example, you only want to use the first seven fields. Highlight the *Phone* field and then click the Re**m**ove Field button. Follow this same procedure to remove the *FAX* field. Click OK when you are finished.

8. You now see the Report Design: New* window, shown in figure 21.15. Note that only the fields you selected are in the report.

9. To preview your report, click the View Data icon on the Toolbar (see fig. 21.16).

10. To print the report, click the Print icon. The Print File dialog box appears. Click OK.

11. Return to Report Design by clicking the Design icon.

12. Choose **F**ile, **S**ave to save the report. The Save File As dialog box appears. Enter the name of your report and click OK. In this instance, name your report **VENDOR**.

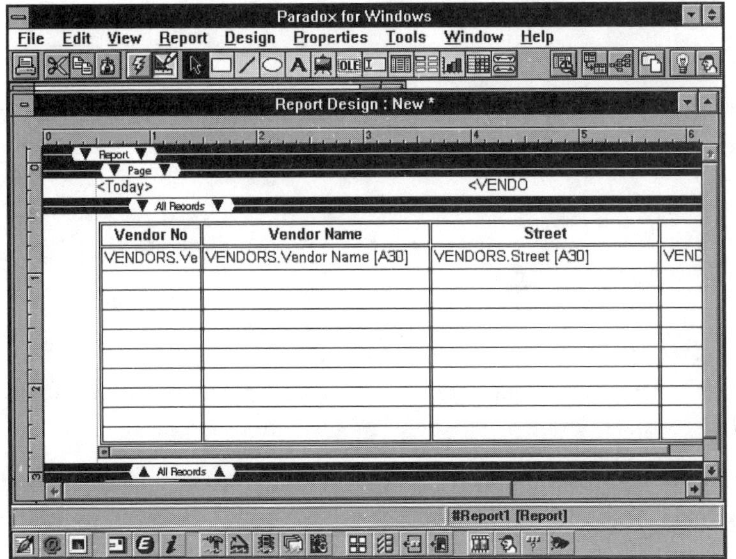

Fig. 21.15
In Report Design you can manipulate your report's appearance and content.

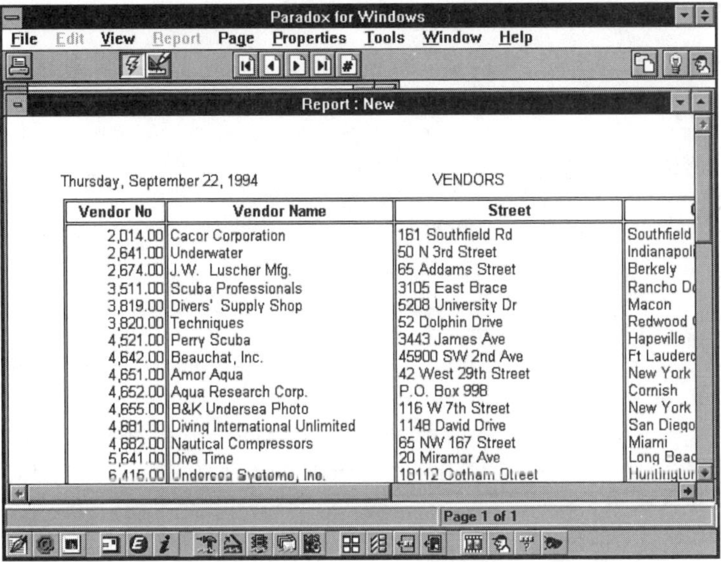

Fig. 21.16
Previewing shows you what your printed report will look like.

You can also create a form following these same basic steps. To create a form, choose **F**ile, **N**ew, **F**orm to access the New Form dialog box.

Note

All objects (reports, forms, data models, queries, and so forth) that belong to the same project should be named similarly. For example, objects relating to the ORDERS table should all have the word *order*, or a derivative of *order* in it, and should in some way explain what the object does or contains. For example, reports that cover distinct geographic areas could be named ORDERUSA or ORDERINTL or a query asking for customers whose accounts were active in 1995 could be called ORDER1995.

Creating a Quick Report or Quick Form

The Quick Report and Quick Form features are a good way to create new documents that contain all the fields in a particular table.

In this example, you create a form based on the CUSTOMER table found in the SAMPLE subdirectory. To create, preview, print, and save this report using the Quick Form feature, follow these steps:

1. While viewing the CUSTOMER table, click the Quick Form icon. You see a preview of your form.

2. Click the Print icon to access the Print File dialog box. In this instance, accept the defaults and click OK to print.

3. Click the Design icon to return to the Form Design window. Choose **F**ile, **S**ave to access the Save File As dialog box. Enter a name for your new table in the New File Name box; in this case, type **CUSTOMER.** Click OK.

Tip

You can't save a design document if you are previewing it (the Save and Save As options on the File menu are dimmed). You must return to Design to save it.

The Quick Form feature is an easy way to create a basic, functional form, which may be all you need if you simply want a simple data entry screen for your table. But in many cases, you may want to select only certain fields, to manipulate, move, or group your data, or to create a form with a more professional design. Although you can do this after you have created a Quick Report, it's easier to use the Data Model dialog box to preselect your specifications.

Once you have created and saved a design document, you can always go back and make changes. To edit a document while viewing its associated table, you must first select the report or form you want to change, and then click the Quick Report or Quick Form icon. To access the report you created earlier in this chapter, VENDOR, while viewing the VENDOR table, follow these steps:

1. Open the VENDOR table by double-clicking its name in the Project Viewer.

2. Choose **P**roperties, **P**referred, **R**eport to access the Choose Preferred Report dialog box.

3. Click the name of the report you created, VENDOR. Click OK to preview your report as you originally designed it.

4. Go back to Report Design by clicking the Design icon. Make any desired changes to the report.

> **Note**
>
> As a shortcut, you also can access a previously created document from the Project Viewer. To reach the appropriate menu, inspect (right-click) the highlighted report or form in the Project Viewer. The menu gives you the following options: **V**iew Data, **P**rint, De**s**ign, Print **W**ith, View Wit**h**, **C**opy, **R**ename, and **D**elete. Double-clicking the selected file automatically performs the first menu item; in this case, viewing the report or form.

Tip

If you select Quick Report or Quick Form without specifying your preferred format, the entire default document is displayed, with all the fields in the table and without any other changes you may have made.

Working with Bands

Paradox reports are divided into four different kinds of bands. These bands are Report, Page, Record, and Group bands. The first three bands are automatically placed in every report; they can't be removed, because they handle basic report functions. A group band is something you create. Figure 21.17 illustrates the three permanent band types in any report. Bands are available only with reports, not with forms.

Paradox uses bands to define the way your report sections repeat. For instance, headers, footers, and summarized and grouped information are all determined by the creation of bands and the placements of objects within them. Here is a more complete definition of the bands that all reports contain:

- *Report Band.* Contains the header and footer of your entire report. The contents of the report band header and footer appear once in a report. By default, the report band precedes the page band.

- *Page Band.* Contains the header and footer of each page. By default, Paradox places the date, the name of the table, and the page number in each page header. These can be changed or deleted if desired.
- *All Records Band.* Contains the records selected for your report and represents the main body of any report.

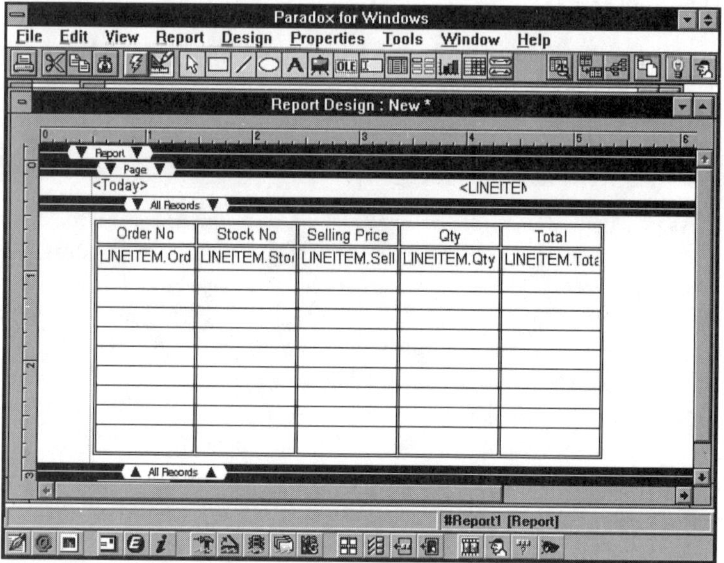

Fig. 21.17 All Paradox reports have three types of permanent bands—Report, Page, and All Records bands.

Selecting and Resizing a Band

To select a band, click the band label or on the white space inside the band. When a band is selected, its label color changes, the status bar states that it's selected, and the left sidebar ruler is darkened along that band.

To resize a selected band, move the pointer over the band until the two-headed arrow appears. Adjust the band size by dragging the double-headed arrow in either direction.

Working with Band Properties

To view a band's properties, right-click a selected band.

The Report Band has two options on the properties menu. Precede Page Header is selected by default; your report header precedes your page header. If you don't want this, click this menu selection to remove the check mark. The Report Band also has Run Time options, which are discussed in more detail later in this chapter.

The Page Band has one menu option. Print on 1st Page, selected by default, enables you to choose whether or not you want the information in the page band printed on the first page of your report.

The Report Band menu has three options including Start Page Number, Run Time, and Sort. The Sort option enables you to sort your report on one or more fields, in either ascending or descending order.

To sort records in a band, follow these steps:

1. Select and inspect the Record Band to access its menu.
2. Select Sort from the menu to access the Sort Record Band dialog box (see fig. 21.18).

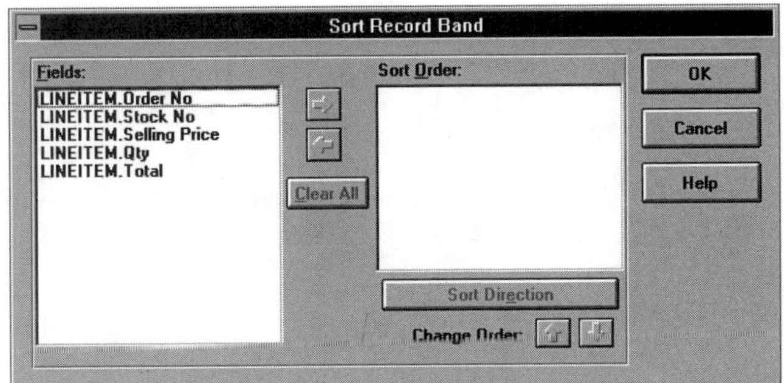

Fig. 21.18
You can sort on one or more fields in the Sort Record Band dialog box.

3. Highlight the field(s) that you want to sort in the **F**ield List, and click the right-arrow button to move the field to the Sort **O**rder list. You also can double-click to achieve the same result.
4. To remove a field from the Sort **O**rder list, highlight and select the left arrow. To start over, select **C**lear All.
5. To change the order of a sorted field, highlight that field and select the up or down arrow to move it.
6. To sort in ascending or descending order, highlight the field and click the Sort Dir**e**ction button. Fields sorted in ascending order, the default, are preceded by a + sign. Descending order is indicated by a – sign.
7. Click OK to sort.

Creating Group Bands

So far you have only displayed the contents of your tables in one long list. Many reports, however, require you to group your data by a specific field. For example, you may want to group a list of customers by city, or group your firm's products by price or type. A group band will let you separate your data into meaningful groups based on common fields. Paradox offers you the option of grouping by one or many fields, or grouping by a set number of records. In the following example, you'll create a group band that groups all the records in the VENDOR table by country. To create this group band, follow these steps:

1. Select the Add Band icon on the Toolbar to bring up the Define Group dialog box (see fig. 21.19).

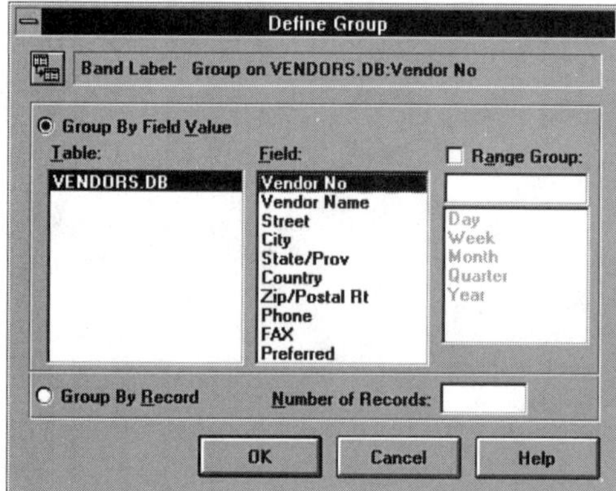

Fig. 21.19
You can add group bands to your report in the Define Group dialog box.

2. You have a choice of grouping by a specific field, or by a certain number of records. In this case, select Group by Field **V**alue.

3. Select a category in the **F**ield list and click OK.

4. When you return to Report Design, you see a new band—Group—on VENDOR.DB:Country, which tells you what the grouping contains.

5. To view the results of your grouping, select the View Data icon. You may need to scroll down to see the first grouping that contains more than one record.

Note

In most cases, you want to employ Group by Field **V**alue if you want to summarize or isolate particular records. If you want to simply group your records together in a specific number, use the Group by **R**ecord selection and enter the **N**umber of Records you want to group. This option is useful, for example, with long reports consisting of many pages, where you may want to group every 10 records or so to give your page some white space and make reading the report easier on the eyes.

Rearranging Group Bands

In some cases you may create more than one group band in a more complex report. To change the position of a group band, select the band you wish to move and drag it to its new location, either above or below the other group band.

Deleting Group Bands

Deleting a group band is a simple procedure. Simply select the band you wish to delete and press the Delete key. Note that you can't delete the Record, Page, or Report bands because they are a permanent part of any report. You can only delete a band you have created.

Note

If you cut one of the three permanent bands in a report, you don't actually delete the band, only the contents of the band. Cutting a group band completely removes it.

Troubleshooting

My report has too much white space.

Resize the appropriate band by selecting and dragging it in order to remove the appropriate amount of undesired white space.

Adding Fields

In most cases, your form or report already contains fields, either all of the table's fields, by default, or those fields you specified in the Data Model or Expert. Sometimes, though, you may want to add fields to an existing document. Some of the reasons you may want to add fields include:

- Creating and adding a summarized field (total, average, minimum, maximum, and so forth)
- Placing a special field (date, table name, and so forth) in your report
- Starting with a blank design window and adding fields exactly as you want to place them (not recommended unless you really want to design something unusual that isn't supported by the three methods described above)

To add an existing field to your document, follow these steps:

1. Click the Field tool icon and drag the cursor to place your field object.
2. Inspect (right-click) the field object to access the properties menu.
3. From this menu choose Define Field to get a list of possible fields. This list contains the names of all the fields in the table.
4. Click the desired field name to place it in the document.

Creating Summarized Fields

One of the most common reasons for using the Field tool is to create summarized fields, usually in a report. Paradox lets you create the following kinds of summarized fields: Sum, Count, Min, Max, Avg, Std, Var, First, Last, and Prev. Not all summary options are available for all field types. For example, summaries involving mathematical calculations (sum, count, and so forth) aren't available for alpha and graphic fields. Paradox also gives you three options for how to summarize: Normal, Unique or Cumulative. These options are explained further in table 21.1.

Tip
Be sure to place your summarized field in the right place in a report. Most summarized fields go in the page footer.

Table 21.1 Summarized Field Options

Option	Result
Sum	Summarizes all records
Count	Counts all records
Min	Displays the minimum value
Max	Displays the maximum value
Avg	Averages all records
Std	Displays standard deviation

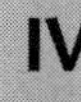

Option	Result
Var	Displays the statistical variation
First	Displays first value
Last	Displays last value
Prev	Displays previous value
Normal	Summarizes current set
Cumulative	Summarizes a running total
Unique	Summarizes only non-duplicate fields

To place a summarized field in your document, follow these steps:

1. Click the Field tool icon and drag the cursor to place your field object.
2. Inspect the field object to access the properties menu.
3. From this menu, choose Define Field to access the Define Field dialog box (see fig. 21.20).

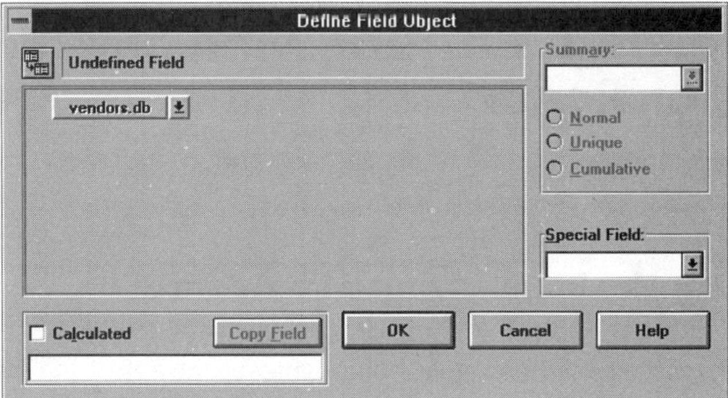

Fig. 21.20
The Define Field Object dialog box enables you to place summarized or special fields in your reports.

4. From the drop-down list on the left, select the field you want to summarize.
5. Choose your summary method from the drop-down Summ**a**ry list.
6. Select **N**ormative, **U**nique, or **C**umulative to determine how you want to summarize the field.
7. Click OK to return to Report Design.

Placing Special Fields in Your Report

Paradox offers the option of placing a number of special fields in your design documents. By default, three special fields are automatically placed in any new report—Today, Table Name, and Page Number. These fields appear in the Page Band of every report, but can be removed by selecting the field and pressing the Delete key.

- *Today*. Displays the current day's date.
- *Now*. Displays the current time.
- *Page Number*. Displays the current page number.
- *Number of Pages*. Displays the total number of pages in the report.
- *Table Name*. Displays the name of the table on which the report is based.

To place a special field in a form or report, create a new field as you did in the previous section. When you inspect the field, choose Define Field to open the Define Field Object dialog box. Select your special field from the **S**pecial Field drop-down list to place it in your document.

Previewing, Printing, and Saving a Form or Report

From the examples earlier in this chapter, you should already be familiar with the basic concepts of previewing, printing, and saving reports.

Changing the Page Layout of a Report

Before you preview or print your report, you may want to change the page layout of your report. For example, you might want to adjust the margins, or switch from portrait to landscape page orientation. To do so, choose **R**eport, **P**age Layout to open the Page Layout dialog box (see fig. 21.21).

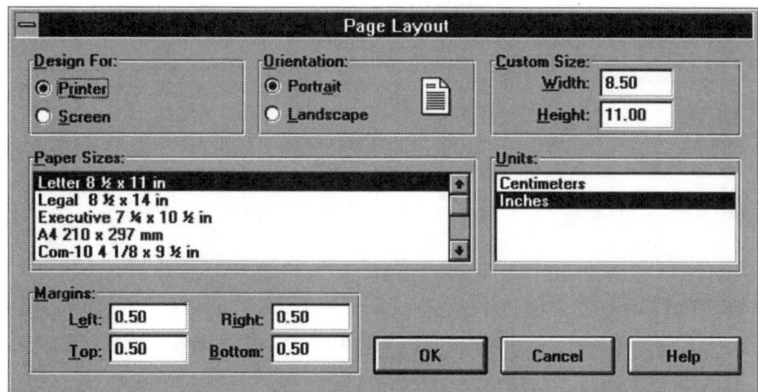

Fig. 21.21
The Page Layout dialog box gives you options for selecting margins, paper size, and orientation.

Previewing a Report or Form

To preview a document you are currently working with in Design, select the View Data icon to enter the Preview mode (see fig. 21.22).

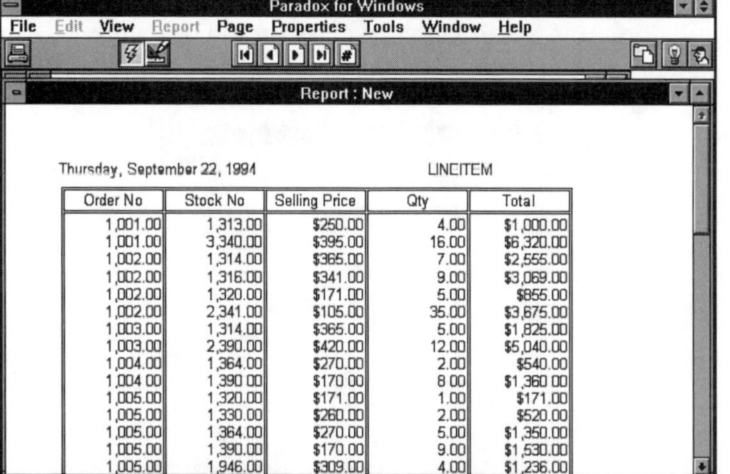

Order No	Stock No	Selling Price	Qty	Total
1,001.00	1,313.00	$250.00	4.00	$1,000.00
1,001.00	3,340.00	$395.00	16.00	$6,320.00
1,002.00	1,314.00	$365.00	7.00	$2,555.00
1,002.00	1,316.00	$341.00	9.00	$3,069.00
1,002.00	1,320.00	$171.00	5.00	$855.00
1,002.00	2,341.00	$105.00	35.00	$3,675.00
1,003.00	1,314.00	$365.00	5.00	$1,825.00
1,003.00	2,390.00	$420.00	12.00	$5,040.00
1,004.00	1,364.00	$270.00	2.00	$540.00
1,004.00	1,390.00	$170.00	8.00	$1,360.00
1,005.00	1,320.00	$171.00	1.00	$171.00
1,005.00	1,330.00	$260.00	2.00	$520.00
1,005.00	1,364.00	$270.00	5.00	$1,350.00
1,005.00	1,390.00	$170.00	9.00	$1,530.00
1,005.00	1,946.00	$309.00	4.00	$1,236.00

Fig. 21.22
Clicking the View Data icon enables you to preview your document.

If you aren't currently working with the document, inspect its name in the Project Viewer and select View Data from the menu. The View Data Toolbar contains many familiar icons, including

 First Page

 Previous Page

Tip
Zoom is also available from the **V**iew menu in Preview mode.

Before previewing your report, you may want to change the zoom option. The default is to show 100 percent, but you might want to see certain objects in more detail and increase the percentage, or view the entire page by reducing the percentage. Paradox also offers automatic adjustment options, such as Fit Width, Fit Height, and Best Fit.

To access the Zoom options, choose **V**iew, **Z**oom to display the zoom submenu.

Printing a Report or Form

To print a document you are currently previewing or designing, click the Print icon to access the Print File dialog box (see fig. 21.23).

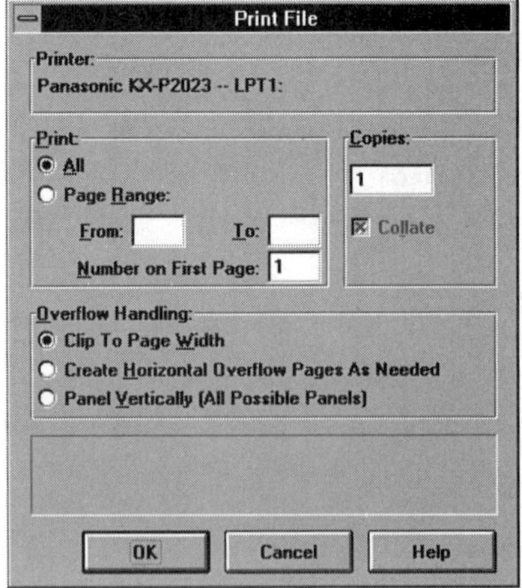

Fig. 21.23
The Print File dialog box gives you options for setting page ranges to print and options for overflow handling.

You also can open the Print File dialog box by double-clicking the report name in the Project Viewer. This dialog box offers the following options:

- ***Print.*** Choose to print either all pages or a selected range of pages. If your selected range does not start at the beginning of the report, you can enter 1 in the **N**umber on the First Page box to start your report at page one. To print your pages in reverse order, enter the last page number of your range in this first range box.

- *Copies.* Enter the number of copies you want to print.
- *Collate.* If you are making more than one copy of a multiple-page report, select this box to print each copy sequentially.
- *Overflow Handling.* Offers three options for handling data that flows over the standard page width:

  *Clip to Page **W**idth.* Cuts off all data that doesn't fit into the designated page margins.

  *Create **H**orizontal Overflow Pages As Needed.* Prints a second page with remaining data immediately after first page.

  *Panel **V**ertically (All Possible Panels).* Prints a second page for each report page, whether or not there is data overflow.

Saving a Report or Form

To save a design document, choose **F**ile, **S**ave. If this is a newly created report or form, the Save File As dialog box appears, which prompts you to enter a name for your document. If you saved it previously, the status bar displays `Report (or Form) Successfully Saved`. To save with a new name (for example, if you made changes and want to save it separately), choose **F**ile, Save **A**s to access the Save File As dialog box and enter a new file name.

Tip

You can't save a report or form if you are previewing it. You must return to Design to save it.

Troubleshooting

The fields in my report exceed the page width.

Although the Print File dialog box offers options for overflow handling, none of these gives you a way to fit all your data on a single page width. Outside of the obvious—limit the number of fields in your report—here are a few other suggestions for manipulating your report so that all your data fits on one page:

Switch to a landscape page layout. choose **R**eport, **P**age Layout to access the Page Layout dialog box. Select the **L**andscape option from the Orientation section.

Extend your margins. Default left and right margins are set at 0.50. These can be extended to 0.25 in the Page Layout dialog box without spilling off the page.

Reduce font size. The standard font size of 10 points can be reduced to 8 points and still produce a readable report. To reduce the font size for all text fields, multi-select all the test fields (shift and select all fields, then inspect to access the font menu).

From Here...

For more details on the information covered in this chapter, refer to the following chapters:

- Chapter 2, "Getting Started with PerfectOffice," covers the basics of copying, moving, formatting, editing, and using menus and dialog boxes.

- Chapter 22, "Working with Design Tools," gives you details on enhancing your reports and forms with Paradox's design tools.

- *Using Paradox for Windows, Special Edition*, also published by Que, covers report and form design in more depth.

Chapter 22

Working with Design Tools

by Patrice-Anne Rutledge

In the last chapter you learned to create basic reports and forms. They are functional, but in many cases you would like to add design elements such as boxes, bolding, and color. The Design window is where you can add, manipulate, and move text, fields, and objects in your report or form. It is your basic canvas for design document creation. Although creating a basic report or form in Paradox is relatively easy, design document creation has many sophisticated options available to users in the Design windows. In this chapter you learn to:

- Work in the report and form design windows
- Use the Design Toolbar
- Understand object properties
- Select, resize, and move objects
- Use palettes
- Work with colors

Using the Design Toolbar

The Report and Form Design Toolbars contain the tools for placing and manipulating objects (text, fields, boxes, and so forth) in your reports and forms. The 27 icons on the Design Toolbar and their uses are listed in table 22.1. With the exception of the Add Band icon, which is available only on the Report Design Toolbar, and the Button icon, available only on the Form Design Toolbar, all icons are available for designing both forms and reports.

Tip
To view the properties menu for any of the tools on the Toolbar, inspect its icon.

◀ See "Copying and Moving Using the Clipboard," p. 290

Table 22.1 Design Toolbar

Icon	Function	Description
	Print	Allows you to access the Print File dialog box and print your document
	Cut to Clipboard	Deletes a selected object and moves it to the Clipboard
	Copy to Clipboard	Copies a selected object to the Clipboard
	Paste from Clipboard	Pastes the current Clipboard contents into the document
	View Data	Previews the document you are creating
	Design	Opens the Design window
	Selection Arrow	Selects a specific object for manipulation
	Box tool	Creates and places a box in your document
	Line tool	Creates and places a line in your document
	Ellipse tool	Creates and places an ellipse or circle in your document
A	Text tool	Places text in your document
	Graphic tool	Places a graphic object in your report. Paradox supports the BMP, PCX, TIF, GIF, and EPS graphic file formats
OLE	OLE tool	Places an OLE object in your document
OK	Button tool	Places a button in your form
	Field tool	Places a field in your document
	Table tool	Places a table in your report
	Multi-Record tool	Creates a multi-record area

Icon	Function	Description
	Graph tool	Places a graph
	Crosstab tool	Creates a crosstab
	Add Band	Adds a group band to your report
	Filter	Filters your report for specific data
	Data Model	Opens the Data Model dialog box
	Object Tree	Displays a schematic of your document, defining the interrelationship of each of your objects (see fig. 22.1)
	Open Project Viewer	Opens the Project Viewer
	Expert	Opens the Experts Control Panel
	Coaches	Accesses the Coaches feature

► See "Understanding Graphs," p. 480

► See "Understanding Crosstabs," p. 471

◄ See "Data Sharing with Client/Server Applications," p. 21

◄ See "Coaches and Experts," p. 11

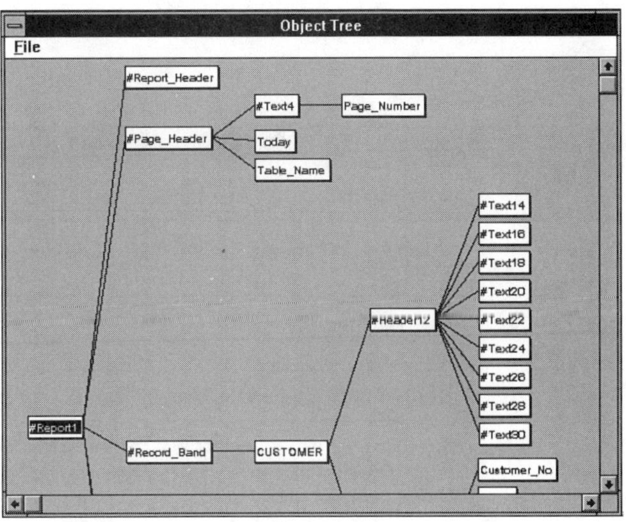

Fig. 22.1
The Object Tree displays a schematic diagram of your report or form, illustrating how each object relates to the others.

Creating and Manipulating a Table Object

In Design, you can create an object as well as move, resize, and change its properties (color, font, pattern, and so forth), including the option to change several objects simultaneously. Inspecting (right-clicking) any object displays the properties menu for that object. This menu is usually the same as the menu you reach by inspecting the corresponding icon on the Toolbar.

Creating and Placing Text and Objects

Placing text and objects—such as boxes, lines, and ellipses—is simple in Design. To place text, select the Text tool and then click where you want to place your text. Type the desired text. You can add style changes to your text, such as a different font, bolding, or italics, as discussed in the "Understanding Object Properties" section that follows.

To place a box in your document, select the Box tool and then click and drag the box to its desired location and size. The Ellipse and Line tools work in much the same way.

Understanding Object Properties

Inspecting an object displays a menu listing of available *properties*—the attributes that can be applied to that object. You will find a list of the property attributes available in Design in table 22.2 below. Not all attributes are available for every object.

Table 22.2 Object Properties

Property	Description
Alignment	Offers a choice of Left, Center, Right or Justified alignment
Attach Header	Reattaches the table header removed with the Detach Header property
Color	Displays the Color palette, seen in figure 22.4
Columnar	Shows a multi-record object in a columnar format
Conditional	Defines when a group header object is displayed
Define...	Used in combination with Field, Graph, Graphic, OLE, Record, or Table, and allows you to make specifications about the object

Property	Description
Delete When Empty	Does not display if field is empty. Selected by default.
Design Sizing	Determines how text objects expand or contract on the window, with the following options: *Fixed Size.* The object remains fixed and does not expand or contract. *Fit Text.* Text expands or contracts to fit. *Grow Only.* Lets object grow, but will not allow it to shrink.
Design	Offers several options for object manipulation in the design window. *Contain Objects.* The object contains any other object placed inside its borders. *Pin Horizontal.* Keeps the object from moving horizontally. *Pin Vertical.* Keeps the object from moving vertically. *Selectable.* Specifies that the object can be selected. *Size to Fit.* Expands or contracts to fit the size of its contents.
Detach Header	Separates the header from the text body
Display Type	Offers a choice of display types, including labeled, unlabeled, drop-down edit, list, radio buttons, and checkbox
Field Layout	In a multi-record object, rearranges the field order
Filter	Opens the Field Filter dialog box
Font	Opens the Font dialog box, where you will find the following options: *Typeface.* Lists all the available typefaces supported by your computer system. *Size.* Lists all available font sizes. *Style.* Offers a choice of Normal, Bold, Italic, Strikeout, or Underline. *Color.* Changes object color.
Format	Changes the object's format
Frame	The menu has the following options: *Style.* Displays the Frame Style palette, shown in figure 22.5. *Color.* Changes frame color. *Thickness.* Offers a choice of the following line widths: Hairline, Half Point, 1 Point, 2 Points, 3 Points, 6 Points, or 10 Points.

(continues)

Table 22.2 Continued

Property	Description
Grid	Offers three options: *Grid Style.* Offers a choice of Single, Double, Triple, 3D, or None for a grid style. *Record Dividers.* Click to select record dividers. *Color.* Changes grid color.
Horizontal Scroll Bar	Click to display a horizontal scroll bar
Line	Offers three options: *Line Style.* Displays the Line Style palette, shown in figure 22.6. *Color.* Changes line color. *Thickness.* Changes line thickness.
Line Ends	Offers a choice of No Arrow, On One End, or On Both Ends to determine if you want arrows at the ends of your lines
Line Spacing	Offers a choice of 1, 1.5, 2, 2.5 or 3 lines
Line Type	Offers a choice of straight or curved lines
Magnification	Offers option of magnifying from 25 percent to 400 percent or to select the best fit for your screen and needs
Method	Attaches an ObjectPAL method to the selected object
Options	Enables you to choose what to display in a graph
Pattern	Displays a menu with the following options: *Color.* Select the color of your pattern. *Style.* Displays the Pattern Style palette, shown in figure 22.7.
Raster Operation	Determines the way a graphic object combines with the screen or another object
Record Layout	In multi-record layout, defines the number of records in each column or row
Report Header	Places the report header on each report page
Run Time	Defines report behavior when it is previewed or printed
Search Text	Opens the Search & Replace dialog box
Update Link	Updates an OLE link
Vertical Scroll Bar	Click to display a vertical scroll bar
Word Wrap	At the end of a line, wraps text to the next line

Note

The term *raster* refers to the group of parallel lines that appear on your CRT (monitor). An image is formed by modulating brightness in these lines. In Paradox, *raster operations* refers to the way a graphic object combines with the screen. Paradox offers eight ways to combine these, each with a different end result.

Troubleshooting

I can't see my entire design document in the design window.

Choose **V**iew, **Z**oom, **B**est Fit to see your entire document in the screen.

I want to remove the double-line grid around my report data.

Select the grid and choose Grid, Grid Style, and None from the menus.

Selecting, Resizing, and Moving Objects

To select an object, point to it and click. A box with handles forms around your selected object. To resize the object, click one of the handles and an arrow appears. Drag the object in the direction the arrow points until you reach the desired size. To move an object, center the pointer in the middle of the selected object, and drag it to the new location.

To select more than one object at a time, or multi-select, press Shift and click all the desired objects. Continuing to press Shift, use the pointer to drag an invisible box around all the selected objects. Inspect any of the objects and choose an option from the properties menu; your selection applies to all the appropriate selected objects. This is an easy way to change the color, pattern, and so forth of a group of objects at once.

In many cases, one object contains another object. For example, if you have placed text inside a box, the box contains the text. You can inspect the container by right-clicking that object and change only its properties, or you can change the container and all the objects it contains by pressing Ctrl and then right-clicking. This opens a menu of penetrating properties, shown in figure 22.2, that penetrate all contained objects. The menu selections may apply to all selected objects or just one. For instance, in a box containing text, color can be applied to both, but the font menu option would apply only to the text.

Fig. 22.2
The penetrating properties menu applies to all selected objects, but not every object may be able to use each property.

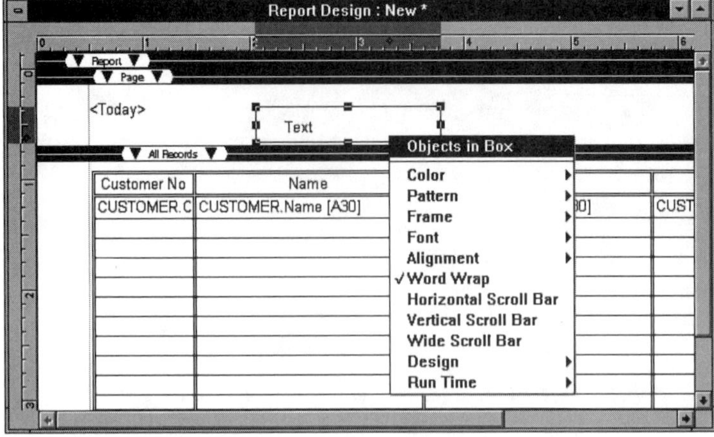

Changing Design Properties

Design also offers the option to set many properties that affect the entire design document. The **P**roperties menu in Design offers the following options:

- *Desktop.* Displays the Desktop Properties dialog box. For more report options, select the Forms and **R**eports... button to access the Forms/Reports Preferences dialog box, illustrated in figure 22.3. This dialog box offers several options:

  New Forms/Report. Enables you to set the default for creating a new report—**N**o default, **A**lways Blank, Always Use **E**xpert, or Always **U**se Data Model.

Fig. 22.3
Use the Forms/Reports Preferences dialog box to predefine how Paradox designs your report.

Open Default. Select the Open **R**eports or Open **F**orms in Design Mode option if this is how you want to open all design documents.

Form Screen Page Size. Select this box to make new reports the size of the desktop. Deselect it to enter specific size information in the **W**idth and **H**eight boxes, and to select **I**nches, **C**entimeters, or Pi**x**els.

Designer Style Sheets. Use the drop-down menus to select screen and printer style sheets.

- ***O**bjectPAL.* Opens the ObjectPAL Preferences dialog box, found only in the form-design screen.
- *Desi**g**ner.* Displays the Designer Properties dialog box, which gives you the following options:

Select From Inside. When you select a contained object, Paradox's default is to select the outer object first. Selecting this option selects the inside object first.

***F**rame Objects.* Frames selected objects with dotted lines.

*Flicker-Free **D**raw.* Helps eliminate screen flickering, but slows object manipulation. This is selected by default.

***O**utline Move/Resize.* Shows you the outline of the object you are manipulating, rather than the entire object. This option is selected by default.

- ***R**eport.* Displays a submenu with the following options:

*Remove **G**roup Repeat.* Select to not display repeated group values.

*Size to **F**it* (default). Automatically sizes the window to fit the report.

*Standard **M**enu* (default). Deselect this box to display a custom menu you've created. To display the standard menu, select the box.

***S**tyle Sheet....* Displays the Style Sheet dialog box, enabling you to change your style sheet.

- *Current Object.* Displays the Properties menu of the object currently selected.

- *Report Options.* Displays a submenu with two options:

  Save Defaults. Saves the current property settings as defaults.

  Restore Defaults. Restores the property settings saved previously.

- *Band Labels.* Selected by default, this option allows you to see your band labels—Report, Record, Page, and so forth. Deselecting it causes your band labels to disappear, but not your bands.
- *Snap to Grid.* Aligns all objects to the grid.
- *Show Grid.* Displays the grid while you are working in Report Design.
- *Grid Settings.* Accesses the Grid Settings dialog box, where you can adjust the scale or measurements of the grid.
- *Horizontal Ruler.* Displays a horizontal ruler.
- *Vertical Ruler.* Displays a vertical ruler.
- *Expanded Ruler.* Displays the expanded ruler, which lets you set the margins, tabs, and spacing of text objects.
- *Show Size and Position.* Displays the size and position of the selected object on the status bar line.

Using Palettes

In some cases, Paradox displays a palette instead of a menu listing for certain properties. A *palette* is a visual display of what a property looks like—rather than a verbal description—and is mostly used in conjunction with the more visual properties such as color, patterns, frame, line, thickness and font. These palettes are displayed in figures 22.4 to 22.7.

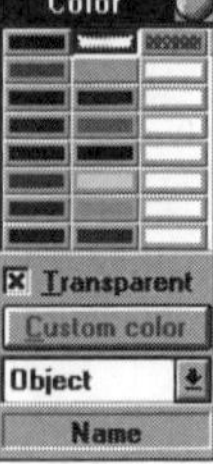

Fig. 22.4
You can select the color of your objects with the Color palette.

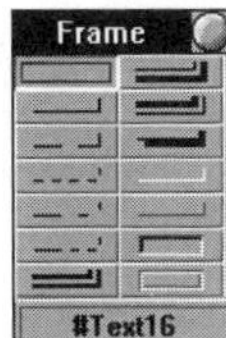

Fig. 22.5
The Frame Style palette offers several frame types from which to choose.

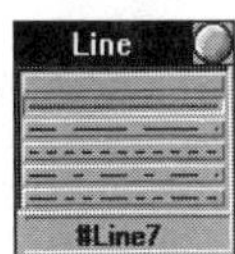

Fig. 22.6
The Line Style palette offers several options for displaying lines.

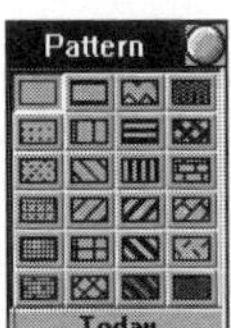

Fig. 22.7
The Pattern Style palette lets you choose the type of pattern you want to apply to your object.

To learn how a palette works, follow these steps to change an object's color:

1. Select an object and inspect (right-click) to open the properties menu.
2. Choose Color to access the color palette.
3. Click your desired color. The palette disappears.

The other palettes work in much the same way as the color palette.

Using a Floating Palette

Paradox offers two kinds of palettes—temporary palettes, such as the one you used in the example above, and floating palettes, which remain on-screen until you remove them. Floating palettes are useful when you want to change the properties of a number of objects, and don't want to continually inspect them to do so.

To float a palette, you must first locate the palette *snap*, a small circle at the top of the palette. Click this snap to float the palette. When you are finished with the palette, click the snap again and the palette disappears.

Working with Transparent and Custom Colors

To create a custom color, follow these steps:

1. Select an object and inspect it to open the properties menu.
2. From the properties menu, choose Color to access the color palette.
3. Click the palette snap to float the palette.
4. Click one of the clear color boxes to display the Custom Color button, and click it. The Custom Color dialog box appears.
5. Adjust the amount of red, green, and blue by moving the scroll bars to create your desired color. You can view it in the area above the scroll bars.
6. Click OK to apply your custom color to the object.

To make a color transparent, select the rectangular box in the lower-right corner of the Color palette. Note that a transparent color in the temporary Color palette is not the same as a transparent color in the floating Color palette. A transparent color from temporary palette appears clear, enabling you to view the color of anything beneath the transparent object. Transparent colors created with the floating palette appear translucent—the color of the background object is viewed through the transparently colored object on top of it.

Troubleshooting

When I click a clear box in the color palette, I can't access the Custom Color button.

You can only create custom colors when floating a palette. Click the palette snap to float the palette.

The color doesn't look the same on paper as it does on the screen.

Because of the way color reacts on your screen, it will never look exactly the same when it's printed. To adjust your color for printing if it doesn't look right, for example if it has too much blue, create a custom color similar to the one that shows on-screen, then reduce the amount of blue in it to look right on paper.

From Here...

For more details on the information covered in this chapter, refer to the following chapters:

- Chapter 2, "Getting Started with PerfectOffice," shows you how to manipulate objects and use toolbars.
- Chapter 21, "Designing Reports and Forms," covers the basics of creating reports and forms.

Chapter 23

Creating Crosstabs and Graphs

by Patrice-Anne Rutledge

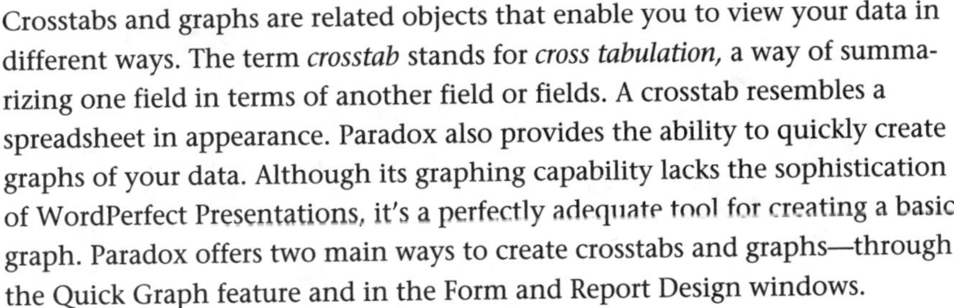

Crosstabs and graphs are related objects that enable you to view your data in different ways. The term *crosstab* stands for *cross tabulation,* a way of summarizing one field in terms of another field or fields. A crosstab resembles a spreadsheet in appearance. Paradox also provides the ability to quickly create graphs of your data. Although its graphing capability lacks the sophistication of WordPerfect Presentations, it's a perfectly adequate tool for creating a basic graph. Paradox offers two main ways to create crosstabs and graphs—through the Quick Graph feature and in the Form and Report Design windows.

In this chapter, you will learn to

- Create one- and two-dimensional crosstabs
- Create multi-table crosstabs
- Create tabular, 1-D, and 2-D graphs

Understanding Crosstabs

Like a spreadsheet, a crosstab contains columns (across the top), rows (along the left margin), and summary data. In a crosstab, a row is also referred to as a category. Paradox offers the ability to create one-dimensional, two-dimensional, and multi-table crosstabs. A one-dimensional crosstab looks at the relationship between two fields in a table. A two-dimensional crosstab looks at the relationship between more than two fields. For example, in the ORDERS table, viewing the total invoice dollars by payment type would create a one-dimensional crosstab. Viewing total invoice dollars by payment type and ship Via would create a two-dimensional crosstab. A multi-table crosstab is derived from fields in more than one table.

Creating a One-Dimensional Crosstab

To create a one-dimensional crosstab summarizing total invoices by payment method, follow these steps:

1. Open the ORDERS table in the SAMPLE subdirectory by double-clicking it in the Project Viewer.

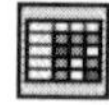

2. Click the Quick Crosstab icon to open the Define Crosstab dialog box (see fig. 23.1).

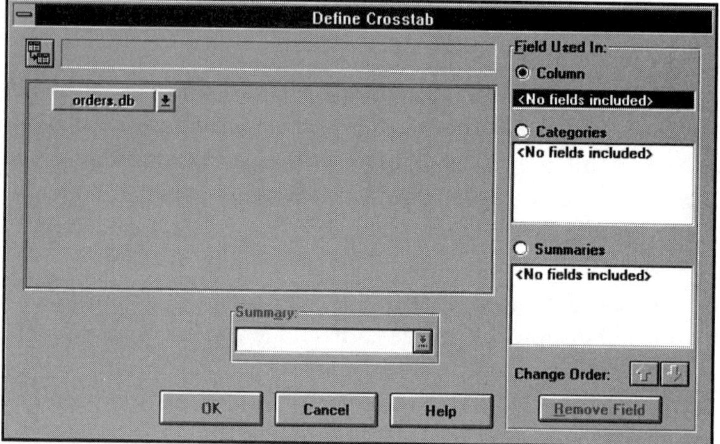

Fig. 23.1
You can specify columns, categories, and summaries in the Define Crosstab dialog box.

3. With the Column radio button selected, click on the field Payment Method from the pull-down menu under the table name, ORDERS.DB.

4. With the Summaries radio button selected, click on the field name Total Invoice from the pull-down menu under ORDERS.DB.

5. Select Sum as the summary method in the Summary drop-down list. Other summary options include Min, Max, Avg, or Count.

6. If you made a mistake, select the field you want to remove and click the *Remove Field* button.

7. Click OK to create your crosstab.

8. You will now view your crosstab as a form (see fig. 23.2).

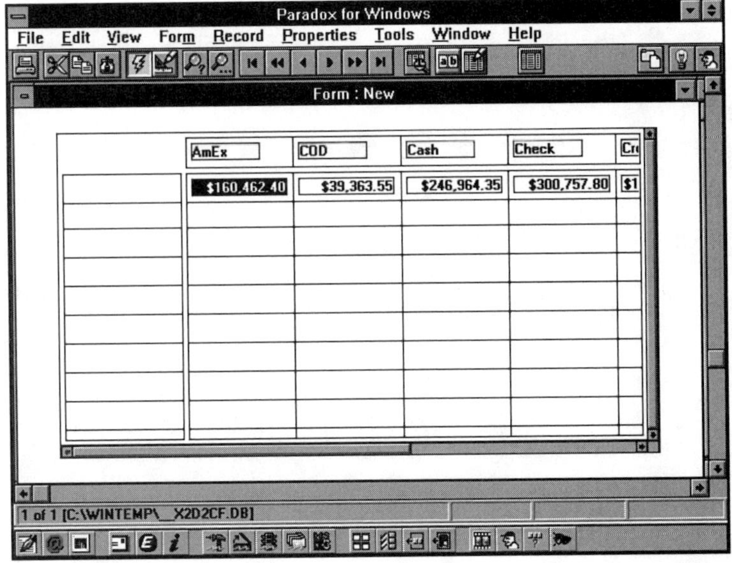

Fig. 23.2
You can now view Total Invoice by Payment Method as a crosstab.

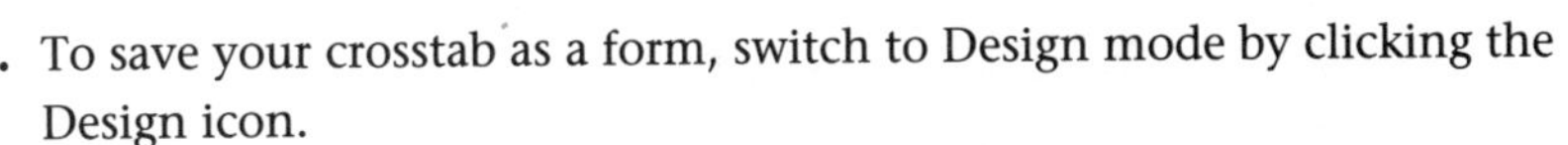

9. To save your crosstab as a form, switch to Design mode by clicking the Design icon.

10. Choose **F**ile, **S**ave to open the Save File dialog box.

11. Enter your desired file name—for example, **ORDERS**—and click OK.

Creating a Two-Dimensional Crosstab

To create a two-dimensional crosstab that summarizes total invoices by payment method and by shipping method, follow these steps:

1. Open the ORDERS table by double-clicking it in the Project Viewer.

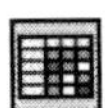

2. Click the Quick Crosstab icon to open the Define Crosstab dialog box.

3. With the Columns radio button selected, click on the Payment Method field from the pull-down menu under the table name, ORDERS.DB.

4. With the Categories radio button selected, click on the Ship Via field from the pull-down menu.

5. With the Summaries radio button selected, click on the Total Invoice field from the pull-down menu.

6. Select Sum as the summary method in the Summary drop-down list.

7. Click OK to create your crosstab.

8. You will now view your crosstab as a form (see fig. 23.3).

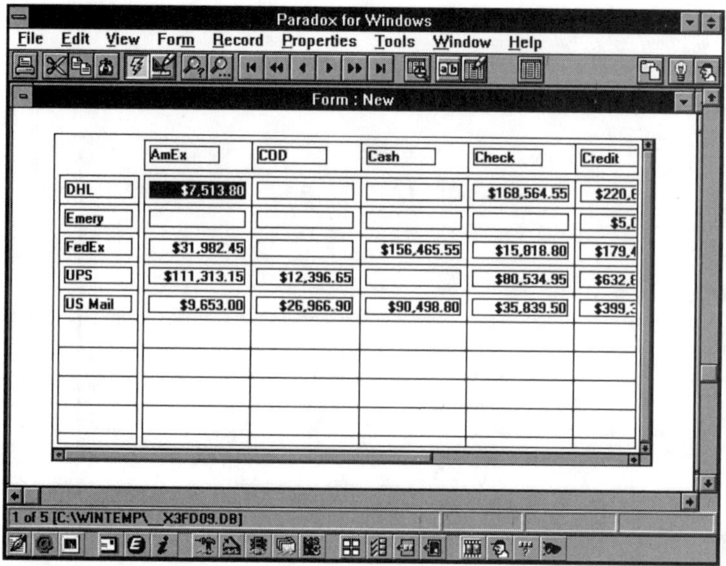

Fig. 23.3
You can now view your crosstab in the form window.

Creating a Multi-Table Crosstab

To create a crosstab that contains fields found in two different tables, you need to create a link between those tables before you can create your crosstab. In Chapter 20, you linked tables to create multi-table queries. To create a crosstab, you need to use the Data Model dialog box to create this same type of link. A Data Model is simply a representation, or model, of how your tables link to each other. To create a crosstab that summarizes the balance due by stock number, follow these steps:

1. Choose **F**ile, **N**ew, **F**orm to open the New Form dialog box.
2. Click the **D**ata Model/Layout Diagram button to open the Data Model dialog box (see fig. 23.4).
3. Double-click on the ORDERS table to select it. You can also highlight the table name and click the right arrow to select.
4. Double-click the LINEITEM table to select it.

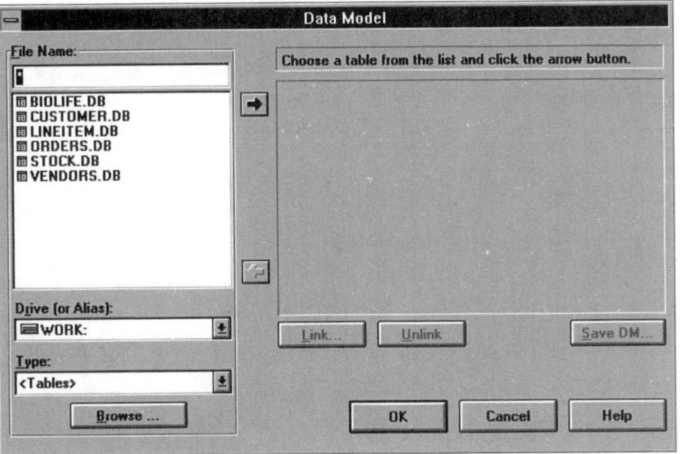

Fig. 23.4
The Data Model dialog box enables you to set links between your tables.

5. To link the two tables, point the pointer to the ORDERS table, and click and draw a line to the LINEITEM table.

6. The Define Link dialog box opens (see fig. 23.5). You will use the default link in this example.

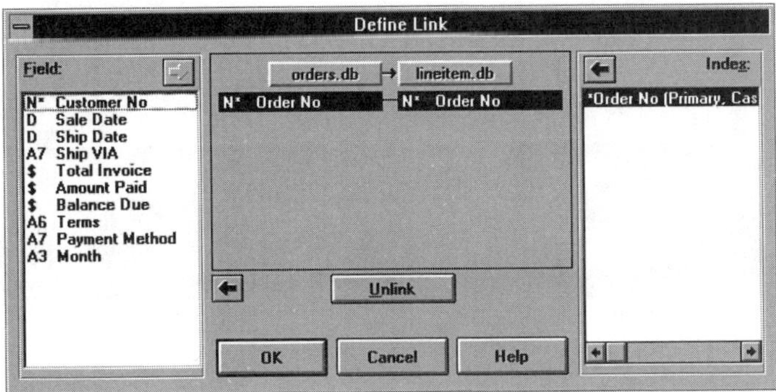

Fig. 23.5
Define how you want to link your tables in the Define Links dialog box.

7. Click OK to return to the Data Model dialog box.

8. Click the Save DM button to save the Data Model. The Save File As dialog box opens.

9. Enter a name for your data model and click OK to continue to the Design Layout dialog box (see fig. 23.6).

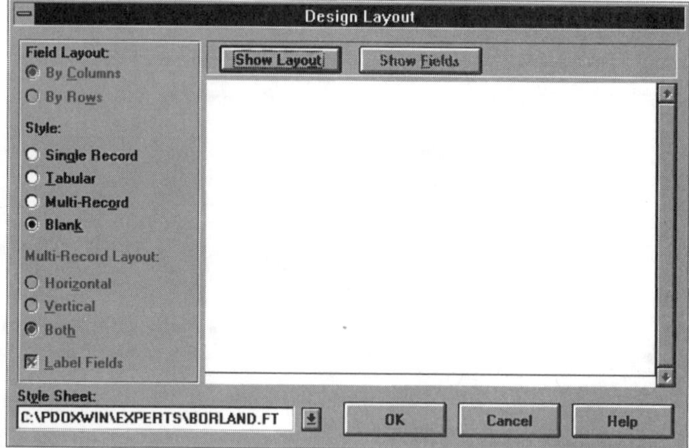

Fig. 23.6
This dialog box enables you to set basic design features for your document.

10. Under Style select the Blank radio button to create a blank form window.

11. Click OK to open a blank Form Design window.

12. Select the Crosstab tool on the Toolbar and click and drag a box on your screen.

13. An empty crosstab appears (see fig. 23.7). Inspect the blank area of the upper-left corner of the crosstab to open the object's menu.

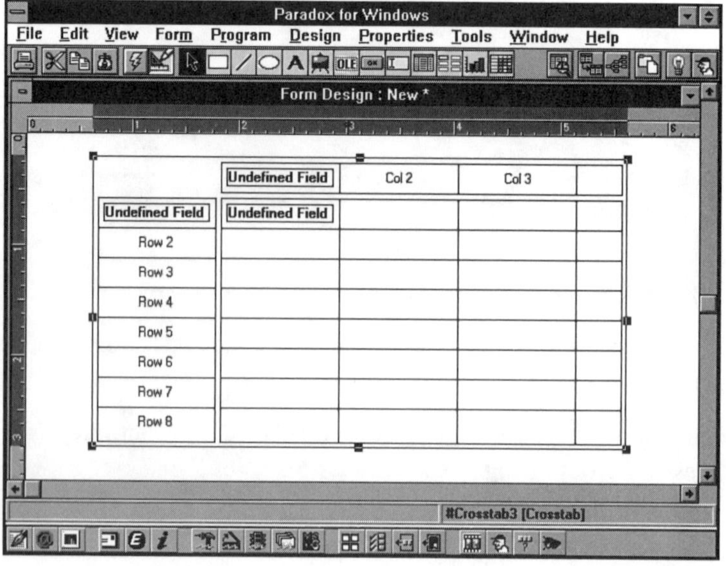

Fig. 23.7
This empty crosstab enables you to choose fields from two tables.

14. Select Define Crosstab and... from the object's menu to open the Define Crosstab dialog box, (see fig. 23.8).

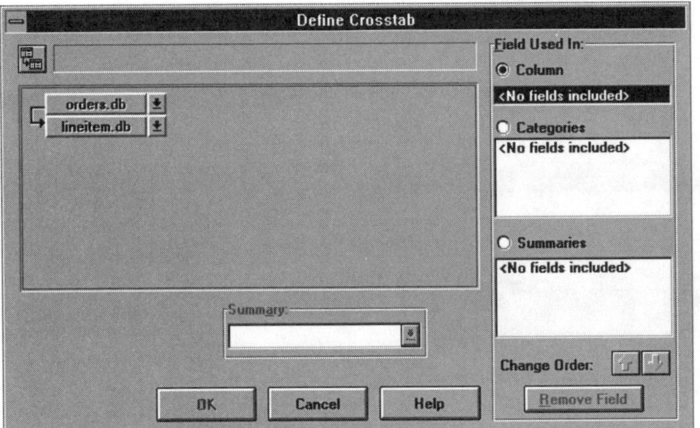

Fig. 23.8
You can define the fields for your crosstab in this dialog box.

15. With the Column radio button selected, use the down-arrow by the LINEITEM.DB to locate and select Stock No. as your column field.

16. With the Summaries radio button selected, use the down-arrow by the ORDERS.DB to locate and select Balance Due as your summary field.

17. Select Sum as your summary method in the Summary drop-down list.

18. Click OK to return to the Design window.

Editing a Crosstab

Once you have created a crosstab, you can edit it later. In the Form Design window, many of the same object properties available for a regular form are available for a crosstab.

Tip
To save a crosstab as a table, choose **E**dit, Save Crossta**b**, and enter the name of the table as you want to save it.

You can edit or add categories (rows), columns, or summaries as well as edit the entire crosstab from the Design window. As an example, to change the category from Ship Via to Terms in the one-dimensional crosstab you created earlier, follow these steps:

1. Select the ORDERS form (if this is the name you chose) in the Project Viewer, inspect it and select Design to open the Form Design window.

2. Select the field ORDERS.DB.ShipVia. The entire field name is somewhat hidden; it is at the top of the category row.

3. Inspect this field to view its menu. Choose Define Field and select ORDERS.DB.Terms from the list. You can also select ... to open the Define field Object dialog box and select your field here.

4. Click the View Data icon to view your new crosstab (see fig. 23.9).

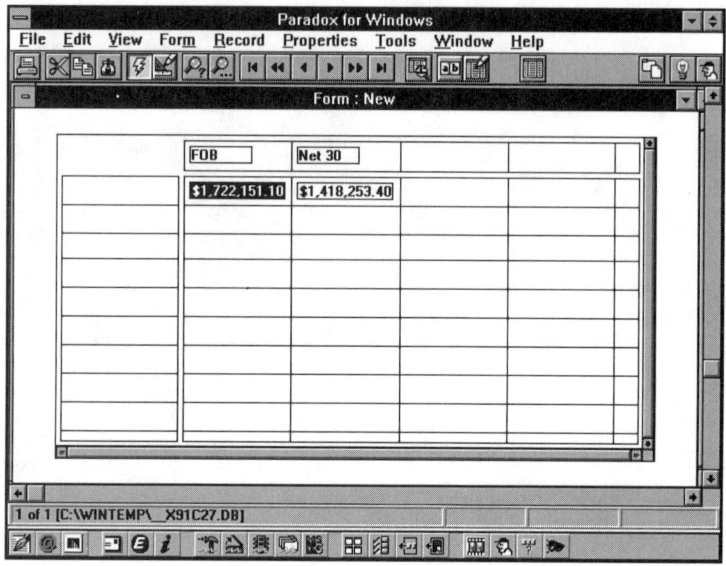

Fig. 23.9
You can now view the crosstab you edited.

Tip
You must inspect the exact area you want to change to access the appropriate menu. For example, if you want to edit a specific field you must inspect it directly; if you want to edit the category, your pointer must be in the row area.

You can inspect and edit each crosstab area—field, category, column, summary, or the entire crosstab—individually to view that area's menu. For a list of all a crosstab's properties see table 23.1.

Table 23.1 Crosstab Elements Properties

Property	Description
Add a Category	Offers a list of available category fields as well as access to the Define Field Object dialog box by selecting ....
Add a Summary	Offers a list of available summary fields as well as access to the Define Field Object dialog box by selecting ....
Alignment	Offers a choice of Left, Center, Right or Justified alignment
Color	Displays the Color palette

Property	Description
Define...	Used in combination with Field, Crosstab, or Column Field, and enables you to make specifications about the object
Design	Offers several options for object manipulation in the design window. *Contain Objects.* The object contains any other object placed inside its borders. *Pin Horizontal.* Keeps the object from moving horizontally. *Pin Vertical.* Keeps the object from moving vertically. *Selectable.* Specifies that the object can be selected. *Size to Fit.* Expands or contracts to fit the size of its contents.
Filter	Opens the Field Filter dialog box
Font	Opens the Font dialog box, where you will find the following options: *Typeface.* Lists all the available typefaces supported by your computer system. *Size.* Lists all available font sizes. *Style.* Offers a choice of Normal, Bold, Italic, Strikeout, or Underline. *Color.* Changes object color.
Frame	Has the following options: *Style.* Displays the Frame Style palette. *Color.* Changes frame color. *Thickness.* Offers a choice of the following line widths: Hairline, Half Point, 1 Point, 2 Points, 3 Points, 6 Points, or 10 Points.
Grid	Offers three options: *Grid Style.* Offers a choice of Single, Double, Triple, 3D, or None for a grid style. *Record Dividers.* Click to select record dividers. *Color.* Changes grid color.
Horizontal	Click to display a horizontal scroll bar
Scroll Bar Method	Attaches an ObjectPAL method to the selected object
Pattern	Displays a dialog box with the following options: *Color.* Select the color of your pattern. *Style.* Displays the Pattern Style palette.
Run Time	Defines report behavior when it is previewed or printed
Vertical Scroll Bar	Select to display a vertical scroll bar

◄ See "Understanding Object Properties," p. 460

Note

Selecting the Blank button from the New Form dialog box isn't the same as creating a blank form using the above steps. Setting up a blank form within the Data Model dialog box enables you to set table relationships. Creating a blank form from the New Form dialog box will create a form without any tables attached to it.

Troubleshooting

My crosstab prints as a blank form.

You printed your crosstab in Design mode. You need to switch to View mode and then print your crosstab.

Understanding Graphs

Tip
In the Report Design window, you can only create a tabular graph.

Before Paradox creates a graph it cross-tabulates the data. Therefore, it's a good idea to understand the basics of crosstabs before you create a graph.

Paradox can create three types of graphs:

- *Tabular.* This is the default graph type. It measures one field in terms of another. The x-value must be a unique key field for this type of graph.
- *One-dimensional.* A one-dimensional graph also measures, or summarizes, one field in terms of another. However, if your x-value isn't unique you need to create a 1-D graph.
- *Two-dimensional.* A two-dimensional graph groups summary data for two fields.

Creating a Tabular Graph

To create a tabular graph listing total invoice by order number in the ORDERS table, follow these steps:

1. Open the ORDERS table by double-clicking it in the Project Viewer.

2. Click the Quick Graph icon to open the Define Graph dialog box (see fig. 23.10).

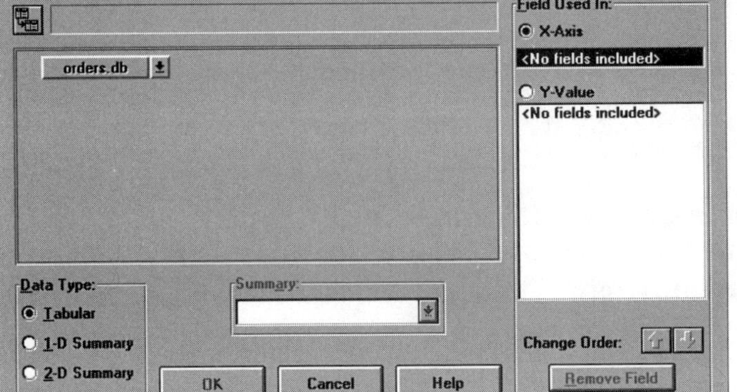

Fig. 23.10
You can specify your graph type in the Define Graph dialog box.

3. Select Tabular under Data Type.

4. With the X-Axis radio button selected, click on the Order No. field from the pull-down menu under the table name, ORDERS.DB.

5. With the Y-Value radio button selected, click on the Total Invoice field.

6. If you made a mistake, select the field you want to remove and click the Remove Field button.

7. Click OK to create your graph.

8. You can now view your graph as a form (see fig. 23.11).

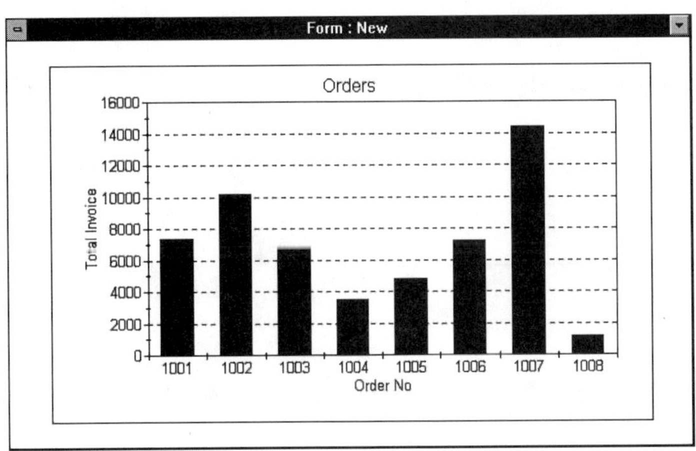

Fig. 23.11
You can now view your new tabular graph.

9. To save your graph as a form, switch to Design mode by clicking the Design icon.

10. Choose **F**ile, **S**ave to open the Save File dialog box.

11. Enter the desired file name and click OK.

Creating a One-Dimensional Graph

To create a one-dimensional graph summarizing total invoices by payment method in the ORDERS table, follow these steps:

1. Open the ORDERS table by double-clicking it in the Project Viewer.

2. Click the Quick Graph icon to open the Define Graph dialog box.

3. Select 1-D Summary under Data Type.

4. With the X-Axis radio button selected, click on the Payment Method field from the pull-down menu under ORDERS.DB.

5. With the Y-Value radio button selected, click on the Total Invoice field from the pull-down menu under ORDERS.DB.

6. Select Sum as the summary method in the Summary drop-down list.

7. If you make a mistake, select the field you want to remove and click the Remove Field button.

8. Click OK to create your graph.

9. You will now view your graph as a form (see fig. 23.12).

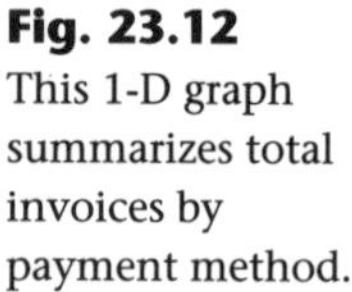

Fig. 23.12
This 1-D graph summarizes total invoices by payment method.

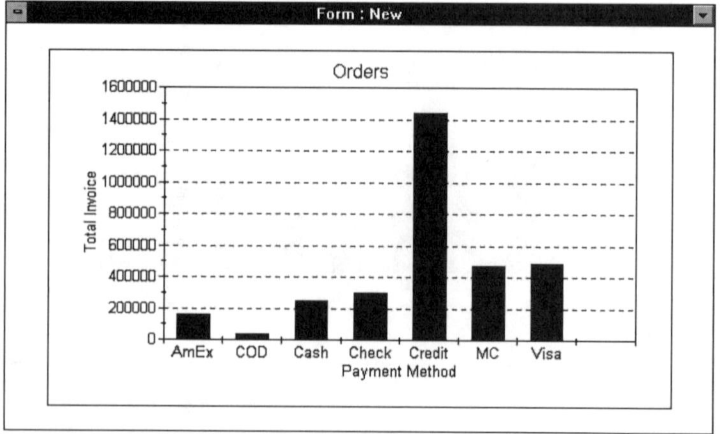

Creating a Two-Dimensional Graph

To create a two-dimensional graph summarizing total invoices by payment method grouped by terms in the ORDERS table, follow these steps:

Tip
You can also create this graph by using the Quick Graph method.

1. Choose **F**ile, **N**ew, **F**orm to open the New Form dialog box.
2. Click the Data Model/Layout Diagram button to open the Data Model dialog box.
3. Double-click on the ORDERS table to select it. You can also highlight the table name and click on the right arrow to select it.
4. Click OK to return to the Data Model dialog box.
5. Click the Save DM button to save the Data Model. The Save File As dialog box opens.
6. Enter a name for your data model and click OK to continue to the Design Layout dialog box.
7. Under Style select the Blank radio button to create a blank form window.
8. Click OK to open a blank Form Design window.
9. Click the Graph tool on the Toolbar and drag a box on your screen in which to place your graph.

10. An empty graph appears, illustrated in figure 23.13. Inspect the blank area of the upper left corner of the graph to open its menu.

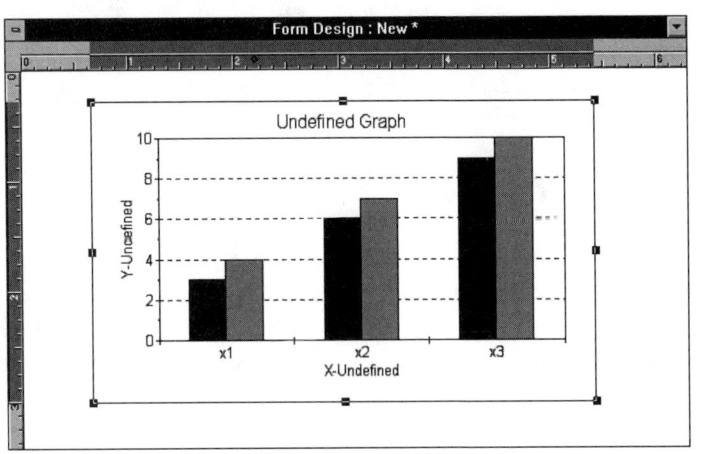

Fig. 23.13
This empty graph enables you to choose fields from two tables.

11. Select Define Graph and... from the graph's menu to open the Define Graph dialog box.
12. Select 2-D Summary under Data Type.
13. With the X-Axis radio button selected, click on the field Payment Method from the pull-down menu under the table name, ORDERS.DB.
14. With the Grouped By radio button selected, click on the Terms field name from the pull-down menu under ORDERS.DB.
15. With the Y-Value radio button selected, click on the field named Total Invoice from the pull-down menu under ORDERS.DB.
16. Select Sum as the summary method in the Summary drop-down list.
17. Click OK to create your graph.

18. Click the View Data icon to view your graph, illustrated in figure 23.14.

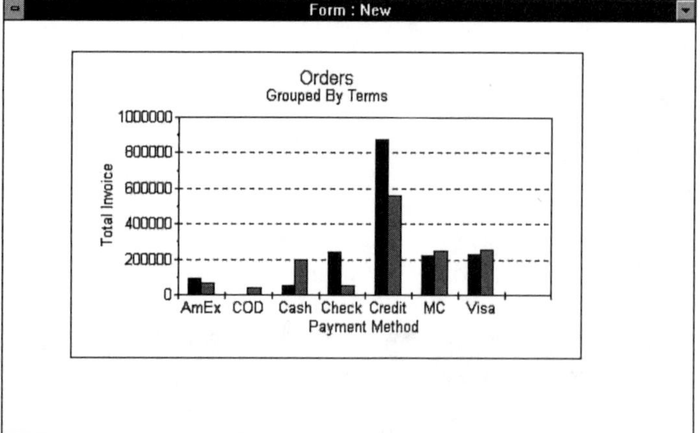

Fig. 23.14
This graph is an example of a 2-D graph.

Editing a Graph

You can edit each part of a graph individually in the Form Design window. The following graph elements can be edited: X-Axis, Y-Axis, Title Box, Background, Graph, and Series. The properties you can edit for each of these are listed in table 23.2. To edit a part of a graph, inspect (right-click) the object to bring up its menu.

Table 23.2 Graph Object Properties

Property	Description
X-Axis	
Define X-Value	Displays a list of available fields
Title	Offers three options: *Text....* Opens the Enter Title dialog box. *Font.* Opens the Font dialog box, where you will find the following options: *Typeface.* Lists all the available typefaces supported by your computer system. *Size.* Lists all available font sizes. *Style.* Offers a choice of Normal, Bold, Italic, Strikeout, or Underline. *Color.* Changes object color. *Use Default.* Uses default settings.
Ticks	Gives you the choice of defining a font or setting alternate ticks
Y-Axis	
Define New Y-Value	Displays a list of available fields
Title	Offers three options: *Text....* Opens the Enter Title dialog box. *Font.* Opens the Font dialog box, where you will find the following options: *Typeface.* Lists all the available typefaces supported by your computer system. *Size.* Lists all available font sizes. *Style.* Offers a choice of Normal, Bold, Italic, Strikeout, or Underline. *Color.* Changes object color. *Use Default.* Uses default settings.
Scale	Offers five options: *Auto-Scale.* Automatically scales the graph. *Logarithm.* Displays the scale as a logarithm. *Low Value.* Sets the lowest value to show on the graph. *High Value.* Sets the highest value to show on the graph. *Increment.* Specifies the increment amount for each grid.
Ticks	Offers two options: *Font.* Opens the Font dialog box, where you will find the following options: *Typeface.* Lists all the available typefaces supported by your computer system. *Size.* Lists all available font sizes. *Style.* Offers a choice of Normal, Bold, Italic, Strikeout, or Underline. *Color.* Changes object color. *Number Format.* Offers several number format options: Windows $, Windows #, Fixed, Scientific, General, comma, Percent, Integer, or DBNumeric.

(continues)

Table 23.2 Continued

Property	Description
Title Box	
Define Graph	Gives you to access the Define Graph dialog box
Title	Offers three options: *Text....* Opens the Enter Title dialog box. *Font.* Opens the Font dialog box, where you will find the following options: *Typeface.* Lists all the available typefaces supported by your computer system. *Size.* Lists all available font sizes. *Style.* Offers a choice or Normal, Bold, Italic, Strikeout, or Underline. *Color.* Changes object color. *Use Default.* Uses default settings.
Subtitle	Offers same options as Title for the subtitle field
Color	Opens the color palette
Pattern	Offers two options: *Color.* Opens the color palette. *Style.* Opens the pattern style palette.
Background	
Color	Opens the color palette
Pattern	Offers two options: *Color.* Opens the color palette. *Style.* Opens the pattern style palette.
Graph	
Define Graph	Opens the Define Graph dialog box
Color	Opens the color palette
Pattern	Offers two options: *Color.* Opens the color palette. *Style.* Opens the pattern style palette.
Frame	The menu has the following options: *Style.* Displays the Frame Style palette. *Color.* Changes frame color. *Thickness.* Offers a choice of the following line widths: Hairline, Half Point, 1 Point, 2 Points, 3 Points, 6 Points, or 10 Points.
Data Type	Offers choices of Tabular, 1D Summary, or 2D Summary

Property	Description
Graph	
Graph Type	Offers numerous graph type options: XY Graph, 2D Bar, 2D Stacked Bar, 2D Rotated Bar, 2D Area, 2D Line, 2D Columns, 2D Pie, 3D Bar, 3D Stacked Bar, 3D Rotated Bar, 3D Area, 3D Surface, 3D Columns, 3D Pie, 3D Ribbon, or 3D Step
Min X-Values	Offers a choice from one to eight. Select ... for numbers greater than eight
Max X-Values	Offers a choice from one to eight. Select ... for numbers greater than eight
Options	Offers the options to display any of the following: title, legend, grid, axes, or labels
Design	Offers several options for object manipulation in the design window. *Contain Objects.* The object contains any other object placed inside its borders. *Pin Horizontal.* Keeps the object from moving horizontally. *Pin Vertical.* Keeps the object from moving vertically. *Selectable.* Specifies that the object can be selected.
Run Time	Defines report behavior when it is previewed or printed
Methods	Attaches an ObjectPAL method to the selected object
Series	
Define Y-Value	Displays a list of available fields
Color	Opens the color palette
Pattern	Offers two options: *Color.* Opens the color palette. *Style.* Opens the pattern style palette.
Remove This Y-Value	Removes series from graph
Type Override	Offers a choice of None (default), 2D Bar, 2D Line, or 2D Area

◄ See "Understanding Object Properties," p. 460

Troubleshooting

I can't see all the series for my tabular graph.

Tabular graphs are best used with tables that contain few records. Because each record becomes a unique graph item, only tables with a small number of records will create a meaningful tabular graph.

I inspected my graph, but didn't get the right menu.

Be sure you inspect the exact location you are trying to edit. If you inspect outside the area you want to edit, you will retrieve the menu for a different area.

Printing a Crosstab or Graph

You print a crosstab or graph just as you would a form or report. Choose **F**ile, **P**rint to access the Print File dialog box. Click OK to print.

From Here...

For more details on the information covered in this chapter, refer to the following chapters:

- Chapter 21, "Designing Reports and Forms," covers the basics of creating reports and forms.
- Chapter 22, "Working with Design Tools," shows you how to work with object properties in the Design window.
- Chapter 24, "Getting Started with Presentations," introduces you to designing charts and graphs in WordPerfect Presentations.

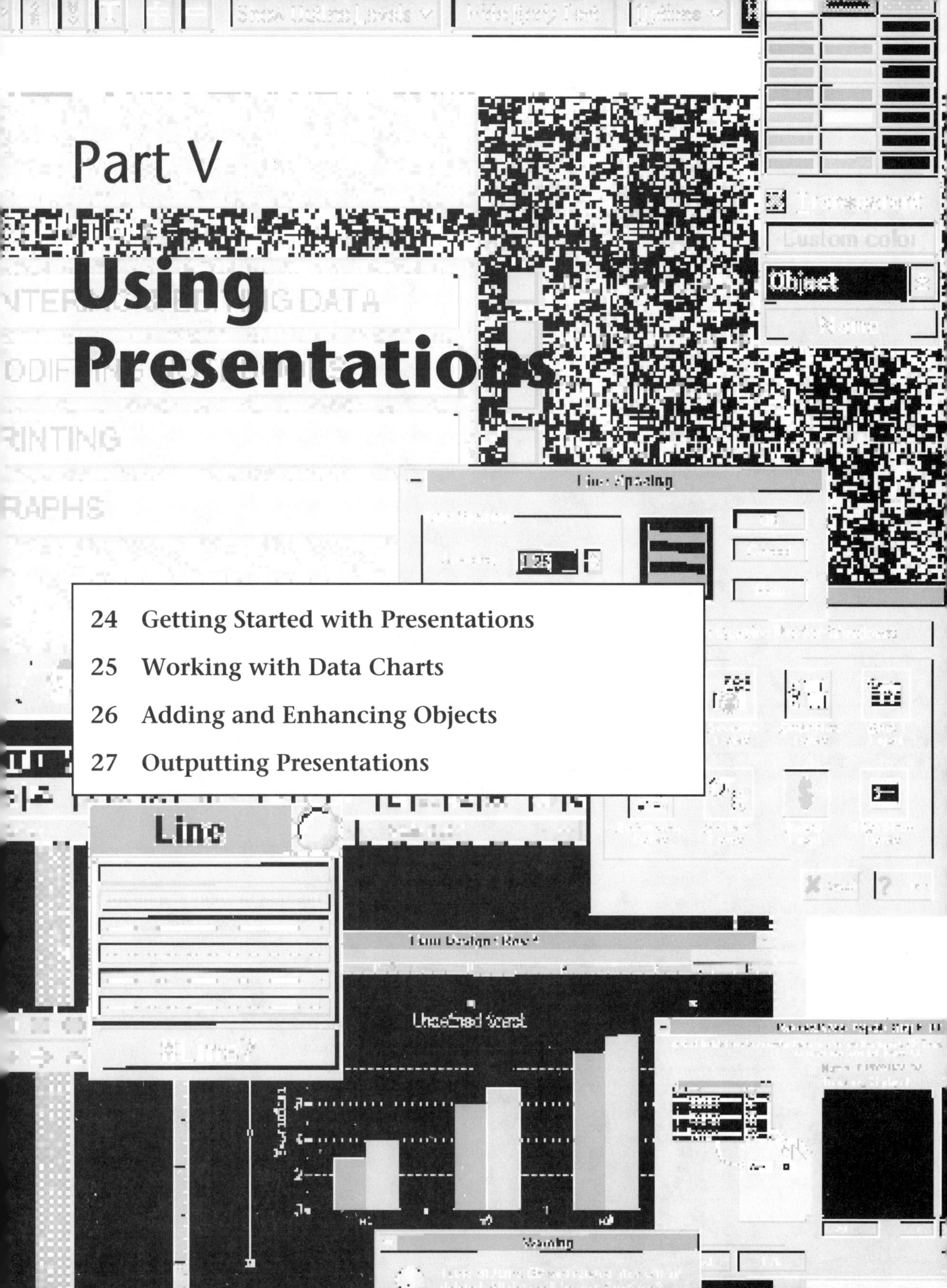

Part V

Using Presentations

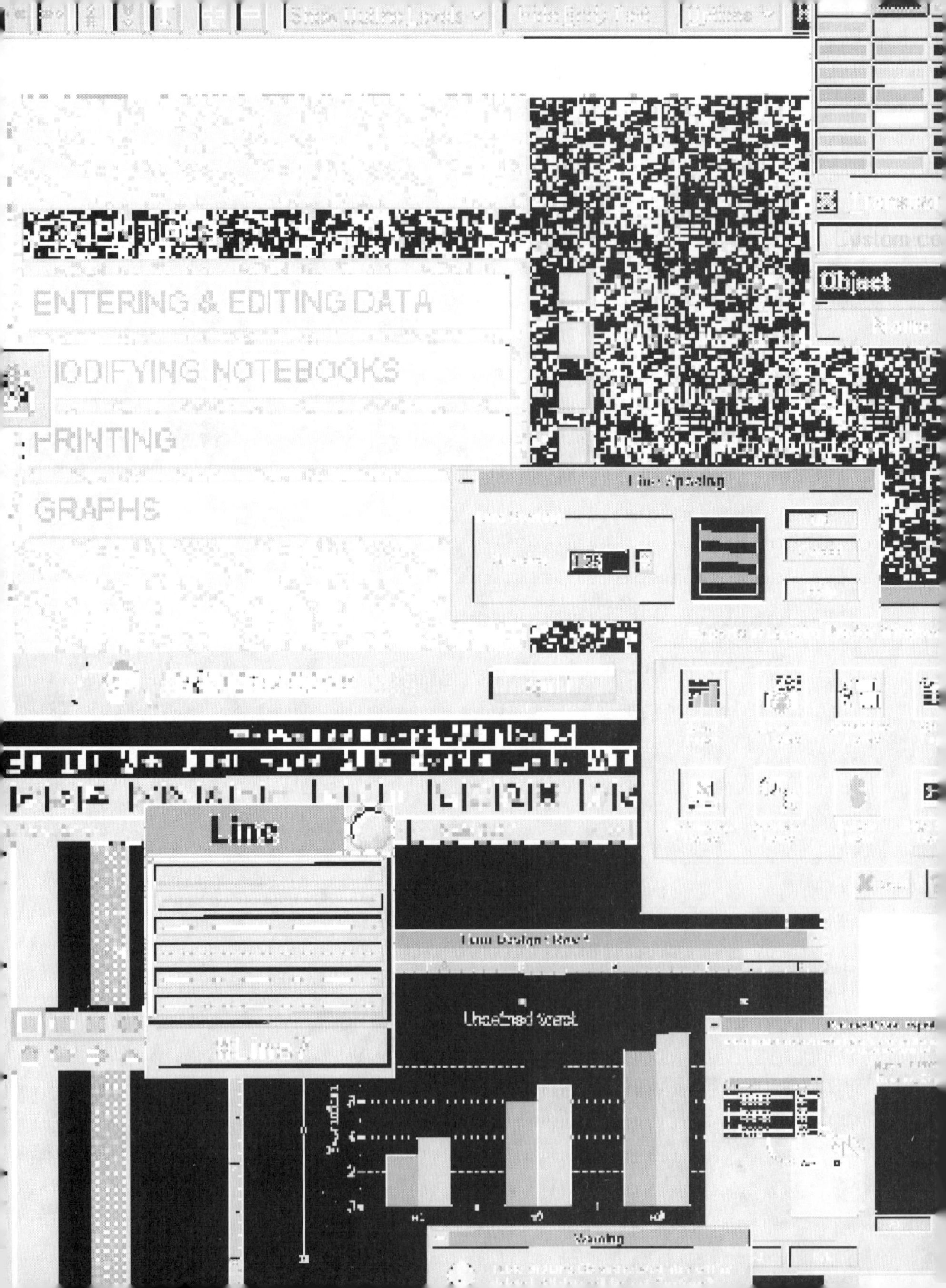
ENTERING & EDITING DATA
IODIFYING NOTEBOOKS
PRINTING
GRAPHS
Line Spacing
Line
Object
Custom co

Chapter 24

Getting Started with Presentations

by Sue Plumley

This chapter introduces WordPerfect Presentations, a program you can use to create professional quality overhead, paper, 35mm slide, or on-screen presentations. In this chapter, you learn how to start Presentations and create a slide show. You also learn the basic steps to entering and editing slide information, and a variety of ways to view the slide screen.

In this chapter, you learn how to

- Start a new presentation
- Change views of the Presentations screen
- Use Outliner to create a presentation
- View slides in the Slide Editor
- List and sort slides

Starting Presentations

You start Presentations like you start any of the applications in Perfect-Office—by double-clicking the program icon in the Program Manager. Additionally, you can start Presentations from the Perfect Office DAD (Desktop Application Director) by clicking the Launch Presentations button. The

Presentations screen displays a dialog box that starts you to work immediately—the Document Selection dialog box. From this box, you choose the document type on which to work: you can start a new presentation, open an existing file, create a slide show, or draw a picture. Depending on your choice, Presentations displays other dialog boxes to help you along the way.

If you choose to start a new presentation, Presentations displays a dialog box from which you can choose slide background and slide type. The backgrounds are made up of various colors, patterns, and graphic lines that make your slides attractive and professional looking. The slide type defines the contents of each slide—bullets, charts, or text, for example.

Selecting a Presentation

When you start Presentations, the Document Selection dialog box appears (see fig. 24.1). From this dialog box, you choose to open or create a file, set preferences, or exit the program. You may or may not want to continue to display this dialog box; Presentations gives you that choice in the Preferences dialog box. Table 24.1 describes the options in that dialog box.

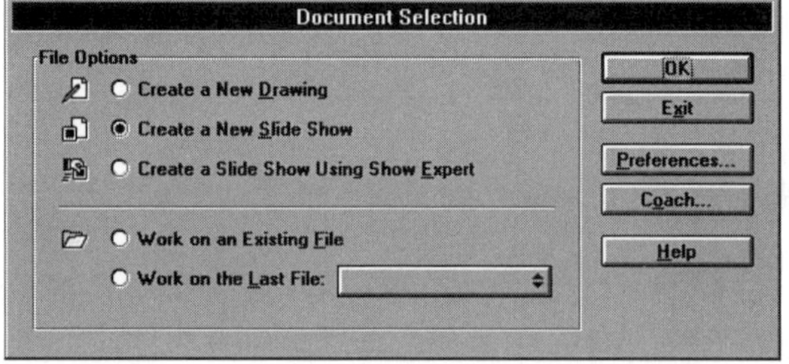

Fig. 24.1
Choose the file to open or create in Document Selection dialog box.

Table 24.1 Document Selection Options

Option	Description
Create a New **D**rawing	Begin a new drawing
Create a New **S**lide Show	Begin a new slide show
Create a Slide Show Using Show **E**xpert	Begin a new slide show using the Show Expert to get step-by-step guidance
Work on an Existing **F**ile	Displays the Open dialog box so you can open an existing file
Work on the **L**ast File	Select to open the last file you worked on; the file name appears in the box to the right of the option

Option	Description
OK	Accept the choice in the File Options area and close the dialog box
Exit	Close Presentations
Preferences	Open the Environment dialog box
Coach	View the Coach file that guides you step-by-step
Help	View Help files describing available choices

If you choose the **P**references command button, the Environment dialog box appears (see fig. 24.2). You can choose various startup options in the Environment dialog box. In the Startup Document Options area, choose **S**lide Show or **D**rawing if you do not want the Document Selection dialog box to appear each time you open the application. Instead, the program opens to a blank drawing screen or a new slide presentation screen. Click OK to close the dialog box and return to the Document Selection dialog box.

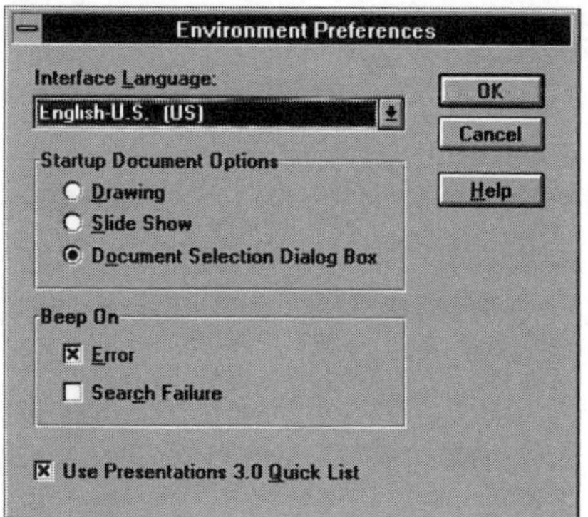

Fig. 24.2
Change the startup options in the Environment dialog box.

Using the Master Gallery

If you choose to create a new slide show in the Document Selection dialog box, the New Slide Show dialog box appears (see fig. 24.3). A *Master* is a background for the slide show that you can apply to one or all slides. Normally, you apply the same Master to all slides in the show to create consistency in the presentation.

Tip
You can change your default Environment Preferences by choosing Edit, Preferences, Environment.

To view the Gallery, click the **G**allery button in the New Slide Show dialog box. The Master Gallery dialog box appears as shown in figure 24.4, with the available backgrounds you can use for your slides. Additionally, the dialog box contains three option buttons you can use:

- ***Import.*** Choose to import other files for use as a Master, such as WordPerfect graphics files (WPG), Paintbrush files (PCX), Tagged Image File Format files (TIF), and so on.
- ***Options.*** Change the setup of the Gallery, such as number of columns in the Gallery dialog box.
- ***Links.*** Use to link, or connect, a new master that you create to the Gallery.

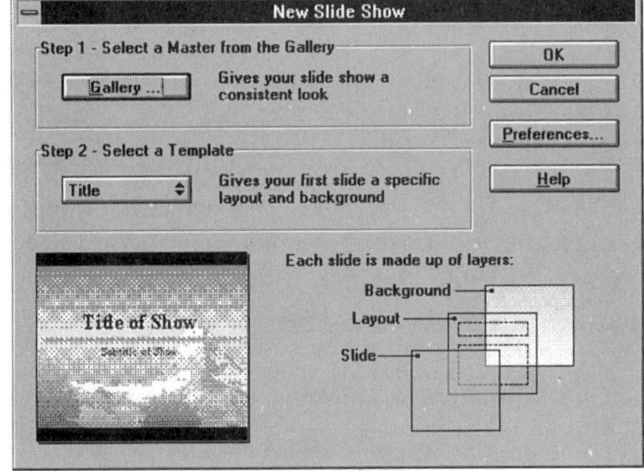

Fig. 24.3
Choose Master in the New Slide Show dialog box.

Choose a Master from the Master Gallery and click Retrieve. The Gallery dialog box closes and returns to the New Slide Show dialog box with the selected Master in the sample box. If you change your mind later, you can always change the Master.

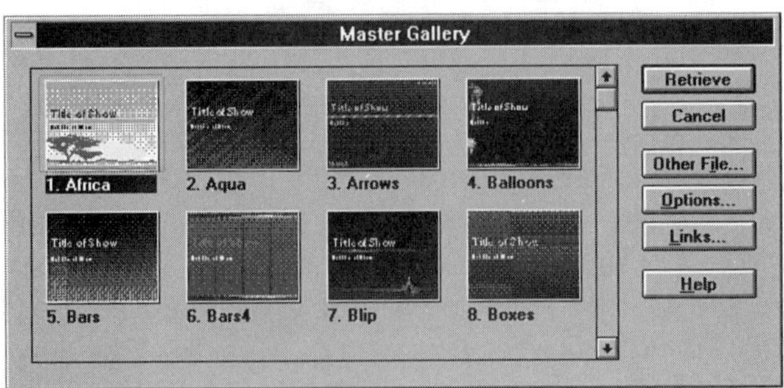

Fig. 24.4
Choose a Master from the Master Gallery dialog box.

Selecting a Slide Type

In step two of the New Slide Show dialog box, you choose the slide type, or layout, you want to use for the first slide. The slide type applies only to the first slide; you select each additional slide's type when you add a slide using the **S**lide, **A**dd Slide command.

In the New Slide Show dialog box, click the box in Step 2-Select a Template. The pop-up list appears (see fig. 24.5); select a slide type. Table 24.2 describes the slide types.

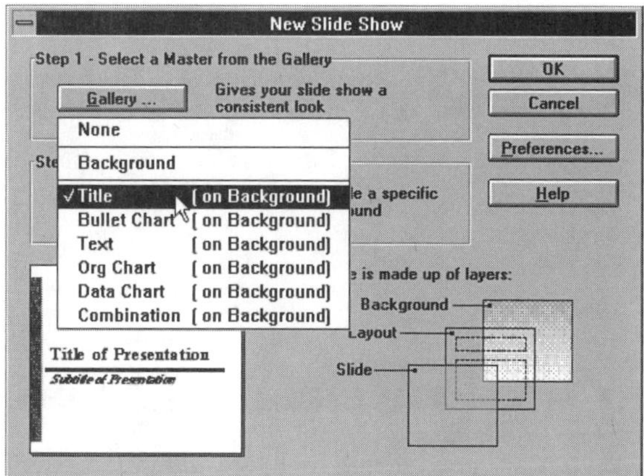

Fig. 24.5
Choose a slide type from the pop-up list.

Table 24.2 Slide Types

Type	Description
None	Plain white background
Background	Background colors and lines only, no text boxes
Title	Background with formatted area for a title and subtitle
Bullet Chart	Background with formatted area for a title, subtitle, and a list of bulleted text
Text	Background with formatted area for a title and paragraph text
Org Chart	Background with formatted area for a title and an organizational chart

(continues)

Tip
To change the slide background anytime during the slide show creation, choose **S**lide, **M**aster Gallery, or click the Master Gallery icon on the Toolbar.

Table 24.2 Continued

Type	Description
Data Chart	Background with formatted area for a title and a data chart
Combination	Background with formatted area for a bulleted list and a data chart

▶ See "Creating a Data Chart," p. 511

▶ See "Creating an Organization Chart," p. 548

After you choose the type of slide you want to use, click OK to close the dialog box and apply the background and layout to the slide on-screen.

Note

If you click the **P**references button in the New Slide Show dialog box, you can change the default options for slide shows, such as starting with a specific slide type, startup view, or page settings.

Viewing the Presentations Screen

Tip
To change the slide type of an existing slide, choose **S**lide, Apply Slide **T**ype.

The WordPerfect Presentations screen includes many elements to help you complete your work. In addition to the common Windows features—Title bar, Menu bar, Minimize/Maximize buttons, and so on—Presentations offers a toolbar, Icon bar, and Power bar to help you perform commands quickly, format your presentation, add elements, and move around your presentation with ease.

In addition to screen elements that help you in your work, Presentations offers a variety of views, or *zooms*, that enable you to look at your work in the best view for you. Although the default view is the full page or slide view, you can, for example, zoom into a specific part of the slide for a closer look.

Figure 24.6 shows the Presentations screen, in full page view, with the screen elements labeled.

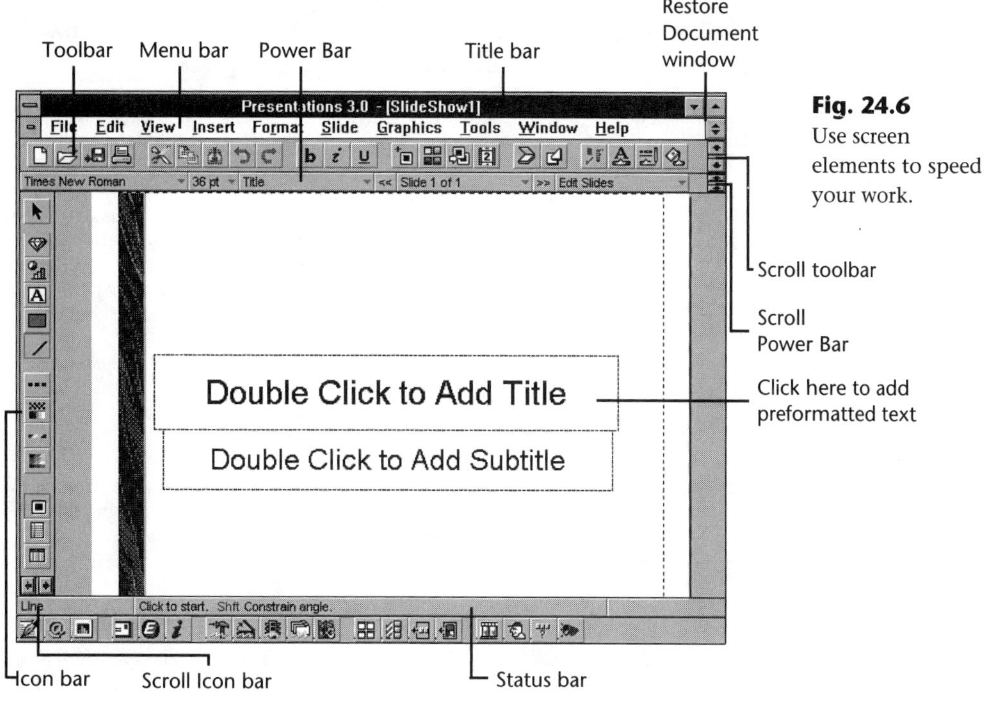

Fig. 24.6
Use screen elements to speed your work.

Using the Toolbar, Power Bar, and Icon Bar

The three icon bars on the Presentations screen help you complete your work by providing formatting, navigating, and command shortcuts you use every day in your work. Using one of the icon bars, for example, you can move to the next slide in the presentation, change text to bold, add a data or organizational chart, and so on.

Toolbar

Table 24.3 lists the icons, or buttons, specific to Presentations and describes their uses.

Tip
Hold the mouse pointer over a button on any of the three bars and a pop-up description of that button appears.

Note

If you cannot view all of the buttons on screen at one time, you can click the scroll bar to display more icons.

Table 24.3 Toolbar Icons

Icon	Button	Description
	Add Slide	Displays the Add Slide dialog box; add one or more slides to the slide show
	Master Gallery	Displays the Master Gallery dialog box; choose a slide background
	Transition	Displays the Slide Transition dialog box; define slide transition and advance options
	Play Show	Displays the Play Slide Show dialog box; choose show options and play the show
	Acquire	Displays the Acquire Image dialog box; scan an image directly into Presentations as a bitmap
	Shadow	Displays the Shadow Attributes dialog box; choose shadow options
	Define Bullet	Displays the Define Bullets/Fonts dialog box; choose bullet options
	Text	Displays the Text Attributes dialog box; choose text options
	Line	Displays the Line Attributes dialog box; choose line options
	Fill	Displays the Fill Attributes dialog box; choose fill options
	Coaches	Displays short tutorials that give you step-by-step instructions on common procedures

Drawing or Icon Bar

Many of the tools on the Icon bar present two or more choices when you click and hold the mouse button down. Table 24.4 lists the Icon Bar buttons and describes each tool. Additionally, when you choose a drawing tool and use it in the work area, the screen changes to the drawing view.

Tip
Hold the mouse pointer over a space in the Toolbar or Power Bar and the pointer changes to a hand; drag the hand to reposition the bar anywhere on the screen.

Note

If you click the scroll bar on the Icon bar, the Slide Sorter View button appears plus extra room for you to insert customized or additional buttons.

Table 24.4 Icon Bar Buttons

Icon	Tool	Description
	Select item	Click on item to select it; after item is selected, you can perform actions such as copying, deleting, formatting, and so on
	Bitmap or Figure Tool	Define the area to draw a bitmap or retrieve an image into a figure area
	Chart Object Tools	Define an area for a data or organizational chart
A	Text Object Tools	Create an area in which to enter a paragraph, one line, or to display a list as bulleted text
	Closed Object Tools	Create a rectangle, rounded rectangle, circle, ellipse, polygon, closed curve, arrow, or regular polygon
	Line Object Tools	Create a straight, curved, or freehand line, a Bezier curve, elliptical arc, or circular arc
	Line Attributes	Choose a line style from the palette
	Fill Attributes	Choose a pattern as fill for a closed object
	Line Colors	Choose a line color from the color palette
	Fill Colors	Choose a fill color from the palette
	Slide Editor View	Change to Slide Editor view
	Outliner view	Change to Outliner view
	Slide List View	Change to Slide List view
	Slide Sorter View	Change to Slide Sorter view

Power Bar

The Power Bar, located directly below the Toolbar, enables you to format text and edit slides. Figure 24.7 illustrates the Power Bar and table 24.5 describes the buttons on the Power Bar.

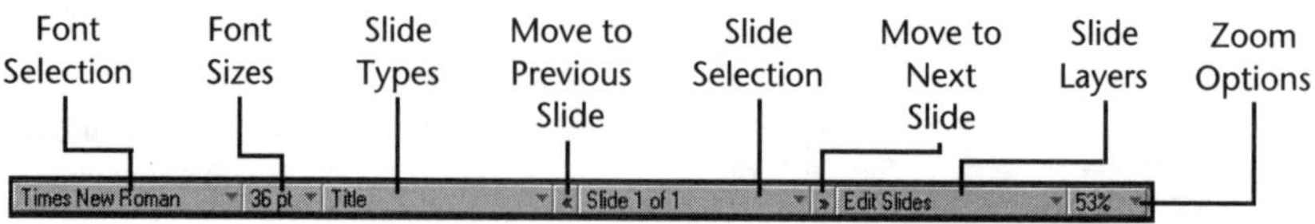

Fig. 24.7
Use the Power Bar to quickly format text and to navigate through your slides.

Table 24.5 Power Bar Buttons

Button	Description
Font Selection	Assign a specific font to selected text
Font Sizes	Assign a font size to selected text
Slide Types	Change the slide type of the current slide
Move to Previous Slide	Go to the previous slide
Slide Selection	Choose the slide you want to move to
Move to Next Slide	Go to the next slide
Slide Layers	Edit the slide background, the slide type, or the text layer
Zoom Options	Change screen view to a percentage, such as 75% or 50%, or to Full Page, Margins, and so on

Viewing the Presentation

The default view in Presentations Slide Editor is Full Page view. You can also change the view to various magnifications. When you zoom or change views, the actual size of the objects, pages, text, and so on does not change; only the view of what you see on-screen changes.

To change the view, choose **V**iew, **Z**oom. A secondary menu appears. Table 24.6 describes each of the available views and lists the shortcuts you can use to switch views.

Table 24.6 Changing Screen Views

Option	Shortcut	Description
Zoom Area	Ctrl+Shift+F5	Magnifies the view of a selected area; drag magnifying glass, drawing a rectangle, across the area you want to enlarge
Full Page	Shift+F5	Displays the entire document
Drawing Area	Alt+F5	Displays the entire drawing area in the drawing window; default view
Selected Objects		Magnifies the view of the selected objects
Actual Size (1:1)		Displays the page as it will look when printed
S**c**reen Size		Displays the page as it will look when you play the slide show
Previous View		Displays the last view before you used Zoom
Zoom **I**n	Shift+PgUp	Magnifies the view by 20 percent each time you use it
Zoom **O**ut	Shift+PgDn	Reduces the view by 20 percent each time you use it

Figure 24.8 shows the screen at Full Page view with the Zoom Area tool.

Note

Another view option is Draft Mode, found near the bottom of the View menu; you can use **D**raft Mode with any of the Zoom views. Draft Mode presents the slides without background color and objects with outlines instead of fill colors, patterns, and other attributes. Use Draft Mode to speed editing and working. To select Draft Mode, choose **V**iew, **D**raft Mode; alternatively, press Ctrl+F5. A check mark appears beside the command in the View menu. To turn Draft Mode off, choose the command again; the check mark disappears.

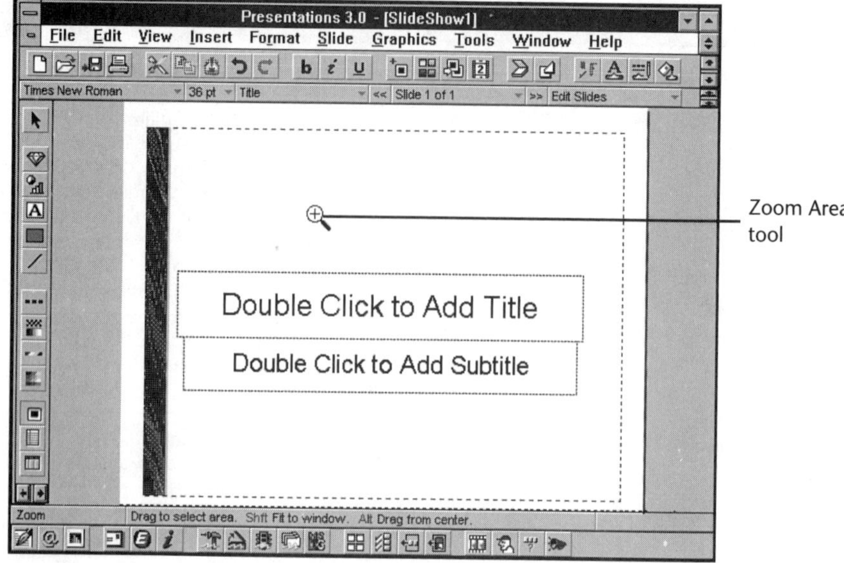

Fig. 24.8 Define an area with the magnifying glass to zoom the area.

Using Outliner

The Outliner view is useful for entering text into your slide show. You can add slides, create titles, text, bullets, and so on in Outliner view, and then convert the outline to the Slide Editor when you are ready to create the slides. Using Outliner view enables you to plan and organize the slide show, rearrange slides, and perfect the show before transferring it to slides.

Tip You can insert a WordPerfect file to use for an outline. Choose **I**nsert, **F**ile and select the document and file type.

To change to Outliner view, click the Outliner view on the Icon Bar or open the **V**iew menu and choose **O**utliner. Figure 24.9 shows Outliner view.

Adding Slides

You can add slides while in Outliner view with either the Toolbar icon or the menu. Additionally, you can delete slides if you choose to. When you add a slide in Presentations, you choose the slide type; alternatively, you can choose to add more than one slide at a time and choose the slide type as you enter the text for each slide.

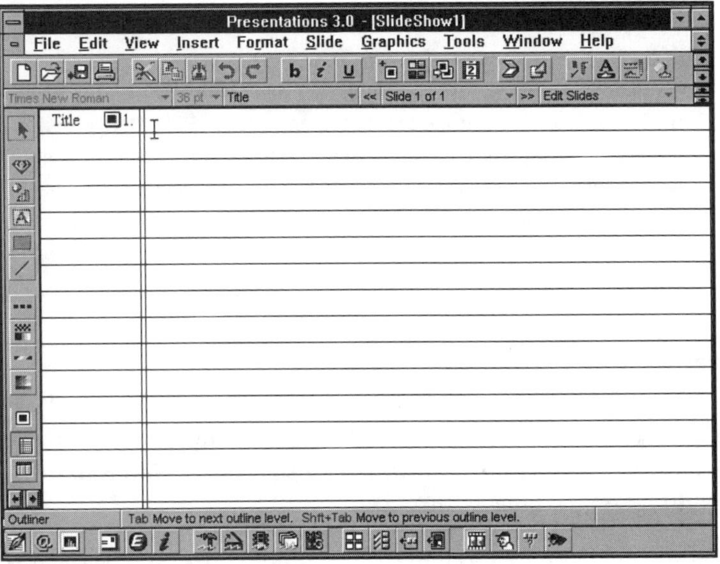

Fig. 24.9
Outliner view looks like a sheet of paper on which you can organize your presentation.

To add a slide to a presentation:

1. In Outliner view, chose **S**lide, **A**dd Slides, or click the Add Slides icon on the Toolbar. The Add Slides dialog box appears (see fig. 24.10).

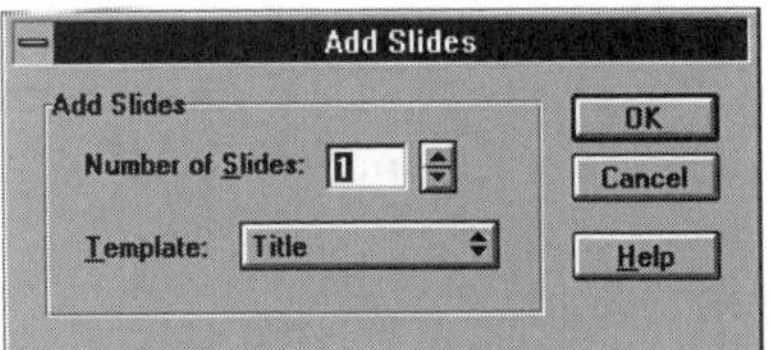

Fig. 24.10
Add a slide to the slide show in Outliner view.

2. In Number of **S**lides, enter or select the number of slides you want to add.

3. In **T**emplate, choose the type of slide you want to add.

4. Click OK to close the dialog box and add the slide(s).

Note

If you add two or more slides, they will all be the same type—Title, for example. You can change the type by clicking the slide number in the Outline and then clicking the Slide Types button on the Power Bar and choosing a type.

Caution

If you add too many slides or change your mind after adding, you can click the line for the slide you want to delete, and choose **S**lide, **D**elete Slides. Presentations displays a message asking if you are sure; click **Y**es to delete or **N**o to cancel. To delete more than one slide, select the lines in Outliner by dragging the mouse, and then select the **S**lide, **D**elete Slides command. When you delete a slide, you delete the entire outline family, including all sublevels.

Entering Text and Assigning Levels

Enter the text for your slides in Outliner so you can easily view, edit, and rearrange the slides before viewing them in Slide Editor view. As you enter the text, or even after entering it, you can assign various levels to the text, such as title, subtitle, bullets, and so on.

To enter text in Outliner, position the insertion point and type the text. The first line of any slide type is a Title. Press Enter to create a subtitle and press Enter again to create bullets. Each time you press Enter after creating the first bullet line, Outliner adds more bullets on the same level.

To change a level, press Tab to move down one level and Shift+Tab to move up one level; for example, to change a bullet to a subtitle, press Shift+Tab. To change the subtitle to a title, press Shift+Tab again. You can create up to six levels of bullets by pressing the Tab key five times. Figure 24.11 shows a sample outline with titles, subtitles, and two levels of bullets.

Rearranging the Slides

As you create your outline, you can rearrange the slide order of the presentation in Outliner view. Change the slide order by dragging the slide title to a new position; all of the slide's text follows the title when you move it.

To move a slide, position the mouse pointer over the slide icon until the pointer changes to a double-headed arrow. Drag the slide up or down to the new position. As you drag, the mouse pointer changes to a slide icon. Additionally, the screen will bump up or down if you drag the icon past the window borders.

Drag the slide icon pointer to a line that holds another slide title. A short, horizontal line appears above the slide title to indicate the new slide will position ahead of it. When you release the mouse button, the slide and the entire outline family slips into its new location. Figure 24.12 illustrates a slide being moved to a new location.

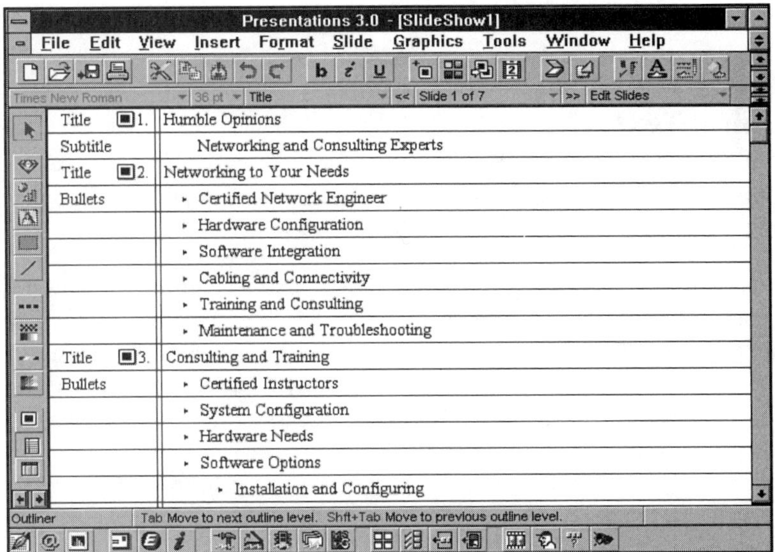

Fig. 24.11
Arrange and rearrange the levels of the slide contents.

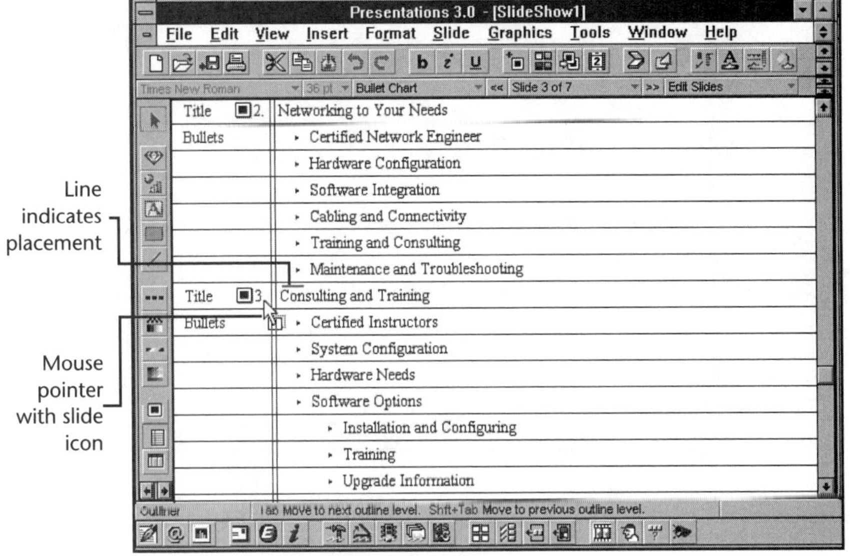

Fig. 24.12
Move a slide and its contents by dragging it to a new position.

Using the Slide Editor

You use Slide Editor to view each individual slide as it will look in the slide show or when printed. You can switch to the Slide Editor after using Outliner to enter your text, or you can create the text and other objects for the presentation directly in Slide Editor view.

To switch to Slide Editor view, choose **V**iew, Slide **E**ditor, or click the Slide Editor View button on the Icon bar to quickly switch views.

Adding Text

Tip
Use the Slide Selection button on the Power Bar to move to other slides as you work with the presentation.

In Slide Editor view, text boxes appear to enable you to enter titles, subtitles, bullets, and so on. You can enter, edit, and format the text in a text box. Additionally, you can move the text box or resize it.

To move or resize a text box, click the box once to select it; small handles appear on the corners and sides of the text box. Drag the box to a new position to move it. To resize the box, position the mouse pointer over any handle; the pointer changes to a double-headed arrow (see fig. 24.13). Drag the handle towards the center to make the text box smaller, or away from the center of the box to make the box larger.

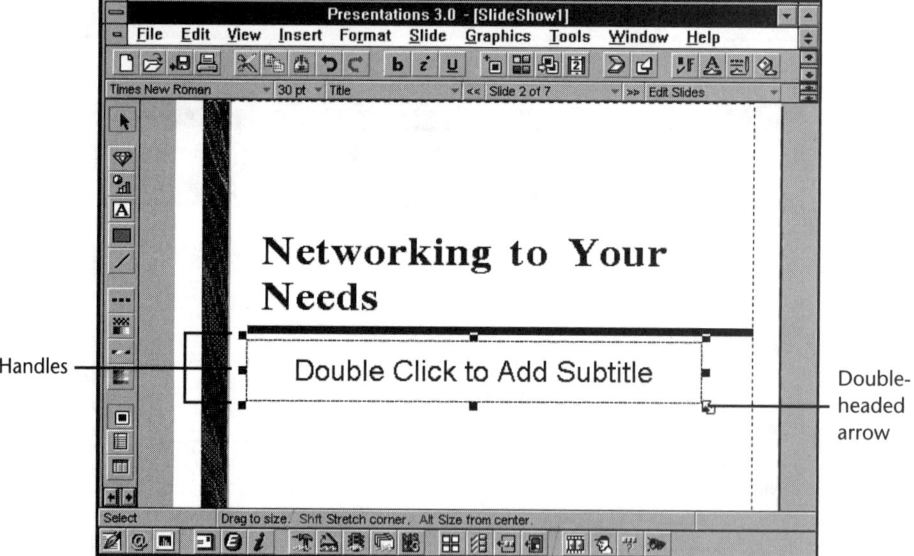

Fig. 24.13
Resize or move a selected text box.

To enter text into a text box, double-click the box. The box changes to a text box with a blinking vertical cursor and a grayed outline (see fig. 24.14). Type the text; when you are done, click outside the text box. To edit the text in a text box, double-click the box and the cursor appears in the text box.

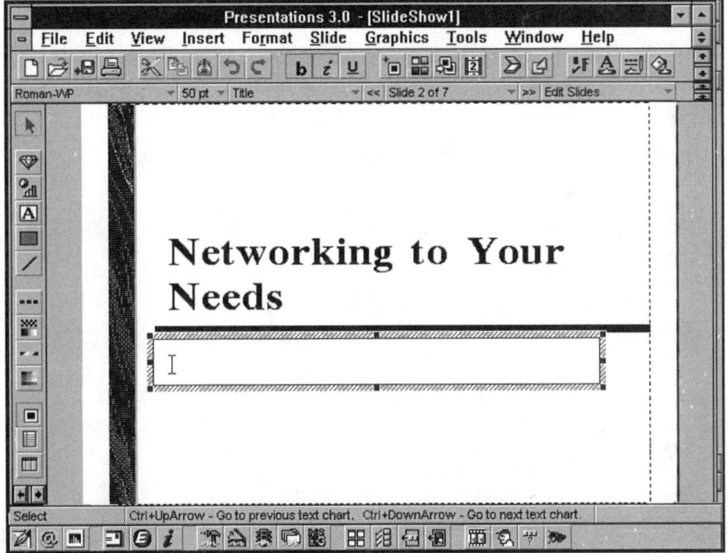

Fig. 24.14
Enter and edit text in the text box.

Tip
When you finish typing in a text box, press the Esc key to indicate you are done typing. The box remains selected for moving or resizing.

> **Note**
>
> Text boxes you do not use will not display during a slide show or print; however, they still appear on-screen in Slide Editor view, and this can be disconcerting. You cannot remove the text box but you can remove the text within it; double-click the box and then click outside of it. The box remains, but at least the text is gone from view.

To create a text box, click the Text Object Tools button on the Icon bar. Select the single line or the paragraph text tool and position the tool in the work area of the slide. The tool looks like a hand holding a rectangle. Drag the hand to create the text block. When you release the mouse button, the new text box appears with a blinking cursor, ready to receive text.

Formatting Text

You format the text in a text box similarly to formatting any text in WordPerfect Office applications. Select the text and choose a font, size, or attribute. In Presentations, you must first double-click the text box and then drag the mouse to select the text; merely selecting the text box will not enable formatting of the text.

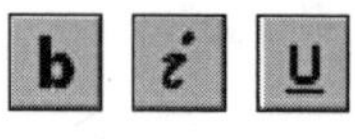

After selecting the text, use the Font Selection and Font Size buttons on the Power Bar to change font and size. Additionally, you can use the Bold, Italic, and Underline buttons on the Toolbar to format text with attributes. Finally, you can use the Fo**r**mat, **F**ont command to format text in text boxes. Figure 24.15 shows the Font dialog box and selected text in the background.

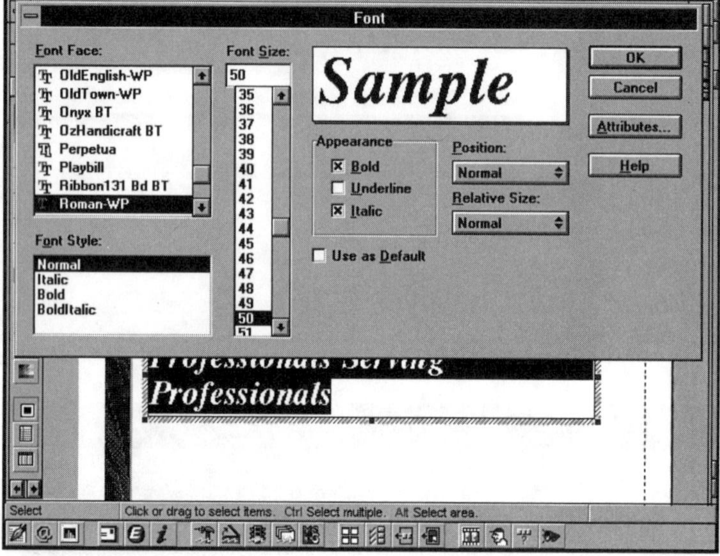

Fig. 24.15
Choose the font, size, and attributes all at one time in the Font dialog box.

Troubleshooting

I switch from Outliner view to Slide Editor view and the text in my titles is too long, thus overlapping other text.

You can do any of three things to solve the problem: change the font size, edit the text, or move the text box on the page so the text does not overlap other text.

I can't move to another slide in Slide Editor view.

If a text box is open—ready for typing by displaying handles and the grayed outline—you cannot move to another slide; click outside of the text box to deselect it and then try again.

Listing and Sorting Slides

Presentations includes two other views—Slide List and Slide Sort—for you to use when creating and organizing your presentation. You will most likely use these two views when you are preparing to play a slide show. Slide List shows each slide's number, title, and other information to help you organize your presentation. Slide Sort shows a mini-gallery of each slide so you can visually organize them.

Using Slide List

In Slide List view, each slide in the presentation is identified by its display number, title, transition effects for moving from one slide to the other, and any advance options, such as a pause before advancing. Figure 24.16 shows Slide List view.

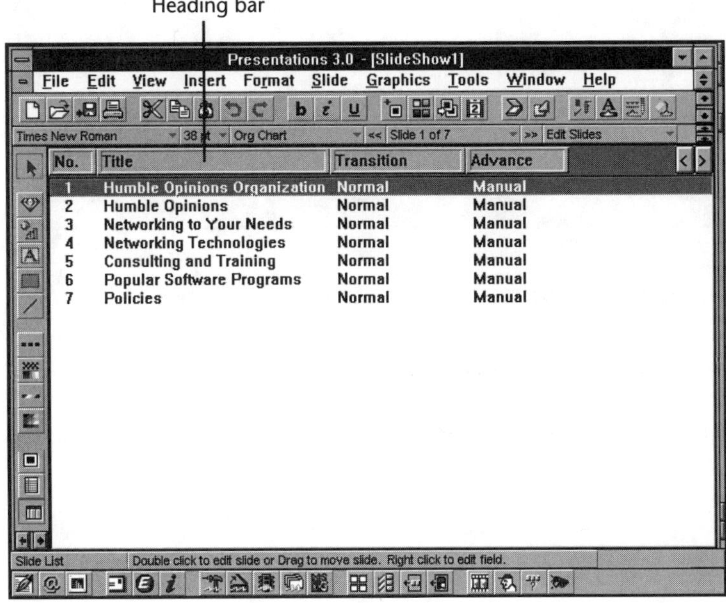

Fig. 24.16
Plan the slide show in Slide List view.

Tip
In Slide List view, change the size of a heading bar and the column by positioning the mouse pointer over the left edge of the heading box and dragging it to the right.

V

Using Presentations

You can rearrange the slides in the Slide List view by clicking the number of the slide and dragging it to a new position. The slide pointer and a horizontal line move to a new position; when you release the mouse button, the slide moves in the list and in the presentation. To edit any slide, double-click while highlighting the slide and the slide appears in Slide Editor view.

▶ See "Running an On-Screen Slide Show," p. 562

Using Slide Sorter

Slide Sorter view displays the slides in your presentation as small slides so you can see the visual impact of the overall presentation. In addition, you can change the order of the slides in Slide Sorter view. To change the view to Slide Sorter, choose **V**iew, Slide Sorter View, or click the Slide Sorter View button on the Icon bar.

Figure 24.17 shows the Slide Sorter view.

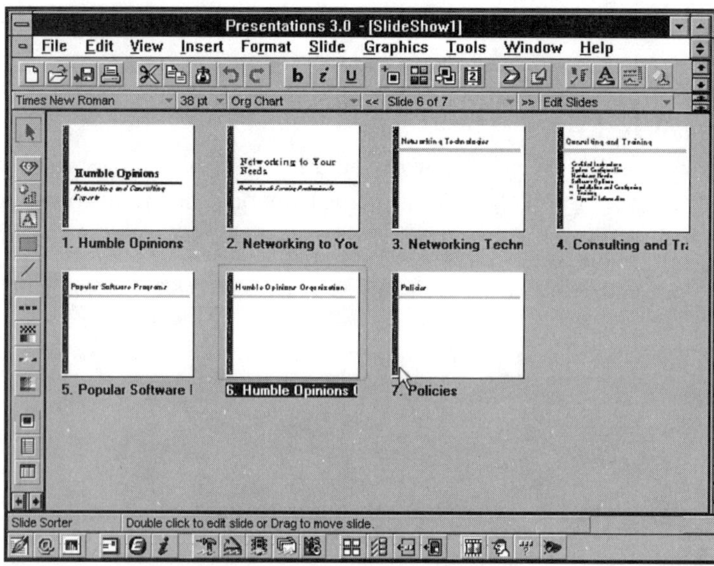

Fig. 24.17 Visually organize the slides in Slide Sorter view.

In Slide Sorter view, you can click and drag a slide to a new position. Additionally, you can select more than one slide to move. To select consecutive slides, click the first slide, hold the Shift key, and click the last slide in the consecutive set of slides. To select non-consecutive slides, click the first slide, press the Ctrl key, and click the other slides you want to move. Drag the selected slides to a new position.

From Here...

This chapter has given you a brief overview of Presentations. For in-depth discussions of specific topics, refer to the following chapters:

- Chapter 25, "Working with Data Charts," describes creating a data chart, adding and editing titles and legends, changing chart types, modifying chart layouts, and changing a chart's grid and axis.

- Chapter 26, "Adding and Enhancing Objects," describes how to add lines and borders to a slide, insert pictures, import and create tables, add an organization chart, and draw in Presentations.

- Chapter 27, "Outputting Presentations," includes information about printing slides, notes, and outlines, as well as preparing a slide show and running it on-screen.

Chapter 25

Working with Data Charts

by Sue Plumley

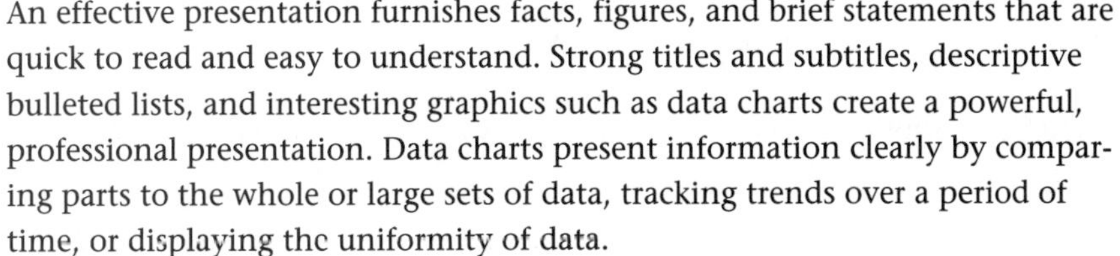

An effective presentation furnishes facts, figures, and brief statements that are quick to read and easy to understand. Strong titles and subtitles, descriptive bulleted lists, and interesting graphics such as data charts create a powerful, professional presentation. Data charts present information clearly by comparing parts to the whole or large sets of data, tracking trends over a period of time, or displaying thc uniformity of data.

In this chapter, you learn how to

- Create a data chart
- Enter and edit data for a chart
- Change chart types
- Modify chart layouts
- Add and edit titles, data labels, and legends

Creating a Data Chart

A data chart is a chart created using figures you enter in a datasheet—similar to a table or spreadsheet. The chart represents the figures visually using column bars, pie pieces, lines, and so on. The chart type you choose depends on the data and how you want to represent it; comparing data, for example, is a common use for pie and bar charts.

Inserting a Chart

You can create a chart using the Data Chart slide type, the Insert menu, or the Chart Object Tool button on the Icon Bar. When you create the chart, you must choose a chart type and then enter the data. Following is a summary of the three methods of inserting a chart into a presentation:

- After defining a slide as a data chart type, then in a Data Chart slide layout, double-click the data chart area; the Data Chart dialog box appears.

- Choose **I**nsert, D**a**ta Chart; the mouse pointer changes to a hand holding a frame. Drag the hand on the slide to indicate the area designated for the chart. When you release the mouse button, the Data Chart dialog box appears.

- Click the Chart Object Tool on the Icon Bar and then click the Data Chart button. The mouse pointer changes to a hand; drag the hand on the slide to create the area for the chart. When you release the mouse button, the Data Chart dialog box appears.

Figure 25.1 shows the Data Chart dialog box and the Chart Object Tool button.

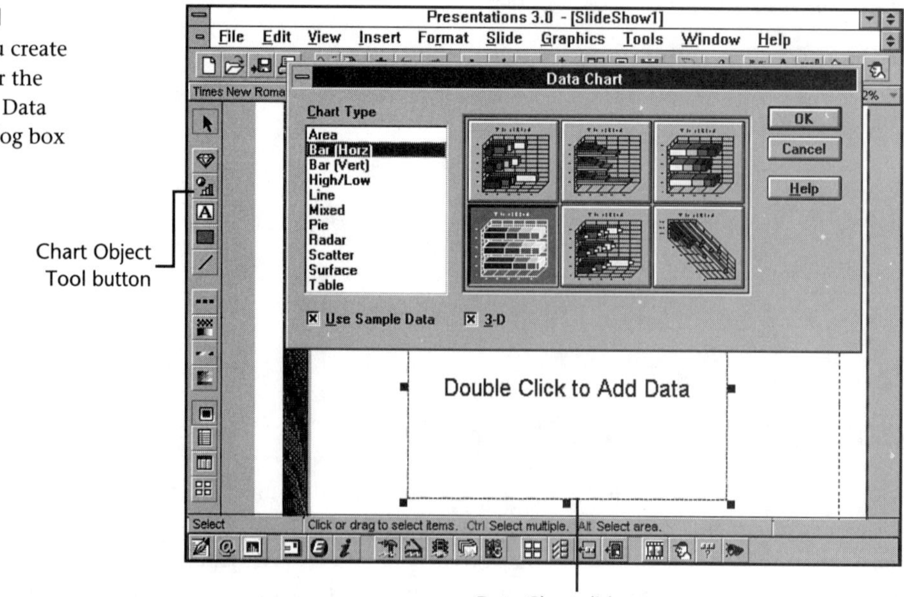

Fig. 25.1 When you create an area for the chart, the Data Chart dialog box appears.

Choosing the Chart Type

You choose the chart type in the Data Chart dialog box and then you enter or import the data for the chart. The type of chart you choose depends on the type of data you are planning to use and how you want to present it. Table 25.1 describes the chart types available in Presentations and their common uses.

Table 25.1 Chart Types

Chart Type	Description
Area	A chart that shows the height of all values with the area below the line filled with color or patterns. Use an area chart to compare several sets of data or trends over a period of time.
Bar	A chart that represents data by the height or length of the columns or bars; you can create horizontal or vertical bars. Use a bar chart to compare one item to another or to compare different items over a period of time.
High/Low	A chart that shows the high and low values compared over time using lines and bars. Use a high/low chart to track fluctuating data (stocks, commodities, and so on) over a period of time.
Line	A chart consisting of a series of data at various points along the axis; the points are connected by a line that indicates a trend or rate of change over a period of time.
Mixed	A chart that combines parts from a line, bar, or area chart so you can plot data in two forms on the same chart. Use a mixed chart to show a correlation between two or more data series.
Pie	A circular, pie-shaped chart with each piece (wedge) showing a data segment and its relationship to the whole. Use a pie chart to sort data and compare parts of the whole.
Radar	A chart that starts from the center using a grid to represent the various data. Use a radar chart to show data over a period of time and to show variations and trends.
Scatter	A chart that plots two sets of data, placing a marker at each point where the data intercept. Use a scatter chart with extremely large amounts of data you want to plot along an interception course.
Surface	A chart that represents values to look like peaks and valleys, or landscape. Solid areas contour to the data to track profits or losses.
Table	Not a graphical chart, but a representation of the data in rows and columns, similar to the data sheet.

Tip

You can change the chart type at any time by clicking the Chart Type button on the Power Bar.

To choose a chart type in the Data Chart dialog box, first choose an option in the **C**hart Type list and then select the view of the chart in the samples (see fig. 25.2). Additionally, you can choose to make a chart three-dimensional by selecting the **3**-D check box at the bottom of the dialog box. Click OK to accept the chart type and close the dialog box. When you close the dialog box, the datasheet appears.

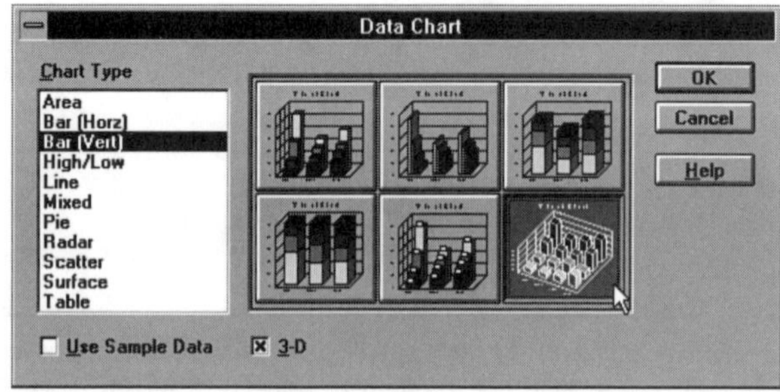

Fig. 25.2
Select chart type options from the Data Chart dialog box.

Tip
Radar charts and tables cannot be created in 3-D.

Note

When you close the Data Chart dialog box, the datasheet appears with sample data already entered, by default. You can delete this data to enter your own, or you can choose the **U**se Sample Data option in the Data Chart dialog box so the option is not checked. If the option is not checked, a blank datasheet appears.

Entering Data

After you choose the chart type, the datasheet appears with sample data (unless you chose to not display the sample data). Figure 25.3 illustrates the datasheet, sample data, and the chart created from the data. Additionally, the Data menu is added to the Menu bar.

Tip
If you cannot see all of the data, you can enlarge the datasheet by positioning the mouse pointer over a corner of the sheet and dragging to enlarge the window.

To enter data in the datasheet, select the cells containing sample data and press the Delete key. The Clear dialog box appears with the **D**ata option selected (see fig. 25.4). Click OK.

To enter the values, enter the legend text, the data labels, and then the values. The *legend* text will appear in a box near the chart and tell what each color or symbol in the chart's *data series* represents. The data series is a range of values in a worksheet and each data series is represented by a marker; for example, a column in a bar chart is a marker, as is a wedge in a pie chart. Data *labels* are names put along the vertical (Y-axis) or horizontal (X-axis) axis to describe the data, such as the year, quarter, dollar amounts, and so on.

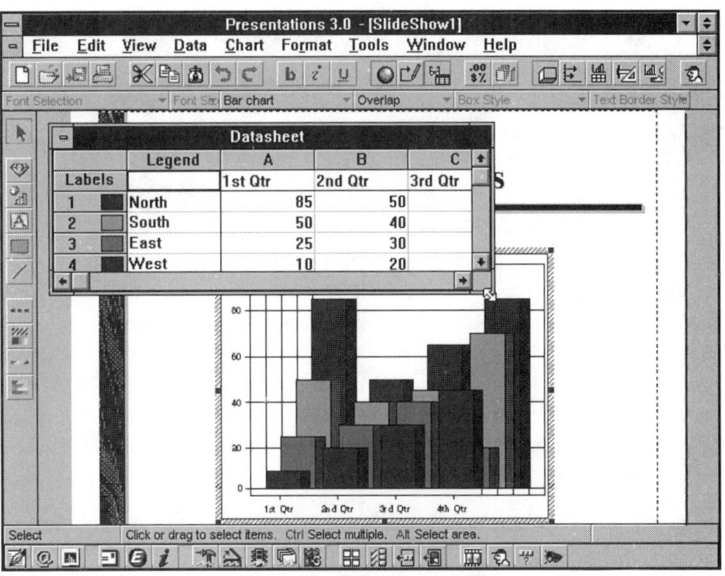

Fig. 25.3
The datasheet looks and acts like a spreadsheet.

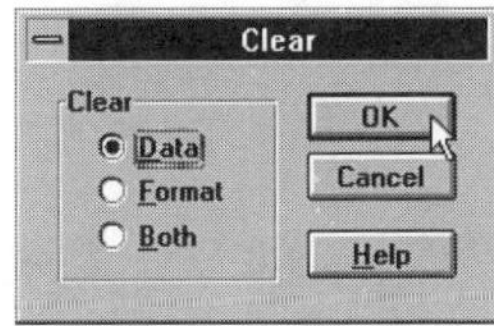

Fig. 25.4
Delete the data from the datasheet and fill in your own.

Figure 25.5 illustrates a sample datasheet after the text and values are added. When you are finished entering the data, double-click the datasheet's Control Menu to close the window. The Control Menu is a small gray box in the left corner of the Title bar of any window.

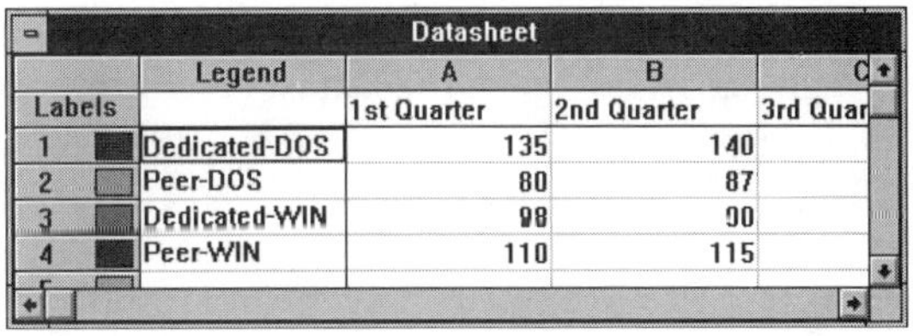

Datasheet

	Legend	A	B	C
Labels		1st Quarter	2nd Quarter	3rd Quar
1	Dedicated-DOS	135	140	
2	Peer-DOS	80	87	
3	Dedicated-WIN	98	90	
4	Peer-WIN	110	115	

Fig. 25.5
Enter the data and close the datasheet window when you are done.

Note

You can import data from a spreadsheet program, such as Quattro Pro, by following these steps:

1. Select the cell in the datasheet to which you want to import the data.
2. Choose **D**ata, **Im**port. The Import Data dialog box appears.
3. Choose the type of data you will import from the **D**ata Type list.
4. Enter the path and file name in the **F**ilename text box.
5. Specify a range, if you want, or you can import the entire worksheet.
6. Click OK. The data imports to the selected cell in the chart datasheet.

Tip
You can edit the data in the datasheet at any-time by clicking the datasheet icon in the Toolbar.

Editing a Chart

Tip
You can quickly and easily transfer data from another program by using the Windows Clipboard.

You can easily edit chart data or other chart options by double-clicking the chart. When you double-click the chart, the chart's border appears as a screened line to indicate it's selected. Additionally, the datasheet containing the charting data appears, the Data menu appears, new options appear on the Toolbar , and several new buttons appear on the Power Bar that pertain only to charts.

Note

If you click a chart once, small black handles appear on the chart's corners and sides, but its border remains a thin black line. When a chart is selected in this manner, you can move, resize, and copy or cut the chart.

Editing Data

To edit the data in a chart, double-click the chart and the datasheet appears; alternatively, select the chart and click the Datasheet button on the Toolbar. Click the cell you want to edit and type the text or value. Press Enter and the chart changes to reflect the new data.

In addition to entering new text or editing text, you can format the values in the chart and sort the data in the cells of the datasheet.

Formatting Values

You can format a cell in a data sheet to contain specific data types, such as numeric, currency, or text.

To format values:

1. Select the values you want to format and choose **D**ata, F**o**rmat, or click the Format button on the Toolbar. The Format dialog box appears (see fig. 25.6).

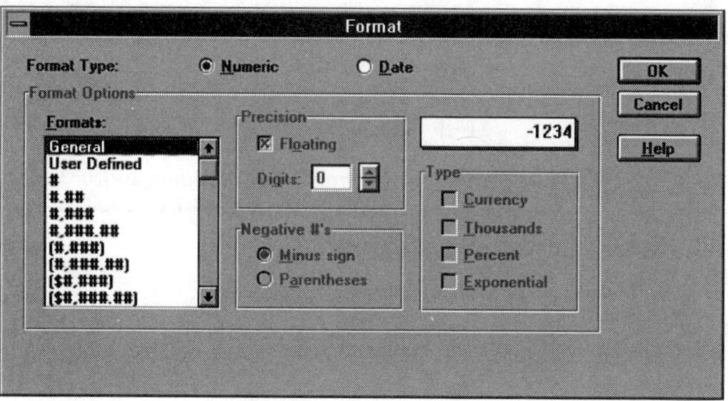

Fig. 25.6
Format the data in selected cells using the Format dialog box.

2. In Format Type, choose either **N**umeric or **D**ate. The options change depending on the Format Type.

3. Select the format you want to use and other options appear.

Numeric Options

Option	Description
Precision Area	Choose only one option
Fl**o**ating	Decimal points and places appear only if needed
Di**g**its	Specify number of decimal places; option is only available if Floating is not selected
Negative #'s Area	Choose only one option
Minus Sign	Displays a minus sign to indicate negative numbers
P**a**rentheses	Displays negative numbers in parentheses instead of with a minus sign
Type Area	Choose any or all options
Currency	Displays values with a dollar sign
Thousands	Displays commas to indicate thousands
Percent	Displays the percent sign with the number

(continues)

Numeric Options Continued	
Option	**Description**
Exponential	Displays the exponent of the values

Date Options	
Option	**Description**
Date Preview	Displays the selected date format
Predefined Formats	Choose a format to display date and/or time

Tip
The numeric format you choose in the Format dialog box changes the axis labels in your chart.

4. Click OK to close the dialog box.

Sorting Data

You can sort the data in a datasheet so that it is in a descending or ascending alphabetical or numerical order. Sorted data is more organized than data that is not sorted, and therefore makes a chart easier to read.

To sort in a datasheet:

1. Select the text or values in the datasheet to be sorted.

2. Choose **D**ata, **S**ort, or click the Sort button on the Toolbar. The Sort Data dialog box appears (see fig. 25.7).

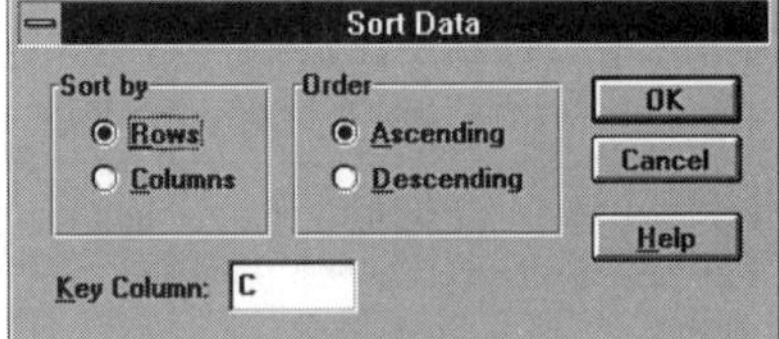

Fig. 25.7
Sort data by rows or columns and in ascending or descending order.

3. In the Sort Data dialog box, choose to sort the data by **R**ows or **C**olumns and in either **A**scending or **D**escending order.

4. Click OK to close the dialog box and sort the data. Changes are reflected in the data chart.

Changing Chart Types

After you create a chart, you may decide a different chart type would better represent the data. You can change the chart type to pie, line, area, or any other available chart. To change a chart type, double-click the chart to select it. Choose **C**hart, Galle**r**y to view the larger variety of chart types or choose the Type command to quickly select a type. Alternatively, click the Data Chart Types button on the Power Bar (see fig. 25.8). Choose the chart type you want and the selected chart changes.

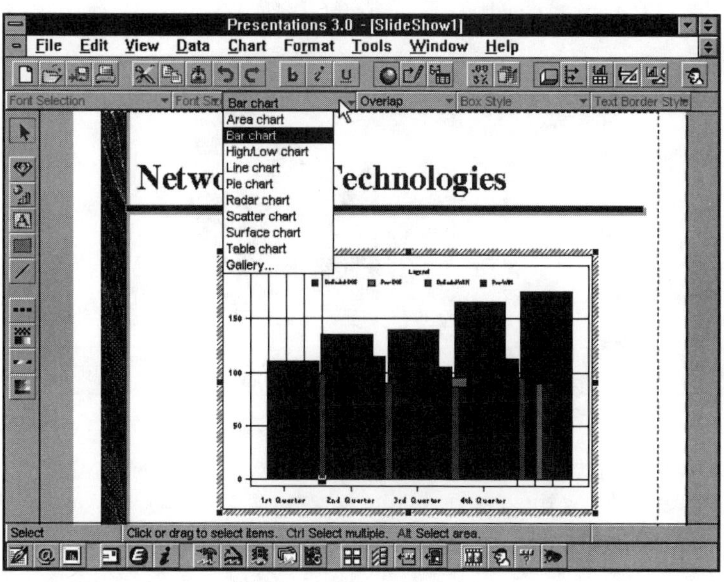

Fig. 25.8
Choose a chart type from the Power Bar list.

Modifying Layout and Series Options

You can edit the layout and the series of a selected chart to further modify the way the data is represented. Layout refers to the style, width, size, and general appearance of the chart's markers. The Layout options change depending on what type of chart you are working on. The Series options refer to each individual data series. You can change the color, type, and even the shape of each series in the chart to further represent the chart's data.

Tip
You can choose the Show Table button to add the data to your chart in table format.

Changing Layout

To change the layout of the chart:

1. Select the chart by double-clicking it.

2. Choose **C**hart, **L**ayout, or click the Layout button on the Toolbar.

3. The Layout dialog box appears (see fig. 25.9).

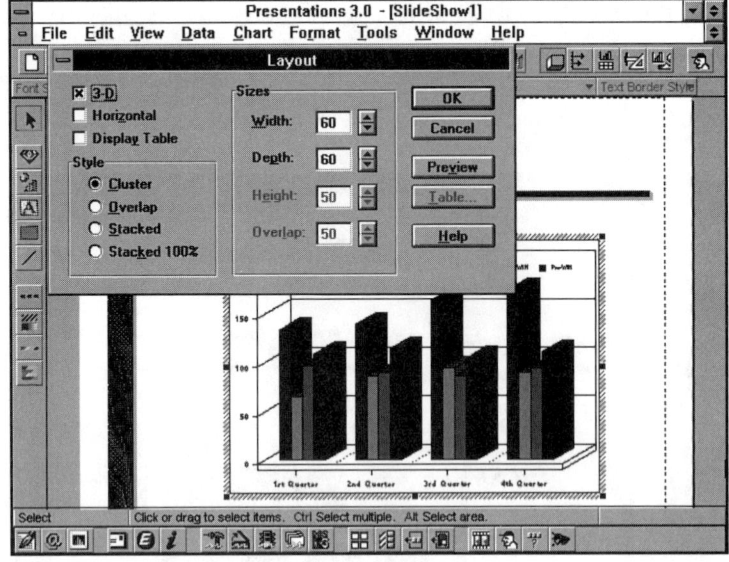

Fig. 25.9
The Layout dialog box appears placed on-screen so you can see the chart and preview changes.

4. Change any of the options in the dialog box and click the Pr**e**view button to view the change before accepting it. Click OK to accept the changes.

> **Caution**
>
> Save your presentation *before* you modify the layout of a chart in case you change your mind about the changes; you can always revert back to the saved copy. Additionally, use the Preview button in the Layout dialog box before accepting the changes you make. If you make many changes, you may never be able to undo them all and the changes may not look good in your chart. If you use the Preview button first, you have the option of canceling the changes and trying again.

Tip
When using the Preview button in the Layout dialog box, click and drag the title bar of the dialog box to move it for a clearer preview.

Table 25.2 Layout Options

Option	Description
3-**D**	Applies a three-dimensional look to the markers in the chart
Hori**z**ontal	Changes the direction of the markers from vertical to horizontal
Displa**y** Table	Displays a table of the data in the chart box

Option	Description
Sizes Area (Area, Bar, Line, High/Low, Scatter Charts)	
Width	Sets width percentages
De**p**th	Sets depth percentages
H**e**ight	Sets height percentages
Over**l**ap	Sets overlap percentages
Style Area (Area, Bar, Line, Radar, Scatter Charts)	
Cluster	Groups each section of markers together so it can be better compared
Overlap	Overlaps the markers
Stacked	Stacks the markers on top of each other
Stac**k**ed 100%	Stacks the markers so they are even along the top and bottom
Type Area (High/Low Chart)	
Line	Changes markers to lines
Bar/Error Bar	Changes markers to bars with error indicators
Error Bar	Changes markers to bars with top and bottom error markers
Area	Changes markers to area markers
Explode Slice Area (Pie Charts)	
Sl**i**ce	Enters a number to indicate which slice you want to separate from the pie
Di**s**tance	Enters the distance from the pie the exploded slice should locate
Pie Options Area (Pie Charts)	
Column	Changes pie slices to bar or column markers
S**o**rt Slice	Changes the positioning of the exploded slice(s)
Link Pies Area (Pie Charts—if more than one)	
Lin**k**	Indicates with lines the relative pieces of each pie
Slic**e**	Indicates the number of slices to link

(continues)

Table 25.2 Continued

Option	Description
Options Area (Radar Chart)	
Radial	Displays on a radial grid
Linear	Displays on a linear grid
Appearance Area (Pie Charts)	
Depth	Sets the thickness of a pie chart
Angle	Rotates the slices
Size	Sets the size of the pie
Tilt	Sets orientation
Colors Area (Surface or Table Charts)	
Blend	Blends colors of the area
Options Area (Surface or Table Charts)	
Label Dividers	Creates a heavy border under the titles row and to the right of the column titles
Range Colors	Displays the table in the range colors
Full Grid	Adds border lines to each cell in table
Fill Color	Sets the color for the entire table chart
Line Color	Sets the line color in a table
Outline Color	Sets the color for the outline of the chart
Outline Contours	Draws an outline around each area

Tip
You can apply a style to a selected chart by clicking the Chart Style button on the Power Bar.

5. Click OK to accept the changes and close the dialog box.

Changing Series

A series is a row of data in a chart. A series is represented by a column, pie slice, line, or other chart marker. You can change how the series looks by setting series options.

To change the series options:

1. Choose **C**hart, **S**eries, or click the Series button on the Button bar. The Series Options dialog box appears (see fig. 25.10).

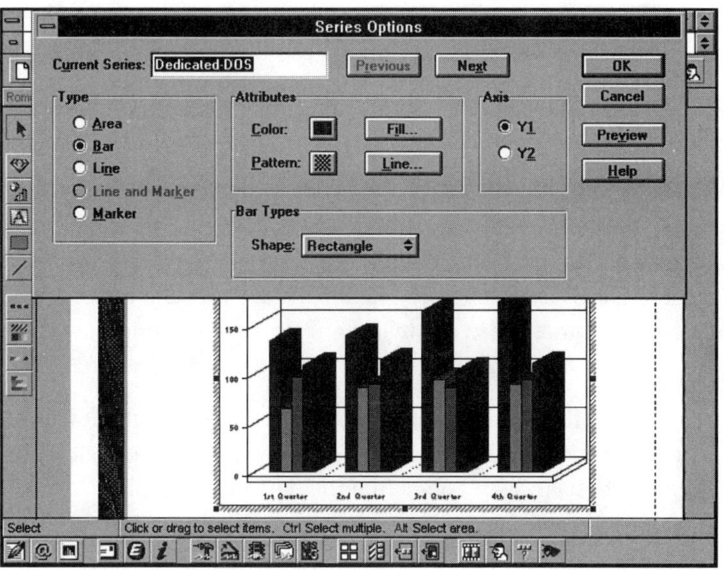

Fig. 25.10
Open the Series Options dialog box to further enhance and modify a chart.

2. In C**u**rrent Series, choose the Ne**x**t or P**r**evious button to select the series you want to edit.

3. In the Type area, choose the type of marker you want to change the selected series to.

4. In the Attributes area, choose **C**olor or **P**attern to display a palette of choices. Select a new choice to apply to the current series.

5. In the Attributes area, choose F**i**ll or **L**ine to change the options for either. Select any other options.

6. Click OK to accept the options and close the dialog box. You can, alternatively, change series options on all markers before closing the dialog box.

Tip
Not all series options are available for all chart types.

Tip
Click the Pre**v**iew button at any time to see how the change looks.

Troubleshooting

I made changes to the Layout or the Series of the selected chart, and I don't like the changes.

Click the Cancel button before closing the Series Options or Layout dialog box. Alternatively, you can click the Undo button on the Toolbar to reverse the changes.

Changing the Grid and Axis

The chart's grid is formed by the horizontal and vertical lines behind the chart's markers. The grid enables you to better see the markers in conjunction with the axes labels and therefore, the lines make the data easier to read. You can add two grids to a chart: the major grid and minor grid. The minor grid further divides the values so you can better read the numbers.

A chart's axes are lines used as reference points for the chart data. The X-axis represents the horizontal line and the Y-axis represents the vertical. You can change axis options to help you define the data on the chart.

Changing the Axis

To change the axis options:

1. Select the chart and then the axis you want to change. Handles appear at either end of a selected axis. Choose **C**hart, **A**xis. The Axis Options dialog box appears (see fig. 25.11).

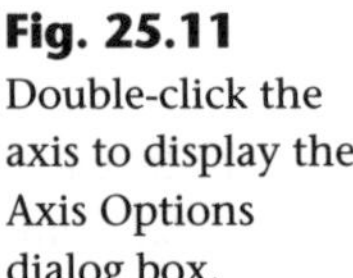

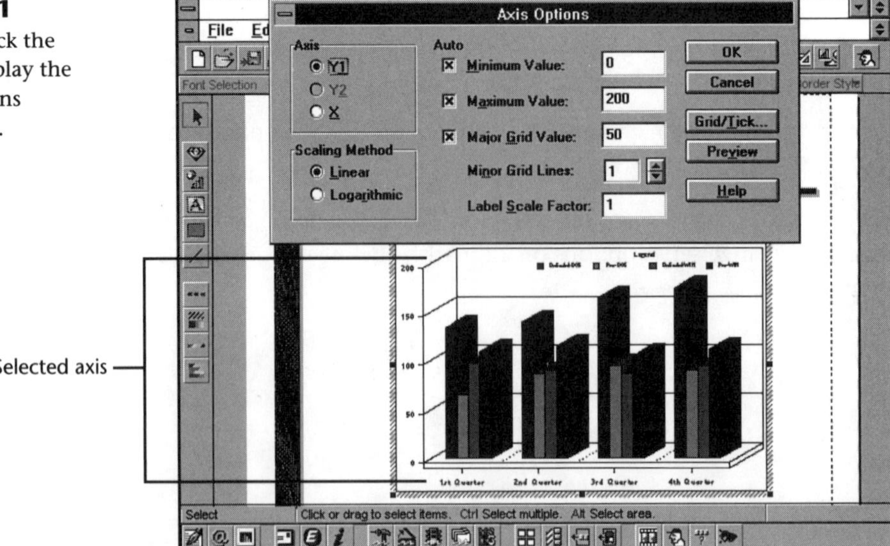

Fig. 25.11 Double-click the axis to display the Axis Options dialog box.

2. In Auto, choose the **M**inimum and M**a**ximum values for the axis values or click the check box to automatically set the values.

3. Enter the Major **G**rid Value or check the box for an automatic setting. Enter the number of Mi**n**or Grid Lines, if you want a minor grid on the chart.

4. Set any other options for the selected axis. Select the other axis in the Axis area and set options for that axis.

5. Choose OK to close the dialog box and accept the changes.

Changing the Grid

The grid in a data chart consists of horizontal and/or vertical lines that help to measure distance between the markers. Ticks are short lines that are used to mark off values, such as dollars, distances, and so on. Major ticks are those lines that fall on a label and minor ticks are lines that fall between labels.

To change the grid and tick options:

1. Select the chart and the axis you want to change. Choose **C**hart, **G**rid/Tick. The Grid and Tick Options dialog box appears (see fig. 25.12). Alternatively, you can double-click the grid on the chart to open the Grid and Tick Options dialog box.

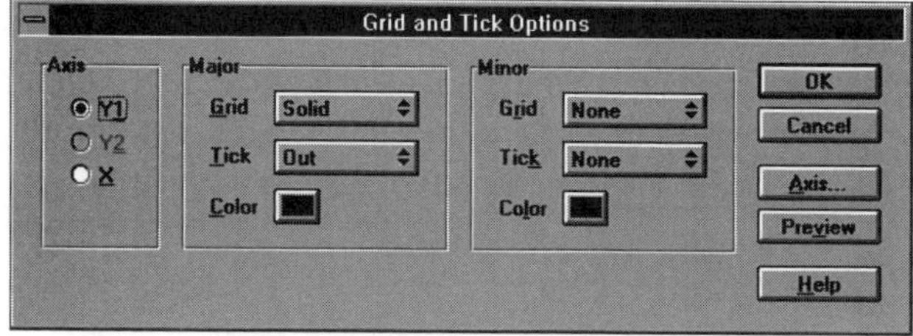

Fig. 25.12
Open the Grid and Tick Options dialog box to change the appearance of the chart's grids.

2. In the Axis area, choose the axis you want to modify.

3. In the Major area, set the options for the **G**rid lines, the **T**ick lines, and the **C**olor of the lines.

4. In the Minor area, set the options for the **G**rid lines, the **T**ick lines, and the **C**olor of the lines, if you want to use minor grid lines.

5. Click OK to accept the changes and close the dialog box.

Tip
If you are already in the Axis Options dialog box, choose the Grid/**T**ick button to open the Grid and Tick dialog box.

V

Using Presentations

Troubleshooting

I cannot see if I have made changes in the Axis Options dialog box when I click the Preview button.

Some options in the Axis Options dialog box are co-dependent on options you set in the Grid and Tick dialog box. Set grid and tick options and then come back to the Axis Options dialog box. Note there is a Grid/**T**ick button in the Axis Options dialog box that you can use as a shortcut; similarly, there is an **A**xis button in the Grid and Tick Options dialog box to bring you back to the Axis Options.

After I make changes in the Grid and Tick dialog box, the axis changes do not look right.

Switch back to the Axis Options dialog box and change some of the options back to automatic by clicking the check box in front of the **M**inimum Value, M**a**ximum Value, and Major **G**rid Value options. The other defaults are Mi**n**or Grid Lines-1 and Label **S**cale Factor-1.

Working with Titles and Legends

You can add and edit chart titles, legends, and data labels to help identify the data in the chart. Titles name the subject of the chart; you also can add a subtitle and axis titles to your chart. The legend lists the colors, patterns, or symbols used for the chart markers and tells you what each represents. You can choose to show or hide the legend in a chart and if you choose to show the legend, you can set its placement, orientation, and various other attributes. Finally, you can edit the data labels in the chart. The labels show the numeric value, time period, or category of the markers.

Adding and Editing Titles

You can add titles to the chart and format the titles so they are easy to read. Editing titles is also quick and easy.

To add or edit titles:

1. Select the chart and choose **C**hart, **T**itles. The Titles dialog box appears (see fig. 25.13).

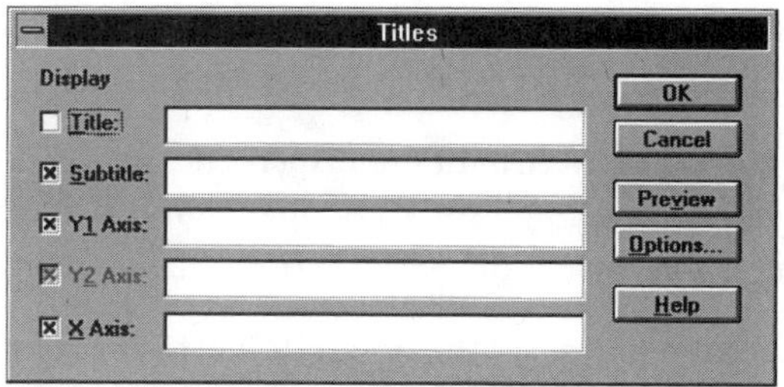

Fig. 25.13
Use the Titles dialog box to enter titles, subtitles, and axis titles.

2. In Display, choose the items you want to display by clicking the box in front of the option so that an X appears in the check box. In the text boxes, enter the text for the various titles.

3. Click the **O**ptions button to format the text. In the Titles Options dialog box, choose to position each title horizontally or vertically. Select each title and set the **F**ont; the Font dialog box appears.

4. Click OK to close the Font dialog box; click OK again to close the Titles Options box. Click OK once more to close the Titles dialog box.

Editing Legends

You can show or hide the legend for the chart. If you choose to show the legend (the default), you can change the position, orientation, box style, and font of the legend box to suit your chart and data.

To modify a legend:

1. Select the chart and choose **C**hart, L**e**gend. The Legend dialog box appears (see fig. 25.14).

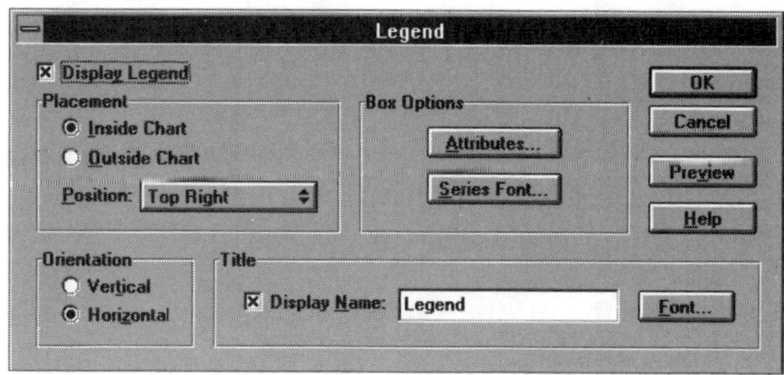

Fig. 25.14
Use the Legend dialog box to modify the legend for your chart.

V

Using Presentations

2. In the Placement area, choose the positioning for the legend; the default is inside of the chart on the top right side.

Tip
With the datasheet on-screen, double-click the Legends button to open the Legends dialog box.

3. In Box Options, click **A**ttributes to display the Box Attributes dialog box in which you choose a box style, and the fill and border color and style. Additionally, you can set the **S**eries Font in the Box Options area.

4. In the Orientation area, set the option to Ver**t**ical or Hori**z**ontal and click OK to accept the changes and close the dialog box.

Editing Data Labels

Data labels are tags that identify the tick marks or grid lines in a chart. You can show or hide the data label, plus change attributes, positions, and the fonts of the labels.

To edit the data labels:

1. Select the chart and choose **C**hart, La**b**els. The Labels dialog box appears (see fig. 25.15).

2. Choose the label you want to display and modify. In the Options area, select Disp**l**ay.

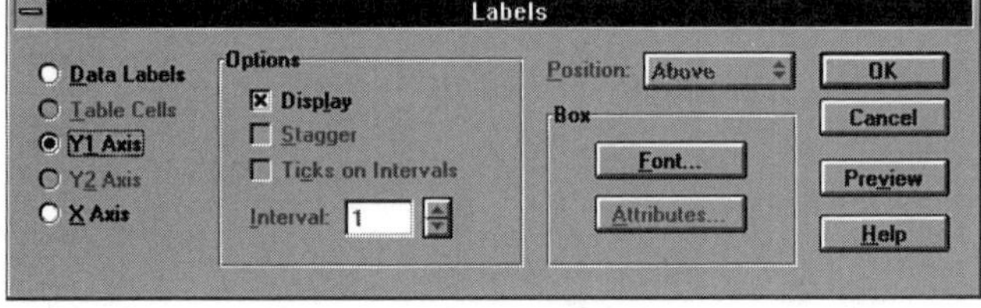

Fig. 25.15
Choose to display the data labels in the Labels dialog box.

Tip
You can double-click a label in the chart to quickly open the Labels dialog box.

3. In **P**osition, choose either Above or Below to indicate the position of the label.

4. In the Box area, click **F**ont to display the Font dialog box and change the font of the selected label. Choose **A**ttributes to display the Attribute dialog box and choose the attribute options.

5. Click OK to close the Attribute or Font dialog box. Click OK again to close the Labels dialog box.

From Here...

Refer to the following chapters for information about adding other object types to a slide and for printing your slide presentation:

- Chapter 26, "Adding and Enhancing Objects," shows you how to add lines, borders, pictures, tables and an organization chart to a presentation. This chapter also shows you how to draw objects in Presentations.

- Chapter 27, "Outputting Presentations," describes how to print slides, notes, and outlines and how to run an on-screen slide show. Additionally, this chapter shows you how to set timing and transitions in a slide show and how to run and save the on-screen slide show.

Chapter 26

Adding and Enhancing Objects

by Sue Plumley

Presentations, whether printed on paper, overhead transparencies, or on-screen, are effective because of their visual impact. Your presentations are more powerful, attractive, and professional-looking when you use brief titles and bulleted lists with charts, tables, pictures, and other graphics that are quick and easy to understand. WordPerfect Presentations enables you to add a variety of graphic objects to your presentations.

In this chapter, you learn how to

- Add lines and borders
- Add pictures and clip art
- Insert and format tables
- Create an organization chart
- Draw using Presentations drawing tools

Adding Lines and Borders

You can add a variety of lines and borders to any slide in your presentation to enhance text or other graphics, such as a logo or clip art picture. After adding the lines or borders, you can choose from a variety of line styles, colors, and thicknesses.

Creating Lines

To draw a line in Presentations, you use the Line Object tools on the Icon Bar. You can draw a curved, arced, straight, or freehand line using the tools; you can also select the line, move the line, or change its attributes.

Drawing Lines

To create a line, click the Line tool, and then choose the line tool you want to use from the pop-up menu. Click and drag the tool in the work area to create a line. Each line tool is similar in its use. You will want to experiment with the tools to get a clear idea of how each works. The Line Object tools are:

Straight. Create a straight horizontal, vertical, or diagonal line. Click the tool once for the beginning of the line and then double-click the tool again at the end of the line.

Curved. Draw soft curves. Click to begin the curve and then at each point you want the curve to change directions, click again. Double-click to end the line.

Freehand. Using the mouse, draw a line in any direction. Click and drag the tool as if the mouse were the pencil. Release the mouse button to end the line.

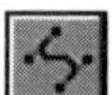

Bezier. Create Bezier curves, or curves with sectors you can edit and move independently. Click to begin the curve, then move the pointer to where the curve changes directions and drag the pointer to display the two handles. Move the handle to change the shape of the curve. Double-click the mouse to end the curve. You can go back and select the curve to display handles; then move the handles to edit the curve.

Elliptical Arcs. Drag the tool to begin the arc. Release the mouse button to complete the arc.

Circular Arcs. Draw arcs that are circular. Click at the beginning of the arc, drag the tool to the end of the arc and then move the pointer to shape the arc. Click to end the arc shape.

Double-click to end any line except the elliptical arc and freehand; the elliptical arc ends when you release the mouse button. Hold down both mouse buttons while drawing any line to reposition the line. Finally, hold the Shift key while drawing a line to constrain the line to a 45-degree angle. Figure 26.1 illustrates each of the line types.

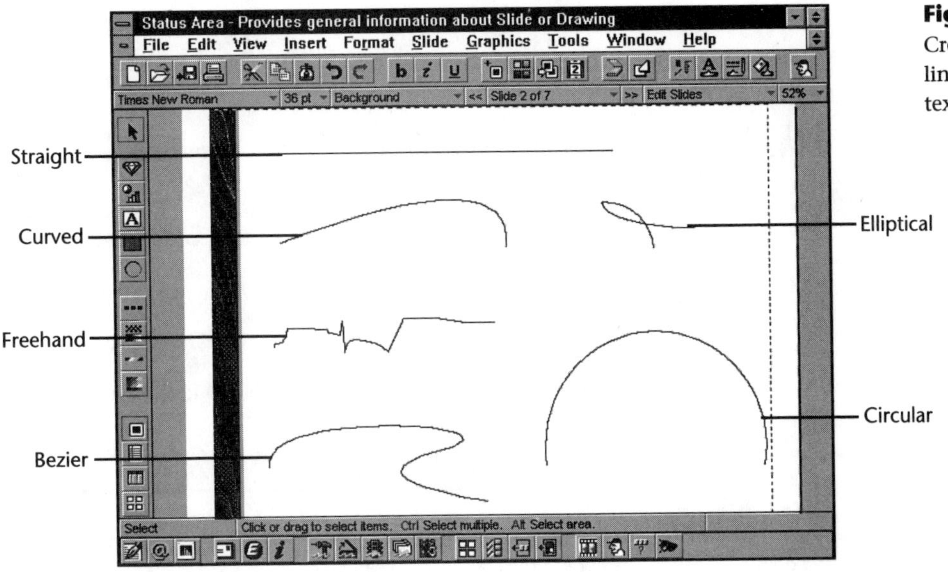

Fig. 26.1
Create a variety of lines to enhance text or graphics.

Modifying Lines

You can change line attributes such as line style, line width, and line color in the Line Attributes dialog box; click the Line button on the Toolbar to open the Line Attributes dialog box. Additionally, you can choose line style and thickness from the Line Attributes button on the Icon Bar.

To change line attributes:

1. Select the line. Choose Format, Line Attributes, or click the Line button on the Toolbar. The Line Attributes dialog box appears (see fig. 26.2).

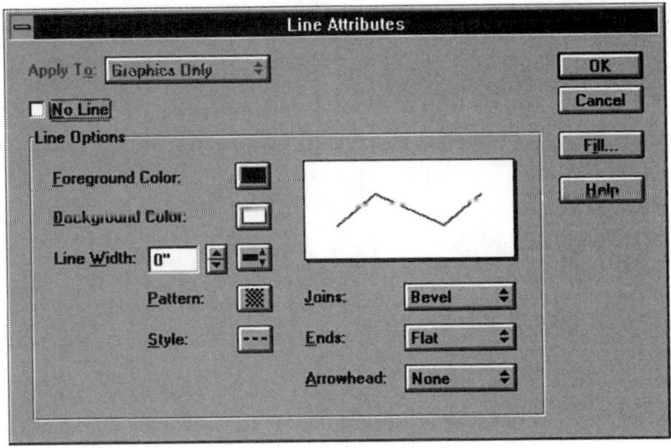

Fig. 26.2
Change line attributes for the selected line.

2. In the Line Options area, choose a **F**oreground color for the line, enter or select a Line **W**idth, and choose a **P**attern and a **S**tyle. You can, additionally, choose from the following options:

   - *Joins.* Choose to join two lines, or angles, with a **B**evel, **M**iter, or **R**ound edge.

   - *Ends.* Choose to make the line endings **R**ound, **F**lat, or **S**quare.

   - *Arrowhead.* Choose to add an arrowhead to the **B**eginning or **E**nding of a line, to B**o**th Ends of a line, or to None.

3. When finished with setting the line attributes, click OK to close the dialog box.

Tip
Joins, ends, and arrowheads are more noticeable when the line thickness is greater than .05 inches.

Troubleshooting

I drew a Freehand line but it turned out too angled and rough.

Freehand lines are very hard to draw smoothly; try using the Bezier curve line tool instead. After you draw the curves, you can click on any handle attached to the curve and adjust the line. You have more control over Bezier than Freehand.

I drew a line but can't see it on the screen.

Click on the Line Attribute tool on the Icon Bar and deselect None so that no X appears in the check box; alternatively, choose Fo**r**mat, Li**n**e Attributes, and choose the **N**o Line option so that no X appears in the check box.

Creating Borders

Many of the objects you draw, such as data charts, clip art, organizational charts, tables, and so on, enable you to add a border; however, you may want to add borders to text or to a drawing you create. You can add a border by using the Closed Object tool on the Drawing toolbar.

Drawing the Border

To draw a border shape, click the Rectangle tool button to display the various closed object tools. You can select any shape after drawing it and drag one of its handles to change the shape. Additionally, hold the Shift key while dragging to create a perfect square, circle, or 45-degree angle. Hold the Alt key while dragging to create the object from a center point instead of the edge.

The Closed Object tools are as follows:

Rectangle. Click the tool and drag to create a rectangle.

Rounded Rectangle. Click the tool and drag the mouse to create the rounded rectangle.

Circle. Click and drag the tool to create a circle.

Ellipse. Click and drag the tool to create an ellipse.

Polygon. Click to begin the shape and move the pointer to create one edge of the shape. Click and the shape becomes closed; however, move the pointer to form the second edge and click again. Repeat until the shape is complete. Press the Shift key while drawing to draw exact horizontal, vertical, or 45-degree angles. Double-click to complete the shape.

Closed Curve. Click once to begin the curved shape. and at each place where the curve changes directions, click again. Double-click to complete the shape.

Arrows. Click once to start the arrow, then move the pointer to where the arrow should end and click again. Releasing the mouse button after the second click creates a straight arrow; however, you can drag after the initial click and create a curved arrow shape.

Regular Polygon. Click the tool and drag to create a five-sided polygon. When you choose Regular Polygon, a dialog box appears in the upper right corner of the screen which enables you to choose the number of sides your image will use.

Figure 26.3 shows an example of each of the closed object shapes you can use for a border.

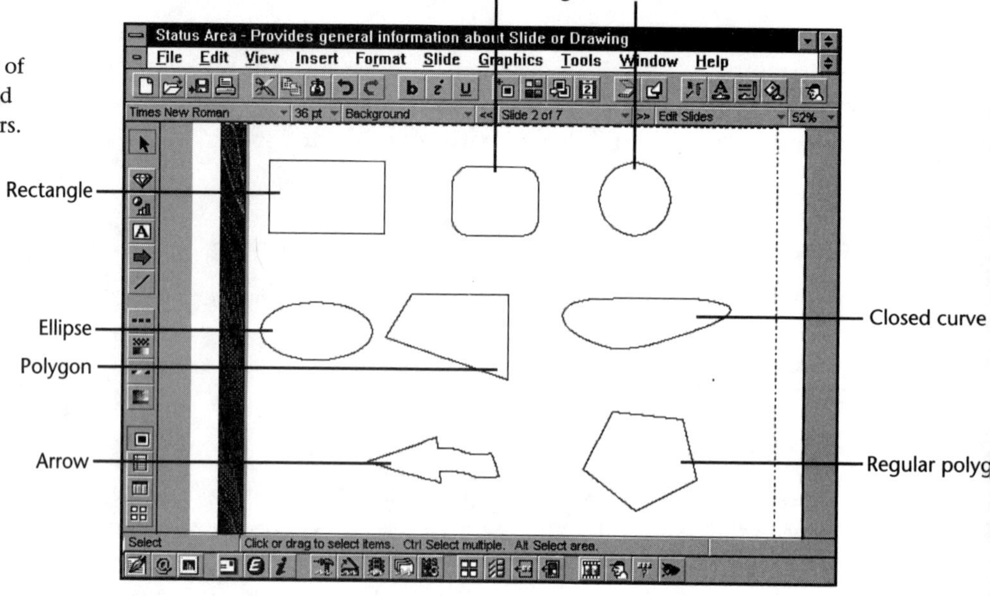

Fig. 26.3
You can use any of these eight closed shapes for borders.

Modifying the Border

When drawing a closed object, you can choose a fill color and pattern before drawing the object, or draw the object, select it, and then choose the fill and pattern. Additionally, you can change the line style, color, and thickness before or after drawing the object.

You can create a shape with no fill, so the shape's border line is all you see on-screen and its inside is transparent. Alternatively, you can create the shape with a fill color or pattern and make the fill transparent or opaque. If the fill is transparent, you can use color and still see what's behind the closed shape; if the fill is opaque, it blocks out what is beneath it but you can place text or other items on top of the closed shape.

To change the fill to none:

1. Select the object. Then choose Format, Fill Attributes, or click the Fill button on the Icon Bar. The Fill Attributes dialog box appears (see fig. 26.4).

2. In Fill Type, choose None. Click OK to close the dialog box.

Tip
When using Gradient fill, use the **A**uto-Step Blending when possible, because it's faster to print than a fixed number of blending steps.

To change the fill to a color or pattern:

1. In the Fill Attributes dialog box, in Fill Type, choose either Pattern or Gradient. Pattern creates a solid color, whereas Gradient produces a blend of two colors.

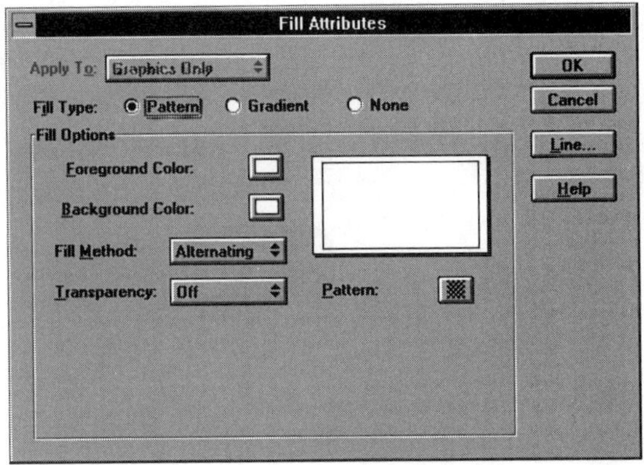

Fig. 26.4
Choose the Fill Attributes dialog box to change the fill type.

2. In Fill Options, if you chose the Pattern F**i**ll Type, choose the **F**oreground and **B**ackground Color. In the **P**attern box, choose the line pattern you want to apply.

   Alternatively, if you chose the Gradient F**i**ll Type, choose both a **C**enter Color and an O**u**ter Color for the fill.

3. If you chose the Pattern F**i**ll Type, you can choose the **T**ransparency option and turn it on or off for the foreground. If you chose the Gradient option, choose from any of the gradient options in the following table:

Option	Description
Fill **M**ethod	Winding fills includes any overlapping areas of the shape. Alternate fills *every other* cell where overlapping occurs; this option applies mainly to table cells.
Type	Refers to the shape of the grade: **C**ircular, **R**ectangular, or **L**inear.
An**g**le	Sets the angle of the rectangular or linear gradient fill.
Auto-Step Blending	Makes the gradient smooth by using automatic blending. Fix**e**d enables you to set the blending steps yourself and shows an example as you enter the fixed number of steps.
X-Offset/**Y**-Offset	Sets the amount (from 0 to 100%) of the offset of the Center color from the center.

4. Click the **L**ine button to display the Line Attributes dialog box. Modify any of the line options, and click OK to close the dialog box.

Figure 26.5 demonstrates various borders and fills with text in them.

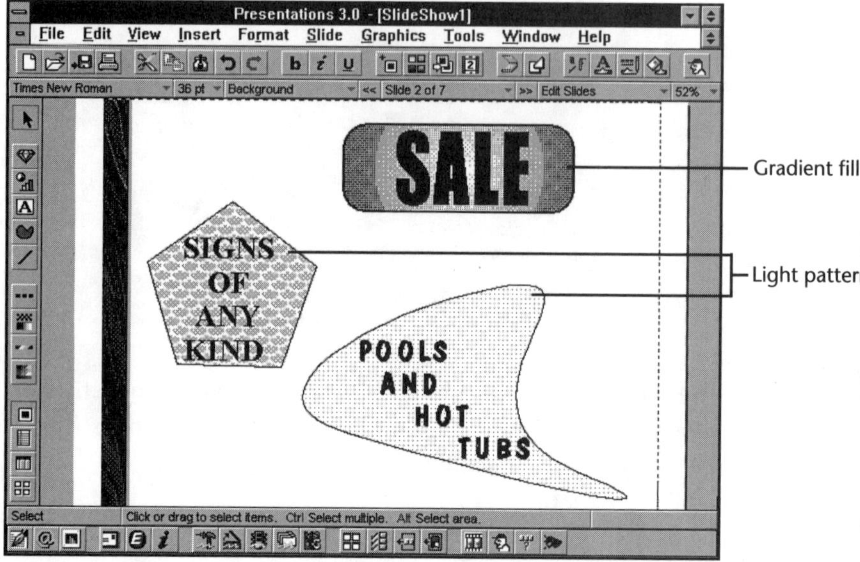

Fig. 26.5 Use borders with fills and patterns to attract attention.

> **Note**
>
> You can move a border around by selecting and dragging it to a new location. Additionally, you can select two or more items, such as a text box and a border, by holding the Shift key as you click on the items. If you have trouble selecting one item that is beneath another, hold the Ctrl key as you click the item.

Adding Pictures

You can add pictures or clip art from the PerfectOffice suite of applications, or from other sources. Pictures help illustrate text and make a presentation more attractive. Presentations includes a QuickArt Gallery that provides various categories of clip art, such as animals, architecture, arrows, and so on. Alternatively, you can insert a file from another program, such as a bitmap or Designer file.

Inserting a Presentations Picture

You can insert a Presentations picture using the QuickArt Gallery. First, you create the area for the picture, and then choose the picture you want to insert.

To insert a Presentations picture:

1. Choose **I**nsert, **Q**uickArt, or click the Figure tool on the Icon Bar. The mouse pointer changes to a hand holding a frame. Drag the hand across the work area to create an area for the picture.

2. When you release the mouse button, the QuickArt Gallery appears (see fig. 26.6).

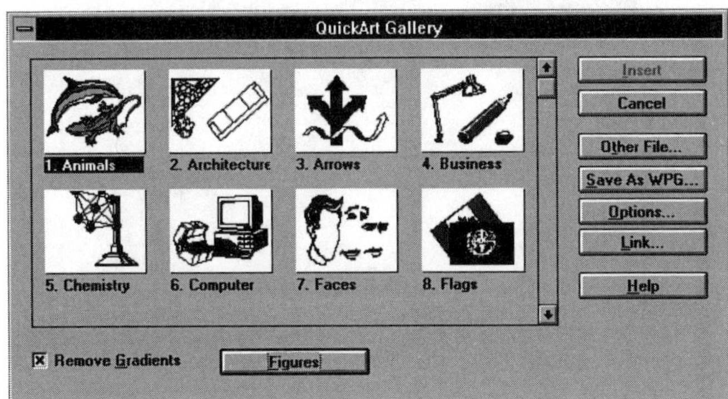

Fig. 26.6
Insert a picture using the QuickArt Gallery.

3. Double-click on a category and related pictures appear. When viewing the items in a category, you can scroll the vertical scroll bar to see more pictures.

4. Choose a picture and choose **I**nsert or click the **C**ategories button to view the categories. When you choose to insert, the picture appears in the work area and the mouse pointer is ready to draw another picture area. To select the picture or continue your work without drawing another area, click the Selection tool on the Drawing toolbar.

Note

You can move, resize, cut and paste, add a border, and otherwise manipulate the picture, as you would any object. To edit individual sections of the image, you may need to separate the image into sections by choosing **G**raphics, S**e**parate.

Inserting a Picture from Another Program

If you have clip art, drawings, or other pictures you want to use from another program, you can insert them to a presentation slide.

To insert a picture from another program:

1. Choose **I**nsert, **Q**uickArt. The hand appears.

2. Draw an area for the art. The QuickArt Gallery dialog box appears.

3. In the dialog box, click the O**t**her File button. The Insert Figure dialog box appears (see fig. 26.7).

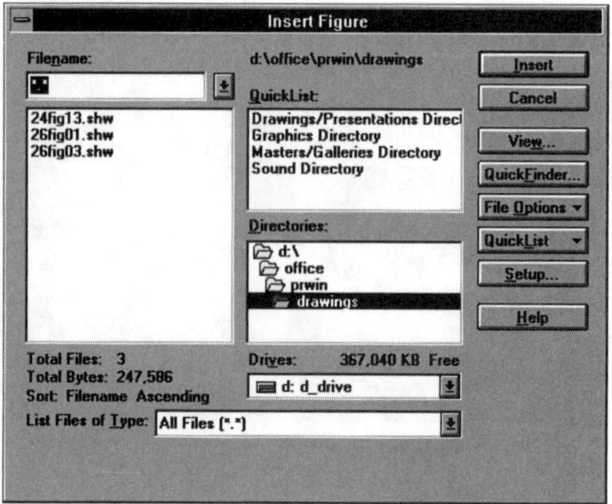

Fig. 26.7
Insert a figure from another application by clicking the Other File button.

> **Note**
>
> It is usually not necessary to specify the file type. Presentations automatically interprets the file type for you. You will normally only use the file type function when you wish to save your file in a format other than .SHW.

4. In List Files of **T**ype, choose the file type of the picture you want to insert. Presentations can import the following file types:

   - AutoCAD (DXF)
   - Bitmaps (BMP)
   - Computer Graphics Metafiles (CGM)
   - Designer (DRW)
   - Encapsulated PostScript (EPS)
   - HP Graphics Language (HPG)
   - Lotus PIC (PIC)

- Macintosh PICT (PCT)
- PC Paintbrush (PCX)
- Tagged Image Format (TIF)
- Truevision Targa (TGA)
- Windows Metafiles (WMF)
- WP Graphics (WPG)
- WP Master (MST)
- WP Presentation (SHW)

5. Select the correct drive and directory, and then choose the file. Click the **I**nsert button and the file inserts to your work area.

Inserting and Formatting Tables

You can create a table within Presentations that enables you to display data in rows and columns. Organizing numerical information in a table format makes it easier to read and comprehend. Additionally, you can display any chart data in table format by choosing Table as the chart type; you can change the table back to a chart when it better suits the presentation. You can also copy a WordPerfect table to the Clipboard and paste it into a Presentations slide.

When creating a table in Presentations, you can choose from six table formats, including outlined, shaded, and plain table designs. Presentations enables you to add titles, subtitles, and range colors, and otherwise format the data within the table.

Adding a Table

You can create a table within Presentations in which you can enter, edit, and format the text, data, labels, and titles. You can also copy a table or table data from another program, such as WordPerfect. After copying the table to the Clipboard, you can paste it into a Presentations slide.

Tip
Make the original table box as large as possible; tables appear small onscreen, although you can enlarge the area later.

To copy a table from another program, create the table. You can format the table text and alignment; however, Presentations does not retain the formatting when it is pasted into a slide. Next, select the entire table and choose

Edit, **C**opy. Switch to the Presentations program and display the slide in which you want to paste the table. Choose **E**dit, **P**aste, and the table appears on the slide. To edit or enhance the table, see the section, "Enhancing a Table."

To create a table within Presentations, follow these steps:

1. Click the Chart Objects Tool. The mouse pointer changes to a hand holding a square.
2. Drag the hand across the slide page to define the area for the table.
3. Release the mouse button. The Data Chart dialog box appears.
4. In **C**hart Type, choose Table. Six table formats appear from which you can choose (see figure 26.8).

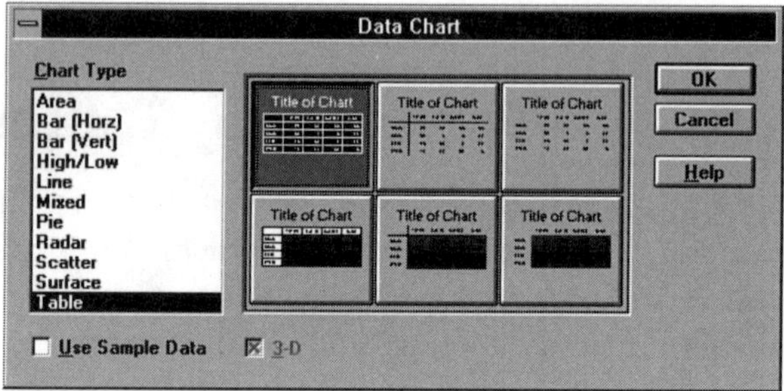

Fig. 26.8
Choose Table as the chart type to view various table formats.

5. Choose a table format and click OK. The dialog box closes and the datasheet appears next to the defined chart area on your slide (see fig. 26.9).
6. Enter the data into the datasheet; you can scroll the window or enlarge it to see more columns and rows.
7. Close the datasheet by double-clicking the window's Control menu. The table appears in the designated area (see fig. 26.10).

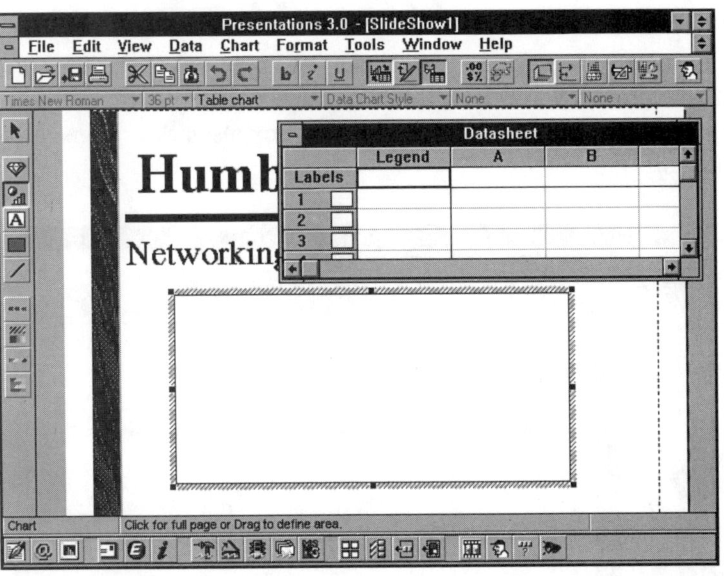

Fig. 26.9
Use the datasheet to define the table's contents.

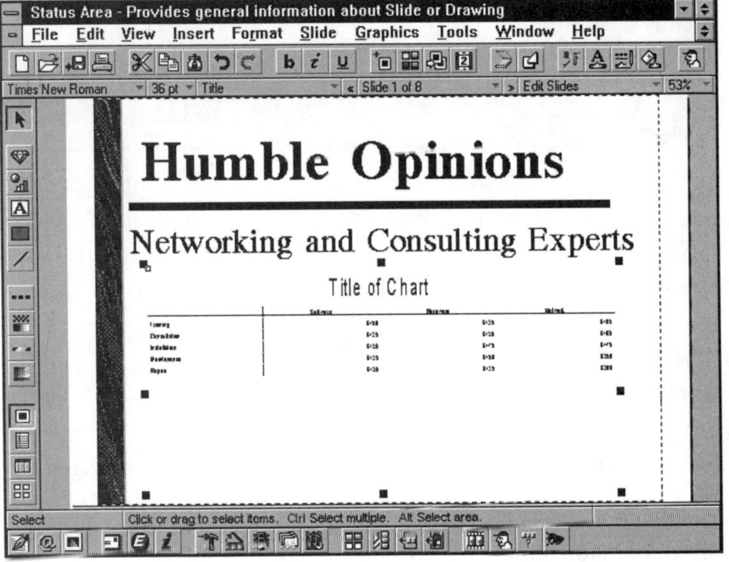

Fig. 26.10
The table appears in the slide when you close the datasheet.

Editing a Table

You can edit the data in a table created in Presentations at any time. You edit the data in the datasheet. To edit the data in a table, double-click the table to activate it. When active, the table's defining box displays a screened border (see fig. 26.11).

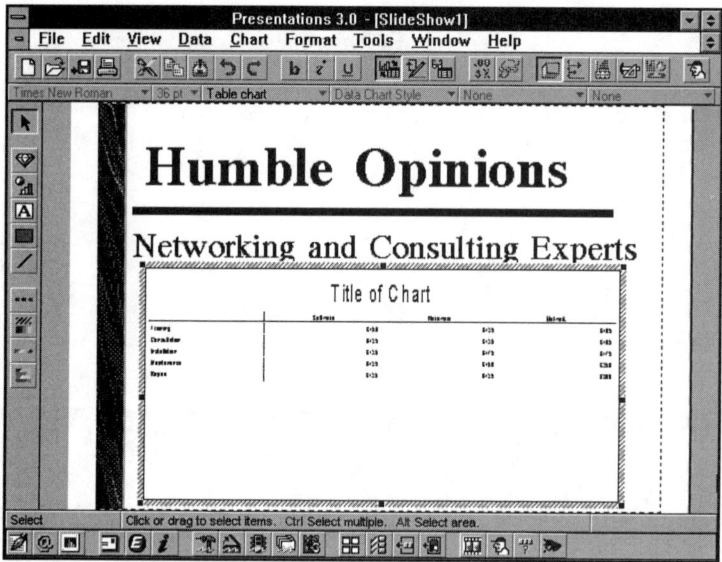

Fig. 26.11
The screened border indicates the table is ready for editing or formatting.

To view the datasheet, click the View Datasheet button on the Toolbar. The datasheet appears. When you are finished editing, double-click the datasheet window's Control menu to close. The edited data appears in the table.

Enhancing a Table

You can format the text and data in a table so the text is large enough to easily read during a presentation. When you format the text or data within the table, all of the text within the table reflects the format changes.

Additionally, you can add titles and subtitles to the table and you can change the color of the table lines, background, font, and so on.

To format the text in a table, follow these steps:

1. Double-click the table to activate it.

2. Choose **C**hart, **L**ayout. The Table/Surface Options dialog box appears (see fig. 26.12).

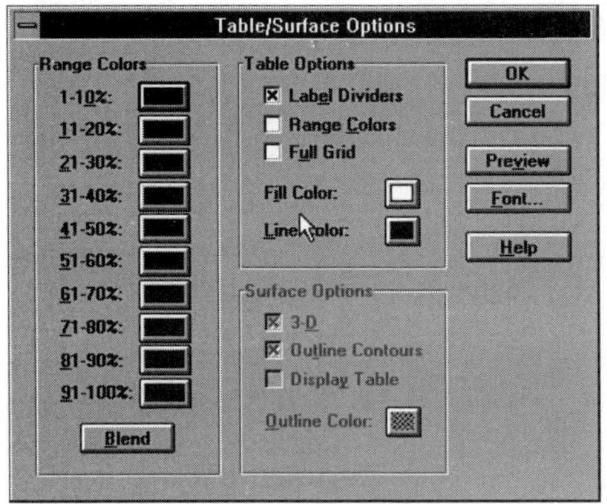

Fig. 26.12
Use the Table/Surface Options dialog box to change the font and other table options.

3. Choose the **F**ont button. The Font dialog box appears.
4. Make any changes in typeface, size, or appearance just as you would in any other Font dialog box.
5. Click OK to close the Font dialog box; click OK to close the Table/Surface Options dialog box. Alternatively, you can choose Pre**v**iew to view the change before accepting it.

Tip
Change the type size to at least 36-point or even larger, so it can easily be read in the presentation slide.

You also can change other table format options in the Table/Surface Options dialog box. Table 26.1 describes the other table options available in the Table/Surface Options dialog box.

Table 26.1 Table/Surface Options

Option	Description
Lab**e**l Dividers	Show or hide the table's formatted grid lines in a table.
Range **C**olors	Show or hide the selected colors to the table cells; this option fills each cell with the selected colors in the Range Colors area of the dialog box.
F**u**ll Grid	Show or hide all grid lines in the table.
F**i**ll Color	Choose one color to use for the table background.
Line Color	Choose one color to use for all grid lines.

Applying Range Colors

Tip
Double-click a selected table to display the Table/Surface Options dialog box.

Presentations includes a useful feature that enables the reader to quickly discern the data in a table: *range colors*. Each range color represents a different value in the table; the range color is applied as background color for each cell. The lowest values, for example, may be represented in a red cell, whereas the highest values could be represented in a yellow cell. Using range colors enables the viewer to quickly see the number of high and low values on the table.

You choose the range colors in the Table/Surface Options dialog box in the Range Colors area (see fig. 26.13). Click on the first color box and a palette appears; choose the color to represent the first range in the table. The first block represents the lowest values on the table and the last block in the Range Color area represents the highest values.

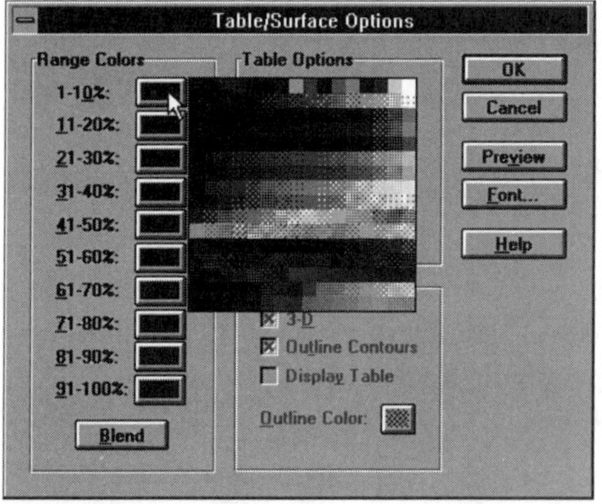

Fig. 26.13
Click each range box to display the palette; choose a color to represent the range.

Tip
Keep the colors light enough so you can read all of the data in the table cells. Try making the text bold if it's hard to read.

You can choose a color for each range block by clicking the block and choosing a color from the palette. Alternatively, you can choose a color for the first range block, and another color for the last range block, and click the **B**lend button. When you click the Blend button, Presentations creates a blend of shades between the two selected colors. Figure 26.14 shows the table with a blend of grays applied to the ranges. Note that you must turn on the Range Colors option in the Table Options area of the dialog box.

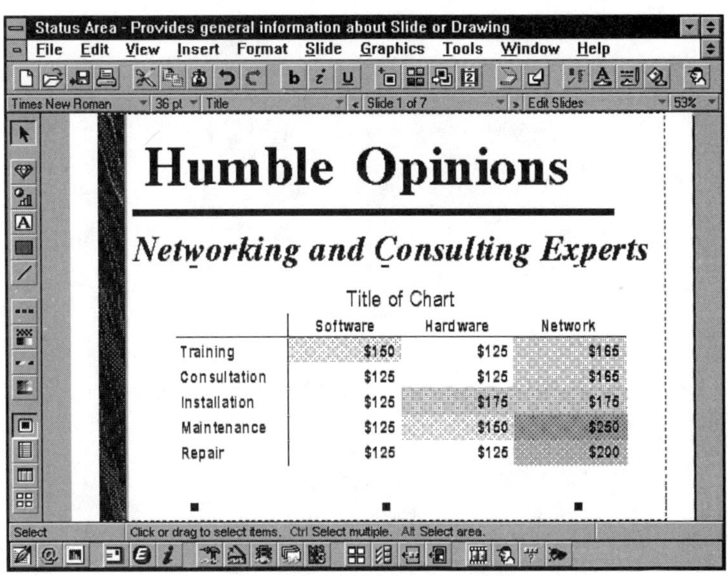

Fig. 26.14
Use grays if you are printing in black and white; use colors if your presentation is on-screen.

Adding Titles and Subtitles

Presentations enables you to add titles and subtitles to your table. You can even format the titles, if you want. When you create a table in Presentations, it adds "Title of Chart" at the top of the table. Using the Titles dialog box, you can enter your own title, add a subtitle, or delete the title text altogether.

To add a title, follow these steps:

1. Double-click the chart to select it.
2. Double-click "Title of Chart." The Titles dialog box appears (see fig. 26.15).

Titles
Display
Title: Title of Chart
Subtitle:
Y1 Axis:
Y2 Axis:
X Axis:
OK
Cancel
Preview
Options...
Help

Fig. 26.15
Use the Titles dialog box to add titles and subtitles.

3. Enter the title in the **T**itle text box; you also can add text in the **S**ubtitle text box.

4. To format either or both titles, choose the **O**ptions button. The Titles Options dialog box appears (see fig. 26.16).

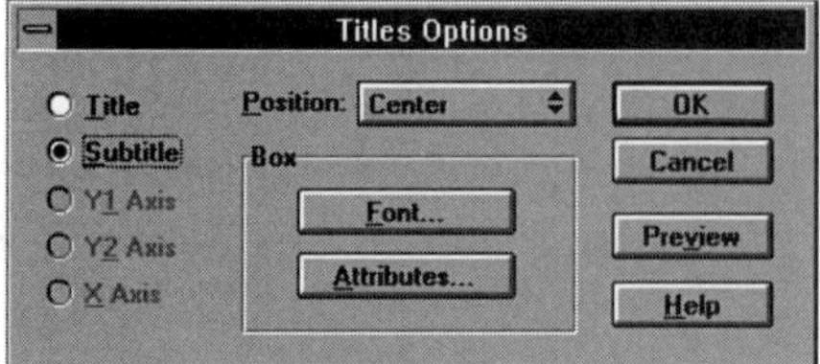

Fig. 26.16
Format the font or position of the titles in the Titles Options dialog box.

5. Choose either **T**itle or **S**ubtitle as the text you want to format; in Box, choose **F**ont. The Font dialog box appears.

6. Choose the typeface, size, and appearance as you would in any Font dialog box. Click OK to close the Font dialog box.

7. In the Titles Options dialog box, choose a new Position for the title, if you want.

8. Click OK to close the Titles Options dialog box; click OK to close the Titles dialog box.

Creating an Organization Chart

Organization charts can be used to show the structure of your organization; you can chart the relationships from the CEO to the office managers, for example, or from the manager to the clerks in her department. To create an organization chart, you choose the layout and then enter the names and titles of the people in the organization. You can easily change layouts, edit entries, promote and demote entries, and perform other such modifications after creating the chart.

Creating the Chart

To create a chart, you must indicate an area on the slide and then choose a layout. You can add the organization chart to your presentation in a variety of ways:

- Using the Organization Chart slide layout, double-click the Organization Chart area to display the Organization Chart dialog box.

- Click the Organization Chart button from the Icon Bar pop-up menu; the pointer changes to a hand. Drag the hand across the slide work area to create an area for the chart. The Organization Chart dialog box appears.

- Choose **I**nsert, **O**rg Chart; The hand appears to draw the chart area. The Organization Chart dialog box appears.

Tip
If you click the charting pointer (the hand) instead of dragging it, the resulting chart fills the window.

Figure 26.17 illustrates the Organization Chart dialog box, from which you choose a chart layout.

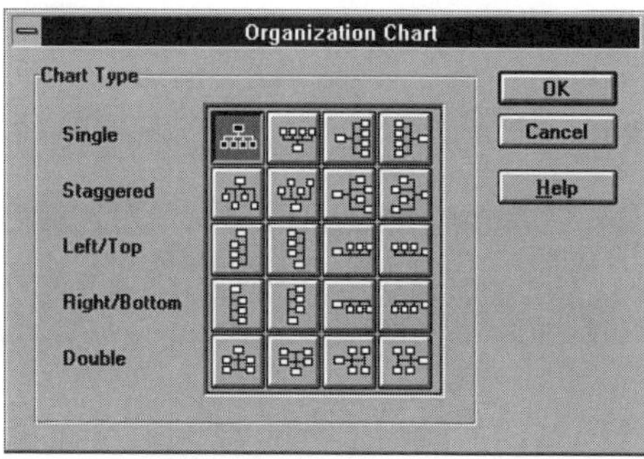

Fig. 26.17
Choose a layout for the chart in the Organization Chart dialog box.

Entering Text

After you choose the chart layout, the Outline window appears (see fig. 26.18). You enter text in the organization chart outline similarly to the way you enter text into the Slide Outliner. As you enter text, the chart on-screen shows the changes.

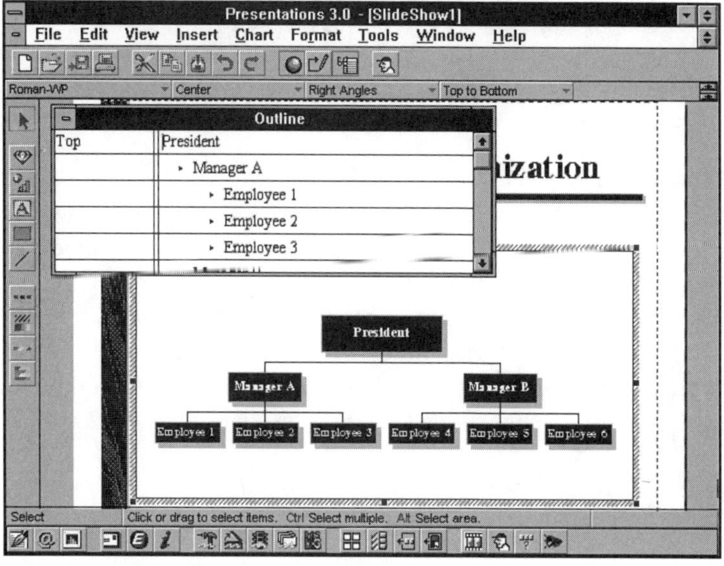

Fig. 26.18
Enter the text in the Outline dialog box to edit the text in the chart.

◄ See "Using Outliner," p. 502

When entering text in the chart outline, you can follow the sample text by entering the president, manager, and employees, or you can enter your own chart structure. The following keys will help you:

- **Enter.** Creates a new box on the same level.
- **Tab.** Demotes one level.
- **Shift+Tab.** Promotes one level.

When you are finished entering the text, double-click the Control menu in the Outline dialog box to close it. The chart appears on-screen, with the charting box selected (see fig. 26.19).

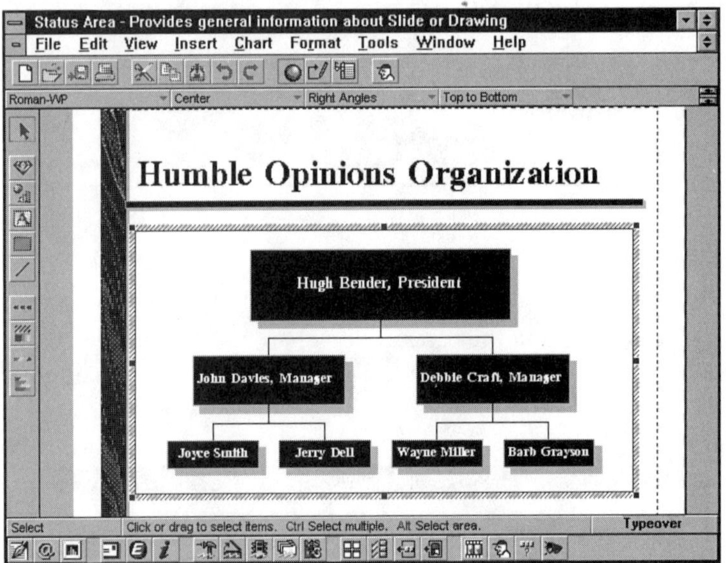

Fig. 26.19
The organization chart appears on-screen, selected.

Tip
You can also edit the chart layout by choosing the **C**hart, **L**ayout command and choosing the options from the Layout dialog box.

Editing the Chart

As with any object, you can edit the text in the chart or the chart colors, layout, and so on. Select the chart and then use the Chart menu and the Toolbar. Additionally, the Power Bar includes six buttons for chart editing when you select the chart: Font Selection, Text Justification, Box Style, Text Border Style, Connector Style, and Chart Orientation. Use the Connector Style button to add lines that connect the boxes in the chart and use the Chart Orientation to change the layout of the chart boxes.

> **Note**
>
> Click the chart once to display the black handles. When the chart is selected in this manner, you can move, cut, copy, and resize the box holding the chart.

Editing Text

To edit the text in the chart, double-click the chart—if it's not already selected—and the Outline dialog box appears; alternatively, select the chart and click the Outline button from the Toolbar. The chart outline appears and you can enter or edit the text as needed.

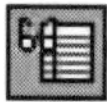

Choosing a Chart Layout

To change the chart layout, choose **C**hart, Galle**r**y. The Organization Chart dialog box appears with a variety of chart layouts. Select one and click OK to close the dialog box and apply the new layout to your chart and text.

Editing Box Attributes

The default chart box is black with a shadow and white, or reversed, text. To change the box attributes:

1. Choose **C**hart, Box **A**ttributes. The Box Attributes dialog box appears (see fig. 26.20).

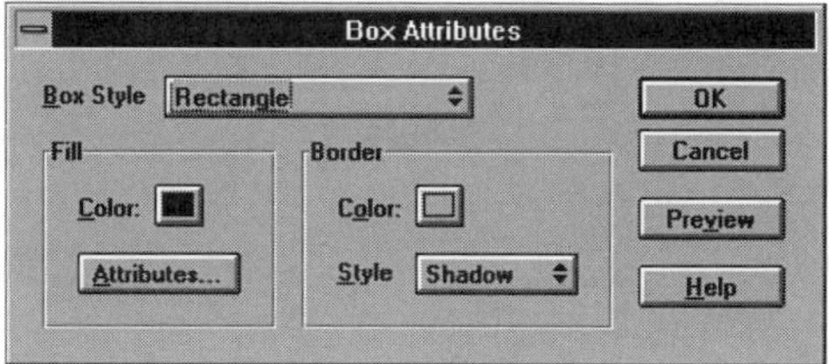

Fig. 26.20
Use the Box Attributes dialog box to choose box style and fill color.

2. In **B**ox Style, choose one of the following: **R**ectangle, Roun**d**ed Rectangle, **O**ctagon, or **N**one.

3. In the Fill area, choose **C**olor and select a color for the box. Choose **A**ttributes to display the Fill Attributes dialog box; choose pattern or gradient fills, and click OK to return to the Box Attributes dialog box.

◄ See "Editing a Chart," p. 516

4. In the Border area, choose C**o**lor and pick a new color for the border. In **S**tyle, choose the border line style you want to use.

Tip
If you want to change the type in the chart box, select the chart and choose Format, Font. To change font color, click the Attributes button.

5. Click Preview to see the changes, and click OK to accept the changes and close the dialog box.

Editing Box Options

You can edit the size of the chart boxes and the text alignment in the Box Options dialog box. To edit the box options:

1. Choose Chart, Box Options. The Box Options dialog box appears (see fig. 26.21).

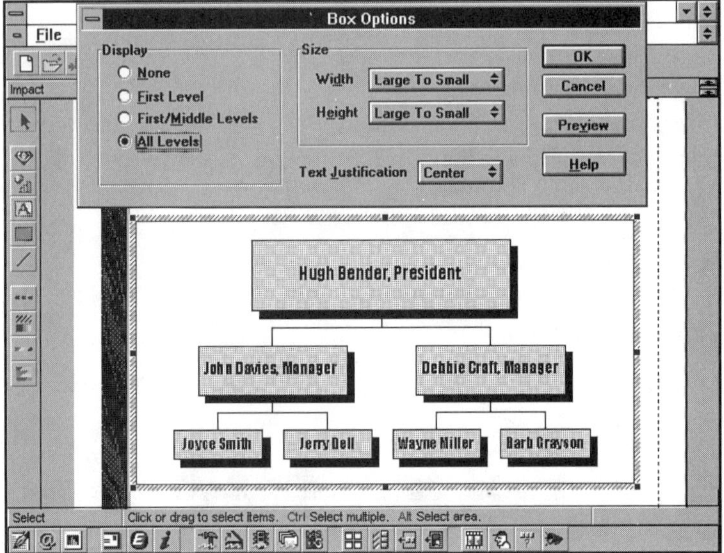

Fig. 26.21
Use the Box Options dialog box to alter box size and text justification.

2. In the Display area, choose the levels you want to show on-screen.
3. In the Size area, choose the Width and Height of the boxes; if you are in doubt of which options to choose, select one and use the Preview button to view it.
4. In Text Justification, choose the alignment you want to use for the in all boxes.
5. Click OK to close the dialog box and apply the changes.

Tip
You can choose the Chart menu and Connectors command to display the Connectors dialog box in which you can choose the style of lines you want to use to connect the boxes.

Drawing with Presentations

With Presentations drawing, you can create your own drawings, trace bitmaps, or add to other picture files, such as imported clip art files. At the beginning of this chapter, you learned to draw with the line and shape tools, as well as how to change fill and line attributes. Those same procedures and dialog boxes apply to many of the other drawing tools in Presentations.

Adding a Drawing Area

To add a drawing area to a slide, click the Bitmap tool from the Icon Bar pop-up menu; the mouse pointer changes to a hand. Drag the hand across the slide work area to create a box for the drawing. The view changes to Drawing view (see fig. 26.22).

Cancel
Return
Select area
Zoom tool
Bitmap Brush Size
Air Brush Density
Zoom
Select area
Eraser tools
Paint tools
Text Object tools
Closed Object tools
Line Object tools
Line Attributes
Fill Attributes
Line Colors
Fill Colors
Foreground and Background Colors
Fill Pattern
Brush Attributes
Bitmap Brush Shape

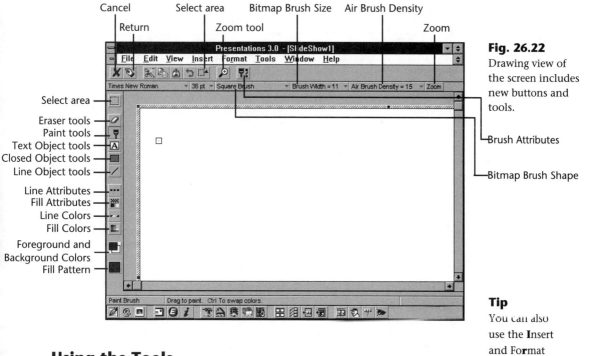

Fig. 26.22 Drawing view of the screen includes new buttons and tools.

Tip You can also use the **I**nsert and Fo**r**mat menus to change drawing tools and modify selected drawn items.

Using the Tools

The Drawing view enlarges just the drawing area from the slide so you can work more easily. Additionally, many tools you can use specifically for drawing appear in the Drawing view. Table 26.2 lists and describes each of the drawing tools.

Table 26.2 Drawing Tools

Tool or button	Description
Cancel	Cancels the drawing and returns to Slide Editor view.
Return	Return to Slide Editor view and update the drawing to the slide.
Select area	Select an area of the drawing, then cut, copy, change attributes, and so on.
Zoom tool	Magnifies the view of the bitmapped drawing; click again to return to normal magnification.
Brush Attributes	Displays the Brush Attributes dialog box from which you can choose brush shapes, brush width, and air brush density.
Bitmap Brush Shape	Choose a brush shape from a drop-down list.
Bitmap Brush Size	Choose a brush size from the drop-down list.
Air Brush Density	Choose the density of the air brush spray from a drop-down list.
Eraser tools	Select either eraser tool to remove painted or drawn items.
Paint tools	Choose from a brush, roller, or spray can to apply paint; also, choose the dropper (paint picker) to select a color of paint already used and then choose a paint tool to apply the color.
Text Object tools	Enter text in the drawing using the text tools.
Closed Object tools	Create a closed object: rectangle, rounded rectangle, circle, ellipse, curved shape, polygon, arrow, or regular polygon.
Line Object tools	Create a line: straight, curved, Bezier, freehand, arc, or circular arc.
Line Attributes	Choose line style and thickness.
Fill Attributes	Choose a pattern or gradient for the fill.
Line Colors	Choose a line color.
Fill Colors	Choose a fill color.
Foreground and Background Colors	Displays the current foreground and background colors.
Fill Pattern	Displays the current fill pattern.

To use a drawing tool, click the tool and move the mouse pointer to the drawing area. Click or click and drag the tool to create the drawing or painting. You can choose the line and/or fill color of an object before you draw, or draw first and then select the object and change its line and fill.

When you are finished drawing, choose the Return button on the Icon Bar or press Ctrl+F4; alternatively, you can choose **F**ile, **R**eturn. To edit a drawing from the Slide Editor view, double-click the drawing.

From Here...

You can now create a slide show or other presentation using text, data charts, and various other objects to make your presentation attractive and effective. Consider the following chapter for some helpful information:

- Chapter 27, "Outputting Presentations," includes information on how to print your presentation, notes, and outline, as well as detailed instructions for creating and running an on-screen presentation, such as setting timing, changing transitions, and running the show.

Chapter 27

Outputting Presentations

by Sue Plumley

You can output a presentation by printing it, or by displaying it on-screen to customers or employees. You can print the slide show itself to paper, film, or transparencies. Additionally, you can print handouts, the outline, drawings, and other documents from the screen. You may also want to show the presentation on-screen. WordPerfect Presentations enables you to run the show automatically, setting timing and transitions between the slides.

In this chapter, you learn how to

- Preview the presentation
- Set printing options
- Select a printer
- Run an on-screen slide show
- Set transitions and timing for the slide show

Printing the Presentation

Before you print your presentation, you can view it in Print Preview; you can click through each slide to see how it will look when printed. When you are ready to print, you can choose the document type you want to print—such as slides, speaker notes, and so on—and you can choose the number of copies, binding offset, and other options before printing.

Previewing the Presentation

Presentations enables you to view the presentation as it will look when printed. You can then make any last-minute changes before sending the presentation to the printer. You must first open the Print dialog box by doing one of the following:

- Choose **F**ile, **P**rint.
- Press F5.

- Click the Print button on the Toolbar.
- Right-click anywhere on the slide to display the QuickMenu and choose **P**rint.

Figure 27.1 illustrates the Print dialog box.

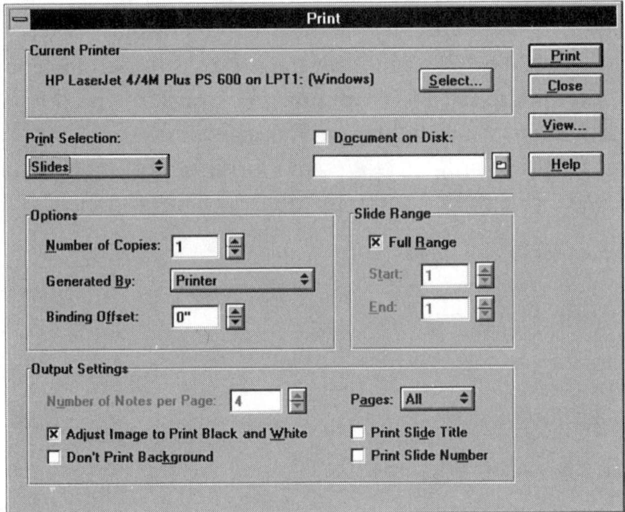

Fig. 27.1
Open the Print dialog box before choosing to preview the presentation.

In the Print dialog box, click the **V**iew button to display the first presentation slide (see fig. 27.2). Click the mouse anywhere on-screen to show the next slide, and so on throughout the remainder of the slides. Press Esc to return to the Print dialog box.

Note

If your printer is a black and white printer, the slides show in preview as black and white. You may want to modify the colors of charts, drawings, or other graphics so the grays or patterns are more discernible.

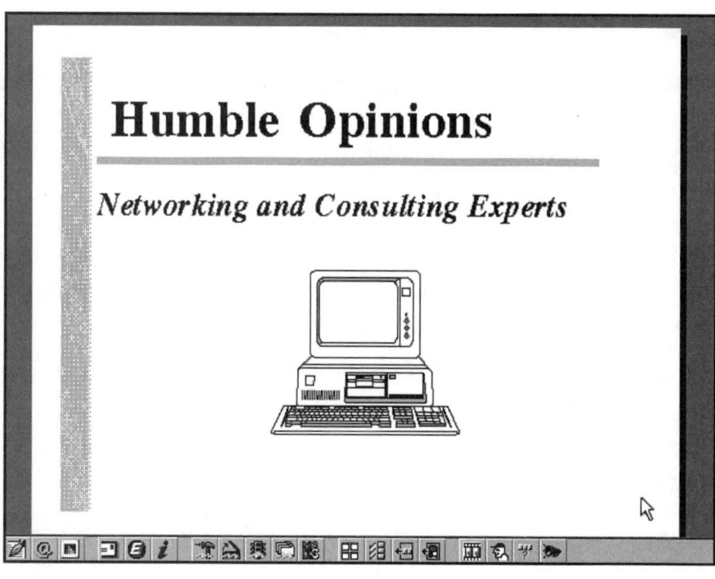

Fig. 27.2
View the slides as they will look when printed.

Choosing Print Options

You can choose a variety of printing options in the Print dialog box, including the number of copies, the slide range, and whether to print the background of the slides. You choose the print options in the Print dialog box.

Tip
If you need to modify any of the slides before printing, choose the **C**lose button in the Print dialog box to return to the presentation.

To choose printing options:

1. Open the Print dialog box. In Pr**i**nt Selection, choose from one of the following options in the pop-up list:

   - ***F****ull Page*. Prints the current page.
   - *Current View*. Prints only what you see on-screen; for example, if you are in a magnified view (zoom), Current View prints only that which is showing.
   - ***S****lides*. Prints all or part of the slide show.
   - *Slide* ***L****ist*. Prints the list of slide titles and options for each slide.
   - ***H****andouts*. Prints the slide show as thumbnails on handout pages so the viewer can make notes as he or she watches the show. Enter the number of slides you want on each page in the Number of Slides per Page text box.
   - *Speaker* ***N****otes*. Prints thumbnails, or small pictures, of each slide with any notes you entered as speaker notes (**S**lide menu, Speaker **N**otes command).

- *Selected Objects.* Prints only the objects you select in the slide.
- *Document on Disk.* Enables you to print a document that is stored on disk instead of opening and displaying the document on-screen first. Enter the path and file name of the document to be printed in the text box.

2. In the Options area of the dialog box, enter the **N**umber of copies you want to print. If you want to set an area on each slide page for binding, enter that amount in the Binding O**f**fset text box.
3. In the Slide **R**ange area, choose either Full **R**ange to print all slides in the presentation or deselect Full **R**ange and the S**t**art and **E**nd text boxes become available. Enter the first and the last slide you want to print in the text boxes.
4. In the Output Settings area, choose from the following options:

   - *Number of Notes per Page.* This option is dimmed unless you are printing handouts or notes. Enter the number of slides to print on each page.
   - *Pages.* Choose to print **A**ll pages in a presentation, or only the **O**dd or **E**ven pages in the presentation.
   - *Adjust Image to Print Black and White.* Choose this option if you are printing to a black and white printer and you want the colors in the graphics to adjust to grays.
   - *Don't Print Background.* Check this option to print the slide without the background colors and designs.
   - *Print Slide Title.* Choose whether to print the slide title on each slide.
   - *Print Slide Number.* Choose whether to print the slide number on the slides.

5. When you have selected the options in the Print dialog box, click the **P**rint button. Presentations sends the selection to the printer and you can continue working.

Troubleshooting

*I want to stop the print job after I choose **P**rint in the Print dialog box.*

Presentations displays the Current Print Job dialog box until the print job leaves the print buffer in Presentations. You can cancel the print job by choosing the Cancel Print Job button in the Current Print Job dialog box. Alternatively, you can use the Windows Print Manager to stop or pause print jobs.

My color graphics and text look an overall gray when I print to a black and white printer.

Choose the Adjust Image to Print Black and **W**hite option in the Output Settings of the Print dialog box. If you are still unhappy with the results, return to the presentation and select the colored graphics you want to change. From the color palettes, you can choose from a variety of grays to assign text, chart markers, lines, fills, patterns, and so on. You may need to experiment with the grays to get the results you want.

◄ See "Working with Files," p. 69

Note

If you have an HPGL plotter or a film recorder connected to your printer, you can print to either the same way you print to a printer. Using the Print dialog box, choose the **S**elect button and from the list of printers, choose your film recorder or plotter. Choose any other options and click **P**rint.

Choosing a Printer

The printer that Presentations uses by default is the printer specified in your Windows setup. You can, however, change that printer through the Print dialog box in Presentations.

To select a printer:

1. Open the Print dialog box. In the Current Printer area, click the **S**elect button. The Print Setup dialog box appears (see fig. 27.3).
2. In the list of A**v**ailable Printers, choose the printer you want to use.

Note

Choose the S**e**tup button to display the Setup dialog box for your specific printer. Use this dialog box to choose page orientation, paper size, and other special features of your printer.

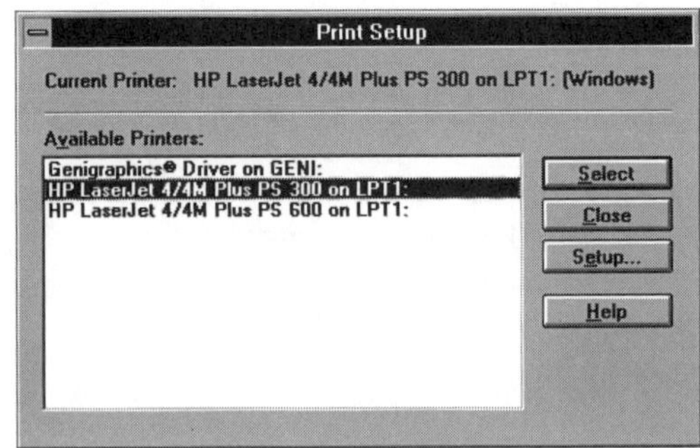

Fig. 27.3
Open the Print Set up dialog box to set up your printer.

3. Choose **S**elect to close the Print Setup dialog box and return to the Print dialog box.

Running an On-Screen Slide Show

With Presentations, you can create a slide show and display that show on-screen for customers, employees, or other interested parties. After creating the slides for the show, you can set slide show options, such as timing and transitions, to make the show professional and effective.

Creating Speaker Notes

When you prepare your slide show, you may want to create speaker notes to accompany the show. You can place speaker notes on a page with thumbnails of the slides in the show and print them to help you remember important points during the show.

To create speaker notes:

Tip
You can use the **V**iew, Slide **S**orter command to view the slides and rearrange them so your presentation is interesting and well-organized.

1. In your open presentation, choose **S**lide, Speaker **N**otes. The Speaker Notes dialog box appears (see fig. 27.4).

2. Using the left and right arrows, select the slide about which you want to add notes.

3. In the text block, enter the notes. You can change slides and enter more notes without closing the dialog box.

4. When you are done, click OK to close the dialog box.

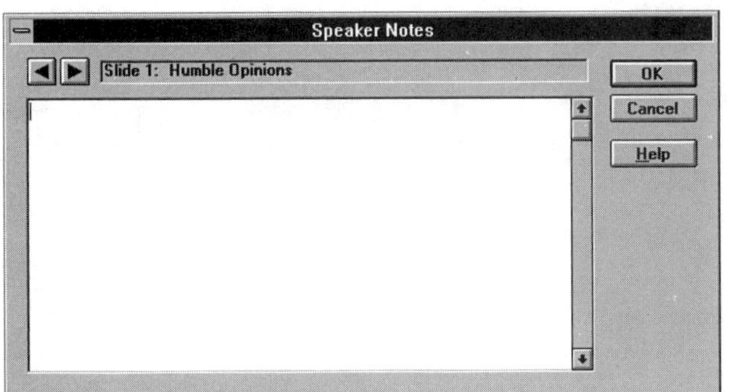

Fig. 27.4
Enter comments and notes on the presentation in the Speaker Notes dialog box.

Setting Slide Show Options

Two important slide show options are timing and transition. Timing refers to how long a specific slide remains on-screen and transition refers to how the program shifts or moves from one slide to another. You can set timing and transition separately for each slide, if you like.

To set timing and transitions:

1. In your open presentation, choose **S**lide, Trans**i**tion. The Slide Transition dialog box appears (see fig. 27.5).
2. At the top of the dialog box, select the slide for which you want to set options. Click the right arrow to move to the next slide and the left arrow to move to the previous slide.
3. Choose the Pre**v**iew button to display the Preview Transition box on-screen with the Slide Transition dialog box (refer to fig. 27.5).
4. In the Transition area of the dialog box, choose **T**ype. The pop-up list contains many different transitions: **N**ormal, **W**ipe, **O**pen, **C**lose, **B**ox, **S**pots, B**l**inds, **J**igsaw, S**n**ake, **D**iagonal, and O**v**erwrite. Choose a transition type.
5. Click the Pre**v**iew button and the transition takes place in the Preview Transition box. Additionally, you can choose the **D**irection in which the transition goes: **I**n or **O**ut; **R**ight, **L**eft, **T**op, or **B**ottom; **V**ertical or **H**orizontal, and so on, depending on the Transition Type you choose.

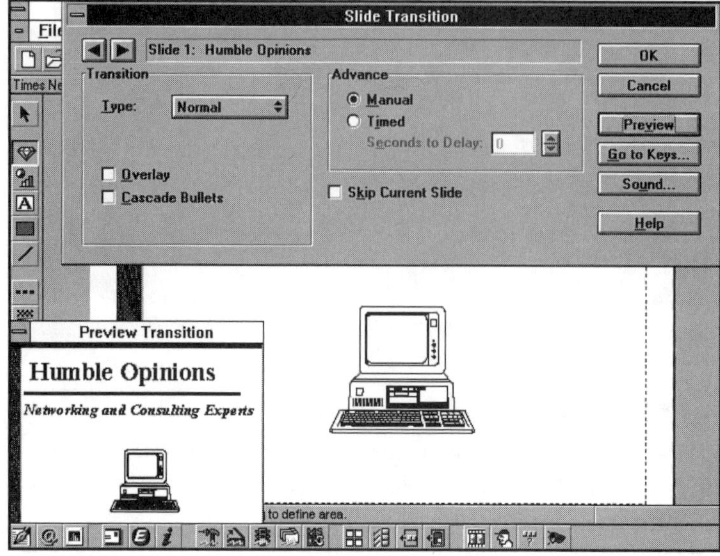

Fig. 27.5
Open the Preview Transition box to preview each transition.

6. Additionally, you can choose two more options in the Transition area of the Slide Transition dialog box:

   - **O**verlay places one slide over another one as each slide appears on-screen.

   - **C**ascade Bullets displays one bullet at a time. Transition **B**ullets Only is an option that appears if you choose **C**ascade Bullets. Choose if you want the transition options you selected to affect bulleted lines.

7. In the Advance area of the Slide Transition dialog box, choose either **M**anual or T**i**med. **M**anual means you click the mouse button to advance the slide when you are ready; T**i**med means you enter the number of **Se**conds to Delay for each slide.

8. Choose OK to close the dialog box and accept the changes in transition and timing.

Tip
Set the seconds to delay higher for slides with a lot of information on them, so the viewer is sure to have enough time to read the information.

Note

You can add sound to a slide show by using MIDI, digital audio, or CD audio sound files to one or more slides, if you have the sound hardware for the job. Choose the So**u**nd button in the Slide Transition dialog box to display the Sound dialog box. Enter any options and click OK to return to the Slide Transition dialog box.

Setting One Slide Transition

You can set the timing and transition to the same setting for the entire slide show, if you want.

To set one slide transition:

1. In the open presentation, choose **S**lide, **O**verride. The Slide Override dialog box appears (see fig. 27.6).

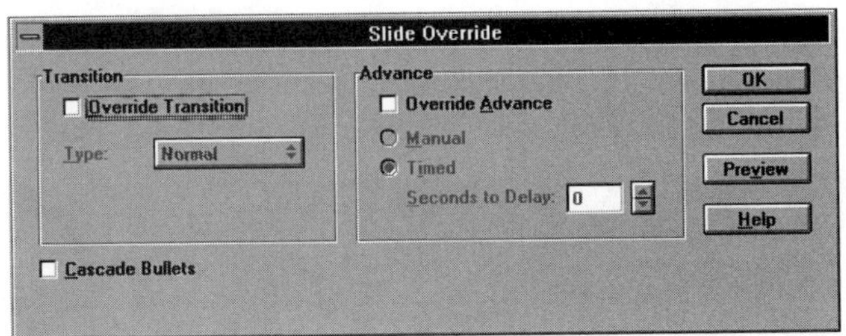

Fig. 27.6
Set one transition and one advance for the entire slide show.

2. In the Transition area, select **O**verride Transition. In **T**ype, choose the one transition you want to use for the entire slide show.
3. In the Advance area, choose Override **A**dvance. Choose either **M**anual or T**i**med and set any other options.
4. Choose OK to close the dialog box or Pre**v**iew to view the transition.

Making a Slide Show Runtime

Making a slide show runtime means to copy the show with all program files to a disk so you can run the show on another computer that does not have WordPerfect Presentations installed.

To make a show runtime:

1. Open the slide show or save the current show.
2. Choose **S**lide, Make **R**untime. The Make Runtime dialog box appears (see fig. 27.7).
3. In the Location to Copy Files area, enter the drive and directory to which you want to copy the show in the **D**irectory text box.
4. In the Slide Show area, enter a name for the show in the **N**ame text box.

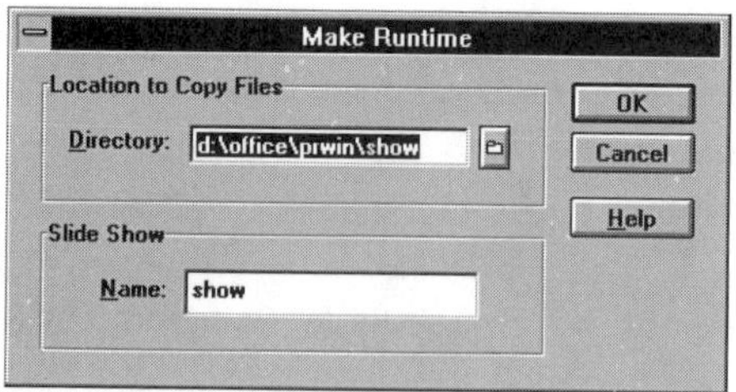

Fig. 27.7
The Make Runtime dialog box enables you to copy your presentation to a disk.

5. Click OK to close the dialog box and copy the show. Presentations displays a message stating it will automatically play the slide show to create a quick file. Choose OK.

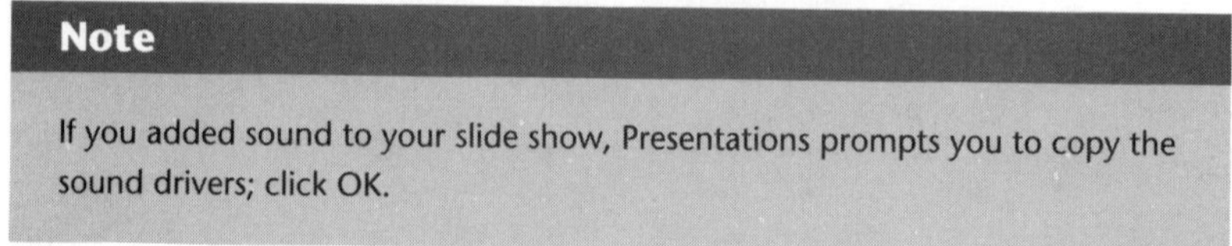

Note

If you added sound to your slide show, Presentations prompts you to copy the sound drivers; click OK.

6. Presentations plays the show, with your transitions and timing selections, copies the files to the specified location, and notifies you when it is finished. Click OK to close the final message box.

Playing a Slide Show

When you run the slide show, Presentations clears the screen of tools, windows, menus, and everything except each slide.

To play a slide show:

1. Open the slide show. Choose **S**lide, **P**lay Slide Show. The Play Slide Show dialog box appears (see fig. 27.8).

Fig. 27.8
Choose to play the slide show and Presentations enables you to make a few last minute changes.

2. In **S**tarting Slide, enter the number of the slide you want to start the presentation with.

3. In Highlighter, choose the **C**olor and the **W**idth of the marker you want to use during the presentation.
4. In Options, choose to **R**epeat Slide Show if you want the show to run continuously.
5. Choose **P**lay to start the show. If the show is set to Manual, click the mouse button when you want to advance to the next slide. Press Esc if you want to cancel the show at any time.

Tip

Use the marker, or highlighter, to draw on-screen during a presentation so you can underline or point out important items.

Note

If the slide show is set to manual, you can click the left mouse button to go to the previous slide and the right mouse button to go to the next slide.

Creating a Quick File

Create a quick file of your slide show to speed up the display. When you create a quick file, you save the slide show as bitmap and thus the display is much quicker; however, the file is much larger than a slide show so make sure you have enough room for the show on your disk.

To create a quick file:

1. Choose **S**lide, **P**lay Slide Show. The Play Slide Show dialog box appears.
2. Choose Create **Q**uick File. Presentations displays a message dialog box stating it will play the show to create the file. Choose OK.
3. When Presentations is finished showing the presentation, it displays a message dialog box stating it is done. Choose OK.
4. Choose **P**lay in the Play Slide Show dialog box to play the show. Click the mouse to speed the show along.

Troubleshooting

I made a change in one of the slides and now the slide show seems slower.

If you saved the slide show as a quick file and then made a change to the show, you must create a quick file again to speed up the display.

I am saving a copy of the slide show to a floppy disk but I am worried the show is too large to fit on one disk.

You can usually fit one slide show onto a high density 3 1/2" or 5 1/4" floppy disk; however, if your show file is larger and fills up the disk, Presentations prompts you to insert a second disk.

From Here...

You now know how to create, edit, print, and show a presentation. You also can use other applications with WordPerfect Presentations. See the following chapters for more information.

- Chapter 9, "Organizing and Formatting Large Documents," describes how to create and edit an outline in WordPerfect. You learn to enter text, edit text, promote and demote heads, and otherwise work with text in an outline. Consider using the WordPerfect outline as a basis for your Presentations slide show.

- Chapter 14, "Building a Spreadsheet," describes how to create a spreadsheet in Quattro Pro. You learn to select and name blocks, copy and move data, fill blocks, use functions, and so on. Consider using a Quattro Pro spreadsheet in your Presentations slide show.

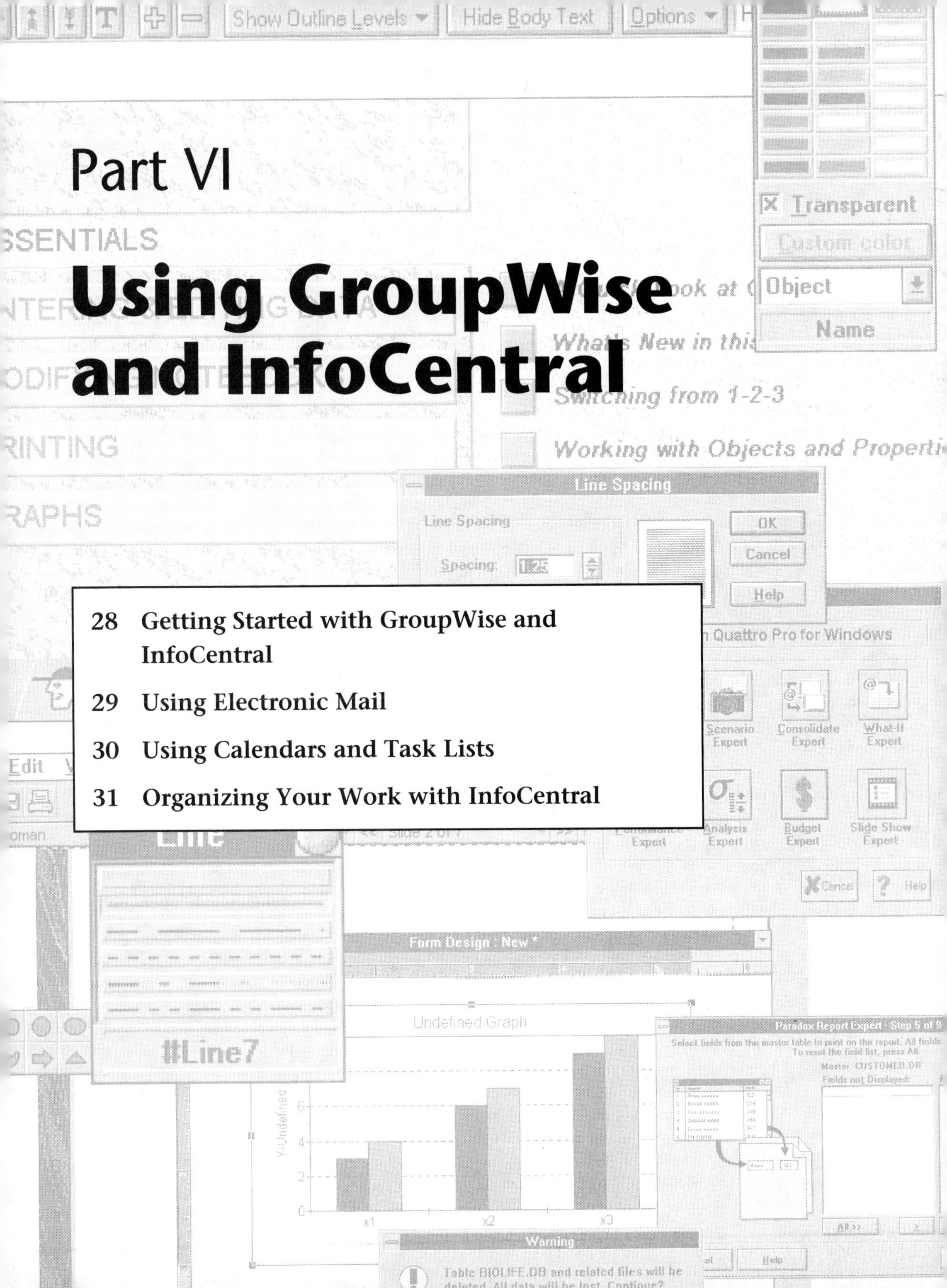

Part VI

Using GroupWise and InfoCentral

Show Outline Levels
Hide Body Text
Options
Transpa
Custom co
Object
Name
ESSENTIALS
ENTERING & EDITING DATA
ODIFYING NOTEBOOKS
PRINTING
GRAPHS
A Quick Look at
What's New in this
Switching from 1-2-3
Working with Objects and Pr
Line Spacing
Line Spacing
Spacing: 1.25
OK
Cancel
Help
Experts in Quattro Pro for Window
Coaches
Quit
WP Presentations - [d:\...\24fig13.shw]
File Edit View Insert Format Slide Graphics Tools Wind
Graph Expert
Scenario Expert
Consolidate Expert
Performance Expert
Analysis Expert
Budget Expert
Line
s New Roman
Slide 2 of 7
Cancel
Form Design : New *
#Line7
Undefined Graph
Paradox Report Expert
Select fields from the master table to print on the re
To reset the field list,
Master: CUSTO
Fields not Disp
Y-Undefined
x1
x2
x3
All >>
Warning
Help
Table BIOLIFE.DB and related files will be
deleted. All data will be lost. Continue?

Chapter 28

Getting Started with GroupWise and InfoCentral

by Bill Bruck

Novell offers two powerful applications that allow you to maintain a personal calendar and keep a to-do list. Whether you choose to use GroupWise or InfoCentral for these functions is up to you. You can even synchronize the data in the two applications whenever you desire.

GroupWise offers extensive messaging capabilities; InfoCentral also offers extensive capabilities to maintain information bases. You'll learn more about these features in this chapter, and then you'll learn how to use each application throughout Part VI.

In this introductory chapter on e-mail, you learn to

- Identify GroupWise's functions and features
- Understand the basic terminology and structure of GroupWise
- See how InfoCentral helps you organize your work
- Understand the concept of information bases

Introducing GroupWise

Novell GroupWise 4.1 is the most powerful e-mail package you can buy. It integrates electronic mail, personal calendaring, group scheduling, and task management. GroupWise may change the way you work, and move you from paper to an electronic orientation.

> **Note**
>
> Novell GroupWise 4.1 is an upgrade to WordPerfect Office 4.0. The product name was changed from Office to GroupWise to alleviate the confusion caused so that the term "Office" could be used for the PerfectOffice suite. The manufacturer's name was changed when WordPerfect Corporation was purchased by Novell.

With GroupWise comes both simplicity and power. GroupWise is easy to use; even beginners can start sending and receiving electronic mail within five minutes of first starting the program. GroupWise's powerful features include folders and filters to organize your work, rules to automatically respond to messages, and auto-dates to schedule ongoing activities.

What You Can Do with GroupWise

From the main GroupWise window, shown in figure 28.1, you can access the main GroupWise functions to:

- Send electronic mail messages
- Send phone messages
- Set personal appointments and make requests for group meetings
- Create personal tasks and assign tasks to others
- View your calendar
- Access your In Box to read messages you receive
- Access your Out Box to see the status of messages you send
- Throw unwanted items in the trash

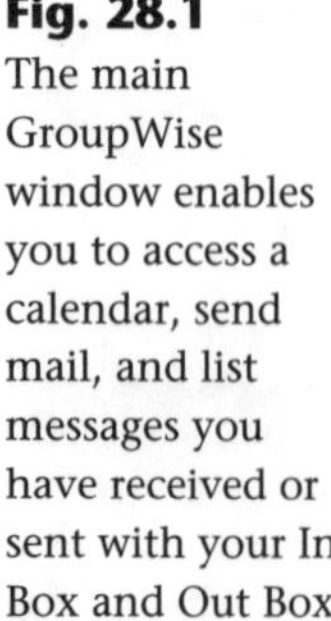
Fig. 28.1
The main GroupWise window enables you to access a calendar, send mail, and list messages you have received or sent with your In Box and Out Box.

Sending Electronic Mail Messages

You send e-mail messages from Mail To: views such as the one pictured in figure 28.2. These views enable you to access an address book to choose participants; attach files from WordPerfect, Quattro Pro, and other applications; attach sound annotations; and set a variety of delivery options.

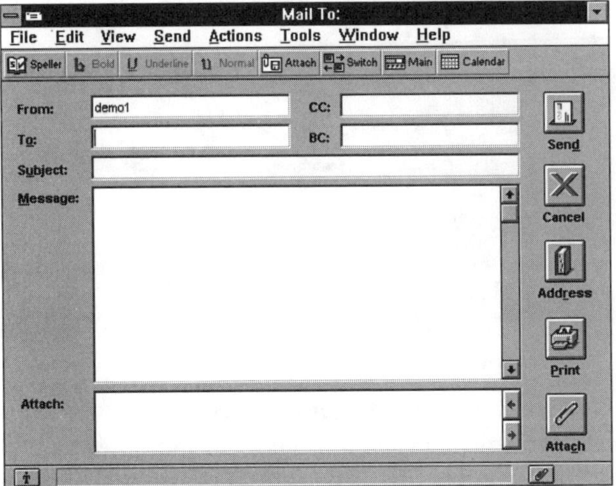

Fig 28.2
You can attach files or sound annotations to a mail message, and use an address book to choose multiple recipients.

Tip
In GroupWise, a *view* is a type of dialog box that cannot be resized.

> **Note**
>
> You may see a little musical note icon at the bottom right of the dialog box. This indicates that you have a sound card installed, and can attach sound annotations.
>
> Neither of these views has boxes for attachments, carbon copies, or blind copies. You can include attachments in either view by clicking the paper clip button, and you can specify carbon or blind copy recipients by selecting the Address Book, as described in the text that follows.

Sending Phone Messages

Phone messages work just like e-mail messages. The Phone To: dialog box resembles the Mail To: dialog box, and offers the same functionality, as seen in figure 28.3.

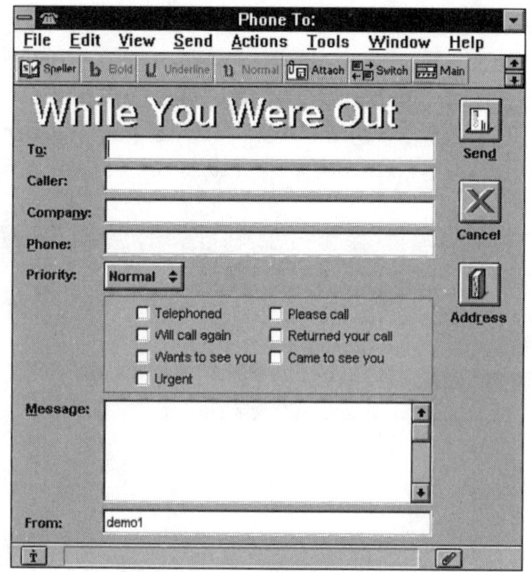

Fig. 28.3
Phone messages resemble their pink paper counterparts, and work the same way as other mail messages.

Setting Personal and Group Appointments

GroupWise integrates e-mail and scheduling to an unprecedented degree. You see that the Appointment To: dialog box shown in figure 28.4 looks just like the others, with the addition of fields for place, date, and time. An auto-date feature makes scheduling repetitive appointments a snap, while the busy search allows you to search through others calendars to find free times for your meeting.

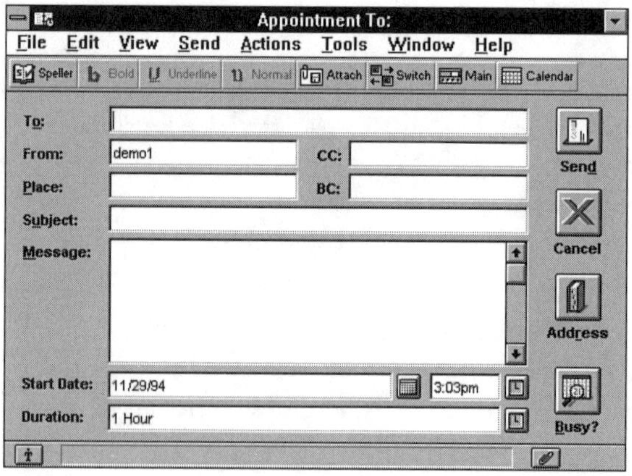

Fig. 28.4
You can create appointment requests that will appear on the calendar of any other GroupWise user, and even conduct busy searches to find free times.

Creating Tasks

You create a personal to-do list with a Personal Task dialog box (not shown). The Task To: dialog box (see fig. 28.5) merely adds the To:, CC:, and BC: fields to allow you to assign the task to others. You can even send notes to recipients on a specified day. Each type of item (mail, phone message, appointment, note, and task) uses the same mail transport system, and operates the same way. This makes it easy to use GroupWise to the fullest to integrate your office features.

Fig. 28.5
The ability to assign tasks to others and track when they are done makes GroupWise a true GroupWare product.

Viewing Your Calendar

GroupWise offers over a dozen calendar views to display your appointments, tasks, and notes. The Day Calendar is one of the most popular (see fig. 28.6). In addition to seeing your calendar and to-do list, you can respond to meeting requests and task assignments, and mark tasks as completed from this view.

Accessing Your In Box and Out Box

Your In Box allows you to read and respond to mail, scheduling requests, and task assignments that you receive. Your Out Box allows you to see the status of all items you send, including when they are delivered, opened, accepted, and deleted. As you can see in figure 28.7, you can even organize your items in folders that you define to suit your work style.

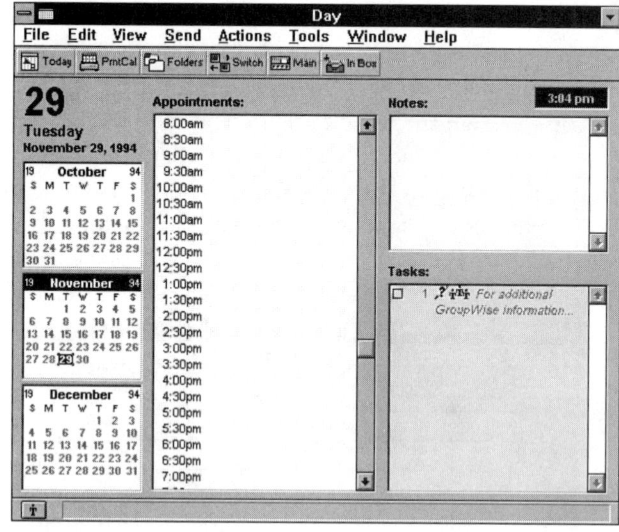

Fig. 28.6
The Day Calendar shows your appointments, tasks, and notes. It is one of many calendars that GroupWise provides.

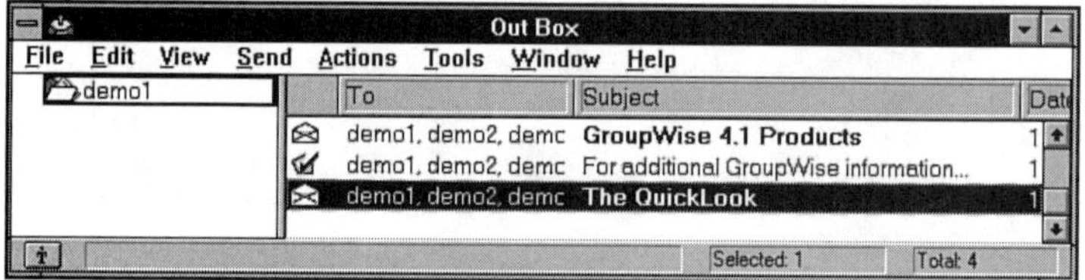

Fig. 28.7
Double-clicking an item in your Out Box enables you to see when that item was delivered, opened, accepted/declined, completed, or deleted.

Understanding How GroupWise Works

Novell describes GroupWise as a "store-and-forward message system." This means that GroupWise is a group of programs that uses directories on a file server to store items sent by a user to other users on the system.

To gain an initial understanding of GroupWise's system architecture, it's worthwhile to examine GroupWise's system components, addressing structure, and system software.

System Components

GroupWise sends *items* to and from *objects* on the system. An *object* is any addressable entity defined within the system that can send or receive messages. In practice, there are four types of objects: users (individuals with user IDs), resources (like conference rooms or overhead projectors), groups (distribution lists of users or resources), or nicknames by which users can be referred.

Items are messages that are sent and stored in the system. These can be electronic mail messages, scheduling requests, task assignments, or notices; and can also include personal calendar items, tasks, and notes.

Items are stored in post offices. *Post offices* are shared directories on a file server where users' items are stored. Each user must belong to a post office.

Just as all users belong to a post office, each post office belongs to a domain. *Domains* are administrative hubs through which post offices are configured and directories are synchronized. Even a small office installation with only one post office must have a domain, because domains are the smallest unit that can be administered separately.

In a GroupWise system with more than one post office, messages are passed from post office to post office via a message server. The *message server* can be thought of as a stand-alone computer that is used to deliver mail between post offices. In fact, a more formal way to define a domain is as a group of post offices directly serviced by a single message server. In large systems, it is common to have multiple domains, each with its own message server and group of post offices.

It is possible to have multiple domain systems arranged in a variety of configurations. All of them are invisible to the end-user, who merely addresses messages to other users anywhere on the system. You can even have systems that include both GroupWise 4.1 and Office 4.0 and Office 3.1; or a GroupWise system that is connected to "foreign" mail systems, like cc:Mail or MCI Mail.

When GroupWise communicates with foreign mail systems, sends your messages out as faxes, or connects to GroupWise Remote via a modem, it uses a gateway. A *gateway* is a piece of software purchased separately from the basic GroupWise system that translates messages from GroupWise to other systems. Gateways are fairly invisible to the end-user, with one exception: To send mail to users on foreign mail may require the use of special addresses, depending on the gateway and the type of mail system involved. Your system administrator will give you necessary instructions if you're using a gateway.

Addressing Structure

Speaking of addresses, you might be interested to know how yours is specified! GroupWise 4.1 uses an absolute addressing system which guarantees that every user on the system has a unique name, so that messages always go to only the correct person.

Your absolute GroupWise address consists of these parts: *domain.po.userID*. This uniquely identifies each object within the GroupWise system. User IDs must be unique within a post office. You can't have two people with the same ID in the same post office, although you could have two JSMITHs on different post offices. Similarly, post office names must be unique within a domain, and domain names must be unique within the system. This ensures that even if multiple users have the same name in different post offices, or post offices with the same name in different domains, mail will always get to where it's being sent.

For most purposes, you won't be too concerned with absolute addressing, because you'll usually pick your users from a list using simple nicknames, or use groups for your common distribution lists. But it's useful to understand conceptually what's going on behind the scenes.

System Software

The admin/server packs contain the programs used to create your mail system. The client software consists of programs that interface with the user to send and receive mail from the post office directories—the end-user software.

Administrative Programs

There are three basic sets of programs that the system administrator uses to install, run, and maintain the GroupWise system:

- *Setup programs*. There are two programs that are used to install the client software for each user—one for DOS (SETUPOF.EXE) and one for Windows (SETUPWIN.EXE). In some installations, the system administrator requests that individual users run these programs the first time they use GroupWise.

- *Administration programs*. There are several programs that are used by GroupWise to route and transfer messages. Most are initiated by GroupWise when you send a message. They run invisibly, in the background. The main administration program that is manually run by the system administrator is AD.EXE—called "Admin." This program enables the administrator to create new domains, post offices, and users; and to run maintenance checks on the GroupWise system.

- *The View Editor program*. This program ships with GroupWise's Windows client. It is used to create customized calendar views, and views for sending various types of items within the Windows client. Depending on the organization, its use might be open to everyone or restricted by the system administrator.

Note

Novell cannot ship a complete mail system with PerfectOffice, complete with administration software. However, Novell wants users to be able to use GroupWise, both to see how its messages work, and to be able to use it for maintaining calendars and to-do lists. Thus, they have created a QuickLook edition. This edition allows you to set up a "mock" post office that has one user—you. You can send messages to yourself, though no one else. You can also maintain your calendar and to-do list.

PerfectOffice also comes with a license for one end-user GroupWise user. Thus, if you belong to an organization that uses GroupWise as its electronic mail system, you'll be able to install GroupWise from the network and have a license to use it.

What Is InfoCentral?

Novell describes InfoCentral as "the innovative personal information manager that is *the perfect way to organize people, places, and things*." In Chapter 31 you'll learn more about how to use InfoCentral, but it's helpful here to find out how information bases are structured and what InfoCentral's features are.

Information Bases

An information base (called an *iBase* for short) is like a super-database. It stores information on objects in a much more flexible manner, and also stores information on the connections between objects.

A traditional database is composed of records and fields. Mary Smith's record, for example, may have fields that include her first name, last name, and phone number. An iBase, by contrast, is composed of objects and object information. Each object ("record") belongs to an object category, and the object information ("fields") for each category may be very different. For example, if Mary is a person (object category), then we may have her first name, last name, home phone number, and birthday. If she is an organization (Mary Smith Cosmetics), we may have the organization name, main phone number, and directions to get there.

However, the additional flexibility offered by using objects and object categories rather than structured records is only one difference between an iBase and a database. The main difference comes when we create relationships between objects.

In a traditional relational database, two databases—sometimes referred to as tables—exist, each with one common field. A relationship is then created between the two, using this common field as an identifier. A common example is an invoicing system. To prevent a data entry person from having to retype a customer's address every time an invoice is sent, each invoice refers to a customer ID. This customer ID then relates the invoice table to a customer address table. While useful in some applications, this type of relationship is very limited, and doesn't parallel the *webs* of multiple relationships that actually characterize real-life objects.

In an InfoCentral iBase, you can think of a *connection* as a type of object. There are connection categories and connection information. For instance, there is a user-definable list of connections between people objects and organization objects. These connections might include employee, student, member, president, and so on. Different connections exist between people, for example, husband-wife, aunt-nephew, or supervisor-employee.

These connections can contain information. This is the hardest concept for a traditional database user to grasp, but some simple examples may bring it to light. A person's home phone number is information about him as a person; so is his birthday and home address. An organization's address, main phone number, and type of business is information about it as an organization. Information about the person's connection to the business, in an iBase, is contained in the connection between them. For instance, a person's direct line at work, his title, and when he was hired is all connection information. It is only relevant to the person as he is associated with the organization.

So, with phone numbers, we can see how object information and connection information work. A person's home phone is part of his object information. An organization's main line, fax line, and toll-free line is part of its object information. A person's direct line, cellular line, and pager number (assuming these are related to the business) are part of the connection information between the person and the organization. To help you visualize this, object information about a person, organization, and connection information are shown in figures 28.8, 28.9, and 28.10, respectively.

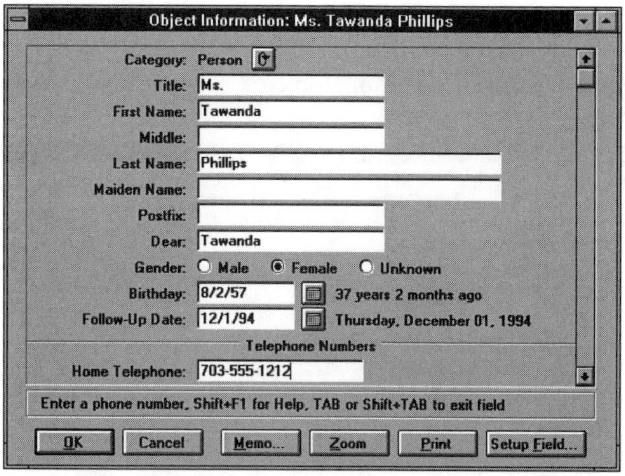

Fig. 28.8
iBases enable you to maintain personal information about people.

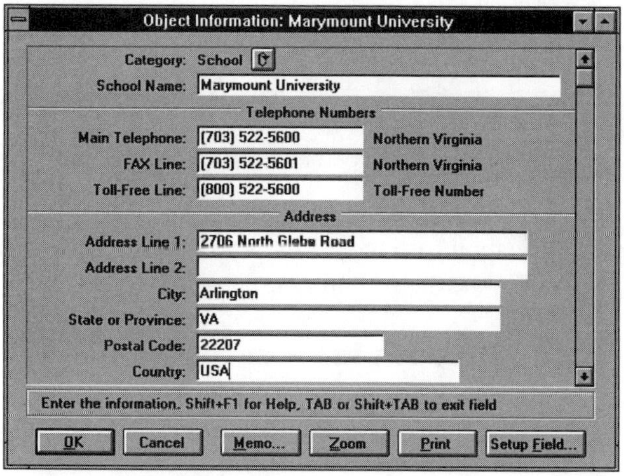

Fig. 28.9
iBases also maintain different information about organizations.

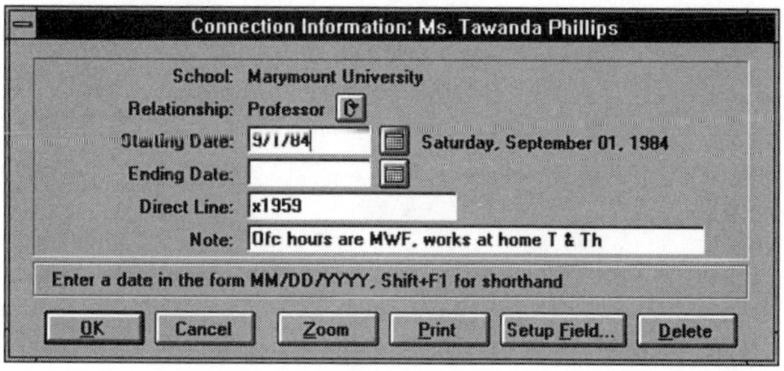

Fig. 28.10
iBases also enable you to maintain information that pertains to the connection between the person and the organization.

InfoCentral becomes very powerful when we add one more concept: Any object can be connected to any and/or every other object in the iBase. We thus see a web of connections among objects, as is pictured in figure 28.11.

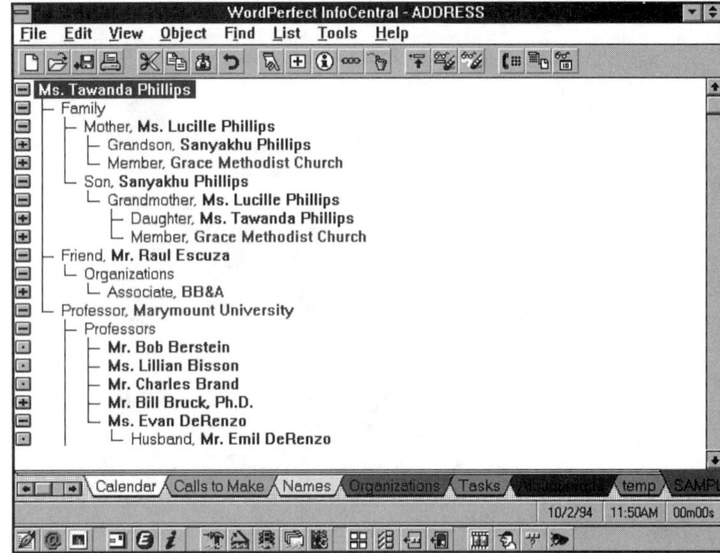

Fig. 28.11
iBases track the complex web of relationships that exist among different objects in the iBase.

Finally, a true information base should allow you to customize every data element within it. As you will see, InfoCentral excels in this.

What You Can Do with InfoCentral

InfoCentral allows you to maintain information bases, calendars, and task lists. It is geared towards being a central point from which all your work can be organized. Its features include the ability to:

- Create lists of objects and connections, so that the manner in which every object in the iBase is connected to every other can be seen
- Easily modify information maintained on objects and connections
- Maintain a calendar with recurring events, connected to other objects in your iBase
- Keep a to-do list of tasks connected to other objects in your iBase
- Associate data files on your disk with iBase objects such as people, clients, or projects

- Launch applications such as WordPerfect or Quattro Pro to create files that are related to iBase objects, and transfer information from those objects (such as names and addresses) into the files being created
- Perform file management functions
- Print information on objects, address books, and mailing labels

From Here...

In this chapter, you learned what GroupWise and InfoCentral are. You were introduced to their features and functions, and you learned the basic terminology and structure of GroupWise. Other chapters that build on what you've learned include:

- Chapter 29, "Using Electronic Mail," discusses how to send and receive electronic mail, set options for your mail messages, and pick recipients from the address list.
- Chapter 30, "Using Calendars and Task Lists," shows you how to use calendars to schedule personal appointments and group meetings. You'll also learn how to use task lists to help you organize your day, and you'll see how easy it is to find free times in others' calendars.
- Chapter 31, "Organizing Your Work with InfoCentral," shows you how to create a personal or company address book so you can save information on clients, staff, or inventories. You'll also learn how to maintain a calendar or task list for personal appointments.
- Chapter 35, "Transferring Data Between Applications," explains how PerfectOffice allows you to transfer information between GroupWise and InfoCentral, and between InfoCentral and other PerfectOffice applications.

Chapter 29

Using Electronic Mail

by Bill Bruck

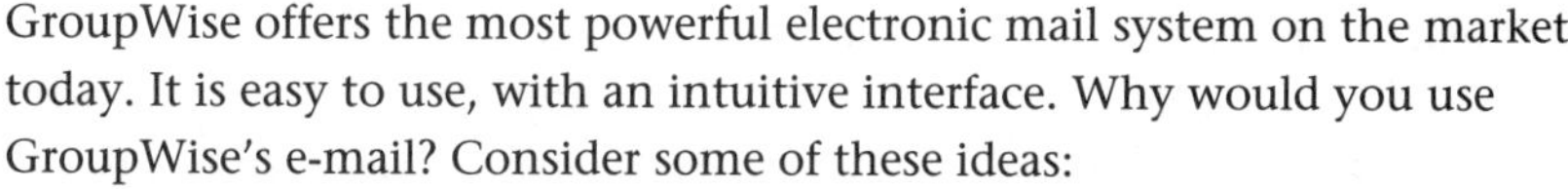

GroupWise offers the most powerful electronic mail system on the market today. It is easy to use, with an intuitive interface. Why would you use GroupWise's e-mail? Consider some of these ideas:

- Get rid of pink "While you were out" slips. Instead, have secretaries or receptionists send *phone messages* to recipients. In addition to saving time and paper, you can pick up phone messages on the road or at home by using Remote GroupWise.

- Set a policy: *All* interoffice memos will be communicated electronically. You'll save trees, reproduction time, and expense.

- Although you want to avoid "junk e-mail," you can post items of general interest to specific groups or everyone on a daily or weekly basis. Some examples include travel schedules of senior officers or summaries of news items affecting your organization.

- Make face-to-face meetings more effective by "matching the medium to the message." For instance, match mail committee reports to meeting participants rather than reading them aloud in staff meetings. Attach supplementary materials to agendas you distribute electronically in advance. Consider which discussions are better held face-to-face, and which ones you can give more thought and time to if you hold them electronically. Remember, electronic discussions give people time to consider their positions and a chance to express them. No more "democracy of the loudest."

As you can see, electronic mail isn't just for passing information on the latest office football pool. It can transform the way your organization does business and, if used wisely, can have an immediate impact on both productivity and efficiency.

In this introductory chapter on e-mail, you learn to

- Use your In and Out Box
- Send a mail message or phone message
- Respond to a mail notification
- Read mail messages addressed to you
- Respond to or forward these messages
- Save and print your mail messages

As you will see in later chapters, GroupWise's e-mail is the transport system to carry you into the electronic office. Not only can you send messages and pass files electronically, this same transport system integrates your group scheduling and task management. It even enables you to use electronic forms.

Using Your In and Out Boxes

Before learning the keystrokes to send mail, it's important that you understand a few ideas related to the way GroupWise handles your mail. GroupWise uses electronic In and Out Boxes to put your mail in, just as you do at your desk. Your In Box holds your incoming items. Your Out Box holds a copy of items you have sent to someone else, along with information that enables you to track these outgoing items.

In the Main window, the In and Out Box icons even look like their physical counterparts. In fact, when you receive a message or request, an envelope appears in your In Box, as shown in figure 29.1.

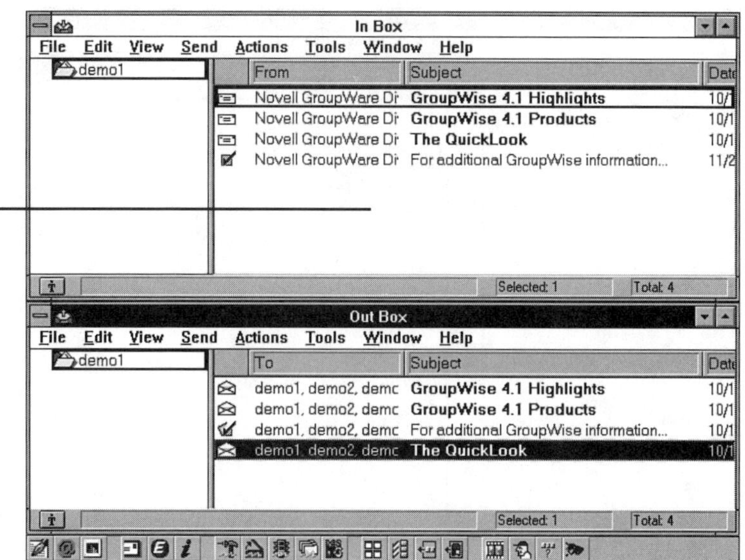

Fig. 29.1
In Box and Out Box enable you to see new incoming items, track the status of outgoing items, and store items in folders.

The In Box

Your In Box is used to manage incoming items—to read, delete, and view information about them. You can tell a lot about items listed in the In Box from symbols or icons that appear before them (see fig. 29.2). Note that the In Box is divided into two sections. On the left, you see a list of folders in which you can store your items. On the right, you see a list of the items in the currently selected folder.

To access your In Box, double-click the In Box icon in the Main window or choose **W**indow, **I**n Box from the menu.

Tip
You also can access the In Box by pressing Alt+Shift+I from the Main window.

You can tell the item type and status from the item type icon to the left of each item:

- *Unopened mail message.* The closed envelope indicates an unopened mail message.

- *Opened mail message.* The opened envelope indicates a mail message you have opened (read).

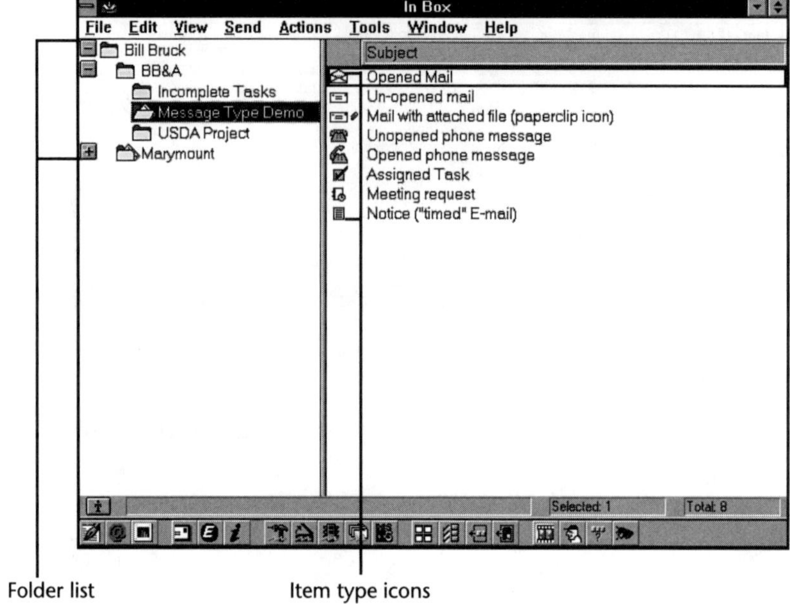

Fig. 29.2 Icons in the In Box (Windows) show you what type of message you have received, and whether you have opened it.

- *Unopened phone message.* The telephone on the cradle indicates a phone message you haven't opened.
- *Opened phone message.* The telephone off the cradle indicates a phone message you have opened.
- *Items in red* are high-priority items.
- *Items in a light blue shading* are low-priority items.

In addition, you might see two other indicators from time to time:

- The paper clip indicates that the message has an attachment—a file that accompanies the message is being copied to your workspace.
- The speaker means that the item has a sound annotation.

The Out Box

Your Out Box provides information on your outgoing items. You can use it for several purposes:

- Tracking the status of items to see whether the item was delivered and whether the recipient opened it

- To resend an item
- To retract an item if recipients haven't opened it
- To keep a record of e-mail you have sent

As with the In Box, the Out Box is divided into two sections. On the left you see a list of folders in which your items can be stored. On the right is a list of the items in the currently selected folder.

To access your Out Box in the Windows client, double-click the Out Box icon, or choose **W**indow, **O**ut Box from the menu. You see an Out Box like the one pictured in figure 29.3.

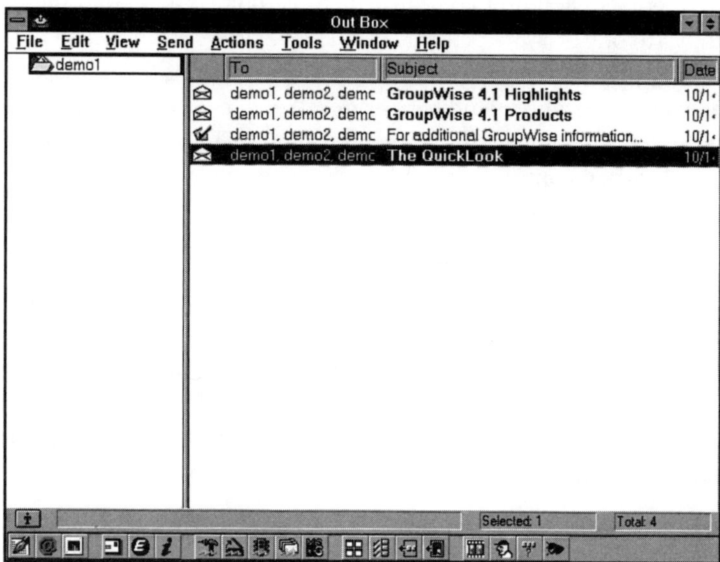

Fig. 29.3
Using the Out Box, you can track when a recipient receives, opens, and deletes your messages.

Troubleshooting

I have so many messages in my In and Out boxes that I can't find anything anymore!

Try getting organized with two tools: First, toss unneeded messages in the Trash by selecting them and pressing the Delete key. Second, sort them to find what you're looking for by choosing **V**iew, S**o**rt.

Sending a Mail Message

Before looking at the steps you use to send a mail message, you need to understand a few terms:

- *Address Book.* Although you can send mail to a person by typing his or her User ID, it is often easier to pick it from a list. This list is called the Address Book. The Address Book offers you the ability to choose users (by name or by User ID), groups (defined by you or by the system administrator), and resources (like conference rooms or overhead projectors, which you use in scheduling meetings).

- *Carbon Copy* and *Blind Copy.* You can send mail to one or more primary recipients. In addition you can send a "carbon copy" and a "blind copy" to one or more persons. People who are "carbon copied" are usually persons who are not directly responsible for the message (or task or event), but who would benefit from knowledge of it. Blind copy recipients only appear in the sender's out box information screen. Primary, carbon copy, and other blind copy recipients of the message are not informed of blind copy recipients.

◀ See "Understanding WordPerfect Basics," p. 86

◀ See "Understanding Quattro Pro," p. 243

- *Attachments.* An attachment is a file you send with your mail message. This file can be a WordPerfect document or a file in another format, such as a Quattro Pro spreadsheet file, a WordPerfect Presentations chart, or an InfoCentral iBase. When a file is attached to a mail message, it is copied from the sender's workspace to a common workspace where you can both access it. When you open the mail message, you can save the attachment to your personal workspace.

To send a message, follow these steps:

1. From the Main window, double-click the Send Mail icon. You see the Mail To window pictured in figure 29.4. Alternatively, you can choose **S**end, New **M**ail from the menu, or press the shortcut key Ctrl+M to access the Mail To window.

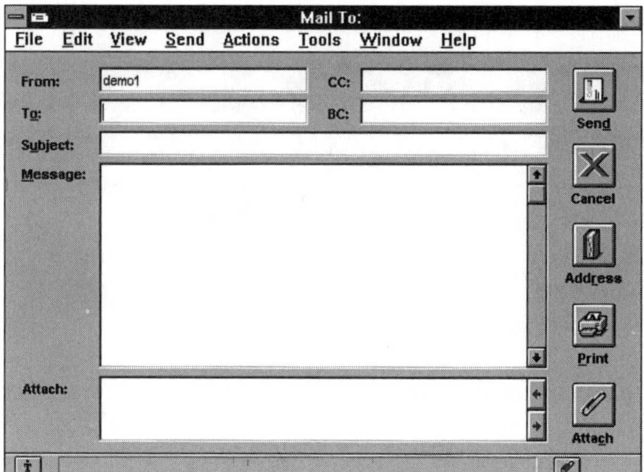

Fig. 29.4
The Mail To: dialog box enables you to specify recipients, type a message, and attach a file to your e-mail.

Note

You can choose from among different Mail To windows that best meet your needs. In addition to the default Mail To window pictured in figure 29.4, there are the Small and the Expanded Mail windows. The Small Mail box displays a smaller window, and the Expanded box displays a larger one for the text of the message itself. (Of course, if the message text is greater than the size of the window, you see scroll bars in any case.)

Neither the Small nor the Expanded Mail view has boxes for attachments, carbon copies, or blind copies. You can include attachments in either view by clicking the Attach button, and you can specify carbon or blind copy recipients by selecting the Address Book as described in the text that follows.

2. Select the recipients in the To, CC, and BC boxes, or use the Address Book/List to select recipients, as described in the next section. You must have at least one recipient in the To box.

3. Specify the subject of the message. The subject is the one-line description visible in your Out Box and the recipients' In Box. The subject is a required field.

Tip
If you do not use the Address Book/List, you must type in recipients' User IDs, not their names.

4. Enter the text of the message.

> **Note**
>
> You can retrieve a WordPerfect or ASCII file into the message by choosing **F**ile, **R**etrieve. You can also retrieve other file types such as Word or Excel. Excel files appear comma delimited. This can be particularly useful if you compose messages on another computer, such as a laptop, and bring them to work on floppy disk.

5. If necessary, you can attach a file to the message, as described later in this chapter.

6. To send the message, click the Send icon. You return to the Main window.

> **Note**
>
> You can mark a message as *Private* if you desire by choosing **A**ctions, Mark Pri**v**ate. This means that anyone who is acting as your proxy will *not* be able to read the message.

Using the Address Book

You can type User IDs of the message recipients if you know them. Many times, however, it's easier to pick them from a list. You can do so with a few keystrokes or mouse clicks in GroupWise. To use the Address Book, follow these steps:

1. From the Mail To window, click the Address button. You see the Address Book window (see fig. 29.5).

2. Highlight the name of the first recipient. You can either use the scroll bars or type the first few characters to quickly bring you to the desired name.

3. With the name highlighted, click the arrow under the recipient type box you want to choose. The person's name appears in the desired list box.

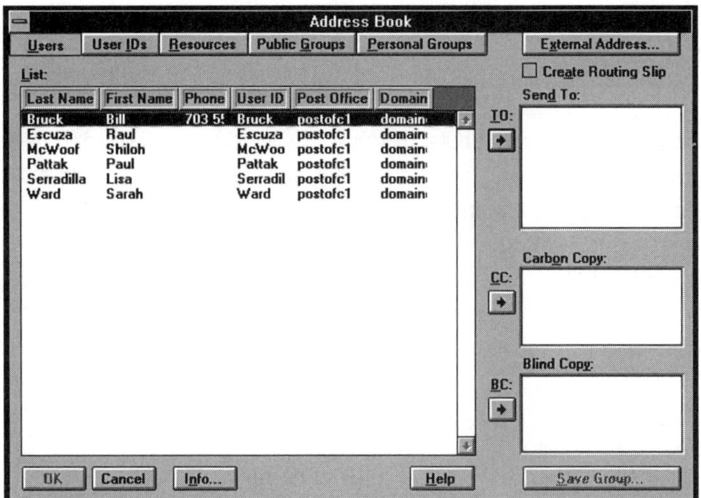

Fig. 29.5
You can double-click a name to quickly move it to the Send To window, or drag-and-drop a name between windows.

Note

A shortcut for choosing a person is to drag his name to the recipient box in which you want him. You can drag a person from one list box to any other in the Address Book. As you click and drag on the name, you see a little icon of a human figure. Alternatively, double-click the name to include that person in the Send To box.

If you're not using a mouse, you can highlight a name and then press Alt+T to move it to the **T**o box; Alt+C for the **C**C box; or Alt+B for the **B**C box.

To remove a person from a recipient list, double-click his name in the recipient list box. The name is deleted. If you are using the keyboard, press Tab until you're in the proper recipient list box, then highlight the name and press the Del key.

4. Continue this process for any other recipients. When you have completed your recipient selection, click OK.

The Address Book offers several options:

- *Users* and *User IDs*. Show the same list of users; the former sorts them by last name and the latter sorts them by User ID.
- *Resources*. Shows you a list of any resources that have been defined on the system, such as conference rooms, equipment, and so on, that can be "checked out" or scheduled. Resources are often used when scheduling appointments and events.

- *Public Groups* and *Personal Groups*. Enables you to send mail to a selected group of people, such as a work group, division, or classification (for example, district managers) to whom you frequently send mail.
- *External Address*. Enables you to enter the address of a recipient on a foreign mail system that can be accessed through your GroupWise system. For instance, some organizations have purchased gateways allowing users to send mail to persons through the Internet, on CompuServe, or via MCI Mail. Sending mail to persons who are on non-GroupWise mail systems requires special addressing procedures. Your system administrator can give you information on the systems accessible through GroupWise and how to use External Address to specify recipients' addresses.
- *Create Routing Slip*. Enables you to send a mail message to several recipients in turn.

Setting Mail Options

Mail options can be set by you or by the system administrator. The system administrator can set your default mail options, or even make some mail options unavailable to you. You can set options for a specific mail message, depending on their availability. To set options for a message, follow these steps:

1. Enter the Send Mail screen, using the procedure listed above.
2. To access the Mail/Phone options dialog box, choose **S**end, Send **O**ptions.

   You see the dialog box for setting options shown in figure 29.6.

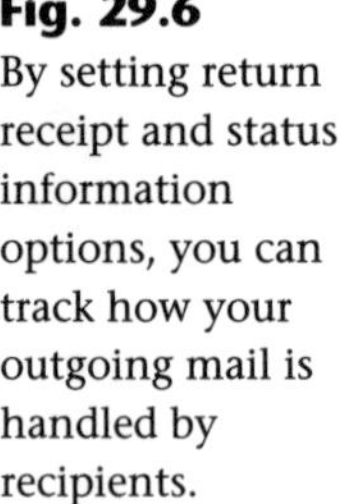

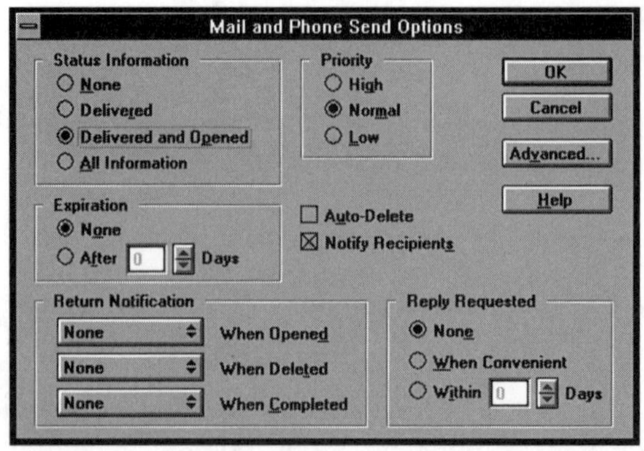

Fig. 29.6
By setting return receipt and status information options, you can track how your outgoing mail is handled by recipients.

Note

Consider putting Send **O**ptions on the Button Bar (**V**iew, Button Bar **P**references, **E**dit). You are much more likely to use options for mail items if you can access the options with one mouse click.

3. Choose options as described in the text that follows.
4. Choose OK to return to the Send Mail screen.

Mail options include the following:

- *Status Information*. This option enables you to specify the amount of information you want to receive about the mail you send. Options include None (you see no status information when you look at information on the message in your Out Box); Delivered (you see the time and date when the message was delivered to each recipient's Post Office); Delivered and Opened (you see when the message was delivered, and when each recipient opened it); All Information (you see when the message was delivered, opened, deleted and, for appointments and tasks, when it was accepted and/or completed).

Caution

Each notification that you request generates another message that the GroupWise system needs to process. Thus, if you want to be notified when the message is delivered and opened, GroupWise generates three mail messages rather than one: the original message, the delivery notification, and the notification that the message was opened. This option can effectively create two to five times as much network traffic than if you set return notification "off."

The network administrator can limit your choices for return notification. Often, if the system is experiencing slowdown because of the amount of network traffic, the administrator might do so.

- *Priority*. You can specify that a mail message is low, medium, or high priority. Mail priority makes a difference in several ways. Users can set their Notify program to tell them about only medium- and/or high-priority items. Recipients also might have created rules based on message priority. If you are using a gateway to a foreign mail system, it may be set to operate only at specific intervals *unless* a high-priority message is being sent. And, of course, the priority determines how the message appears in the recipient's In Box.

- *Expiration.* You might want to indicate that your message should automatically expire after a certain number of days. Then, if the message has not been opened within this time frame, it is removed from the recipient's In Box automatically. This feature is particularly useful for messages dealing with time-sensitive events. Keeping recipients' In Boxes free of messages that are not relevant unless they are read before a certain time is a courtesy to your recipients.

- *Return Notification.* You can ask to be notified when the message is opened, deleted, or completed. You may request notification via the pop-up Notify box and/or a return mail message. This option is particularly helpful when you are assigning tasks or when your message is important.

- *Reply Requested.* If receiving a response is important to you, you can indicate it here. The two options are When Convenient and Within xx Days. When you choose this option, included in each of your recipient's messages is the fact that you want a reply when convenient or within the number of days specified. The fact that a reply has been requested is also indicated by the icon the recipient will see in their In Box.

- *Auto-Delete.* This option moves the item from your Out Box into your trash after all recipients have deleted the item and discarded it from their trash. If one or more recipients do not delete the item or do not clean out their trash periodically, the item is not deleted from your Out Box.

- *Notify Recipients.* This option enables you to specify whether recipients should be notified via the Notify program when they receive your mail. In any case, recipients must be running Notify to be notified of your incoming mail.

In addition, choose Ad**v**anced to access the options (see fig. 29.7).

- *Insert in Out Box.* When you select this option, mail you send is inserted in your Out Box. Many users prefer to keep this box selected so that they can track outgoing mail from their Out Box.

- *Conceal Subject.* If you choose this option, the subject of the message does not appear either in the recipient's notification box or in the list of received messages in the recipient's In Box. This option can be helpful when a recipient works in an area where passersby might be able to see a pop-up notification.

- *Deliver Item After xx Days.* You can specify a number of days to delay delivery. This option delays the delivery of the message until the requisite number of days have passed or the specific date has been reached. This option can be useful when you want to tell a group of recipients about an event in the future but want to remind them two or three days in advance rather than right now.
- *Security.* This option includes a notice stating the security classification in the message.

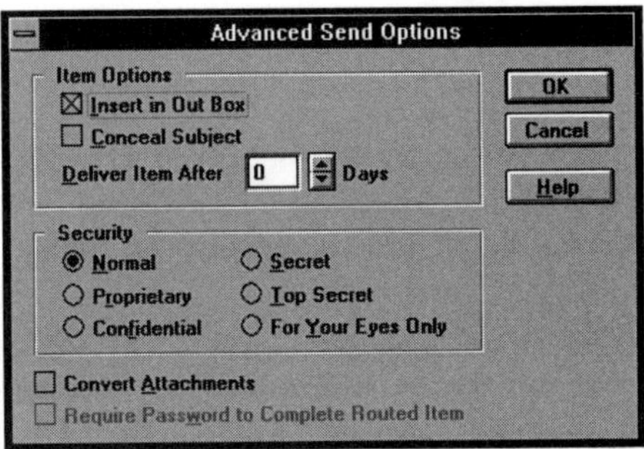

Fig. 29.7
You can set a security mark on messages; however, this does not encrypt or protect the message to any greater extent than normal messages.

Caution

The Security option may be misleading because it merely prints the classification. It does not encrypt the message, stop proxies from reading it, or take any steps to ensure the message's security.

- *Convert Attachments.* This option converts messages and attachments that are being sent through a gateway to a foreign mail system.

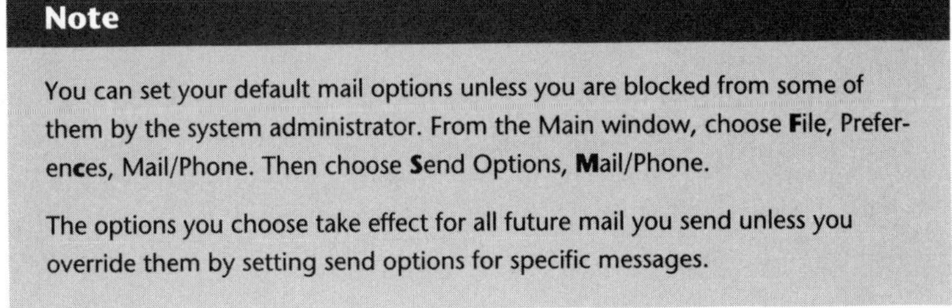

Note

You can set your default mail options unless you are blocked from some of them by the system administrator. From the Main window, choose **F**ile, Preferen**c**es, Mail/Phone. Then choose **S**end Options, **M**ail/Phone.

The options you choose take effect for all future mail you send unless you override them by setting send options for specific messages.

Attaching Files

You'll find that attaching files to messages becomes an integral part of the way you work as you move to an electronic office environment. Some common uses for file attachments include the following:

- Sending drafts for review and approval
- Forwarding copies of spreadsheets so that managers can review budget figures
- Forwarding a chart to a person doing a presentation or briefing
- Sending a manuscript, legal memo, or report to a client

When you start using file attachments effectively, you take your first giant step toward a paper-*lite*, if not a paper-*less*, office. To attach a file, follow these steps:

1. From the Mail To window, click the Attach button. You see the Attachments dialog box (see fig. 29.8). This dialog box lists all the files you're sending with your mail message.

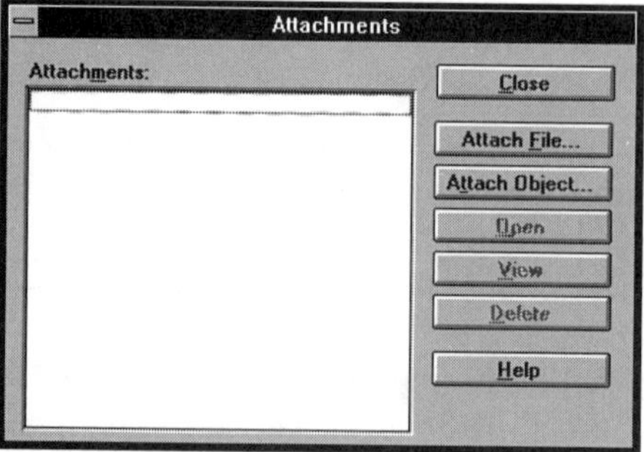

Fig. 29.8
You can attach files as well as OLE objects to a GroupWise message.

◄ See "Saving, Opening, and Closing Files," p. 59

2. Choose Attach **F**ile. You see the Attach File dialog box (see fig. 29.9).
3. Select the proper directory by using the Directory list box; then highlight the desired file in the Files list box. If you want to attach several sequential files, you can click the first one, then hold down the Shift key and click the last file. All files are highlighted. You can highlight several nonsequential files by holding down the Ctrl key and clicking them.

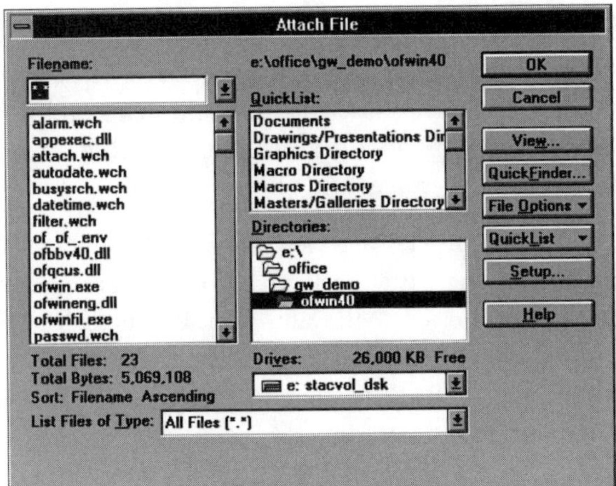

Fig. 29.9
The Attach File dialog box provides all PerfectOffice file management features, including QuickLists and QuickFinder.

4. After you have highlighted the desired file(s), choose OK. You return to the Attachments dialog box, and the file(s) are listed (see fig. 29.10). If you want to add more files, repeat steps 2 and 3.

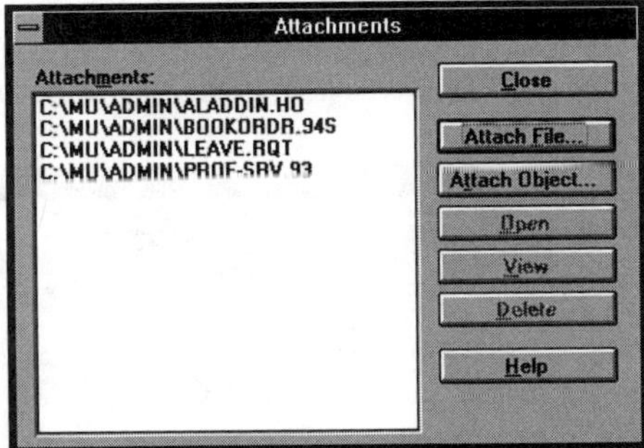

Fig. 29.10
Many files can be attached to the same mail message.

> **Note**
>
> The Add Attachment dialog box is a standard Open File dialog box used throughout PerfectOffice. From within it, you can view, move, or copy files, and create or remove directories. A Quick List feature enables you to have a list of descriptively named directories or file groups you can access quickly. The Find File feature includes the QuickFinder that indexes all the files on your disk so that you can readily find a file with any word or phrase in it—anywhere on your disk.

Sending Phone Messages

Tip
The date and time the phone message was sent appear at the bottom of the phone message form when you open it (but not when you send it).

Phone messages are just another type of mail message. The screens might look a little different and have somewhat different fields on them, but the messaging concepts and steps are the same. The following list includes some differences between mail messages and phone messages:

- Fields added in Phone Message views include Caller, Company, and Phone number, along with check boxes for standard phone message information: Telephoned, Will Call Again, Wants to See You, Please Call, Returned Your Call, Came to See You, and Urgent. In addition, the Windows WYWO (While You Were Out) form enables you to choose the message's priority on-screen.
- Phone forms do not have a field for carbon copies or blind copies. However, these are accessible through the Address Book.

To send a phone message, follow these steps:

1. From the Main window, double-click the Phone Message icon. You see a WYWO (While You Were Out) dialog box (see fig. 29.11). (Alternatively, you can choose **S**end, New **P**hone Message from the menu, or press the shortcut key Ctrl+P to access the WYWO dialog box.)

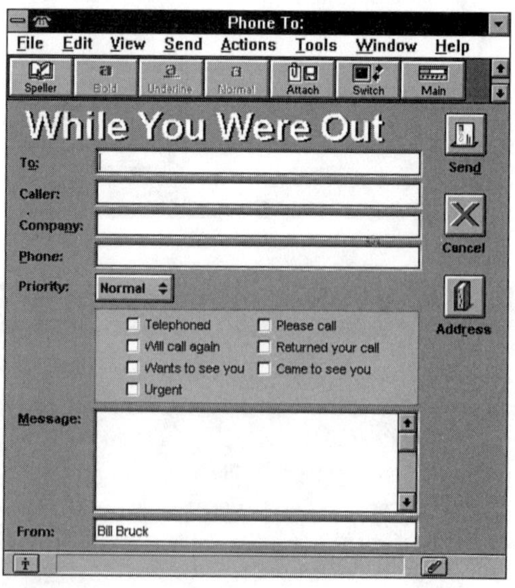

Fig. 29.11
The telephone message is an example of the way that mail forms can be customized.

Tip
The To: field is the only required one.

2. Fill out the To, Caller, Company, and Phone information, and check off any appropriate boxes such as Telephoned, Will Call Again, and so on.

3. Enter the text of the phone message.

4. Send the message by clicking the Send icon. You return to the Main window.

Troubleshooting

When I send a message to Frank Burns, the computer tells me that he isn't on the system, even though I know he is!

Remember that you must address messages to a person's UserID, not to his name. For instance, rather than addressing the message to Frank Burns (his name) you may need to address it to FBURNS (his UserID).

Receiving Mail

Unfortunately, like regular mail, e-mail is seductive. It's enticing to drop whatever you're doing and switch over to your In Box to see what you've received. Thankfully, GroupWise provides tools to help filter and manage your incoming mail. These include the ability to block notification of some or all mail messages, depending on priority, and a rules-based mail-management system that enables you to automatically file or respond to classes of mail messages.

Before getting into these advanced features, however, you need to learn the basics of handling incoming mail. In this section, you learn how to:

- Respond to mail notification
- Read incoming mail
- Save and print mail messages
- Respond to e-mail
- Forward messages to other people
- Read attached files

Receiving Notification of Incoming Mail

The Notify program is a separate GroupWise application that you will usually leave running while you are at your workstation. While it is running, a pop-up window appears when you have incoming mail (or scheduling requests or tasks). This window tells you who sent you the item, the item type (message, scheduling request, phone message, and so on), and the subject of the message. You can then choose to switch to GroupWise and read the incoming item, if you desire.

When PerfectOffice is installed, Notify may automatically open when you enter Windows. If this is not the case, load Notify by double-clicking the Notify icon.

The notification window is pictured in figure 29.12. When you see this window pop up, you can clear one or all notifications, or you can choose **R**ead to switch to GroupWise to read your message.

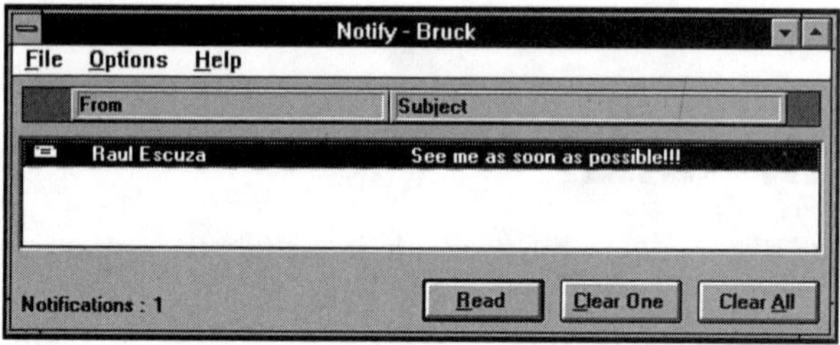

Fig. 29.12 Choose Read to jump directly to GroupWise to open your mail.

Tip You also can copy the Notify icon to the Startup group to ensure that Notify will always be running when you enter Windows.

Troubleshooting

Sometimes I get a notification of a mail message that I've already read! What's going wrong?

Nothing, really—this is the way the Notify program works. By analogy, a registered mail package arrives at the post office, and the postal carrier is given a notice telling you to come to the post office (the Notify program). You happen to go to the post office for other business, and pick up the registered letter. That afternoon, the carrier will still bring your notice to your door, even though you already got the package. There is a similar timing issue that occasionally occurs with the Notify program because it only polls the system every so often for new messages.

Reading Your Mail

Your In Box shows you the messages you have received. From the In Box, you can choose the messages you want to read.

Note

The Shelf on the Main window shows an icon for unopened items. Clicking on this icon shows you only the unread items in your In Box. This is an example of the use of a *filter*. In this case, it is the In Box filtered to show items that are not opened or not accepted.

To select the messages you want to read from the In Box, follow these steps:

1. Access the In Box by double-clicking the In Box icon from the Main window. You might want to maximize the In Box window, because the default size only shows two or three items. Remember that an unopened envelope indicates an unread item.

2. Double-click the first item you want to read, or highlight the item and press Enter. You see a Mail window (see fig. 29.13).

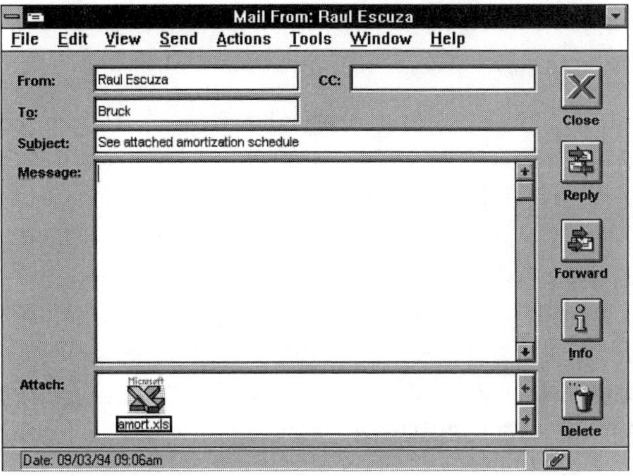

Fig. 29.13 Double-click an attachment icon to quickly view it.

3. Read the message. If you want to save it, print it, respond to it, forward it, or read attached files, follow the instructions outlined in the next sections.

4. When you finish reading the message, you have the following options:

- *Delete.* You can delete the message by clicking the Trash icon. The next message in the In Box appears on your screen, and the deleted message is removed from your In Box.

> **Note**
>
> You can double-click the Trash icon on the Main window to open your Trash. From the Trash window, you can undelete items by selecting them and choosing Edit, Undelete or by dragging the item back to your In Box. You can empty your trash by choosing Edit, Empty Trash.

- *Close.* Closing brings you back to the In Box and marks your message as having been read. In the Windows client, you can close by clicking the Cancel icon (the large X), or by double-clicking the control menu box at the top left corner of the Mail To window. You can also leave the Mail To window open, and switch to the In Box window by clicking in the In Box window.

- *Move.* Move between messages by choosing **A**ctions, Read **N**ext or **P**revious, or press Ctrl+up arrow or Ctrl+down arrow to move between messages.

Saving Mail Messages

When you save a message you have received, you are transferring it, in effect, from a common workspace to your workspace (which you control). The same is true when you save attached files. This is one of the most powerful uses of GroupWise as a transport system—to copy files from one person to another, so that everyone who needs a file can access it. Save messages you receive by following these steps:

1. Follow the steps outlined earlier to access your In Box and read the message you want to save.

2. Choose **F**ile, **S**ave. You see the Save Message Entries dialog box (see fig. 29.14).

3. If more than one item is listed, highlight the item you want to save. For instance, if you receive a message with an attachment, the message and the attachment are separate items you can save.

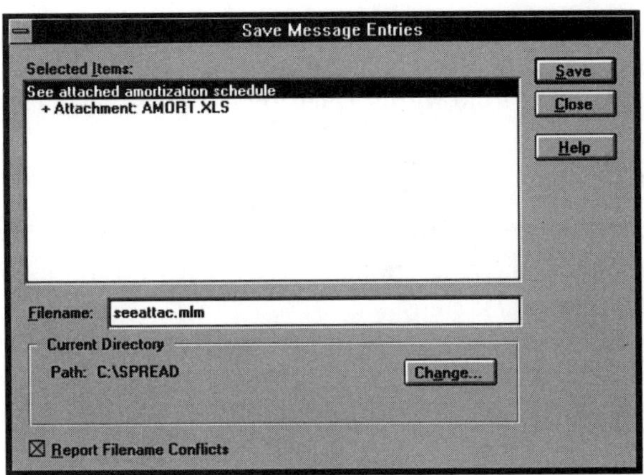

Fig. 29.14
You can quickly save received messages, attachments, or both to your personal workspace.

4. Change the default directory, if necessary, by choosing Ch**a**nge, selecting an alternate directory, then clicking OK. Change the default file name if desired by choosing **F**ilename, then typing a different file name.

◄ See "Using Directory Dialog Boxes," p. 63

5. Choose OK. The selected entry is saved in the directory with the name you specified.

Tip
You can change the default directory for saved files from the Main window by choosing **F**ile, Preferen**c**es, **L**ocation of files, **S**ave Directory.

Printing Mail Messages

GroupWise prints items in three ways: through the GroupWise program itself, through an associated application (like WordPerfect), or through a Fax/Print gateway—a program, purchased separately, that enables you to send faxes through GroupWise and any printer to be used for printing. To print a message, do the following:

1. Have the message to be printed in the active window.

2. Choose **F**ile, **P**rint from the menu of the Mail From dialog box.

◄ See "Printing," p. 146

Note

You can also click the Print button if the Button Bar is visible. If it is not visible, you can show the Button Bar by choosing **V**iew, **B**utton Bar from the menu.

You might also want to change the printer setup options by choosing **F**ile, Print S**e**tup. You can then select a specific printer to use for the print job, as well as a default font.

3. You can choose to print attached files from the application associated with them. This can be helpful, for example, if you want to print Quattro Pro files from within Quattro Pro rather than GroupWise.

Responding to and Forwarding Mail

Two of the most common things you will do with mail (other than file it and delete it) are *respond* to it and *forward* it to someone else. To respond to and forward mail, follow these steps:

1. Have the appropriate message on-screen.

2. Click the Forward or Reply icon.

   If you choose Reply, you can choose to reply to all recipients or just to the sender, and you can also choose to include the sender's original message in the reply.

   If you choose Forward, you are placed in a mail window in which you can enter the new recipient's address (including multiple recipients) and add a message to include with the forwarded e-mail. If you choose Reply, you are again placed in a mail window in which you can enter your reply. In either case, you can also send the message to additional recipients with the Address Book.

Viewing and Opening Attached Files

When you receive mail that has a file attached, you can *view* the file by using GroupWise's built-in viewers, or you can *open* the attachment, thereby launching the application program associated with it.

To *view* an attachment is to look at it without seeing all of its formatting, and without being able to edit it. Files made by spreadsheets, databases, charts, clip art, and word processors are saved in very different formats. A *viewer* is a program that detects what type of format a given file is in and the application that created it and is able to decipher files from a number of different formats to enable you to look at their contents. GroupWise has a viewer that works for many common application programs.

If you want to be able to edit the attachment or see all of its formatting characteristics, you will probably want to use the application program that created it (or another similar program) to actually retrieve or *open* the file in that application. Then you can edit the file, make comments on it, and save the changed version.

GroupWise determines the correct application to run by creating *associations*. GroupWise associates files and applications in two ways—first by extension, and then by file type. For instance, if a file has a QBW extension, you can set GroupWise's preferences to automatically run QuickBooks for Windows. If no extension association is set, GroupWise looks at the file itself, tries to determine the file type, and then runs the appropriate application.

Thus, to take full advantage of GroupWise's attached files, you want to be able to accomplish four tasks:

- View an attached file
- Open attached files
- Define associations when opening attached files (Windows)
- Define permanent associations in Preferences

To view attached files, follow these steps:

1. Access your In Box and select an incoming message with an attached file.
2. Access the View Attachment window (see fig. 29.15) in any of the following ways:
   - Double-click the attachment's icon, if the Attach box is in the mail view you are using.
   - Right-click the attachment to access the QuickMenu, then choose View.
   - Choose **F**ile, Vie**w** Attachment.
   - Click the View Attachment button on the Button Bar.

3. If you see the attachment displayed in the View Attachment window, you can use the scroll bars to see parts of the file that do not appear in the window. GroupWise automatically recognizes many different file types and selects the correct viewer for them.
4. If you do not see the attachment displayed, you see the message Conversion needed to view. Click OK. The file *might* convert, or you might see the message `File conversion failed`. In this case, you have to open the application that created the file (or any other application that can read the file).

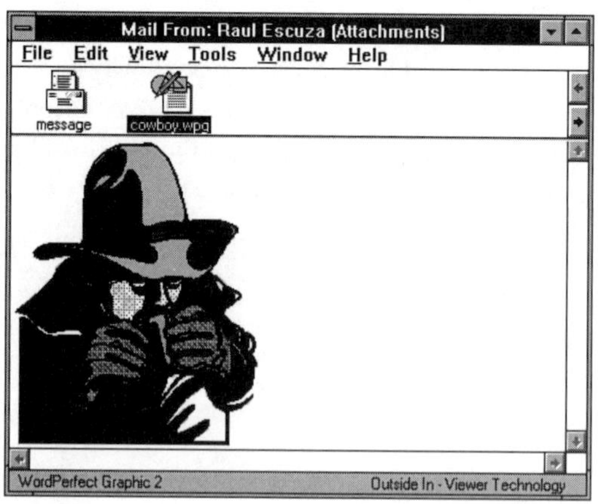

Fig. 29.15
You can view text, graphics, and spreadsheet attachments directly from within GroupWise.

To *open* an attachment in Windows, follow these steps:

1. Access your In Box and select an incoming message that has an attached file.

2. The shortcut you use next depends on whether or not the mail view you are using shows the Attach box. (In either case, you can choose **F**ile, A**t**tachments to access the Attachments dialog box, as shown in figure 29.16.)

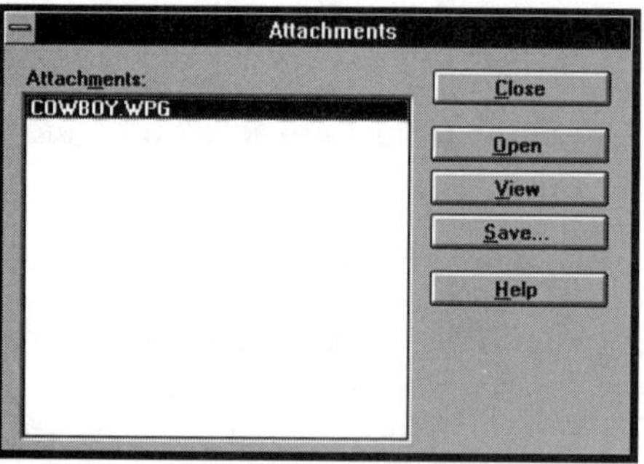

Fig. 29.16
This dialog box enables you to open, view, or save any or all of your attachments.

If the view does display the Attach box, position the mouse pointer on the icon of the attachment to be opened. Right-click to access the QuickMenu, and choose Open.

If it does not open, click the Paperclip icon to access the attachments dialog box, highlight the desired attachment, and choose **O**pen.

3. If you can determine an association for the attached file, you might be asked to confirm that this is the proper application, and then the application runs. You can use this application to examine or edit the attachment. When you are finished, exit the application. You return to the Mail From dialog box.

4. If you can't determine an association for the attached file, you see an Attachment Association (Unknown) dialog box. You are asked what application to run. Provide the path and file name—for example, `C:\OFFICE\PRWIN\PRWIN.EXE` to run WordPerfect Presentations. You also have an opportunity to specify that the association be made permanent when opening or printing this file. The application then runs as in step 3.

To create a permanent file association in Windows, follow these steps:

1. From the Main window, choose **F**ile, Preferen**c**es, Associations. You see the Associations dialog box (see fig. 29.17).

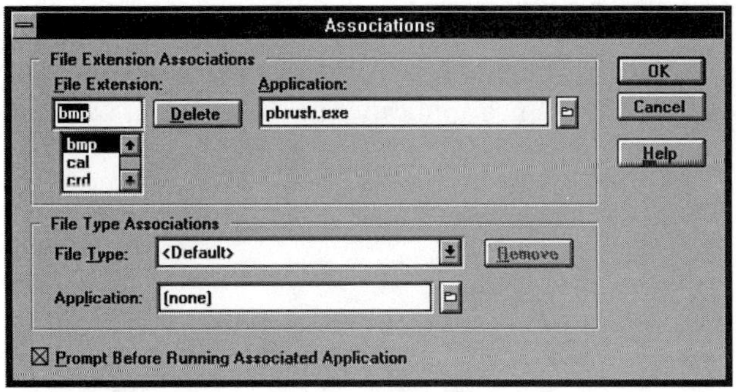

Fig. 29.17
You can specify which application will be used to open attachments that have specific extensions.

2. To set an association by file extension, choose **F**ile Extension and specify the file extension to be associated, such as QBW.

   Then choose **A**pplication and type the path and file name of the application that should be opened when a file with this extension is selected—for example, `C:\QBOOKSW\QBW.EXE`.

3. To set an association by file type, select File Type, and scroll down the list until you find the file type for which you want to create an association, such as Ami Pro 3.1; then choose Application and specify the application to use.

The associated application might not be the one in which the file was created. For instance, you might use both WordPerfect 6.1 and Ami Pro in your organization, but you personally only use WordPerfect. Whenever you receive an attachment written in Ami Pro, you might want to have WordPerfect opened, knowing that the Ami Pro file will automatically be converted.

From Here...

In this chapter, you learned how to send and receive a mail message. Other chapters that build on what you've learned include:

- Chapter 30, "Using Calendars and Task Lists," shows you how to schedule personal appointments and group meetings. See how easy it is to find free times in others' calendars. You'll also learn how to maintain a to-do list to help you organize your day.
- Chapter 31, "Organizing Your Work with InfoCentral," shows you how to create a personal or company address book, and save information on clients, staff, or inventories.
- Chapter 32, "Using QuickTasks," discusses how electronic mail works with other PerfectOffice applications to accomplish common office tasks.

Chapter 30

Using Calendars and Task Lists

by Bill Bruck

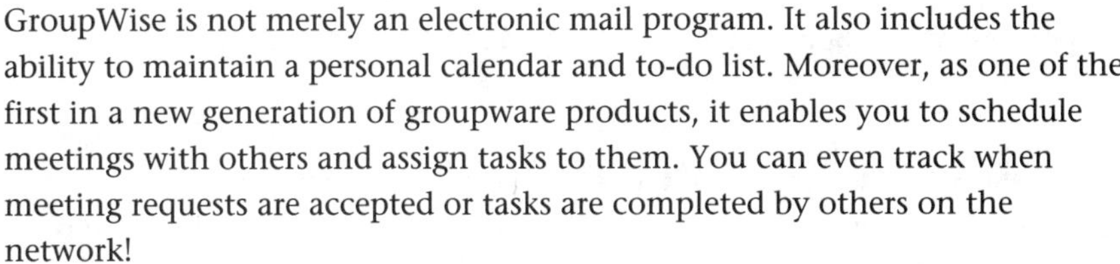

GroupWise is not merely an electronic mail program. It also includes the ability to maintain a personal calendar and to-do list. Moreover, as one of the first in a new generation of groupware products, it enables you to schedule meetings with others and assign tasks to them. You can even track when meeting requests are accepted or tasks are completed by others on the network!

In this chapter, you learn to

- Schedule appointments and meetings
- Maintain a calendar
- Use a to-do list
- Assign tasks to others

Scheduling Appointments and Meetings

At first, keeping your personal calendar electronically may seem to be more trouble than it's worth. As you move into the electronic office environment, however, you start to find many advantages to organizing your work this way:

- You can quickly print the calendar in a number of attractive formats, including the popular day organizer, detailed weekly schedule, or month-at-a-glance. Unlike paper calendars, you can make all three printouts to keep with you, and you can always print a fresh, up-to-date copy without the inevitable scratch-outs.

- You can easily schedule regular, recurring appointments.
- You can include notes to yourself or even attachments to provide background information that you need for an appointment.
- You always have a record of your appointments that you can search electronically—for example, to find out when you met with Ms. Smouthers last month.
- You can easily keep a calendar for another person. This feature of electronic calendaring can be a boon to professionals and executives.

◀ See "Sending a Mail Message," p. 590

The procedures and forms used to schedule appointments and meetings are very similar to the ones you learned for sending an e-mail message. To schedule an appointment or meeting, you need to choose an appropriate Personal Appointment or Appointment To: view, then schedule the appointment or meeting.

Choosing an Appointment View

The message views used to schedule personal appointments and meetings resemble the Mail To: view that you use to send e-mail. You can choose between two views for creating personal appointments, and two views for creating group meeting requests.

To make a personal appointment or group meeting, look at the word in the pop-up list button under the Schedule icon on the main menu. If it says Personal A..., double-clicking the Schedule icon brings up a Personal Appointment view. If it says Meeting, double-clicking the Schedule icon brings up an Appointment To: view (to schedule a meeting with others).

If you want to change the default appointment type, click and hold down the left mouse button on the pop-up list button under the Schedule button. A menu appears while you hold down the mouse button, as shown in figure 30.1. Move the mouse pointer to the view you want and release the button. This not only opens the chosen view, it makes this view the default.

Tip
You can also access the default appointment view by choosing **S**end, New **A**ppointment.

The name of the default appointment view appears in the Main Window under the word Schedule. It may be one of the two personal appointment views or one of the two group appointment views. When you double-click the Schedule button, the default view is displayed. Whether double-clicking the Schedule button brings up a personal appointment or a meeting depends on the default view.

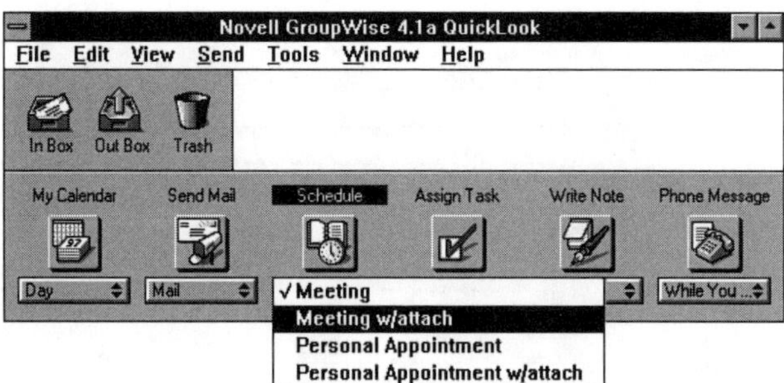

Fig. 30.1
Change the default appointment view by using the pop-up list of schedule views.

While in a Personal Appointment or Appointment To: view, if you want to switch to another view, choose **V**iew, S**w**itch View. The Switch View dialog box shown in figure 30.2 appears. Notice the list of alternative appointment views (both Group and Personal). You can even switch the item type to an e-mail item, a task, or a note. Information you have entered into the view, such as the subject or message, is saved in the new view—unless, of course, the new view has no corresponding field (for example, starting time).

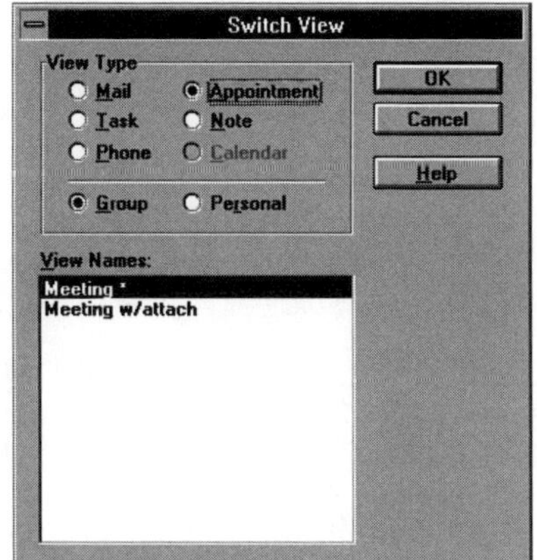

Fig. 30.2
While creating an appointment, you can switch between appointment views or even switch to another type of item entirely.

Scheduling Personal Appointments

To create an appointment that appears only on your personal calendar, follow these steps:

1. From the Main Window, choose a Personal Appointment view as described above. The Personal Appointment dialog box appears (see fig. 30.3).

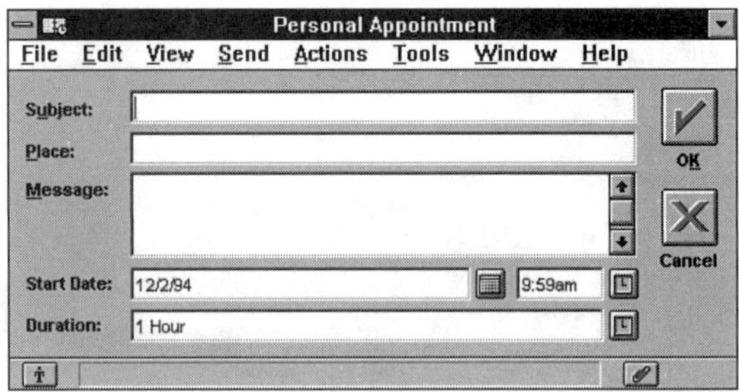

Fig. 30.3
The Personal Appointment dialog box shows options to be filled in when creating a personal appointment.

2. Fill in personal appointment options:

   *Subject and **M**essage.* These items are identical to information entered in mail messages. ***P**lace* is optional and for your information.

   Start Date. Either enter a date or click the Calendar icon to display the Set Date dialog box pictured in figure 30.4.

Fig. 30.4
You can easily choose an appointment's date by clicking it, or choose another month by using the arrow buttons.

   Click the desired date, or choose another month using the arrow buttons. Choose OK to return to the Personal Appointment dialog box.

   Start Time and *Duration.* You can type in these entries, or click either of the Clock icons to display the Time Input dialog box shown in figure 30.5.

   Click and drag the green arrow on the left to set an appointment's starting time, and the red arrow on the right to set the ending time. The starting time, ending time, and appointment duration appear. Verify the times by reviewing the start and end time postings on the right side of the box. Choose OK to return to the Personal Appointment dialog box.

3. Choose OK to record the personal appointment you have set in your calendar.

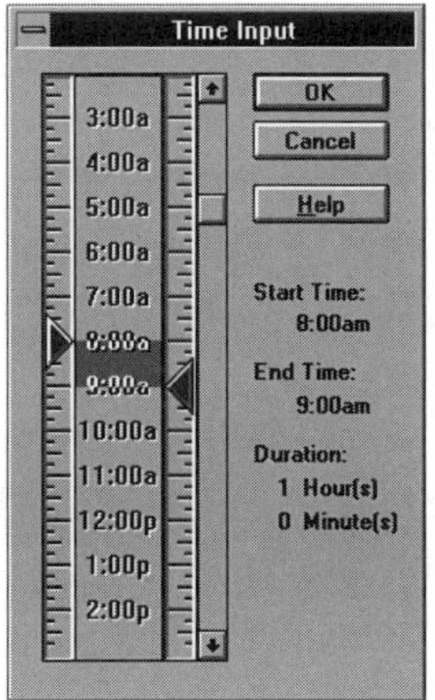

Fig. 30.5
Drag the left and right arrows to set an appointment's beginning and ending time.

Scheduling Meetings

Scheduling a meeting is like scheduling a personal appointment, with two additions. First, you specify the people who attend the meeting. Second, you can optionally search all your calendars for common free times.

Tip
Remember to include yourself as a meeting participant. You will not automatically be included in a meeting unless you so specify.

Follow these steps to schedule a meeting:

1. Choose an Appointment To: view as described previously. The Appointment To: dialog box appears (see fig. 30.6).

2. Fill in appointment options as you did for personal appointments in the preceding section. Additionally, complete the T**o**, **C**C, and **B**C options as you would for an e-mail message. Remember that you can use public or personal groups or the Add**r**ess Book for specifying recipients of the scheduling request.

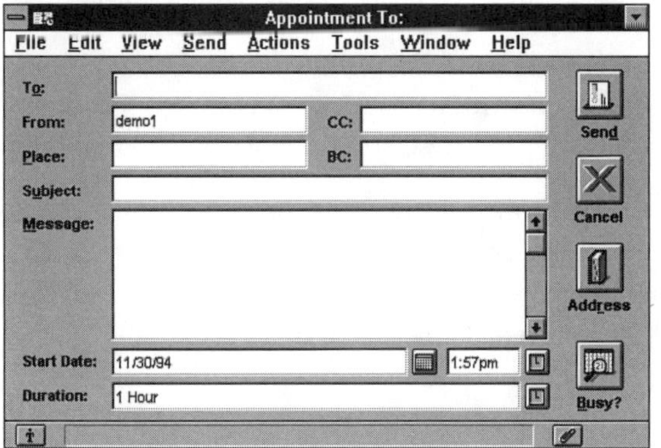

Fig. 30.6
The Appointment To: dialog box shows options to be filled in when scheduling a group of people.

3. Check busy times. Choose **S**end, Busy Searc**h**; or click the Busy icon. The Busy Search Settings dialog box appears (see fig. 30.7).

Fig. 30.7
You can search for a block of free time on specific days of the week, certain times of the day, and within a certain date range.

◄ See "Using the Address Book," p. 592

4. Fill in options for the search:

   Days to Search. Specify which days of the week should be searched. By default, weekends are skipped.

   Range and Time to Search. Enter the earliest date for the meeting, the possible range of times, and how many days to search.

   *Sho***w** *Appointment Information.* Shows what conflicting appointments participants have. You must have read access to each participant's calendar to see their appointment information.

Tip
Default options appearing in the Busy Search Settings dialog box can be changed. From the Main Window, choose **F**ile, Preferen**c**es, Busy Search.

5. Choose OK. The Choose Appointment Time dialog box appears (see fig. 30.8).

6. The dialog box has Time Selection boxes. The upper box, in the line labeled Combined Time, represents the appointment time you can choose. The lower box, in the area for participant information, shows you which participants are free and which are busy.

   Use the horizontal scroll bars or the left and right arrows to scroll across the days and times you have selected. Note any white areas on the Combined Time bar. These are the times when all participants are free.

7. Move the upper time selection box to a white area large enough to accommodate the box, and choose OK. You return to the Appointment To: dialog box, and the date, starting time and meeting duration you selected is displayed in the dialog box.

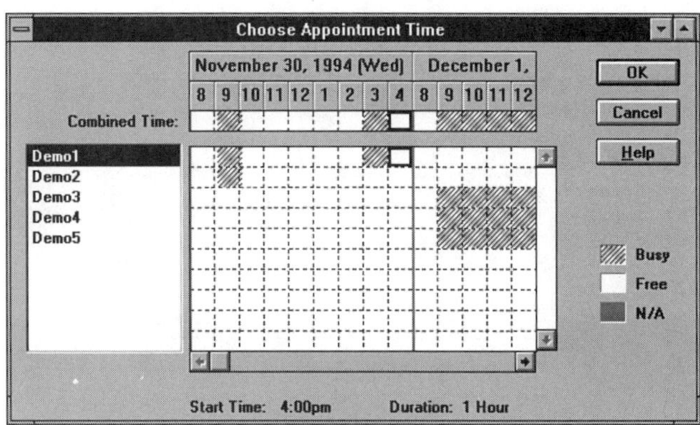

Fig. 30.8
By looking at the top Combined Time line, you can quickly identify free times for meetings.

8. Click the Sen**d** button to send a scheduling request to all participants.

Responding to Scheduling Requests

When someone schedules you for a meeting, the scheduling request appears in your In Box as an unopened item. When you open the item, you can choose to accept the request, decline it (with an optional comment), or delegate it to someone else. Your decision (and comment) is recorded as part of item information in the sender's Out Box.

> **Note**
>
> Unopened scheduling requests also appear as tentative appointments in your calendar. You can also open and respond to them from the calendar, as discussed below.

To respond to a scheduling request, follow these steps:

1. Access your In Box.
2. Open the scheduling request. Meeting requests appear as appointment books with a little clock in front of them.

3. When you open the scheduling request, you see the sender's request, as shown in figure 30.9.
4. Take one of these actions:

   Close. You return to the In Box. The request remains in the In Box, marked open, but you have not acted on it.

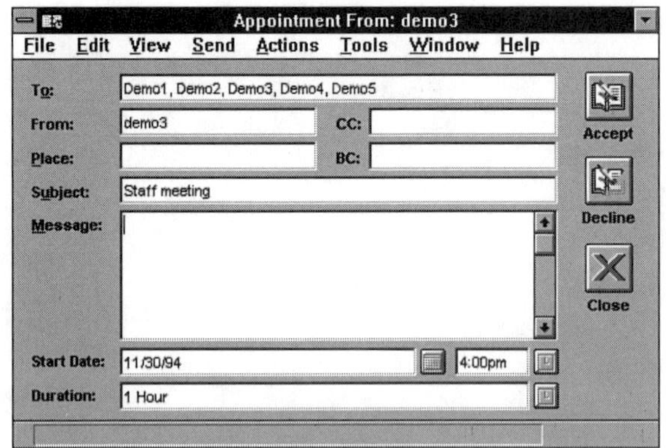

Fig. 30.9
You can accept or decline a received appointment request, or close it and decide later.

Accept. You return to the In Box. The request is removed from your In Box and inserted as an appointment in your calendar.

Decline. You are asked whether you want to include a comment, and then you return to the In Box. The request is moved from the In Box to trash. (You can access your trash if you change your mind until you either empty your trash, or the sender retracts the request.)

Delegate. You can specify a person to delegate this meeting to by choosing **A**ctions, D**e**legate. You see the Delegate dialog box. Specify the person to whom you want to delegate the meeting by typing their User ID or using the Address Book/List. You can also attach a message to the recipient and the sender. The item is removed from your In Box, notification is placed in the sender's Out Box, and a scheduling request is placed in the In Box of the person to whom you are delegating this meeting. This person then has the same options.

Maintaining a Calendar

◀ See "Using Your In and Out Boxes," p. 586

◀ See "Sending a Mail Message," p. 590

In previous chapters, you learned about two types of views that you can access from the Main Window:

- In and Out Boxes that list incoming and outgoing items
- Message views that enable you to create e-mail and meeting requests that are sent to others

This chapter introduces the third major type of view that GroupWise provides: the calendar view. Over a dozen different calendar views are available with GroupWise, and you can add other views as desired.

Calendar views can contain different elements, arranged and sized in different ways. The Day view in figure 30.1, for example, includes a calendar, appointment list, note list, and task list. The Week view in figure 30.10 has no calendar, but does include multiple appointment, note, and task lists. The Week view also has buttons that are missing in the Day view that enable you to move between weeks.

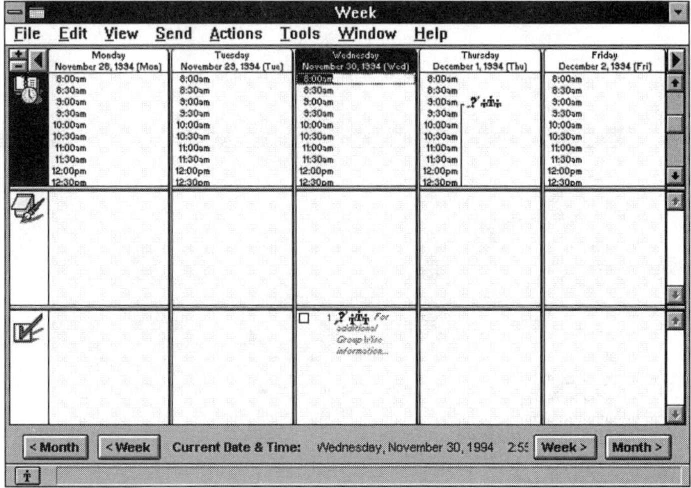

Fig. 30.10
The Week view shows appointments, notes, and tasks for several days at once.

Group appointments that you accept are indicated by a *group* icon. Pending appointment requests are indicated by a question mark to the left of the group icon. These appointments are also in italic.

All calendar views contain some or all of the following elements:

- Monthly calendars
- Daily appointment lists
- Task list boxes
- Note list boxes

Use the calendar to select days and to provide the same information that a paper calendar provides. Use the appointment list to view, create, and edit appointments; respond to scheduling requests; and set alarms.

You see the default calendar view in the Main Window, under the words, My Calendar. When you double-click the My Calendar button, the default view displays. Similarly, you can access the default appointment view from the menu by choosing **W**indow, **C**alendar.

To choose another calendar view from the Main Window, click and hold down the left mouse button on the pop-up list beneath the My Calendar button. A menu appears, as shown in figure 30.11. Move the mouse pointer to the view you want and release the button. This action not only opens the chosen view, it also makes this view the default.

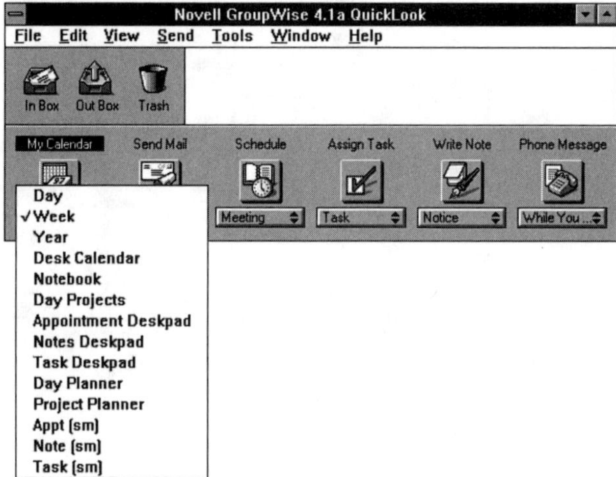

Fig. 30.11
Choose a default calendar view by using the pop-up list of views.

Switch from one calendar view to another by choosing **V**iew, S**w**itch View or by clicking the Switch button on the toolbar. The Switch View dialog box appears (see fig. 30.12).

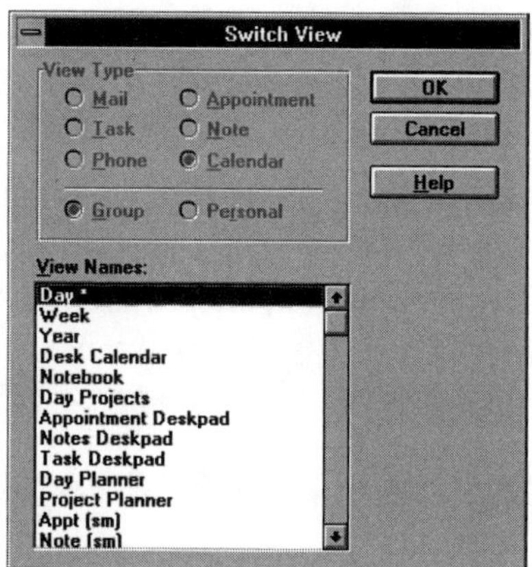

Fig. 30.12
You can switch from one calendar view to another by choosing View, Switch View to access this dialog box from any calendar view.

> **Troubleshooting**
>
> *When I double-click the My Calendar icon in the Main window, I see the wrong calendar. What's wrong?*
>
> When you use the drop-down list under the My Calendar icon to choose a different calendar, you are changing the default calendar view. Use this drop-down list to change the default back to your preferred calendar. In the future, to switch calendars without changing the default, choose **V**iew, S**w**itch View from the calendar.

Tip
Using the toolbar to switch between views doesn't change the default view.

Moving from Date to Date

In order to effectively use your calendar, you'll need to be able to go to specific dates to review and modify your appointment.

To move from date to date, take one of the following actions:

- If a monthly or yearly calendar window is part of the calendar view you are using, click the desired date.

- If Date Change buttons are available in the calendar view, use them to move to the next day, week, month, or year. (The Date Change buttons may have different labels, depending on the view you use, but their use is obvious from the context.)

Tip
You can access a Day calendar view from a Year calendar view by double-clicking the desired day.

Creating and Editing Appointments

You can create new appointments or edit existing ones from any view that shows a daily appointment list.

To create or edit an appointment, double-click a displayed time in the Appointments list. You can also tab to the Appointments list by using the cursor keys to highlight the desired time and press Enter. The Appointment To: dialog box appears (see fig. 30.13). (If the appointment was a personal appointment, you will see a Personal Appointment dialog box instead.)

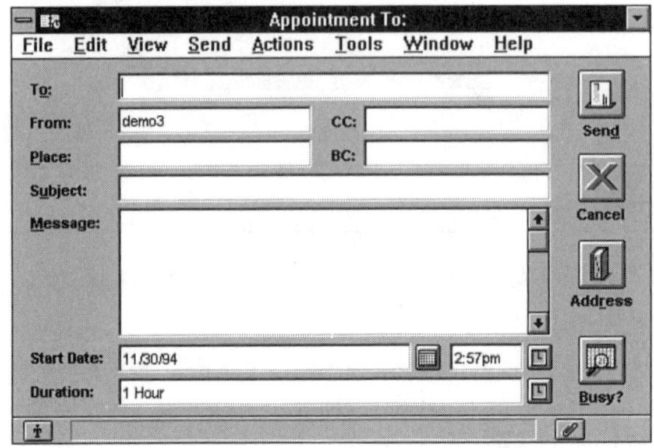

Fig. 30.13 A quick way to make an appointment is to double-click an empty time in an appointment window. An appointment dialog box like this one appears.

Setting Alarms

Tip If you double-click a calendar time to create an appointment and see the wrong appointment view, change the view by clicking the Switch View button or choosing **V**iew, S**w**itch View.

To set alarms from the calendar, select the appointment by highlighting it with the arrows or clicking the appointment with the mouse.

In Windows, choose **A**ctions, **S**et Alarm; or access the QuickMenu with the right mouse button, and then choose Set Alarm. The Set Alarm dialog box appears (see fig. 30.14). Specify the number of hours and minutes prior to the event that you want the alarm to sound and (optionally) any program that should run at this time.

> **Troubleshooting**
>
> *When I try to set an alarm, the program won't accept it. What's wrong?*
>
> You can't set an alarm for an appointment that occurs before the current date and time.

Fig. 30.14
You can set alarms or even schedule an application (such as a backup or communications program) to be run at a specific time with the alarm feature.

Responding to Requests

You can respond to scheduling requests from the calendar by following these steps:

1. Highlight an appointment request in the Appointments list. Pending group appointments show a question mark to their left and are in italics.

2. Double-click the appointment or press Enter. A dialog box similar to figure 30.15 appears.

3. Accept or decline the appointment. An accepted appointment appears in the calendar as do other accepted group appointments. If you decline the appointment, it is removed from the calendar and moved to the trash. In either case, the sender is notified of your action, assuming that notification is enabled.

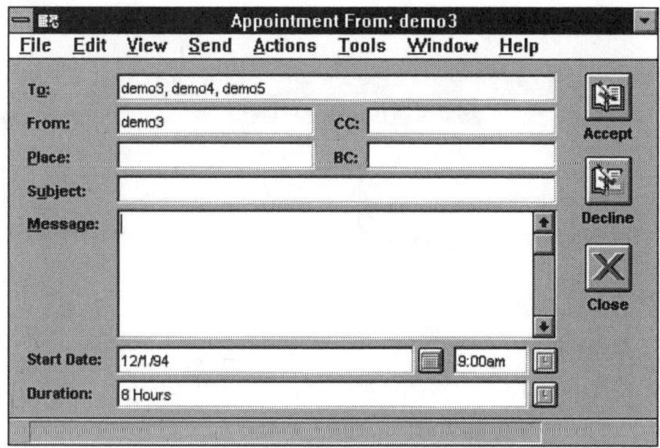

Fig. 30.15
When you double-click an appointment request in your calendar, you see this dialog box that enables you to accept or decline the appointment.

Moving Appointments

You can take advantage of GroupWise's drag-and-drop capabilities to move appointments. You can move an appointment's time in any view that has an appointment list. Just click and drag the desired appointment to the new time, as shown in figure 30.16.

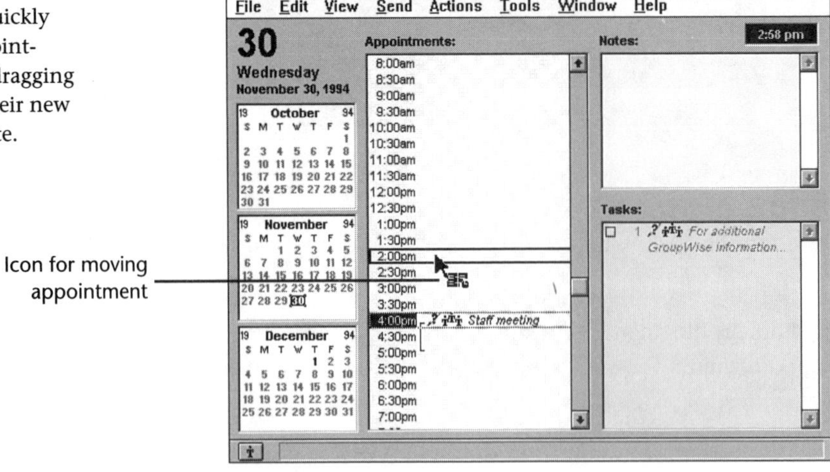

Fig. 30.16
You can quickly move appointments by dragging them to their new time or date.

You can also move an appointment from day to day in Windows if the view has both an Appointments list and a calendar. Drag the appointment from its place in the Appointments list to the calendar, and drop it on the new day.

In this way, you can move personal appointments easily. You cannot move a group appointment, however, that you didn't schedule. If you *did* schedule the group appointment, moving it sends another scheduling request to all recipients, who must accept the changed appointment.

Note

When dragging appointments, you'll see a No symbol in place of the mouse pointer where you cannot drop the appointment, such as in the area between windows.

Printing Your Calendar

GroupWise enables you to rapidly and easily print the calendars you make, in a variety of formats. A Day Organizer printout, for example, is shown in figure 30.17.

To print a calendar, follow these steps:

1. Choose **F**ile, Print Ca**l**endar. The Print Calendar dialog box appears (see fig. 30.18).

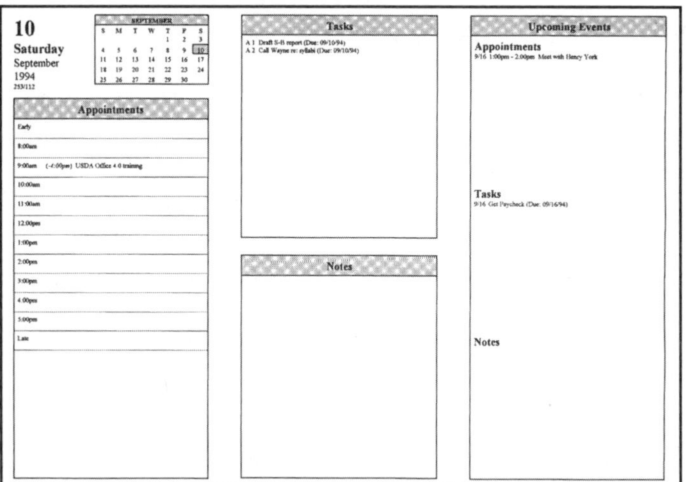

Fig. 30.17
A Day Organizer printout, showing calendar printing capabilities of GroupWise.

2. Choose the calendar type to print. You see the format of the chosen calendar in the dialog box.

3. Choose the starting date and number of days, months, or years you want printed (depending on the type of calendar that you print).

4. Choose the attributes, contents, and paper size, using options provided in the dialog box.

5. Make sure that Windows **P**rinting is selected.

6. Choose OK to print the calendar.

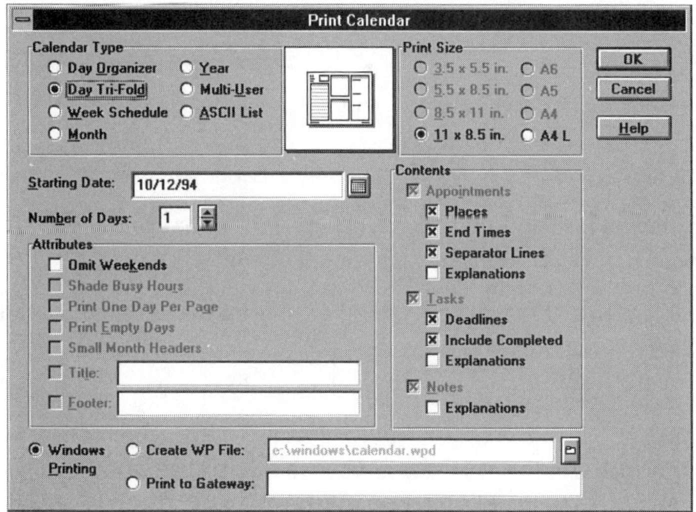

Fig. 30.18
The Print Calendar dialog box, showing options for calendar printing.

Using a To-Do List and Assigning Tasks

GroupWise's task lists offer a host of features that enable you to manage your work and that of the people who work for you:

- Tasks can include messages and attached files, and start/end times.
- Tasks appear on the calendar the day they are scheduled to be started.
- Tasks can be marked as completed; unfinished tasks will carry over to the next day.
- You can assign tasks to other people and track when they have been opened, accepted/declined, completed, and deleted.
- Tasks and notes use the same transport system that e-mail and meetings use, and offer similar options and data-entry procedures.

Creating and Editing Personal Tasks

You can create a task from the Main Window or from a calendar view that shows a task list:

- From the Main Window, check the default task view by looking at the name on the pop-up list under the Assign Task icon. If the default view is Personal Task or Personal Task w/Attach, choose **S**end, New **T**ask, or double-click the Assign Task icon.

  Alternatively, if the default view is Task or Task w/Attach, use the pop-up list under the Assign Task icon to select a personal task view.

- From a calendar view that contains a task list, choose **S**end, New **T**ask, or double-click an empty line in the task list.

Tip
To switch between a personal task and an assigned task, click the Switch Task button or choose **V**iew, **Sw**itch View before you record the task by selecting OK.

In either case, you see a Personal Task dialog box (see fig. 30.19).

Fill in personal task options and then choose OK to record the task and place it in your calendar. Options include the following:

- S**u**bject and **M**essage are identical to information entered in mail messages.
- Use Start Date to indicate the date on which this task should be started. The task appears on the calendar, starting on the date for which it is scheduled. Set the start date as you would the date of a scheduled appointment, by typing the date or using the calendar icon to select a date.

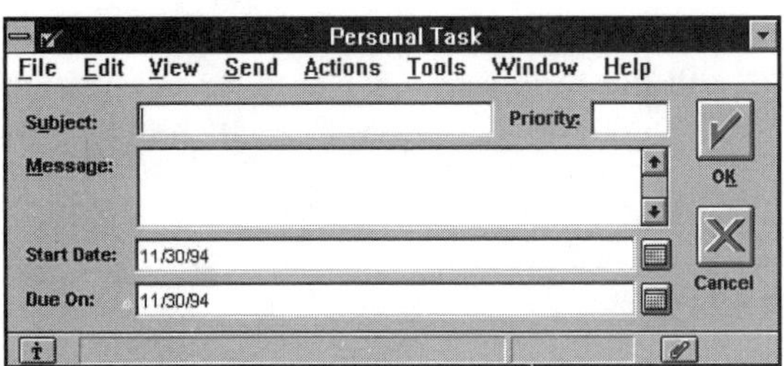

Fig. 30.19
Creating a personal task is like sending mail or setting a personal appointment.

- Use Due On or Due Date to indicate the date the task must be completed. By default, this is the same as the starting date. If a task is carried over in your calendar past its due date, it appears in red, indicating that it is overdue.
- You can assign Priorit**y** with a letter (A, B, C), a number (1, 2, 3), or both (A1, A3, B1). Tasks are sorted by their priority in the task list.
- You can add an attachment to the task the same way you add it to an e-mail message or an appointment.
- You can mark the task as private by choosing **A**ctions, Mark Pri**v**ate.

Assigning a task to another person is almost as easy as creating a personal task. (One might argue that it's even easier, because you don't have to do the task yourself!)

To assign a task, follow these steps:

1. Select a Task view (rather than a Personal Task view) from the pop-up list under the Assign Task icon in the Main window. You see a Task To: dialog box similar to the one in figure 30.20.

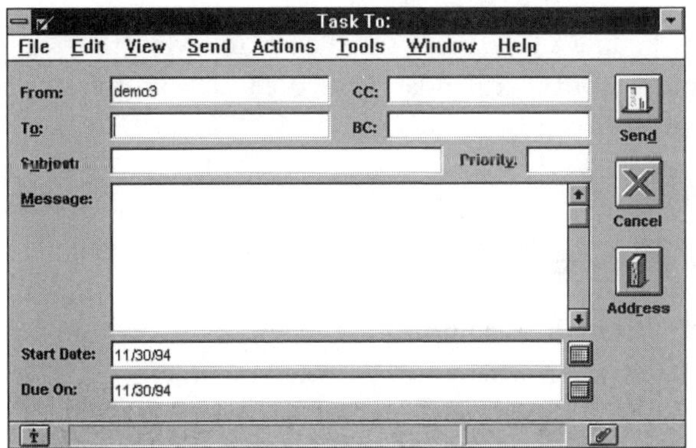

Fig. 30.20
When you assign tasks, you address them just as you would a mail message.

◀ See "Sending a Mail Message," p. 590

2. Fill in task options as you did for personal tasks. Additionally, complete the T**o**, **C**C, and **B**C options as you would for an e-mail message. Remember that you can use public or personal groups, or the Address Book/List.

Using Task Lists

Many of the calendar views contain task lists, including the project views, day planner views, task desk pad, and week view. Some just show today's tasks, and some (like the desk pad and week views) show tasks for future days as well.

You can obtain information about specific tasks by examining the icons in front of them. A group of figures represents a "group task"—one that was assigned to you. If it has a question mark and is in italic, you have not accepted it yet. A task in red is overdue, and one with a check mark has been completed.

You can use the task list to create new tasks, edit tasks, mark them complete, or reschedule them. Each of these options is explained in the text that follows:

Tip
Mark tasks done when you complete them or at the end of the day so they won't be brought forward to the next day. If you mark them done at the beginning of the next day, they appear on any printouts you make of things to do that day.

- To create new tasks from the Windows task list, double-click an empty area in the task list box. You see a task dialog box; fill it in as described previously.
- To edit a task in the task list, double-click it. You see a task dialog box, and can edit the information on the task.
- To mark a task as complete, click the check box to the left of the task. You see a check mark to the left of the task, indicating that it is complete. This task won't be brought forward to the next day.
- To reschedule a task, make sure you're in a view that shows both a task list and a monthly calendar. Drag the task from the task list to the new day on the calendar.

From Here...

In this chapter, you learned how to send and receive a mail message. Other chapters that build on what you've learned include:

- Chapter 31, "Organizing Your Work with InfoCentral," shows you how to create a personal or company address book, and how to save information on clients, staff, or inventories. You also learn an alternative method for keeping a calendar and to-do list.

- Chapter 32, "Using QuickTasks," discusses how electronic mail works with other PerfectOffice applications to accomplish common office tasks.

- Chapter 36, "Customizing Toolbars, DAD Bars, and Menus," teaches you how to edit GroupWise's toolbars and set default preferences.

Chapter 31

Organizing Your Work with InfoCentral

by Bill Bruck

Novell describes InfoCentral as "the innovative personal information manager that is *the perfect way to organize people, places and things.*" More than this, however, InfoCentral enables you to organize your work. It provides tools to organize information, maintain a calendar and task list, and launch applications related to specific subjects.

In this chapter, you learn to

- Identify the basic parts of an Information Base (iBase)
- Use iBases that come with InfoCentral
- Add and edit data in an iBase
- Find information in an iBase
- Modify the structure of an iBase
- Create documents using your iBase
- Maintain a calendar and to-do list with InfoCentral

Introducing Information Bases (iBases)

InfoCentral organizes information in Information Bases (iBases), which store information on both objects (things like people or organizations) and connections between them.

This information is displayed in two different ways. *Outline views*, such as the one shown in figure 31.1, display lists of objects and connections between them in an outline format. *Calendar views*, such as the one shown in figure 31.2, display certain categories of objects: events, tasks, and notes. While these latter types of objects can also be displayed in outline views, calendars enable you to organize yourself by dates.

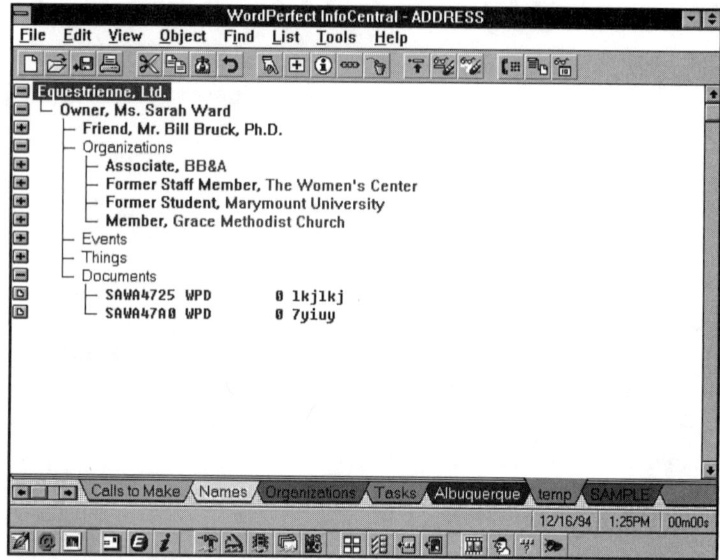

Fig. 31.1
Outline views displays lists of iBase objects and connections between them.

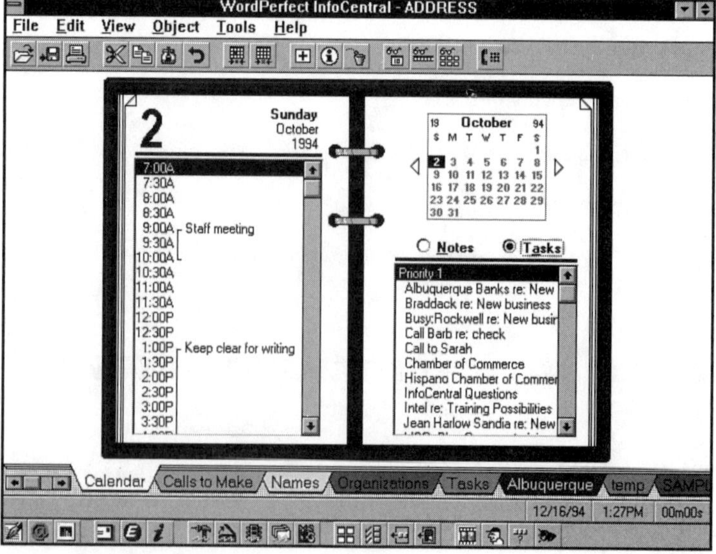

Fig. 31.2
Calendar views show your appointments, tasks, and notes.

> **Note**
>
> The calendar view resembles GroupWise's day calendar, and in fact works in much the same way. These products offer you two alternatives for maintaining calendars and to-do lists. InfoCentral even enables you to import and export calendars and to-do lists to and from GroupWise by choosing **F**ile, **G**roupWise Update, as is explained in the text that follows.

To learn how you can organize your work with InfoCentral, it is first necessary to understand how an iBase works. The remainder of this section will show you the power of this unique way of organizing objects and relationships between them. In the next sections, you will learn to work with the outline view to display your iBase information and maintain customized lists of related objects. You will learn to add objects or relationships, and find out how easy it is to modify the structure of your iBase.

Following this, you will learn two specialized applications for an information base: how to create documents, spreadsheets or graphics that relate to projects, people or other objects in your iBase, and how to maintain a calendar and to-do list with InfoCentral.

For now, let's start with learning what an information base really is.

Information Bases and Databases

Information management theorists teach that there is a difference between data and information. Information is *meaningful* data. Knowing that your company grossed $375,000 in product sales this year is data. Knowing that this is a 25% increase over last year is information. It's data that you can do something with.

There is usually one basic difference between data and information. You know how information relates to other information. A piece of information isn't an isolated fact; it has a context that gives it meaning.

Traditional databases are aptly named. They store data as isolated elements. The only relationships that databases store are the pre-defined relationships that are built into the record/field structure. Thus, they are *data* bases, not *information* bases.

InfoCentral offers a new concept in information management. InfoCentral not only stores *data*, it stores *relationships* between data. Thus, it does not store *databases*, it stores *information bases* (abbreviated as iBases).

What's the difference? Consider one example:

Tawanda Phillips is a pretty typical person. She has a family, a job, and friends. She lives in a web of relationships. Her relationship to Mrs. Phillips is daughter-mother; to Sanyakhu it is mother-son. Her relationship to her superior at work is employee-employer. With her next-door neighbor it is friend-friend. An iBase enables us to capture data on all these people, and in addition to capture Tawanda's relationship with all of them, as can be seen in figure 31.3.

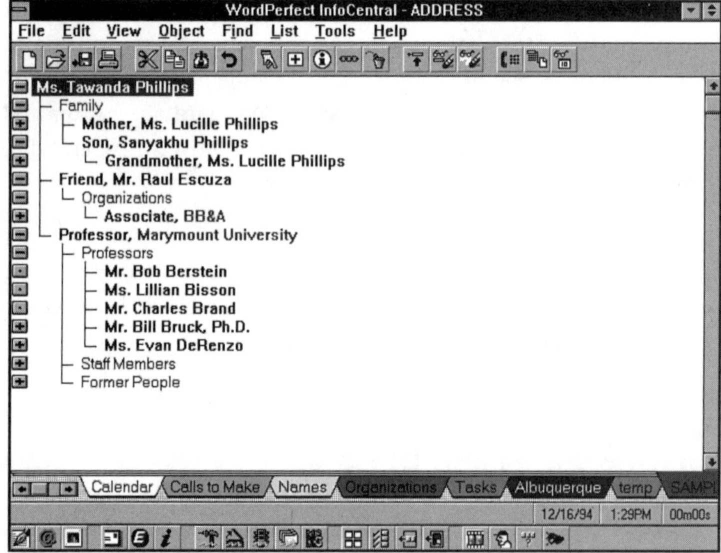

Fig. 31.3
InfoCentral enables you to display not only objects, but all of the connections that one object has with other objects.

Each of these relationships has data that is specific to the relationship. For instance, friend-friend relationships might have a source (college, childhood, former job), and starting date. Employer-employee relationships might have a starting date, ending date, job title, and direct line.

Thus, some data may be stored with a person (home phone number); some with a company (main phone number); and others with the person's relationship to the company (direct line).

As we expand the information we have about a person, we see a widening web of relationships, and we can see the way more and more objects such as people, companies, schools, institutions, restaurants, hotels, and so forth, are related to that person. Moreover, we can start with an event or any other object and similarly expand all other people, organizations, and so forth, that are associated with it until eventually we can see every piece of data in the iBase and how it relates to every other piece of data.

However, objects can be more than physical things like schools or companies. Objects can also be events like phone calls, appointments, or meetings. They can be home products like recipes, or work products like projects or files on your PC.

Thus, the iBase concept can be extended to encompass the relationships between people, the things they do, and the other people involved in these events. Of course, relationships change, and the information you need to store about objects and their relationships change as well. You may find that you should have a "directions" field for Organizations, because you never remember how to get to places. Or you may find that you need two fields for direct phone lines, rather than one. An information base should enable you to customize every data element within it. As you will see, InfoCentral excels in this.

An iBase can thus be used as a simple database. It can also be used to track the entire web of relationships between people, organizations, physical objects, events, and products. Its ability to track relationships makes it effective as a project management tool. Its capacity to store information on files and launch applications makes it an effective document management tool.

Information Base Elements

To understand how an iBase works, it is important to understand the terminology used to describe iBase elements. These include objects, connections, lists, views, and tabs.

Objects

An *object* is a thing or an event about which information is maintained in an iBase, and which can be related to other objects. Examples of objects are Sam Smith, Loyola College, Cincinnati, and 10:00 meeting. Each object belongs to an *object category*. Examples of object categories include people, places, events, telephone calls, tasks, companies, schools, cities, and restaurants. The information maintained about an object is called, appropriately enough, *object information*. The information maintained on an object varies by the object's category. For instance, persons have telephone numbers, whereas cities do not.

Connections

A *connection* is the relationship between two objects. For example, the connection between John Jones and ABC corporation is employee. The connection between John and Mary Jones is husband-wife. Available connections between two objects depend on their object categories. For instance, different connections are available between two people than between two organizations. Connections are user-definable.

InfoCentral recognizes one-way and two-way connections. For instance, husband-wife is a two-way connection. John's connection to Mary is husband; Mary's connection to John is wife. Connections between two persons, two organizations, two things, two events, an organization and a thing, and an organization and an event are all two-way connections. On the other hand, employee is a one-way connection. Connections between persons and organizations and things and events are both one-way.

Tip
There are two types of views in InfoCentral. Outline views list objects and connections. Calendar views display calendars, lists of appointments, and task lists.

Each connection contains information on the connection, called *connection information.* Examples of connection information for students might be start date, graduation date, and dorm phone number.

Lists, Views, and Tabs

InfoCentral displays iBase information in an outline format as shown in figure 31.4. As you can see, some parts of the outline are collapsed so that only the person's name is shown; and some parts are expanded to show other objects and connections to a specified object. These outlines are termed *lists.*

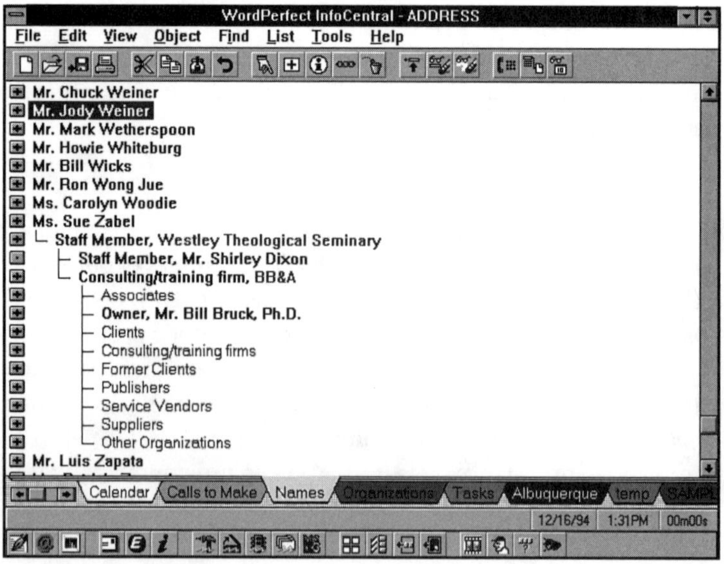

Fig. 31.4
A plus sign indicates that an object has related objects that are not displayed. A dot indicates that the object has no connections.

A list of objects and connections is termed an *outline view.* You may create different views of an iBase. You can save lists that you use frequently in *tabs* that you see at the bottom of the screen (see fig. 31.5).

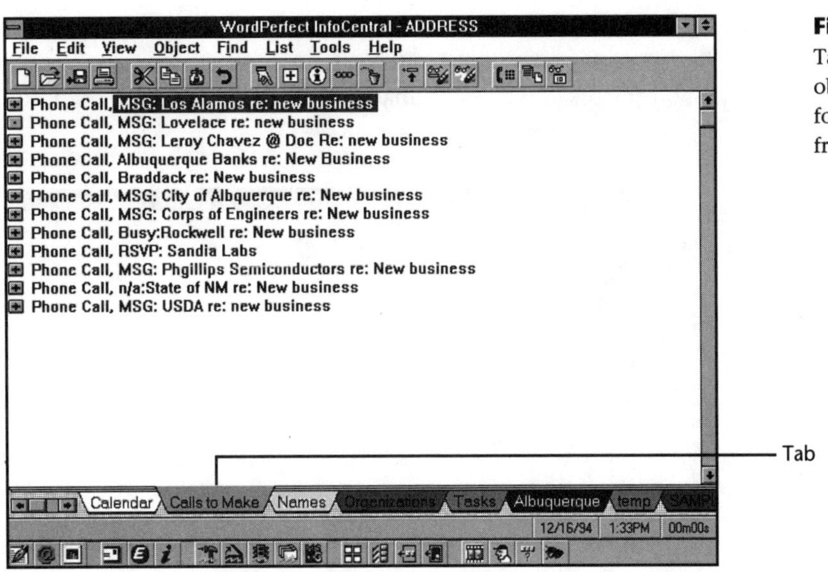

Fig. 31.5
Tabs are lists of objects in outline form that you use frequently.

InfoCentral Screen Elements

The InfoCentral screen has many elements common to all PerfectOffice applications, including a title bar, menu bar, toolbar, scroll bar, and status bar. For information on using these common features, refer to Chapter 2, "Getting Started with PerfectOffice," and Chapter 3, "Using Common PerfectOffice Tools."

A typical InfoCentral screen is displayed figure 31.6. Screen elements that are unique to InfoCentral that can be seen in this screen include:

- *Main Window.* The screen that you see in an InfoCentral iBase is not a data entry screen. It is a screen that displays objects that you select and their relationships.
- *Object icons.* Each listed object has one of three icons:

Icon	Description
	Indicates that the listed object has related objects that are not displayed
	Indicates that the listed object has related objects that are displayed
	Indicates that the listed object has no related objects

- *Tabs.* Tabs are used to switch between different lists of objects in an iBase. Tabs are also available to switch into a calendar view that lists appointments and tasks. A small scroll bar allows you to scroll to tabs which are not visible on the screen.

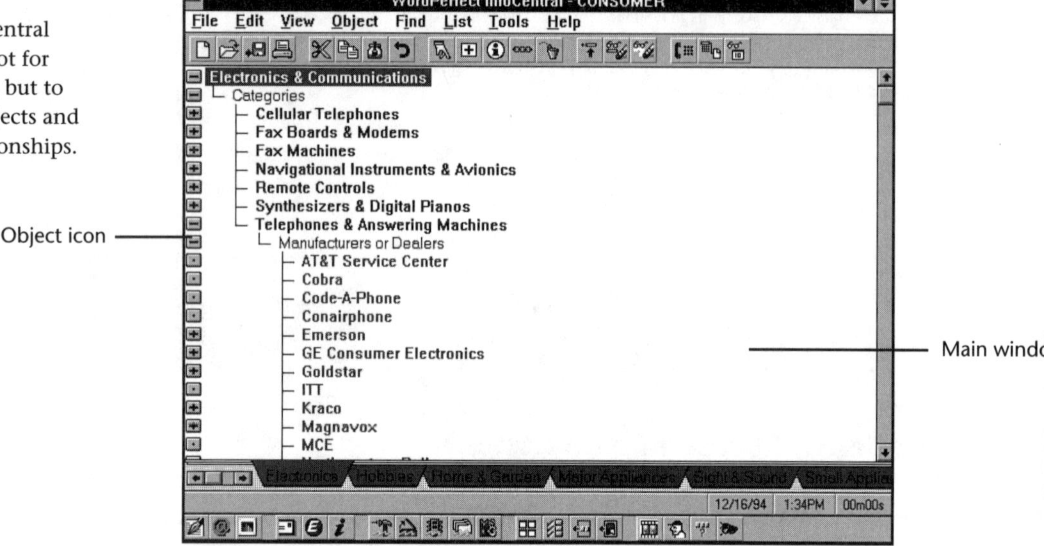

Fig. 31.6
The InfoCentral screen is not for data entry, but to display objects and their relationships.

Shipping iBases

Two types of iBases ship with PerfectOffice: Content iBases and Templates.

Content iBases are information bases that contain useful data. Content iBases that ship with PerfectOffice include:

- *ComputerCentral.* This iBase contains information about computer manufacturers, including products they make and support telephone numbers.

- *WineCentral.* This iBase provides the gourmets among us with information on wines by international region, including vineyards, wineries, labels, and prices.

- *ConsumerCentral.* For the shoppers in our midst, the ConsumerCentral iBase lists hundreds of companies that provide products and services including electronics, appliances, home and garden, hobbies, and sight and sound.

- *TravelCentral.* This iBase is geared toward the business traveler, and lists information on restaurants, hotels, airline and car rental companies, as well as information on regional destinations.

Templates are empty iBases which can be used for common tasks. They contain object categories, predefined connections, object information dialog boxes, and connection information dialog boxes. Templates that ship with PerfectOffice include templates for collecting (stamps, CDs, videos), auto and gardening templates, and an iBase for maintaining rental properties.

Displaying iBase Information

In order to use iBases effectively, you need to know how to open an iBase, view lists of objects and relations, and view information on an object or connection.

Open InfoCentral by double-clicking the InfoCentral icon in the PerfectOffice program group.

When you are finished using InfoCentral, close the application by choosing **F**ile, E**x**it. Your data is saved automatically, and you need not save your iBase file separately.

◄ See "Introducing DAD," p. 27

Opening iBases

To open an iBase, use the following steps:

1. From the InfoCentral main window, choose **F**ile, **O**pen. You see the Open iBase dialog box.

2. Move to the appropriate directory using the directory list box.

3. Double-click the appropriate content iBase or template.

> **Note**
>
> Your iBase is automatically saved when you exit InfoCentral. You may, however, save your iBase at any point in time by choosing **F**ile, **S**ave. You may rename it by choosing **F**ile, Save **A**s.

Tip

By default, content iBases are saved in the \WPIC\IBASES directory. Templates are saved in the \WPIC\IBASES \TEMPLATE directory.

Moving Between Tabs

At the bottom of the InfoCentral screen, you see a list of tabs. These enable you to move between the calendar views and outline views that have been created for your iBase. To move to a tab, click it.

If the tab you wish to move to is not visible, use the small tab scroll bar until you can see the desired tab, then click it.

Viewing and Editing Object Information

To view or edit information on objects, follow the procedure below.

1. Access the appropriate iBase and list of objects as described previously.
2. Use the scroll bar, if needed, until the object you want to view is on the screen.

3. If the object has connections to other objects which are not shown, a + icon will appear to the left of the object. To see these connected objects, click the + icon. You see the specified object and its connected objects.
4. Right-click the object. You see a QuickMenu.
5. Choose **I**nformation. You see a dialog box displaying the information categories that pertain to the object.
6. View or edit the information as desired, then click OK to return to the object list.

Tip
You can also view item information by choosing **E**dit, **I**nformation.

Note

You will see different information in the Object Information dialog box depending on the Object's category.

Viewing and Editing Connection Information

To view or edit information on objects, follow the procedure below.

1. Access the appropriate iBase and list of objects as described above.
2. Use the scroll bar, if needed, until the object with the desired connection is on-screen.

3. If the object's connections are not shown, click the + icon to the left of the object. You see the object's connections and connected objects.
4. Right-click the line connecting the two objects. You see a QuickMenu.

Note

You can also right-click the connection name if there is only one connected object. If there is more than one connected object, right-clicking the name will give you the opportunity to specify how the plural form of the connection name should be spelled.

5. Choose **I**nformation. You see a dialog box displaying the categories that pertain to the connection.

6. View or edit the information as desired, then click OK to return to the object list.

Tip
You will see different information in the Connection Information dialog box depending on the Connection's category.

Troubleshooting

I can't find a person's work phone number. There doesn't even seem to be a place for it in the iBase.

A person's personal phone numbers are stored as part of their object information. The main phone number of their employer is stored as part of its object information. A person's direct line at work is a function of their job—that is, the connection between them and their employer. Thus, their direct work phone line is stored in the connection information.

Maintaining Object Lists

Sometimes, the objects you wish to view or edit do not appear on existing lists of objects. You can easily create new tabs (lists of objects). You can then use any of several ways of finding objects and adding them to tabs. These include FastFind, List-by-Example, and List-by-Connection.

Tip
If you use a long tab name, you will see a long tab, which prevents you from seeing a lot of other tabs on the screen.

Creating Tabs

A *tab* is a list of objects that can be maintained and manipulated independently of other tabs in your iBase. Empty tabs appear at the right of your tab list. To create a new list of objects:

1. Right-click an empty tab, then choose Tab **P**roperties. The Tab Properties dialog box appears (see fig. 31.7).

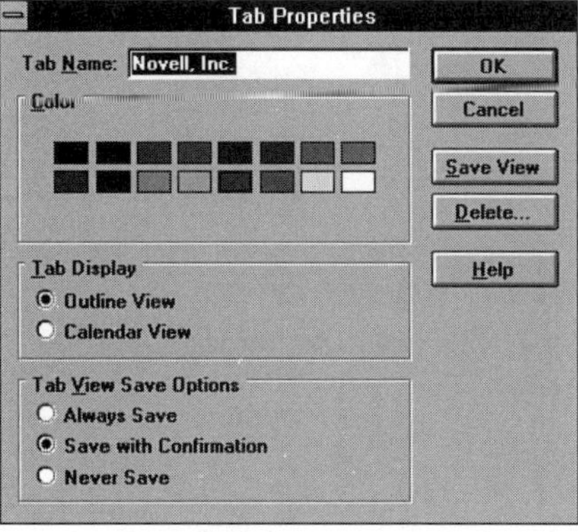

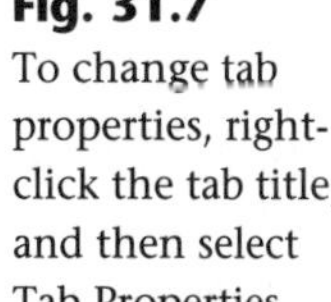

Fig. 31.7
To change tab properties, right-click the tab title, and then select Tab Properties.

VI Groupwise and InfoCentral

2. Type in a short tab name.

Tip
You can also edit the color or text of an existing tab by following these steps.

3. Click a color for the tab.

4. Choose tab options as desired. For a list, you choose an outline view rather than a calendar view. Choose Tab **V**iew Save Options as desired.

5. Click OK when you are finished. You see the newly created empty object list.

6. Add objects to the tab using any of the methods described in the sections that follow.

Saving and Clearing Tabs

Whether the tab's object list will be saved when you exit InfoCentral or move to a different tab depends on the Tab View Save options discussed in the preceding section.

- If the save option is set to Always Save, the object list will be saved whenever you exit the Tab; InfoCentral will not prompt you to save.
- If the save option is set to Save with Confirmation, you must choose to save the object list or not.
- If the save option is set to Never Save, the object list will not be saved when you exit the tab, and you will not be prompted or warned. You can save the tab manually, however, by choosing **F**ile, **S**ave before exiting the tab.

You can clear the entire tab by clicking the Clear View tool. You can remove a line from a tab by clicking the Clear Line tool. This removes the selected object and any related subsidiary objects from the tab.

Note

When you clear objects from a tab or do not save a tab, the information in those objects is not lost. You are merely not displaying these objects in this particular list of objects.

Listing Objects Using FastFind

When you want to list objects whose names you know, use the FastFind function, as described here:

1. Move to the tab in which you want to display the objects.

2. Click the FastFind tool. Alternatively, choose F**i**nd, **F**astFind. You see the FastFind dialog box (see fig. 31.8).

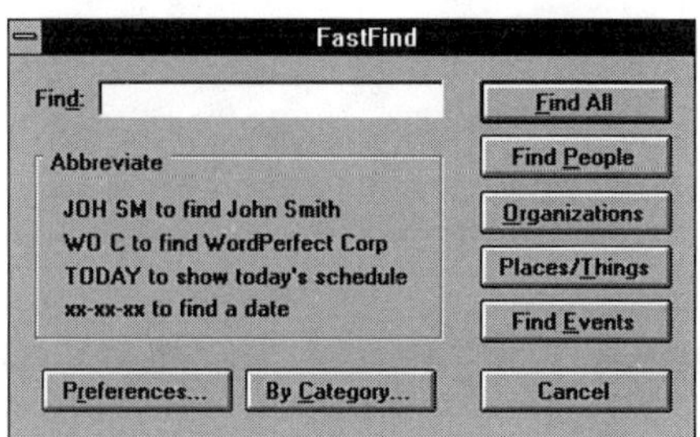

Fig. 31.8
You can quickly find objects or list categories using the FastFind feature.

3. Type the first few letters of the object's name. If the name contains more than one word, you can type the first few letters of each word.

4. Choose which categories of objects you want to find: Find **P**eople, **O**rganizations, Places/**T**hings, or Find **E**vents. If you want to find all objects no matter what the category, choose **F**ind All.

5. Objects meeting the criteria that are not currently on the tab will be added to the tab. The selected object will be the first existing or new object that meets the selection criteria.

Tip
To search through less common categories, choose By **C**ategory, and then choose the category to be searched.

Listing Objects by Example

Sometimes you wish to list objects within a specific category with a finer degree of control, by specifying objects whose object information meets certain criteria. In this case, use Find-By-Example as described here:

1. Move to the tab in which you want to display the objects.

2. Choose F**i**nd, Find-By-**E**xample. You see the Find-By-Example dialog box, listing all available object categories (see fig. 31.9).

3. Select the desired category, then click OK. You see the Find-By-Example dialog box for entering criteria.

4. Add criteria in any or all of the available fields. For instance, you may wish to find all organizations located in Virginia (State or Province = "VA") with an 800 number (Toll-free Line = "(800)*"). Then click OK.

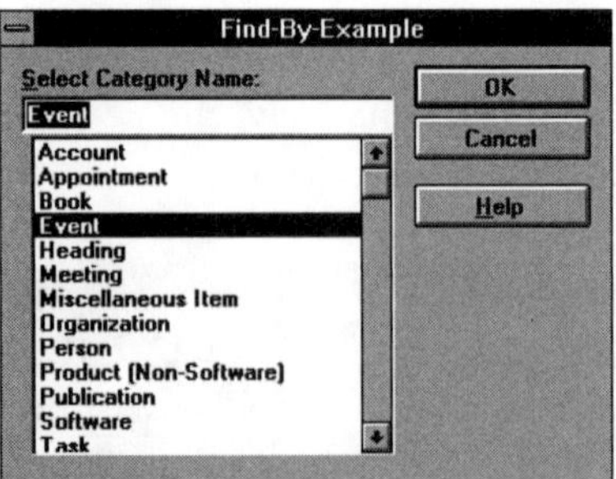

Fig. 31.9
Find-By-Example is a powerful search tool enabling you to specify criteria for objects to be displayed on a tab.

> **Note**
>
> You can use the ? and * wildcards to specify criteria. ? replaces exactly one character in a name. * replaces any number of characters in a name. You can also mix characters. For example, **alb*** represents any name that starts with *alb*. ***alb** represents any name that ends in *alb*. ***alb*** represents any name that has *alb* anywhere in it.

5. Objects meeting the criteria that are not currently on the tab will be added to the tab. The selected object will be the first existing or new object that meets the selection criteria.

Listing Objects by Connection

On occasion, you may want to find objects that have specific connections with other objects. For instance, you may wish to list all realtors, uncles, products, suppliers, and so forth. To do this, use Find-by-Connection as described here:

1. Move to the tab in which you want to display the objects.
2. Choose F**i**nd, Find-By-**C**onnection. You see the Find-By-Connection dialog box, which enables you to choose the object categories that the desired connection is between.
3. Choose the two object categories that the connection is between and click OK. You see the Describe Connection dialog box.
4. The available connections between the two object categories are shown. Choose the connection you want to search for, then choose **A**dd to View.

5. Objects meeting the criteria that are not currently on the tab will be added to the tab. The selected object will be the first existing or new object that meets the selection criteria.

Note

You can also list all object categories by choosing **V**iew, **A**ll Categories. This adds a list of categories to your tab. You can then click the icon to the left of a desired category to list all objects belonging to this category.

Troubleshooting

My tab keeps growing every time I do a FastFind. I'm messing up my iBase!

Think of the tab as a temporary method of displaying the data. You can add objects, delete lines, or clear the whole tab. Unless you save the changed information, it will not affect the way the tab shows in the future. It's often best to be prompted when you leave a tab as to whether or not you want your changes saved. To set this option, right-click the tab title and choose Save with Confirmation from the Tab Properties dialog box.

Maintaining Objects and Connections

In order to add and edit items in your iBase, you will need to be able to work with both objects and connections.

Adding an Object to an iBase

Adding a new object to an iBase consists of three primary steps: categorizing the object, filling in information about the object, and (optionally) connecting the object to other objects, as shown in the following procedure:

1. Open the appropriate iBase, and move to the Tab in which the object should appear, as described in the preceding section.

2. Click the Add button, or choose **O**bject, **A**dd. You see the Add New Object dialog box (see fig. 31.10).

3. Select the category of the object, then choose OK.

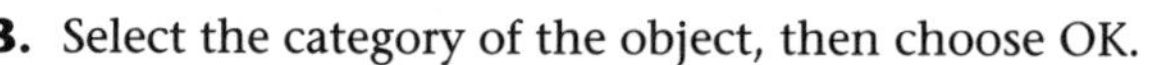

4. You see a dialog box that asks you for the name of the new object. Provide a name and click OK.

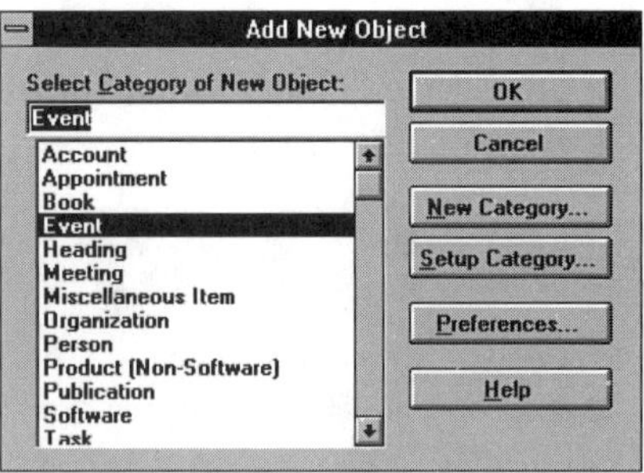

Fig. 31.10
Adding new objects to a list is simple with the Add New Object dialog box.

> **Note**
>
> When entering an object name, you do not need to capitalize it. InfoCentral will intelligently capitalize the first letter of each word. InfoCentral will also check the iBase to ensure against duplicate name entry. If a duplicate name in the same category is found, you will be warned, and can opt to proceed or cancel the operation.

Tip
You can also type a new category name then choose **N**ew Category to set up a new category. This is described more fully in the text that follows.

5. You see an Adding A... dialog box. You will see different object information fields depending on the category of the new object. Fill in the object information and click OK.

6. An Attention InfoCentral dialog box will appear. You will be asked if you wish to add a connection between the new object and existing objects in the iBase. If you choose Yes, add a connection as described in the next section. After you add the connection, or if you choose not to add a connection, you will return to the outline view and will see the new object.

Adding Connections

You can easily connect an object to any number of other objects, and modify existing connections. As you create connections, you determine which objects appear as subsidiaries under other objects in outline views. To create a new connection, follow these steps:

1. Select the object to which you want to add a connection and click the Connect button, or choose **O**bject, **C**onnect. (Alternatively, you can add a new object and choose to add a connection as described previously.) The regular mouse pointer turns into a Connection Pointer.

2. Your next step depends on the status of the object to which you want to add the connection (the *destination object*):

- If the destination object is displayed in the current tab, double-click the object.
- If the destination object is displayed in another tab, click the appropriate tab, then double-click the destination object.
- If the destination object is not displayed in another tab, or if you would like it to be displayed in the currently selected tab, use any of the methods described previously to find and list the destination object. Then double-click it.

Tip
You may cancel adding a connection by pressing the Esc key when you see a connection pointer.

3. You see a Describe Connection dialog box. The available connections will depend on the categories of the two objects being connected.
4. Choose the appropriate connection description and click OK.
5. You see a Connection Information dialog box (see fig. 31.11). The information in this dialog box will depend on the connection. Fill in the connection information fields and click OK. You return to the outline view.

Tip
You can create a new connection type by choosing **N**ew Description, as discussed in the following text.

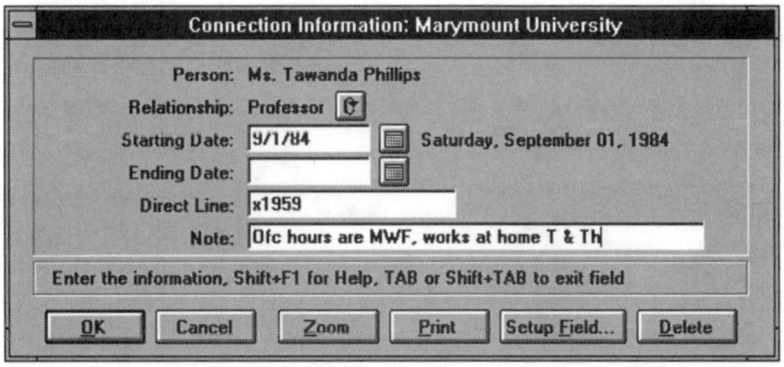

Fig. 31.11
Connection information refers to information such as hire date that is pertinent to the relationship between two objects, rather than to either object individually.

Note

To delete a connection, right-click the connection lines to access the QuickMenu, then choose **D**elete. You will be prompted to confirm the deletion. To change a connection, delete the old one, then create a new one. Be aware that the old connection data will be lost. When a connection has ended, it's better to put an end date in the connection information rather than to delete it. Then the objects will be listed as "former student" or "former employee."

Modifying the Structure of an iBase

One thing that makes iBases so powerful is that their structure can be modified on-the-fly, to better provide you with information on objects and their relationships. In addition to being able to create tabs that list selected objects, you can easily customize the fields that define object and connection information, and create new object and connection categories.

Editing Fields

You can edit the fields that contain information on both objects and categories. InfoCentral enables you to add or delete fields, re-order fields, and change field properties. To edit fields, follow these steps:

1. Open the appropriate iBase, and list the Object or Connection whose fields you want to edit.
2. Right-click the Object or Connection, then choose **I**nformation from the QuickMenu. You see an Object Information or Connection Information dialog box displaying the information fields on the Object or Connection.
3. Select the field to be edited.
4. Click Setup **F**ield. You see a QuickMenu offering choices for editing the fields.
5. Choose the editing option you desire:
   - *Field Properties*. You see the Field Properties dialog box (see fig. 31.12). Choose the appropriate field type for the data you are entering. You will then see a dialog box enabling you to specify defaults and data ranges for the field, as described in the following section.

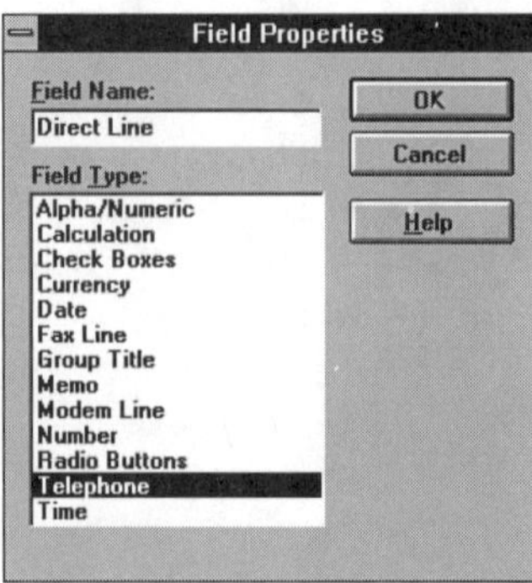

Fig. 31.12
Each field has a field type that determines the type of information that will be stored in it.

- *Add New Field.* You see the Field Properties dialog box (see fig. 31.13). Type a name for the new field, then click OK. Specify defaults for the field as described in the next section.

- *Move Field.* You return to a modified Information dialog box Use the arrow keys to move the selected field up or down, then press Enter.

- *Delete Field.* The selected field is deleted from the iBase and information in it is lost.

- *Select Different Field.* You return to a modified Information dialog box. Use the up and down arrow keys to move to the desired field, then press Enter to select it.

Tip
To rearrange fields without using Move Field, simply drag the field name to the desired placement in the dialog box and drop it in place.

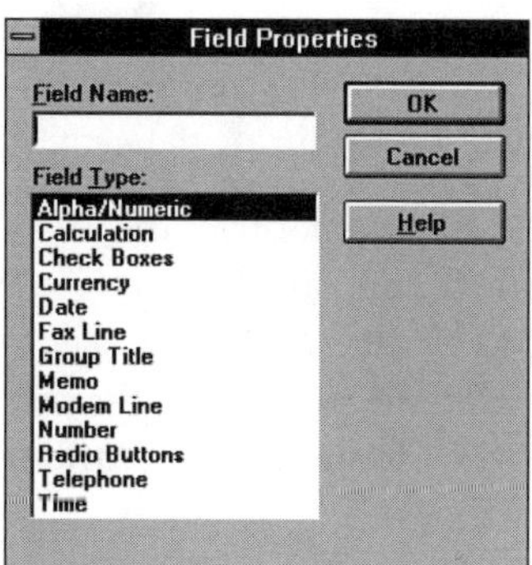

Fig. 31.13
You can add new fields to objects or connections at any time, and specify the properties of these new fields.

- *Field Trash Can.* You see a Field Trash Can dialog box listing all deleted fields. Select a field, then choose **U**ndelete to restore the field to the database.

6. After you specify field defaults, you return to the Object Information or Connection Information dialog box.

Tip
Fields may not be available to be undeleted. If a field can be undeleted, information in it will be restored.

Editing Field Type Specifications

When you add a new field or choose a new field type for an existing field, you will see a dialog box named with the name of the field (see fig. 31.14). The contents of this dialog box vary with the type of field chosen. Some of the common options in these dialog boxes include:

- *Contextual Hint.* A short descriptive statement that appears at the bottom of the dialog box when the field is selected.

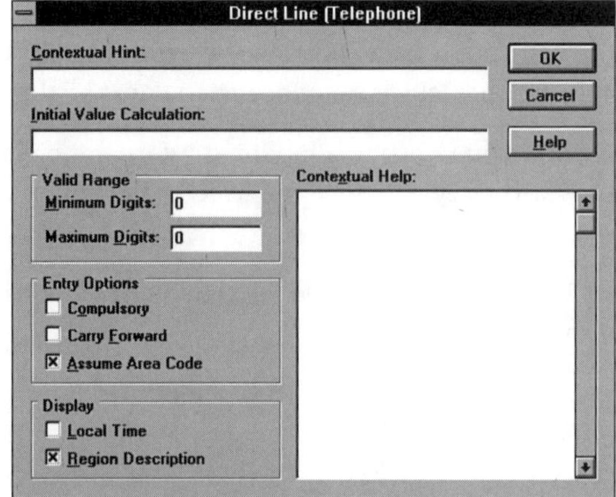

Fig. 31.14 Contents of object dialog boxes vary with the information stored in that object. People dialog boxes have several phone numbers, while organization dialog boxes have a directions field.

- *Conte**x**tual Help.* A help paragraph you write for the user that can be accessed by pressing Shift+F1 during data entry.
- Template Format. A template controls the way that data is displayed. For instance, a phone number template might resemble (###) ###-####. For text templates, # indicates an entered character, while other characters like , or - will print as entered. For numeric templates, # indicates degree of precision. For example, $###.## will produce currency figures that include two decimals.
- *Entry Options.* These include C**o**mpulsory entry, Carry **F**orward (use last entered value as default), address field, numbers only, display only, and **A**ssume Area Code.
- *Valid Range.* These can be starting and ending dates, numbers, size of memo field, or minimum/maximum number of characters, depending on the field type.
- ***I**nitial Value Calculation.* This is the default value that the user will see when entering data.
- *Justification.* These include right, left, and center. This option only appears with certain field types.
- *Case.* Options include as entered, capitalized (will automatically capitalize all words), and upper and lower (will convert entered text to uppercase or lowercase).
- *Description & Default.* Radio buttons and check boxes enable you to enter text for the buttons and a default button state.

After you make your selections, click OK to return to the Information dialog box.

Creating and Editing Object Categories

InfoCentral comes with over 15 object categories, including Person, Phone Call, Property, Restaurant, Task, and so on. On occasion, you may find it easier to create a new category than to modify field properties in an existing category to best describe information in your iBase. To create a new object category, follow these steps:

1. From the main InfoCentral window, choose **E**dit, C**a**tegories. Alternatively, when viewing object information, choose Category. In either case, you see the Select Category dialog box (see fig. 31.15).

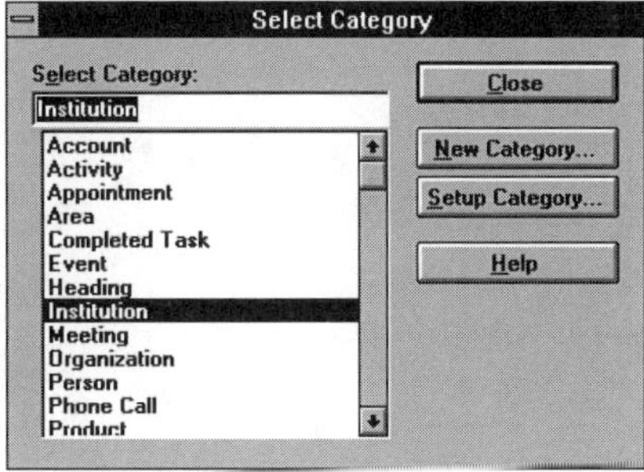

Fig. 31.15
You can create new categories or edit old ones, but you can only delete categories if you access the dialog box from the Main window.

2. To create a new category, click **N**ew Category. To edit an existing category, select the desired category and choose **S**etup Category. In either case, you see the Setup Category dialog box.

3. Enter or edit the category name. Choose a category type and a display color. When you are finished selecting options, click OK. You return to the Select Category dialog box.

Tip
You can delete a category only if you access the Select Category dialog box from the main InfoCentral window. To delete a category, select it, choose **S**etup Category, then choose **D**elete.

> **Caution**
>
> If you delete a category which has entries associated with it, InfoCentral will warn you of the consequences of performing the delete. Deleting a category with associated entries will cause those entries to be permanently deleted; they are not recoverable from the trash can.

VI

Groupwise and InfoCentral

Creating and Editing Connection Descriptions

InfoCentral provides a variety of connections between each type of object. Occasionally, however, you will wish to add or edit connection categories to fine-tune the relationships in your iBase. To create a new connection description, follow these steps:

1. From the main InfoCentral window, choose **E**dit, C**o**nnections. You see the Setup Connections dialog box.

2. Choose the two object categories that the connection is between, then click OK. You see a Describe Connection dialog box such as that shown in figure 31.16 or figure 31.17, depending on whether the connection is a one-way or two-way connection.

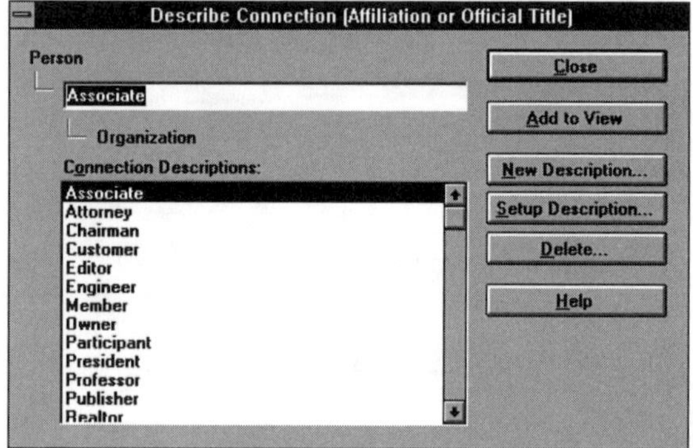

Fig. 31.16
Some connections between objects are one-way.

Fig. 31.17
Others are two-way.

> **Note**
>
> Whether a one- or two-way connection appears depends on the object categories. People-People connections are two-way (for example, father/son) whereas People-Organizations are one-way (for example, employee). In either case, however, the modification options remain the same.

Tip
Access the Describe Connection dialog box when viewing connection information by choosing Relationship. The delete option is not available when you access the dialog box in this way.

3. Choose connection options as desired:

- ***A**dd to View.* Select a connection, and then choose this option to add all objects with the selected connection to the current outline view.

- ***N**ew Description.* This option enables you to create a new connection between objects of the selected type (see fig. 31.18).

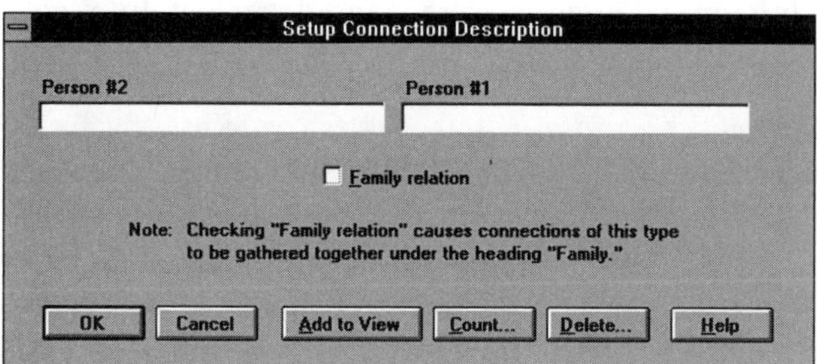

Fig. 31.18
You can create new connections once you specify the two types of objects to be connected.

- ***S**etup Description.* You edit a current connection after selecting a connection by using this option, which displays the same dialog box as the New Description, but with the connection information displayed. Note that you can also count the number of connections in the iBase using this option.

- ***D**elete.* Select a connection, and then choose this option to delete it from the list. If any objects have this connection, you will be warned that their connection will be deleted.

- ***H**elp.* This option in the one-way connection dialog box provides context-sensitive Help on the Describe Connection process.

Tip
Remember that you can access context-sensitive Help by pressing F1 if no Help button appears in the dialog box.

4. Click **C**lose when you are finished choosing options. You return to the Setup Connection dialog box. Click Cancel to return to the main view.

Managing Your Documents with InfoCentral

iBase objects can include files on your disk. WordPerfect documents, Quattro Pro spreadsheets, or Presentations slideshows can all be included in your iBase. These objects can be related to other objects, including people, projects, and clients. InfoCentral can be used as a central repository that organizes and manages your documents.

In fact, InfoCentral offers special features to help you do just this. These include:

- *Launching applications automatically.* This feature enables you to create related files—files that are related to the person or project you have selected. When creating related WordPerfect files, you can use WordPerfect templates and automatically export related information from InfoCentral into the WordPerfect document. InfoCentral will even name the document for you and store summary information on it.

- *Managing disk files.* InfoCentral enables you to list directories in outline views as you would any other objects. You can copy, move, or delete files from your outline view, or add descriptive memos to files or directories. Further, InfoCentral provides tools to create connections between files or groups of files and other objects in your iBase.

- *Making connections.* With InfoCentral, you can connect existing disk files with persons, organizations, or projects. This enables you to view all files that are connected with a given person, and launch them as needed. You can even create tabs that deal with specific projects or clients.

Tip
Create a connection between a file and another object by selecting the file in an outline view, clicking the Connections button, then double-clicking the object to which you want it connected.

Creating Related Files

After you select a person, client, project, or other object, you can create a file that is connected to that object. Creating a related file accomplishes three tasks:

- It launches the relevant application, such as WordPerfect.

- It transfers appropriate data from the person or client into the new file (such as return address or signature block information).

- It names the file, records summary information, and establishes a connection to the new (file) object within InfoCentral.

The first time you create a related file, you see an InfoCentral Personalizer information dialog box. After you choose OK, you will see a series of dialog boxes asking you for the names of your word processor, spreadsheet, and graphics programs. You may specify the path to these programs, or InfoCentral will search local and/or network drives to find them for you. You will see the Create a Related File dialog box; you can then create a related file as discussed below.

To create a related file, follow these steps:

1. Select the person or other object to which you want to connect the file.

2. Choose **O**bject, Create **R**elated File, or click the Create Related File button. You see the Create a Related File dialog box (see fig. 31.19).

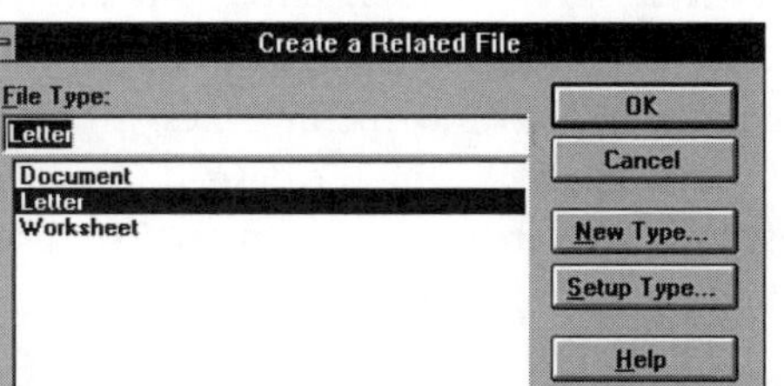

Fig. 31.19
You can create letters, memos, or spreadsheets that are connected to people or projects from within InfoCentral.

3. Select the file type, and click OK. You may be prompted to select a related organization. If so, select the appropriate organization and click OK. This allows InfoCentral to know what information should be exported to the application, such as home address or work address for a letter.

4. You will be prompted for a description of the new file. Provide a concise description, using full words and spaces if desired.

Tip
The description you provide will be displayed along with the filename and date in tabs that list this file.

5. The appropriate application will be launched, and information from InfoCentral inserted as appropriate. When you are finished creating the file, save your work. You may then exit the application or leave the application active and switch back to InfoCentral by pressing Alt+Tab until you see InfoCentral. The file will be listed in the tab as an object connected to the original object you selected.

Note

From the Create a Related File dialog box, you can choose **S**etup Type to edit options regarding how InfoCentral creates a selected document type, or choose **N**ew Type to create a new type of document. In either case, you will see a Setup File Type dialog box that enables you to specify the file type, Windows application to be launched, and the connection description. A Default **T**ext option enables you to customize what text or InfoCentral fields are exported into the new document. An **A**dvanced option enables you to specify files to be launched, and even keystrokes that can be used to fill in WordPerfect Templates.

Copying, Moving, Deleting, and Opening Files

You can use InfoCentral to do basic file management functions such as listing, copying, moving, deleting, and opening files. All file management functions require that you begin by listing the desired file(s) in a tab. There are several ways to list files in a tab with InfoCentral. Two of the most common are using View All Drives and FastFind.

Choose **V**iew, All **D**rives to see a listing of all disk drives on your system. Click the Drive icon to see directories within each drive. Click a Directory icon to see files within the directory.

Tip
The DOS wildcard ? stands for 1 character; * stands for any number of characters, to the end of the filename.

To list files using FastFind:

1. Move to the desired tab or create a new tab as described earlier.
2. Choose F**i**nd, FastFind F**i**les.
3. Type a valid pathname or file specification. You may use the * and ? wildcards. The files matching your specification are shown on the selected tab.

Tip
You can also open a file by double-clicking it, or by right-clicking, and then choosing Open from the QuickMenu.

To perform file management tasks:

1. Ensure that you are in the correct tab, and then select the desired file.
2. Choose **F**ile, File Proper**t**ies.
3. Choose **O**pen, **C**opy, **M**ove, **D**elete, **R**ename, or **A**ttributes. You will see a dialog box providing the options necessary to accomplish the specified task.

Note

You can only perform file management tasks on one file at a time using InfoCentral. Use QuickFiles with DAD to perform more advanced file management functions. Other InfoCentral options enable you to undelete a recently deleted file, create a directory, rename a directory, and remove an empty directory.

Keeping a Calendar and To-Do List

InfoCentral offers two types of data views: outline views and calendar views. So far in this chapter, you have worked only with outline views. The calendar view, shown in figure 31.20, resembles GroupWise's calendar. However, the technology behind its operation is very different. Appointments are shown on the schedule on the left, notes and tasks are displayed on the list to the right.

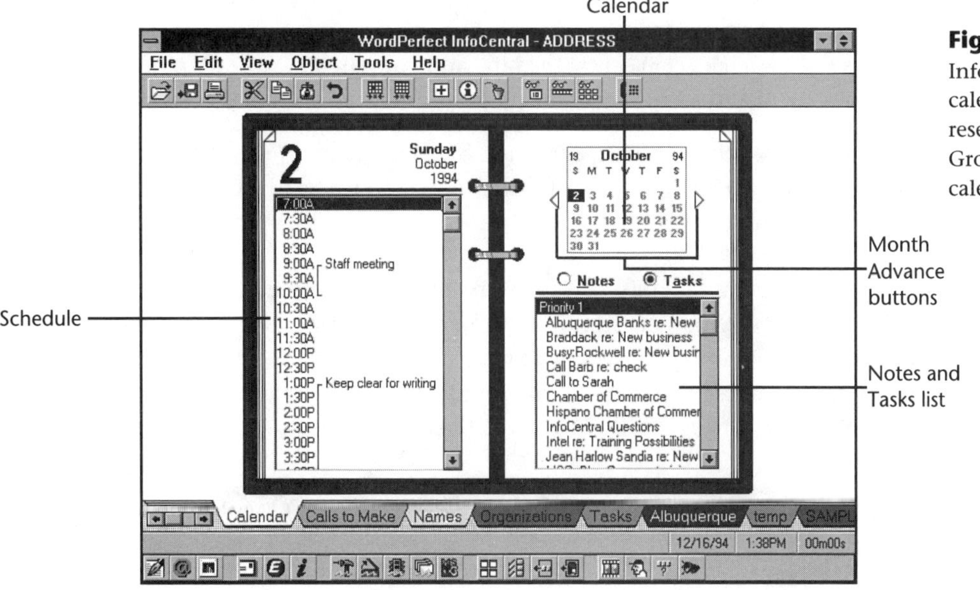

Fig. 31.20
InfoCentral's calendar view resembles GroupWise's calendar view.

You move between days of the current month by clicking the desired day in the calendar. Move between months with the Month Advance buttons.

Tip
You can also move to the next and previous day by clicking the down-turned page corners at the top of the notebook pages.

Events that you have created are displayed on your schedule in the calendar, whether you create them from within the calendar view or from within an outline view. Similarly, tasks you create from the calendar or an outline appear in the task list.

Note

All objects that have "event" as their category type will appear on the calendar. In the default iBases, these include appointments, events, meetings, and (oddly enough) telephone calls. Objects that have "task" as their category type will appear on the task list. Adding an object with "notes" as its category type will *not* insert it into the notes section of the calendar.

You can create a new task or event in several ways:

- From an outline view, add an object as described earlier. Make sure that the object has a category whose type is event or task.
- From the calendar view, add an event by selecting the appropriate time, then double-clicking, or right-clicking and then clicking the Add button. Add a task from the calendar view by clicking the Add button. You see an Add New Object dialog box, and you can add the new object as you would in an outline view.
- From the calendar view, add notes by selecting the **N**otes radio button to display the Notes text box. Click in the Notes text box and type the desired note. It will remain with the calendar for that day.

To edit a note, display the Notes text box, then edit the displayed notes as you would any other text. To edit a task or event, double-click it. You will see an Object Information dialog box (see fig. 31.21). Edit the information as desired, and choose OK. To delete an event or task, select it, then choose **O**bject, **D**elete.

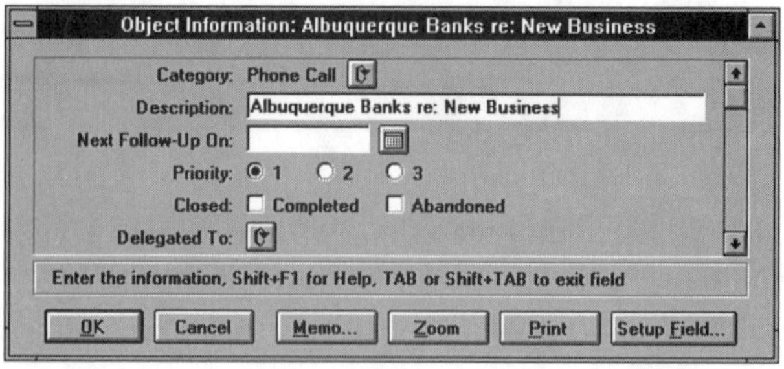

Object Information: Albuquerque Banks re: New Business

Category: Phone Call
Description: Albuquerque Banks re: New Business
Next Follow-Up On:
Priority: 1 2 3
Closed: Completed Abandoned
Delegated To:
Enter the information, Shift+F1 for Help, TAB or Shift+TAB to exit field
OK Cancel Memo... Zoom Print Setup Field...

Fig. 31.21
To edit an event or task, double-click it from the calendar view.

Note

You can schedule limited types of recurring events within InfoCentral. Alternatively, use GroupWise for recurring events, then synchronize your GroupWise and InfoCentral calendars as described below. To schedule a recurring event, choose **T**ools, **R**ecurring Event. Choose whether the event is an appointment, event, or meeting, then choose how many times the event should recur. After creating a description for the event and the date of the first occurrence, you can specify whether the event should recur weekly, monthly, yearly, or for a specified number of days.

The Notes text box displays notes that you enter from the calendar for a specific day. Notes are not iBase objects like others that have properties and can be connected to other objects. They are more like a yellow sticky note that reminds you of something for that day only.

The Tasks text box displays tasks that are incomplete. No matter what day you move to, you will see the same list of incomplete tasks. When you mark a task complete, it disappears from the task list. It does not remain on the list for the day on which it was completed.

To mark a task complete, right-click it to edit it, then check the Completed check box in the Object Information dialog box.

Troubleshooting

I need to display my completed tasks. How can I do this?

From an outline view, choose F**i**nd, Find-By-**E**xample. Choose Task as the category name. In the Find-By-Example Enter Criteria dialog box, check Completed as the status, then click OK. Your completed tasks will be added to the currently displayed tab.

Printing Lists and Synchronizing Data with GroupWise

Printing calendar data is not one of InfoCentral's fortes, at least in its current version. You cannot print a calendar, but only a list of your tasks, notes, and appointments for a range of days you specify. For this reason, many users may prefer to export their data to GroupWise, and then use the Print Calendar feature from that application.

Printing Lists

To print data from an outline view, move to the desired tab. Using any of the techniques described above, display only the items you want to print. Expand any of the connections that you want to print. Then click the Print button, or choose **F**ile, **P**rint, Current **T**ab. You see the Print Current Tab dialog box. Set print options as desired, then choose **P**rint.

To print data in a calendar view, move to the calendar tab. Click the Print button, or choose **F**ile, **P**rint Calendar Info. You see the Print Calendar Information dialog box. Set the date range and print options as desired, then choose **P**rint.

You can also print information about objects in your iBase. To print information about one object, select it. To print information about several, display only these objects in a tab. Then choose **F**ile, **P**rint, **O**bject Info. You see the Print Object Information dialog box. Choose the appropriate range of objects, printing options, and then choose **P**rint. The printout will contain the same information as you see in the Object Information dialog box used to edit an object.

InfoCentral enables you to print an address book as well. Move to an outline view and, if desired, select only those objects to be printed. Choose **F**ile, **P**rint, **A**ddress Book. You see the Print Address Book dialog box. Choose the appropriate range of objects, printing options, and whether to print connections as well as objects. You can also choose to only see names of persons you have telephoned recently. Choose **P**rint. The printout will contain the same information as you see in the Object Information dialog box used to edit an object.

Finally, you can also print labels by choosing **F**ile, **P**rint, **M**ailing Labels. The Print Mailing Labels dialog box (see fig. 31.22) enables you to choose a type of label, then prints labels for all objects in the tab.

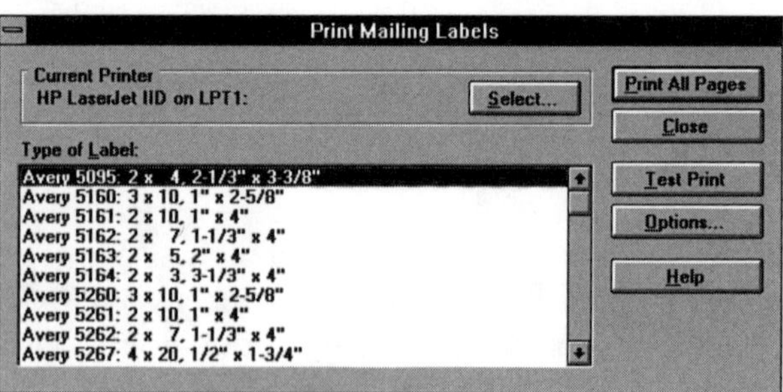

Fig. 31.22
InfoCentral enables you to print labels in any of several popular formats.

Synchronizing with GroupWise

GroupWise and InfoCentral can both be used as Personal Information Managers (PIMs). Each has advantages and disadvantages. For instance, your GroupWise calendar is not in one file that can easily be transported between machines. On the other hand, InfoCentral is weaker than GroupWise on printing and scheduling recurring tasks. For this reason, you may wish to use both products to schedule appointments and track tasks. If you do, you will appreciate the ability to synchronize your InfoCentral iBase with your GroupWise mailbox.

To synchronize the two sets of data, follow these steps:

1. Ensure that you can access GroupWise from the machine you are using.

2. Open InfoCentral.

3. Choose **F**ile, **G**roupWise Update. You see the GroupWise Import/Export dialog box (see fig. 31.23).

4. Choose whether to import or to export appointments and tasks.

5. Choose a time period for the import or export, then choose OK.

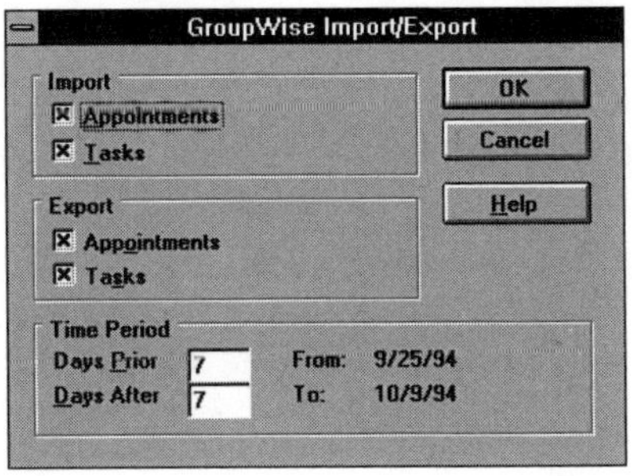

Fig. 31.23
You can import and export tasks, events, meetings, and appointments to synchronize your iBase with your GroupWise calendar.

InfoCentral will scan the iBase for appropriate items, then will launch GroupWise. The appropriate items will be imported to and from GroupWise with no further action needed on your part.

From Here...

You have now learned how to organize people, places, and things using InfoCentral. From here, you can learn more about common PerfectOffice features and customizing PerfectOffice applications by referring to the following chapters:

- Chapter 35, "Transferring Data Between Applications," explains DDE and OLE, and defines the differences between linking and embedding data.
- Chapter 36, "Customizing Toolbars, DAD Bars, and Menus," teaches you how to set personal preferences for all these elements.

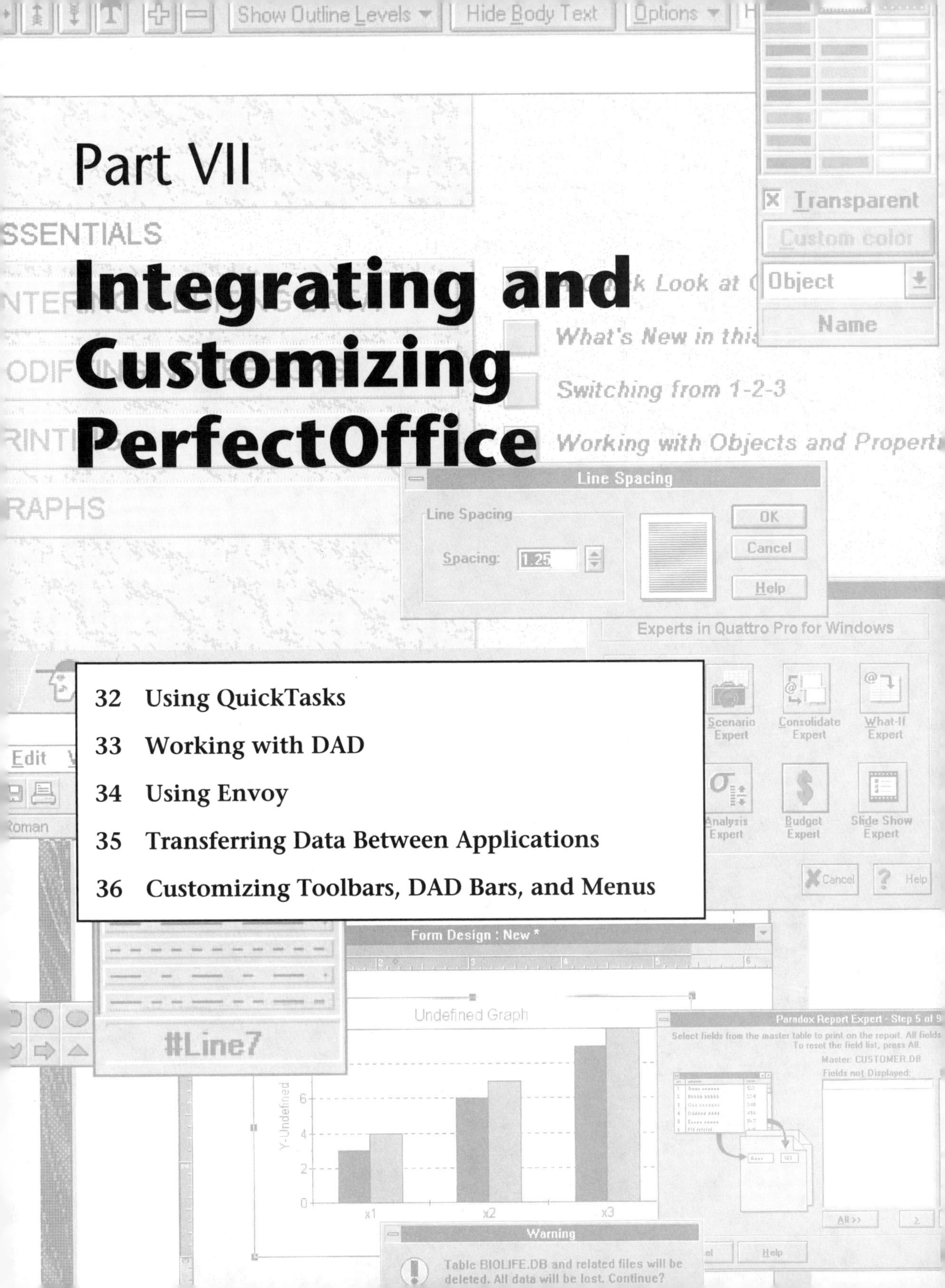

Part VII

Integrating and Customizing PerfectOffice

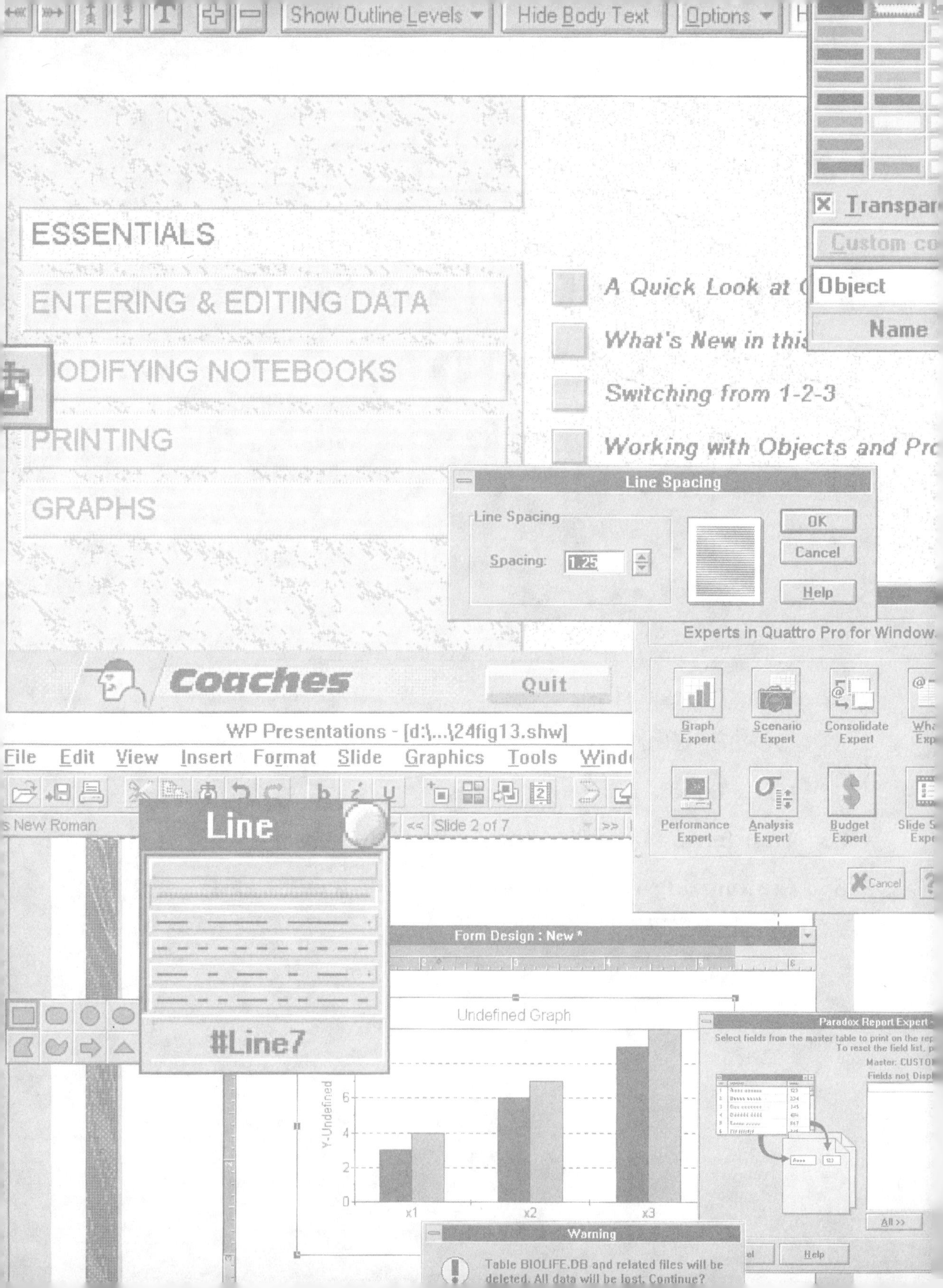
Show Outline Levels
Hide Body Text
Options
Transpar
Custom co
Object
Name
ESSENTIALS
ENTERING & EDITING DATA
ODIFYING NOTEBOOKS
PRINTING
GRAPHS
A Quick Look at
What's New in this
Switching from 1-2-3
Working with Objects and Pro
Line Spacing
Line Spacing
Spacing:
1.25
OK
Cancel
Help
Experts in Quattro Pro for Window
Graph Expert
Scenario Expert
Consolidate Expert
Performance Expert
Analysis Expert
Budget Expert
Cancel
Coaches
Quit
WP Presentations - [d:\...\24fig13.shw]
File
Edit
View
Insert
Format
Slide
Graphics
Tools
Slide 2 of 7
Line
#Line7
Form Design : New *
Undefined Graph
Y-Undefined
x1
x2
x3
Paradox Report Expert
Select fields from the master table to print on the rep
Master: CUSTO
Fields not Disp
All >>
Help
Warning
Table BIOLIFE.DB and related files will be deleted. All data will be lost. Continue?

Chapter 32

Using QuickTasks

by Steve Mann

Part of what makes PerfectOffice the "perfect way to work" is its task orientation. For you, this means that as you use PerfectOffice you should be able to focus on getting your work done, rather than on learning specific applications. Instead of focusing on features of WordPerfect for Windows or Quattro Pro, for example, you can think about the job, or *task*, that you need to accomplish.

The principle technique for performing tasks in PerfectOffice is QuickTasks. PerfectOffice contains over 60 QuickTasks that automate many of the day-to-day tasks you commonly do.

In this chapter, you learn to

- Access QuickTasks from DAD
- Use QuickTasks that automatically link to either 1-2-3 or Excel
- Use a QuickTask to write a letter
- Schedule a trip and update your GroupWise or InfoCentral calendar
- Easily "finish" any document
- Merge Paradox data into WordPerfect
- Automate tasks you perform at the beginning of each day

Learning QuickTask Essentials

At the heart of PerfectOffice is the concept that a suite is more than just a box full of otherwise unrelated products. Suite products need to be *integrated*. In the past, integration meant more work for you. Yes, integrated products could "talk" together, but it was up to you to start the conversation.

Refereeing the conversation required you to learn the nitty-gritty details of cross-application communication, such as DDE. Just the terminology is enough to make a person search for the Excedrin bottle.

While most of us enjoy technology, we *use* software to get our work done—not simply for technology's sake. QuickTasks reflect your need to do the work.

So what is a QuickTask? It is an automated routine that does work for you. It takes you through the task, step-by-step, from start to finish. Most QuickTasks involve two or more applications—but to you it is application-independent. You don't need to know which applications are required. You need not start the applications at all. You simply choose a task, click its button, and the QuickTask does the work for you.

Accessing QuickTasks

You access QuickTasks from a special button on DAD. When you click the QuickTasks button, DAD displays a special toolbar which contains all of the available QuickTasks (see fig. 32.1). Each button represents one QuickTask.

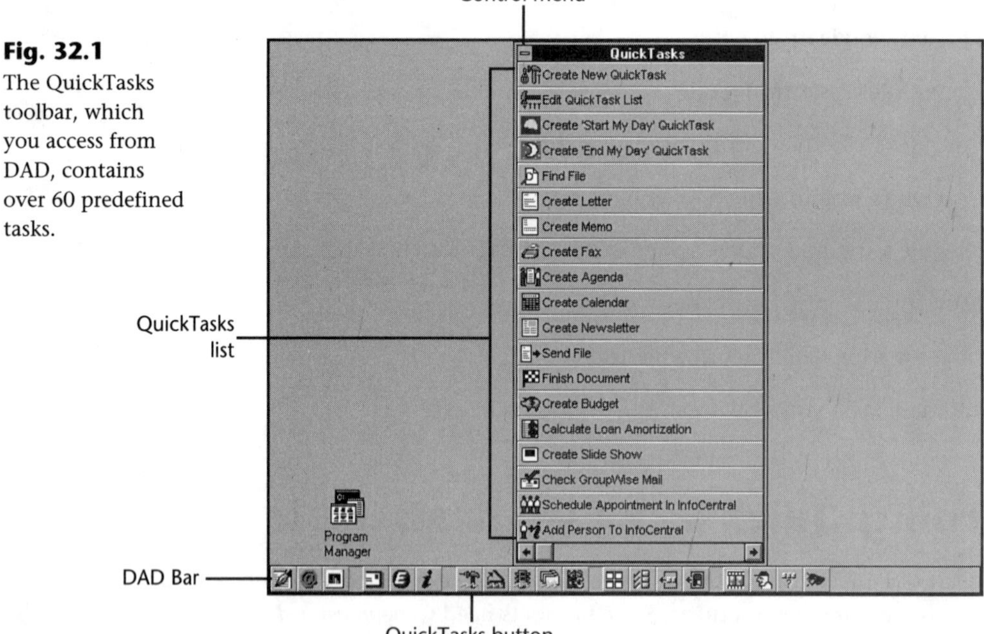

Fig. 32.1
The QuickTasks toolbar, which you access from DAD, contains over 60 predefined tasks.

Even though you only see about 20 items on the toolbar, it contains all of the PerfectOffice QuickTasks. (The exact number of tasks you'll see varies depending on the resolution of your monitor.) At the bottom of the toolbar is a scroll bar. When you click one of the arrows on the scroll bar, a full column of new QuickTasks appears. This enables you to quickly scroll through all of the available QuickTasks.

◄ See "Introducing DAD," p. 27

Using the QuickTask Toolbar

The QuickTask toolbar behaves pretty much like other DAD bars, with four notable exceptions:

Tip
To see more QuickTasks on the toolbar, widen the toolbar to show more columns of QuickTasks. Simply drag the toolbar borders as you do with other windows.

- With other DAD Bars, you can add, delete, and reorder buttons to your heart's content. However, the first two QuickTasks on the bar cannot be removed. Create New QuickTask and Edit QuickTask List are special QuickTasks that always occupy these reserved spots.
- Standard DAD Bars display as icons only, text only, or both icon and text. QuickTask buttons always appear with both icons and text; the other display options are disabled. However, you can edit the QuickTasks' button text to make the descriptions more meaningful to you or to shorten them.
- Unlike DAD itself, you can't embed the QuickTasks toolbar on the sides of the desktop, it must always take the form of a floating palette. You move the palette by clicking the title bar and dragging the palette around the screen.
- The QuickTask toolbar remains in front of other windows until you choose a QuickTask or close it by double-clicking the control menu (see fig. 32.1). The box does not have a menu, so there is no Close menu item.

► See "Customizing Toolbars and DAD Bars," p. 740

► See "Setting Toolbar and DAD Bar Preferences," p. 741

Using Third-Party Products with QuickTasks

Several QuickTasks make use of a special PerfectOffice technology called *PerfectLinks*. This capability extends QuickTasks even beyond PerfectOffice's own products, enabling you to link in certain third-party products. PerfectLinks surfaces in two specific areas of QuickTasks: spreadsheets and e-mail.

Several spreadsheet-centered QuickTasks automatically detect which spreadsheet you use, and then funnel the work to the proper program. For example, say you install Quattro Pro as your spreadsheet, but a co-worker already uses Excel. The same PerfectLinks QuickTask will accomplish its goal for both of you—without any customization by either of you. QuickTasks that use PerfectLinks to support 1-2-3 and Excel are shown in table 32.1 below.

Similarly, e-mail tasks work with Novell's GroupWise as well as cc:Mail and MS Mail.

Reviewing PerfectOffice's QuickTask Table of Contents

PerfectOffice includes more than 60 QuickTasks to automate your work. The tasks are listed in table 32.1 in the order the QuickTasks appear on the toolbar.

Table 32.1 PerfectOffice QuickTasks

Button	Button Text	Application
	Create New QuickTask	Varies
	Edit QuickTask List	Varies
	Create "Start My Day" QuickTask	Varies
	Create "End My Day" QuickTask	Varies
	Find File	None
	Create Letter	WordPerfect
	Create Memo	WordPerfect
	Create Fax	WordPerfect
	Create Agenda	WordPerfect
	Create Calendar	WordPerfect
	Create Newsletter	WordPerfect
	Send File	GroupWise
	Finish Document	Varies
	Create Budget	WordPerfect

Button	Button Text	Application
	Calculate Loan Amortization	Quattro Pro, Excel, 1-2-3
	Create Slide Show	Presentations
	Check GroupWise Mail	GroupWise
	Schedule Appointment In InfoCentral	InfoCentral
	Add Person To InfoCentral	InfoCentral
	Schedule A Trip	Quattro Pro, Excel, 1-2-3
	Extra Payment Analysis	Quattro Pro, Excel, 1-2-3
	Plan Project Schedule	Quattro Pro, Excel, 1-2-3
	Sync. GroupWise And InfoCentral	GroupWise, InfoCentral
	Create InfoCentral Phone List In WP	WordPerfect, InfoCentral
	Merge InfoCentral Addresses Into WP	WordPerfect, InfoCentral
	Create Brochure	WordPerfect
	Create Business Card	WordPerfect
	Create Certificate	WordPerfect
	Create Envelope	WordPerfect
	Create Expense Report	WordPerfect
	Create Card	WordPerfect
	Create Idea List	WordPerfect
	Create Invoice	WordPerfect
	Create Pleading	WordPerfect
	Create Press Release	WordPerfect

(continues)

Table 32.1 Continued

Button	Button Text	Application
	Create Purchase Order	WordPerfect
	Create Report	WordPerfect
	Create Resume	WordPerfect
	Create Term Paper	WordPerfect
	Create Sign	WordPerfect
	Create Balance Sheet	WordPerfect
	Create Cash Flow Statement	WordPerfect
	Create New Template	WordPerfect
	Index File	None
	Archive File	None
	Perform "What-If" Analysis	Quattro Pro
	Perform Spreadsheet Scenario Analysis	Quattro Pro
	Calculate Statistical Analysis	Quattro Pro
	Create Chart In Quattro Pro	Quattro Pro
	Perform Spreadsheet Consolidation	Quattro Pro
	Merge Paradox Data Into WP	WordPerfect, Paradox
	Create Form In Paradox	Paradox
	Print Labels From Paradox	Paradox
	Create Report In Paradox	Paradox
	Link Quattro Pro Table To Paradox	Quattro Pro, Paradox
	Open Document As Copy	WordPerfect
	Open Spreadsheet As Copy	Quattro Pro

Button	Button Text	Application
	Change Network Password	NetWare
	Map Network Drive	NetWare
	Detach Network Server	NetWare
	Hold Network Print Job	NetWare
	Delete Network Print Job	NetWare
	View Network Print Job Status	NetWare

Taking a Guided Tour of Some QuickTasks

Enough about how QuickTasks work—or do your work for you. Now it's time to experiment with a few of the more common QuickTasks. We'll take a guided tour through five specific tasks. We'll start with a few simple ones, and then progress to QuickTasks that automate more complex processes.

QuickTask #1—Create a Letter

The Create a Letter QuickTask guides you through writing a letter from start to finish:

1. To start the Letter QuickTask, select the Create Letter button on the QuickTasks list. The task will start WordPerfect and display a dialog box from which you choose the letterhead type for your letter. As you click each radio button, you'll see a preview of the corresponding letterhead format in the graphic area on the left (see fig. 32.2).

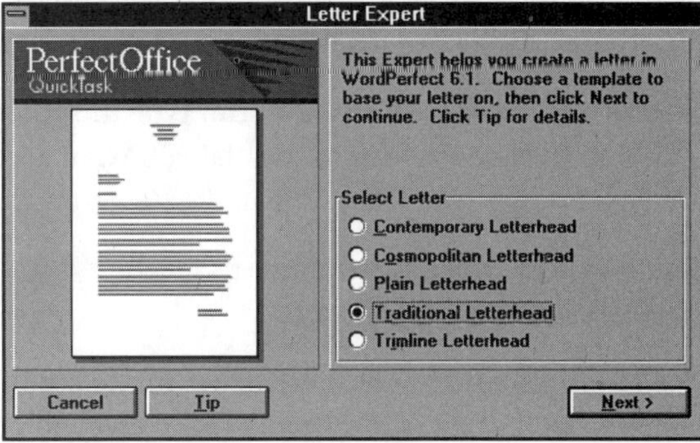

Fig. 32.2
The first step in creating your letter is to choose one of the five letterhead types.

Click the **T**ip button on any QuickTask dialog box to replace the graphic panel on the left of the dialog box with additional text describing the purpose of the dialog box and the steps you should take in the dialog box. Click the **T**ip button again to return to the graphic panel. Click the **N**ext button to continue.

2. If you have not already entered the "Personalize Your Template" personal information, you will be prompted to do so. Enter this information and click OK.

3. Choose the specific formatting of your letter (see fig. 32.3). The formatting elements you set are:

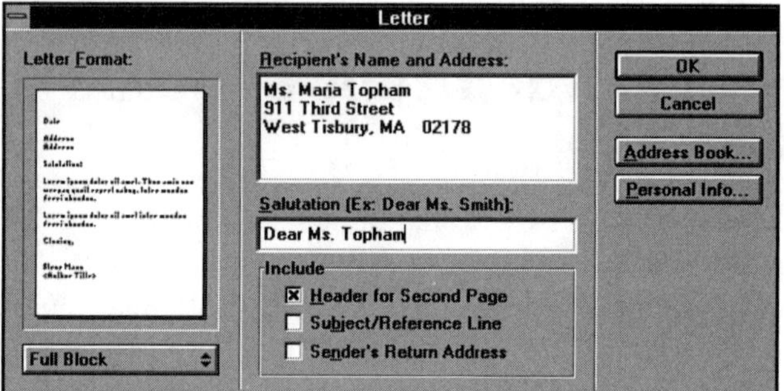

Fig. 32.3
The Create a Letter QuickTask enables you to make specific formatting choices for your letter.

- *Letter **F**ormat.* This format determines placement of the date, recipient's address, and the letter closing. The predefined letter formats are Full Block, Modified Block, Semi-Block, and Simplified. When the dialog box appears, Full Block is selected. To choose another format, click the Letter Format button at the bottom left of the dialog box, holding down the mouse button. Move the mouse pointer, and highlight bar, down the list to your new choice. Release the mouse button to complete the selection. The button text changes to reflect your new choice, and the letter preview area updates to display the new format.

- ***R**ecipient's Name and Address.* You can type this information directly into the address area of the dialog box, or access previously entered addresses by clicking the *Address Book* button.

- ***S**alutation.* Here you enter the letter's greeting, such as *Dear Ms. Topham*, or an informal *Hi Maria.*

- *Special Include items.* Three check boxes in the bottom center give you the option to include a header for the second page, a subject/reference line, and the sender's return address information.

The second page header option adds the recipient's name, page number, and date to the top left of each subsequent page. If you check the Subject/Reference line, a `RE:Subject` line is added on the line above the salutation. The return address information appears at the top of the letter, above the recipient's address.

- *Personal Information.* The first time you use any QuickTask that involves WordPerfect for Windows, the task requests that you enter your personal information (see step 2). Subsequent QuickTasks use that same information. The **P**ersonal Info button on this dialog box gives you access to that information. Choose it to edit existing entries or add new information.

After selecting all of your letter's format options, click OK.

4. An informational dialog box instructs you to look for a small Continue dialog box that will sit out of the way while you edit your letter in WordPerfect (see fig. 32.4). Read the text in the dialog box (remember the **T**ip button if you want more instructions), and then click **N**ext.

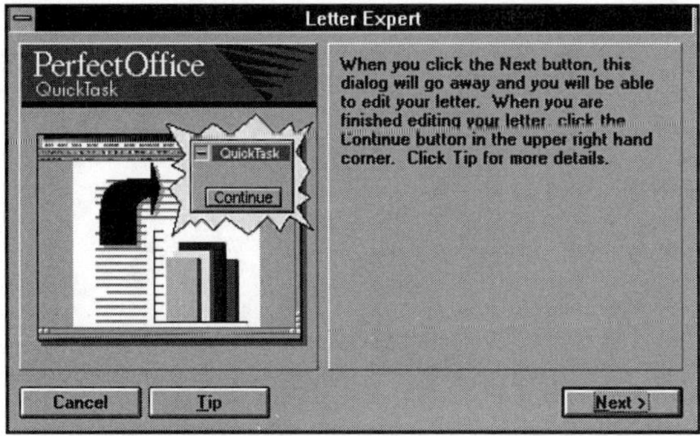

Fig. 32.4
QuickTask informs you that although you'll be able to edit your letter in WordPerfect, it will be waiting to help you with more steps.

5. Write your letter. All the features of WordPerfect are at your disposal. QuickTask's Continue dialog box waits in the upper-right corner (see fig. 32.5).

Fig. 32.5
This small dialog box waits in the upper-right corner of your screen, staying out of your way while you edit your letter.

6. When you have finished writing your letter, click the **C**ontinue button in the QuickTask dialog box.

7. With the body of the letter complete, you're ready to add the letter closing (see fig. 32.6). Like the formatting options in step 2, you have several choices:

   - *Co**m**plimentary Closing.* Click and hold down the mouse button, then move the mouse pointer over the specific text closing. There are 13 different items from which to choose.

   - *Include items.* Check the boxes for writer's initials, typist's initials, and enclosures. For each check you make, be sure to fill in the information to the right of the check box (initials or number of enclosures). These are standard items for most business letters.

   - *Cou**r**tesy Copies To.* This item is the CC you find at the bottom of many business letters and memos. If you are sending copies of the letter to individuals other than the recipient, add their names to this list. The **S**ave Group and Se**l**ect Group buttons are tools to manage multiple groups.

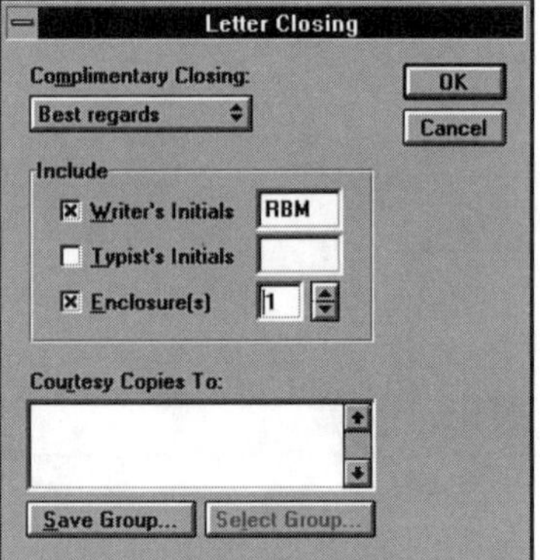

Fig. 32.6
The letter closing completes the body of your letter.

8. Completing the letter itself usually doesn't finish your work. You created the letter to do something with it. The Letter Expert dialog box anticipates several actions you might want to take (see fig. 32.7). Simply check the box next to each action you want the QuickTask to perform and then click **F**inish.

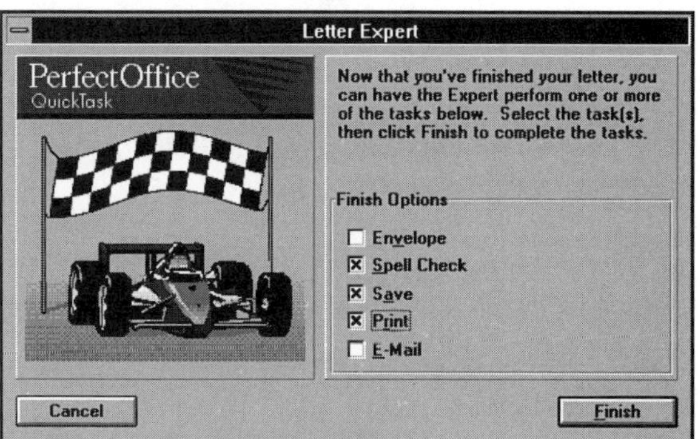

Fig. 32.7
Use the Letter Expert dialog box to complete the process of creating a letter.

Note

The items on the Letter Expert dialog box appear in the order they are actually carried out. Selecting **S**pell Check, **S**ave, and **E**-Mail will cause the QuickTasks to spell check before saving, then mail the document. This applies to all Letter Expert dialog boxes, regardless of the specific items in the list.

Troubleshooting

When I run a QuickTask, the dialog box flashes on the screen and then disappears.

If a QuickTask's window or dialog box disappears, it is usually just hidden behind another window, typically the application's main window. Use the Alt+Tab keys to find and switch to "Desktop Application Director."

QuickTask #2—Schedule a Trip

The Schedule a Trip QuickTask gathers information about your trip, then schedules your time away in InfoCentral, GroupWise, or both.

The Create a Letter QuickTask demonstrated how QuickTasks automate a work process from start to finish. Although creating the letter involved several steps and options, only WordPerfect is required. Schedule a Trip makes use of several applications: Quattro Pro, InfoCentral, and GroupWise. It is also one of the PerfectLinks QuickTasks—meaning that it will automatically detect which Windows spreadsheet is installed and use it to schedule your trip. So you can add Excel and 1-2-3 to the list of applications involved in the task.

Tip
As with all QuickTasks, the introductory dialog box lets you read about the purpose of the task before getting too far into it. If you decide not to run the task, click the Cancel button.

Follow these steps to schedule a trip:

1. Click the Schedule a Trip button on the QuickTask toolbar to display an introductory dialog box describing the task (see fig. 32.8). To continue, choose **N**ext.

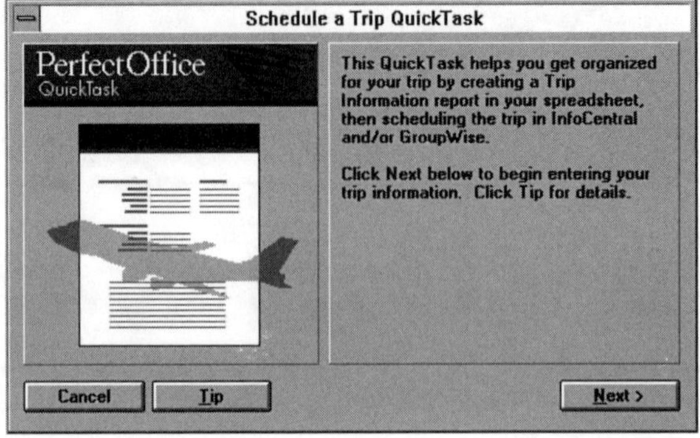

Fig. 32.8
Each QuickTask informs you of the task's purpose before starting its work.

Tip
QuickTasks make it simple to back up a step. If you need to correct spelling mistakes, enter new information, or review descriptions from a previous step, click the **P**revious button.

2. Fill in each of the fields with the specifics of your trip including your name (or the person who is going on the trip), destination, and the hotel's name, address, and phone number (see fig. 32.9). When you are finished, click **N**ext.

3. Enter your departure information. Figure 32.10 shows the handy calendar icon next to the Date edit box, which makes it easy to enter dates. Click the calendar icon to pop up the current month's calendar. The double arrows on the calendar advance or back up a year at a time; the single arrows move a month forward or back. Select an airline, either from the drop-down list, or by typing directly into the edit box. When you've entered all the information, click **N**ext.

4. Enter your return information. The dialog box is identical to the one in figure 32.10. Remember, this QuickTask only needs to know your departure and return flights to schedule the trip in your calendar—it doesn't need to know about connecting flights, layovers, or other intermediate details.

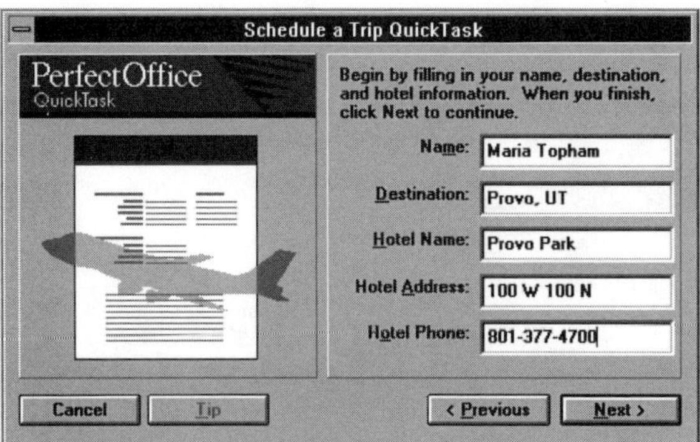

Fig. 32.9
The Schedule a Trip QuickTask first gathers information about where you'll be going and where you'll stay.

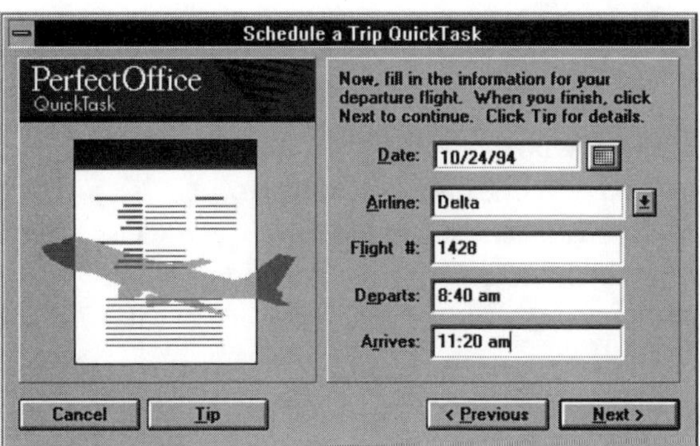

Fig. 32.10
Once you've entered where you're going, you need to supply information about when you'll leave and return.

5. This is the PerfectLinks part of the task. If you have two or more Windows spreadsheets on your hard disk, the dialog box in figure 32.11 appears asking you to choose one. Of course, Quattro Pro is the default, because it is a key component of PerfectOffice. If you want QuickTasks to always use the same spreadsheet, even if you have more than one installed, check the box labeled Make Current Selection the Default, and QuickTasks won't prompt you next time. For single spreadsheet users, the QuickTask will skip this step.

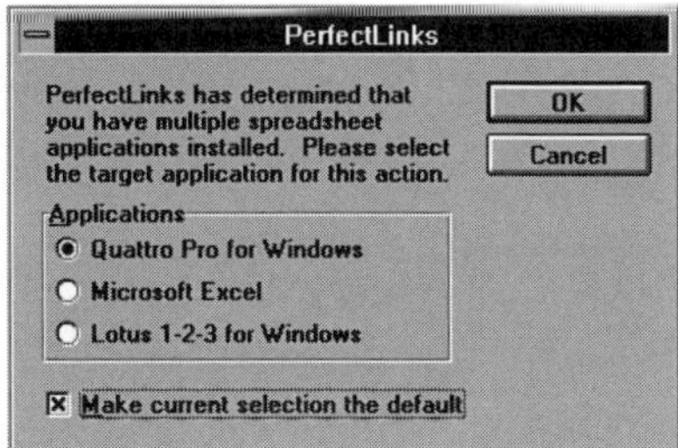

Fig. 32.11
If you have more than one spreadsheet installed, PerfectLinks will ask you which spreadsheet you wish to use to complete the QuickTask.

6. The task proceeds, creating a spreadsheet notebook which summarizes your trip information (see fig. 32.12). You can edit the information, and then click **C**ontinue in the dialog box in the upper-right corner.

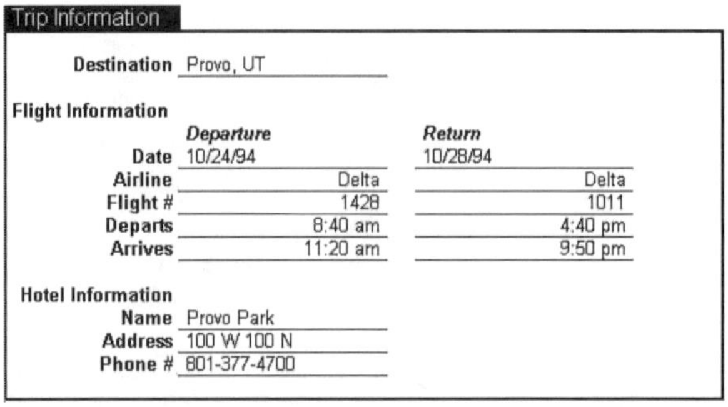

Fig. 32.12
Your trip schedule appears so you can make any changes before continuing to the last step.

Trip Information

Destination Provo, UT

Flight Information

	Departure	***Return***
Date	10/24/94	10/28/94
Airline	Delta	Delta
Flight #	1428	1011
Departs	8:40 am	4:40 pm
Arrives	11:20 am	9:50 pm

Hotel Information

Name Provo Park
Address 100 W 100 N
Phone # 801-377-4700

◄ See "Scheduling Appointments and Meetings," p. 611

7. The Finish dialog box (see fig. 32.13) then gives you four options: **P**rint Worksheet, **S**ave Worksheet, Schedule **G**roupWise, and Schedule **I**nfoCentral. If you schedule in GroupWise, the task schedules an appointment which blocks out the days that you'll be gone. InfoCentral scheduling enters the trip in your InfoCentral calendar.

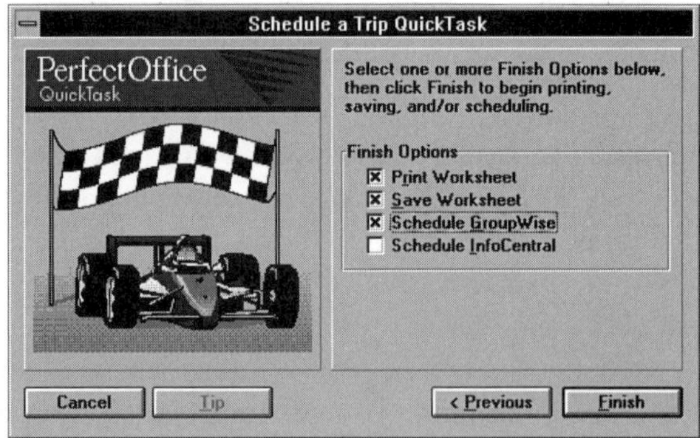

Fig. 32.13
The Schedule a Trip QuickTask concludes with a Finish dialog box that helps you to print or schedule your trip in either GroupWise or InfoCentral.

QuickTask #3—Finish Document

The Finish Document QuickTask automates tasks you typically do once your document is complete.

Both the Create a Letter and Schedule a Trip QuickTasks incorporate a final step called the Finish dialog box. What if you want to "finish" a document (or spreadsheet, slideshow, or other type of file) that was not created by a QuickTask? Your third QuickTask answers that question. While the concept is simple, this QuickTask is actually quite powerful and can involve several applications. As usual, for you the whole process is application-independent. Here are the steps to finish a document:

1. Choose the Finish a Document QuickTask from the QuickTasks toolbar.

2. The QuickTask detects which PerfectOffice applications are running and asks whether you want to use a document from an open application or from a file on disk. Select the check box for the proper document type (see fig. 32.14).

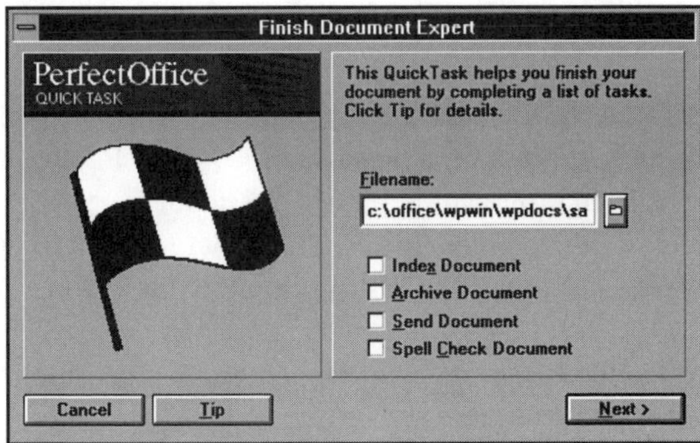

Fig. 32.14
The Finish a Document Quick-Task operates on any disk file or document currently open in WordPerfect, Quattro Pro, or Presentations; and as any file on disk.

If you choose a file from disk, you'll need to enter the document name or click the file browser. Move to step 3 *before* choosing **N**ext.

◄ See "Saving, Opening, and Closing Files," p. 59

3. Finish has a large list of actions it can perform on the document (see fig. 32.15). Some of these actions are simple, some complex. Some of the actions, such as Index and Archive, are complete QuickTasks by themselves. Rather than trace through the dialog boxes for each of these actions, they are described in the text that follows:

   - *Spell check.* If the file is a WordPerfect document or a Quattro Pro spreadsheet, the task will run the Spell Checker, just as if you had chosen Spell Check from the application's menu.

   - *Save.* If you choose a currently open document, this causes the document to be saved to disk.

   - *Print.* Prints the document to the default Windows printer.

   - *E-mail.* The QuickTask looks for an existing e-mail system and sends the document. This is another example of PerfectLinks, because the Finish dialog box supports both cc:Mail and MS Mail.

If you installed the GroupWise QuickLook that comes with PerfectOffice, try using e-mail to send a document to yourself.

- *Fax.* This action is enabled only if the QuickTask finds a fax driver installed on your system. If one is installed, the QuickTask faxes through your fax driver.

► See "An Overview of Envoy," p. 701

- *Publish to Envoy.* "Prints" the document to Envoy for sharing with others in a work group.

◄ See "Finding Files with QuickFinder," p. 79

- *Index.* Adds the document to a QuickFinder index for rapid searching and retrieving of the file at a later date. There is a separate Index QuickTask that Finish uses to complete this action.

- *Archive.* Makes a backup copy of the file to an archive location you specify, often on a network drive, with simple versioning control—in other words, archiving the file repeatedly does not overwrite the previously saved file. There is a separate Archive QuickTask that Finish uses to complete this action.

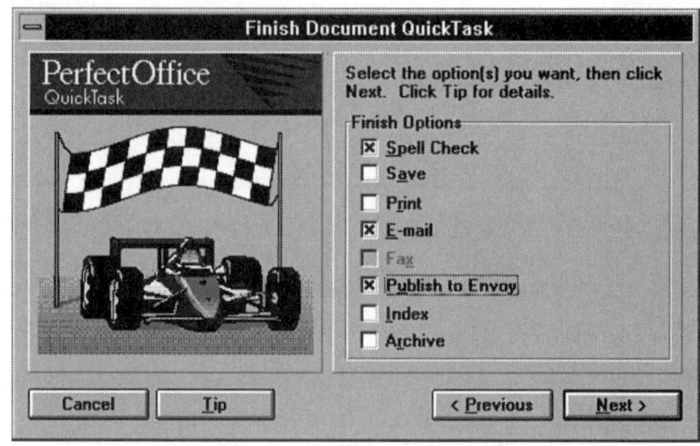

Fig. 32.15
The Finish a Document QuickTask gives you a simple way to "finish" a file. Finishing means any task you would perform with a completed file, such as printing, e-mailing, or indexing.

4. Select the boxes for the actions you want, and click **F**inish. Each action is then carried out in sequence. The specific dialog boxes you'll encounter depend on the steps you choose.

QuickTask #4—Merge Paradox Data into WordPerfect

The Merge Paradox Data in WordPerfect QuickTask makes quick work of merging or importing any type of Paradox database into WordPerfect for Windows.

One of the most common types of data integration is between a database and a word processor. Typical merges are to merge customer lists from a database into a form letter created in the word processor, or to make a nicely formatted table in the word processor from a list in the database. The Merge QuickTask makes pulling data from Paradox into WordPerfect a snap. Here you'll take some Paradox data into a WordPerfect table:

◄ See "Using Merge," p. 226

1. Click the Merge Paradox Data into WordPerfect QuickTask on the QuickTask toolbar.

2. Select the merge type. As figure 32.16 shows, your choices are

   - **M**erge Only
   - **I**mport Only
   - Import **a**nd Merge

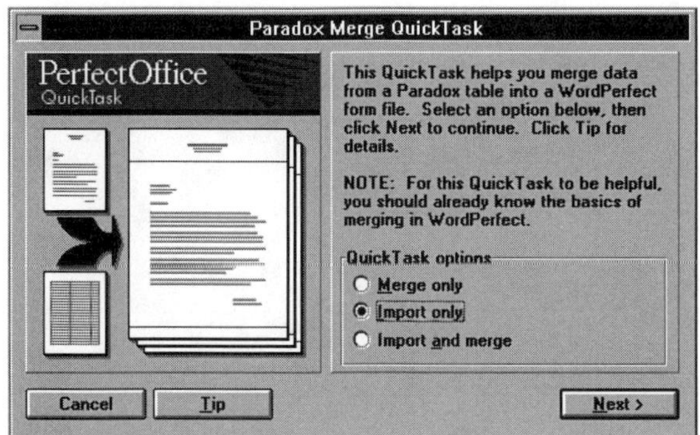

Fig. 32.16
Merge combines the Paradox data with a WordPerfect form to create new documents. Import brings the Paradox data into WordPerfect as either a table or a ready-to-be-merged data file.

   Merge combines the Paradox data with the WordPerfect form (usually a form letter) right now. *Import* brings the Paradox data into WordPerfect in either a table or a file ready to be merged, but doesn't actually perform the merge right now.

3. If Paradox is running, you can choose to merge or import the currently selected table in Paradox. Otherwise, choose Paradox **T**able on Disk (see fig. 32.17). Type in a filename or use the Browse button. The Paradox sample file CONTACTS.DB is a good example to demonstrate a table import. The file is located in the Paradox sample directory (usually C:\OFFICE\PDOXWIN\SAMPLE).

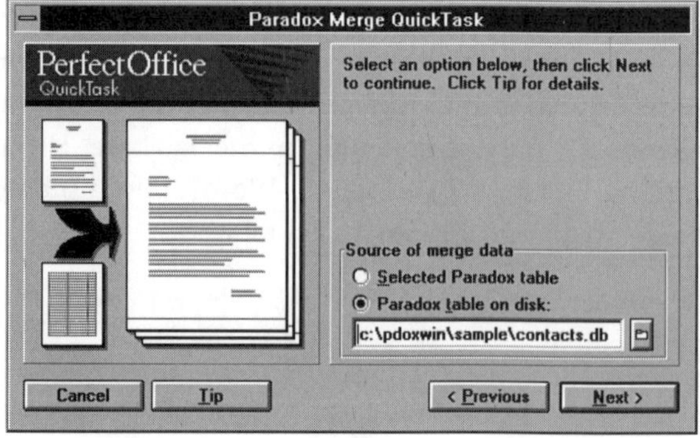

Fig. 32.17 You can merge either an open database in Paradox or a Paradox database file from disk with the Merge QuickTask.

4. When importing, your final choice is the type of import (see fig. 32.18):

   - Import as WordPerfect **T**able
   - Import as WordPerfect **D**ata File

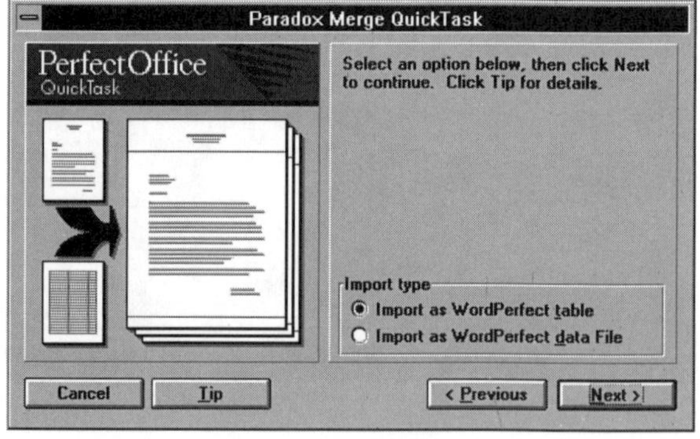

Fig. 32.18 When importing, you specify to import as either a WordPerfect table or data file. Use a data file if you intend to merge the data later.

The task has gathered all the information it needs, so it starts up Paradox, reads in the CONTACTS.DB database, then starts WordPerfect for Windows and begins to extract the data from Paradox into WordPerfect for Windows.

5. The QuickTask will inform you when the import is complete. Click OK to exit the QuickTask.

QuickTask #5—Create a "Start My Day" QuickTask

The fifth, and final, QuickTask in this guided tour is the Create "Start My Day" QuickTask. As the title indicates, this task is a little different from the others you've experienced so far. The unique aspect of this task is that its sole purpose is to create another QuickTask!

The goal is to make a QuickTask that you can run every morning—a task that starts your day. The problem is that every PerfectOffice user starts the day a little differently. Rather than try to define a one-size-fits-all QuickTask for this purpose, PerfectOffice supplies a way for you to create your own "Start My Day" QuickTask. If that sounds a little confusing, don't worry; it's really quite simple. Let's look at it step-by-step and see how it works:

1. Start the Create "Start My Day" QuickTask by clicking the button on the QuickTasks toolbar.

2. This introductory dialog box gives more detail on the purpose of this QuickTask (see fig. 32.19). Click **N**ext.

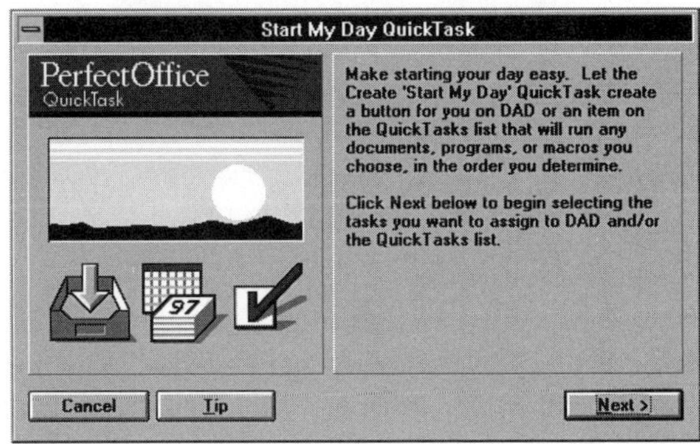

Fig. 32.19
Like other QuickTasks, Create "Start My Day" begins with an introductory dialog box that explains that QuickTask's purpose.

3. Figure 32.20 shows a list of predefined actions you might choose to start your day. Activate an item by clicking its description or the small check box to the left of the description.

   To add your own items to the list, click the Add button. For each item you add to the list, you'll need to enter the program name and a description name that will appear in the list. Add programs, macros, or documents from the dialog box shown in figure 32.21.

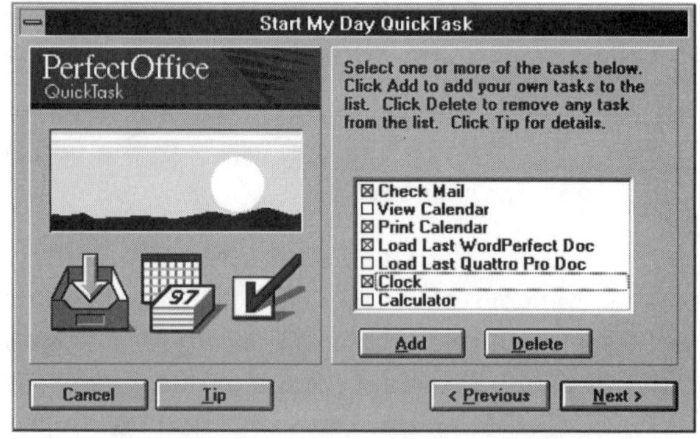

Fig. 32.20
The check boxes next to the list items indicate whether that item will be included in your customized "Start My Day" QuickTask.

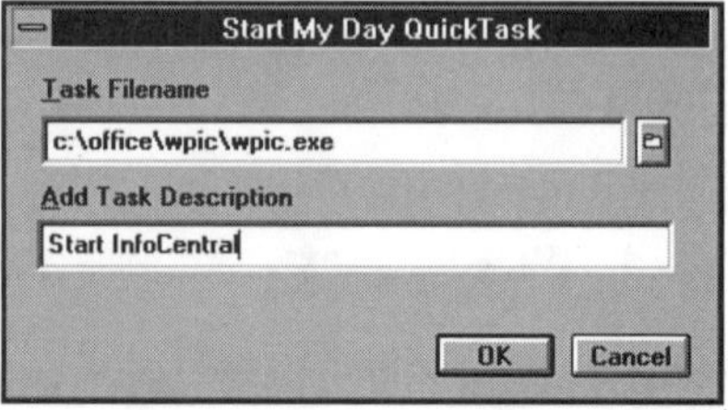

Fig. 32.21
The list of "Start My Day" actions can be extended by adding your own items, such as programs, macros, or documents, to the list.

The Delete button enables you to remove items from the list. However, you usually don't need to delete items, because you can uncheck them in the list. Deleting an item removes it from the list permanently. When all items are chosen and added, choose **N**ext.

4. The next step is to determine the order in which the items should execute. Only the items that are selected in the list in the previous dialog box will appear in this step (see fig. 32.22). The top-most item will occur first, then progress sequentially down the list. To move an item up in the order, click it to highlight it, and then choose Move Up (or Move Down to push it toward the bottom of the list). Continue moving items up or down until they are in the order you want, and then click **N**ext.

5. Now for the most unique part of this QuickTask. Choosing **N**ext doesn't run anything. Instead, it brings you to a Finish dialog box with only two options (see fig. 32.23):

   - Add as Button on **D**AD
   - Add to **Q**uickTask List

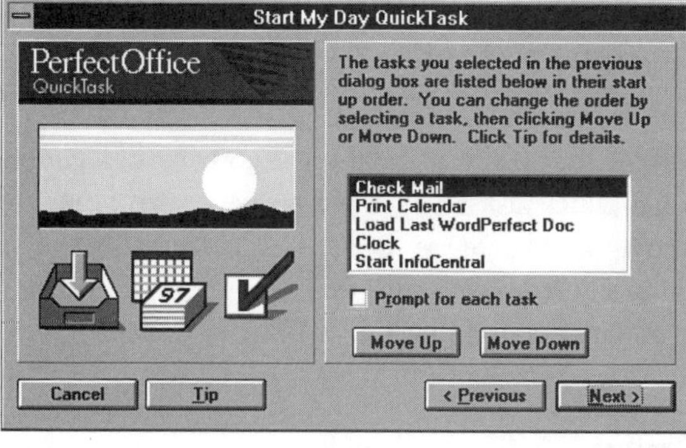

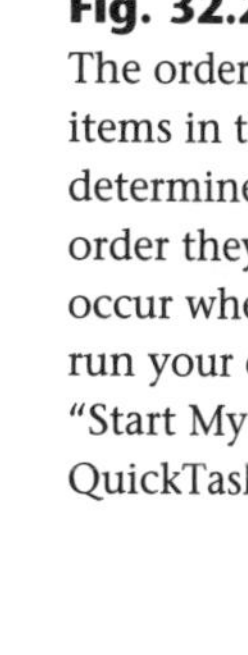

Fig. 32.22
The order of the items in the list determines the order they will occur when you run your own "Start My Day" QuickTask.

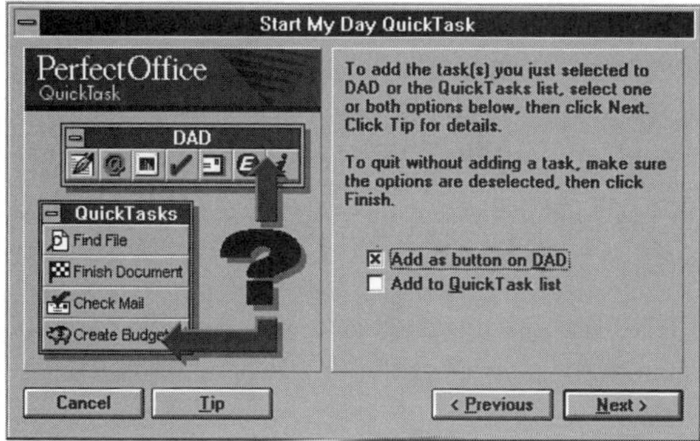

Fig. 32.23
You choose whether to place your new Quick-Task on DAD or on the QuickTask toolbar.

What do they mean? Let's review. You created a customized QuickTask that performs certain actions to start your day. You went through a list of predefined actions and had the chance to add some of your own. You picked several actions that appealed to you.

It wouldn't be very effective to go through this process at the beginning of every day—too much work. What would be better is to save the choices you've made up to this point, and then automatically run those choices when you are ready to start a new day. All you need is a way to indicate when you want that event to occur.

This Finish dialog box tells you that it is going to save your list of actions and make a way for you to run that list. That method will be either a new button on the DAD bar, or a new task button on the QuickTask toolbar (or both!). The QuickTask will ask you to enter a descriptive name for your customized task (for example, **Brenda's Start My Day Task**) and then will generate a filename for you. You can edit the filename if you choose. Choose **A**dd and your task will be added.

Try adding a new button to DAD. The button will have the description you enter. When you click it, it will run the exact list of actions you selected.

It is important that you understand the concept of a QuickTask that creates other QuickTasks. As you experiment with other QuickTasks, you'll discover that there are several that perform similarly. You run them, define a custom sequence that you prefer, and then save that sequence on DAD or as a new QuickTask.

From Here...

You've learned how to use QuickTasks to get your work done more effectively. From here, you can learn more about creating new QuickTasks to automate your own work. Look in the following chapters:

- Chapter 31, "Organizing Your Work with InfoCentral," shows you how to create a personal or company address book, and save information on clients, staff, or inventories.
- Chapter 36, "Customizing Toolbars, DAD Bars, and Menus," shows you how to change the contents of your QuickTask toolbar.

Chapter 33

Working with DAD

by Steve Mann

Chapter 2 introduced you to the Desktop Application Director, or *DAD*, the hub of PerfectOffice. Although you can use PerfectOffice without DAD, you'll get the most integration from PerfectOffice by using it. This chapter will focus on how you can get the most from DAD's special capabilites. In this chapter, you learn how to

- Use DAD's QuickFiles for file management
- Open recently used files directly from DAD with QuickOpen
- Launch programs, scripts, or open files by specifying commands or file names with DAD's QuickRun
- Tile the PerfectOffice applications, making it easier to work with more than one application at a time
- Add your own applications to the list of PerfectOffice applications that DAD tiles
- Access Windows Control Panel applets from DAD's Control Panel toolbar
- Share data easily between PerfectOffice applications with DAD's Data Sharing toolbar

Understanding PerfectFit Technology

Many of DAD's capabilities build on PerfectFit technology, the underlying foundation for much of PerfectOffice. PerfectFit, as first explained in Chapter 1, enables PerfectOffice applications to share common components, such as dialog boxes, toolbars, menus, and tools like the Spell Checker and QuickCorrect.

DAD takes these PerfectFit components and makes them available from the desktop, independent of any application. Because DAD builds on the same PerfectFit components as the applications, many of DAD's capabilities will already be familiar to you. For example, the shared toolbar component of PerfectFit gives DAD and the PerfectOffice applications common methods for moving and resizing their toolbars: adding buttons to launch applications and scripts, removing buttons, and changing the text on buttons. Once you've learned to edit DAD's toolbars, you already know how to edit the toolbars in WordPerfect.

▶ See "Customizing Toolbars and DAD Bars," p. 740

DAD has the usual capabilities you expect from a toolbar—the ability to launch programs and scripts, for example—but it also has several special "Quick" capabilities unique to DAD and available directly from DAD's default toolbar (called the PerfectOffice toolbar.) The most prominent of these special capabilities are QuickTasks (the subject of the last chapter), QuickFiles, QuickOpen, QuickRun, and a tiling feature specific to PerfectOffice applications (see fig. 33.1). These special features are the subject of this chapter.

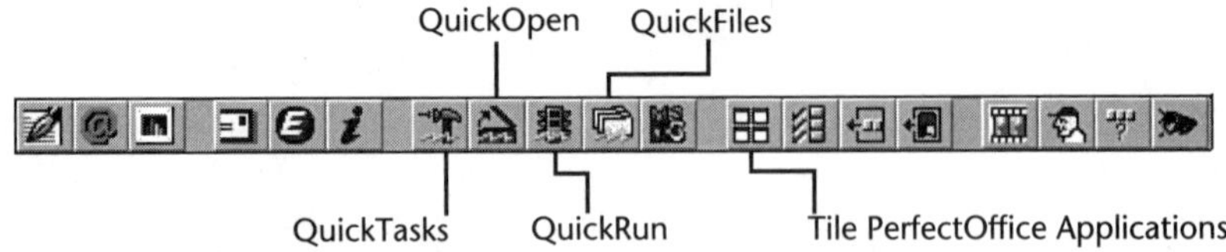

Fig. 33.1
A key to working effectively with DAD is understanding DAD's special features.

Using QuickFiles

DAD gives you all of the capabilities of a file manager right from the QuickFiles button. When you select QuickFiles, you see what should be a familiar dialog box—the directory dialog box from PerfectOffice applications (see fig. 33.2). All of the features available from the directory dialog boxes are also available from QuickFiles.

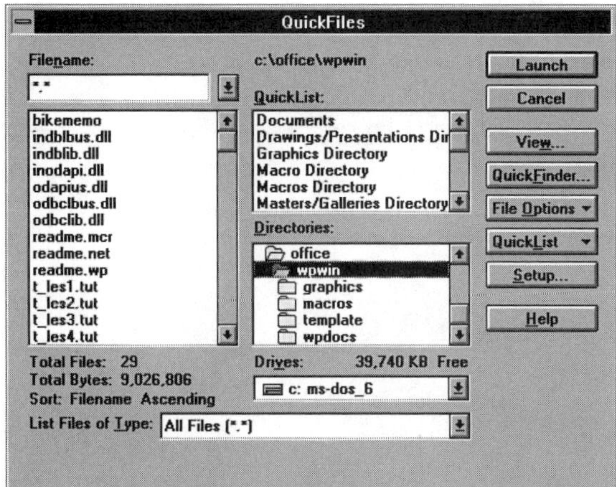

Fig. 33.2
The QuickFiles dialog box gives DAD the same file management capabilities that PerfectOffice applications share in their directory dialog boxes.

Note

While the QuickFiles dialog box is active, you cannot use other DAD features or buttons, but you can switch to other applications. To switch, simply click the application's window (if it is visible), or press Alt+Tab until you see the application you want. To switch back, use Alt+Tab to select the Desktop Application Director (DAD). The QuickFiles dialog box will come forward with DAD.

◄ See "Using Directory Dialog Boxes," p. 63

QuickFiles is a powerful tool for managing files, and it includes many hidden treasures, like the QuickFinder, QuickList, and viewer. Be sure to spend the time to familiarize yourself with QuickFiles. The time will be well spent.

Tip
Right-click the file name, QuickList, or directories list box to display a QuickMenu full of additional commands that apply to that list box.

Using QuickOpen

QuickOpen is a shortcut for you to get back to work on the files you have recently worked on. The idea is simple. You are probably familiar with the list of recently-opened files on the File menu of most applications. DAD looks for these lists of files for each of the applications in PerfectOffice as well as Excel and Lotus 1-2-3. This saves you the steps of launching the application, then choosing the file from the application's File menu. With QuickOpen, you go right to the file you were working on, and DAD handles the details of getting the application up and loading the right file.

When you click the QuickOpen button, you see a list of the last opened files from each of the applications, as well as the icon of the application that file is associated with (see fig. 33.3). To launch the appropriate application already loaded with the file, just click that file's button in the QuickOpen list. The files are listed by application, with the most recently used files first.

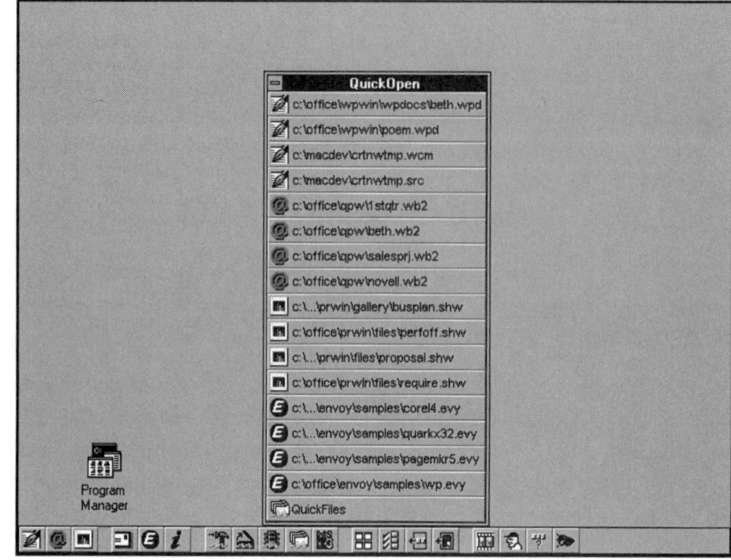

Fig. 33.3
DAD's QuickOpen list gives you fast access to the files you last worked with in any of the PerfectOffice applications.

Tip
QuickOpen is the fastest way to get back to your files in the morning or after restarting Windows. Just click QuickOpen, choose the document you were last editing and you're right back to work!

► See "Setting DAD Bar Display Preferences," p. 744

Unlike QuickFiles, which brings up a directory dialog box, the QuickOpen list is a special type of DAD toolbar called a *palette*. This particular palette always stays in front of other windows. If you Alt+Tab to another window, or launch a program, the QuickOpen toolbar will stay in front. You can either click one of the QuickOpen's buttons to open a file, or double-click the Control menu box on the title bar. You'll notice that there is no Control menu, but double-clicking the Control menu box will close the toolbar.

Using QuickRun

QuickRun is a fast way to launch programs, scripts, or even documents with their associated applications that are not already on DAD as buttons. When you choose the QuickRun button, you see the dialog box shown in figure 33.4.

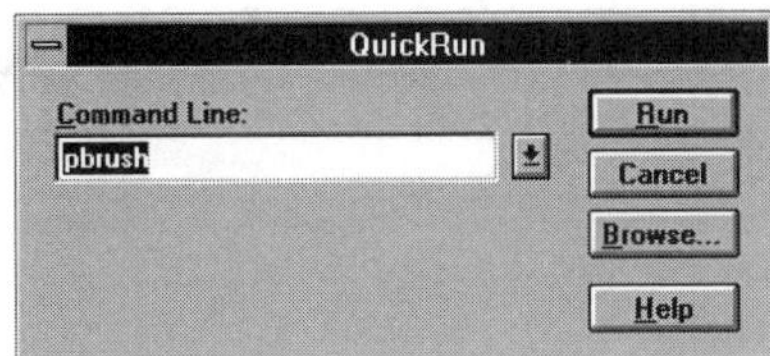

Fig. 33.4
QuickRun is DAD's shortcut for launching programs, scripts, or documents that don't already have a DAD button.

You can enter a file name, with or without a complete path, or choose the **B**rowse button to search for the item you wish to run. Clicking **B**rowse in the QuickRun dialog box gives you the same capability as choosing QuickFiles from DAD. Not only can you search for a file, you can also rename, copy, or delete files or directories while in QuickRun's Browse dialog box. After you enter or select a file, choose **R**un.

◄ See "Using QuickFinder," p. 76

When you enter a program name, QuickRun automatically searches for the file in the directory you specify (if any), and then looks in the DOS current directory, your Windows directory, and in all the directories in your DOS PATH.

If you enter a document name, QuickRun makes use of the Windows associations, based on the three letter extension of the file name. These associations are part of Windows that you access from the Windows File Manager, under **F**ile, **A**ssociate. Many Windows applications also register a default extension, or association, in the system registry file when the product is installed. These associations are not visible in the Windows File Manager.

For example, the file extension WPD is associated with WordPerfect. If you enter the file name C:\OFFICE\WPWIN\WPDOCS\MYDOC.WPD, QuickRun will know to start up WordPerfect with MYDOC.WPD loaded.

The default extensions registered for the PerfectOffice applications are shown in table 33.1.

Table 33.1 PerfectOffice Default File Types and Their Associated Extensions

File Type	Default Extension
WordPerfect for Windows document	WPD
WordPerfect for Windows template	WPT
WordPerfect graphic	WPG

(continues)

Table 33.1 Continued

File Type	Default Extension
WordPerfect form	FRM
WordPerfect data file	DAT
Quattro Pro 6.0 notebook	WB2
Quattro Pro 5.0 notebook	WB1
Paradox database	DB
Presentations slide show	SHW
Presentations master	MST
InfoCentral iBase	ICA
Envoy document	EVY
PerfectScript script (macro)	WCM
PerfectScript coach	WCH
AppWare project	PRJ

Tip
When browsing or using QuickFiles to launch a document, use the View button to make sure you've got the right file before running or opening it.

One very convenient feature of QuickRun is the history list, which you access by clicking the down arrow next to the **C**ommand Line text box (see fig. 33.5). QuickRun remembers the last ten QuickRun commands, even across sessions.

Like the QuickFiles dialog box, you cannot access other DAD features until you close the dialog box, either by choosing Run or Cancel, but you can Alt+Tab to other windows. Just remember to Alt+Tab to the Desktop Application Director to get back to the QuickRun dialog box.

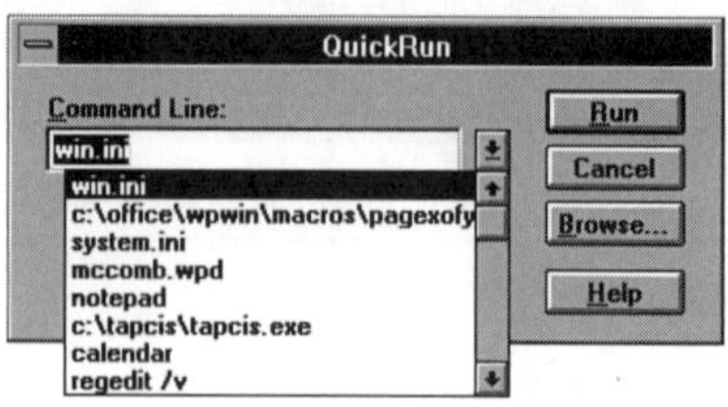

Fig. 33.5
QuickRun's history list remembers the last ten commands you issued from the QuickRun dialog box.

Troubleshooting

I enter a document name in QuickRun, but it doesn't launch WordPerfect. What am I doing wrong?

QuickRun can only launch an application based on the three letter extension of the file name. If you give your WordPerfect documents an extension other than WPD, QuickRun will not know which application to launch.

If you don't like the WPD default extension, or you want more than one extension to be associated with WordPerfect, you'll need to add a new association. The easiest way to create a new association is from the Windows File Manager (WINFILE.EXE). Run File Manager (use QuickRun!), and then choose the **F**ile, **A**ssociate command. Enter the new extension and select WordPerfect Document in the **A**ssociate With list box. Click OK and your new association is set up for QuickRun.

Tiling PerfectOffice Applications

When you are working with PerfectOffice applications, you may find that DAD's Tile button is more useful than the tiling available from Windows.

Tiling from Windows

To tile from Windows, you have to press Ctrl+Esc (or double-click the Windows desktop) to bring up the Task List, and then choose the **T**ile button (see fig. 33.6).

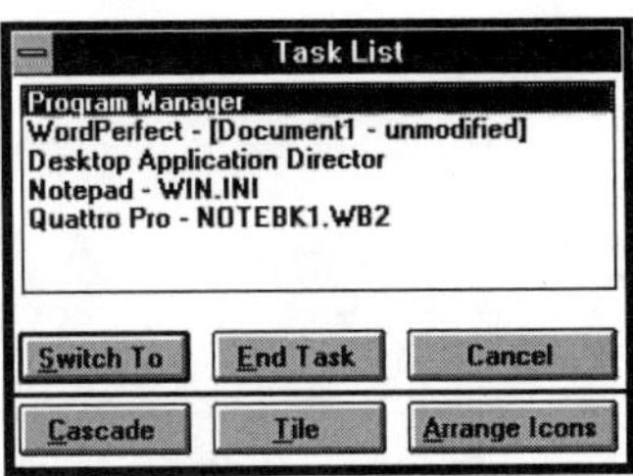

Fig. 33.6
You can tile all open applications from the Windows Task Manager by pressing Ctrl+ESC, then choosing Tile.

When you choose Task List's **T**ile button, the screen is divided equally between all of the items in the Task List; the windows are resized and placed side by side (except for minimized applications). This procedure will often tile applications you don't want tiled—like Program Manager (see fig. 33.7).

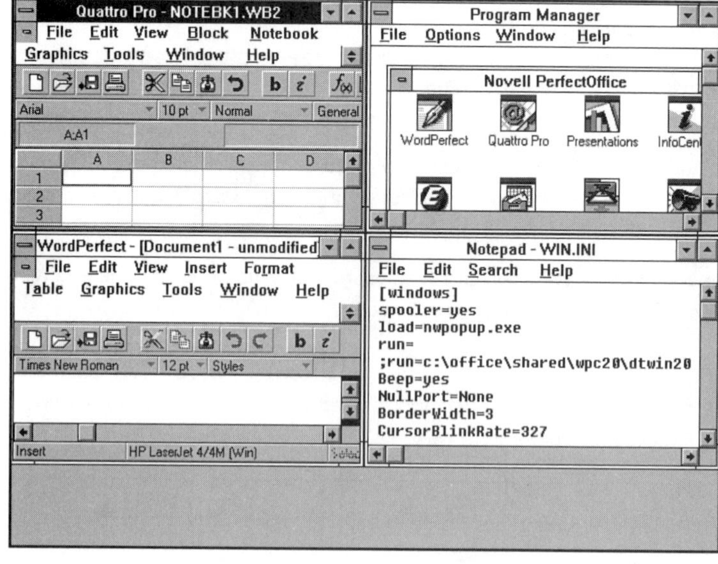

Fig. 33.7 Task List's Tile option often includes applications you don't want tiled, such as Program Manager.

Tip Tile applications horizontally—top-to-bottom instead of side-by-side—by holding down the Shift key while choosing the DAD Tile button.

Tiling from the DAD Bar

More often, you want only the major applications you are working with to be tiled. For example, if you are using WordPerfect and Quattro Pro, you might want to transfer a Quattro Pro chart into WordPerfect using cut and paste, or OLE drag-and-drop. Or, you might want to review a WordPerfect document while creating a slide show in Presentations.

When you click the Tile button on the DAD Bar, you tile as shown in figure 33.8. Only the open (non-minimized) PerfectOffice applications are tiled.

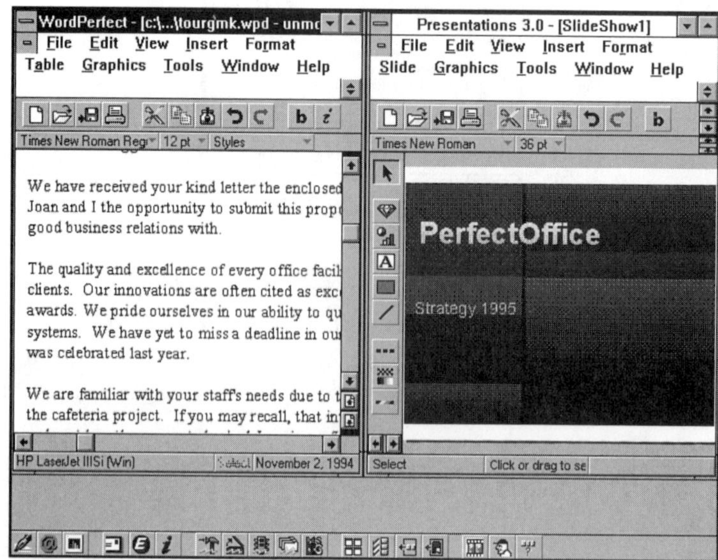

Fig. 33.8 DAD's tile function only tiles open PerfectOffice applications, making it easier to share data between applications.

Adding Applications to DAD's Tile List

By default, only the following applications are tiled by DAD: WordPerfect for Windows, Presentations, Quattro Pro, Paradox, Envoy, and InfoCentral. GroupWise is not tiled, because its main window is a fixed size.

Although there is no option to change the tile list from DAD, you can add additional applications by editing the WIN.INI file. Follow these steps to change DAD's list of tile applications:

1. Choose QuickRun, then type **WIN.INI** in the **C**ommand Line box. By association, NotePad will launch and open the WIN.INI file from your Windows directory so you can edit it.

2. Search for Desktop Application Director (DAD) by selecting **S**earch, **F**ind, then entering **Desktop App** in the Fi**n**d What line. Choose **F**ind Next to begin the search. Finally, choose Cancel to remove the Find dialog box. You should see a section of the file that matches the lines below:

```
[Desktop Application Director]
      .
```

(there may be other lines here)

```
      .
TileApp1=qpw.exe
TileApp2=wpwin61.exe
TileApp3=prwin30.exe
TileApp4=pdoxwin.exe
TileApp5=envoy.exe
TileApp6=wpic.exe
```

3. Remove an application by deleting its line and renumbering the TileApp# lines below it.

4. To add an application, add a TileApp# line, placing the next number in place of the #. You must enter the actual program name (for example, **WPWIN61.EXE** instead of **WordPerfect 6.1**) without a directory path. For example, to add the Windows Paintbrush program, you would add the following line to the section shown above:

   ```
   TileApp7=pbrush.exe
   ```

   The order that the applications are listed in the WIN.INI makes no difference, as long as the numbers are sequential. The order that you launch the applications determines the ordering during tiling—the first application launched appears left-most when tiled.

5. Choose **F**ile, **S**ave to save the revised WIN.INI file from Notepad.

In this way you can build custom lists of the applications you work with and want to have DAD tile. Adding or removing lines from this section of WIN.INI affects only the functioning of DAD's Tile button.

Caution

Misnumbering the TileApp statements causes all lines following the misnumbered line to be ignored. After adding or deleting from the TileApp list, double-check for sequential numbering. Do not leave any blank lines. A blank line is used to indicate the end of the section, in this case the `[Desktop Applications Director]` section.

Using Multiple DAD Bars

When you installed DAD, the PerfectOffice toolbar was set up for you, with buttons for the PerfectOffice applications, Quick features, and housekeeping tasks such as exiting DAD. The PerfectOffice installation also created other toolbars with specialized functions, but you may not have discovered these other toolbars.

Figure 33.9 shows DAD's QuickMenu, which you can activate by right-clicking DAD. The menu contains three sections. Our primary interest is the top section of the list, which shows a list of available DAD toolbars: Control Panel, PerfectOffice, and Data Sharing.

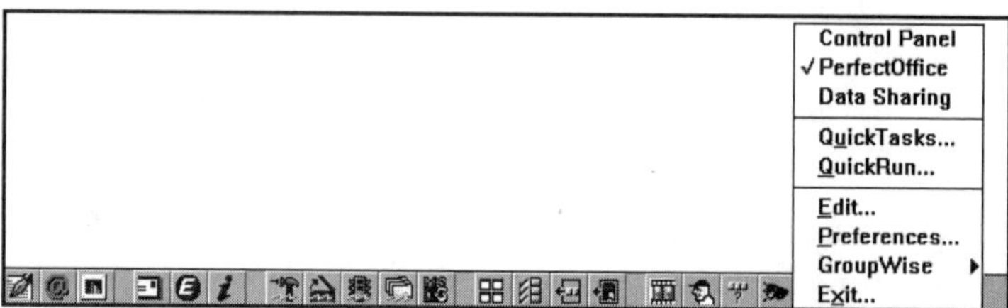

Fig. 33.9 Right-clicking DAD brings up a QuickMenu from which you can change among DAD's toolbars.

Tip

Although Quick-Run is a button only on DAD's default Perfect-Office toolbar, you can access Quick-Run from any toolbar through DAD's right-click QuickMenu.

To change to another toolbar, right-click DAD, and then, while holding down the right mouse button, move the highlight bar to the toolbar you want to select. When you release the mouse button, DAD will switch to the highlighted toolbar.

The Control Panel Toolbar

DAD's Control Panel toolbar makes many Windows settings easily accessible (see fig. 33.10). The following are items on the toolbar: Colors, Fonts, Ports, Mouse, Desktop, Keyboard, Printers, International, Date/Time, Network,

Volume, Recording, Sound, Drivers, and 386 Enhanced. These items are the same ones you can access from the Control Panel application in the Main program group in Windows.

Fig. 33.10
DAD's Control Panel toolbar contains buttons for many of the icons in Windows' Control Panel application.

You can use the Control Panel toolbar's Desktop button to try out PerfectOffice's two screen savers: Button Bounce and Wandering Buttons. Follow these steps:

1. Right-click DAD and choose Control Panel.
2. From the Control Panel toolbar, click the Launch Desktop button.
3. From the Desktop dialog box shown in figure 33.11, click the down arrow for the Screen Saver N**a**me. You see two new screen savers: Button Bounce and Wandering Buttons.
4. Click either one, then click the T**e**st button to get a preview of these new screen savers.

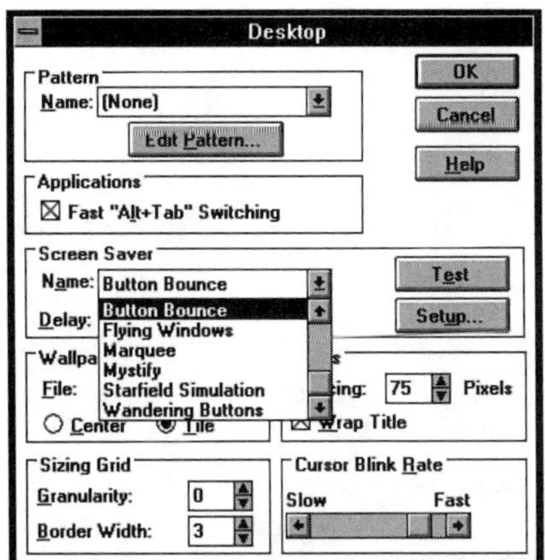

Fig. 33.11
Clicking the Desktop button on DAD's Control Panel toolbar brings you directly here, where you can try out PerfectOffice's two screen savers.

Note

Although the Control Panel toolbar is created in all installations of PerfectOffice, the two new PerfectOffice screen savers are not installed if you perform a minimum install.

The Data Sharing Toolbar

Application integration is a key message of PerfectOffice. The Data Sharing toolbar contains six buttons that simplify integration by sharing data between applications (see fig. 33.12). To display this toolbar, right-click the PerfectOffice toolbar and choose Data Sharing. The first three buttons are the common Clipboard cut, copy, and paste functions. While these abilites are available from many applications' toolbars or menus, having them on DAD makes it easy to use the Clipboard while switching between applications.

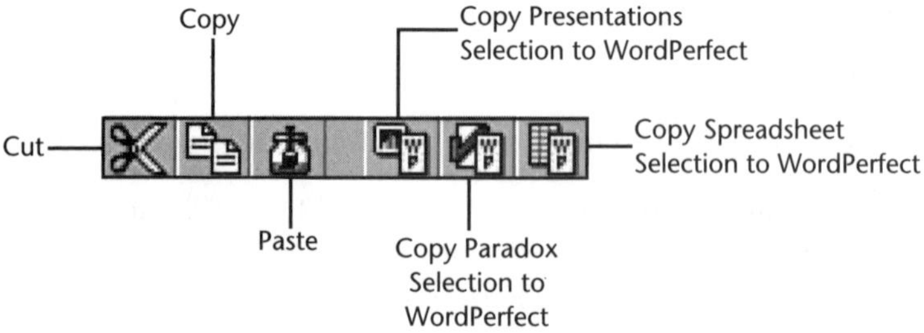

Copy
Copy Presentations Selection to WordPerfect
Cut
Copy Spreadsheet Selection to WordPerfect
Paste
Copy Paradox Selection to WordPerfect

Fig. 33.12
The Data Sharing toolbar makes it easy to share data between PerfectOffice applications.

For example, if you tile WordPerfect for Windows and Quattro Pro using DAD's Tile button, you can select data in one application, and cut or copy the data using DAD's buttons (see fig. 33.13). You then switch applications, either by clicking the application's window or by pressing Alt+Tab. To place the cut or copied object, position the cursor and click the Paste button.

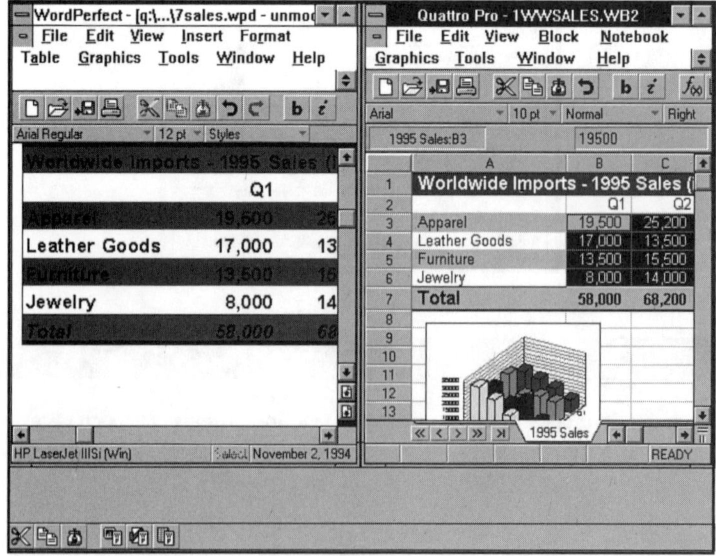

Fig. 33.13
When you combine DAD's ability to tile applications with Cut, Copy, and Paste, you get simple, yet powerful, data sharing.

The whole process sounds more difficult than it really is. Once you try out the Data Sharing toolbar, you'll quickly find it a powerful and fast method for moving data between applications. This method is especially useful when you want to copy several items.

In Chapter 36, you'll learn how the Cut, Copy, and Paste buttons can be added to other toolbars, including the PerfectOffice toolbar. If you find that you're using these features frequently, you may want to place them on your favorite toolbar, so that switching toolbars is not required to access them. The other three Data Sharing buttons automate copying—or optionally linking or embedding—data from Presentations, Paradox, or Quattro Pro into WordPerfect.

► See "Using the Data Sharing Toolbar," p. 737

From Here...

You've learned how to work more effectively with DAD, using QuickFiles, QuickOpen, QuickRun, and DAD's default Control Panel and Data Sharing toolbars. There's plenty more you can learn about customizing DAD—adding your own buttons, creating new toolbars from scratch or from Program Manager groups, and using DAD's advanced display options. There is also much yet to cover on data sharing, including using OLE 2.0 to link and embed data.

Here are chapters you should consider from here:

- Chapter 35, "Transferring Data Between Applications," explains DDE and OLE, and defines the differences between linking and embedding data.
- Chapter 36, "Customizing Toolbars, DAD Bars, and Menus," shows you how to edit, create, and customize DAD toolbars.

Chapter 34

Using Envoy

by Bill Bruck

PerfectOffice positions itself as a total office solution. An important part of this total solution is *document publishing*. Document publishing means distributing a document electronically, in a form that is easily readable no matter what computer is used to read the document. Novell Envoy is the document publishing application of PerfectOffice.

In this chapter, you learn how to

- Create an Envoy document
- Use the Envoy Viewer to read an Envoy document
- Annotate an Envoy document
- Add bookmarks and hypertext links to an Envoy document

An Overview of Envoy

Using Envoy, you can create a document that

- Can be read on both PCs and Macintoshes
- Cannot be changed by readers
- Can, however, be annotated by reviewers
- Includes objects such as sound files or animated pictures
- Contains bookmarks and hypertext links to help readers move through the document

For example, you may want to maintain a technical manual that includes text, diagrams, and pictures. It is probably vital that users not make changes to this document, but it is equally important that they be able to jump quickly to procedures of interest.

Alternatively, you may wish to route a contract via GroupWise to a variety of attorneys and representatives of the contracting parties for comment. It is important that the original document not be altered, but that reviewers be able to highlight important parts, put "sticky" notes on it, read others' comments, and identify who has made which comment.

In either of these cases, Envoy provides the solution.

Envoy consists of two parts. The Envoy printer driver is used to convert a document from its original format into an Envoy document. This driver enables you to create an Envoy document from any application that can send a job to a Windows printer. It even enables you to embed the original document's fonts in the Envoy document, to ensure that exact formatting is maintained.

The second part is the Viewer. The Viewer enables the document to be read and annotated. It provides document security, allowing the creator to choose whether the document can be annotated, printed, or password protected against even being viewed. The Viewer is also the part of Envoy that enables the document creator to add bookmarks and hypertext links, and permits readers to annotate and/or highlight the document.

Creating Envoy Documents

You can easily create an Envoy document from any Windows application, once Envoy has been installed. You can even create a runtime Envoy document, so that the reader does not need to have Envoy on his machine in order to read the document (the reader does, however, need to open the runtime Envoy document from within Windows).

Creating Envoy Documents from within an Application

To create an Envoy document from within an application, follow these steps:

1. Open the application you want to use to create the Envoy document.

2. Open or create the document to be made into an Envoy document.

3. Use your application's commands to select the printer to which the document will be printed. For instance, in WordPerfect, it is **F**ile, **P**rint, **S**elect, whereas in Word 2 it is **F**ile, P**r**int Setup.

4. From the list of available printers, choose Envoy Driver on EVY.

5. Print the file as you normally would from the application—often, by choosing **F**ile, **P**rint. For example, figure 34.1 shows a newsletter ready to be printed from WordPerfect.

Note

When the Envoy printer driver is chosen, printing a document does not actually send it to a printer. Instead, it creates an Envoy file out of it.

Tip

If the Envoy printer driver does not appear on the list, Envoy has not been correctly installed. Reinstall it from the distribution disks or see your system administrator.

Fig. 34.1
You can convert any document that can be printed from Windows into an Envoy document.

You are taken into the Envoy Viewer, and your printed document is created as an Envoy file, as shown in figure 34.2.

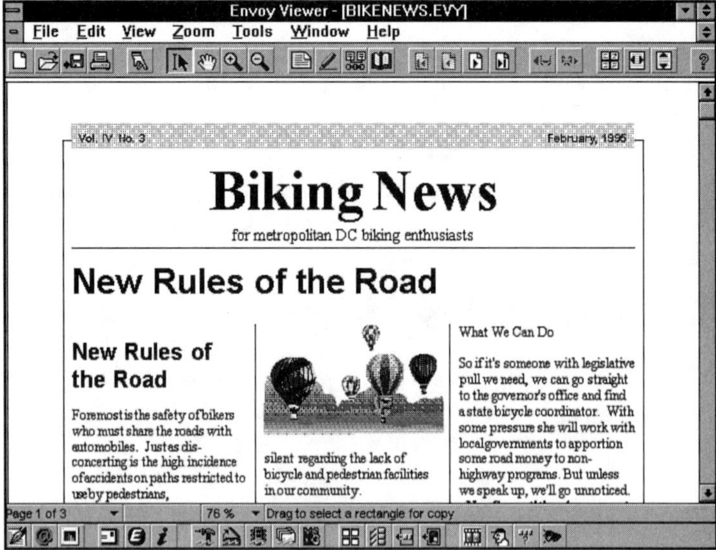

Fig. 34.2 The Envoy document resembles its original counterpart almost exactly.

6. Save the file as described in "Saving Envoy Files" later in this chapter, and close Envoy. You return to your application.

Creating Envoy Documents from within the Envoy Viewer

You can also create Envoy documents from within the Envoy Viewer itself. To do so, follow these steps:

1. Open Envoy by clicking the Envoy button on the DAD Bar.

2. Choose **F**ile, **I**mport, **F**ile. You see an Import Document dialog box (see fig. 34.3).

3. Choose the file to be imported.

> **Note**
>
> To import properly, the document must have an extension that is registered in the Windows registration database. For instance, WordPerfect documents must have the extension .WPD; Presentations drawings must have the extension .WPG.

◀ See "Using QuickRun," p. 690

4. The application that created the file opens with the desired document loaded, and you see the Print dialog box of the application. Print the file, making sure that you are using the Envoy print driver.

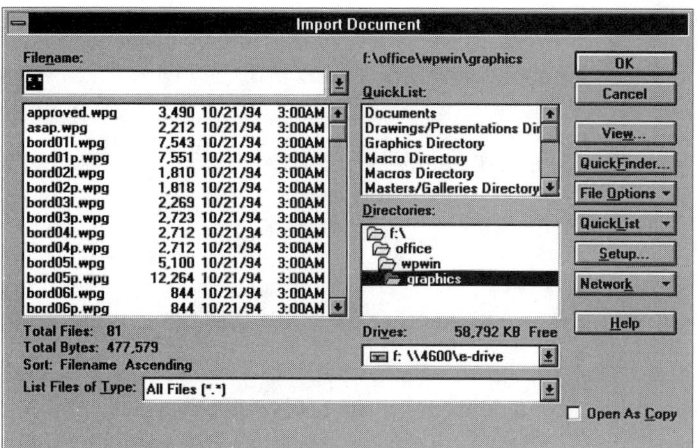

Fig. 34.3
The Import Document dialog box enables you to convert other documents into Envoy format from within the Envoy Viewer.

The application closes, and you see the new Envoy document in the Envoy Viewer.

5. Save the file as described in "Saving Envoy Files" later in this chapter.

Creating Envoy Documents with Drag and Drop

You can also create Envoy files with a drag-and-drop method. To do so, follow these steps:

1. Open the Windows File Manager and make sure that it is not maximized.

2. Open Envoy (either minimized or in a window).

3. Drag the file of your choice from the File Manager onto the Title bar or Menu bar area of the Envoy window, onto the minimized Envoy icon, or onto the text area of the Envoy screen if there isn't a document currently open.

Tip
If you drag the file into the text area of an existing Envoy file, you may create an OLE object in that file, rather than creating a new Envoy file. (See "Inserting OLE Objects" later in this chapter for more details.)

Note

This method works best with files created by other PerfectOffice applications. Often files created with earlier versions of WordPerfect—or with major applications from other vendors—will not import using this method.

4. The application that created the file opens (minimized) with the desired document loaded, and you see the print dialog box of the application.

Print the file, making sure that you are using the Envoy print driver.

The application will close, and Envoy will open with the new document in it.

5. Save the file as described in "Saving Envoy Files" below, and close Envoy.

Saving Envoy Files

You save Envoy files as you do other files in PerfectOffice applications:

1. Choose **F**ile, **S**ave. If the file has previously been saved, the modified file will replace the old file on the disk with no further prompting. Alternatively, if you want to save an existing file with a new name, choose **F**ile, Save **A**s.

   If this is the first time you have saved the file, or if you chose Save **A**s, you see the Save As dialog box (see fig. 34.4).

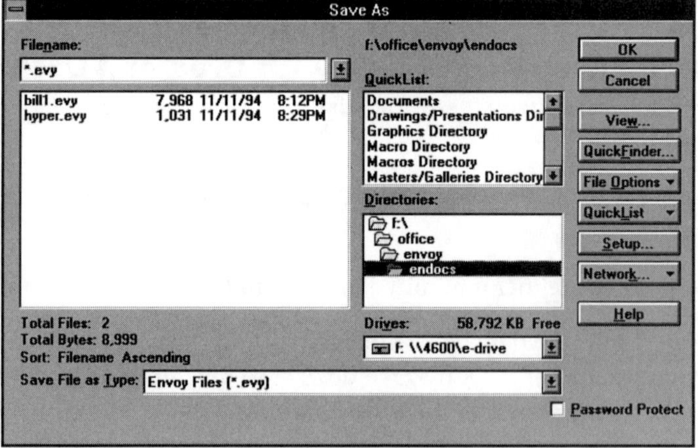

Fig. 34.4
You should save Envoy documents with an .EVY extension from the Save As dialog box so that Envoy can easily locate them.

2. If you want to set security options, choose **P**assword Protect. (Security options are discussed in the next section.)

3. Enter the filename and, if necessary, select a different drive or directory, and then choose OK.

Setting Security Options

If you choose **P**assword Protect when saving a document, you see the Security Settings dialog box after you choose OK. You may choose from the following options:

- ***P****assword.* Users will be prompted for a password when opening the file, and will not be able to open the file without it.
- *Document Access*. Unrestricted access is the default. Users can annotate the document and save their changes, and print the document. If you choose View and Print only, users can annotate the document, but they cannot save their changes. If you choose View Only, they will also not be able to print it. In either case, they will not be able to copy contents to the Clipboard, nor can they use **F**ile, Save **A**s to save it with a different name.

Caution

Restricting document access makes permanent changes in the document that you cannot undo. Always save a copy of the document with no restrictions before saving a restricted version.

Creating a Runtime Document

Sometimes, you may want to provide your Envoy document to a person that does not have Envoy on his computer. You can do this by saving the file as a runtime document. When you do this, a runtime version of the Envoy Viewer is saved with the file. The runtime Viewer works just as the full Viewer does, with a few exceptions:

Tip

Saving a file as a runtime document adds approximately 475K to its size.

- The help files are reduced.
- Only the document saved with the Viewer can be viewed.
- You cannot create new Envoy files with the runtime Viewer.

To create a runtime document when you save an Envoy document, follow these steps:

1. Choose **F**ile, Save **A**s. You see the Save As dialog box (see fig. 34.5).

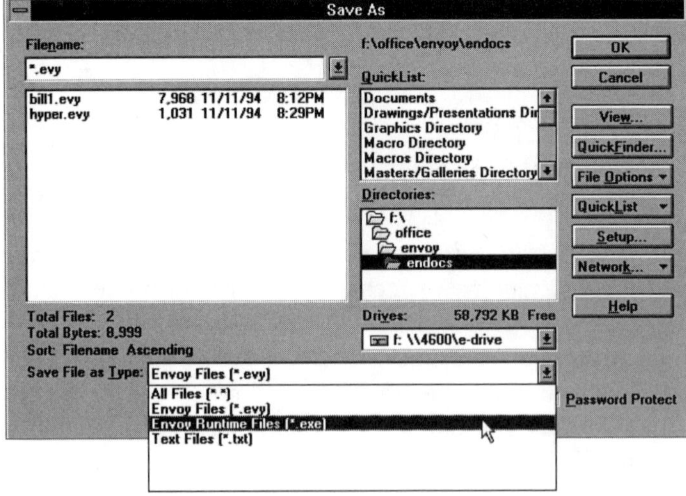

Fig. 34.5
You can create runtime Envoy documents by choosing Envoy Runtime Files as the file type from the Save As dialog box.

2. Choose Save File as **T**ype.
3. Choose Envoy Runtime Files (*.EXE).
4. Enter the filename.
5. Choose OK.

Open a runtime Envoy document just as you would any other Windows application, by using any of the following methods:

- Double-click it from File Manager.
- From the Program Manager, choose **F**ile, **R**un and specify the path and filename.

- Click the QuickRun icon on the DAD Bar, and then type the path and filename in the Command Line text box.
- Create an icon of it from Program Manager by choosing **F**ile, **N**ew.

Embedding Fonts in Envoy Documents

Sometimes, it is vital that the exact fonts the document was created with are used in viewing it—even if users don't have those fonts on their system. In this case, you can embed the original fonts in the Envoy document by following these steps:

1. Open the application from which you want to create the Envoy document, then open or create the document.

2. Use your application's commands to select the printer to which the document will be printed. For instance, in WordPerfect, it is **F**ile, **P**rint, **S**elect, whereas in Word 2 it is **F**ile, P**r**int Setup.

3. From the list of available printers, select Envoy Driver on ENV. Do not exit this dialog box.

4. From the dialog box in which you select the printer, choose **S**etup. (Depending on the application, you may have to choose **O**ptions, then **S**etup.) You see the Envoy Driver Setup dialog box (see fig. 34.6).

Tip
If you don't embed fonts, Envoy will use intelligent font mapping to choose the font with the closest typeface and size to the original. Embedding fonts significantly adds to the size of the Envoy document.

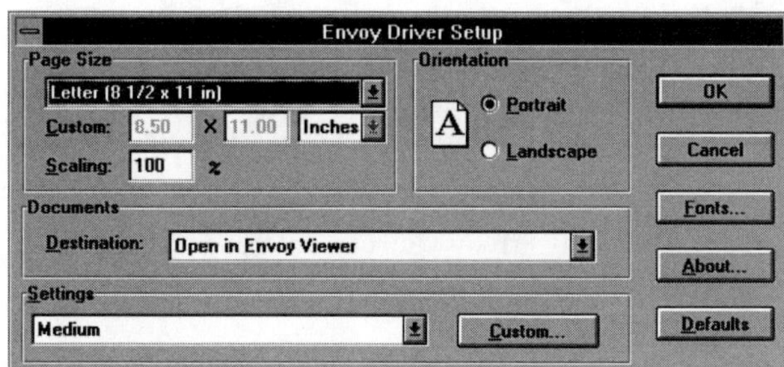

Fig. 34.6
You can embed original fonts within an Envoy document by choosing **F**onts from the Envoy Driver Setup dialog box.

5. Choose **F**onts. You see the Envoy Driver True Type Font Embedding Options dialog box.

6. Choose each font that you want to save (embed) with the document, and then click the right arrow to add it to the Embed list. Alternatively, choose **N**on Standard to embed all fonts that are on your Windows system that are not standard Windows fonts. (This option will add significantly to the size of your document and the speed of its loading.)

7. When you are finished, choose OK to return to the Envoy Driver Setup dialog box, and then choose OK again to return to the dialog box from which you selected the Envoy printer driver. Choose OK or Close (depending on the dialog box options) to return to the application.

8. Print the file as you normally would from the application. For example, figure 34.7 shows a newsletter being printed from WordPerfect.

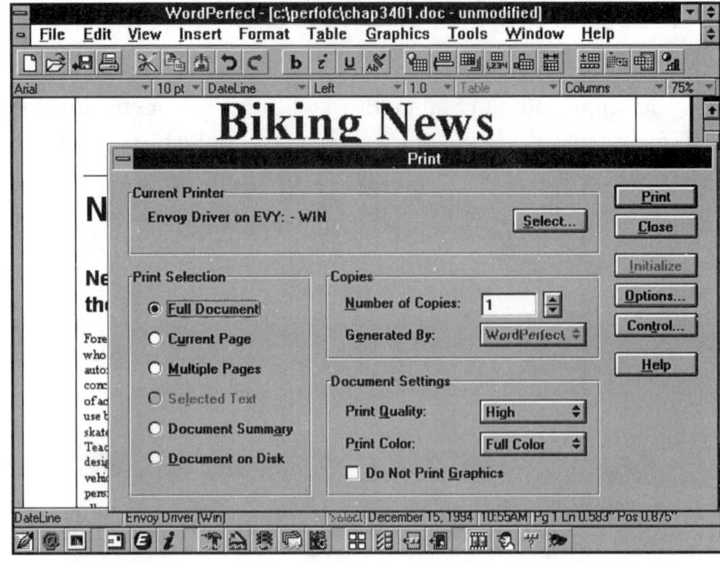

Fig. 34.7
To create a file from the application, you print as you normally would, except to the Envoy printer driver.

You are taken into the Envoy viewer, and your printed document is created as an Envoy file (see fig. 34.8).

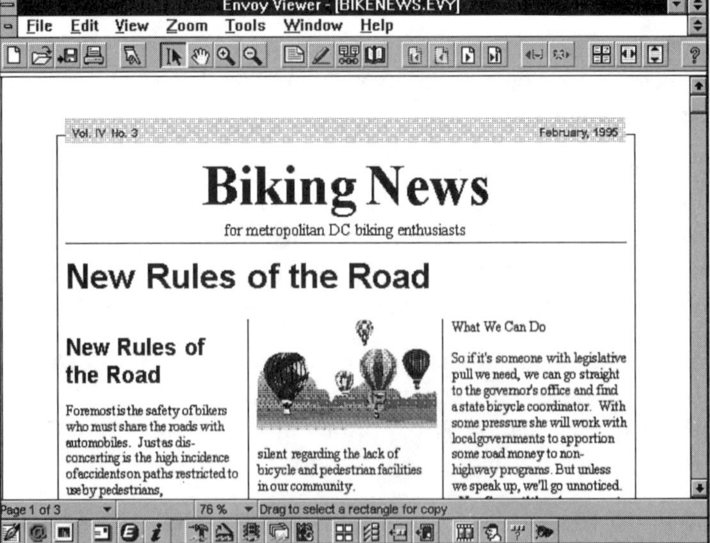

Fig. 34.8
The printed document is created as an Envoy file, and you are taken into the Envoy Viewer to save the new Envoy document.

9. Save the file as described in "Saving Envoy Files," and close Envoy. You return to your application.

Viewing and Annotating Envoy Files

When you distribute an Envoy file, users may read, print, and/or annotate it, depending on the security options you have specified. Users need to know how to do several things to effectively use the Envoy Viewer:

- Open, close, and print Envoy files
- Set environment options
- Move through the document
- Annotate the document with highlights and notes
- Add bookmarks, hypertext links, and OLE objects to the document

Opening and Closing Envoy Files

You may open an Envoy file from the File Manager or from Envoy itself. To open an Envoy file from the File Manager, open the File Manager, then double-click the Envoy file from the appropriate directory listing. (To open a runtime Envoy file, refer to "Creating a Runtime Document" earlier in this chapter.)

To open an Envoy file from the Envoy Viewer, follow these steps:

1. Click the Envoy button on the DAD Bar to open Envoy. (To review making a DAD Bar visible, see Chapter 2, "Getting Started with PerfectOffice.") You see the Envoy Viewer (see fig. 34.9).

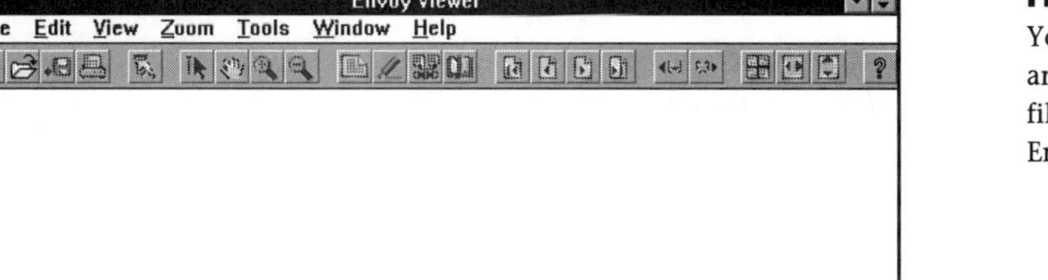

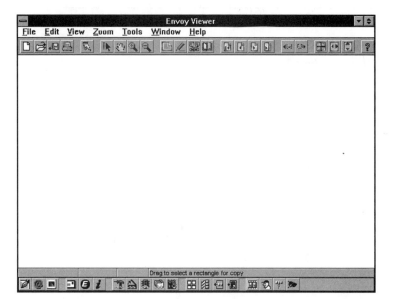

Fig. 34.9
You will view and annotate Envoy files from the Envoy Viewer.

2. Choose **F**ile, **O**pen or click the Open icon. You see the Open dialog box, as shown in figure 34.10.

Fig. 34.10
The Open dialog box enables you to open Envoy files.

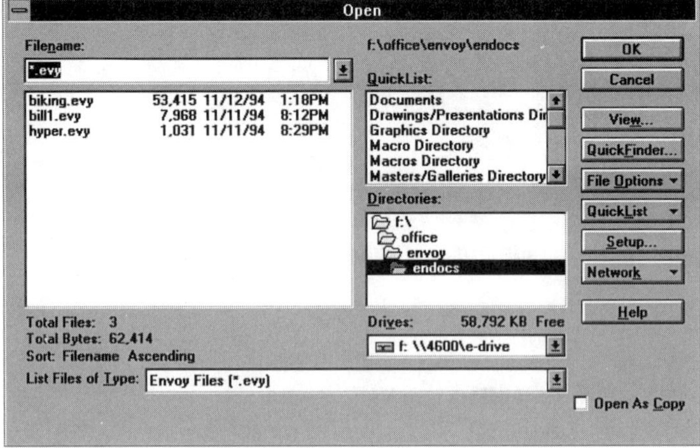

3. Choose the appropriate drive and directory, then double-click the file to open it. The file is opened in the Envoy Viewer.

◀ See "Saving, Opening, and Closing Files," p. 59

To close a file, choose **F**ile, **C**lose. If you have added annotations to the file, you will be asked if you want to save it before closing. If you respond **Y**es, the file will be saved, replacing the old version with no further prompting.

Troubleshooting

When I view an Envoy file at home, equations are all messed up. The symbols are shown as boxes. What might be wrong?

Apparently, you don't have the fonts at home that were used to create the document at work, and there are no similar fonts. You will need to recreate the Envoy file, embedding the appropriate fonts in it as described in "Embedding Fonts in Envoy Documents" earlier in this chapter.

Printing Envoy Files

To print an Envoy file, follow these steps:

1. Open the file in Envoy, as described in the preceding section.

2. Choose **F**ile, **P**rint. You see the Print dialog box (see fig. 34.11).

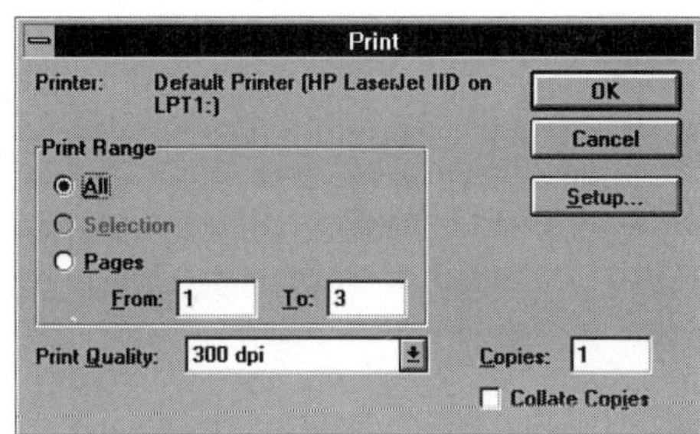

Fig. 34.11
You can print Envoy documents from the Envoy Viewer, providing there are no security restrictions against printing.

3. Choose **S**etup, if necessary, to select a different printer.

4. Set the Print Range, Print **Q**uality, and number of **C**opies, if desired.

5. Choose OK to print the document.

Changing the Viewer Environment

You can set environment options that determine how your file will look in the Envoy window, including the zoom factor and display of thumbnails.

Setting the Zoom Factor

The zoom factor is the degree of magnification that the Envoy file has on the screen. You can show an entire page, or just a few letters.

The quickest way to change the zoom factor is by using the Fit Width and Fit Height buttons on the toolbar. The Fit Width button calculates the proper zoom factor to show the entire width of the page from side to side, including the white margins. The Fit Height button functions similarly, but shows the entire height of the page from top to bottom, including the white margins. When you click the Fit Height button, smaller text may be represented by shaded lines rather than letters. Often, the Fit Height button is used to show entire page layout or larger graphics, rather than regular text.

You can also set the zoom factor by choosing **Z**oom on the Menu bar. You can then choose specific zoom factors, such as 25%, 50%, 75%, 80%, 90%, and so forth.

Finally, you can use the Zoom In and Zoom Out buttons on the toolbar to magnify selected areas of the document in two ways:

- Click the Zoom In or Zoom Out button, and then click in the document window. The document will zoom in or out by selected amounts each time you click the button.

Tip
After you click the Zoom In or Zoom Out button, the status bar reminds you of the options you have and the current Zoom percentage.

- Click the Zoom In button, and then drag a rectangle in the document window. The document will be magnified so that the rectangle you drew occupies the entire window.
- Click the Zoom Out button, then drag a rectangle in the document window. The contents of the document window will shrink to fit into the rectangle that you drew.

Displaying Thumbnails

Thumbnails are small representations of each page of a document that can be shown at the top or left of the Envoy screen.

To show thumbnails, click the Thumbnails button on the toolbar. Repeatedly clicking this button scrolls you through the thumbnail display options. The first time you click, thumbnails appear at the top of the window (see fig. 34.12). The second time, they appear at the left. The third time, they disappear.

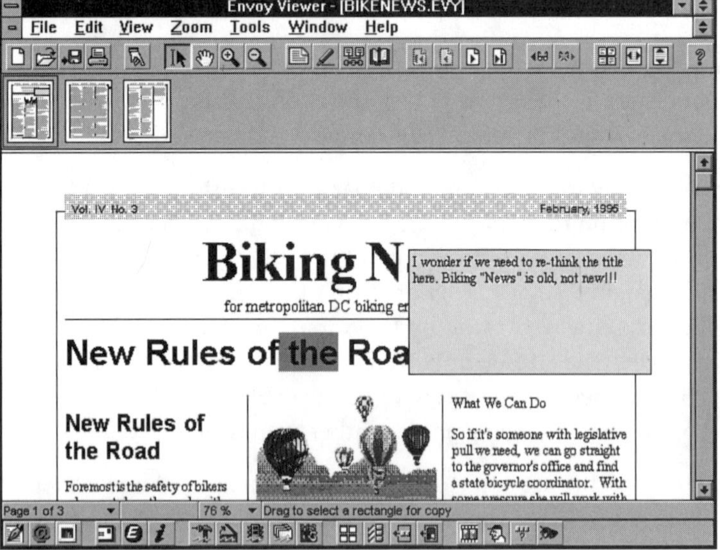

Fig. 34.12
Thumbnails are small pictures of each page. They can appear at the top or left of the Envoy Window.

You may also show the page numbers below the thumbnails while thumbnails are displayed by choosing **V**iew, **T**humbnails, Show **P**age Numbers. (If page numbers are already displayed, the last command changes to Hide **P**age Numbers.)

Moving Through Envoy Files

You can move through Envoy files in several ways:

- Using the scroll bars
- Using the toolbar or menu
- Using thumbnails
- Using the Scroll tool
- Using the Find command

Perhaps the easiest way to move through the Envoy document for Windows users is by using the scroll bars.

You can also move between pages easily using the First Page, Previous Page, Next Page, and Last Page buttons on the toolbar. Alternatively, you can choose **V**iew, then **L**ast Page, **P**revious Page, **N**ext Page, **L**ast Page, or **G**o To Page.

If thumbnails are displayed, you can go to a specific page by double-clicking the appropriate thumbnail.

You can also scroll through a document using the Scroll tool. When you choose the Scroll tool, the mouse pointer changes to a hand. You can then drag the page in any direction. Thus, if you drag it down, the text (and/or pages) above the current position starts to show. The Scroll tool is most useful when you want to show a little more of the document than is displayed in the window.

Alternatively, you can search for specific text within the document or annotation. Choose **E**dit, **F**ind. You see the Find dialog box (see fig. 34.13). Choose whether to look in **T**ext, **N**ote, **H**ighlight, **O**LE Object, H**y**pertext Source, or **B**ookmark. Type the text to be searched for in the Find Text box and, then choose **F**ind Next.

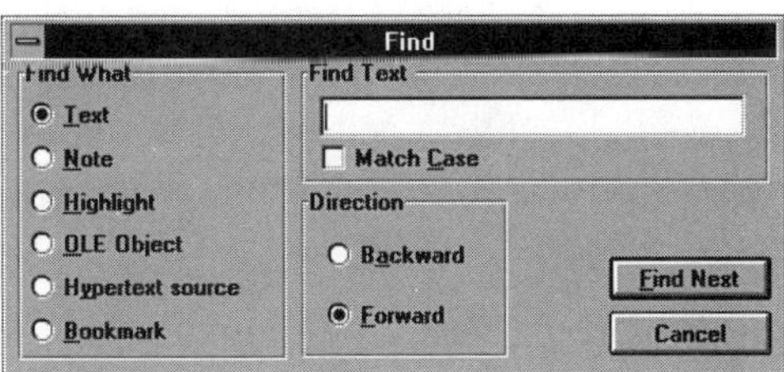

Fig. 34.13
You can search Envoy documents for selected words in the text or in annotations.

Highlighting Text

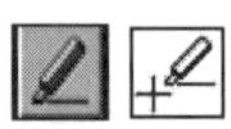

You can highlight text while you are reading an Envoy document almost like you are doing it by hand with a highlighter. To highlight text, click the Highlight button on the toolbar. The mouse pointer changes to a miniature highlighter. Drag the mouse pointer over the text to be highlighted. The highlighted text changes color, just as a paper copy would (see fig. 34.14). Alternatively, you can drag over an area of the document that does not contain text. In this case, a rectangular area is selected.

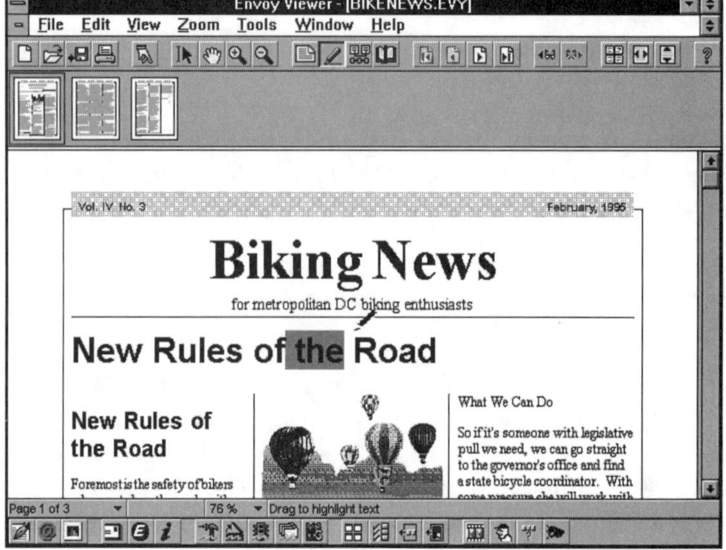

Fig. 34.14
Dragging the Highlight mouse pointer over text highlights it just as it would on paper.

To clear highlighting, make sure the Highlight tool is selected. Click anywhere in an area of highlighted text. The entire highlighted text is selected. Press the Delete key to remove the highlighting. Alternatively, you can right-click highlighted text, then choose **C**lear.

Tip
By default, the highlight author is the person who logged in (or installed PerfectOffice in the standalone version).

To change highlighting options, make sure the Highlight tool is selected, then right-click any area of highlighted text to see a QuickMenu. Choose Highlight **P**roperties. You see the Highlight Properties dialog box (see fig. 34.15). You can change the highlight color or, if your printer prints it better, choose to have highlighted text struck out rather than colored. You can also change the name of the highlight author.

Any changes you make become defaults affecting the present and future highlighted text—even in future work sessions. They do not, however, affect text that is already highlighted in the document.

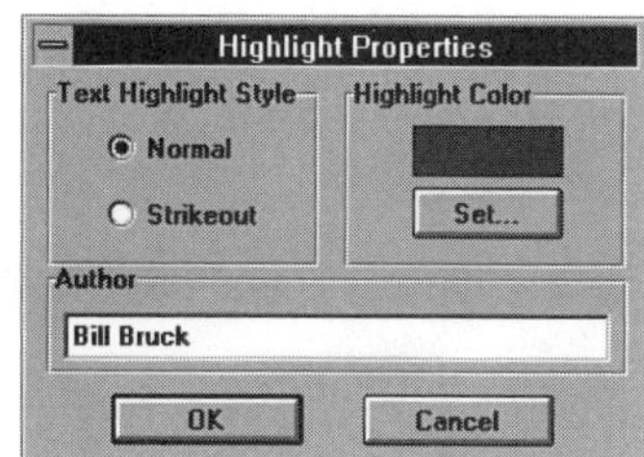

Fig. 34.15
You can change highlight color using the Highlight Properties dialog box.

Attaching Notes

You can annotate Envoy document by attaching what look like yellow sticky notes to them, as seen in figure 34.16. These notes can be any size, and you can move and resize them at will.

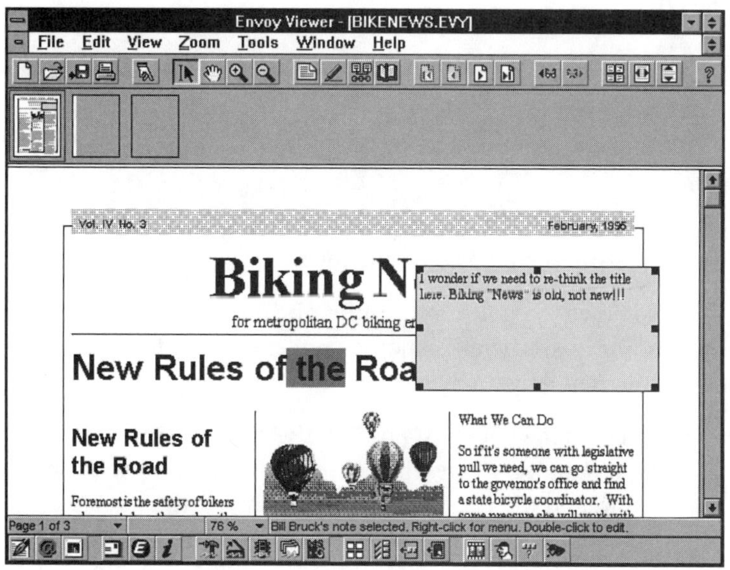

Fig. 34.16
You can attach "yellow sticky notes" to Envoy documents to annotate them.

To create a note, follow these steps:

1. Click the Insert Note button on the toolbar. The mouse pointer changes to a note—a sheet of paper with the edge turned over.

2. Click at the position you wish the note to appear. A standard size yellow note box appears. (You can create custom-size notes by dragging the mouse pointer over the area the note should occupy, rather than clicking where the note should appear.)

3. You see a blinking insertion point within the note box. Type the text of the note. Don't worry if there's too much or too little text for the note box—you can resize the box later.

4. When you are finished, click anywhere outside the note box.

To edit the note, click the Select button on the toolbar. Rapidly double-click the mouse pointer anywhere inside the note box. You see a blinking insertion point, and can edit your text as you like.

You can also move or resize a note box by using the following procedure:

1. Click the Select button on the toolbar.

2. Click anywhere in the note box. You see handles around it (see fig. 34.17).

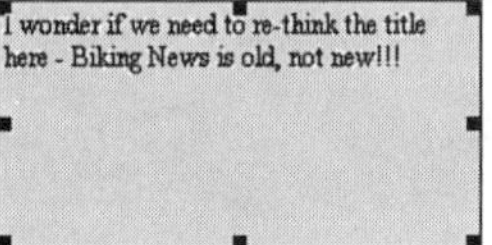

Fig. 34.17
You can move or resize note boxes by using their handles.

3. Move or resize the note box using the following procedures:

   - To move the note box, position the mouse pointer in the middle of the box, where the mouse pointer changes to a 4-headed arrow, and then drag it to its new position.

   - To resize the note box, position the mouse pointer on one of the eight handles, where the mouse pointer changes to a 2-headed arrow, and then drag the handle to change the box size.

4. Click anywhere outside of the box to deselect it.

You can also delete a note box. Select the box by clicking it with the Select tool, and then press the Delete key.

Caution

There's no Undo command in Envoy. Be careful!

You may not want to see these yellow boxes all over a document you are viewing. You can close a note, leaving only a note icon in the document to indicate where the note is. To close a note, right-click it with the Select tool, then choose Close Note. To open a closed note, double-click the note icon with the Select tool.

To change note box options, make sure that the Select tool is selected, then right-click the note box to see a QuickMenu. Choose Note **P**roperties. You see the Note Properties dialog box (see fig. 34.18). You can change the justification, font and color of the text, the background color, and the author's name. You can also choose the icon to be displayed if the note is closed.

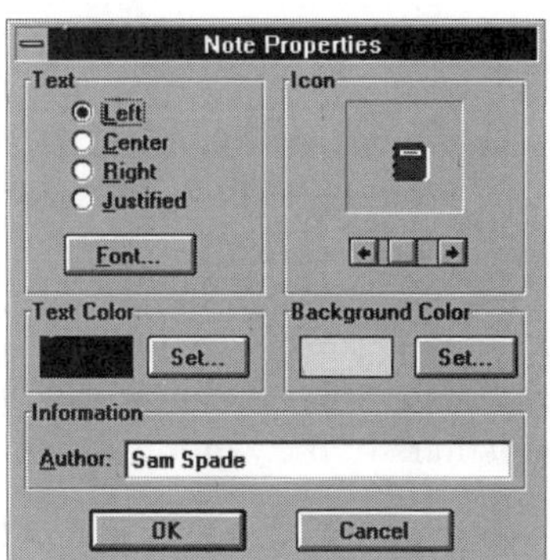

Fig. 34.18
You can reset the default note color, text font and color, and author's name with the Note Properties dialog box.

You can use the color and icons to easily show who is annotating a document. Just make sure that each reviewer uses a unique color (for open notes) and icon (for closed ones).

Tip
You can easily see who wrote a note by positioning your mouse pointer on it. For a note written by Frank Owen, the status line will say, "Click to select Frank Owen's note. Double-click to edit it."

Note

Any changes you make in the Note Properties dialog box become defaults. They will affect future notes written in this document, and notes you enter from now on in other documents, until you reset the note properties again.

Adding Bookmarks

Bookmarks are an alphabetical list of *jump terms*—terms that enable you to move quickly to pre-defined places in your Envoy document. The creator of an Envoy document often creates bookmarks prior to saving the document to assist readers in finding important places.

To effectively use bookmarks, you need to know how to create them, use them, and set bookmark options.

To create a bookmark, follow these steps:

1. Click the Bookmark button on the toolbar. The mouse pointer changes to a bookmark—a book with a place marker in it.

2. Mark the position to which you want the user to move when the bookmark is selected in one of two ways:

   - Position the mouse pointer inside text until the bookmark pointer displays an insertion point, then drag over text to select it.

   - Position the mouse pointer where there is no text until the bookmark pointer displays crosshairs, then drag a rectangle to select it.

3. You see the Bookmark Properties dialog box (see fig. 34.19). Fill in options as needed:

   - Type a label for the bookmark. (If you selected text, the first words of the selected text will be the label, unless you change it.)

   - When you jump to the bookmark, choose whether the bookmark text should be centered in the window (Center Bookmark in Window) or whether the window should zoom to the size needed to fit the bookmark in the window (Fit Bookmark to Window).

   - If you want the content of the bookmark to be selected after you jump to it—perhaps so that the reader can easily copy it to the Clipboard—choose Select Bookmark Content After Jump.

Fig. 34.19
You can change default bookmark options with the Bookmark Properties dialog box.

4. When you are finished selecting options, choose OK. The bookmark is added to the list, and the mouse pointer remains as a bookmark pointer. Create another bookmark or select a different type of pointer for another action.

To edit the properties of an existing bookmark, follow these steps:

1. Click the Bookmark button on the toolbar.

2. Right-click anywhere inside the text of an existing bookmark to display a QuickMenu.

3. Choose Bookmark **P**roperties to display the Bookmark Properties dialog box. You can edit the options of existing bookmarks with the Bookmark Properties dialog box.

4. Change options as needed, and then choose OK.

To jump to a bookmark, choose **V**iew, Go To **B**ookmark, or click the Bookmarks button on the status bar at the bottom of the window. You see a list of available bookmarks. Click the desired one. You will jump to the area of the document defined in the bookmark.

Adding Hypertext Links

Hypertext links are buttons or jump terms within the document that allow you to jump to predefined places in your Envoy document. The creator of an Envoy document often creates hypertext links prior to saving the document. This is most easily done if the original document contains a table of contents, list of figures, index, or other logical place for hypertext links. You can even create hypertext links whenever an unfamiliar term exists in a document—assuming that you have the term defined somewhere else.

To effectively use hypertext links, you need to know how to create them, use them, and set their options.

To create a hypertext link, follow these steps:

1. Click the Hypertext button on the toolbar. The mouse pointer changes to a hypertext pointer.

2. Choose from either of the following procedures, depending on whether you want to create a jump term or a hypertext button:

   - To create a jump term (a word or phrase that the user can click to jump through the link), position the mouse pointer inside text until the hypertext pointer displays an insertion point, then drag over text to select it.

   - To create a hypertext button, position the mouse pointer where there is no text until the bookmark pointer displays crosshairs, and then drag a rectangle the size of the button.

   In either case, on the status bar, you see the message `Go to the destination, then drag the link on main view or thumbnails.`

3. Move to the position that you want to jump to, and then click the mouse.

4. To set options, right-click in the text, then choose Hypertext **P**roperties. If you do not want to set options, skip to step 6.

5. Depending on whether you selected text or a rectangle, proceed as follows:

- If you selected text, you see the Hypertext Properties dialog box shown in figure 34.20. Select the source text style as colored, underlined, or underlined and colored. Choose the source text color. When you jump through the hypertext link, choose whether the text should be centered in the window (**C**enter Destination in Window) or whether the window should zoom to the size needed to fit the text (**F**it Destination to Window). When you are finished selecting options, choose OK.

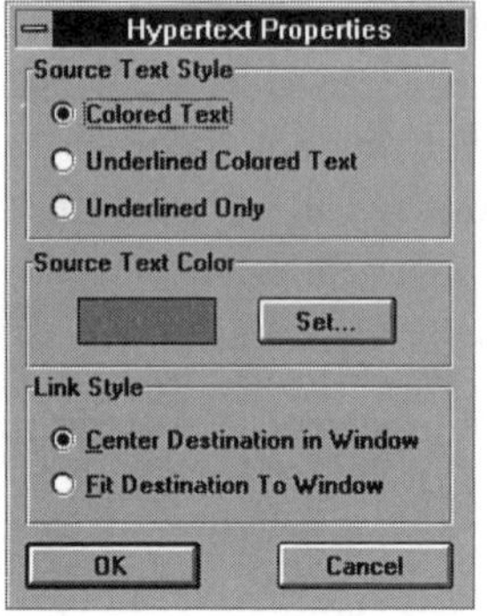

Fig. 34.20
The Hypertext Properties dialog box for text enables you to change the color and underline of jump terms.

Tip
Make jump terms resemble jump terms in Windows help: green and underlined.

- If you selected a rectangle, you see the Hypertext Properties dialog box (see fig. 34.21). Select the source text style as an **I**nvisible Rectangle, Framed **R**ectangle, or Button. If you chose Framed **R**ectangle, choose the rectangle color. If you chose Button, use the button scroll bar to choose from predefined button types. When you jump through the hypertext link, choose whether the text should be centered in the window (**C**enter Destination in Window) or whether the window should zoom to the size needed to fit the text (**F**it Destination to Window). When you are finished selecting options, choose OK.

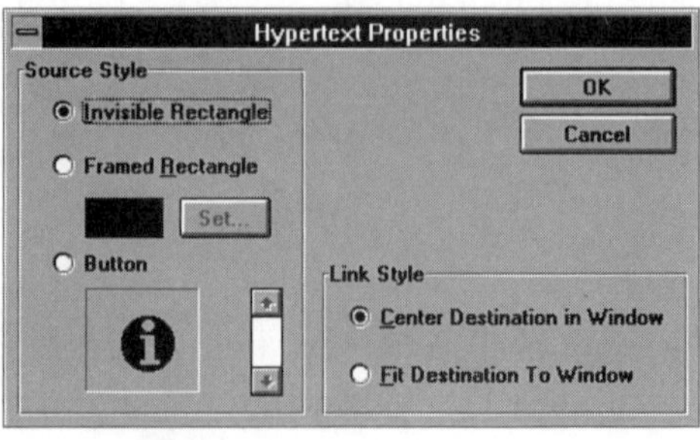

Fig. 34.21
The Hypertext Properties dialog box for rectangles enables you to specify the rectangle as colored, invisible, or a button.

6. The hypertext link is created, and the mouse pointer remains as a hypertext pointer. Create another link or select a different type of pointer for another action. (You can choose invisible rectangles to make graphic objects in your documents into jump terms.)

To edit the properties of an existing hypertext link, follow these steps:

1. Click the Hypertext button on the toolbar.

2. Right-click anywhere inside the text of an existing hypertext source. You see a QuickMenu.

3. Choose Hypertext **P**roperties. You see the appropriate Hypertext Properties dialog box.

4. Change options as needed, and then choose OK.

Whenever your selection pointer is positioned on a hypertext source, it will change to a hand. This is true whether the source is text, a colored box, an invisible box, or a button.

To jump to a hypertext link, position your selection pointer on a hypertext source. When the mouse pointer changes to a hand, click. You will jump to the area of the document defined in the hypertext link.

Inserting OLE Objects

You can insert objects—such as sound clips, animated pictures, or links to spreadsheets and databases—into your Envoy document by using Object Linking and Embedding (OLE).

► See "Understanding Data Transfer," p. 726

However, one special consideration applies to using OLE with Envoy documents: Using OLE, you can create a Link to the object (for instance, to a sound file), or you can embed the sound file in the Envoy document. When you create a link, the sound file exists on the disk, and when you click the sound file icon in the Envoy document, it reads the file from the disk. When you embed the sound file in the Envoy document, a copy of the sound file is placed in the Envoy document itself.

In most applications, linking is preferred much of the time, for two reasons: Linking keeps the Envoy file relatively small, whereas embedding can make the Envoy file rather large. Linking also ensures that you are reading the latest version of the file, whereas embedding "locks" the then-current version of the file into the Envoy document.

Tip
For you "techies" who are into the details of OLE: Envoy is OLE 1.0-enabled, not OLE 2.0-enabled.

However, many times, Envoy documents are distributed via WAN, disk, or other medium to viewers who may have no access to the disk to which an OLE object is linked. If you are creating an Envoy document that will be distributed in this manner, you may want to embed, rather than link, your OLE object.

From Here...

You have now learned most of PerfectOffice's integration features. You can finish learning about integration by reading the next chapter, or move into customizing PerfectOffice with Chapter 36:

- In Chapter 35, "Transferring Data Between Applications," you learn about OBEX, OLE and DDE. You are introduced to the datasharing DAD bar, and learn about QuickTasks that automate the data sharing process.
- In Chapter 36, "Customizing Toolbars, DAD Bars, and Menus," you learn how to make PerfectOffice work for you by creating new toolbars, DAD Bars, and menus, and placing items on existing ones that invoke features, launch applications, play scripts, or run macros.

Chapter 35

Transferring Data Between Applications

by Bill Bruck

One of the benefits of working within a suite environment is the ability to think about your work, rather than the applications that you are using to get your project done. Behind the scenes, however, data often needs to be transferred between applications for you to obtain a finished result. For instance, a final report may be a WordPerfect document incorporating a Quattro Pro spreadsheet, Presentations chart, and item list maintained in Paradox.

In this chapter, you'll find out more about how to transfer data between applications. Specifically, you learn about

- The difference between copying, moving, embedding, and linking data
- Shortcuts for moving and copying data between applications
- How to create data links between applications
- How to embed an object in another application
- How to use the Data Sharing DAD Bar

As you begin to use more than one PerfectOffice application and integrate applications to do your work, you'll find that you need more information about what occurs when data is transferred from one application to another. Here's where to get it!

Before talking about "how to do it," however, it's vital that you understand what's going on with data transfers, and the three very different ways that data is transferred.

Understanding Data Transfer

◀ See "Editing Text," p. 93

◀ See "Copying and Moving Data," p. 289

There are three basic ways that data can be transferred between documents: moving/copying, linking, and embedding. Before you learn the different commands and methods used to transfer data, it's a good idea to get a conceptual understanding of what's happening with the different processes.

Understanding Moving and Copying

Most people are familiar with moving and copying data using the cut-and-paste metaphor. When you move a sentence from one WordPerfect paragraph to another, or move a Quattro Pro cell to another location, you do two operations. First, you cut the data, which removes it from the original location. Then, you paste the data to its new location. Copying works the same way, except that a copy of the data is left in the original location as well. You move data by copying it to the Clipboard, then pasting it where you want to move it.

Note

When you cut or copy data, it goes to the Windows Clipboard. This is a temporary storage area that holds the last thing that you cut or copied. The data stays in the Clipboard until you either exit Windows or copy something else into the Clipboard. There are a couple of important implications of this:

- The same Clipboard is used in all Windows applications, enabling you to move data from one application to another.
- Because the Clipboard only holds one thing, if you put something else in the Clipboard, the first thing is erased.
- You can paste the same copy of the data from the Clipboard multiple times—until you copy something else into the Clipboard.

Moving and copying data between applications works the same way as it does within applications. The data is moved or copied to the Windows Clipboard, from which it is retrieved when you paste the data in the destination application.

Note

When you move or copy data using the drag-and-drop method discussed later in this chapter, the data is not put into the Clipboard, nor are the contents of the Clipboard affected. However, since the data is not in the Clipboard, you cannot repetitively paste multiple copies of it.

Understanding Linking

Linking data adds another dimension to the copying process. For example, when you link a range of cells in Quattro Pro to a WordPerfect document, the Quattro Pro information is displayed in the document, but it is not actually saved there. Rather, the WordPerfect document maintains link information that specifies where the linked data is to be obtained: the application that created it, the path and filename, and the selected information in that file. When you link data, you create a "pointer" from the file where you want the data to appear to the file in which the data exists.

> **Note**
>
> You might want to become familiar with the technical terminology used for linked and embedded data (see the following table).
>
> In this chapter, the terminology *source application* and *destination application* are used, rather than *server* and *client*, for purposes of clarity.

Term	Refers to
Object	The data that is linked or embedded
Source File	The file from which the object comes
Source Application	The application in which the source file is created
Server	Another term for source application
Destination Application	The application in which the object appears
Client	Another term for the destination application
Destination File	The file in which the object appears

Because a link consists of a pointer to a source file, the object that appears in the destination file is always the latest version. When you or someone else changes the source file containing the object, the object in the destination file changes. For example, if someone changes the Quattro Pro file, which affects the cells that are linked to WordPerfect, the Quattro Pro cells appearing in your WordPerfect document immediately reflect this change.

Alternatively, you can specify that the link be updated manually. In this case, the object remains static unless you manually update it.

Tip
When creating a link, first ensure that your source document has been saved so that information about the link can be stored. If the document has not yet been saved, you won't be able to create the link.

There are different technologies that Windows applications use to create links. Three of the most common are DDE, OLE 1.0, and OLE 2.0. DDE, the oldest, stands for Dynamic Data Exchange. It allows for linking, but not embedding. DDE was later subsumed under OLE, Object Linking and Embedding. The major differences between OLE 1.0 and 2.0 are that OLE 2.0 allows for dragging and dropping data between applications, and allows you to edit the source data from within the destination application. PerfectOffice applications support OLE 2.0 where possible. However, you may have links to other applications that only support OLE 1.0. If you double-click a linked object, you stay in the destination application, and the menus change to those of the source application, then the link is an OLE 2.0 link. If, on the other hand, you double-click and the original application opens up, the link may be OLE 1.0 or 2.0.

Note

OLE and DDE are quite complex; usually the method being used for linking and embedding is immaterial to the user. However, if you *are* interested in the details, WordPerfect 6.1 is an OLE 2.0 server, meaning that you can link WordPerfect information to Quattro Pro or Presentations, for example. It is *not*, however, an OLE 2.0 in-place server. Thus, when you double-click WordPerfect objects that are embedded in Quattro Pro, you will not be able to use in-place editing.

Understanding Embedding

Embedding data is like copying it, with one difference. When you embed an object, a copy of it is stored in the destination file, just as it is when you copy it. However, because OLE is used to transfer the data, you can edit the embedded data using the source application by double-clicking it. For example, if you have a Quattro Pro spreadsheet embedded into a WordPerfect document, you can double-click the spreadsheet inside WordPerfect, then use Quattro Pro to edit it.

Depending on the specific applications involved, when you double-click an embedded object to edit it, a window may open, enabling you to edit the object using its source application. Alternatively, the title bar, toolbar, and menus may change to those of the source application, enabling you to edit the object in-place. For instance, when you double-click an embedded Quattro Pro object within WordPerfect, the title bar, menu bar, and toolbar change to those of Quattro Pro, enabling in-place editing. However, when you double-click an embedded WordPerfect object within Quattro Pro, you see a WordPerfect pop-up menu, enabling you to edit the WordPerfect object.

This is because, while WordPerfect 6.1 is an OLE 2.0 server, it is not an "OLE 2.0 in-place server" that allows for in-place editing.

Comparing the Methods of Transferring Data

In summary, the differences between the three methods of transferring data can be seen in the following table.

Method	Copies Data to Destination	Allows Editing Using Source Destination Application	Updates When Source Changes
Copying/Moving	yes	no	no
Linking	no	yes	yes
Embedding	yes	yes	no

Tip
When you copy or move data between two OLE 2.0-compliant appli-cations such as WordPerfect 6.1 and Quattro Pro 6.0, you are actually embedding, rather than copying or moving, the data.

Having looked at the principles behind the three methods of transferring data, let's see how to actually do it!

Techniques for Moving and Copying

There are several methods that you can use to move or copy data between applications. These include using menus and toolbars, drag and drop, and the Data Sharing DAD Bar.

Tip
You can also use hot keys for cutting and pasting: Ctrl+X for cut, Ctrl+C for copy, and Ctrl+V for paste.

Moving and copying data using the menus and toolbars is the same whether you are transferring the data within or between applications:

1. Open the source application, and select the data to be moved or copied.
2. Choose **E**dit, Cu**t** or Edit, **C**opy; or click the Cut or Copy button on the toolbar, if one is visible. Alternatively, right-click the data to be moved, then choose **C**ut or C**o**py from the QuickMenu that pops up.

3. Open the destination application, and place the insertion point where the data should go.
4. Choose Edit, **P**aste, or click the Paste button on the toolbar, if one is visible. Alternatively, right-click at the insertion point, then choose **P**aste from the QuickMenu that pops up.

Techniques for Linking and Embedding

To effectively work with linked and embedded data, you need to be able to:

- Create links and embedded data
- Edit a linked object
- Edit the link itself

Creating Links and Embedding Data

Creating links and embedding data are both a little slower than merely copying data, but you'll soon find that you can accomplish them efficiently by following these steps:

1. Open the source application and select the data to be linked or embedded.

2. Choose Edit, **C**opy; or click the Copy button on the toolbar, if one is visible. Alternatively, right-click the data to be moved, then choose C**o**py from the QuickMenu that pops up. A copy of the data is placed in the Windows Clipboard.

Tip
You can also use Ctrl+C to copy the data into the Clipboard.

3. Open the destination application and place the insertion point where the data should go.

4. Choose **E**dit, Paste **S**pecial. You see the Paste Special dialog box (see fig. 35.1).

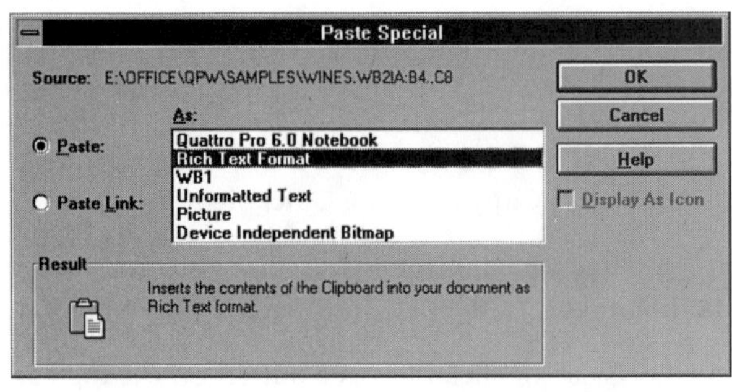

Fig. 35.1
The Paste Special dialog box allows you to both embed and link objects, as well as specify the object type.

5. To embed the data, choose **P**aste; to link it, choose Paste **L**ink.
6. Select a data type and, if desired, **D**isplay As Icon as discussed below, then click OK. The data appears in your destination application.

You can also drag selected text or objects from one application to another by following these steps:

1. Open both the source application and the destination application.
2. Ensure that a DAD Bar is visible and, if necessary, switch to the PerfectOffice DAD Bar.

◄ See "Exploring DAD," p. 30

3. Click the Tile PerfectOffice Applications button. You see your active applications tiled on the window.

4. Select the text or object in the source application, and position your mouse pointer inside it.
5. Embed the object by holding down the Ctrl key while dragging the object to the appropriate position in the destination application. Alternatively, link the object by holding down Ctrl+Shift while you drag the object to the destination application (see fig. 35.2).

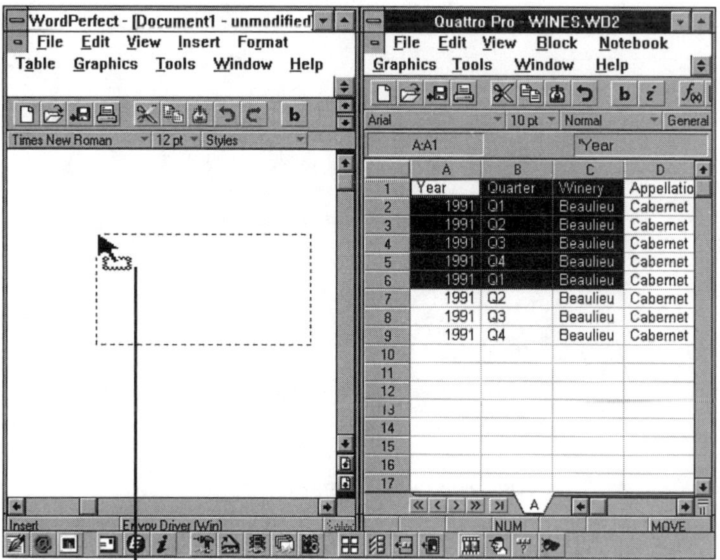

Fig. 35.2
An easy way to embed objects is to open both application windows, select the data, then hold down the Ctrl key while dragging the data from one window to the other.

Troubleshooting

Why is it that sometimes I can drag text from a non-PerfectOffice application into WordPerfect, and sometimes I can't?

If the other application is OLE 2.0-compliant, you can drag and drop objects into WordPerfect (which also is OLE 2.0-compliant). If it is not, you may still be able to cut and paste data using the Edit menu. However, some Windows applications do not use the Windows Clipboard in a standard way. You won't be able to move or copy data from these applications.

Tip
If the Data Sharing DAD Bar is visible, you can also use the Cut, Copy, and Paste buttons on it to transfer data from one application to another.

Choosing Data Types

When you are linking or embedding an object in the Paste Special dialog box, you see a number of different object types from which you can choose. The list you see depends on the characteristics of both the source and destination application.

Tip
When you choose OLE 2.0 data types, the **D**isplay As Icon option becomes active. This is useful when you attach sound files or background text files to a document.

In general, the first data type on this list is the file type of the source application. Thus, when you link or embed a Quattro Pro file into Presentations, the first data type on the list is Quatto Pro 6.0 Notebook, as you see in figure35.3. Similarly, when you link or embed a Presentations drawing into WordPerfect, the first entry on the list is Presentations 3.0 Drawing. Choosing this option is often advantageous, because it offers full OLE 2.0 functionality.

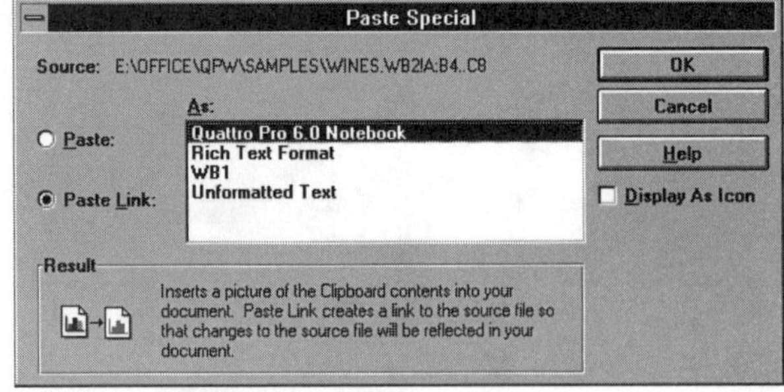

Fig. 35.3
The first data type listed usually provides the best way of linking data. If the Display As Icon option is active, it indicates that the data type provides an OLE 2.0 link.

Other data types that you can choose may include:

- *Rich Text Format.* This data type is useful in transferring data from one word processor to another, when you want to retain the maximum formatting information possible.

- *Unformatted Text.* This data type is useful in opposite situations, when you want to merely transfer text without formatting.
- *Picture, Metafile, or Device Independent Bitmap.* These options convert the object into different graphic formats.
- When embedding an object, you'll also often see options such as WB1, WordPerfect 6.0, WPG10, or WPG20. These options allow you to paste the object into your document in a slightly different, often earlier, format than that of the current version of the source application.

Note

You often have more options when embedding a file with the **P**aste option than when linking it with Paste **L**ink. This makes sense, because a link must usually be established with the file in its original format.

Inserting Objects

You can also embed an object by choosing **I**nsert, **O**bject from the menu of PerfectOffice applications such as WordPerfect and Presentations. You see the Insert Object dialog box shown in figure 35.4. (In Quattro Pro, choose Edit, Insert **O**bject.)

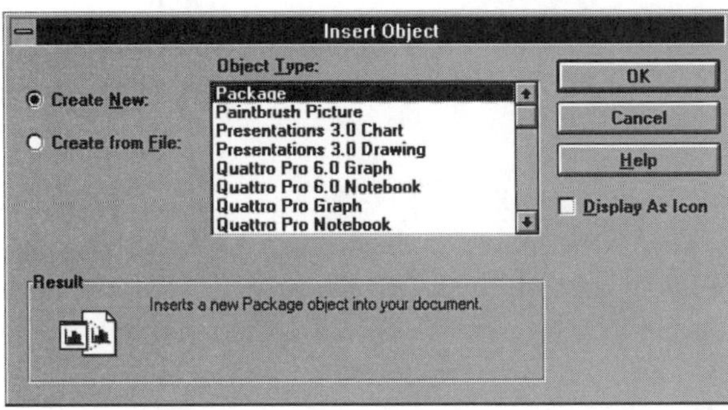

Fig. 35.4
The Insert Object dialog box allows you to create new embedded objects in your file using a variety of OLE-compliant applications, by choosing Create New.

This dialog box provides two choices for embedding an object. If you choose Create **N**ew, you see a list of OLE object types that are supported on your system. If you have installed applications from other vendors that are OLE compliant, they may also appear on this list.

This option enables you to create a new object using one of the listed types of objects. When you choose an Object **T**ype, the appropriate application opens. If the source application is an OLE 2.0 in-place service, you use in-place editing. Otherwise, it opens in its own window, and you can create the new object there. See the next section for details on editing linked objects.

You may also want to embed an object that already exists as a file on the disk. In this case, choose Create from **F**ile while you are in the Insert Object dialog box. The dialog box changes to the one shown in figure 35.5. You can type the name of the desired file, or use the Browse button to see a Select File dialog box, then choose the file from there.

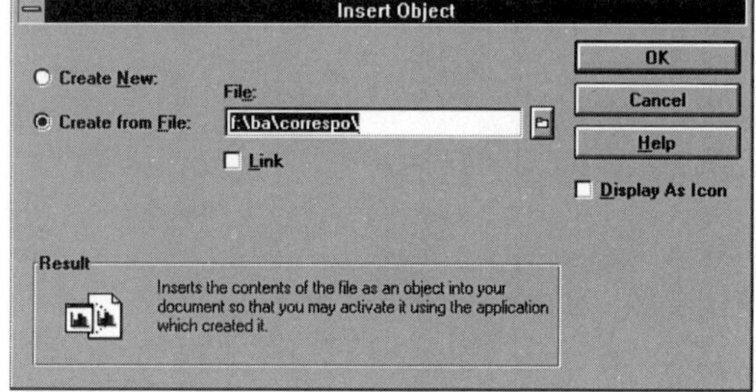

Fig. 35.5
You can embed an entire file into your document by choosing Create from File in the Insert Object dialog box.

Editing a Linked Object

Tip
When you create an object from a file, you have the options of creating it as a link rather than embedding the object, or displaying it as an icon.

One of the nicest things about linking objects is that you can "go back through" the link to edit the source file in the source application that created it.

When you double-click a linked object, another application window opens on the screen. This is the source application that created the object, and you see the source file in that window. Edit the object within the application window and save it as you normally would. When you're finished, choose **F**ile. There is an option such as the one shown in figure 35.6 that enables you to exit and return to the destination application.

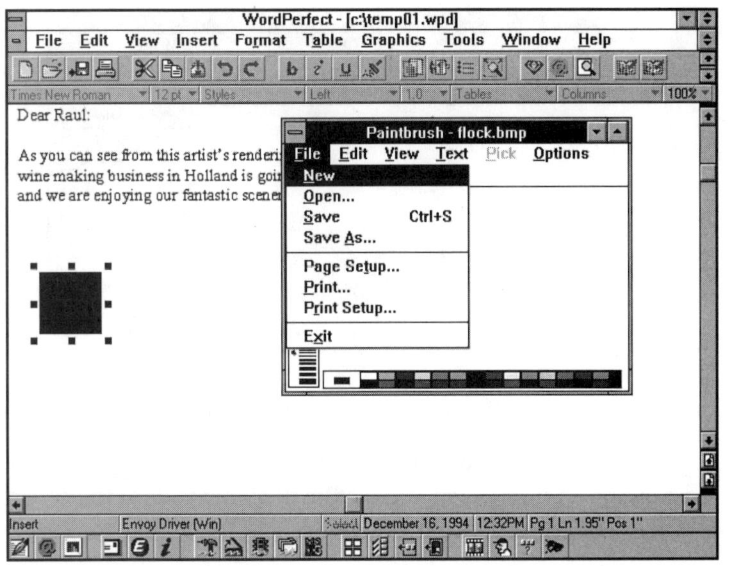

Fig. 35.6
When you edit a linked object, that object's application window opens, allowing you to edit it. An option on the File menu returns you to your original application.

Editing a Link

When you have linked one or more objects into your documents, you can edit the linked information. You may want to edit the links in your document for a number of reasons:

- To redefine the link if the source file is renamed or moved
- To break the link so that the object no longer changes in your document
- To change the link from automatically updated (whenever the source file changes) to manually updated (when you specify)
- To update a manual link

To edit a link in WordPerfect or Presentations, choose **E**dit, Lin**k**s. The Links dialog box appears (see fig. 35.7). All the links in your document are listed.

The Links dialog box provides the following options which affect links that you have selected:

- *Automatic and **M**anual.* Choosing **A**utomatic causes objects to be updated as soon as they are changed. Choosing **M**anual causes objects not to be updated until an Update command is given.
- ***U**pdate Now.* This option causes all selected manual links to be updated—that is, the objects are refreshed from the latest versions of the source files.

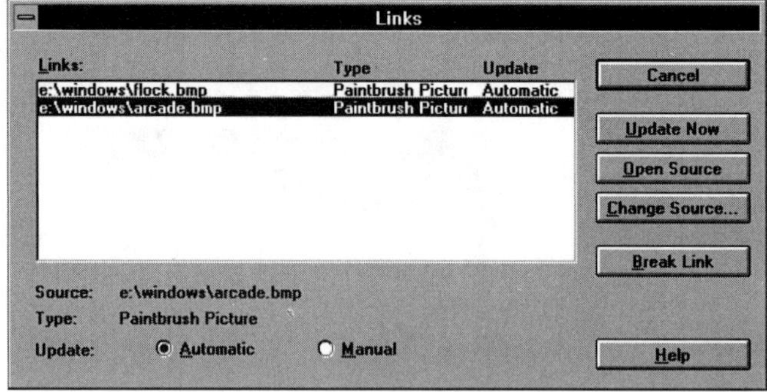

Fig. 35.7
The Links dialog box lists all links in your document, and allows you to edit them, break them, or specify them as manual or automatic.

- ***O**pen Source*. This option opens the source file in the source application.
- ***C**hange Source*. When you choose this option, the Change Source dialog box appears. You can then change the filename and (in the case of spreadsheets) the cell range.
- ***B**reak Link*. This option breaks the link between the object and its source file. The object then becomes an embedded object in the destination file.

Troubleshooting

*Why is the Lin**k**s option grayed out on the Edit menu?*

The Lin**k**s option is only active if you have links in your document. If you have embedded objects, rather than linked objects, the option is not active.

Why is it that changes in my source document sometimes aren't reflected in my destination document?

The source document may not be available, either because it no longer exists, has been moved, or you cannot establish a connection to it on the network. In this case, the last copy of the object will display in your destination document.

Alternatively, the link may be one which is manually updated, rather than updated automatically.

In either case, you can examine the link information and make necessary changes.

Using the Data Sharing Toolbar

PerfectOffice ships with a Data Sharing DAD Bar, shown in figure 35.8. The Data Sharing DAD Bar allows you to cut, copy, and paste data. It also provides QuickTasks for embedding and linking data between PerfectOffice applications.

◄ See "Using Multiple DAD Bars," p. 696

Fig. 35.8
You can cut, copy, and paste data using the Data Sharing DAD Bar.

The toolbar has buttons that you use to cut, copy, and paste data, as discussed in an earlier section, "Techniques for Moving and Copying." It also has three buttons designed for embedding and linking data between PerfectOffice applications:

Button	QuickTask
	Copy Presentations Selection to WordPerfect
	Copy Paradox Selection to WordPerfect
	Copy Spreadsheet Selection to WordPerfect

These buttons invoke QuickTasks that help to automate the processes discussed in this chapter. For instance, when you click the Copy Spreadsheet Selection to WordPerfect, you see the Copy Data dialog box (see fig. 35.9). This remains on-screen until you have selected cells in the spreadsheet and click Continue.

◄ See "Learning QuickTask Essentials," p. 665

Fig. 35.9
The Copy Data dialog box stays on-screen while you select the spreadsheet cells to be copied

When you click Continue, WordPerfect opens, and you see the Paste Special dialog box shown in figure 35.10. You can choose to **P**aste (embed) or Paste **L**ink your data, and select the appropriate format. When you choose OK, the embedded or linked object is created, and the QuickTask ends. (The Copy Spreadsheet Selection QuickTask also works with Excel and Lotus 1-2-3, if they are installed.)

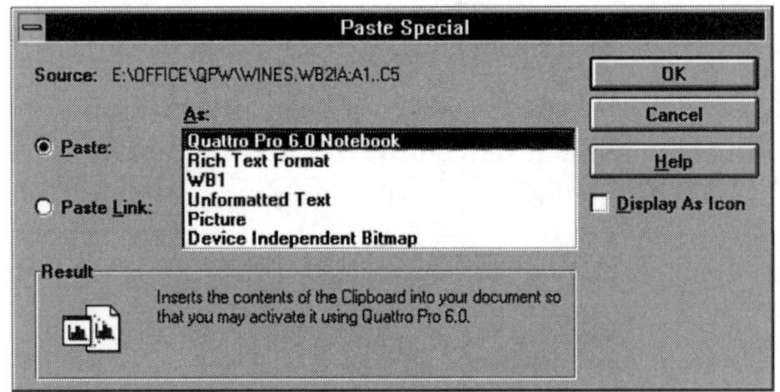

Fig. 35.10
The Copy Spreadsheet Selection to WordPerfect QuickTask takes you directly to the Paste Special dialog box, where you can choose to embed or link the spreadsheet selection.

From Here...

You have now learned how to copy, move, link, and embed data between PerfectOffice applications. From here, you can learn more about customizing PerfectOffice applications by referring to the following chapters:

- Chapter 31, "Organizing Your Work with InfoCentral," shows you how to create a personal or company address book, and how to save information on clients, staff, or inventories.

- Chapter 32, "Using QuickTasks," discusses the multifaceted QuickTasks, and how they can help you work more efficiently.

- Chapter 36, "Customizing Toolbars, DAD Bars, and Menus," shows you how you can customize PerfectOffice to the way you work by creating and editing your own toolbars and menus.

Chapter 36

Customizing Toolbars, DAD Bars, and Menus

by Bill Bruck

One of the things that makes PerfectOffice the perfect place to work, as Novell states in its literature, is that it can be customized to such a great degree. In this chapter, you learn to

- Set toolbar and DAD Bar display preferences
- Move toolbars and DAD Bars on the screen
- Customize toolbars, DAD Bars, and menus
- Create and edit toolbars and DAD Bars
- Create and edit menus

Certain PerfectOffice applications, like WordPerfect, Presentations, and GroupWise, enable you to create and edit toolbars in an identical manner, with a few variations. You can even create and edit menus in WordPerfect and Presentations in a similar manner.

Some of the applications, however, behave quite differently. InfoCentral, Quattro Pro, Paradox, Envoy, and AppWare were not originally designed by WordPerfect Corporation. In this first version of PerfectOffice, they have not been fully integrated at the level of modifying menus and toolbars, although their toolbars and menus look like those in other applications.

This chapter discusses how to modify "standard" PerfectOffice toolbars and menus, such as those found in WordPerfect, Presentations, and GroupWise. In future versions of PerfectOffice, other applications will most probably utilize these standard settings.

◄ See "Using Multiple DAD Bars," p. 696

In this chapter, you also learn how to customize the DAD Bar. In Chapter 33, "Working with DAD," you learned how to use the powerful features contained in the Desktop Application Director (DAD). These features can be made even more useful when you customize DAD to your own working style. As you will see, you customize DAD Bars like you do other toolbars.

Note

Novell applications are moving away from using WordPerfect's original term *button bar* and toward the more generic term *toolbar*. GroupWise 4.1, however, is in the midst of this transition. As a result, you will see the term "button bar" in many GroupWise dialog boxes and help screens, and the term "toolbar" in others. Whether GroupWise dialog box titles say toolbar or button bar, they function identically to toolbar dialog boxes found in WordPerfect and Presentations.

Customizing Toolbars and DAD Bars

Major PerfectOffice applications such as WordPerfect, Presentations, and GroupWise enable you to create multiple toolbars, edit their buttons, and position them in several different places on-screen.

To effectively customize your toolbars or DAD Bars, you need to know how to:

- Display and hide toolbars or DAD Bars
- Select different toolbars or DAD Bars
- Access the Toolbar Preferences or DAD Preferences dialog box
- Control toolbar or DAD Bar display options
- Position the toolbar or DAD Bar in the window

Displaying, Hiding, and Selecting Toolbars

You can control the display of the toolbar by choosing **V**iew, **T**oolbar. There will be a checkmark by the Toolbar entry if the toolbar is displayed.

Tip

To hide a toolbar, right-click it, and then choose **H**ide Toolbar.

To select a different toolbar to display, ensure that a toolbar is displayed, then right-click it. You see a pop-up QuickMenu that displays the names of available toolbars. Click the name of the toolbar that you want to display.

Setting Toolbar and DAD Bar Preferences

To control toolbar and DAD Bar display options, or to create, edit, copy, rename, or delete a toolbar or DAD Bar, you must access the Toolbar or DAD Bar Preferences dialog box. To do so, use the following procedure:

1. Make sure that the toolbar or DAD Bar is displayed, and then right-click it. You see a QuickMenu that displays the names of available toolbars or DAD Bars, and selections including Edit, Preferences, and Hide Toolbar.

2. Select **P**references. You see a Toolbar Preferences dialog box (see fig. 36.1) or DAD Bar Preferences dialog box.

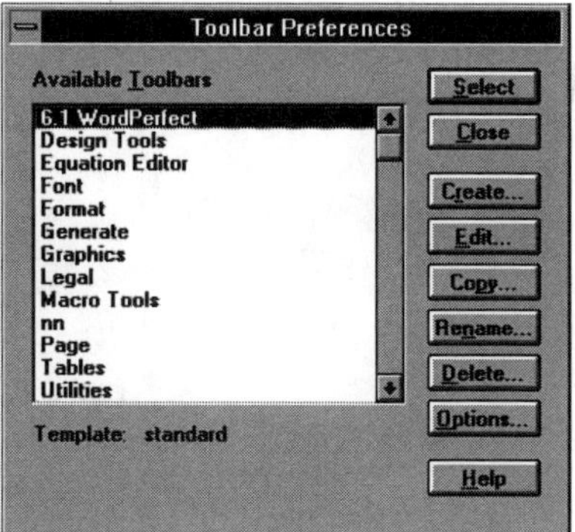

Fig. 36.1
You can select different toolbars, as well as create and edit new ones, from the Toolbar Preferences dialog box.

3. If necessary, highlight the toolbar that you want to select, edit, copy, rename, or delete.

4. Choose an option from the following list:

   - ***S**elect.* Use this to display the selected toolbar or DAD Bar.

   - *Close.* This option will complete any operations you have made and return you to the application.

   - *C**r**eate.* Use this option to create a new toolbar or DAD Bar (see "Creating Toolbars, DAD Bars, and Menu Bars," later in this chapter).

   - ***E**dit.* Use this option to edit an existing toolbar or DAD Bar (see "Editing Toolbars, DAD Bars, and Menu Bars," later in this chapter).

   - *Co**p**y.* Use this option to copy an existing toolbar. The option works slightly differently depending on the application. It is not available for DAD Bars.

In Presentations, you see a Copy Toolbar dialog box that merely asks you for the name of the new toolbar.

In WordPerfect, toolbars are stored in templates. When you choose Co**p**y, you see the Copy Toolbar(s) dialog box (see fig. 36.2). You specify the template containing the toolbar you want to copy, and then specify the toolbar in that template to be copied. Finally, you specify the template to copy the toolbar to. If the copying operation will result in overwriting the name of an existing toolbar, you will be prompted to overwrite the toolbar or provide a new name for it. (You see this prompt, for instance, when you copy a toolbar to the same template it comes from.)

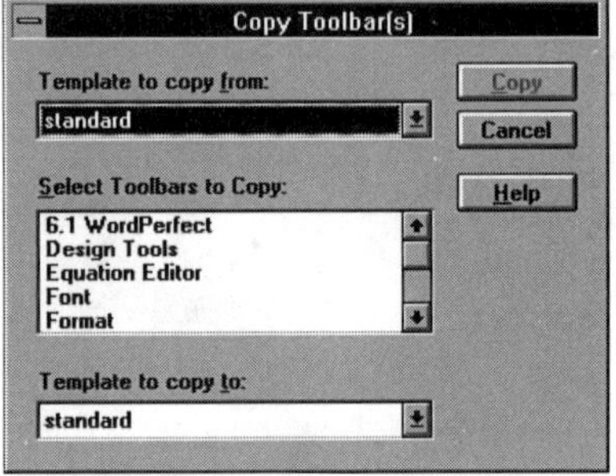

Fig. 36.2
In WordPerfect, you copy a toolbar from one template to another using the Copy Toolbar(s) dialog box.

In GroupWise, toolbars are stored in a toolbar file (for example, WPOFUS.BTN). The copy operation copies a toolbar from one toolbar file to another.

Tip
You can quickly edit the currently displayed toolbar from the QuickMenu by choosing **E**dit.

- *Re**n**ame*. This option enables you to rename an existing toolbar or DAD Bar.
- ***D**elete*. Use this option to delete a toolbar or DAD Bar. Certain default toolbars noted with <> symbols cannot be deleted.
- ***O**ptions* (toolbars only). This option enables you to set display preferences, as described in the following section, "Setting Toolbar Display Preferences."
- ***D**isplay* (DAD Bars only). This option enables you to set display preferences as described in "Setting DAD Bar Display Preferences."
- ***H**elp*. This option provides context-sensitive Help.

Setting Toolbar Display Preferences

You can specify options regarding the appearance and location of your toolbars. The selections you make will affect any toolbar that you select, and will be retained in future work sessions until you reset them. To set display preferences, use the following procedure:

1. Access the Toolbar Preferences dialog box by right-clicking a toolbar, then choosing **P**references.

2. Choose **O**ptions. You see the Toolbar Options dialog box (see fig. 36.3).

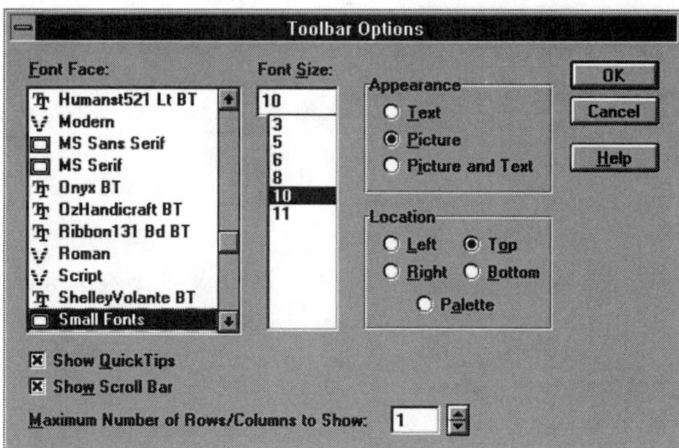

Fig. 36.3
The Toolbar Options dialog box enables you to change the appearance and location of your toolbar.

3. Select display preferences (note that not all preferences are available in all applications):

   - *Font Face and Font **S**ize*. Choose the font and size for toolbars that display text.

   - *Appearance*. Toolbars can display **T**ext (text only), **P**icture (icon only), or P**i**cture and Text.

   - *Location*. You can specify that toolbars display to the **L**eft, **R**ight, T**o**p, or **B**ottom of the window, or as a floating P**a**lette.

   - *Show **Q**uick Tips*. Click this checkbox to have a description appear when you position your mouse pointer on a toolbar button.

   - *Sho**w** Scroll Bar*. Click this checkbox to have a scroll bar appear on the toolbar so that you can have more buttons than appear in the window.

   - ***M**aximum Number of Rows/Columns to Show*. You can display more than one row or column of buttons by entering a number greater than 1 in this option.

Tip
If you choose **T**ext or P**i**cture and Text, display your toolbars at the left or right side of the window; otherwise, you will not have room for many buttons.

4. When you are finished selecting preferences, choose OK. You return to the Toolbar Preferences dialog box.

5. You can now set further toolbar preferences or choose **C**lose to return to the application.

Setting DAD Bar Display Preferences

You may choose to display DAD Bars in five locations: at the top, bottom, left or right of the screen, or as a floating palette.

> **Note**
>
> The DAD Bar should not overwrite part of the active application window if you display it at the top, bottom, left, or right. Instead, any maximized window will be reduced in size so that sufficient space is left for the DAD Bar. Thus, if the DAD Bar is displayed at the top or bottom of the screen, the application's title bar or status bar should not be obscured.
>
> With non-Novell applications, occasionally the status bar will be obscured. To solve this, drag the DAD Bar to the middle of the screen, then back to the bottom of the screen (as described in the following section, "Moving Toolbars and DAD Bars with the Mouse").

In addition, the Desktop Application Director has three display modes:

- *Always in Front.* The DAD Bar will always display, no matter what window is active.

Tip
In the Auto Hide and Normal modes, the DAD Bar will obscure part of a maximized window when it is displayed.

- *Auto Hide.* The DAD Bar does not appear on-screen while you use your Windows applications. It pops up as you move the mouse pointer to the edge of the screen where the DAD Bar is located. Thus, if the DAD Bar is positioned at the bottom of the screen, move the mouse pointer to the bottom of the screen to make the DAD Bar appear. As you move the mouse pointer away from the DAD Bar, it disappears from view.

- *Normal.* The DAD Bar behaves as any other application window. To switch to the DAD Bar, hold down the Alt key, then repeatedly press the Tab key until the Desktop Application Director is selected; or use any of the other standard Windows methods for switching between applications.

You can select the appearance, location, and display mode of your DAD Bars. The selections you make will affect any DAD Bar that you select, and will be retained in future work sessions, until you reset them. To set display preferences, use the following procedure:

1. Access the DAD Preferences dialog box by right-clicking a DAD Bar, and then choosing **P**references.

2. Choose D**i**splay. You see the DAD Display Preferences dialog box (see fig. 36.4).

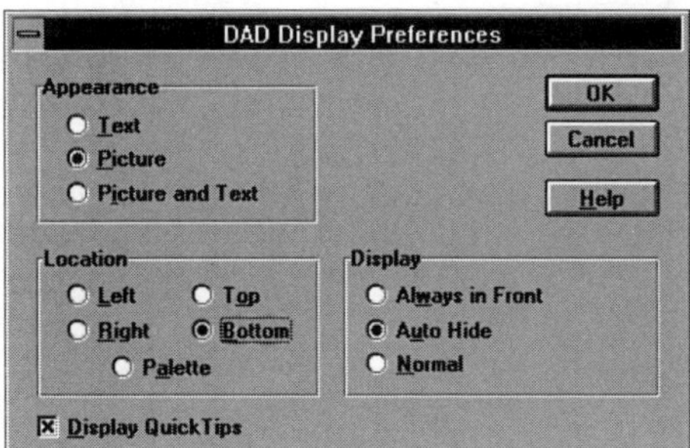

Fig. 36.4
The DAD Display Preferences dialog box enables you to change the appearance, location, and display mode of your DAD bar.

3. Select the desired display preferences. Note that the Appearance, Location, and **D**isplay QuickTips options work just as they do for any toolbar, as described earlier. Choose any of those options, or choose any of the Display options that were described earlier in this section.

4. When you are finished selecting preferences, choose OK. You return to the DAD Preferences dialog box.

5. You can now set further DAD preferences or choose **C**lose.

Moving Toolbars and DAD Bars with the Mouse

Another easy way to position toolbars or DAD Bars is by moving them with the mouse, as outlined in the following steps:

1. Ensure that the toolbar or DAD Bar is visible on the screen.

2. Position the mouse pointer in an area of the toolbar or DAD Bar that does not contain buttons—either in the space between buttons or below or after the buttons. The mouse pointer changes to a hand.

Tip
You can also move a toolbar that appears as a palette in the middle of the screen by dragging its title bar, or close it by double-clicking its Control menu box.

3. Drag the toolbar or DAD Bar to the desired edge of the window. Alternatively, display the toolbar or DAD Bar as a palette by dragging it into the middle of the window.

4. When you release the mouse button, the toolbar or DAD Bar moves to its new position.

Customizing Menu Bars

In WordPerfect and Presentations, you can create multiple menu bars and edit their contents—just as you can with toolbars and DAD Bars. Expect other PerfectOffice applications to include this functionality in future releases.

Tip
In WordPerfect, you can hide the menu bar and all of the toolbars by choosing **V**iew, **H**ide Bars. To restore the menu bar, press the Esc key.

To effectively customize your menus, you need to know how to:

- Select different menu bars
- Access the Menu Preferences dialog box
- Create and edit menus

Selecting Menu Bars

To select a different menu bar to display, right-click the current menu bar. You see a QuickMenu that displays the names of available menu bars (see fig. 36.5). Click the menu that you want to display.

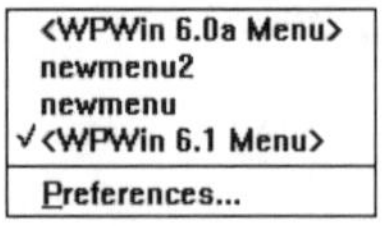

<WPWin 6.0a Menu>
newmenu2
newmenu
✓<WPWin 6.1 Menu>
Preferences...

Fig. 36.5
When you right-click a menu bar in WordPerfect or Presentations, this QuickMenu enables you to choose different menus or set menu preferences.

Setting Menu Preferences

To create, edit, copy, rename, or delete a menu, you must access the Menu Bar Preferences dialog box. To do so, use the following procedure:

1. Right-click the menu. You see a QuickMenu.

2. Choose **P**references. You see a Menu Bar Preferences dialog box (see fig. 36.6).

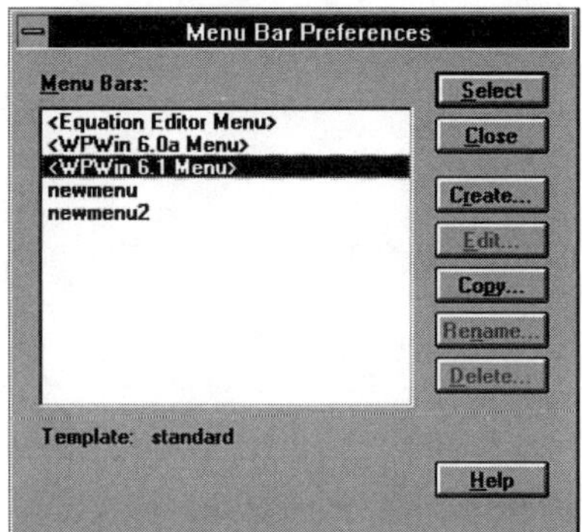

Fig. 36.6
Use the Menu Bar Preferences dialog box to customize menus just as you customize toolbars.

3. If necessary, highlight the menu that you want to select, edit, copy, rename, or delete.

4. Choose an option from the following list:

   - ***S**elect*. Choose this to display the selected menu.

   - ***C**lose*. This option completes any operations you have made and returns you to the application.

   - *C**r**eate*. Choose this option to create a new menu. See "Creating Toolbars, DAD Bars, and Menu Bars" on the following page for details.

   - ***E**dit*. Choose this option to edit an existing menu. See "Editing Toolbars, DAD Bars, and Menu Bars" later in this chapter for details.

   - *Co**p**y*. Choose this option to copy an existing menu. The option works slightly differently depending on the application. In Presentations, you see a Copy Menu Bar dialog box that merely asks you for the name of the new menu. By default, the new menu will have the same entries as the menu selected in the **M**enu Bars list.

     In WordPerfect, menus are stored in templates. When you choose Copy, you see the Copy Menu Bars dialog box (see fig. 36.7). You specify the template containing the menu you want to copy, then specify the menu in that template to be copied. Finally, you specify the template to copy the menu to. If the copying operation will result in overwriting the name of an existing menu, you will be prompted to overwrite the menu or provide a new name for it. (You see this prompt, for instance, when you copy a menu to the same template it comes from.)

Tip
Menus that are enclosed in angle braces (<>) are default menus that cannot be edited, renamed, or deleted. You can copy these menus, however, and then edit them.

Tip
In Presentations, you can quickly edit the currently displayed menu by right-clicking the menu, and then choosing **E**dit from the QuickMenu.

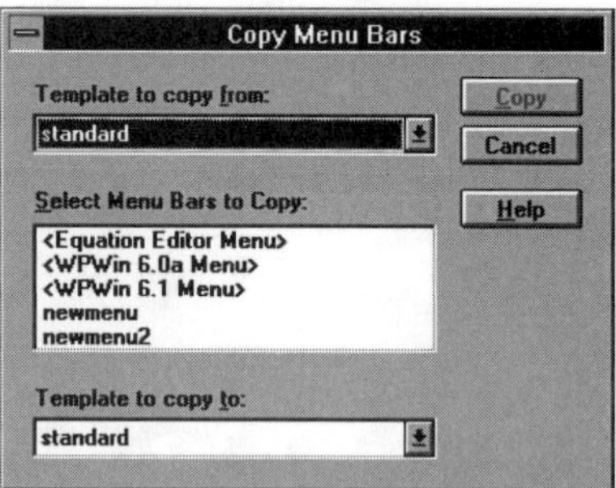

Fig. 36.7
The Copy Menu Bars dialog box in WordPerfect enables you to copy menus from one template to another.

- *Rename*. This option enables you to rename an existing menu.
- *Delete*. Choose this option to delete a menu from the list of available menus.
- *Help*. This option provides context-sensitive Help on menus.

Creating and Editing Toolbars, DAD Bars, and Menu Bars

Although on the surface it would not seem obvious, the process of creating and editing toolbars and DAD Bars is almost identical to creating and editing menus. This is because the same elements can be added to toolbar buttons and DAD Bar buttons as to menu items.

Creating Toolbars, DAD Bars, and Menu Bars

Creating a new toolbar, DAD Bar, or menu bar involves two basic steps: giving the toolbar, DAD Bar, or menu bar a name, and then adding buttons or items to it. To create a new toolbar, DAD Bar, or menu bar, follow these steps:

1. Access the Toolbar, DAD Bar, or Menu Bar Preferences dialog box by using the procedure outlined earlier.

2. Choose Create. You see a Create Toolbar, Create DAD Bar, or Create Menu Bar dialog box.

   When creating a DAD Bar, the Create DAD Bar dialog box enables you to create a new (empty) DAD Bar, or to create a DAD Bar from an existing program group, such as one that contains all your frequently used applications.

3. Give the toolbar, DAD Bar, or menu a descriptive name, and then choose OK.

Note

In WordPerfect, toolbars and menu bars are saved in a template, rather than as a separate file on the disk. You can specify which template the new toolbar or menu will be saved in by choosing **T**emplate from the Create Toolbar or Create Menu Bar dialog box. In the resulting Toolbar or Menu Bar Location dialog box, you can specify either the current document's template or the default template. If you choose the latter, your toolbar or menu will be available in all documents.

4. You see the Toolbar Editor dialog box similar to the one in figure 36.8, or a similar Menu Bar Editor dialog box.

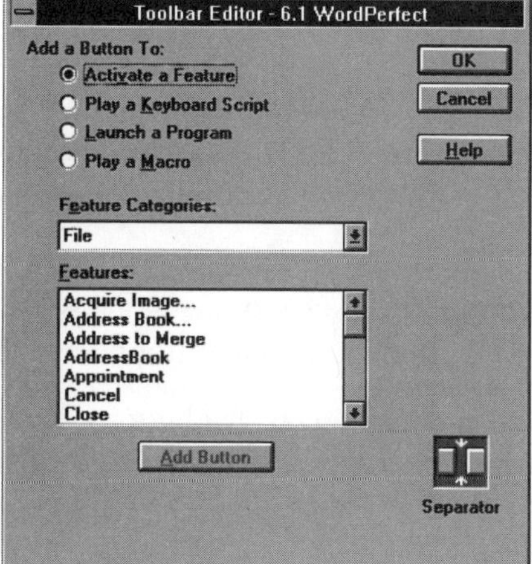

Fig. 36.8
You can add, move, and delete buttons from a toolbar using the Toolbar Editor dialog box.

5. Add, move, and delete buttons as described in "Editing Toolbars, DAD Bars, and Menu Bars" on the next page. When you are finished, choose OK. You return to the Toolbar, DAD Bar, or Menu Bar Preferences dialog box. Your new toolbar, DAD Bar, or menu is on the appropriate list.

6. You can set further preferences, or choose **C**lose to return to the application.

Troubleshooting

Sometimes I don't know what the toolbar buttons mean. On my office mate's machine, she gets a little yellow prompt when she puts her mouse pointer on a button. How can I do that?

Right-click a toolbar, then choose **P**references. From the Toolbar Preferences dialog box, choose **O**ptions, Show **Q**uickTips.

Editing Toolbars, DAD Bars, and Menu Bars

Editing a toolbar, DAD Bar, or menu bar involves adding, deleting, moving, and customizing buttons or items. To edit an existing toolbar, DAD Bar, or menu bar, follow these steps:

1. Access the Toolbar, DAD Bar, or Menu Bar Preferences dialog box as described earlier.

2. Select the toolbar, DAD Bar, or menu to be edited.

3. Choose **E**dit. You see a Toolbar or Menu Bar Editor dialog box similar to the one shown in figure 36.9. (The Toolbar Editor for DAD Bars and the Menu Bar Editor, not shown, have similar functionality.) You can now do the following:

   - Add buttons to the toolbar or menu items as described in "Adding Toolbar Buttons, DAD Bar Buttons, and Menu Items."

   - Move toolbar buttons, DAD Bar buttons, or menu items by dragging them to a new position on the toolbar, DAD Bar, or menu.

   - Delete buttons or items by dragging them off the toolbar, DAD Bar, or menu.

   - Customize buttons and items as described in "Customizing Toolbar Buttons, DAD Bar Buttons, and Menu Items," later in this chapter.

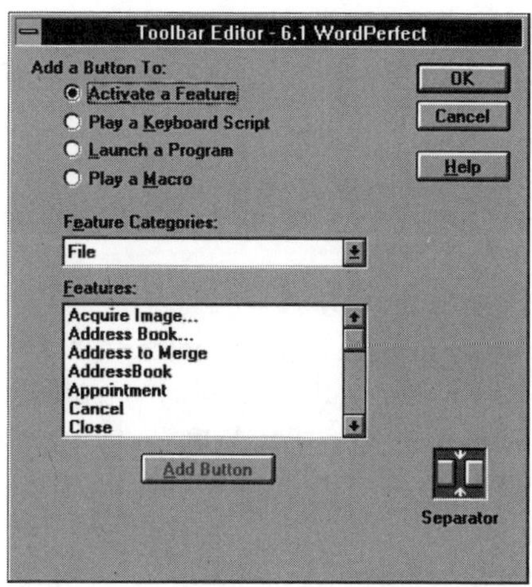

Fig. 36.9
Using the Toolbar Editor dialog box, you can add, move, delete, or customize buttons.

4. When you are finished editing the toolbar, DAD Bar, or menu bar, choose OK. You return to the Toolbar or Menu Bar Preferences dialog box.

5. You can now set further preferences or choose **C**lose to return to the application.

Adding Toolbar Buttons, DAD Bar Buttons, and Menu Items

Toolbar buttons, DAD Bar buttons, and menu items are extremely powerful. One of their simplest uses is to invoke program features. But toolbar buttons, DAD Bar buttons, and menu items can perform four different types of tasks:

- *Activate a feature.* Each application has specific features that can be assigned to a toolbar button or menu item. These are the features that are seen on the default menus of the application. This option enables these menu items to be assigned to toolbar buttons, and permits menus to be rearranged to your liking. In addition, DAD has features of its own (like QuickTasks) that can be assigned to DAD Bar buttons.

- *Play a keyboard script.* You can use a keyboard script to store a sequence of keystrokes. These keystrokes are played back when you click the button or choose the menu item that contains the keyboard script. Keyboard scripts can contain text and extended characters. They can also contain function-key and hot-key keystrokes. Thus, you can record simple macros that do anything which can be done by a series of keystrokes (but not mouse movements or mouse clicks).

- *Launch a program.* Toolbar buttons, DAD Bar buttons, and menu items can launch any application on your disk—both PerfectOffice and non-PerfectOffice programs.
- *Play a macro.* You can also create a button or menu item that will run a macro. (The macro must already have been created and saved on the disk.)

In order to add a button or item to your toolbar, DAD Bar, or menu, access the Toolbar or Menu Bar Editor dialog box by creating or editing a toolbar, DAD Bar, or menu as described earlier. What you do next depends on what type of button or menu item you want to add.

Adding a Button for a Feature

To add a button for a feature, follow these steps:

1. From the Toolbar or Menu Editor dialog box, choose Acti**v**ate a Feature. The Toolbar or Menu Editor dialog box shows options for F**e**ature Categories and **F**eatures.
2. Select F**e**ature Categories, and click the down arrow to the right of the Feature Categories text box. You see a list of available Feature Categories (see fig. 36.10). These parallel the main menu options. Some applications may have additional feature categories.

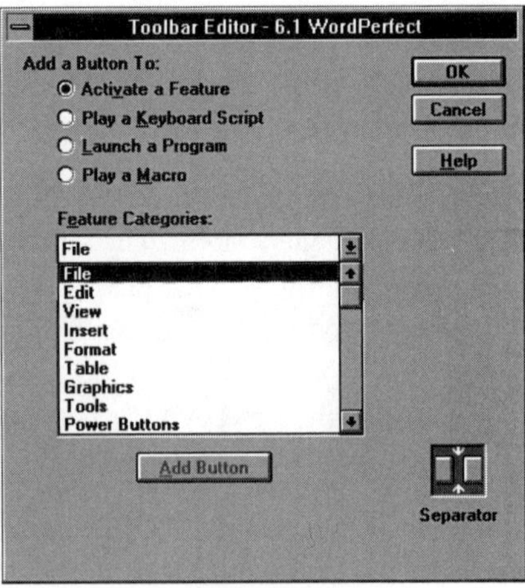

Fig. 36.10
You can assign buttons or menu items to application features that parallel default menu items.

3. Depending on the category you select, a different list of features will appear. Select the feature you want to associate with the button, then choose **A**dd Button or **A**dd Menu Item. A new button or item appears on the toolbar or menu, and you remain in the Edit Toolbar or Menu Bar Editor dialog box so you can make further additions.

Tip
New menu items are added as main selections on the menu bar. Move them by dragging them to their appropriate place on a menu.

Note

Feature categories for adding DAD Bar buttons include DAD, Integration, Tasks, Data Sharing, Control Panel, and all other DAD Bars. DAD features enable you to access QuickTasks, QuickFiles, QuickRun, QuickOpen, cascade and tile applications, and close DAD and/or Windows. Integration features enable you to copy information between applications, and open common GroupWise windows. Tasks enable you to put any existing QuickTask onto a button. Data sharing offers options for copying data between applications. Control Panel provides access to the common elements of the Windows Control Panel. Select any of the other DAD Bars to copy buttons from one DAD Bar to another.

Tip
By default, a new keyboard script menu item has the name of the first word in the script. To change this name, double-click the menu item while you are editing the menu bar.

Adding a Keyboard Script to a Button or Menu Item

If you want to add a keyboard script to a button or menu item, follow these steps:

1. From the Toolbar or Menu Bar Editor dialog box, choose Play a **K**eyboard Script. The Toolbar or Menu Bar Editor dialog box shows a text box for the keyboard script (see fig. 36.11).

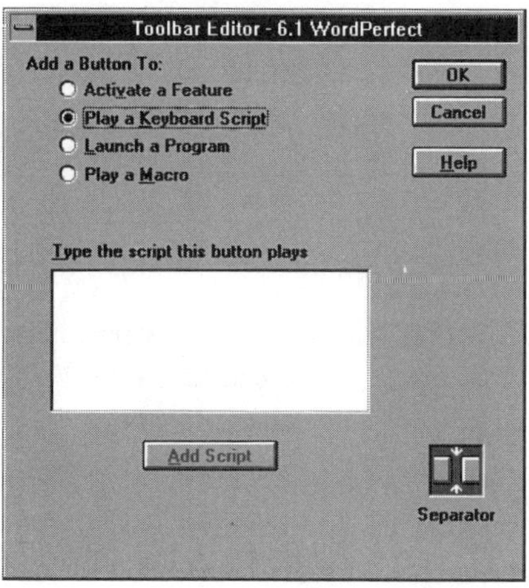

Fig. 36.11
Toolbar buttons and menu items can contain scripts that play text, function keys, or menu choices.

2. Choose **T**ype the Script This Button Plays. An insertion point appears in the text box.

3. Type the keystrokes that the button should play. Function keys are entered with braces—for example, **{Shift+F7}**.

4. When you are finished, choose **A**dd Script. A new button or item appears on the toolbar or menu, and you remain in the Toolbar or Menu Bar Editor dialog box so you can make further additions.

Tip
By default, a new application launch menu item has the name of the application. To change this name, double-click the menu item.

Creating a Button or Menu Item to Launch a Program

To create a button that will launch a program:

1. From the Toolbar or Menu Editor dialog box, choose **L**aunch a Program.

2. Click the Select File button that now appears in the dialog box.

3. You see the Select File dialog box (see fig. 36.12).

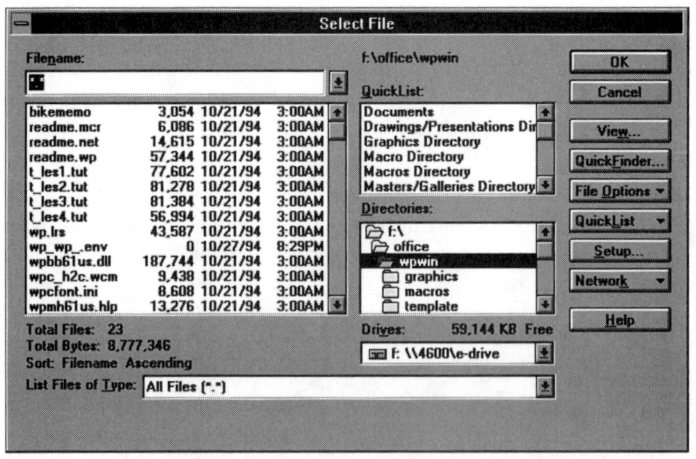

Fig. 36.12
Assign an application to a toolbar button or menu item using the Select File dialog box.

◄ See "Saving, Opening, and Closing Files," p. 59

4. Select the appropriate drive, directory, and file from this dialog box.

5. When you are finished, choose OK. A new button or item appears on the toolbar or menu, and you return to the Toolbar or Menu Bar Editor dialog box so you can make further additions.

Running a Macro from a Toolbar Button or Menu Item

If you would like to assign a macro to a toolbar button or menu item, follow these steps:

1. From the Toolbar or Menu Bar Editor dialog box, choose Play a **M**acro.
2. Click the **A**dd Macro button that now appears in the dialog box.

> **Note**
>
> In WordPerfect, you can also choose Add **T**emplate Macro. This adds a macro that is stored in a template to a button or menu item, as opposed to one stored on the disk. In this case, you see a list of macros stored in the current template, and you can choose a macro from this list.

3. You see a directory dialog box like the one shown in figure 36.13, enabling you to choose the macro to be assigned to the button or menu item. (WordPerfect's dialog box is called Select Macro; GroupWise's is called Select File. They both offer identical functionality.)

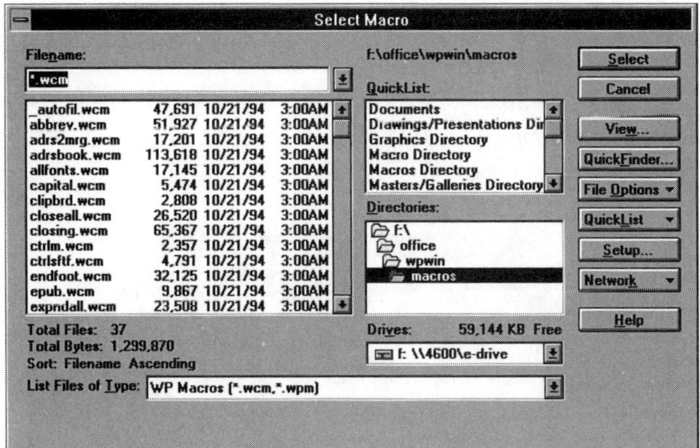

Fig. 36.13
You can also assign macros to toolbar buttons and menu items.

4. Select the appropriate drive, directory, and macro file from this dialog box, and then choose OK. A new button or item appears on the toolbar or menu, and you return to the Edit Toolbar or Menu Bar dialog box so you can make further additions.

Adding a Macro to a DAD Bar

If you would like to run a macro from a button on a DAD Bar, the methods differ slightly if the macro is to be found on the disk, or contained in DAD itself:

1. From the Toolbar Editor dialog box, choose Play a **M**acro.

2. Click the **A**dd Macro button that now appears in the dialog box. You see the Select Macro Source dialog box shown in figure 36.14.

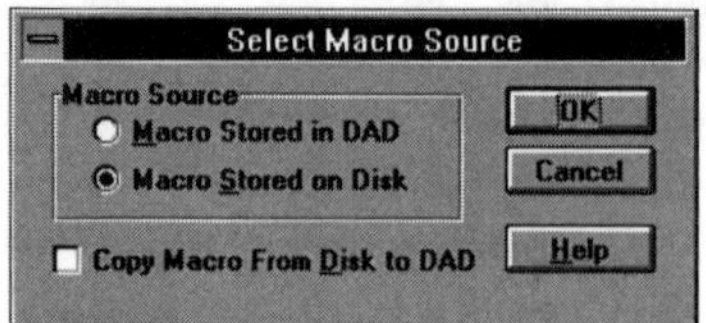

Fig. 36.14
You can assign two types of macros to DAD buttons: macros stored on the disk, or macros stored with DAD itself.

3. Select **M**acro Stored in DAD or Macro **S**tored on Disk. If you want to copy a macro from the disk to DAD, choose Macro **S**tored on Disk, and also select Copy Macro from **D**isk to DAD.

4. Choose OK.

5. If you chose **M**acro Stored in DAD, you see the Select Macro dialog box shown in figure 36.15. A list of macros that are stored in DAD is displayed in the **M**acros in DAD list box. Select the desired macro and choose **S**elect.

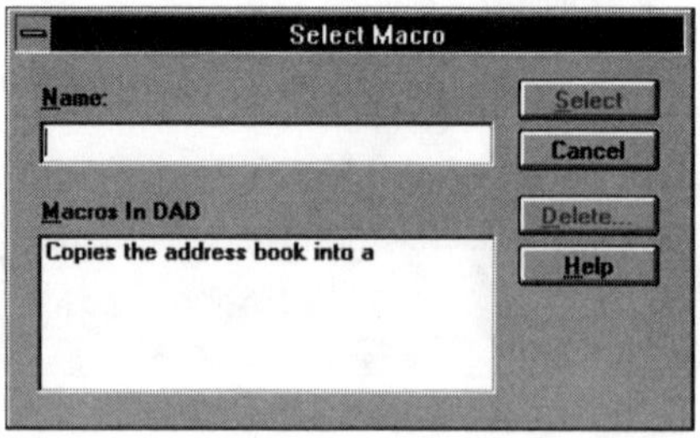

Select Macro
Name:
Macros In DAD
Copies the address book into a
Select
Cancel
Delete...
Help

Fig. 36.15
If you chose to select a macro in DAD, you can only choose macros that are already in the Desktop Applications Director.

Or, if you chose Macro **S**tored on Disk, you see an Add Macro dialog box (see fig. 36.16). Select the appropriate drive, directory, and macro file from this dialog box, then choose OK.

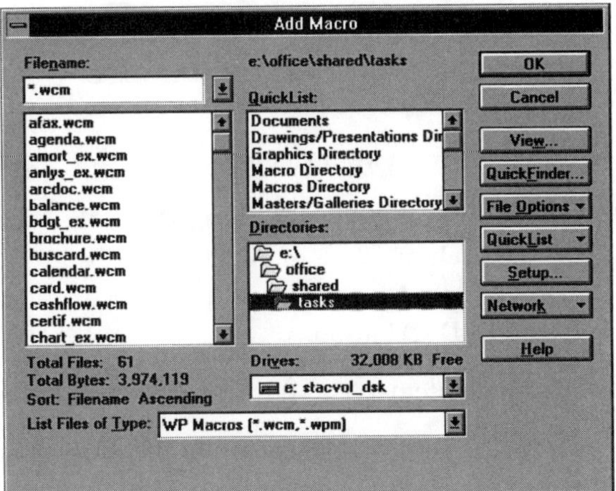

Fig 36.16
Add a macro on disk using the Add Macro dialog box.

6. A new button appears on the DAD Bar, and you return to the Edit Toolbar dialog box so you can make further additions.

Customizing Toolbar Buttons, DAD Bar Buttons, and Menu Items

You can customize a button or menu item by double-clicking it while you are editing or creating a toolbar, DAD Bar, or menu bar. You see a Customize Button dialog box (see fig. 36.17) or an Edit Menu Text dialog box (see fig. 36.18).

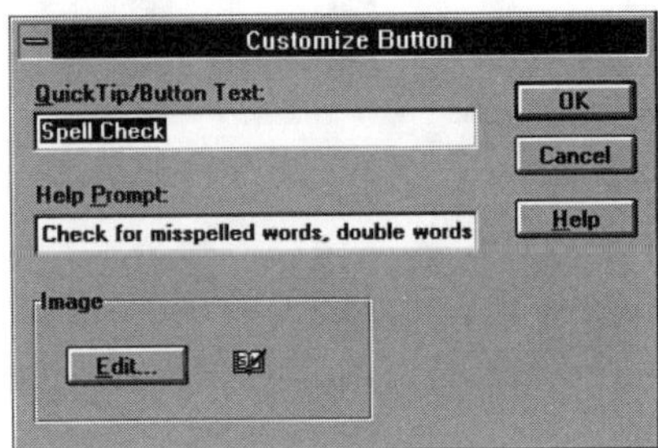

Fig. 36.17
The Customize Button dialog box enables you to change the properties of the toolbar or DAD Bar button.

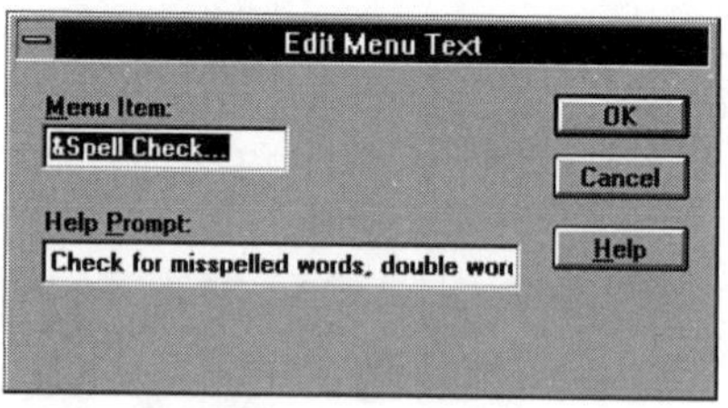

Fig. 36.18
The Edit Menu Text dialog box enables you to change the text of the menu item and the help prompt that appears on the title bar.

These dialog boxes provide options including:

- ***Q**uick Tip/Button Text* (for toolbar buttons). This is the text that shows when (a) you have selected **T**ext or P**i**cture and Text in your toolbar display options, and (b) **D**isplay QuickTips is selected, and you hold the mouse pointer on a DAD button.
- ***M**enu Item* (for menu items). This is the text of the menu item.
- *Help **P**rompt*. This is the text that appears in the title bar when you position your mouse on a button or menu item.
- ***E**dit* (for toolbar buttons). This option enables you to edit the image of the button. Choosing **E**dit displays an Image Editor dialog box (see fig. 36.19). Select the colors that you can paint with the left and right mouse buttons by clicking the appropriate colors with the respective buttons.

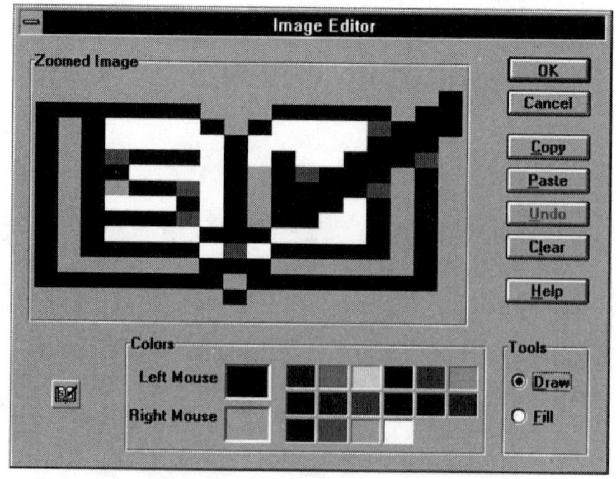

Fig. 36.19
PerfectOffice includes a bitmap editor that enables you to change the appearance of toolbar buttons.

If **D**raw is selected, click either button to fill small rectangles with the appropriate color, one at a time. If **F**ill is selected, clicking a cell will change the color of that cell and all contiguous cells of the same color.

You can also use the **C**opy and **P**aste commands to copy images from one button to another.

Troubleshooting

Now I've created three toolbars that I like. Can I show them all on the screen at once?

Unfortunately, only one toolbar can be displayed at a time in most applications. Toolbars can, however, display more than one row or column of buttons. In WordPerfect, there is another special toolbar called the Power Bar that can also be displayed while a "regular" toolbar is displayed. The Power Bar can be edited just like any other toolbar. In Presentations, there is also a second toolbar showing buttons specific to the mode you are in. This toolbar can be moved, but not edited.

Setting Additional Properties for Buttons and Menu Items

When you edit toolbars, DAD Bars, and menu bars and double-click a button or menu item, you may see a Properties button.

This option enables you to change certain aspects of the command invoked by the button or menu item. How it works depends on what the button or menu item does.

- For buttons or menu items that invoke a feature, no Properties option is available. There is also no Properties option available for DAD Bar buttons that invoke macros stored in DAD, or WordPerfect toolbar buttons that invoke macros stored in the template.

- If the button or menu item plays a keyboard script, choosing Properties displays a Script Properties dialog box that enables you to edit the script.

- Choosing Properties for buttons or menu items that launch a program displays an Application Launch Properties dialog box (see fig. 36.20). You can use this dialog box to specify the **C**ommand Line, **W**orking Directory, and whether to run the program minimized.

- Choosing Properties for buttons that launch macros located on the disk enables you to edit the path and name of the macro.

Fig 36.20
The Application Launch Properties dialog box enables you to set options for launching programs from buttons or menu items.

Troubleshooting

Now I've created three DAD Bars that I like. Can I show them all on the screen at once?

Unfortunately, only one DAD Bar can be displayed at a time. However, if you right-click a displayed DAD Bar, you can easily choose another by clicking it in the QuickMenu.

From Here...

You have learned basic skills for using all the PerfectOffice applications, and in this part of the book, you also learned how to customize common PerfectOffice application elements. If you haven't already looked at the chapters on individual applications, you will probably want to do so now:

- See Chapter 5, "Getting Started with WordPerfect," to learn how to use WordPerfect to create common business and personal documents. See how to edit and format documents and use several shortcuts that will help you automate your word processing work.
- In Chapter 12, "Getting Started with Quattro Pro," you discover how to create everything from simple home budgets to complex spreadsheets involving data analysis and charts.
- Chapter 19, "Getting Started with Paradox," explores how to use Paradox to create databases for home and business use. Learn how to create queries, design reports and forms, and create crosstabs and graphs.

- In Chapter 24, "Getting Started with Presentations," you can learn all about Novell's premier graphics and presentations program. See how to create slide shows, make charts, and use drawing objects.
- Chapter 28, "Getting Started with GroupWise and InfoCentral," teaches you how to use GroupWise to send e-mail, schedule meetings, and assign and track tasks within a work group. You'll also learn about InfoCentral—Novell's Personal Information Manager.

Index of Common Problems

(continues)

(continues)

If you're having trouble with...	You'll find help here...
WordPerfect Continued	
Can't remember syntax for commands when editing macro	p. 225
Can't tell what macro does by looking at new toolbar button	p. 225
City, state, and ZIP code are jammed together in the inside address after mail merge	p. 238
Envelopes aren't there after merge	p. 238
Keyboard merge didn't move to next place for input	p. 239
Quattro Pro	
Screen shows NOTEBK2.WB2 instead of NOTEBK1.WB2	p. 245
Cell selector disappears when using the scroll bars	p. 248
Some Ctrl+letter shortcut keys don't perform properly	p. 250
When Coaches are active, can't switch to another Windows program	p. 254
Asterisks are displayed instead of the number entered in a cell	p. 265
Get "wrong password" message when trying to open password-protected notebook file	p. 276
Don't know password and can't open password-protected files	p. 276
Need help finding command necessary to perform a task	p. 282
Want to use old, familiar Quattro Pro for DOS command menus	p. 282
Block name table doesn't seem to show correct addresses for some blocks	p. 289
Some formulas don't show correct results even though they appear to contain correct block names	p. 289
The Tabs option doesn't appear in the SpeedFill dialog box	p. 301

(continues)

Index

Symbols

A

B

C

E

G

H

I

J-K

L

M

N

O

P

Q

R

S

T

U

V

W

X-Y-Z